Princely Gardens

KENNETH WOODBRIDGE

Princely Gardens

The origins and development of the French formal style

with 315 illustrations

THAMES AND HUDSON

Frontispiece Versailles: Le Nôtre's north *parterre*, detail of a painting by Allegrain. In the foreground are Louis XIV, Louvois and Le Nôtre with a group of courtiers.

Designed by Pauline Baines

Filmset in Great Britain by Tameside Filmsetting, Ashton-under-Lyne, Lancs.
Printed and bound in Hungary.

Contents

Preface · 7
Introduction · 9

I Origins

1 *The medieval legacy* · 13

The literary image · The practical tradition · Burgundian and early Valois gardens · Provence-Anjou: the gardens of 'Le Roi René'

2 *The early-Renaissance background* · 23

Literary sources · Renaissance theory · Italian gardens of the later fifteenth century

II The French Renaissance Garden

3 *Early Italian influence* · 39

Historical background: 1494–1515 · Amboise · Blois · Gaillon · Le Verger · Bury

4 *Italian theory and French practice: Leonardo to Philibert de l'Orme* · 51

Historical background: 1515–1559 · Fontainebleau · Serlio and Philibert de l'Orme: Ancy-le-Franc and Anet · Chenonceaux · Chantilly

5 *Gardens, politics and religion, 1560–94* · 77

Historical background · The gardens of Catherine de Médicis · Garden festivals · The mannerism of Jacques Androuet du Cerceau and Bernard Palissy

6 *The vegetal component: French gardening in the sixteenth and seventeenth centuries* · 97

Gardening principles · Medicinal and botanic gardens · The flower garden and the *parterre* · The Tuileries: the garden and the gardeners

III The Classical Tradition

7 *Between mannerism and classicism* · 121

Historical background: Henri IV and Louis XIII · Hydraulics: the Francini and Salomon de Caus · Saint-Germain-en-Laye · The Luxembourg · Liancourt

8 *Richelieu's gardens and the alternative tradition* · 143

Richelieu · Saint-Cloud and Rueil · The picturesque image

9 *François Mansart and the gardens of the new financial elite* · 161

Montjeu · Wideville · Tanlay · Brécy · Berny · Balleroy · Maisons · Gesvres · Fresnes · Petit-Bourg · Jacques Boyceau and André Mollet: *Le Jardin de Plaisir*

10 *Vaux-le-Vicomte* · 181

Mazarin and the surintendance · Abel Servien and Meudon · Nicolas Fouquet · Saint-Mandé · Le Vau and Le Nôtre · Vaux-le-Vicomte

11 *Versailles* · 197

The structure of Versailles, 1661–88 · The *bosquets* · Sculpture · Water · The Potager du Roi · Versailles in perspective

12 *The Royal Gardens under Louis XIV* · 225

Organization · Trianon · Marly · Fontainebleau · Saint-Germain-en-Laye · The Tuileries

13 *Le Nôtre and the Genius of the Place* · 247

Chantilly · Dampierre · Saint-Cloud · Sceaux · Meudon · Maintenon · Anet · Castries

IV The Legacy of Le Nôtre

14 *The Theory and Practice of Gardening* · 267

Le Nôtre codified · J.-F. Blondel · *Le Jardin Anglais* and the *style paysager*, 1770–1880

15 *The Classical Revival 1875–1935* · 279

Les Jardins de l'Intelligence · Henri and Achille Duchêne · Courances · Voisins · California Ferdinand Duprat: La Roche-Courbon · Villandry · The revival reassessed

Notes to the text · 292
Appendix A. Plants used for ornamental purposes · 300
Appendix B. Plants for *parterres* in the French version of *Hypnerotomachia* · 306
Appendix C. Chronological table: monarchs and gardens · 307
Glossary · 308
Bibliography · 309
Sources of illustrations · 313
Index · 315

Preface

THE RESEARCH in which this book originated was begun in 1972 with the aid of a Leverhulme Research Fellowship. My purpose was to explore the links between the English and French traditions of garden design. It soon became apparent that although the gardens of Le Nôtre were well known, their sources in sixteenth- and seventeenth-century theory and practice had not been studied to the same extent. Professor Dora Wiebenson was working on the relation between English and French theory and practice in the eighteenth century, and her book *The Picturesque Garden in France* was published in 1978. Initially therefore my research was concentrated on the pre-Le Nôtre garden. The work of Le Nôtre was a logical conclusion to this. Histories of the French garden have tended to conclude with the Revolution. So, although the nineteenth- and twentieth-century development is a subject in itself, two summary chapters have been added to round off the story of the French formal garden and bring it up to date.

The unfailing welcome I have received in France and the friends I have made are in themselves a reward for writing this book. I owe a particular debt to the experience and advice of Monsieur Jean Feray, Inspecteur Principal des Monuments Historiques at the Ministère de la Culture; and to the librarian, Mme. Françoise Bercé. Mlle. Rosaline Bacou of the Musée du Louvre and Mme. Françoise Jestaz of the Bibliothèque Nationale have been especially helpful over the illustrations; and in Stockholm I was greatly assisted by Dr. Runar Strandberg and the staff of the National Museum. Among the many other keepers, archivists and librarians to whom I am indebted are: Mme. F. Chapard at the Musée Condé, Chantilly; Mme. Sylvie Béguin, Louvre; Mlle. Josiane Sartre, Musée des Arts Decoratifs; Mme. Tissier de Mallerais, Blois. The late Vicomte de Noailles, himself a gardener of distinction, was very kind in providing me with introductions to private owners.

Denis Lambin, besides commenting on the manuscript at various stages, has shared with me his enthusiasm for gardens. His friendship and that of Jacques Carré and Michel Baridon has enriched my experience of their country in many ways. Finally, I am grateful to Mlle. Monique Mosser for the stimulus of her enthusiasm and for involving me in various interesting projects.

In England I owe much to the encouragement of Professor J. B. Trapp and Robin Middleton. Sandra Raphael has given me advice on the plant identifications. Elizabeth Johnson has worked on the index. J. R. K. Davie and J. E. Hancock have helped in the photography. I have also to thank the editor, copy editor and designer at Thames and Hudson.

The work of gathering and assembling the material for this book would hardly have been possible without the assistance of Joan Woodbridge to whom, more than anyone, its successful completion is due. She fell ill three days after delivering the final proofs, and died on March 25th, 1985. The book is her memorial.

NOTE

Before the metric system was introduced in 1801, the currency unit was the *livre*, representing a pound of silver. There were twenty *sols* to the *livre*, and twelve *deniers* to the *sol*. The measures of length were *toise* (six *pieds*), *pied* and *pouce* (the twelfth part of a *pied*), corresponding to our feet and inches. In conformity with present-day practice these have been converted to metres, unless they form part of a quotation.

pallas
Juno
Venus
Nature
deduit

Introduction

A CERTAIN TOLERANCE of definition is required in speaking of the art of gardens, for what, in the first place, is a garden? A
1 simple description such as 'an area of ground enclosed for cultivating plants', as opposed to a park, 'an area enclosed for
2 conserving animals', is satisfactory initially when these uses are distinct. But as the size of the area set aside for ornament or pleasure increases, and is controlled by some unifying concept of design, the question becomes more confused. In the eighteenth century William Shenstone used the term 'landskip-gardening' as distinct from 'kitchen' and 'parterre' gardening. 'It consists', he wrote, 'in pleasing the imagination by scenes of grandeur, beauty or variety. Convenience merely has no share here; any farther than as it pleases the imagination.' He was of course referring to his own brand of gardening, which was virtually abolishing the garden and setting the house in a park; but his definition could be applied equally well to a great French garden such as Meudon or Chantilly. On the other hand, some garden historians have implied that landscape gardening is just a question of laying a garden open to a view.[1] Shenstone distinguishes between 'landskip' and 'prospect', 'the former as expressive of home scenes, the latter distant images. Prospects should take in the blue distant hills; but never so remotely, that they be not distinguishable from clouds. Yet this mere extent is what the vulgar value.' To consider gardening as an art must imply a measure of aesthetic control of all the elements within the bounds; and, if what is outside is to be included, an element of selection in what is to be seen, or at least in the choice of site for other than purely practical reasons. Crescenzi, for instance, gives instructions for siting and planting gardens according to the prevailing winds of Italy;[2] and while such considerations are clearly of great importance, they cannot be said to be governed by aesthetic motives.

In certain arts it is very difficult to disentangle the aesthetic and the functional, or to identify precise use. And indeed why should we? The pattern of the fields in the French countryside today, the ordered rows of vines and the commercial groves of poplar planted in quincunx, are as satisfying to the eye and mind, often more so, than many elaborate parterres. Nevertheless the prime aim in this book will be to trace the formal and symbolic aspects of the art of gardening, and to deal with horticultural matters only in so far as they relate to these; remembering, however, that the distinction between the *jardin de plaisir* and the *potager* was not always as apparent as it became in the gardens of the wealthy, particularly after 1600. The very use of the word *verger* in connection with a fifteenth-century pleasure garden indicates that the orchard was a pleasant place to retire to and became embellished for that purpose.

In this context 'formal' is used in the general sense of 'pertaining to the visible form, arrangement, or external qualities' of a garden, regardless of style; whereas 'formal style' in the title of the book conveys the widely accepted sense of 'regular or geometric', a style where the form of the garden is determined by a pre-ordained framework of paths, walks or rides in which the straight line predominates. But, as Sir Reginald Blomfield wrote (*The Formal Garden in England*, 1892), 'The formal system of gardening is a question-begging name. The formal treatment of gardens ought, perhaps, to be called the architectural treatment of gardens, for it consists of the extension of the principles of design which govern the house, to the grounds which surround it'. There is, however, another sense of 'formal': 'ceremonious' or suited for formal occasions in which conventional behaviour is appropriate. 'Formal' in this sense may very well be applied to the design of classical French châteaux and their immediate surroundings as it developed in the sixteenth and seventeenth centuries, with emphasis on the axial approach to the house, through a hierarchy of courtyards with the garden as a climax; a scheme calculated to demonstrate the status of the owner.

Garden design is a composite art in which plants do not always predominate. Some features, such as terraces and canals, are functional before they are ornamental. Water is so essential that a spring or fountain conveniently placed at the centre of the garden has become identified with the source of life, deeply imbued with symbolic meanings, and one of the first artificial features to be elaborated. Cascades or waterfalls, appealing to the eye and ear, and sheets of water exploited for their reflecting quality, are an important part of the Western tradition. Water organs, automata, and other ingenious toys also belong to it, although perhaps marginally. Caves or grottoes have associations with gardens going back to Classical times; the architectural grotto may be an important element in the design. Buildings are inseparable from the art of gardens. The function of casinos, temples and pavilions in

1 Dame Nature admitting the poet to an enclosed garden, from *Le Livre des Echecs amoureux*, late fifteenth century.

2 Park from *Le Livre des Echecs amoureux*, late fifteenth century.

the social life for which the garden is a setting is not limited to use. They may have symbolic overtones, serve as goals or stages along a path, or be so intimately related to the structure that garden and building are indistinguishable, as in the Mannerist confusion of architectural and garden space in the Villa Papa Giulio. But while their place in garden design must be considered, a detailed discussion of the style of buildings belongs to the history of architecture. In the same way the style and content of statues belongs to the history of sculpture; but garden sculpture cannot be omitted on the grounds that it is furniture, for it often serves as a focus to give meaning to the whole design.

Art history has tended to be dominated by the concept of nationality, which inevitably has strong territorial associations. Thus the art of gardening particularly attracts feelings of national rivalry. This was the case in the eighteenth century when the dominant French style was challenged by *le jardin anglais*. Ideas of the opposition of the natural to the artificial, or of freedom as opposed to control, in which this style originated, are deeply embedded in the European tradition, and were current in France, as much as in England, before the eighteenth century. Nevertheless, by the end of the seventeenth century André Le Nôtre had put his stamp on a style of garden recognizably *à la française*, which the French, on the whole, continue to regard as the embodiment of the national genius. Le Nôtre did not invent the style. Most of the elements originated outside France. Italian gardeners introduced beds laid out in ornamental figures, and regularity of design about a central axis followed from Italian theory; but when the same principles were submitted to the influence of French social conditions, topography and climate, something different resulted.

Important French gardens were made in relation to royal houses or seats of the nobility. Great Italian gardens of the sixteenth century were associated with villas, and existed in their own right even without a residence. They were sited in the hills; summer retreats, where there was abundant falling water for elaborate fountains and cascades. French sites were flatter. Like the great rivers, gardens seemed to spread. Anet is French; Lante is Italian; Castello is Italian; the garden of the Tuileries is French, and it is not just a matter of situation. Nor should we suppose a simple influence of one country's art on another's; the interaction of French and Italian culture, particularly in the sixteenth century, was too complex for that. Among the aims of this book is to record that interaction, and otherwise to assemble and verify (mainly from printed sources) what is known about the development of the regular, architectural or formal style of garden in France, and to put it in some historical perspective.

PART I

Origins

LE IARDIN CLOS OU CRVT LE VRAY LORIER

I

The medieval legacy

The literary image

TWO VISUAL METAPHORS dominate the medieval image of the garden: the *hortus conclusus* and the *hortus deliciarum*. The first derives from the Song of Songs:

> A garden inclosed is my sister, my spouse;
> a spring shut up, a fountain sealed.

3 This becomes the symbol of the Church with the Virgin presiding over a 'well of living waters'.

The second, whose prototype is Eden, is the symbol of the
4 pleasures of the world, and particularly concupiscence. The most famous literary *hortus deliciarum* is that of Déduit in *Le Roman de la Rose*.[1] The poem is an allegory of the dangers of idolatrous love. Dreaming that he is walking by the river on a fine spring morning, the poet sees a garden enclosed by a crenellated wall. Seduced by the singing of birds he seeks an entrance, and is admitted by a young woman, the description of whose copper-coloured hair, tender flesh, sparkling eyes and scented breath establishes the poem's erotic tone. 'Even in Jerusalem there would not be found a woman whose neck was more beautiful, or soft and smooth to touch', says the poet, making the analogy with the Shulamite maiden. Her dress and appearance are those of a high-born lady in the height of fashion. She wears gloves to keep her hands white. 'I am called Oiseuse [Idleness]by those who know me', she says. 'I am a rich and powerful woman; for most of the time I have only to amuse myself, and comb and do my hair. I am a close friend of Déduit [Pleasure], the kind and gracious owner of this garden, and who had these trees brought from the country of the Alexandrines and planted in this orchard. When the trees were big he enclosed them by the wall which you see all round.' Hate, Treachery, Infamy, Covetousness, Greed, Envy, Sadness, Old Age, Hypocrisy and Poverty, whose images are painted on the wall outside the garden, are excluded from it. Within, the gracious Déduit relaxes with
5 his chosen companions, Youth, Beauty, Riches, Candour, Courtesy, Liberality and the God of Love himself. They dance, sing and dally in the shade. 'Heavens, what a fine life they lead!' sighs the poet, and wanders off to explore the place, followed at a distance by Cupid with his bow. In a remote spot he comes upon a fountain, situated beneath a pine tree. An inscription on the marble basin associates it with Narcissus. It is thus quite the opposite of the Virgin's 'well of living waters', for Narcissus died of self-love, the most barren illusion of all. Peering into the water the poet sees the whole garden reflected as in a crystal; and, among a thousand other things, a rose garden surrounded by a hedge. He seeks it out; and while he stands lost in admiration of one rose more beautiful than all the rest, he is pierced by an arrow from Cupid's bow, significantly through the organ of sight. From that moment he must possess the object of his unreasonable passion despite all obstacles and arguments against it.

If the sermon on the vanity of an earthly paradise had been heeded, the history of the French garden would have been different. As things are it is arbitrary but convenient to begin with such a story as the *Roman*. For one thing, as the names of the characters Déduit and Oiseuse imply, its history is bound up with the changing preoccupations of a leisure class. Déduit's garden is a literary invention with only slender roots in fact. The poem tells us nothing about a thirteenth-century French garden. Nor do the illustrations help, for in early copies they are little more than tokens of emblematic but not representational significance. Only with the spread of Flemish realism in the mid-fifteenth century, assisted by the patronage of the dukes of Burgundy, do credible portrayals of parks and gardens begin to appear with increasing frequency.

The practical tradition

It may be assumed that a practical tradition of gardening was established in France by the Romans and probably preserved in the monasteries. The ancestor of the French Renaissance garden enclosed by galleries was the peristyle via the cloister. The Crusades provided an opportunity for direct experience of Islamic gardens, and were responsible for the introduction of new trees and other plants into Europe. Guillaume de Lorris implies this in his *Roman de la Rose* when he refers to 'trees brought from the country of the Alexandrines' for Déduit's orchard. About the time that Jean de Meun completed Lorris's unfinished poem between 1268 and 1278, Pietro de Crescenzi was writing *Opus Ruralium Commodorum*, based on Classical texts such as Varro's *Res Rusticanae*, from which it became known in France as *Le Rustican*.[2] It was

3 Virgin and child in an enclosed garden (*hortus conclusus*), from *Livre des chants royaux*, fifteenth century.

4 A miniature from Henri de Suso's *Horloge de Sapience*, *c.* 1447–60. A mystical revelation in a garden while surrounded by the pleasures of the senses – music, hawking and hunting.

5 A dance in Déduit's garden, from the *Roman de la Rose*, *c.* 1485. Here Déduit (Pleasure) relaxes with Youth, Beauty, Candour, Courtesy, Liberality and Love.

6, 7 Orpheus and Narcissus, two miniatures ▷ by Jean Miélot from Christine de Pisan's *Epître d'Othéa*, 1455–61. Compare Orpheus's seat with ill.95.

translated into French in 1373 by the order of Charles V. Fifteen manuscript copies are on record; and fourteen printed editions appeared between 1486 and 1540.[3] It spread the knowledge of an ancient text at a time when the original was not available; and was the most important, if not the only, treatise on agriculture, until it was superseded by the work of Charles Etienne [4] and Olivier de Serres[5], or by the antique texts themselves. The eighth book concerns 'vergiers, jardins et choses délectables'. Plants are not only useful, but are appreciated for their scent, and because their colours delight the eye. Indeed gardens are made for enjoyment and health, for pleasure rather than produce. In all gardens there should be a shady seat under a tree; and even in those of moderate size it is best to have a fountain of running water. Gardens of from two to four acres or more should be surrounded by a ditch and hedges of thorn or rose, pomegranate, nut, plum or quince according to the climate. Where it is appropriate, there should be arbours or pavilions made of trellis-work. There are those for whom the only limit to doing what they want is the art and science to do it. The pleasure grounds of kings and great noblemen will be places where they can retire to refresh themselves after giving satisfaction to their subjects. The windows of the palace will overlook the gardens, with a clear view of the animals in the park. There will be fishponds, a wood for wild animals, and trees near the house will be caged in net of brass wire to contain many kinds of bird. Crescenzi gives detailed instructions for making green battlemented walls of poplar or elm to surround an orchard, and how to cut and bend them to form floors and roofs of summerhouses, which look forward to Bernard Palissy,[6] and all the elaborate artifice associated with the Renaissance gardening tradition.

Although Crescenzi was an Italian from Bologna, his book was dedicated to Charles II of Anjou. The connection was that Charles's father had been invested with the kingdoms of Naples and Sicily by Pope Urban IV in order to gain his support against the emperor, Frederick II. The Angevin claim to the throne of Naples and Sicily was a major factor in the relations of France and Italy for two hundred years. Direct contact with Arab–Norman culture must have had its effect in France. Robert II, Comte d'Artois, regent in Naples after his uncle Charles's death, was doubtless familiar with the gardens at Palermo, where Roger II had 'hills and woods near the town enclosed by a stone wall, and planted with a variety of trees to make a delightful park, where deer, stags and wild boar roamed at will; and where he built a palace served by fresh spring water brought in underground canals'.[7] Before his death in 1302, not long after the publication of Crescenzi's book, Robert d'Artois enclosed the park of his domain at Hesdin,[8] in the Pas-de-Calais, by a wall 13 kilometres long, and installed a gallery of automata worked by water, which almost certainly derived from Arab versions of the treatise of Heron of Alexandria.

Burgundian and early Valois gardens

The period from the mid-fourteenth to the mid-fifteenth century, when war and near-anarchy prevailed over large parts of France, was hardly a time for the art of gardening to flourish. Hesdin, whose automata had been maintained for over a century, was sacked by the English. It was protected from their depredations when it became part of the domains of the dukes of Burgundy through the marriage of Charles V's brother, Philip the Bold. Robert d'Artois' famous gallery of automata was restored in 1433,[9] and new ones added. They included figures which could be made to squirt water, and other devices for dousing, or covering people with soot or flour. Some of the tricks were relatively harmless: a fountain in which the water mysteriously came and went; a room which produced rain, thunder, lightning and snow; a talking hermit made of wood. Others were almost beyond a joke, such as machines which struck people in the face or beat them. The automata were contained in a building referred to as Le Pavillon des Engiens. La Salle du Marais[10] seems to have belonged to the park rather than to the castle; and there was also a place called La Gloriete or La Gayole, where there was a tree with artificial birds also capable of squirting water. These are the forerunners of those more elaborate automata so popular in Italian and French gardens of the sixteenth and early seventeenth century, at Pratolino and Saint-Germain-en-Laye, for example. When Philip the Good was negotiating with the English on behalf of his cousin Louis XI, the Burgundian chronicler Chastellain[11] reported that the ambassadors were taken to the park, 'where there was one of the most beautiful fountains ever seen'. The chief negotiators had their table in a summerhouse which could be turned on wheels to face in any direction. And there were other marvels in the park, like the giant sundial of painted lead, supported by six savages and six seated lions. Since the style and needle was crowned with a ball and cross, it sounds as if it was more like an obelisk. If diplomacy was not likely to be advanced by dousing and bags of flour, we may at least suppose that some minion was submitted to these indignities for the amusement of the principals.

It has been suggested that books made for Duke Philip in the studio of Loyset Liédet, who was a native of Hesdin, represent the park; even a style of landscape gardening.[12]
Orpheus sitting on a turf-and-wattle seat in the stories from 6
Ovid by Christine de Pisan,[13] might be the duke himself
viewing the animals of his menagerie. The fountain of 7
Narcissus has a literary pedigree at least back to *Le Roman de la Rose* although doubtless based on an original. But the probability is that the roundness of the bushes, the neatness of the trees and the straightness of the avenues in the story of Pyramus and Thisbe, owe more to artistic convention than to topiary.

A copy of Crescenzi's book, probably made at Bruges about 1473,[14] has a picture of Charles V receiving a translation, and represents the scene a hundred years after the event. The memory of his own gardens at the palace of Saint Pol in Paris, is preserved in street names such as 'rue des Jardins', 'du Parc-Royal', 'des Rosiers', 'du Beautrellis', 'de la Cerisaie', 'des Lions'. The records of the gardens were studied by the seventeenth-century lawyer, Henri Sauval, and published in his *Histoire et Recherches des Antiquités de la Ville*

8 Enclosed garden in a castle precinct, from the *Roman de Renaud de Montauban*, 1468–70. Note the plants in majolica containers.

de Paris in 1724. The gardens were a complex of enclosures covering many acres, and including orchards and vineyards. Some were surrounded by the apartments of the palace or by galleries supported on stone pillars. The gallery of the queen's apartment was painted to represent a long terrace overlooking woods, the branches of the trees reaching up into the vault which was painted blue and white to represent the sky in daytime. Other gardens were surrounded by *tonnelles* made of trellis covered with vine, hop or some other climbing plant, with elaborate pavilions also made of trellis at each corner.

> The pavilions were round or square, or one or the other alternately; within, all round, were turf seats, raised on footrests of similar construction: the trellises surrounding them were crenellated or finished in fleurs-de-lis: the battlements ended in tabernacles, roughly like a clock-tower crowned with a big apple, and from which sprang a weathervane painted with the arms of France. As for the diamond shapes of the ordinary trellis, they were filled with fleurs-de-lis, and sometimes folded so that they represented the arms of France, those of the royal children and the princes of the blood.
>
> In the middle of the garden, often instead of an open courtyard [*préau*], there was a fountain in a basin of stone or marble, which spurted water through the mouth of a lion, or some other wild beast.
>
> (Sauval II, p. 283)

The ornamental planting of a garden frequently included a labyrinth or Maison de Dédalus, like that in the neighbouring garden of the Hôtel des Tournelles, which was uprooted by John, Duke of Bedford, when he was regent of France in 1431, in order to plant 5913 elms.[15] But the aesthetic appeal of all medieval gardens was incidental to their function of providing fruit, vegetables and medicinal herbs. Within the castle precincts they were carefully restricted, each garden being surrounded by a low fence and frequently consisting only of a patch of grass with a raised turf seat on a brick base such as often occur in the illustrations of the time. This practice persisted well into the sixteenth century, with
flowering shrubs or rare flowers placed about in majolica 8
containers. Larger gardens outside the castle walls, often planted with fruit trees and hence called *vergers*, were also walled. Because they were pleasant places in which to sit, many were provided with a summerhouse or something more elaborate, as appears in the illustrations to the month of April in the famous Book of Hours made for Jean, Duc de Berry, by Pol de Limbourg about 1416, with the duke's château of Dourdan on the banks of the Orge in the background. A similar walled garden is shown in *Le Livre des*
Echecs Amoureux,[16] a book deriving closely from *Le Roman de* 1
la Rose, in which the garden is shown divided into the familiar square or rectangular plots, with the taller flowers against the wall. A garden with another substantial pavilion is illustrated in *L'Instruction d'un Jeune Prince*,[17] made for

9 The author of *L'Instruction d'un Jeune Prince*, *c.* 1470, offers his work to his patron in a garden with a pavilion.

Charles, duke of Burgundy, in 1470. It shows the author
9 offering his work to the young prince. The garden has raised beds and a plant trained round a circular frame growing in one of those majolica containers. It is open to the landscape on one side, which gives it another dimension.

Provence-Anjou: the gardens of 'Le Roi René'

René, the last independent duke of Anjou,[18] was a compulsive builder, and in his later years addicted to gardens. A younger son of Louis II of Anjou, he obtained the title of the duchy of Bar through the offices of his redoubtable mother, Yolande. Unfortunately the power of Burgundy supported another claimant, and in the subsequent conflict René was defeated and spent four uncomfortable years as a prisoner in Dijon. While still in captivity he became duke of Anjou and Provence through the death of his elder brother; and three months later he inherited the kingdom of Naples and Sicily from Queen Jeanne II. He was released in 1437, for a ransom which crippled his finances for the rest of his life. He was equally unsuccessful in sustaining his title to Naples; and, after being forced to leave in 1441, spent most of the remainder of his life in Anjou or Provence although he continued to style himself king of Jerusalem, Naples and Sicily, and hence was known as 'le Roi René'. After 1442 his chief residences were at Angers and Aix-en-Provence; and until he finally settled in Provence in 1471 he divided his time between them. Anjou had suffered badly during the English wars, and had been besieged as late as 1443. René did much to assist the revival of agriculture, and to restore the economy, interceding with his brother-in-law, Charles VII, to allow some tax relief to his hard-pressed subjects. Provence had been spared these privations. It was, moreover, a cultural centre of some importance due to the establishment of the papal court at Avignon, with the resulting traffic between France and Italy.

The chronicler Bourdigné credits René with the introduction of the mulberry to the south of France, and the naturalization in Anjou of roses from Provence. He was particularly interested in viticulture, acclimatizing muscat vines brought back from southern Italy, and filling the nurseries of Lorraine with stock from the Loire. References to his gardens in Anjou occur frequently in letters and accounts after 1450;[19] and as the court moved from place to place his people received instructions to get them ready. The ducal house at Angers was in the western corner of the great thirteenth-century citadel, with its seventeen towers, built by Saint Louis on a rock overlooking the Maine. One garden
10 certainly occupied the area southwest of what is now called the Logis Royal; the others might have been outside the walls; or, if inside, to the north of the *logis* where there is a gallery said to have been built by René adjoining the chapel.[20] Despite the view of René's nineteenth-century biographer, Lecoy de la Marche, that the garden had something of 'the natural and picturesque appearance of modern *jardins anglais*',[21] the evidence is that they did not differ much from those shown in miniature paintings of the time, with small fenced enclosures, square or round; raked walks; trellised arbours or *tonnelles* covered with vine, rose or other creepers; and turf seats. Indeed, with all the castle services, there would have been no space for an extensive pleasure garden within the precincts. But René had other gardens in the neighbourhood. He made one at Chanzé on a rocky outcrop, about 90 metres (280 *pieds*) long and varying from 10 to 30
metres (30 to 85 *pieds*) wide, jutting into the Maine. He 11
acquired vineyards, gardens and houses adjoining it in 1452;[22] and in 1453 built a small lodge with a hall, gallery and rooms for his daughters and their attendants. He used it as a retreat, and established a religious community there, with a hermitage in imitation of the grotto of Sainte Baume in

10 Site of René of Anjou's garden within the citadel of Angers, in the Cour des Seigneurs.

Provence; hence the place became known as La Baumette. It later had the distinction of receiving Rabelais as a novice.[23] There is no doubt that the chief attraction for René was the site, where the river makes a wide turn, with views over the meadows, and up to the castle of Angers in the northeast.

René also had manors at Ponts-de-Cé, La Reculée, Rivettes and, 20 kilometres away, La Menitré. The Ponts-de-Cé bridges the Loire where it divides into three streams south of Angers. The château is on the Isle de Saint Aubin, commanding the crossing. In 1454,[24] with the other work done in preparation for René's return to Anjou for his second marriage to Jeanne de Laval, a contract was made for repairing the big garden of the castle and for making another small garden near the entrance.[25] There was to be a large *préau*, and another one with a pavilion, *tonnelles* and aviaries. Roses were to be planted and *accoudoirs* made, those wooden railings surrounding the planted areas which are shown in most pictures of the time. Between his infrequent visits things evidently were neglected; five years later, when he was back in Provence, he was told the hedges were broken down so that the pigs had got in and spoiled everything. He therefore ordered the whole area to be walled; and at the same time he ordered a little building, with a fireplace and a lattice window looking down on the bridge, so that he could eat there when he felt inclined.[26] 'Try to find some money,' he wrote to his treasurer, 'for otherwise the gardens could all go to ruin, which will be a pity.'[27]

About 40 kilometres east of Angers was the old castle of Baugé, ruined during the English wars but repaired by René's mother, Yolande, in 1430. René made considerable restorations in 1455; and in 1465 he bought four adjoining gardens. Even after he had left Angers for good, he saw to its upkeep. Perrinet de Vainucourt, who is described as 'fruitier et concierge du chastel', was paid to feed the birds and remake the *dédalus* in 1477,[28] attentions which support a story of René's predilection for the place. But in fact he seems to have favoured it as a residence only in the late 1460s, and then for short periods. He finally took his leave of it in the autumn of 1471.

The greater part of René's time in Provence was spent in his residence at Aix, especially during the last years of his life from 1472 to 1480. Here he built a lodge with a variety of comfortably furnished rooms, and he preferred to live there, surrounded by his flowers and trees, rather than in the old castle. Many communications are addressed from 'Jardin d'Aix', 'Verger d'Aix', or 'Bastide d'Aix', rather than just

11 The hermitage called 'La Baumette', founded by René of Anjou in a picturesque bend of the Maine (1453), and adorned by him with gardens and vineyards. This drawing is of 1696.

Aix. Right up to his last days he was improving it, as entries in his accounts testify. Thus, in 1478 and 1479 Nicolas, sometimes called 'du jardrin', sometimes Gienot, was paid as much as a hundred florins for work, 'en la grant gallerie que le roy fait faire en sa bastide près Aix, le long du jardrin,' or 'ladite gallerie, qui regarde sur le jeu de paume'.[29]

The Abbé Arnaud d'Agnel suggests that the old king must have had this great gallery built as much to watch tennis in comfort as to be able to look at his garden when the weather was bad. From the sums of money mentioned we can suppose it to have been a fine piece of work, truly deserving the epithet 'grant'. The abbé also notes that the Bastide d'Aix was beside the River Arc, a little distance from the castle which was destroyed in 1786. He also dismisses as a legend rather than history the tradition of René's experiments in horticulture. René's early biographers[30] say that the garden of Aix contained many varieties of pinks, roses, nutmeg trees and other plants which he is credited with propagating; but only one item in the accounts refers to ornamental flowers, when 3 florins 10 gros were paid for the purchase of *giroflies et graines*. At Gardanne south of Aix, which he acquired in 1454, he replaced the old castle on a hill with a house more conveniently situated. It was called 'La Maison du Verger', and was built near a stream on the edge of the town. Steps were made to the top of a hill called Captivel so that he could watch the departure of the hunt.[31] Captivel is a flat-topped ridge, now largely built over, in the centre of the present town, and reached by narrow streets of steps. From the top there are views all round over a landscape full of incident and variety. But despite the attachment which René is said by some writers to have had for Gardanne he does not seem to have stayed there for long at any time, and he was inclined to visit it at short notice. In July 1474[32] his bailiff complained that he had only three days to prepare the place for the king, queen and their court, together with their son, the duke of Calabria, who had never been there. The gardens were in a bad state because he had to attend to the harvest, the vines and other matters. In the end they only stayed one night. On another occasion René had all the furniture moved from Gardanne to Aix in order to accommodate a party of lords and ladies on the spur of the moment.[33]

René was unquestionably interested in practical horticultural and pastoral pursuits. Not only did he encourage the cultivation of traditional crops, but he introduced new ones. Unfortunately the profits were thin; the expenses of the vineyards regularly exceeded the receipts, and staffing was lavish. The royal flock was attended by ten shepherds dressed in liveries of red and white embroidered with his arms. Although heavily in debt he continued to indulge his taste for building and making pleasure gardens up to his death in 1480. But while none of them have survived, his reputation lives in literary works in which pastoral themes and landscape play an important part. His strong aesthetic sense was first expressed in organizing tournaments and fêtes, in the details of which he took a personal interest. The last and most famous was *Le Pas de la Bergère*, at Tarascon in 1449. Unlike the usual chivalrous displays this had a pastoral theme. The victors received their prizes from Isabeau de Lenoncourt in the guise of a shepherdess; while many of the knights themselves were dressed in shepherd's garments. Following the death of his wife, Isabelle de Lorraine, in 1453 René married Jeanne de Laval who was twenty-one. *Regnault et Jeanneton* is the story of their courtship thinly disguised as a pastoral idyll. His book, *Le Mortifiement de Vaine Plaisance*,[34] is the story of the penitent soul tormented by the heart given to idle enjoyment. Fear and Repentence seize the heart and deliver it to Supreme Love, True Hope and Firm Faith (*Souveraine Amour, Vraye Esperance, Ferme Foy*), who nail it to the Cross in order to unite it for ever with the passion of its Saviour; while Divine Grace (*Grace Divine*) gives it the final thrust to kill earthly desire for ever. One of the illustrations shows this scene taking place in a garden, as a symbol of earthly pleasure. 12

12 In René's *Le Mortifiement de Vaine Plaisance*, the medieval walled garden is used as a symbol of earthly pleasure in an allegory of repentence: Love, Hope and Faith nail the penitent heart to the Cross of Christ.

René's most celebrated work is *Le Livre du Cueur d'Amour Espris*, a treatise on profane love in the manner of *Le Roman de la Rose*, but of mixed prose and verse. A copy now in Vienna[35] has some of the most perfect miniature paintings of the period, notable not only for their landscape settings, but for the poetic moods which they evoke. It is interesting to find united in a man of his time a sensitivity to mood in landscape painting and a love of gardening, a combination more often associated with patrons of the eighteenth century. It is evidence at least that the tradition is much older.

2

The early-Renaissance background

Literary sources: 'Hypnerotomachia Poliphili'

THE MEDIEVAL AND RENAISSANCE traditions had already met in René of Anjou's lifetime. We have only to be reminded that the future Julius II, creator of the Vatican Belvedere Court, was known to him as Giuliano della Rovere, bishop of Carpentras and later of Avignon. It is generally realized that what we call 'the Renaissance' was not a sudden change in the climate of thought, but a process already advanced when René's contemporary, Leone Battista Alberti, was born. The Classical themes of the pictures in books such as *Recueil des histoires de Troye*, made for Philip, duke of Burgundy, in
14 1464, are combined with Gothic forms. The fountain in 'The Judgment of Paris' is a Gothic ancestor of the well-known fountain of the Three Graces, which appears in its
15 Renaissance dress in Colonna's *Hypnerotomachia Poliphili*, written at the same time, although not printed until 1499.
16 The Roman Venus presides over an enclosed garden, which is
17 also a *hortus deliciarum*. But despite obvious affinities with *Le Roman de la Rose*, *Hypnerotomachia* is a very different book. It may belong in the same allegorical tradition – Poliphilus seeks his love in a dream, and finds consolation in a garden setting – but there the resemblance ends. *Hypnerotomachia* is a story of the discovery of the antique world, from the huge unintelligible fragments in the landscape where Poliphilus first wanders, to the monuments, inscriptions, triumphs, legends and rituals revealed to him by Polia after he has chosen to enter the door marked 'EROTOTROPHOS'. The book is therefore a major source of the romantic cult of Classical remains; the world discovered and recorded by the early Renaissance antiquaries.

Hypnerotomachia is the richest Renaissance source of garden imagery. The gardens Colonna describes can hardly be thought to resemble actual places, so information about garden design in Italy in the latter part of the Quattrocento has to be gleaned from a mass of fantasy, allegory and literary precedents. His main descriptions are those of the gardens of the palace of Queen Eleuterilyda, where Poliphilus is received at the beginning of his quest; and those of the island of Cythera, where the love of Poliphilus and Polia is ritually consummated in the Temple of Venus at its centre. The palace of Queen Eleuterilyda is approached by a drive lined with cypress trees, leading to a courtyard surrounded on three sides by a hedge of orange and lemon, cut to form an arched entrance. In the centre is the fountain with the statue of the Three Graces. On either side of the drive are parterres made of blue periwinkles. Gardens on the other side are fantasy, being made with glass and silk; or rather, they perhaps describe some elaborate artefact in miniature or embroidery. Even so they probably reveal their sources in actual gardens: of beds in which cypress and box trees are planted alternately; an enclosure consisting of an arcade with pillars entwined with convolvulus; a level parterre laid out in compartments of knots.[1] In another garden the parterre, instead of being laid out in knots, was a piece of green velvet like a fine lawn in April; and, in the middle, a bower of trellis covered with simulated roses 'so like nature that they might be judged more beautiful than the real ones'. All round the insides were seats of red jasper; and the floor was a single piece of yellow jasper, so clear and polished that the whole garden could be seen reflected in it. While these last words are almost exactly those Lorris uses of the fountain of Narcissus in *Le Roman de la Rose*, Colonna's garden is more than a literary convention. The laying out of beds in figured patterns is evidently of ancient origin; although Colonna is the first Renaissance writer to give details, we may suppose he spoke from experience. We recognize the rectangular compartments, the trees in tubs, the piece of fine turf, the trellis arbours, as familiar features of fifteenth-century gardens. So too is the labyrinth which stands between two of Queen 18
Eleuterilyda's gardens, although its form surpasses probability, and is possibly derived from another fictitous labyrinth described by Colonna's contemporary, Antonio Averlino (known as Filarete) in his *Trattato di Architectura* written between 1460 and 1464. Both have seven circuits formed by watercourses; but Filarete's is square and Colonna's circular. And whereas Filarete offers no symbolic interpretation, Colonna makes the allegory explicit; seven circuits are the seven ages of man. At the beginning of each circuit stands a tower where a choice has to be made. Some circuits are more difficult than others; but progress is in one direction only, towards the central tower where dwells a

13 Lorenzo di Credi places the *Annunciation* in a loggia open to the landscape.

14, 15 The theme of the Three Graces in a medieval and Renaissance setting. In the *Recueil des histoires de Troyes* (above) made for Philip, Duke of Burgundy in 1464, the classical scene of the Judgement of Paris includes a fountain in the Gothic style. Colonna's *Hypnerotomachia Poliphili*, 1499 (right) shows the Three Graces in a Renaissance style fountain.

16, 17 The garden of Venus in the *Hypnerotomachia* is clearly a profane version of the Virgin's *hortus conclusus*, a parallel made explicit in the scene of the worship of Venus and her child (above, from the original Italian edition of 1499). Another engraving (right, from the French edition of 1546) shows the garden again as a symbol of earthly pleasures.

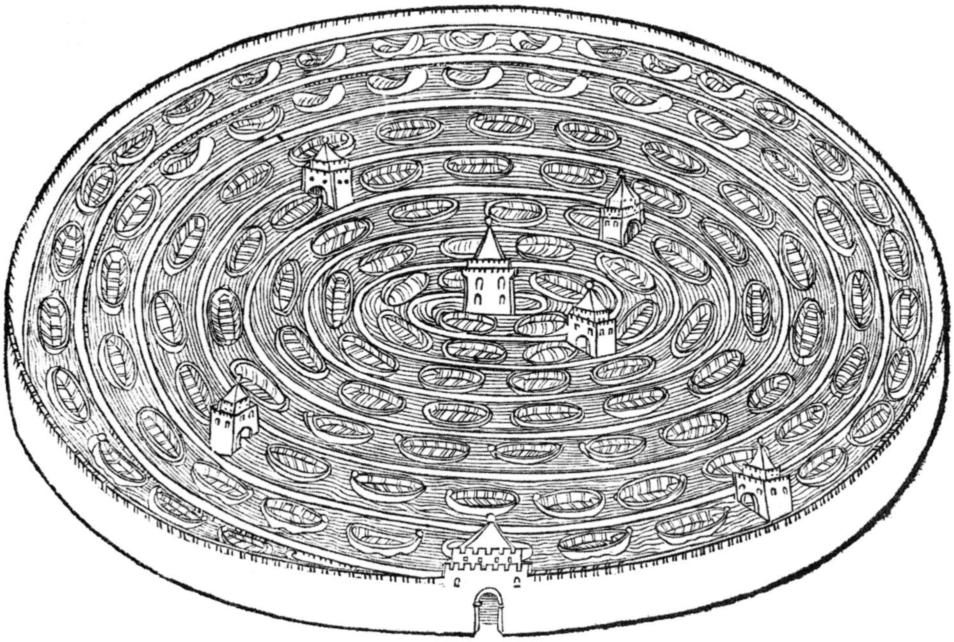

18 Labyrinth from the French *Songe de Poliphile*, 1546. The seven circular watercourses, each with a tower at the beginning, represent the seven ages of man.

19 The fourth garden of Queen Eleuterilyda (*Songe de Poliphile*, 1546), made up of mystical Hermetic elements – the circle, the square and the triangle – standing for celestial harmony.

monster in whose mouth all those who enter the maze inevitably fall. Indeed he may devour them at the entrance, or swallow them in any of the revolutions.[2]

The philosophic overtones are more originally displayed
19 in the fourth garden, for which an explanation can only be found in the Hermetic mysticism of the times. The impression given is of a place of great antiquity. It is enclosed by a circular arcade of a hundred arches made of bricks, but so thickly covered with ivy that these cannot be seen. In every arch is an altar of porphyry bearing the statue of a nymph in gold, each with a different dress and posture. All face inwards towards a golden pyramid, triangular, supported on the backs of three sphinxes. These in turn stand on a base consisting of a square pedestal, a circular plinth and a triangle. As Logistica, his guide, explains to Poliphilus: 'in these three figures, the square, the circle and the triangle, celestial harmony consists'.

The most detailed passages concerning gardens are reserved for the island of Cythera, to which the lovers are taken in Cupid's barque, and in whose amphitheatre the final rituals are performed. Cythera is at first reminiscent of other literary paradises: orchards and groves planted with fruitful and fragrant trees, watered by springs, with all manner of tricks and surprises to make people laugh. There are no rocks or hills; no gloomy shades, or paths without the song of birds; no undue wind, heat, frost or fog; but a climate always conducive to the riches nature can produce, an abode of the gods and the blessed spirits. What distinguishes it from its precedents is the emphasis on architectural embellishment and proportion. There is also so much circumstantial detail that we must assume some first-hand experience on Colonna's part, unless we are to credit him with a high degree of originality. There are, after all, not only descriptions but a wealth of illustration. We know from Crescenzi and other writers that topiary was an ancient art;
and we can see it represented in paintings by Mantegna and 20
other contemporaries of Colonna. We may also suppose that intricate parterres were not purely his invention and that by 1467 the planting of such designs was already a highly developed art.

20 Renaissance topiary in an allegorical setting: Mantegna's *Wisdom overcoming the Vices*.

21 Arcade in the gardens of Queen Eleuterilyda, one of the illustrations added to the French version of *Le Songe de Poliphile* in 1546.

22 Temple colonnade on the island of Cythera, with topiary between the columns, from *Le Songe de Poliphile*, 1546.

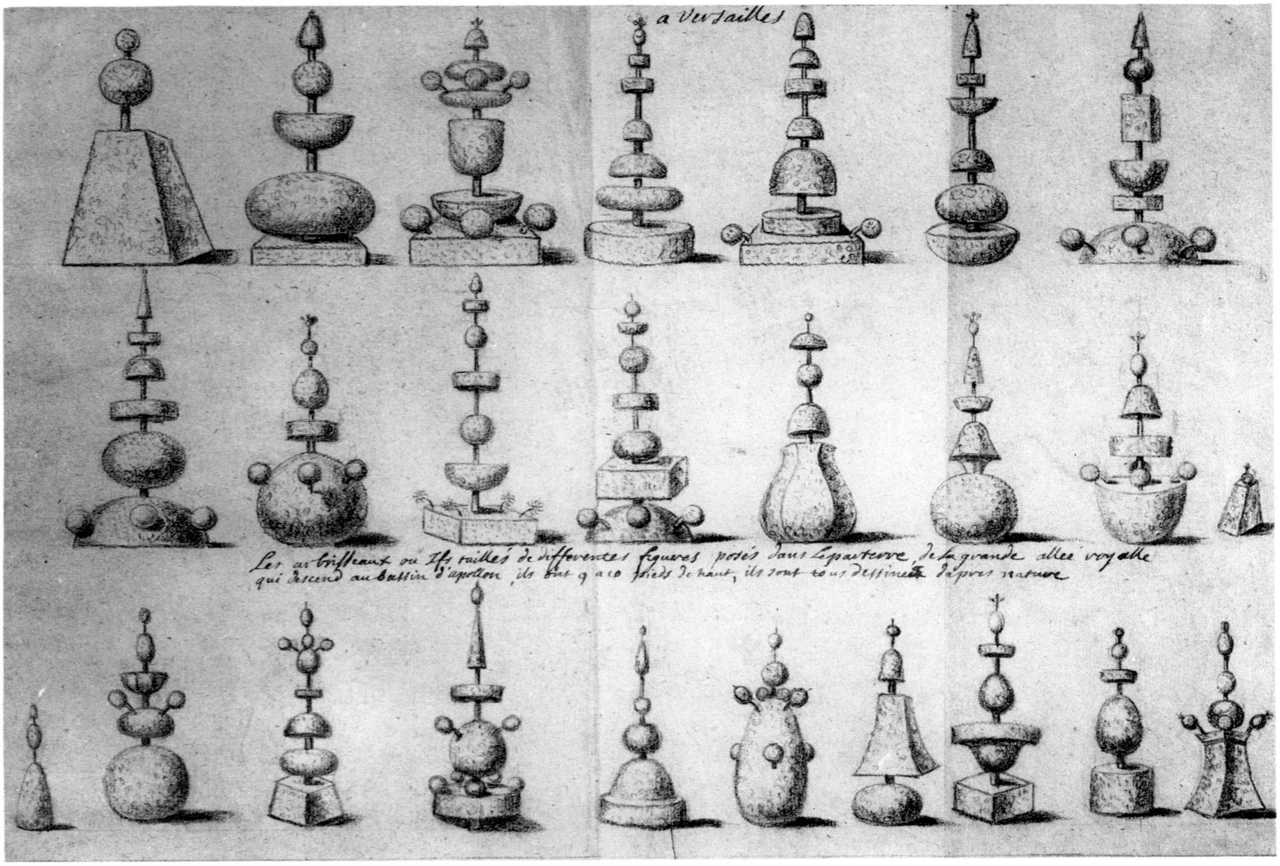

23 Seventeenth-century designs for topiary at Versailles. Compare with topiary between the columns in ill. 22.

When Jean Martin published the French version in 1546,[3] the illustrations were redrawn and others added, mostly to
21 enlarge on the architectural features of the garden. Its popularity lasted well into the seventeenth century, stimulating the fashion for elaborate artifice in topiary and intricate parterres. It was known to Bernard Palissy; and the mannered fountain designs of Du Cerceau probably owe something to its inspiration. A more direct comparison may be made between the description of a hedge surrounding the second terrace at Cythera, cut into shapes representing towers, ships and soldiers fighting, huntsmen and hounds and so on, and the drawing by Israel Silvestre of a somewhat similar feature at the château of Marimont-en-Hainaut; or the sculpture crowning the arcaded court at Raray (Oise).
22 The elegant circular arcades and peristyles have no parallel in any sixteenth-century French gardens; although Blunt
23 suggests that they may have inspired Hardouin-Mansart's
24 colonnade at Versailles over a hundred years later.[4] The later popularity of *Le Songe de Poliphile* would undoubtedly have reinforced a general attitude to the laying out of grounds. But it would probably be mistaken to regard *Hypnerotomachia* as a point of departure. In the arts particularly, theory may modify practice but rarely precedes it. One of the reasons why books like Colonna's loom so large in historical perspective is that so little evidence of the ephemeral art of gardening survives. In the circumstances, our knowledge of Italian gardens of the Quattrocento comes from a few literary sources, and from painting, mostly of the latter part of the century.

As Luigi Dami says, the sentimental and idyllic views of nature which flow from some of the early literary expressions, where everything is held in a moment of transitory perfection, are abstractions, unnatural and a little ridiculous.[5] Boccaccio's gardens, coming between those of *Le Roman de la Rose* and *Hypnerotomachia Poliphili*, share something of their unreality. The garden described in the introduction to the third day of the *Decameron* is an enclosed garden bordered and traversed by straight walks covered with trellis of vine, the fountain at its centre. The water in channels round the lawn slides 'down towards the plain', suggesting a garden on a hill with views over the surrounding countryside. Paintings show gardens viewed through loggias. Filippino Lippi's *Annunciation* has a walled
garden with regular parterres. Lorenzo di Credi's *Annun-* 13
ciation of the early sixteenth century has a loggia with a vista stretching to the horizon, and trees and shrubs growing naturally; quite a new sense of openness.

24 Hardouin-Mansart's colonnade at Versailles, possibly inspired by the *Hypnerotomachia Poliphili*.

Renaissance theory: Alberti

Behind Colonna's architectural fantasies and his obsession with measurement lay Renaissance theories of the arts. For the laying out of grounds the most significant was the publication of Alberti's *De re Aedificatoria*,[6] not for the little he had to say on gardens so much as for the implication of the famous dictum on the classical concept of beauty as congruity, 'the harmony of all the parts, in whatsoever subject it appears, fitted together with such proportion and connection that nothing could be added, diminished, or altered but for the worse.' There were two important aspects of the theory: reference to antiquity and the concept of the natural. The idea that painting and sculpture should represent appearances in a lifelike manner was accepted by the time of Alberti's birth in 1404. This was justified in theory by what was known of the practice of the ancients, and by the concept of art as an imitation of physical things. There was, however, another tradition inherited from the late Roman world, particularly from the neo-Platonic school of Plotinus, which held that appearances corresponded imperfectly to a spiritual reality which lay behind them. According to Plotinus: 'If anyone condemns the arts because they create by way of imitation of nature, we must first observe that natural things themselves are an imitation of something further; and next we must bear in mind that the arts do not simply imitate the visible, but go back to the reasons from which nature comes.'[7]

Parallel with this way of thinking about the arts of painting and sculpture was a method of interpreting literary texts as allegory, so that myths were held to conceal rational and didactic meanings. Early Christian exegetists found moral and mystical truths behind the concrete imagery of the Bible; thus the enclosed garden of the Song of Songs becomes a symbol for the Church. A spiritual realm lay beyond human understanding, but its nature was hinted at by objects of sense. A hierarchy of values was assumed, from material to spiritual; and a hierarchy of beings from beast to angel, increasingly free from the exigencies of a bodily existence. Hierarchies also extended to the heavenly host, so that while the lower orders of Principalities and Angels were involved in human affairs, the highest, the Seraphim, speculated eternally on the order and providence of God. It followed that the contemplative life was superior to the active, and that those whose activity was purely intellectual were superior to craftsmen who were inevitably involved with matter.

Alberti's theory was concerned with the status of the arts in this context. In *Della Pittura* he affirmed the theory of art as imitation of nature, but he made the definition more precise by his theory of perspective. Whereas, before Alberti, Flemish painters, for instance, created an illusion of depth by capturing the visual appearance of things, diminishing in size as they receded from the eye, Alberti's method made it possible to regulate the sizes of all objects in the picture, and the relative distances between them proportionally, and hence, it was thought, with greater realism. This, of course, has no direct connection with the design of gardens, but it is related to Alberti's main theoretical work in *De re Aedificatoria* in which gardens are specifically included.

A theory which held that the aim of art was to imitate nature could not include architecture if 'imitation' were interpreted as 'copying' a physical object. A building would have to imitate nature in a purely symbolic way. The basis for such a view already existed in the Platonic idea, stated in the *Timaeus*, that the stability of the cosmos was due to the primacy of numbers. The primary bodies out of which the world is composed were conceived of as building materials, 'put together in the perfect geometrical proportions of squares and cubes (1:2:4:8: and 1:3:9:27). . . . According to this composition, the world's body, consisting of the four primary bodies, whose quantities are limited and lead to the most perfect proportions, is in unity and concord with itself and hence will not suffer dissolution from any internal disharmony of its parts; the bond is simply geometrical proportion.'[8] Since geometry was nature's order, beauty was a matter of proportion. It was exemplified in the proportions of the human body, and in the Pythagorean discovery of the mathematical basis of musical intervals. So far as architects were concerned, these were embodied in Classical aesthetic theory by Vitruvius in *De Architectura.* As members of the body corresponded to each other, so should the parts of a building. As the ratios of the intervals in the musical scale represented 'natural' harmony, so should the measurements of parts of a building be in harmonic ratio with one another. Vitruvius's writings had been known and respected at least since the time of Charlemagne. Augustine had sanctified harmonic proportion as the source of all aesthetic perfection; and for this reason music, above all, and after that architecture, were able to give 'intimations of that ultimate harmony which the blessed will enjoy in the world to come'. The theory of harmonic proportions was certainly put into practice by the builders of the Gothic cathedrals in northern France. The builders of the Italian Renaissance gave new life to the theory by returning to the sources; Brunelleschi, in particular, undertaking a methodical study of Roman architectural remains, building up a repertory of Classical forms which he applied in designs governed strictly by the theory of harmonic ratios.

Alberti's close association with Brunelleschi between 1434 and 1436 must therefore be reckoned as one of the most important influences leading to the *De re Aedificatoria*, the first book of its kind since Vitruvius, and a bible of Renaissance architecture. The details of Alberti's theory and his extension of the concept of harmonic proportion are not strictly necessary to a discussion of garden design; the importance lies in the spirit rather than the letter. His theory of beauty is contained partly in the sixth but mainly in the ninth book. It relates particularly to building, but the underlying principle has wider implications, for instance in distinguishing between judgment and taste. Taking beauty in woman as an example, one, he says, may prefer her 'slender and fine-shaped'; another 'plump and fleshy'; and a third 'would neither have her so thin as to seem wasted with sickness, nor so strong and robust as if she were a ploughman in disguise', but 'would have her such a beauty as might be formed by taking from the first what the second might spare'. There may be some hidden reason for such taste, but this would not be a reason to pronounce one more beautiful than the other; for 'the judgment which you make that a thing is beautiful, does not proceed from mere opinion, but from secret argument and discourse implanted in the mind itself.' That is to say, while taste is irrational, judgments proceed from reason. 'Every body', says Alberti, 'consists of certain peculiar parts, of which if you take away any one, or lessen or enlarge it, or remove it to an improper place, that which gave the beauty and grace to this body will at once be lamed and spoiled. There are three things principally of which the whole of what we are looking into consists; the Number [*numerus*], and that which I have called the Finishing [*finitio*], and the Collocation [*collocatio*].' Continuing the analogy with the body, by *numerus* Alberti means the natural preference for even or uneven numbers, such as two eyes, two arms, two legs, but one nose and one mouth. To these he adds other numbers favoured by philosophers, such as seven, being the number of the planets; nine, the spheres of heaven; four, dedicated to the deity, so that solemn oaths were made four times; also, for various reasons, six, eight and ten, the latter considered by Aristotle the most perfect of all 'because its square is composed of four continued cubes put together'.

Finitio is proportion: the measure of the head, for instance, in relation to the height of the body, or the hand in relation to the arm. Alberti gives more attention to the principles which should govern the proportion of the parts than to either *numerus* or *collocatio*. He adopted the Pythagorean discovery that musical consonances could be determined by the ratio of the length of vibrating strings, and the belief that such ratios represented a 'natural' order extending throughout the cosmos:

> The rule of these proportions is best gathered from those things in which we find nature herself to be most compleat and admirable; and indeed I am every day more and more convinced of the truth of Pythagoras's saying, that nature is sure to act consistently, and with a constant analogy in all her operations: from whence I conclude, that the same numbers, by means of which the agreement of sounds affects our ears with delight, are the very same which please our eyes and our minds. We shall therefore borrow all our rules for the finishing of our proportions, from the musicians, who are the greatest masters of this sort of numbers, and from those particular things wherein nature shows herself most excellent and compleat.
>
> (*De re Aedificatoria* IX, 5, trans. Leoni, 1726)

Collocatio is the arrangement of the parts, so that nothing can be differently placed without injuring the whole. As Alberti says, it is 'much easier to conceive where it is ill-done, than it is to lay down exact rules for the doing it. . . . The very smallest parts . . . of the work, if they are set in their right places, add to the beauty of the whole; if they are placed in mean or improper situations, though excellent in themselves, they become mean.' Thus in nature, a man with one foot bigger than the other appears deformed. Indeed it is clear in what follows that, for Alberti, *collocatio* is associated with the symmetry of the body; and this part of his theory is of direct relevance to the development of garden design.

> So agreeable it is to nature, that members of the right side should exactly answer the left: wherefore the very first thing we are to take care of must be, that every part, even the most inconsiderable, lie duly to the level and plumb-line, and be disposed with an exact correspondence as to the Number, Form and Appearance; so that the right may answer to the left, the high to the low, the similar to the similar, so as to form a correspondent ornament in that body whereof they are parts. Even statues, pictures, or any other ornaments of that sort with which we embellish our work, must be so disposed as to seem to have sprung up naturally in their properest places, and to be twins.
>
> (IX, 7)

One other thing is necessary to perfection, 'for by nature we desire things perfect', says Alberti. This he calls Congruity (*concinnitas*). It is the quality which unites *numerus*, *finitio* and *collocatio* so that nothing can be added or taken away, decreased or enlarged, or differently placed without detracting from the beauty and grace of the whole. *Concinnitas* amounts to a law of beauty which is apprehended by reason. It 'runs through every Part and Action of Man's Life, and every Production of Nature herself, which are all directed by the Law of Congruity, nor does Nature study anything more than to make all her works absolute and perfect, which they could never be without this Congruity, since they would want that Consent of the Parts which is so necessary to Perfection.'

The application of such principles was of course most evident in architecture, yet extended to the laying out of grounds insofar as architects were concerned with them. Alberti's views about the arts are related to his general belief that public interest is paramount and that princes and private citizens alike are bound to it. Even the houses of the noblest citizens should not exceed temples and public buildings in splendour. The magnificence of the building may be adapted to the dignity of the owner; indeed it is natural to wish to procure honour for one's country and one's family. But, says Alberti, 'I should rather, in private edifices, that the greatest Men fell rather a little short on Ornament, than they should be condemned for Luxury and Profusion by the more discreet and frugal. Whoever considers the true Nature of ornament in Building will be convinced, that it is not Expence so much that is requisite, as Taste and Contrivance. I think no prudent Man in building his private House should willingly differ too much from his Neighbours, or raise their Envy by his too great Expence and Ostentation.' (IX, 1)

It is in the context of the above views that Alberti's remarks on gardens should be read; for these concern particulars rather than general principles. There are a number of observations throughout the *De re Aedificatoria* which could be taken to relate to gardens in a general sense. For instance the kind of association at which later garden-makers deliberately aimed is recommended by Alberti in his discussion of the numinous, expressed in Book VI,4. He gives many examples of religious custom which add 'greater Air of Dignity and Awefulness to a Place'. Among the adornments are those which nature offers, 'for we frequently meet with Circumstances extreamly noble and surprising, such as Promentories, Rocks, broken Hills vastly high and sharp, Grottoes, Caverns, Springs and the like . . . nor should there be wanting in the Prospect Remains of Antiquity. . . .' And among things commonly done to add to the beauty of the situation he mentions 'Columns, Obelisks and Trees left by great men in order to strike posterity [with] veneration'. He notes, in Book VIII, 2, the associations between gardens and funerary customs in antiquity. 'The Alexandrians, in the time of Strabo the Historian, had Gardens and Inclosures consecrated wholly to the Burial of the Dead. . . . Augustus's sepulchre in Rome was built of marble, shaded with evergreens, and at the top stood his statue. In the island of Tyrina . . . the sepulchre of Erythraea was a great Mound of Earth planted with wild palm trees.' His remarks on chapels, pyramids, columns, towers and incriptions are of particular interest in view of the proliferation of such objects in eighteenth-century landscape gardens. In Leoni's English translation of *De re Aedificatoria* in 1726 we read that the building of 'lofty Towers placed in proper situations . . . afford a most beautiful Prospect'. Indeed, so rich a source is Alberti's book, it is possible to find a precedent for many trends in architectural and garden design in the three hundred years following its publication.

What Alberti has to say specifically on gardens is mainly included in Book IX, 2 and 4, about the adornments of houses. He distinguishes between town houses, where neighbours have to be considered, and houses in the country 'where all the gayest and most licentious Embellishments are allowable'. What he really favours is the country villa near a town, with the advantages of both. Aesthetic considerations weigh more than others in the siting of the house. It should make 'a cheerful Appearance to those that go a little way out of town to take the air. . . . I would have it stand pretty high, but upon so easy an ascent, that it should hardly be perceptible to those that go to it, till they find themselves at the top, and a large prospect opens itself to their view. Nor should there be any want of pleasant Landskips, flowery Meads, open Champains, shady Groves, or limpid Brooks, or clear Streams and Lakes for swimming. . . .' Another advantage of the country is that there is no necessity 'for setting one house upon another', as Alberti puts it, for he abhors changes of level necessitating stairs. Once the guests have entered the house let them 'be in doubt whether they shall for pleasure continue where they are, or pass further to those other beauties which tempt them on. Let them be led from square rooms into round ones, and again from round into square, and so into others of mixed lines, neither all round nor all square; and let the passage into the very innermost appartments be, if possible, without the least ascent or descent, but all be upon one even floor, or at least let the ascents be as easy as they may be.'

It seems clear that Alberti thought of the garden proper as continuing this pattern of a sequence of rooms 'thrown into those figures that are most commended in the platforms of the house, Circles, Semi-circles, and the like, and surrounded with Laurels, Cedars, Junipers with their branches intermixed and twining one into another'. In accordance with his concept of *collocatio*, 'the trees ought to be planted in rows exactly even, and answering to one another exactly in straight lines'. Walks should be terminated by evergreens. Where the sole aim is relaxation, many things are permitted to delight and amuse; porticos to enjoy either sun or shade; vine covered arbours supported on marble columns, as was the custom of the Romans; vases, and even 'ridiculous statues' provided they are not obscene. Gardens should be enriched with rare plants; and among the ancients, gardeners traced their masters' names in box, or sweet smelling herbs, in parterres. 'Our minds are delighted in a particular manner with the pictures of pleasant landskips, of havens, of fishing, hunting, swimming, country sports, of flowery fields and thick groves.' Even pictures of springs, cascades and streams can relieve the fevered mind; and those who cannot sleep, by turning their imagination to the memory of clear waters, 'shall presently be moistened and a pleasant forgetfulness shall creep unto them'. Thus, by implication, the sight and sound of water is an important element in the garden, 'bursting out in different places where least expected'.

Alberti recalls the artificial caverns of the ancients, with walls lined with 'pumice', and sometimes daubed with green wax in imitation of mossy slime. He saw one, it is not known where, 'with a clear spring of water falling from it, and walls composed of various sorts of sea-shells, lying roughly together, some reversed, some with their mouths outwards, their colours being so artfully blended as to form a very beautiful variety.' The first recorded use of tufa is by Giulio Romano at the Palazzo del Tè at Mantua, between 1526 and 1534. One of the earliest descriptions of a Renaissance grotto is contained in a letter written in 1538, concerning Cardinal Giovanni Gaddi's garden in Rome.[9] Many of Alberti's ideas on gardens seem to come from Classical texts such as the younger Pliny's descriptions of his villas, paraphrased, modified and interspersed with observations of his own. Like Pliny he recommends box for hedges where it is sheltered from the wind and the salt spray of the sea; and warns against its use in exposed places. For Pliny's plane trees draped with ivy, Alberti says 'nor let there be wanting cypress trees clothed with ivy'.

Perhaps the most original Quattrocento contribution to garden design is Alberti's concept of the garden as similar in plan to a house, an ordered series of connected rooms about an axis. The Italian garden has, in general, retained this human scale of a place to live in out of doors; unlike the vast expanses covered by French gardens, much of which could only have been used to look upon. There may be a connection with the scale of French and Italian landscapes; the difference between the Loire and the Tiber. However, at the time of which we write, there was no question of gardens of great size in either country. It is clear from his general observations on the siting of a villa, that Alberti fully appreciated the pleasures of the countryside and what we might call the 'natural' landscape. While regularity is justified by natural principles, in another sense concepts of art and nature are opposed. Nature is related to garden design in two special senses: first, because of the materials with which the gardens are made; second, because a garden stands in direct relation to what surrounds it. The very idea of a garden presupposes nature controlled in some degree by art. The house envisaged by Alberti would be set in fields rather than the wilderness, despite the natural adornments he advocates: rocks, hills, caverns, springs, and the like. Nevertheless, Venus and Priapus were never far from the Latin soul; Italy was, and is, peopled with local deities of woods, streams and caves. And until the power of falling water was turned to modern uses, generations of Italians built their villas within earshot of the thundering, spray-filled gorge at Tivoli. The sophisticated view of life in the country as a contrast to the pressures of life in the city and the court received ultimate expression in the idea of Arcady; a community of shepherds living and behaving in a natural way with the minimum of artifice. Sannazaro's *Arcadia*,[10] written in the fifteenth century, contrasts the pleasures of the 'natural' landscape with princely gardens: 'Great spreading trees produced by nature on the high mountains are more agreeable to the beholder than plants carefully tended by experienced gardeners in gardens of delight . . . A spring edged with greenery and coming naturally from the living rock is as cheerful a sight as a fountain of variegated and many-coloured marble.'

The arcadian idea was kept alive by successive dramatic and literary works such as Tasso's *Aminta*, Guarini's *Il Pastor Fido* and D'Urfé's *Astrée*. There is a continuity in courtly masquerade which links René of Anjou's *Le Pas de la Bergère* at Tarascon in 1499 with Marie Antoinette's Hameau at Trianon and her dairy at Rambouillet. The close proximity of the forest was one of the main attractions of Fontainebleau. The development of French garden design in the direction of greater regularity was not due to the lack of an alternative tradition.

Direct influences: Italian gardens of the later fifteenth century

Hypnerotomachia and Alberti's *De re Aedificatoria* did not become widely known in France until Martin's translations in 1546 and 1553 respectively. Meanwhile, Frenchmen had direct experience of Italian culture through embassies, trade and the invasions launched from time to time in support of claims to Italian titles, from the thirteenth century, until François I's defeat at Pavia in 1525 put an end to them. By the end of the fifteenth century France had acquired an administrative and territorial unity almost commensurate with the modern state. The duchies of Burgundy and Anjou had been absorbed; only Navarre and Brittany remained independent. The latter came under the crown in 1488 by the marriage of Anne de Bretagne to Charles VIII. Italy, on the other hand, was a land whose people shared a common language and some consciousness of an imperial past; but politically it was a collection of diffuse and warring entities, the chief of which were the Venetian and the Florentine republics, the Papal States, the kingdom of Naples and Sicily, and the duchy of Milan. Smaller states dependant on one or other of them included the marquisate of Mantua and the duchy of Ferrara.

Among leading patrons of the new learning were the popes and cardinals in Rome and the Medici family in Florence. These centres exerted a continuing influence in France. Rome, of course, was the source of the cult of antiquity, whose remains were everywhere in evidence, and increasingly revealed as Roman sites were developed to make gardens or *vigne* for wealthy churchmen. Pope Pius II (Aeneas Silvius Piccolomini) was deeply susceptible to the nostalgia of ruins. Many years before Colonna's book was published, he recorded in his *Commentaries* how he explored the shores of lake Nemi; and he was one of the first to investigate the remains of Hadrian's Tibur. 'Walls once hung with the rich tapestries and cloth of gold are now clothed with ivy; thorns and brambles usurp the seats of purple-robed tribunes, sumptuous dwelling places of queens have become the abode of serpents.'

Between 1459 and 1462 Pius rebuilt his native village of Corsignano, putting into practice ideas of planning which were being expressed in writing by Alberti and Filarete. He called the new town 'Pienza'. Incorporated in the plan was the Palazzo Piccolomini built round a courtyard, with a small square garden beyond, overlooked by a three-tiered loggia. The level area of the garden is built up by terrace walls against the hillside, with spectacular views of the wild Val d'Orcia. While the site of Corsignano, like many Italian hill towns, was originally defensive, Pius's decision to develop it was evidently governed by his appreciation of the magnificent view and its aesthetic possibilities. In such situations massive walls were necessary to create a level site; but it was probably the Italian example that led the French to choose places to make massive terrace gardens, when the terrain provided more opportunities for sites on the level. Even at the end of the sixteenth century, Montaigne, observing the gardens of the cardinals in Rome, remarked how hilly, deformed and irregular sites had been transformed by art into pleasure gardens of uncommon beauty, taking advantage of diversity to give a charm impossible to imitate on the level sites of France.[11] Pius's contemporary, René of Anjou, may well have been stimulated to make gardens where he did through his experience in Italy.

The architect of Pienza was Bernardo Rossellino, a Florentine who worked with Alberti in Rome for Pope Nicolas V between 1450 and 1457. The axial arrangement of entrance, courtyard, loggia and garden, culminating in the view over the landscape, represented the ideas which Alberti was expressing. No gardens are attributed to Alberti himself, although the Rucellai garden,[12] described in Giovanni Rucellai's *Il Zibaldoni Quaresimale* has been thought to owe something to his inspiration. The garden no longer exists; and the account of it gives only a fragmentary picture. Despite this, the main feature of the design is apparent. A fine barrel-shaped pergola made of oak, a hundred yards (braccia) long and eight wide, on the axis of the house, is extended to the Arno by an avenue of the same width and six hundred yards long. The writer describes how this vista stretches from the centre of the four doors leading into the garden, so that when he is seated at table he can see the boats passing on the river. It is not clear how other parts of the garden relate to this axis. There is a gate between the pergola and the avenue; and 'at the head of the pergola' another door leading to a very pleasant lawn, surrounded by walls, with box trees cut into various shapes: giants, centaurs, steps and vases. One large box tree is cut into fifteen stages one above the other (as in Leonardo's *Annunciation*). Elsewhere the garden is said to be enclosed by a hedge four hundred yards long, with seats in it shaded by laurel; and along the edge 'a fine path which is always swept'. The hedge is varied with trees and shrubs which are a pleasure to those who walk along it. Within this enclosed area are a rose-garden and an exedra of clipped laurel, with seats round it, and a carved stone feature on a pedestal in the middle. Pius's view of the Val d'Orcia at Pienza differs from that of Rucellai in that the latter is controlled, extending the axis of the garden into the landscape, and is connected with a new interest in mathematical perspective. It is an open question whether the idea of the Rucellai garden derived from Alberti's approach to and gradual revelation of an architectural theme, or whether they are both expressions of tendencies widely diffused and arising from a variety of causes. One of these was doubtless a revived interest in antiquity. But although new gardens were laid out on old Roman sites, so far as we know at present the tradition had to be recreated from literary sources. Nevertheless, in constructing actual gardens a literary description cannot by itself serve as a model.

Medici villas such as Poggio a Caiano, near Florence, were 25
centres of family life. The gardens were productive and Utens's paintings (although done over a century later) show how small a part was set aside for pleasure. Elsewhere, elaborate rural retreats were made in the latter part of the fifteenth century. Belriguardo, at Ferrara, enlarged by Ercole I, was altogether marvellous. There was a succession of gardens, orchards, forests, woodland, pleasant valleys, and steps which descended on all sides to the river, where there were bathing places in the shade of fine trees. The park was stocked with a great variety of birds, and wild and domestic animals, as much to delight the eye as for the hunter. It was at this place that Renée, daughter of Louis XII, friend of Calvin and protectress of the Reform, spent summers in her early years as duchess of Ferrara. The princely gardens which Sannazaro decried might well have been those of his patron, the king of Naples.

25 Poggio a Caiano, one of several Medici villas near Florence (painting by G. van Utens). Only a small part of the gardens was devoted to pleasure.

The most famous was at Poggio Reale. The site at Doliolum was a few kilometres east of the walls of Naples, on the road to Capua, at the top of a marshy slope leading to the bay. It was the confluence of the Bolla water system, which in antiquity carried the waters of the Sebeto and other streams into Naples. Alfonso II's restoration of the cisterns and canals was described in an allegorical poem, *Lepidina*, composed in 1496 by Giovanni Pontano, in which Doliolum becomes the marriage bed of Parthenope, the legendary queen who founded Naples, and Sebethus. 'Parthenope's bath', writes George Hersey,[13] 'is the cleansing and restoration of the city by these waters. The new fountains [of Poggio Reale] are the nymph's white breasts. . . . the caves and tunnels, and above all Parthenope's black gaze which pulls Sebethus to her, are the conduits.' In the poem the whole landscape becomes an erotic metaphor. Vesuvius's dark breasts are 'covered with violets, and veined with milky streams'. Posillipo's cavern is 'a black mole' on her white body. Capri's flanks are covered with prickly bushes that hide her grottoes. Parthenope herself has a double role, for besides the good queen she was also the siren who tried to lure Ulysses to his death. 'Alas,' says Lepidina's husband, 'lest she should turn that look on me and I be torn from these arms.'

Pontano's poem is an indication of the associations which Poggio Reale evoked. Apart from the cleansing function of the waters, the villa and gardens were built purely for entertainment. It seems generally agreed that the Florentine, Giuliano da Maiano (1432–90), was the architect; and if Lorenzo de' Medici did not have a hand in it, there is evidence of his interest. In August 1487, two models for the design of a palace were sent from Florence to Naples; and after Giuliano da Maiano's death in 1490, Lorenzo recommended Luca Fancelli as architect-in-chief. Pietro Summonte, writing in 1524, said that the eminent humanist and architect Fra Giocondo from Verona was summoned to Naples in 1494. It is suggested that he supervised the work at Poggio Reale; but by 1494 this apparently had stopped. However, Fra Giocondo was in Naples before that. He visited antiquities at Pozzuoli and Gaeta with Sannazaro in 1489 and 1492. Fra Giocondo is of interest because he was among those invited to France by Charles VIII in 1494.

Poggio Reale has long ceased to exist. Reconstructions are based almost entirely on two unscaled sketch plans made in the early sixteenth century by Baldassare Peruzzi. Sebastiano Serlio, who wrote enthusiastically of Poggio Reale in his *Third Book of Architecture*, never went to Naples. He could have heard of it from Peruzzi, with whom he was intimate. But he could have derived his idea from two contemporary descriptions; one by Jean Burchard in 1495; and another by Marcantonio Michiel in 1509. Hersey says he used the latter. In 1488 Giuliano da Maiano was reported working on fountains and columns for the lower gardens. In 1489 a new

26 Poggio Reale, in a reconstruction by Bastiaen Stoopendael, late seventeenth century.

road lined with poplars was under construction from Santa Caterina a Formello to the villa. The French ambassador was entertained there towards the end of 1490, when it may be assumed to have been complete.

An idea of the appearance of the whole can be got from a
26 late-seventeenth-century engraving by Bastiaen Stoopendael, after the canals had been filled in and parts of the garden covered with outbuildings. The site on the hillside was laid out in terraces with views over the Bay of Naples. While the details are uncertain, all are agreed that the house was nearly square, arranged about an arcaded courtyard, having square towers at the corners containing rooms and staircases, a form for which there were precedents going back to Roman times. The upper terrace was occupied by the house and a garden of canals in the form of a cross, with a fountain in the centre; the lower terrace by a square garden of four compartments, adjoining the house, and a large rectangular fishpond. Between these two areas ran a pergola, and at right angles to it an arched loggia opened onto a balustraded platform surrounded on three sides by water. It was here that much entertaining took place, and it is referred to in a contemporary journal as 'a grotto beside a pool'. The effect must have been spectacular, looking down first on the garden and then coming to the loggia along the pergola, with the water below, and beyond all this a huge park sloping away to the sea. Poggio Reale was indeed a *hortus deliciarum*. When Charles VIII and his victorious army arrived in the spring of 1495, they were seduced.

PART II

The French Renaissance Garden

3

Early Italian influence

Historical background, 1494–1515: Charles VIII to the death of Louis XII

When Charles VIII succeeded Louis XI, France had acquired an administrative and territorial unity almost commensurate with the modern state. The duchies of Burgundy and Anjou had been absorbed by the crown. Only Navarre and Brittany remained independent. The latter, on the death of the duke in 1488, was left in the hands of his young and marriageable daughter Anne, on whose choice of husband its allegiance depended. Charles VIII settled the matter by invasion, with a wedding as the price of peace. Despite the manner of the wooing, Anne de Bretagne does not seem to have resented the attachment. In an age of political marriages, she appears to have been well endowed with a sense of what the situation demanded. 'The queen is seventeen', wrote the Venetian envoy, Contarini. 'She is small and thin, and is clearly lame in one foot although she uses pattens; very far-seeing for her age, so that what she has set her mind on she must have at all costs, either by smiles or tears. She is excessively jealous of the king, to the point that, since she has been his wife, few nights have passed when she has not slept with his majesty. She has done this to good purpose for she is eight months pregnant'.[1]

The portrait of Charles from the same source is hardly prepossessing. 'The king of France is twenty-two; small and ill-formed; a plain face, with big white eyes, much more apt to see evil than good; an aquiline nose, too long and thick to be agreeable; the lips are also thick, and he keeps them continually open; he has certain very awkward nervous movements of the hand, and his speech comes slowly. His beard is thin, inclining to red. . . . In my opinion, which could be wrong, I believe he amounts to little either in mind or body. However, everyone in Paris praises his skill at tennis, hunting and the joust, activities to which, for good or ill, he devotes much time.' Contarini adds that it was said that some of his decisions showed high intelligence; but he clearly had reservations. The general impression from himself and others is of an impassive, obstinate and secretive personality. If such a man was instrumental in introducing Italian Renaissance culture into France it was only on a superficial level. In the annals of the French garden, Anne de Bretagne's name is the more memorable.

Until François I's defeat at Pavia in 1515, the invasion of Italy was the main preoccupation of three successive kings. The ostensible reason for Charles VIII's adventure was a revival of the Angevin claim to Naples; and, with Naples as a base, vague dreams of yet one more crusade to gain Jerusalem for Christendom. He was encouraged by the fears and rivalries of the Italians themselves; in particular by Ludovico Sforza, ruler of Milan during the minority of his nephew; and Cardinal Giuliano della Rovere (the future Julius II), arch-enemy of the reigning Pope Alexander VI (Rodrigo Borgia).

Charles's army (variously estimated at between 15,000 and 40,000, but probably nearer the smaller figure) entered Italy in August 1494. Charles was received by Ludovico at Milan. By agreement with Pietro de' Medici, he agreed to pass peaceably through Tuscany. The French entered Florence triumphantly on 17 November; but meanwhile the Medici had been expelled, and the Medici palace sacked by the mob. Charles only remained there seven days, before leaving for Rome, where he arrived at the end of December. Alexander VI shut himself up in the Castel Sant'Angelo. On 16 January, Charles wrote to Monseigneur de Bourbon that he had moved into the Vatican palace which was a very fine dwelling, as well-furnished as any palace or castle he had ever seen. 'And after dinner,' he continued, 'the Holy Father, who was in his castle of Sant'Angelo, came to the palace, and we met and saw one another in the garden surrounding the covered walk by which one goes to the castle'.[2]

The French reached Naples in February; Alfonso II having fled to Sicily, leaving garrisons in the Castel Nuovo and the Castel del Uovo. Before entering Naples, Charles spent a night at Poggio Reale. A letter to Guillaume Briconnet, bishop of Saint Malo,[3] said it was situated as far from Naples as Plessis was from Tours; and approached on all sides by great paths and *allées*. It was surrounded by orange and other fruit trees. The garden was enclosed by square walls, and round about the house were fair fountains and enclosures full of strange birds. On the other side was a fine park with an abundance of animals, a warren of rabbits and hares, and another of pheasants, partridges and suchlike. It was to

27 Fenced garden with carved gate, from *Chants royaux sur la conception*, early sixteenth century.

28 Pavilion of Anne de Bretagne at Blois in the early seventeenth century.

Poggio Reale that Charles retired when taken ill after the fall of the Castel del Uovo. He wrote to the cardinal de Bourbon on 28 March that he had measles. And immediately following: 'What's more, you would not credit the fine gardens I have in this town. For by my faith only Adam and Eve seem lacking to make them an earthly Paradise, so beautiful are they and so full of good and remarkable things, as I hope to tell you when I see you.' It only needed love for his euphoria to be complete. This, according to *Le Vergier d'Honneur*, a poem celebrating the Naples expedition, appeared in the form of Leonore de Marzano, who was presented to Charles by her stepmother the duchess of Malfi. His susceptibility to feminine beauty was well known, and also his love of horsemanship. Leonore is said to have excelled in both, so that she soon became his mistress. These associations were therefore added to those he brought back to Amboise from Italy. Circumstances contribute greatly to the impression made by works of art; and for gardens in particular, conditions during the arduous progress through Italy would not have been propitious to their enjoyment. The uncertain outcome of the enterprise and the winter months would have been against it. Perhaps the gardens of Naples were indeed far superior to any that the French had seen; but that they made so much of them must have been due in part to the success which gave them the leisure to enjoy.

Charles VIII's occupation of Naples was short-lived. The league formed against him by the Aragonese, the Pope and the Venetians, included Ludovico Sforza, whose treachery was not forgotten by the French. However, the French army escaped and Charles returned to Amboise in October, bringing with him Italian artists and craftsmen,[4] among them 'Dom Pasello, jardinier' and Fra Giocondo from Verona.[5] Pasello is identified as Pacello de Mercogliano, who was in charge of the gardens of Blois in the subsequent reign. Fra Giocondo, as we have seen, was associated with the building of Poggio Reale. No architectural work in France can safely be attributed to him,[6] but he had published Vitruvius, and lectured on him in Paris between 1500 and 1504. Among his other publications were works on agriculture by Cato, Columella, Varro and the 4th-century Palladius. Therefore his influence should not be discounted, for it was among young men then in infancy, that Italian theory took hold and made itself apparent.

Charles died in 1498, having collapsed after hitting his head on the lintel of a door at Amboise. If his own contribution to the development of domestic architecture was minimal, many of the French nobility and gentry had direct experience of Italian Renaissance art and architecture, and the charm of Italian gardens. Among them were men who, in the subsequent reign, played a substantial part in cross-fertilizing the French and Italian architectural traditions, out of which the classical French style of garden design was to grow. Indeed Pierre de Rohan, maréchal de Gié, in command of the French forces who entered Naples in February 1495, had seven years previously entertained Charles in his newly built château of Le Verger, northeast of Angers, which incorporated gardens in a regular plan. Georges d'Amboise, archbishop of Rouen, must be placed high on the list of those Frenchmen who accompanied Charles and were seduced by the beauty of Italian palaces and gardens. He became Louis XII's chief minister; and when he was made cardinal in 1498, the hat was brought to Chinon by Cesare Borgia in person. He had ambitions to be supreme pontiff; and in this he was defeated at the papal election of 1503 by Giuliano della Rovere, who became Julius II. His rebuilding of the château of Gaillon and the making of its splendid gardens between 1502 and 1506 was almost exactly contemporaneous with Bramante's creation of the Belvedere Court for Julius.

Florimond Robertet was secretary to Charles VIII during the Naples campaign. Letters from Italy are signed 'Charles. Robertet'. He was about the same age as Georges d'Amboise, on whose death in 1510 he became Louis' chief minister. Not only did Robertet know Poggio Reale at first hand, but he later visited Italy on Louis XII's behalf, twice in 1502, and again in 1507 and 1509. After Louis' death in 1515 he accompanied François I to Italy; and acted as Louise de Savoie's chief adviser when she was regent during the king's captivity from 1525 to 1526. The château of Bury, west of Blois, begun in 1511, was important as a precedent not only in French château planning, but in placing the garden as the climax of an axial approach. It also had the distinction of receiving a copy of Donatello's David[7] to ornament the forecourt.

Charles VIII, being without issue, was succeeded by his cousin the Duc d'Orléans, who became Louis XII, and who hastened to have his marriage annulled so that he could marry Charles's widow, Anne de Bretagne, and so keep her duchy united with the crown. Although not obsessed by dreams of grandeur, he inherited Charles's ambition to possess Naples, to which he added his own claims to the duchy of Milan. Louis completed what Charles had begun at Amboise; but his most important architectural enterprise was the enlargement of his ancestral home at Blois, and the creation there of gardens which, at least in size, were a notable advance in the art of garden design in France. The
28 'Jardin de la Reine'[8] contained the Pavillon d'Anne de
Bretagne, described by Gebelin[9] as a veritable 'casino à la Italienne', but in a flamboyant style. Anne is said to have had
29 a predilection for gardens. Her *Book of Hours*,[10] decorated by
30 Jean Bourdichon with about three hundred paintings of flowers and fruit, is a major source of information on plants of the Renaissance garden, besides being a masterpiece of the French illuminated book.

29, 30 Camomile and forget-me-not, two details from Anne de Bretagne's *Book of Hours* decorated by Jean Bourdichon.

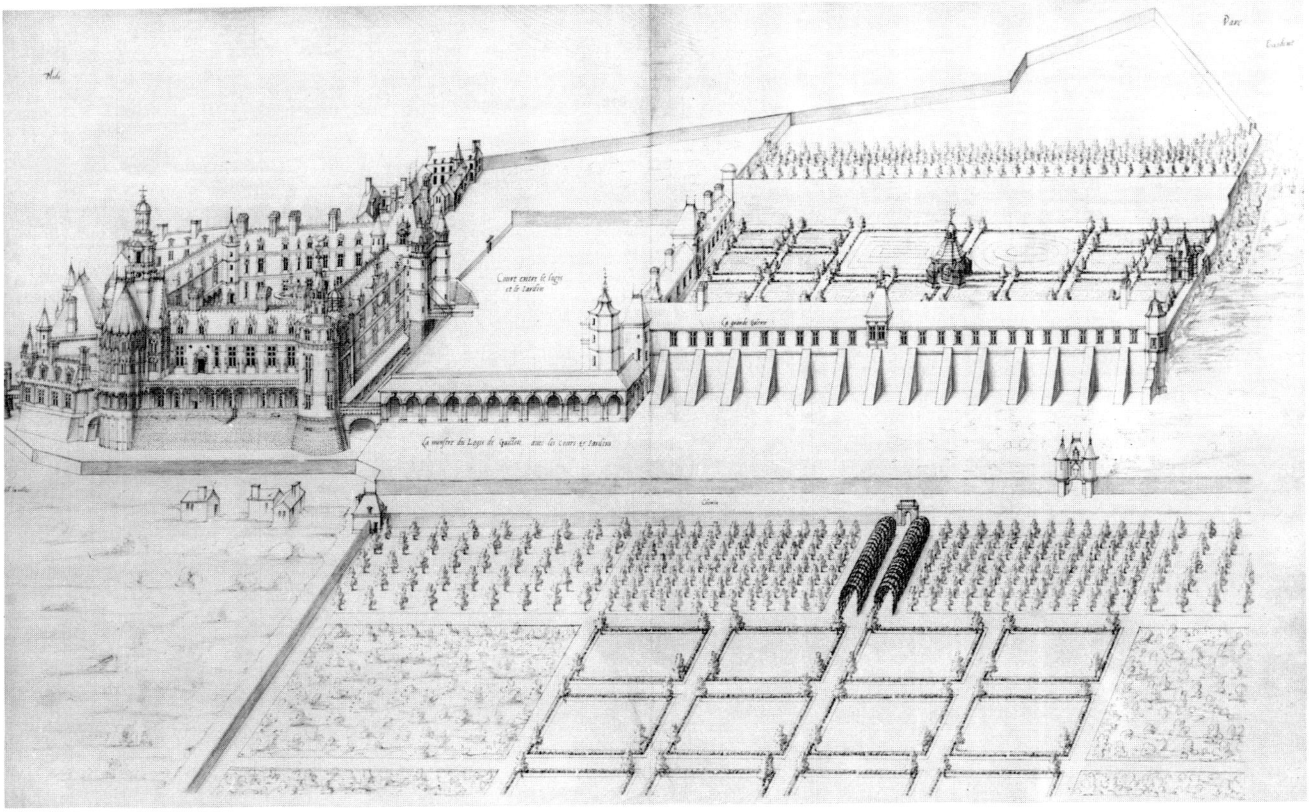

33 The château and garden of Gaillon.

malicious winds. This shelter is in the garden; above are the apartments of the gardener-priest[18] to whom this function has brought big profits and who has become rich compared to what he was.' This seems to be the first reference to an *orangerie* in France.

In 1505 land was bought to make an upper garden, which became known as 'Le Grand Jardin'.[19] It was trapezoidal in shape, and its terraced wall supported the gallery on the west
32 side of the lower or main garden. Du Cerceau's drawing shows a large building in the southeast corner which was not built until the reign of Charles IX (1560–74), and the beginning of the great avenue made at that time, leading from the northwest corner into the forest. In 1599 a new arcade was built against the wall of the upper garden, with a gallery above having a central pedimented feature surmounted by a lantern and dome, giving a new architectural focus to the lower garden.

It seems that the upper garden served a mainly practical purpose; although it is doubtful at this period if there was a clear separation between ornament and use. As we have seen, one of Pacello's main functions was the cultivation of exotic fruits. In his description of Blois in 1517 Beatis wrote: 'Almost all fruits which grow in cultivated ground can be seen there; even fig trees, but in small numbers; and their figs, very small, rarely reach maturity . . . There are also many plants and herbs for salad, endives and cabbages as fine as those in Rome.'

It is possible that Pacello de Mercogliano introduced into France the practice of laying out beds in elaborate patterns, as shown in Du Cerceau's drawings. It is well known that symbolic mazes or knots were made in gardens for at least a century or more before. Jacopo d'Atri's description of Gaillon in 1509 (discussed below) mentions a bed planted to represent the arms of France. Du Cerceau's drawings were obviously embellished with details of his own invention. In many cases there are marked differences in the ornamental patterns between drawings and engravings. There is no reason to doubt, however, that the gardens at Blois were laid out from the start as relatively simple geometric figures, made of low-growing herbs or even vegetables. The drawing of Anne de Bretagne's pavilion in Félibien's 28
manuscript of 1681 shows that at that time the garden was used for growing vegetables.

Pacello de Mercogliano was made canon of Saint-Saveur in June 1503; and was given the *seigneurie* of Château Gaillard in May 1505. Three years later the chapter of Saint-Saveur granted him land at La Regnardière, for his lifetime and thirty years after, to build a house. In 1510 he contracted to make a well in the upper garden; and his name appears on receipts until 1531. He appears to have had charge of the lower garden, called Le Jardin de la Reine, for which he received 300 *livres* a year 'par manière de pension, gages et entretènement à cause du gouvernment général, cultiviage et reparacions des dits jardins'. From 1526 the upper garden was in charge of Jherome (Jérome) de Naples, who also received 300 *livres* a year. Jérome died in 1532, and the two gardens were combined under Pacello de Mercogliano's management. He died in 1534, aged about eighty.

GAILLON

33 Georges d'Amboise acquired the château of Gaillon[20] with the archbishopric of Rouen in 1494. He was contemplating its reconstruction in 1499, but the work was not seriously undertaken until 1507, after the campaigns in Italy. The site
34 commanded magnificent views over the valley of the Seine; and from 1502 to 1506 master masons from Georges d'Amboise's native Touraine were employed in reconstructing the old château, and building a huge level terrace for the garden, 180 metres long, half as long again as the lower garden at Blois and over twice as wide, carved out of the hillside 'with untold labour and expense'. It adjoined the courtyard of the castle to which access was by a drawbridge across the moat.

From 1506 to 1509 craftsmen from the Rouen area worked under the instructions of Italians. The garden itself was totally enclosed. Galleries – panelled, paved, and roofed with slate – ran along the northeast and southeast sides, with arcades of oak – painted green, blue and gold – open to the garden. On the side overlooking the valley, the walls were decorated with frescoes showing the king, cardinal and other French nobles hunting birds with nets and falcons. A large wooden pavilion was placed over the intersection of *allées* at the 35
centre, facing the entrance. Like the one at Blois it was octagonal in plan, with arched openings in the Italian style. Half-domed bays alternated with the openings. The central dome was roofed with slate and crowned by a lantern. Jacopo d'Atri, the Mantuan envoy to the French court who visited Gaillon in 1510,[21] says it was richly decorated with coats of arms and other motifs; Dom Antonio de Beatis in 1517 says it was painted blue and gold. The end of the garden, opposite the entrance, was enclosed in wire to form an aviary, with running water and trees, 'in so great a space', d'Atri says, 'that the birds appeared to be at liberty'. Terminating the central *allée*, at the gate into the park, was a garden room set aside for the cardinal's private use; according to Beatis, for resting at midday during the summer. He says it was octagonal, made of brick with wooden panelling, roofed with slate, and with stained-glass windows on every side. D'Atri says it was of wood and painted green.

Beatis and d'Atri agree in the essentials about the planting and arrangement of the garden. It was divided by *allées* into square compartments (d'Atri says there were four), each surrounded by railings of wrought timber, painted green, with handsome gates. Each square was differently planted; some with flowers or trees, especially fruit trees (d'Atri mentions peach, apple, pear, cherry; and says that the garden contained all kinds of fruit except fig and melon); others with box and rosemary cut into the forms of horses, ships, birds

34 The garden of Gaillon, looking from the right-hand side of the previous picture, with the château in the distance as it appeared in the mid-seventeenth century.

35 The upper garden of Gaillon, looking from the gate towards the central pavilion.

36 The second fountain of Gaillon, made for the pavilion above. It was commissioned from Genoese artists in 1506.

and other animals. One square had the arms of France with a motto in antique letters 'avec de toutes petites plantes'; another was in the form of a fine labyrinth. These descriptions confirm what may be deduced from other sources, that gardens of this period combined useful, decorative and symbolic elements.

The credit for the design of the gardens has hitherto gone to Pacello de Mercogliano, who is not mentioned in the Gaillon accounts[22] before April 1506, when he was paid expenses for coming to look at the garden. This was after the main work of construction was completed; and would support Lesueur's view[23] that Pacello was concerned only with horticulture and the laying out of beds. On the other hand, Pierre Valence, a master craftsman from Touraine, who was both a joiner and hydraulics expert, was employed at Gaillon from the beginning of 1503, when he was mainly concerned with the small independent pleasure garden in the park, known as Le Lydieu. But he was also responsible for the panelling of the galleries in the main garden, and had charge of the work in connection with the fountains. There were two of these, both made in Italy. One, which stood in the main court of the castle, was a gift from the Venetian Republic. It was shipped by sea to Honfleur, and erected at Gaillon in April 1508. The second, destined for the garden, 36
was commissioned from Agostino Solario and two associates at Genoa in 1506.[24] In view of his established functions, and in the absence of any other candidate, it would seem reasonable to credit Valence with the huge pavilion harbouring the garden fountain. His Touraine origins, and the similarity of the work at Gaillon to what was done at Blois, suggest he might have been responsible for all the woodwork at both places.

Le Lydieu was a retreat in the park, some distance from the 37
château and approached by a road from the main garden along the hillside. Its situation might have been determined by the presence of springs, and the need, as occurred in many places, to build a tank to make a head of water for pressure to the fountains in the garden. The fact that Pierre Valence, an acknowledged hydraulics expert,[25] was occupied with it from the start supports this supposition. Between 1502 and 1504 the park proper was enclosed by a wall of about 8 kilometres in circumference. At the same time a pond was dug on the site of an existing vineyard; and the vines removed in order to make 'une allée et pavillons'. Between 1503 and 1506 a small complex arose in this area which included a chapel, a garden about 32 metres square, with a fountain, pavilion and trellis arbours. D'Atri mentions 'two beautiful decorated houses' in the park, for eating or for sheltering from the rain; a church, not too big but 'ben devota'; a solitary hermitage and many other places for amusement. Some of this undoubtedly refers to Le Lydieu. The accounts mention the hermitage in 1508. Jacques Androuet du Cerceau's drawing shows Le Lydieu after 1550, with the canal and sumptuous Renaissance casino known as La Maison Blanche. At the southeast end of the canal he 38
shows 'l'Hermitage': a chapel in the Gothic style, an artificial rock, and a garden of four square compartments with a

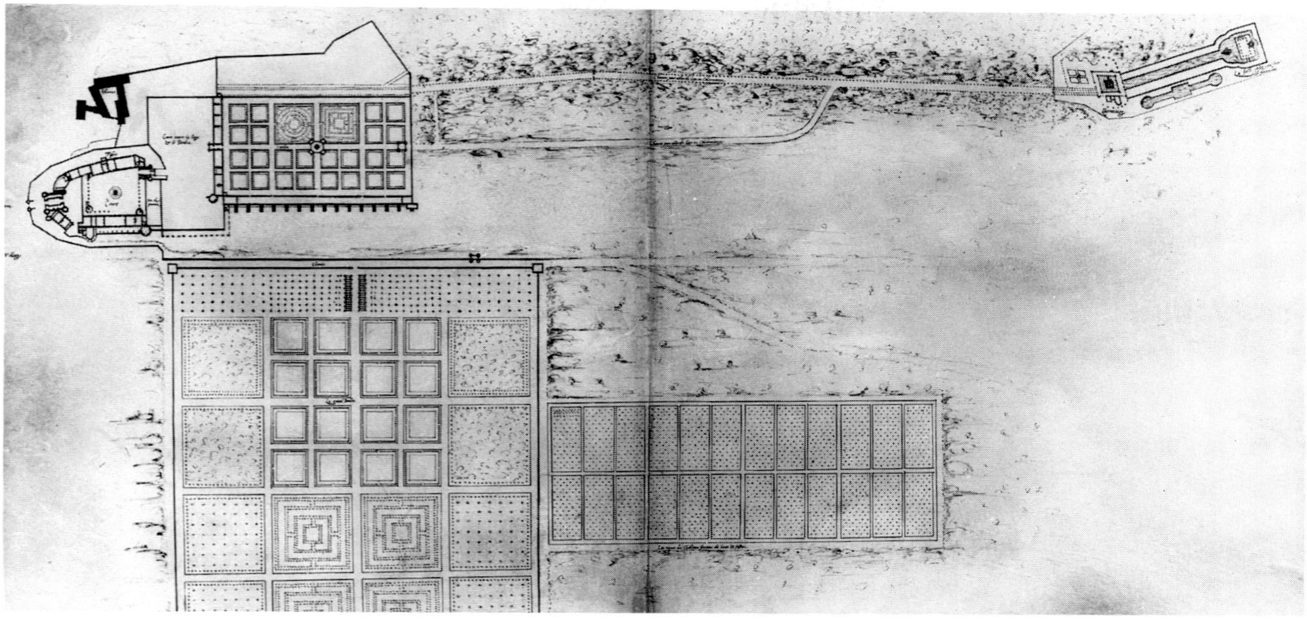

37, 38 Plan of the château and garden of Gaillon with (below) a detail of Le Lydieu, a retreat at the extreme east end of the park, top right on the plan, which included La Maison Blanche.

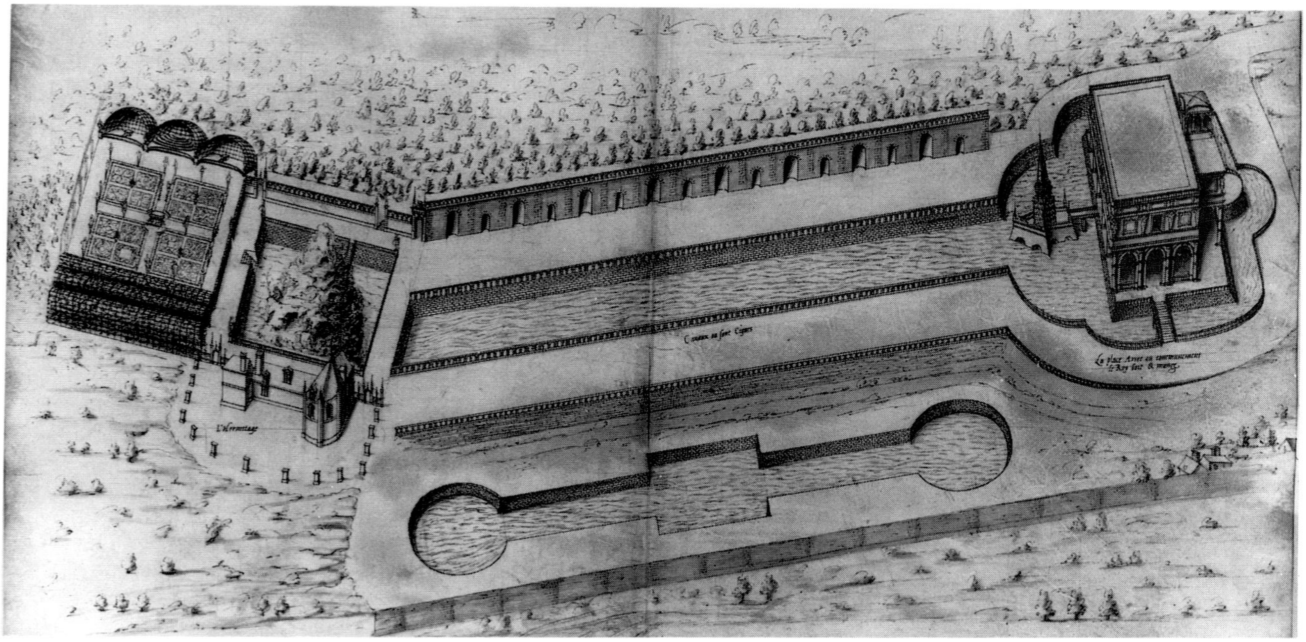

fountain at the centre. There is no reason to doubt that the chapel and garden are those referred to in Georges d'Amboise's accounts. It is assumed by Chirol that the *rocher d'hermitage* was added by the cardinal de Bourbon, but there is no evidence either way. Le Lydieu suggests the inspiration of the *vigne* of the Roman cardinals. There is nothing like it in French sixteenth-century garden design. Du Cerceau's drawings of the main garden also show it after the cardinal de Bourbon's transformation, particularly the handsome stone gallery along the northeast side of the garden. The large walled garden below was also made in the cardinal de Bourbon's day, doubtless for fruit and vegetables, thus removing the useful function from the upper garden. There are differences of detail between Du Cerceau's drawing and engraving, particularly in the ornamental treatment of the beds. This is not of great importance if the main features of the garden are accurate, but it does mean that Du Cerceau's evidence should be received with caution.

39 Le Verger in the early seventeenth century.

LE VERGER

Le Verger was one of the first châteaux to show a new concern with symmetry, incorporating gardens within a regular plan. The site was without any of the defensive or spectacular advantages of Amboise, Gaillon or even Blois; a gentle rise behind, open fields in the front, the pleasant little River Loir not far away. What Pierre de Rohan, Maréchal de Gié, erected in place of the old castle, which he pulled down, is not quite what its name would suggest; nevertheless, despite its six round machicolated towers with pointed roofs, linked by curtain walls with a battlemented walk and surrounded by a moat, the sumptuous house was not a fortress. There were two courts; the first, entered across a drawbridge between two round towers, was flanked by living quarters; opposite the entrance was a second moat, surmounted by an open balustrade, and a second drawbridge leading to the court with the private apartments. Tree-covered *allées*, some 800 paces (*pas*) long, led from the entrance to the Loir on the west, and a little pleasure-house called La Maison Neuve. On the opposite side, towards the east, were other gardens called Les Carreaux, a name which is self-explanatory. These opened on to the park, a walled enclosure of 4 kilometres round, with ponds, woods and springs, and stocked with animals and birds 'et autres deduitz
39 et plaisures'.[26] The engraving published by Israel Henriet about 1650 obviously includes later additions.

BURY

There is an apocryphal story that Florimond Robertet was given the *chatellenie* of Bury by the king (presumably Louis XII) as a reward for his honesty in refusing a gift of 30,000 francs offered by the Venetians after he had concluded a treaty with them. Madame Tissier de Mallerais[27] considers that this was on the occasion of the treaty with Venice in 1513, when Giovanni de' Medici became Pope Leo X. But a deed shows that Robertet bought the land at Bury from Germain de Bonneval for 4000 gold crowns on 2 January 1511. The deed states: 'ladite seigneurie est de present en ruyne quant au manoir et il n'y a aucune demeurance ou habitation.' Madame Tissier de Mallerais thinks that the building was begun almost immediately, although a clause enabling the vendors to go back on the contract on repayment of the purchase money was renounced only in December 1513. The initial 'L' on the façade indicates that the building was far advanced by Louis' death in 1515; while 'C' and 'F' on the façade facing the garden suggest that it was finished in the following reign. François I visited Robertet at Bury sometime before 1524, so the château must be assumed completed by that date.

Bury was more modest than Gaillon. It is said to have resembled Le Verger,[28] but this applies only to the style and arrangement of the buildings, for the site is altogether different. The way in which the garden has a place in the whole architectural scheme is something new. The château 40
was built on high ground overlooking the valley of La Cisse, a few kilometres west of Blois. The final approach from the west was level; on the east the ground sloped steeply. The seigneural block was self-contained; the main courtyard was

square, closed on the west by a crenellated wall low enough to reveal the façade of the *corps de logis* beyond. Although apparently defensive, it could not effectively serve this purpose; and in fact was a terrace supported within by a gallery, faced with an elegant arcade in true Italian Renaissance style. On entering the main courtyard the visitor was faced with the principal façade of the *logis*, more richly decorated than the others, and rising in the centre into a central pavilion of two or more storeys crowned with a high four-sided roof. The main decorative emphasis was thus on the line of approach. Proceeding along the main axis through the building, the visitor would emerge on a platform with steps into the garden, a level terrace some 5 metres (16 *pieds*) below, at a lower level than the main courtyard. If this was decorated with beds laid out in the manner shown by Du Cerceau the effect must have been dramatic. And this was not all, for it was the foreground of an extensive view over the forest. We may assume from the unity of the design that all this was intended from the start. The termination of the main axis, in the centre of the terrace wall supporting the garden to the east, was marked by a chapel. The corner towers at each end were kept proportionately low. The choice of a new site so near the hillside, where the fall of the ground restricted the size and necessitated a substantial terrace wall, points to its intended effect as the climax to the approach. As the main rooms of the *corps de logis* overlooked the garden, some ornamental treatment may be presumed, although we do not know if it was laid out as Du Cerceau represents it. As is usually the case, the patterns of the squares shown in his drawings differ from those in the engravings.

The terrace was extended to the south by a second garden of the same size, the land for which was bought in 1518. Du Cerceau's engraving shows it decorated like the first. This was not the case in the drawings, and it was probably the *potager*, communicating directly with the *basse-cour*. The perspective drawing shows it entirely surrounded by a pergola with a flat trellis top, presumably for vines. The east side is open to the view. The engraved perspective does not show the trellis walk on the *basse-cour* side, while the plan shows it only on the east side overlooking the valley.

The designer of Bury is unknown. The arcade of the portico is a pure Renaissance design. The pilaster treatment of the inner façade recalls some of the work of Giuliano da Sangallo. The *perron*, with its double flight of steps leading to the garden, the uniform plan, the symmetry and the axial arrangement, were well established in Italian practice. Despite these features, the predominant style of the buildings is that of the French masons, who could well have had their instructions from Robertet himself. From his youth he was familiar with Renaissance culture. Like Pierre de Rohan, Maréchal de Gié, and Cardinal Georges d'Amboise, he had acquired a taste for Italian art. The copy of Donatello's *David* which he acquired after the Maréchal's disgrace was intended for the courtyard of his town house at Blois; but Du Cerceau shows a statue resembling the *David* on a column in the main courtyard at Bury.

40 The château and gardens of Bury.

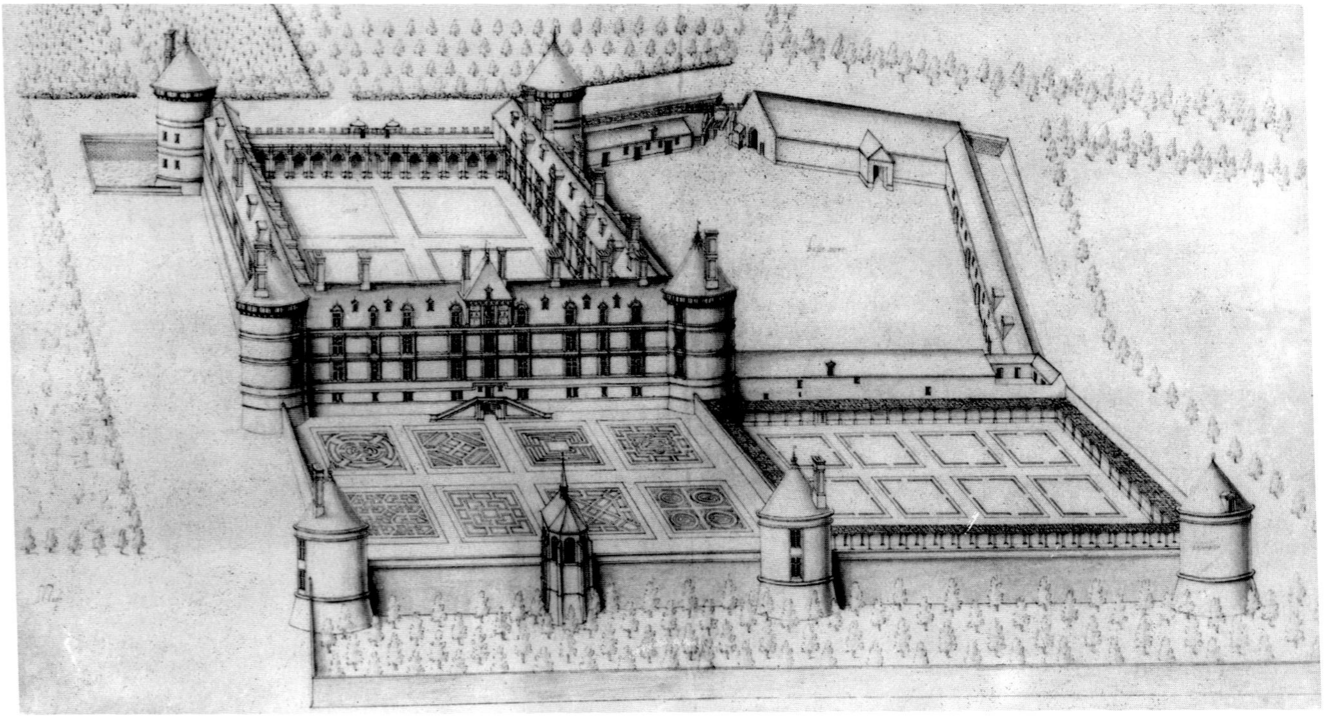

4

Italian theory and French practice: Leonardo to Philibert de l'Orme

Historical background

LOUIS XII'S HEIR was his nephew François, son of Charles Comte d'Angoulême and Louise de Savoie. Anne de Bretagne had two daughters, Claude and Renée. Claude's marriage to her cousin François was politically desirable to keep Brittany united with the rest of France. Renée became duchess of Ferrara in 1528, and thus sister-in-law of Ippolito d'Este, then eighteen years of age. The court at Ferrara was noted for its culture; and the summer palace of Belriguardo, where Renée went shortly after her arrival, was famous for its gardens. Ippolito had both taste and charm, and an inclination to extravagance; qualities he shared with François, to whose court he was introduced by Cardinal Jean du Bellay. François immediately took to him. Ippolito was already archbishop of Milan at a very early age. Du Bellay arranged with François that he should be granted his abbey of Breteuil in Picardy. To this François added other favours, making him councillor of state, obtaining for him a cardinal's hat in 1538; and in 1540 the bishopric of Lyon. Ippolito's diplomatic skills were much valued. He had a house at Fontainebleau, designed by Sebastiano Serlio; and he was closely associated with the court of France until his death in 1572. Diplomacy, the arts and collecting went hand in hand. Ippolito d'Este's commission of a salt-cellar from Benvenuto Cellini, and his introduction of the goldsmith to François, are well known, thanks to Cellini's own account. His best-known monument, the Villa d'Este at Tivoli, was made at the end of his life, after François' death; but it is unimaginable that they did not discuss such projects.

Both François and his sister, Marguerite d'Angoulême, were strongly influenced by their mother, Louise de Savoie, who had a leaning towards Italian culture. She had a strong dislike of Blois where once, in the previous reign, she and her children had been virtually held prisoners. Pierre de Rohan, Maréchal de Gié, who had custody of them at the time, persuaded Louis XII to transfer them to Amboise, on the pretext that Blois was full of builders and therefore not safe. It was thus that Amboise was the royal residence at the beginning of François' reign, which opened with a successful attempt to reestablish the French claim to Milan. At Marignano, the young king gained a reputation for martial valour. It was at Amboise that he received the aged Leonardo da Vinci, whom he invited to France after the capture of Milan, installing him at the nearby château of Cloux.

Whatever Leonardo did for François it cannot have been much, due to his age and the short time he had to live. It has been suggested that Chambord may have been influenced by his ideas.[1] He certainly made sketches for the canalization of the Sauldre and the rebuilding of the château of Romorantin which belonged to Louise de Savoie. Its site, in the flat lake-strewn area of Sologne south of Orléans, is very different from those of Blois and Amboise. In the region of Romorantin the Sauldre spreads out to form a number of islands. Leonardo's idea was to contain the river in regular canals, the main one forming an axis about which the new château would be built; and at the same time to link it with the Cher and make it navigable. The extensive grounds were to be laid out with avenues, squares and fountains. Since the court would go there only from time to time to enjoy the hunting, Leonardo proposed that prefabricated wooden houses should be made, to be erected and dismantled as required, in 'a vast camping ground, half park, half garden', as Heydenreich put it. The whole plan, contained in its rectilinear canals, recalled Filarete's concept of an ideal city, with which Leonardo must have been familiar.

The project for Romorantin was abandoned due to the plague;[2] instead, a new site was sought, away from towns. This was found at Chambord, in the forest some 40 kilometres to the north, where a vast new hunting lodge was begun. Work was in full swing by 1522, and went on intermittently until François' death in 1547 when it virtually ceased. There were no gardens to match the grandeur and scale of the château. The Cosson meandered by a number of streams across the marshy site, creating stagnant pools under the castle walls. And thus the grounds remained until Hardouin-Mansart's scheme to canalize the river and create a 237
grand parterre about 1683.[3]

As a residence Chambord has always been almost completely useless. As an object in the landscape it is a monumental folly which dwarfs anything that Filarete or Colonna could have imagined. The roof terrace, which is its

41 Garden pavilion in Renaissance style at Les Baux, Provence.

most remarkable feature, has aesthetic implications. Together with others at La Muette,[4] Challuau and Saint-Germain-en-Laye, it invites not only views of the chase but the visual pleasures of the prospect itself.

François I's ambition to be emperor, and his military adventures in Italy, came to an end with his defeat and capture by Charles V at Pavia in 1525. His subsequent imprisonment in Spain was a watershed. When he returned to France in 1526 he abandoned the châteaux of the Loire, associated with his previous existence, and favoured the region near Paris: Fontainebleau, Saint-Germain-en-Laye, Villers-Cotterets, the château of Madrid.[5] Hunting replaced war as François' main preoccupation; and there was nothing much to recommend these sites for building, beyond the proximity of the forest. This was the main attraction of Fontainebleau, which François established as one of the most favoured royal palaces. For him it was central. It was there he invited Primaticcio, Vignola, Serlio, establishing the French version of the Italian High Renaissance and Mannerist style of what has become known as the School of Fontainebleau. Moreover, by favouring Italians he touched the pride of Frenchmen. It was under this stimulus that the French classical style was formed; particularly by Philibert de l'Orme in the following reigns. For the fortunes of Italians and Frenchmen fluctuated according to the political influences round the throne. In this connection an event took place in 1518 which had unforeseen and far-reaching consequences.

Giovanni de' Medici had succeeded Julius II as pope in 1513. At the same time he appointed his brother's only son, Lorenzo, as his representative in Florence. In 1518 he arranged Lorenzo's marriage to Madeleine de la Tour d'Auvergne, a distant relative of the young king of France. It was celebrated at Amboise, together with the christening of François' first son, and was followed by a month of festivals, to which the aged Leonardo no doubt contributed. Madeleine died the following April, having given birth to a daughter, Catherine. During her formative years in Rome and Florence, an orphan and hapless victim of the fortunes of her family, Catherine developed two of her notable characteristics, the ability to survive and a taste for expensive building. The first she was compelled to exercise all her life; she had to wait forty years to indulge the second. In 1533, at the age of fourteen, she was married to François' second son, Henri, who on the death of his elder brother in 1536 became heir to the throne. During her married life as dauphine and queen, Catherine lived in the shadow of Henri's mistress, Diane de Poitiers, widow of Louis de Brézé, Grand Sénéchal de Normandie, and eighteen years older than Henri. The rebuilding for Diane of the Brézé family home at Anet by Philibert de l'Orme in the 1540s was a significant architectural event.

De l'Orme was born at Lyon, sometime between 1505 and 1510. His father, Jean de l'Orme, was a master mason. Philibert was a product of the French building tradition and the new learning disseminated by the printing presses of Lyon. A practical interest in building, an acquaintance with the Classics, coupled with a precocious intelligence and a strong belief in his own superior ability, inevitably led to Italy. Between 1533 and 1536 he studied Roman antiquities; not only those which were standing, but the pieces being unearthed at the Villa Adriana and elsewhere. It is probable that it was here he met Serlio, who was similarly engaged and who became his friend.

De l'Orme reports in *Le Premier Tome de l'Architecture* (1568) that one day, two years after his arrival in Rome, while he was measuring the arch of Titus, he was approached by a party of noblemen and cardinals. It was thus he met Marcello Cervini (the future Pope Marcellus II) who introduced him to his circle of artists, humanists and collectors, one of whom was undoubtedly the young Ippolito d'Este. But more significant for Philibert de l'Orme's future was the presence in Rome during 1535–6 of Cardinal Jean du Bellay, accompanied by his doctor, François Rabelais. Rabelais remained De l'Orme's friend, and mentions him by name in chapter sixty-one of the fourth book of *Gargantua and Pantagruel*. Cardinal du Bellay gave De l'Orme his first important architectural commission.

As bishop of Paris he possessed the abbey of Saint-Maur. He obtained a papal bull to secularize this, and replace the monks by a dean and nine canons, one of whom was Rabelais. For himself, as dean, he planned a new residence on a slightly elevated site overlooking the Marne, with ground sloping gently to the river. Rabelais described it as 'paradis de salubrité, aménité, sérénité, commodité, délices et tous honnestes plaisirs de agriculture et vie rustique'. Du Bellay had in mind those vineyards and villas on the hills of Rome belonging to his fellow cardinals. The house De l'Orme designed for him, a one-storey Italianate building occupying four sides of a court, could have been inspired by the recently completed Palazzo del Tè at Mantua. The significance of Saint-Maur-les-Fossés in the history of garden design lies in the choice of site and the villa concept, rather than in what was actually achieved. The building was incomplete when Cardinal du Bellay was sent to Italy again at the beginning of the new reign in 1547. It was acquired from Cardinal du Bellay's heirs by Catherine de Médicis in 1563. Du Cerceau's engravings show the garden front as redesigned to her order, but it is doubtful if the garden was ever laid out as he shows it.

On his succession Henri II appointed Philibert de l'Orme superintendent of the royal buildings, giving him greater powers of control than any of his predecessors, so that his function was for the first time equivalent to what is now understood by 'architect'. He was immediately commissioned to design a tomb for François I at Saint-Denis, and to supervise the building of Diane de Poitiers' new château at Anet. Saint-Germain-en-Laye was one of the royal châteaux for which he was responsible. The old castle, restored by 42
François I, stood well back from the Seine. A few hundred metres to the south a steep escarpment descended to the river above Le Pecq with panoramic views over the country towards Paris. In 1557 De l'Orme signed a contract for a new château on this site (near the menagerie built by him in 1548), known as 'La Maison du Théâtre' and subsequently just 'Le

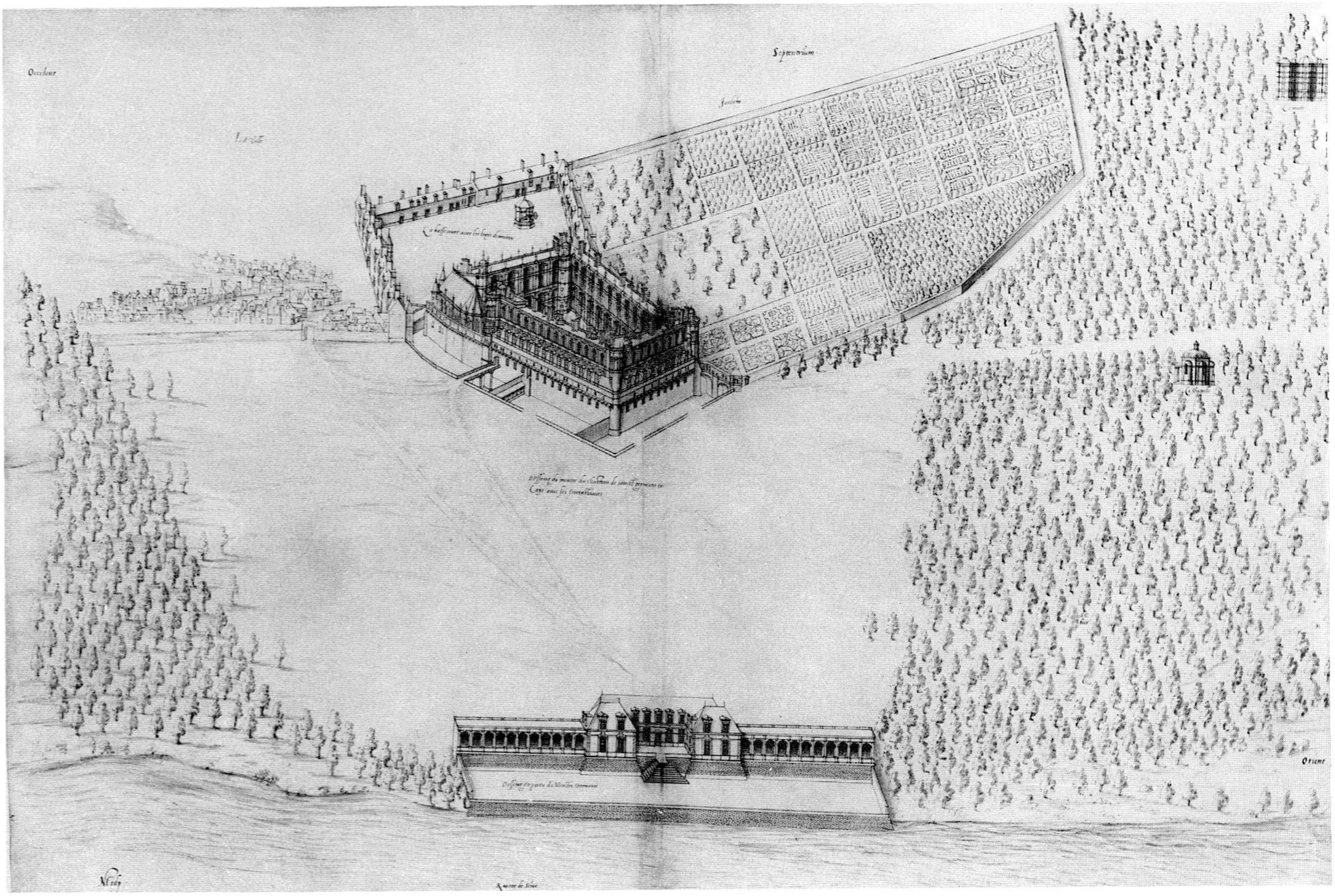

42 The old château of Saint-Germain-en-Laye, with Philibert de L'Orme's Maison du Théâtre (Château-Neuf) in the foreground.

Château Neuf'. It was to be a place of entertainment rather than a residence, with one big room almost 17 metres long (8 *toises*, 2 *pieds*), pavilions at four corners, and a square courtyard with four semi-circular bays enclosed by a wall. On the south side a flight of steps led to a terrace. He seems to have envisaged terraces and gardens descending to the river, where, again in his own words, 'the king wished to make . . . a bridge of one arch as wide as the river, which would be the most magnificent work ever seen'. Whether De l'Orme's scheme would have been anything like what was done after 1594 is not known. The Tivoli gardens were being planned at the time De l'Orme made his contract. He would certainly have known about them, possibly from Cardinal Ippolito d'Este personally. It is reasonable to suppose that he had something similar in mind, although not on the scale of what was ultimately done. Du Cerceau's perspective view shows the Château Neuf as De l'Orme designed it, with a single terrace actually bordering the Seine, which gives quite a wrong impression, for the château was built some 80 metres above the river. The sudden death of Henri II in 1560, from a wound in the eye received while jousting, was a disaster for Diane de Poitiers, and for Philibert de l'Orme who had to give up his appointment and leave his work at Chenonceaux and Saint-Germain-en-Laye incomplete.

The period from 1526 (when François I returned from captivity) to 1560 was one of internal peace, before the wars between Catholic and Huguenot factions in the second half of the century, and the personal power struggle associated with them. Many of the nobility took the opportunity to rebuild or in some way adapt their old defensive castles in accordance with a more sophisticated style. Anne de Montmorency was one of the dominant personalities of the sixteenth century. He shared François I's captivity, and his successful defence of Provence when Charles V invaded Italy earned him the office of Constable of France. When war broke out again in 1557 he was defeated and captured at Saint

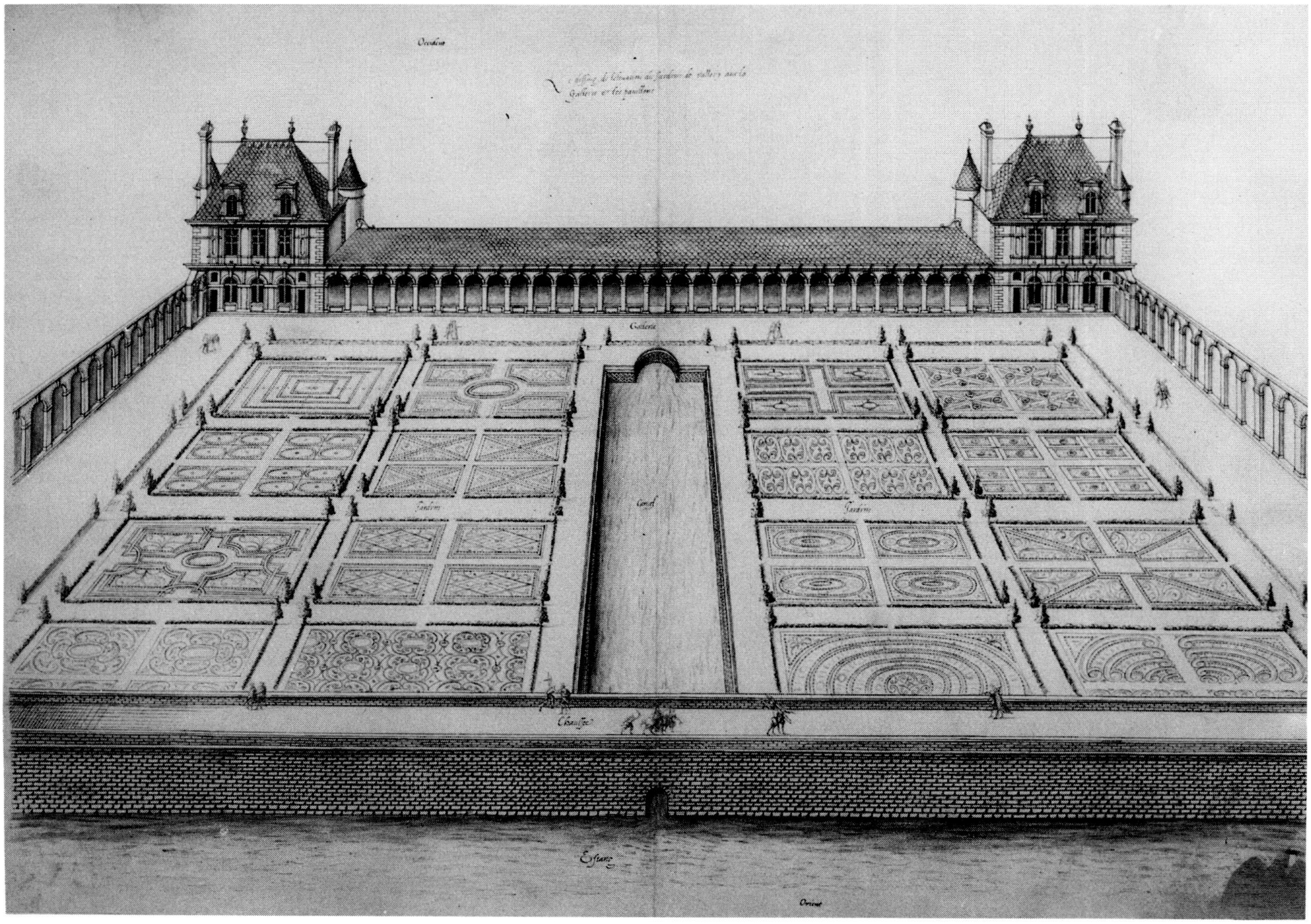

43 The garden of Vallery showing the canal and Italianate gallery.

Quentin; and only released after a year in captivity on the payment of a huge ransom. His son and nephews, the Chatillon, were leaders of the Huguenot party. Anne de Montmorency himself was not tolerant of the reformed religion; and in 1561 he formed an alliance with his old rival François, Duc de Guise, and Jacques d'Albon, Maréchal Saint André, to direct the policy of the Catholic party. In the civil wars which followed he was badly wounded at Dreux in 1562; and died fighting at Saint-Denis in 1567. During his lifetime Montmorency had periods of almost unrivalled power. He was fanatically loyal to the crown, and ruthless in dealing with sedition. But like others of his time he had a great respect for learning, and a taste for ostentation. He lavished his accumulated wealth on his châteaux of Ecouen and Chantilly, where he employed leading architects, painters and sculptors. His collections included not only antiquities, but two *Slaves* in marble by Michelangelo from the tomb of Julius II. A man with such inclinations did not neglect the art of gardens.

Maréchal Saint André's father, Jean d'Albon, was one of the governors of François I's children, and it was thus that a warm friendship was formed between his son and Henri II, who made him Maréchal de France. In 1548 he bought the
old castle of Vallery, halfway between Nemours and Sens, 43
where he made an enclosed and independent garden with an elegant Italianate gallery and an ornamental canal. He died in the battle of Dreux in 1562, at the same time as Montmorency was wounded.

René II, Duc de Lorraine, fought with the French at Marignano. His son Claude was created Duc de Guise by François I. About 1546 he built a pleasant house beside the Marne at Joinville, as an alternative to the old fortified castle

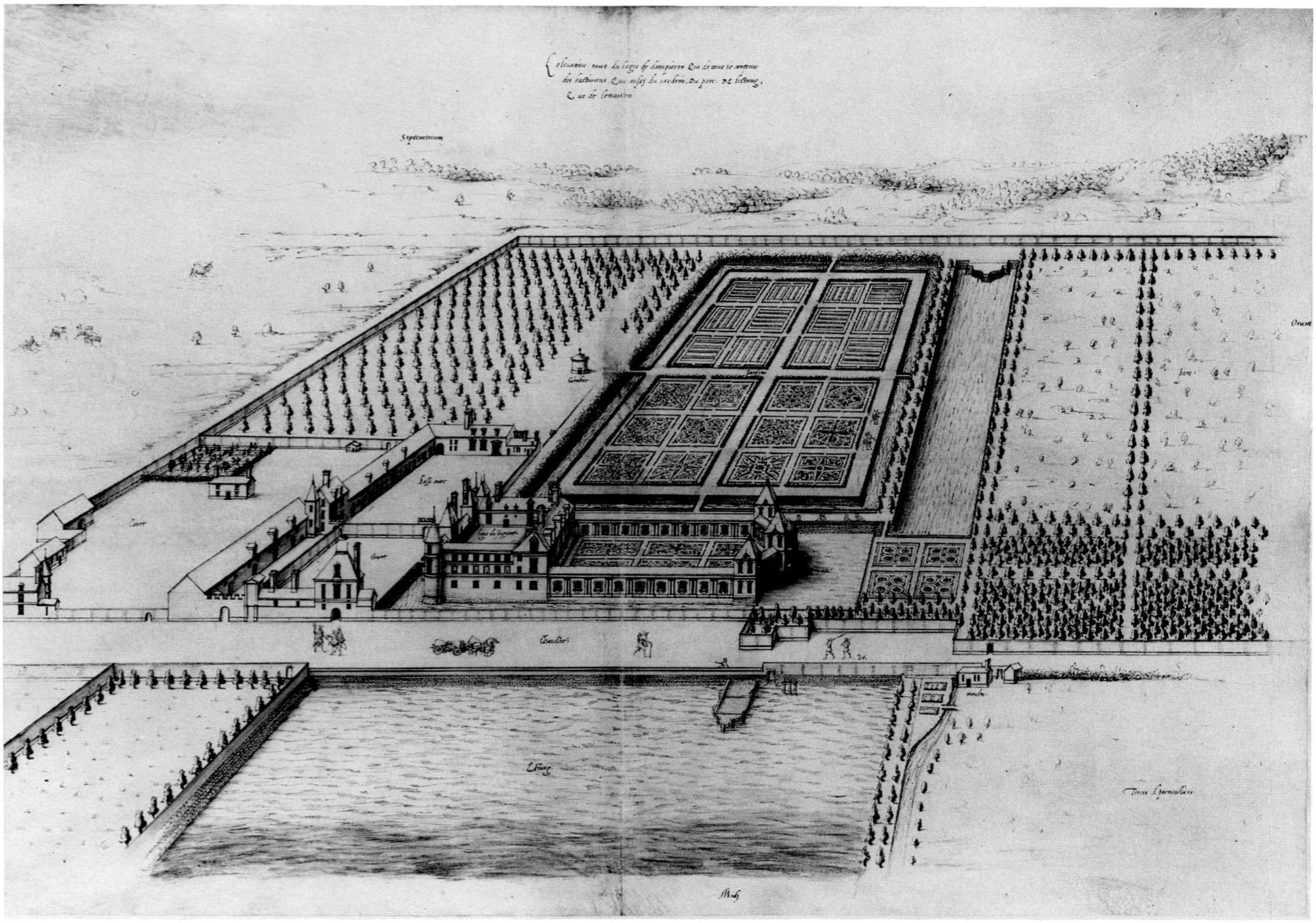

44 The château and garden of Dampierre.

on the hill. It became known as Joinville-le-Grand-Jardin.
Claude's sons, François and Charles, became leaders of the
Catholic faction in the wars of religion. Their sister Marie
married James V of Scotland, and was the mother of Mary
Stuart who married François, eldest son of Henri II and
Catherine de Médicis. Charles de Guise became cardinal of
Lorraine, and in 1552 acquired two properties which
subsequently have a distinguished place in the history of the
44 French garden: Dampierre (Yvelines), built by François I's
treasurer Jean Duval sometime before 1550; and Meudon,
where he employed Primaticcio to design a casino in the
Italian manner on a spectacular site southwest of Paris. It had
a room for dining in the central pavilion, supported on a
45 heavily rusticated basement. It was called the Grotte de
Meudon because the basement room was furnished as a
nymphaeum. In Vasari's words,[6] 'below is a large room with
fountains decorated with stucco and full of figures in relief,
and with shells and other marine objects of marvellous
beauty'. The floor was of polychrome mosaic, white, red,
green and grey; the vaults were ornamented with painted
stucco by Domenico del Barbiere (Dominique Florentin);
while water flowed abundantly from lions' masks into bowls
in niches round the walls, or spurted from hidden jets to
surprise the unwary visitor. A similar room was built at La
Bastie d'Urfé (Loire). Claude d'Urfé was ambassador to the
Holy See from 1549 to 1551. He brought back pictures,
marble bas-reliefs and inlaid woodwork from Italy, and
rebuilt his house in the Italian manner, including the shell-
work grotto and a garden temple in Italian style. It is only 46
necessary to look at François Gebelin's *Châteaux de la
Renaissance* to see the extent to which, in varying degrees, the
Italian Renaissance style had penetrated the houses of the 41

45 The Grotte de Meudon, designed by Primaticcio for Charles de Guise. The grotto proper was in the basement.

46 Garden temple in the Italian style at La Bastie d'Urfé.

nobility; and undoubtedly these included gardens which have left no memorial. The most important were recorded by Jacques Androuet du Cerceau in *Les Plus Excellents Bastiments de France*.

Fontainebleau

The *raison d'être* and perennial attraction of Fontainebleau is
the strange rock-strewn forest. A royal castle (or hunting
lodge) was in existence by the twelfth century; and a religious
community (the Couvent des Mathurins) was established
there by Louis IX (Saint Louis), with a chapel and a hospital.
François I's rebuilding of the château began in 1528, with 47
alterations to the building surrounding the courtyard (the
Cour Ovale) under the direction of a French master mason,
Gilles le Breton. At the same time a new entrance was made
in the southwest corner, with a pavilion (known as the Porte
Dorée) composed of three bays, one above the other. It was
to be approached by a causeway lined with elms,[7] forming
the eastern boundary of a trapezoidal lake, fed by a spring.

This lake is central to the design, which is determined not
by some ideal concept, but (as is so often the case with
gardens) according to the logic of the situation. The lake was
the focus of a courtyard, whose axis was the centre of a new 48
gallery in the Italian manner and a fountain jutting into the
lake; hence its name, the Cour de la Fontaine. Over the
fountain was erected Michelangelo's *Hercules*, in white
marble, which François' agent had managed to buy in 1529.
The general plan shown by Jacques Androuet du Cerceau in 50
his drawings of the 1560s, after Catherine de Médicis'

alterations, was established in its essentials by 1540. The ground east of the causeway was acquired sometime before 1535, to form what was called the Grand Jardin, a roughly square area divided into two unequal parts by a canal. The north part consisted of twelve rectangular islands; the part south of the canal contained two large areas for the Jeu de Balle and the Jeu des Barres (prisoners' base). Indeed, although the Grand Jardin was laid out as a parterre at the end of the century, the whole of this area was a provision for outdoor exercise and games, intermediate between the castle and the forest. North of the Cour Ovale was a private garden with access from the royal apartments.

In 1528 Gilles le Breton was instructed to make all the walls for enclosing the gardens; and in 1534 he was paid for works of masonry on the causeway, two sides of the pond, and about the canals in the *Grand Jardin*.[8] The following year Jossé Maillard was paid for carpentry work in pavilions and buildings at three corners of the garden; Pierre Toustain for work about the springs; and a contract was made with Michel Vallance, fountain maker.

To the west, between the lake and the town, was an irregular piece of ground tapering from north to south. This was the area containing the spring which gave Fontainebleau its name. Formerly an orchard, it was levelled between 1535 and 1538, canals dug, and a network of straight walks constructed.[9] This garden became known as the Jardin des Pins, on account of trees identified by Jean Guillaume as Maritime Pine (*Pinus pinaster*).[10] In 1538 some 2000 willows were planted along the canals, supplementing those already growing beside the pond. All this work was done under the direction of the gardener, Claude de Creil.[11] His contract (March 1538) required him to enlarge the garden, laying it out in square beds and walks as he had been shown, to plant currant bushes and roses round the balustrades[12] and little willow hedges to enclose the enlarged garden, as well as round the spring and fishpond. He was to plant vines along a section of the wall near the offices; form a *berceau* by bending willows planted along the central path of the small garden, and sow the seeds of pine in various places as instructed.[13]

One of the main functions of the garden was to provide for the royal table; and in 1538 Jehan Geoffroy (or Geuffroy), described as 'arboriste', brought fruit trees from Provence.[14] Elsewhere these are specified as 'orangiers et autres arbres', not only for Fontainebleau but for the garden being made at Villers-Cotterets.[15] Perhaps the importance of this aspect is summed up in the commission to Girolamo della Robbia for

47 The Fontainebleau of François I and Catherine de Médicis. In the centre the Cour de la Fontaine faces south over the pond. Behind is the private garden (Jardin de la Reine) which Catherine enclosed by moats. The Cour Ovale is on the right with its entrance, the Porte Dorée. On the left the new Galerie d'Ulysse encloses the south side of the Cour du Cheval Blanc, with the Grotte des Pins on the extreme left.

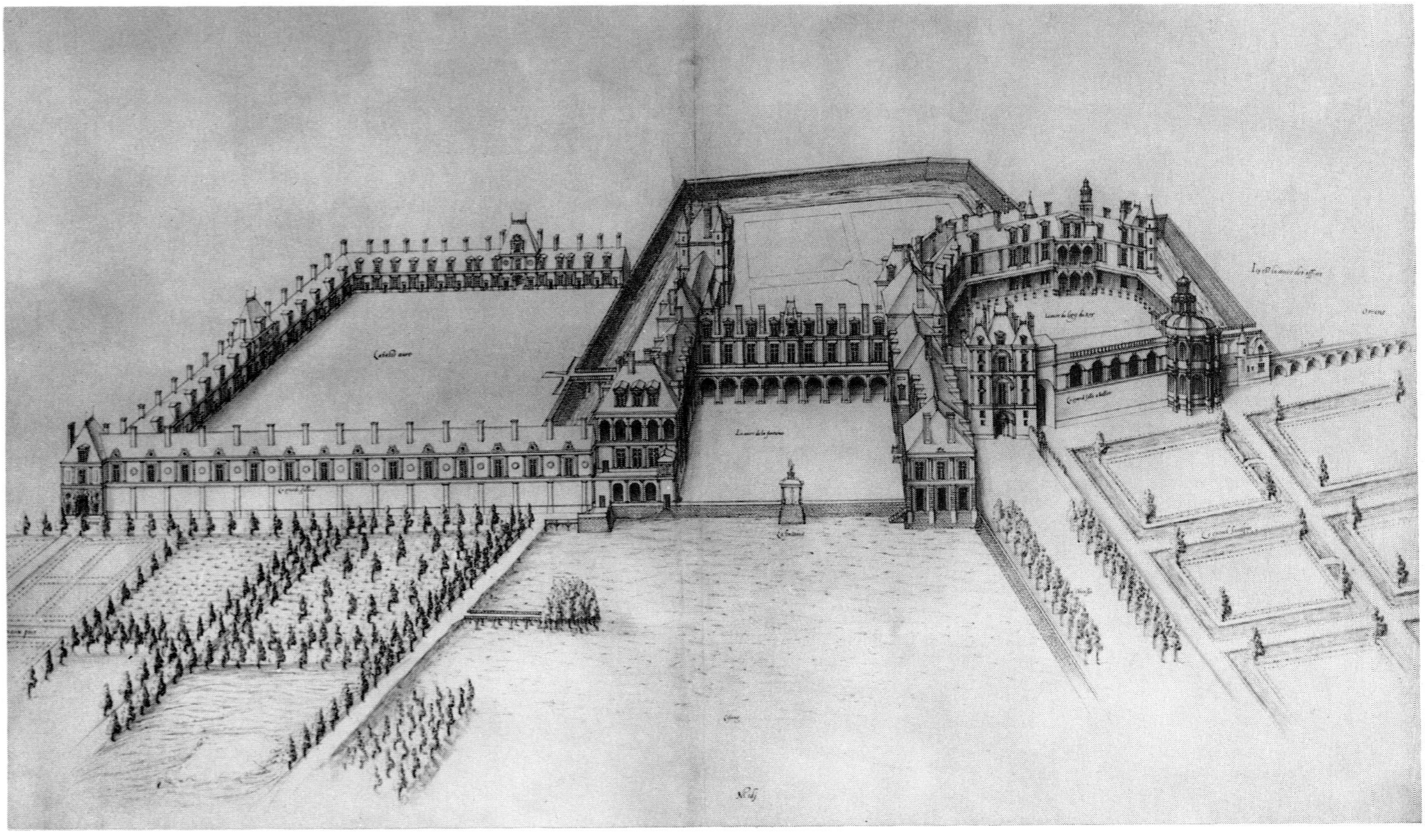

48, 49 Fontainebleau: the Cour de la Fontaine from south of the lake (above) and the Grotte des Pins (left).

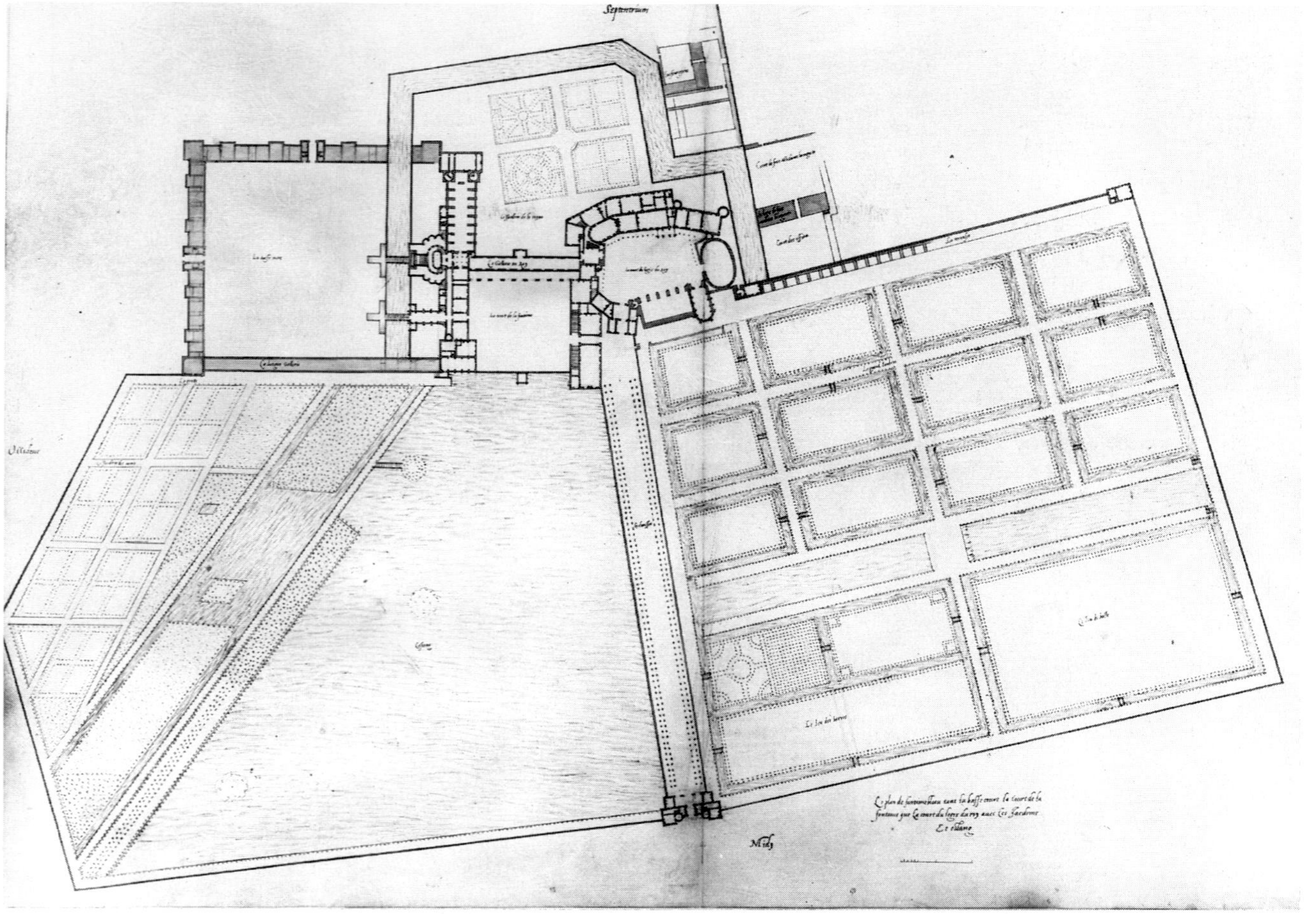

50 Plan of Fontainebleau. In the foreground, from left to right, the Jardin des Pins, the lake, the elm-lined causeway leading to the Porte Dorée, and the Grand Jardin.

'A big round enamelled terracotta plaque on the porch and entrance . . . decorated with a big triumphal crown all round, filled with several sorts of leaves and flowers, melons, cucumbers, pineapples, pomegranates, grapes, poppies, artichokes, lemons, oranges, peaches, frogs, lizards and snails and several others.'[16]

The Italians at Fontainebleau

The Florentine painter Gian Battista di Jacopo, called Il Rosso, came to Fontainebleau in 1530 to direct the decoration of the Grande Galerie. The following year Francesco Primaticcio was sent by the duke of Mantua to assist him. Primaticcio was only twenty-eight, and had been assisting Giulio Romano at the Palazzo del Tè. When Rosso died in 1541, Primaticcio was in charge of the works at Fontainebleau. As Vasari reports, Rosso lived more like a prince than an artist, with numerous servants and horses, his house furnished with tapestries, silver and other valuable furniture. Primaticcio, who was made abbot of Saint Martin, did the same. During the reign of Henri II, Philibert de l'Orme had the direction of all the building; but on Henri's death Catherine de Médicis again put Primaticcio in charge, a position he held until his death in 1570.

Rosso was hardly concerned with the gardens; and Primaticcio primarily with their architectural and sculptural ornament. In 1540 another gallery (the Galerie d'Ulysse) was built, continuing the line of the north side of the lake westwards, and forming the south side of a new *basse-cour* (later known as the Cour du Cheval Blanc). The ground floor of the terminal pavilion of this building was made as a grotto, opening onto the Jardin des Pins; if not the first, one 49
of the earliest architectural grottoes in France. It was built shortly after 1540, and is attributed by Blunt to Primaticcio.[17] The three-arched portico with crude figures of giants emerging from the rock could, he suggests, have been inspired by the Sala dei Giganti in the Palazzo del Tè at Mantua, painted by Giulio Romano between 1530 and 1535. The earliest recorded Italian Renaissance grottoes are those in the *giardino segreto* at the Palazzo del Tè (*c.*1532), and in the garden of Giovanni Gaddi at Rome (before 1538).[18] The Fontainebleau grotto does not resemble either of these. It seems to have been a purely architectural feature, not a fountain grotto. It is difficult to conceive, as some have done, how it could be used for bathing. Dimier says, 'the truth is that no one ever bathed in this grotto, any more than in that of Apollo at Versailles.'[19]

51 The Grotte des Pins and the Pavillon de Pomone at the north-west angle of the Jardin des Pins.

52 Drawing of a garden gallery by Vredemann de Vries. The gallery built by Primaticcio for Catherine de Médicis in the area north of the Cour Ovale (the Jardin de la Reine) was probably in this style.

Father Pierre Dan wrote in the early seventeenth century: 'In one of the corners of this garden, at the end of the Grande Galerie, is a square pavilion erected by the great king François, as shown by his monogram and motto, in which are two big pictures painted in fresco by the Sieur Rosso, where the loves of Vertumnus and Pomona are represented.'[20] The exact date of the Pavillon de Pomone is uncertain, but must be before Rosso's death, so is about 1540. It was in the northwest angle of the wall, between the Jardin des Pins and the street, just west of the grotto. It is shown in a
51 seventeenth-century engraving by Silvestre, and a drawing by Patel the elder. At first sight it would appear to be a curious place for such a building, until it is realized that its function was to protect frescoes by Primaticcio and Rosso; and that these in turn were in the nature of *trompe-l'oeil* paintings to terminate the vistas when approaching along paths from east and south. This also accounts for the composition which, in both cases, includes a *tonnelle* or pergola in perspective. Rosso's painting, representing the seduction of Pomona, goddess of orchards, by Vertumnus disguised as an old woman, is recorded in an engraving by Antonio Fantuzzi; [21] Primaticcio's in an engraving signed 'L.D.'.[22] It represents a gardening scene, with a Priapus on the pedestal of which is engraved 'A fontenebleau'.

It was about the same time that Giacomo Barozzi, called Vignola, was called upon to model and cast in bronze copies of ancient statues to ornament the private garden. These included Laocoon, Apollo Belvedere, and the sleeping Ariadne. The private gardens, north of the Cour Ovale (called on Du Cerceau's plan, Le Jardin de la Reine) were the main scene of work done for Catherine de Médicis under Primaticcio's supervision mostly between 1560 and 1563. It included surrounding the whole area with a moat; the building of an elaborate carved and painted wooden gallery; and ornamenting the garden with sculpture and decorated parterres. The gallery, shown in Du Cerceau's engravings parallel to the gallery of François I, was made between February 1560 and March 1561. Ambroise Perret, carpenter, received 250 *livres* for twenty-four large wooden columns; and at the same time five carvers were at work on it; including Germain Pilon who, among other things, provided four figures representing Mars, Mercury, Juno and Venus. The gallery was painted green and gilded. Its construction would have been similar to the contemporary gallery at Montargis, shown in Du Cerceau's engraving; but
52 more ornate, like the structures shown in the drawings of Vredemann de Vries.

Apart from construction work, large sums were spent on the gardens. The payments ordered by 'maistre Francisque Primadicis [Primaticcio], abbé de Saint Martin', included the purchase of 'several sorts of plants', and payments to 'gardeners, labourers, woodcutters, carters and others'.[23] Altogether 21,628 *livres* were spent at Fontainebleau in 1560–1, compared with 7329 *livres* in 1562. This last sum included work on a pleasure-house in the park called Mi-Voye, 'where there is a fine garden and several fountains and canals', says Pierre Dan. 'Catherine de Médicis, the queen mother, bought this place where she has a menagerie set up with a few cattle, and a beautiful "dairy", in order to go and amuse herself, keep cool and take dairy produce during the summer.' This retreat in the park, east of the Grand Jardin and north of where the great canal was later made, was ornamented, painted and gilded like all the rest. Among the painters was Niccolo dell' Abbate; and one, Renoult (or Renoud) called Fondet, who did grotesques. The sculptor Firmin Rousset modelled signs of the zodiac in plaster, three stories in stucco bas-relief, and a figure of Cybele in wood for the newell of the spiral stair between the queen's study and her chamber. All this has disappeared but its character may be imagined from what still survives at Fontainebleau.

Serlio and Philibert de l'Orme: Ancy-le-Franc and Anet

Sebastiano Serlio was the most important Italian architect to have worked in France hitherto. Vignola, although he came to Fontainebleau with Primaticcio a year before Serlio, was over thirty years younger, and his original contributions to garden architecture (at the Villa Papa Giulio, and probably the Villa Lante and Caprarola) were in the future. Nevertheless, Serlio's books on architecture were more influential than his buildings. *Regole Generali di Architettura*[24] was published in Venice in 1537. It was a book directed towards practice, in which the drawings and diagrams were of equal, if not more importance than the text; and as a manual it superseded all previous works. Among other things it was the first book of its kind to give patterns for the laying out of gardens in the form of labyrinths or other regular figures. The next volume[25] was published in Venice in 1540. It set down the results of his study of the buildings of antiquity in Rome and elsewhere, as well as those of his immediate predecessors, particularly Bramante. It included drawings of the exedra in the Belvedere Court of the Vatican; and a plan and section of Poggio Reale which, in its general form, is related to the only existing building associated with Serlio in France, the château of Ancy-le-Franc, near Tonnerre, in Burgundy. The book was dedicated to François I; and it was François' sister, Marguerite d'Angoulême, who gave the order to the treasurer to pay 'à Sebastiano Serlio de Boullogne, architecteur du roy', an annual salary of 100 *écus d'or*, beginning 1 January 1540 (OS) and to continue as long as it shall please her. He dedicated his fifth book to her.

In 1541 Serlio is described as 'paintre et architecteur ordinaire au faict de nos dicts édiffices et bastiments audit Fontainebleau'. As long as Primaticcio was in charge all went well for Serlio; but when, after François' death, Philibert de l'Orme was in control of the royal buildings, he was no more than tolerated. About 1550 he went to Lyon; but returned to Fontainebleau where he died in 1554.

At the best of times he does not seem to have acted as more than an advisor. He designed an open loggia overlooking the Cour Ovale on one side and the garden (presumably the Grand Jardin) on the other. This was not made. Serlio wrote, 'but I who was in that place, and lived there continuously,

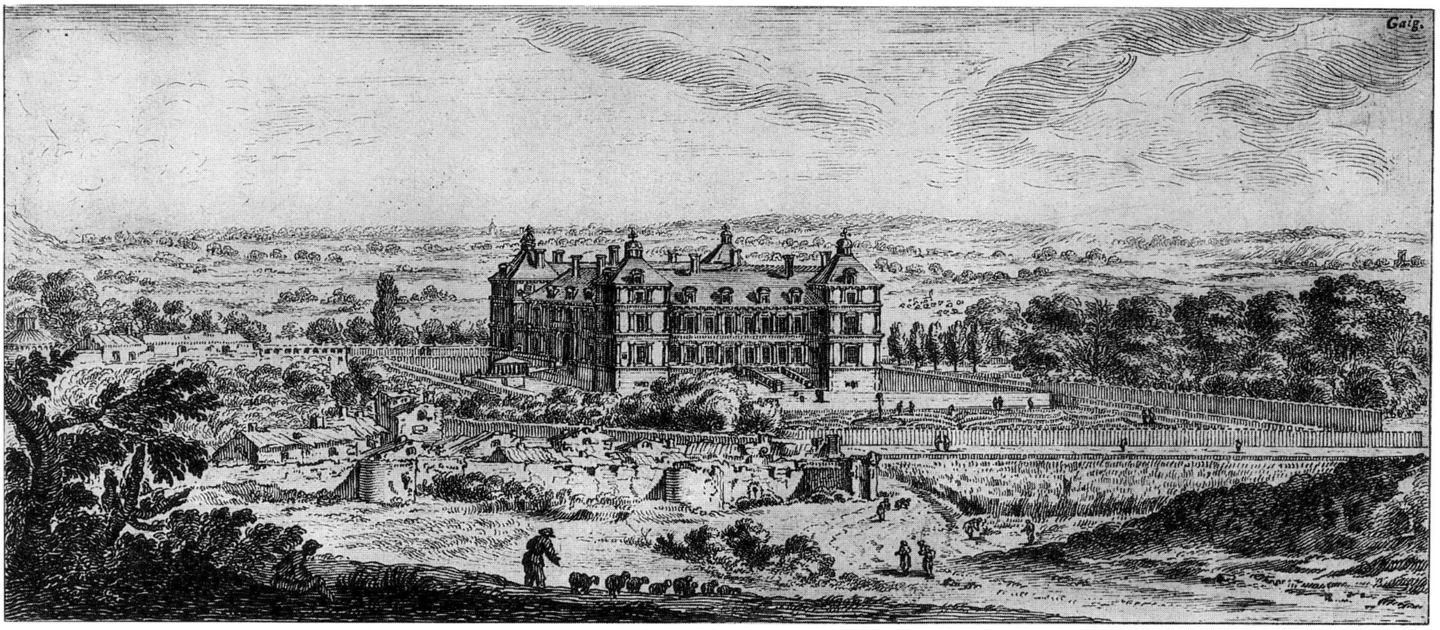

53, 54, 55 Ancy-le-Franc: a mid seventeenth-century view showing the garden in a semi-derelict state (above), an early eighteenth-century plan for a restored garden and park (below left) and an aerial photograph (below right).

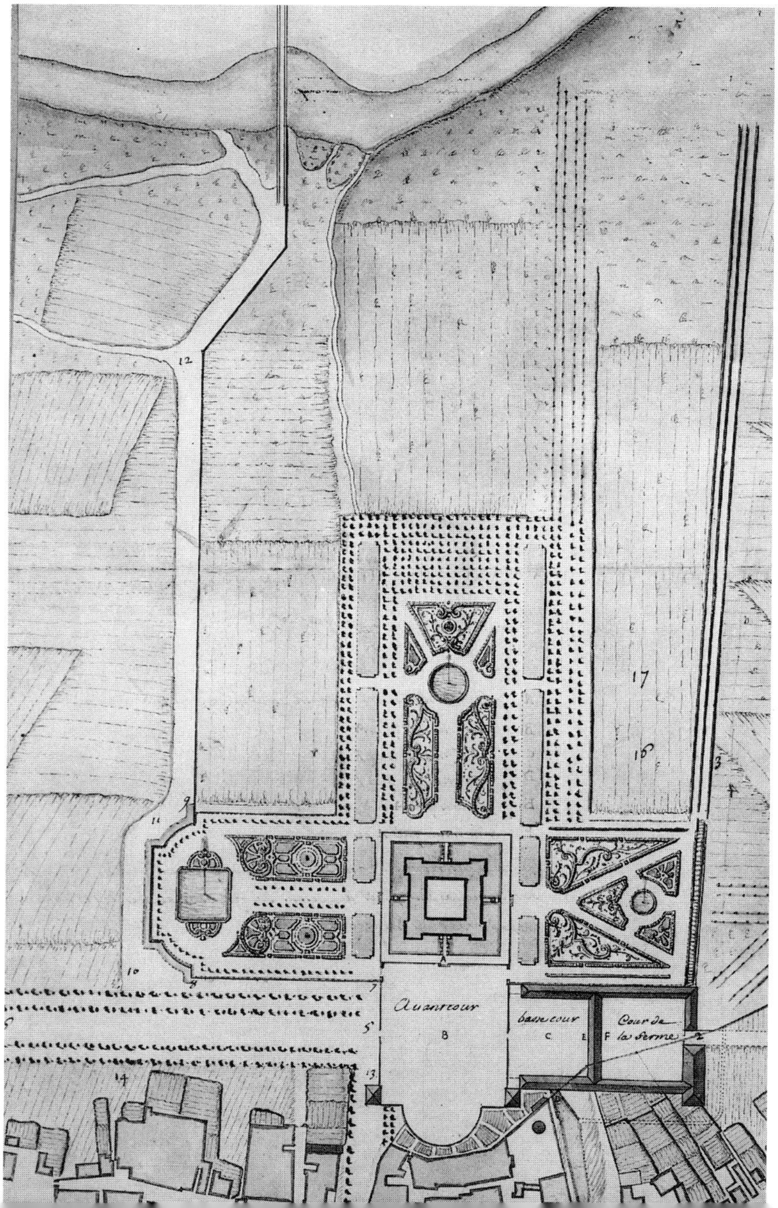

was not asked for the least advice.' He continued with his treatise on architecture, however. Books I and II were published in Paris in 1545, with texts in Italian and French. The French translation was by Jean Martin, who also made the first French translation of Colonna's *Hypnerotomachia Poliphili* (called *Le Songe de Poliphile*) published in 1546; and of Vitruvius's *De Architectura* in 1547, the year when Serlio's fifth book was also published. There are two manuscripts for an unpublished sixth book, one at Columbia University, the other at Munich.[26] These contain designs for the cardinal of Ferrara's house at Fontainebleau, known as the 'Grand Ferrare', the Louvre, and the château of Ancy-le-Franc. The first is destroyed with the exception of a doorway; the second was never built; the third still exists.

ANCY-LE-FRANC

The date 1546 is inscribed over the door in the rear façade at Ancy. Professor Guillaume has argued[27] that it probably indicates the beginning rather than the end of the work; and that although the château was begun to Serlio's design, it was completed by another architect who was probably French. Serlio gave his designs in the manuscript of his unpublished sixth book. The finished building differs considerably from them. On the other hand Jacques Androuet du Cerceau's drawings, published some thirty years after the house was 56
begun, show the whole disposition of house and grounds. This represents a completely integrated and regular house and garden plan. Du Cerceau says that it is so pleasing to look at that it might have been made in one day. He knows of nothing like it. The château was surrounded by a raised terrace about 6 metres wide ('trois toises') outside the moat and 4 metres ('deux toises') above it, from where there is a view over the garden. From the centre of the south side of the terrace, steps led to the entrance of the garden, which lies opposite the steps across a strip of grass. The garden itself is surrounded by a hedge and a canal and is divided into twelve equal rectangular areas. Opposite the entrance, at the far end of the central axis, is another opening leading to a *bosquet* which closes the whole of the walled area to the south. Within the *bosquet* is a walk at right angles to the centre axis, leading on either side to green rooms, called on the drawn plan: 'Cabinets tous couverts de buissons' (B.M.48).

56 The château and garden of Ancy-le-Franc.

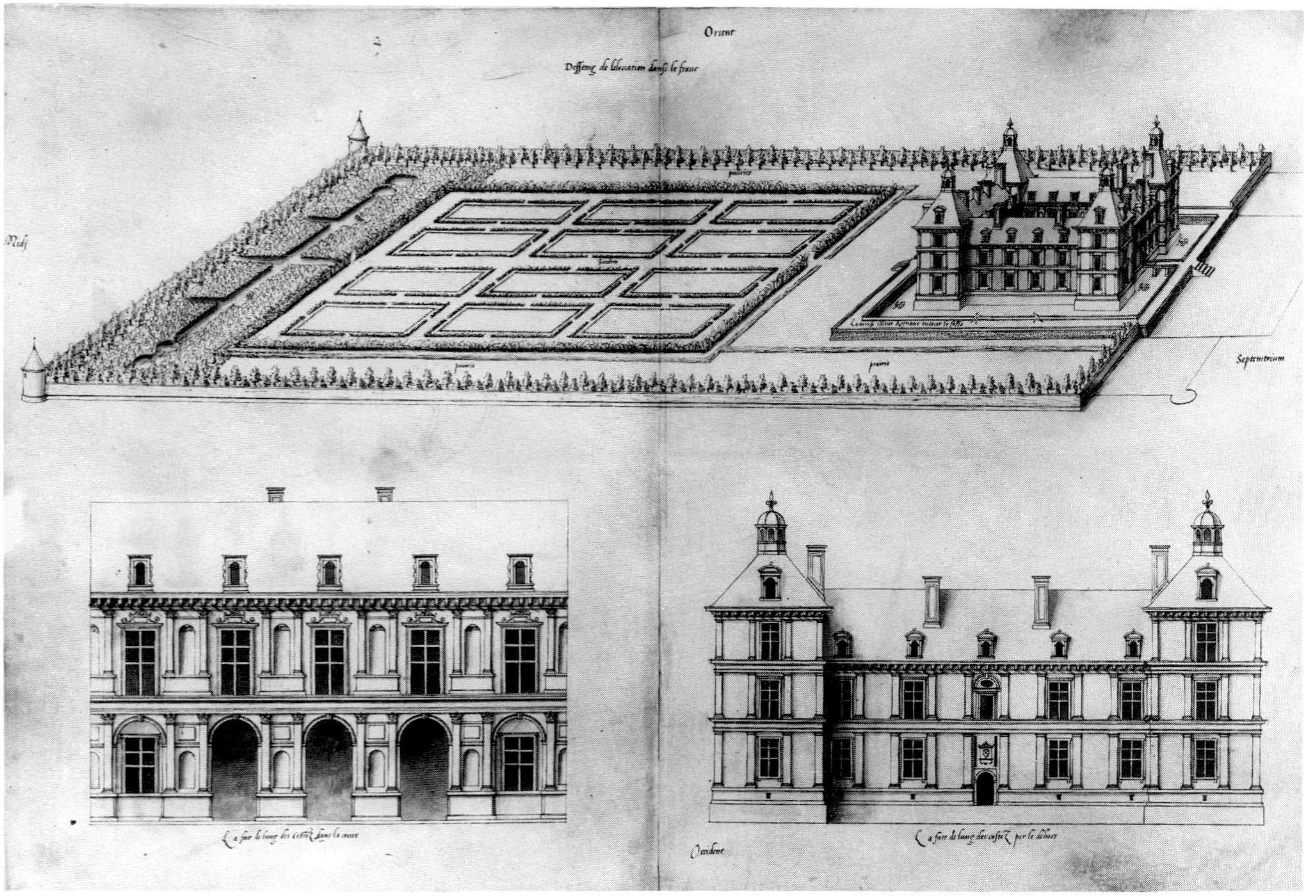

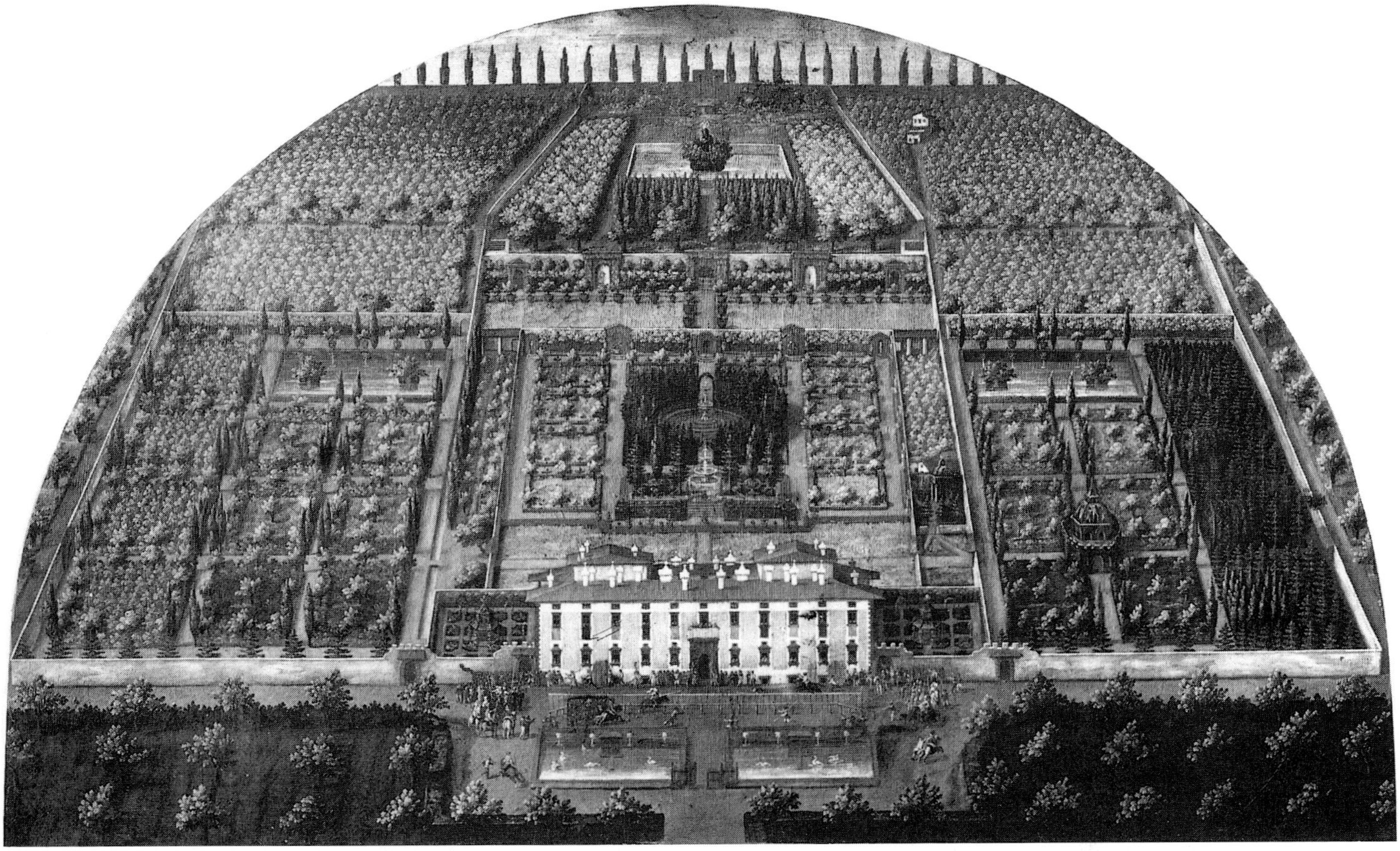

57 Castello, a Medici villa near Florence (painting by Utens), contemporary with Ancy-le-Franc.

57 There are parallels with the contemporary garden plan of Castello designed by Tribolo for Cosimo de' Medici, the first duke of Tuscany, in the 1540s. Both gardens are laid out symmetrically about the extended axis of the house. At Castello the main garden is separated from the house by a level strip, possibly grass; so it is at Ancy. In each case the garden ends in a *bosquet* – a common feature in Italy, but new in a French garden. However, the resemblance ends with the general disposition of the parts. The sites are quite different. Ancy is completely flat, while the ground at Castello rises gently and is terraced. The treatment is also dissimilar, for at Castello the middle of the garden was planted with 'high and thick cypresses, laurels and myrtles growing wild, and forming a labyrinth surrounded by a hedge'; whereas at Ancy, according to Du Cerceau's drawing, there were no trees in the garden, whose twelve rectangular divisions have the appearance of flat and unvaried regularity.

Although it is no more than conjecture, the similarity of Serlio's general plan of Ancy-le-Franc to the section of Poggio Reale in his third book, may be of significance. Evidently Serlio had no direct experience of Poggio Reale; 26
and according to Hersey[28] based his drawings on descriptions by Marcantonio Michiel written in 1509. But his friend Peruzzi left rough sketch plans which have been variously interpreted. Hersey's own interpretation, excluding the lower garden and fishpond, may be compared with Du Cerceau's version. Moreover, it appears that Du Cerceau had seen Serlio's unpublished projects for Ancy-le-Franc,[29] and may therefore have been aware of more than we now know.

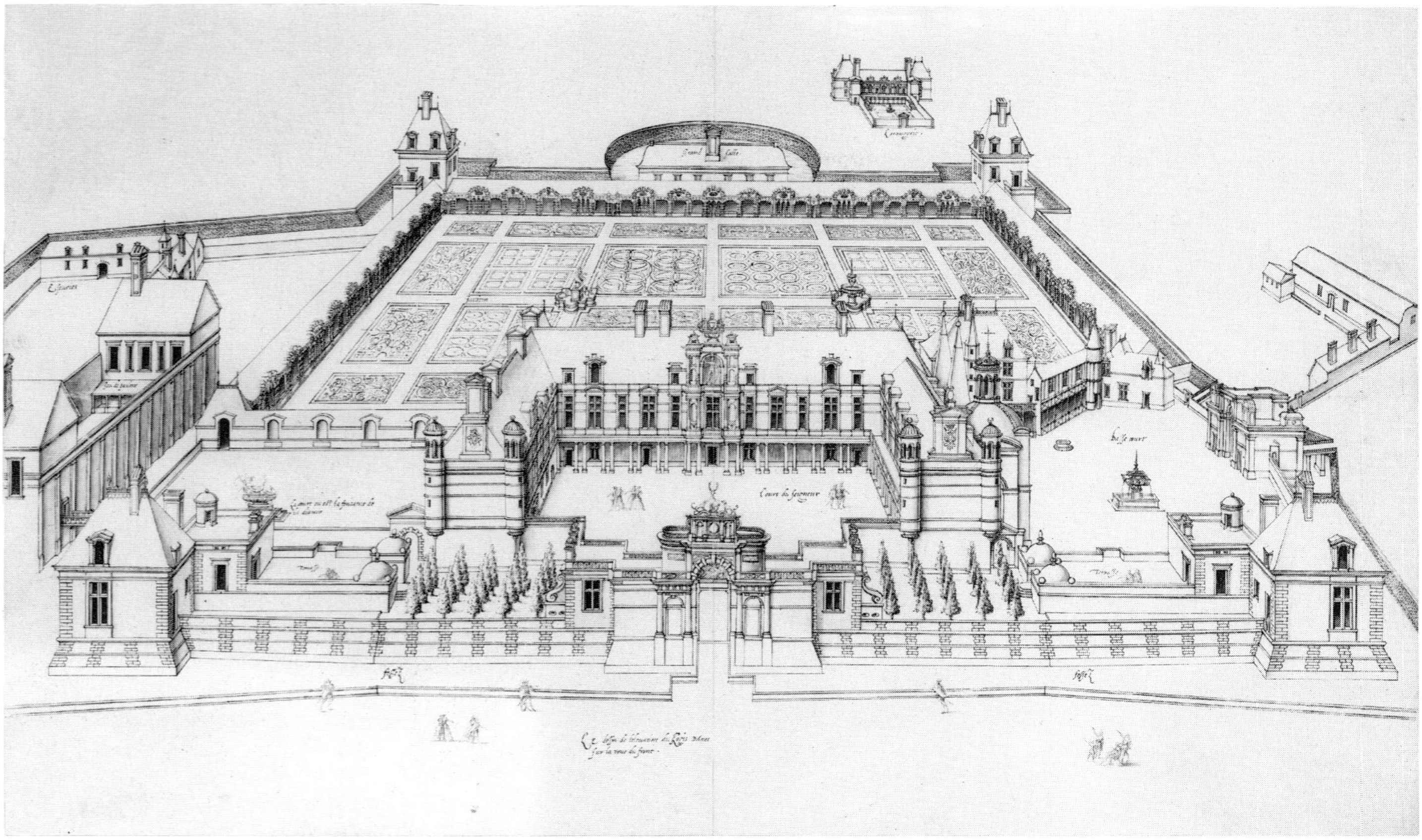

58 The château and garden of Anet. The Fontaine de Diane stands in the left-hand courtyard.

ANET

Ancy-le-Franc was without precedent in France. The French tradition was continued at Anet, where the formal axial approach established at Bury was developed. Philibert de l'Orme was Serlio's heir in more senses than one. He literally succeeded him as superintendent of the royal buildings on François' death; and *Le Premier Tome de l'Architecture* (1568) followed Serlio's treatise, a French answer to the Italian's work. De l'Orme was also the first Frenchman to work out a consistent style marrying the traditions of the past with new
58 lessons from Renaissance Italy. Anet incorporated the garden within an architectural whole in an original way, paralleled by Vignola's almost contemporary design for the Villa Giulia in Rome, although of course, the French and Italian projects are quite dissimilar in scale and conception.

Anet was the family home of Diane de Poitiers' husband, Louis de Brézé, Grand Sénéchal de Normandie. Jacques de Brézé, Louis' father, had been condemned to death for killing his wife's lover. He was reprieved for a fine of 100,000 gold crowns, in lieu of which he offered his estates. He was pardoned by Charles VIII, but abandoned his lands and titles to his son Louis, Diane's husband. On Louis' death an order was made to seize Anet again for the crown. This was disputed by Diane, who was granted its use and the enjoyment of its revenues for herself and her daughters. Immediately on his accession in 1547, Henri made Diane the gift of Anet, and created her duchesse de Valentinois, a title to which her family had long laid claim. Anet was the place Diane loved best. Its rebuilding was at the same time a celebration and a memorial; the one was symbolized by the ubiquitous monogram DH; the other by the sarcophagi (they are in fact chimneys) which decorate the entrance gateway and the terrace at either side. Although not a royal building, De l'Orme says in his *Instruction*[30] that the king was more interested in what was being done at Anet than in all his royal houses, and got cross when De l'Orme did not go there often enough.

There is some dispute about when the rebuilding of Anet began. The evidence has been summarized by Heliot,[31] and on balance it seems that De l'Orme started there about 1546, and that the main part of the work was finished by 1552, the date over the entrance gate. He was required to preserve the old house of the Brézé. As he himself put it: 'at the château of Anet, . . . for allowing me to do what I wanted in the conduct of the new building, I neatly incorporated the old house, which was as difficult and tiresome a thing to do as may be imagined.' In *Architecture* book III, chapter 65, he sets out the problem of a nobleman who wants to build a fine new house

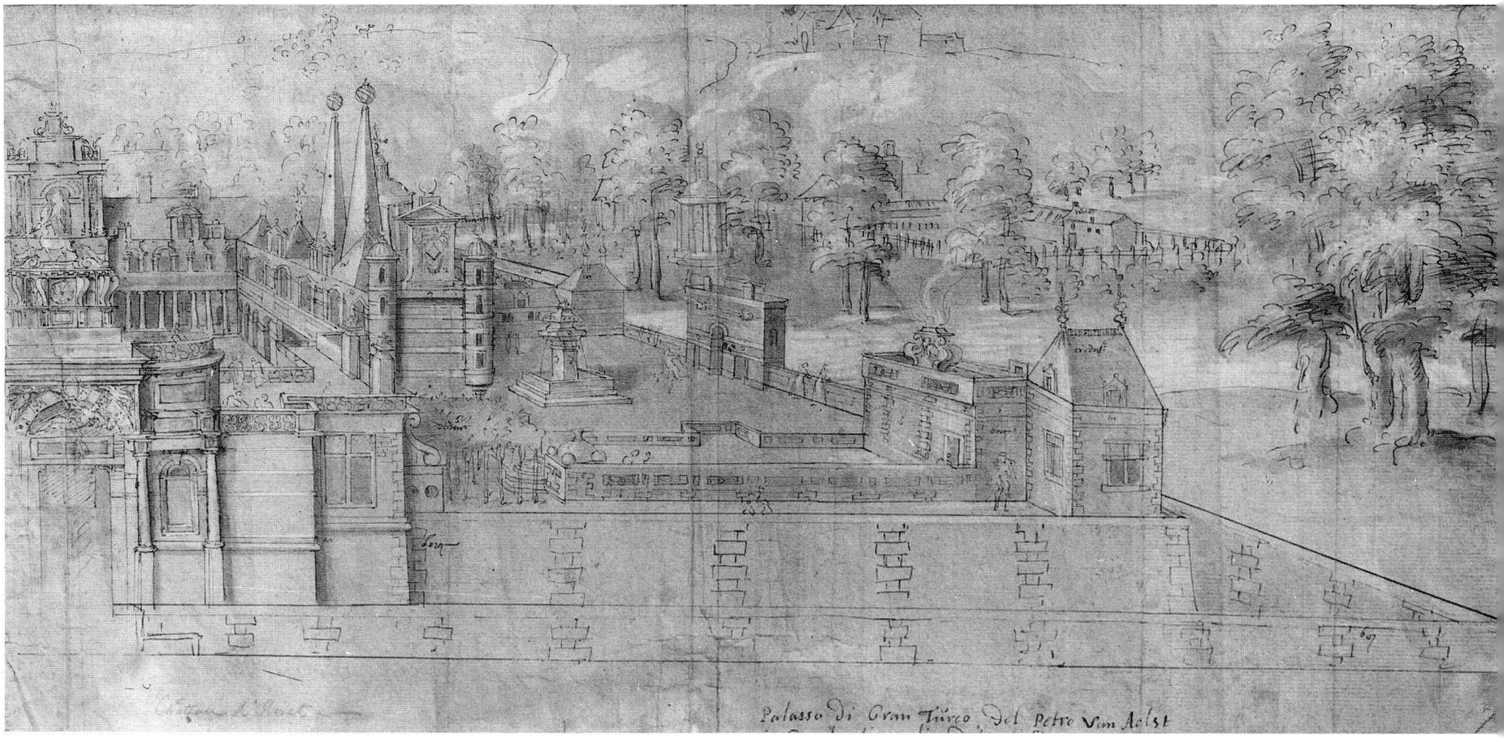

59 The right-hand side of the château of Anet, with the gatehouse on the left and the right-hand pavilion. Note the classical open temple in the park on the right. An anonymous sixteenth-century drawing.

while preserving the old one. In the first place, says De l'Orme, he needs an architect of good judgment, who will not straightway tell him to pull everything down and build afresh; and, of course, one who will incorporate the irregularity of the old into a regular plan, as required by the principles of Vitruvius and Alberti. 'This place seems to me to be most suitable, the better to show the use of geometric lines and the convenience which they offer in avoiding obstacles one can sometimes meet; and also for incorporating old dwellings in new ones . . . and that the work requires it for its beauty, perfection and decoration.' All this he learned at Anet where, despite the freedom he says he had, there were difficulties in doing exactly what he wanted. For one thing he was not always on the spot, and on returning he would find the workmen had not obeyed instructions. 'If they had not made me work so much, I would have thought up many more beautiful works than there are there', he wrote (fo. 12v.).

De l'Orme's solution was to plan a new symmetrical layout with a central axis. The main buildings were designed around three sides of a courtyard; the fourth was closed by a grand entrance gateway. The scale was such that it dwarfed the old irregular buildings[32] incorporated round a courtyard adjoining the east wing, while another courtyard balanced it on the west. The extension on either side of the gatehouse, flanked by identical pavilions, stretched the whole width of
the three courtyards, giving a symmetrical appearance to the
front. Two small architectural gardens,[33] each consisting of a 59
grove planted as a quincunx and a terrace, linked the
gatehouse with the pavilions. The terrace, which was in fact
the roof of a cellar or store, was approached from the grove
by a flight of oval steps, based on Bramante's design in the 60
Belvedere Court of the Vatican. They were flanked by broad, squat pillars with hemispherical domes. The wall closing the terrace was surmounted by a sarcophagus. The little garden was thus a memorial to the dead Louis de Brézé; and in contrast to the symbolism elsewhere which recalled the status and ancestry of the family, it was a reminder of mortality. The importance given to the gateway and to the centrepiece of the main Corps de Logis marked the axis of approach which led through the house to a terrace which overlooked a garden enclosed on the three remaining sides by galleries or cloisters, with pavilions at the northeast and northwest corners. A building used for entertainment and bathing jutted into a crescent-shaped basin formed from the moat, and terminated the main axis at the end of the garden. This repeats the scheme at Bury: buildings round three sides of a court, the fourth closed by a wall and gateway; an axial approach marked by the gateway and the central pavilion of the main Corps de Logis, with the garden as a climax. But the scale and importance of the garden at Anet was immeasurably greater. The enclosed part alone (and there

60 Anet: view looking right from the gatehouse, up the oval steps towards the wall surmounted by a sarcophagus.

61 One of the marble fountains of Anet, not in its original position.

were subsidiary gardens in the park) was larger than the area occupied by all three courtyards of the château. The galleries enclosing the garden were in the tradition of Blois and Gaillon, although grander and more substantial. The terrace had no precedent in France. It was made over a cryptoporticus contained between the projecting east and west wings of the château. Du Cerceau lovingly describes the terrace 'from which . . . one views the garden, which is given beauty seen from here'. A double flight of steps in the shape of a crescent descended to the level of the garden and echoed the shape of the basin terminating the main axis. The basin could not, of course, be seen from the terrace, but the gallery which hid it on the far side of the garden would not have obscured views of the countryside beyond. The cryptoporticus has been fully discussed by architectural historians and its original appearance with the steps was reconstructed by A. Bourgeois.[34] Parts of it can still be seen in a ruinous state. Its original function was to strengthen the foundations of the main building (which has now disappeared) by a system of vaulting; its secondary purpose – to serve as a loggia open to the garden and to support a terrace – made a virtue of necessity, one of the things De l'Orme says in his treatise that a good architect should do. Precedents existed in Italy, and Blunt specifically mentions the Villa Madama,[35] where the loggia forms part of the villa, but where the terrace of the *giardino segreto* is carried on vaults.

According to Du Cerceau's plan and perspective view, the garden was divided into twenty-four rectangular beds: eight squares in two rows of four in the central part, bordered by half squares, and with quarter squares in the corners. Two
61 marble fountains were placed symmetrically at the intersections of the paths. One of these was rediscovered and now stands at the entrance to the modern garden, north of
62 the surviving west wing. The famous Fontaine de Diane, illustrated by Du Cerceau, stood in the west courtyard. Du Cerceau does not show the decoration of the parterres; but Olivier de Magny (*c.*1529–*c.*1560), in an ode in praise of the gardens of Anet, says that some of them were in the form of

> monograms and mottoes
> the whole in plants so well feigned
> one would almost say that it was painted.

Despite the sycophantic tone of the poem, it is given credibility by the specific reference to some of the designs. It would be entirely in keeping with Diane's character, and the decoration of the rest of the château, that they were emblematic references to her own ancestry and to her connection with the royal house of France. It would also be in accordance with what is known of practice elsewhere.[36] As might be expected there was a crescent with the letter H and the arms of France. Beside it were the Médicis arms quartered with three fleurs-de-lys, and the crescents of the Poitiers, Coultron and Saint-Vallier families. Surrounding the lozenge figure was an interwoven band of knots, surmounted by a ducal crown, all composed of small different-coloured flowers.[37] These figures were probably made in the squares nearest the terrace, so that on arriving from the entrance the visitor was faced with the status and ancestry of the owner rather than an invitation to view a garden.

Claude Mollet in *Le Théâtre des Plans et Jardinages* writes of the large number of flowers and medicinal herbs grown at Anet when his father, Jacques Mollet, was gardener there; but this was after 1576 when the château passed to Charles II of Lorraine, Duc d'Aumale, son of Diane's second daughter Louise. Mollet records that the first *parterres de broderie* in France (see Chapter 6) were made at Anet on the instructions of Etienne du Perac, when he was employed by the Duc d'Aumale after 1582.[38] De l'Orme's gallery, a traditional feature of French Renaissance gardens, was nevertheless more permanent and elaborate than its predecessors; and it probably provoked the cardinal de Bourbon to add a fine one to his garden at Gaillon (Anet and Gaillon are not far from one another) sometime after 1550. Du Cerceau's drawing of Anet shows that the roof was supported on the garden side by pillars with bands similar to De l'Orme's French order. The gallery was destroyed in the course of the seventeenth-century alterations, but a fragment of the paving, a mosaic of brick and stone, survives in the present grounds. De l'Orme invented a particular kind of roof which he used for the pavilions at the northeast and northwest corners. Of these he wrote: 'I had it made at the château of Anet . . . at the two little pavilions which are in the park on the river, where players of *small horns*, trumpets and other instruments could be placed, to give pleasure to the king and princes when they were in the said park.' The idea of a building jutting into the semicircular basin between these two pavilions recalls the garden loggia of Poggio Reale; but De l'Orme says it was intended as a cellar. When it was roofed its use was changed to a room for games and entertainments, and as a place for bathing. In his *Nouvelles Inventions*, De l'Orme describes it as 'the room in front of the baths near the galleries of the big parterre of the garden'. The room was about 10 metres wide and 40 metres long. A description of Anet in 1640 says it was a building of two storeys, 'from where a secret descent behind leads within to a very big basin of water which is esteemed very pure, healthy and suitable for bathing'.

De l'Orme was justly proud of Anet. Among references to it in his *Architecture* is one on canalization. When an architect has to build on marshy ground, he says, he must show intelligence and imagination in draining it. The little canals which are necessary to do this may collect the water in basins of various forms, to give pleasure or to breed fish or for some other profitable use, 'as I had done from necessity in the park of the château of Anet where the place was so waterlogged that one could not go there: nevertheless I made it as delightful and pleasant as any park or garden one may see, provided it is well maintained . . .'(*Architecture*, fo. 46). This is a clear indication that De l'Orme was as much concerned in the design of grounds as of buildings. Du Cerceau, in the description of Anet in the second volume of *Les Plus Excellents Bastiments de France*, says that the park outside the garden was walled and divided into distinct areas separated by tree-lined walks (*allées*) or canals. Some of the areas were planted as orchards, others were meadow, thicket, wood or

62 The Fontaine de Diane, Anet. Engraving by Du Cerceau.

warren. Immediately adjoining the northeast corner of the garden was the Orangery, a single-storey block linking two pavilions of two storeys with high-pitched roofs. It was self-contained, within a walled garden of its own. A design for the entrance door, crowned with two crescents, is given in *Architecture* (fo. 244v. and plate fo. 248). On the extreme right of Du Cerceau's bird's-eye view, at the northeast corner of a group of outbuildings, is the aviary described as a room with a semicircular vault. An anonymous sixteenth-century
59 drawing of this area shows an open temple of columns
supporting a shallow dome, crowned with Diane de Poitiers' crescent emblem. It is similar to the rotundas common in English landscape gardens from the early part of the eighteenth century. North of the aviary was the heronry, a fairly simple cage astride a canal.

Within thirty years of Diane de Poitiers' death the gardens of Anet were in decay. Because of the treason of her grandson, Charles of Lorraine, Duc d'Aumale, Anet was condemned to be razed. Aumale saved himself by flight; Anet was reprieved by Henri IV, and sold in 1614. The grounds were completely redesigned by Le Nôtre, or more probably by his nephew, Claude Desgots, for Louis-Joseph de Vendôme between 1681 and 1688. These later developments are not within the scope of the present chapter, but a comparison of Du Cerceau's view and Desgots' plan
with a modern aerial photograph reveals how small a grand 279
Renaissance garden was, compared with the grandiose schemes of the late seventeenth century. All Diane de Poitiers' park buildings lay in a third of the area occupied by the huge seventeenth-century parterres. Her garden occupied only the central part of the parterre nearest the house in Desgots' scheme. In the aerial photograph the limits of the gallery are shown by a small white mark, a surviving fragment of the pavement between the curved path and the château. The huge areas covered by seventeenth-century garden planning made symmetry topographically impossible. The plans show clearly the open asymmetrical balance which replaced the Renaissance ideal of closed symmetry. Closure on such a scale was virtually pointless. Thus, Diane de Poitiers' gallery and her other garden buildings were swept away. Her gardens had long been neglected, and were ruinous anyway.

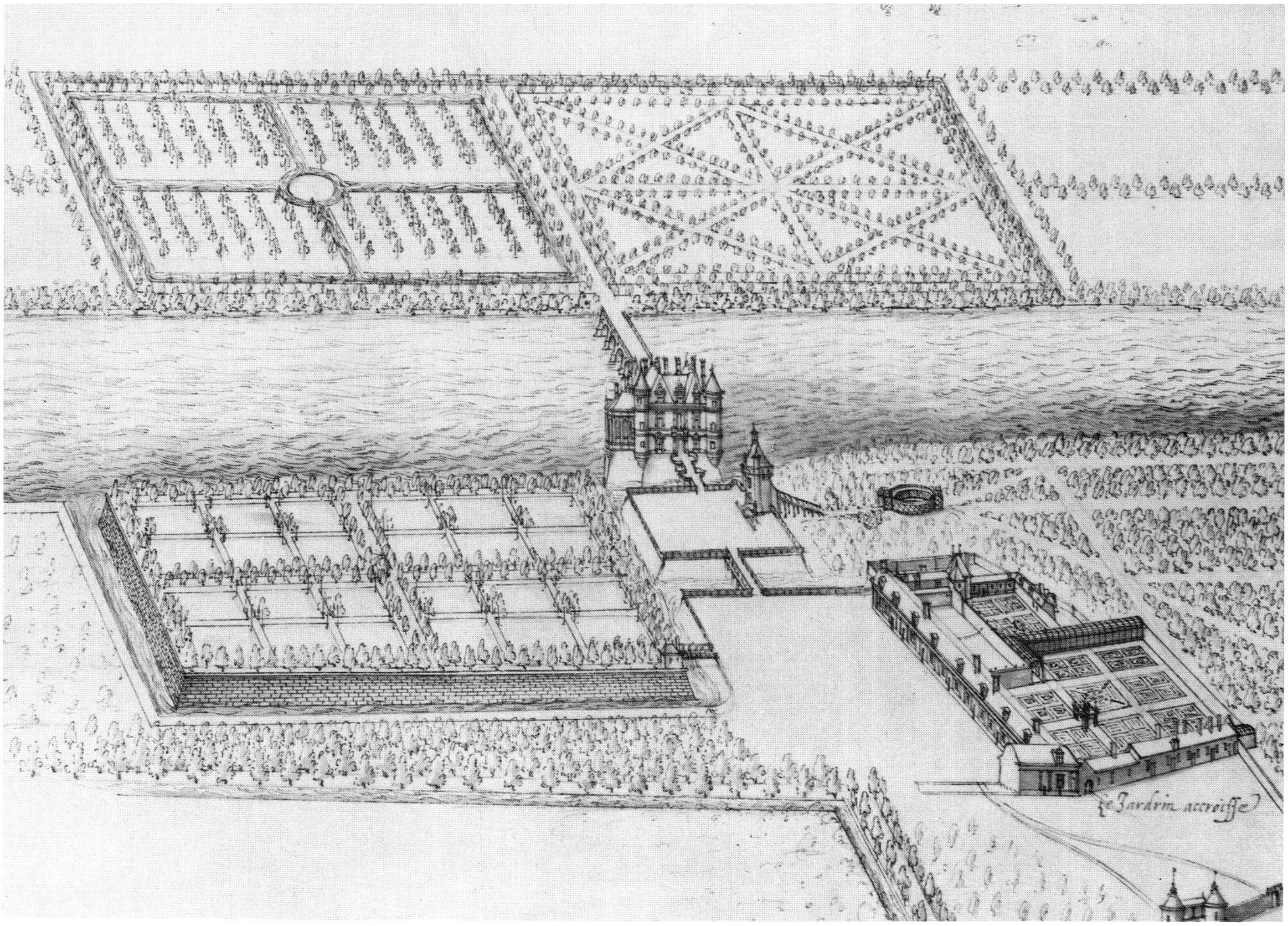

63 The château and garden of Chenonceaux. Detail of a drawing by Du Cerceau. The round structure to the right of the château is the trellis surrounding the Fontaine de Rocher. See ill. 77.

CHENONCEAUX

De l'Orme was also associated with Diane de Poitiers' garden at Chenonceaux, the making of which is very well recorded, thanks to the work of Abbé Casimir Chevalier in publishing Diane's accounts and other documents. These give the most complete picture we have of gardening practice in mid-sixteenth-century France. Early in the fifteenth century a castle belonging to the Marques family on the banks of the River Cher was razed to punish the owner for having received a garrison of English. In 1432 Jean Marques II obtained permission to build the *donjon* which still stands on the west side of the forecourt, near the entrance of the present château. This was originally built by Thomas Bohier, who acquired Chenonceaux in 1512. The credit for thinking of a house actually standing in the river, on the foundations of a mill, is his. Bohier was a financier; and during the early part of François I's reign he was called upon to administer the revenues of the duchy of Milan. After his death an enquiry into the conduct of the financiers resulted in his heir, Antoine Bohier, being declared debtor for 190,000 *livres* to the treasury; and to liquidate this Chenonceaux was ceded to the crown. Henri II gave it to Diane de Poitiers, at the same time as he created her duchesse de Valentinois and gave her Anet. The queen, Catherine, immediately questioned the legality of the gift; and in order to establish Diane's title, an elaborate legal comedy was started, in which the ownership reverted to Bohier. Diane ultimately bought it for 50,000 *livres*. Although she enjoyed the revenue of the estate from the start, and repaired the buildings, she does not seem to have used it. None of her published letters are addressed from Chenonceaux.

Bohier had left one garden, the Jardin du Pavillon, apparently on the west of the entrance, near the old *donjon* called La Tour des Marques. It was presumably on the site

63 shown in Du Cerceau's drawing (B.M.90), although the range of buildings lining the forecourt were added after Diane had ceded Chenonceaux to Catherine de Médicis. Vines were grown there, for much attention was given in 1548 and 1549 to repairing and making trellis. This was work of a fairly substantial kind, for 'grand Jehan Rasteau, maistre cherpentier, demeurant d'Amboise' was paid 50 *livres tournois* 'pour la façon des treilles de cherpenterye qu'il a faictes au jardin du pavillon'. There is also mention of a fountain.

64 In 1551 Diane set about making a new garden on the north bank of the Cher, east of the château forecourt. Responsibility for this was given to the abbot of Pontlevoy, Bernard de Ruthie, who was also Grand-Aumonier of France. Pontlevoy was only 15 kilometres to the east, and the work was supervised by the maître d'hôtel of the abbey, Benoit Guy, Sieur des Carroys, with the help of the steward of Chenonceaux, André Bereau. The specification is given in the accounts.[39] The garden was to be an enclosed area of about $2\frac{1}{2}$ acres (*arpents*); a rectangle with the longer side running east-west, bounded on the south by the river, on the north by the warren, on the east by the arable fields belonging to the château farm. It was to be protected from flooding by a wall of earth, held together and reinforced by a wooden frame and faced with stone. This was to go all round the garden, forming a raised terrace (*levée*), in turn surrounded by moats, the water being controlled by a sluice in the southeast corner. Construction began in the spring of 1551, and continued on and off until the winter of 1554, with work on the walls, moats and garden overlapping. The *allées* of the garden were laid out early in 1552; and 200 fruit trees from the garden of the archbishop of Tours at Saint-Avertin were delivered by boat. They are not named, but plum, cherry and pear trees were bought later. In the spring of 1553, 100 willows were planted between the river and the garden wall; and Bereau collected 150 white mulberries from monseigneur de la Bourdaisière in Tours. These were associated with the newly introduced culture of the silk worm.

Unfortunately the Cher flooded in April 1555, making breaches in the wall and carrying away all the turf on the river side. In September, grass and weeds were knee high on the terrace, and the castle yard was also in need of clearing of bushes, brambles and thorns. A great deal of work was needed to put right the damage in the garden. In January 1557 the archbishop of Tours sent his own gardener from Vernou to supervise the work. He brought 27 unspecified fruit trees, 6 apricots, 300 'pomyers de Paradis' (a dwarf apple cultivated at Tours), 8 bundles of currants, 100 musk roses and lily bulbs. Charlot Guérin, who had been gardener at Chenonceaux since 1552, died later in the year, and his place was taken by Jacques Dutertre. He was regularly assisted by two other men, Guillaume Martin and Lois Dagault, with

64 Chenonceaux, the garden of Diane de Poitiers.

others as the occasion demanded. They hoed the peas, artichokes and onions, and prepared new beds. The archbishop's gardener left a boy 'pour tendre les plants des parterres'. This evidently referred to ornamental planting, since parts of the garden were laid out in the form of a labyrinth and other figures. The labyrinth was uprooted in 1557, and the white mulberries were transplanted to the warren. Indeed, the main purpose of the garden was to provide fruit and vegetables (artichokes, leeks, onions, cucumbers, spring cabbage, melons and currants). Violets and strawberries were planted in large quantities; but apart from lilies and musk roses, no other flowers are mentioned. Du Cerceau's bird's-eye view shows the garden divided at right angles by two main *allées*, with the four quarters subdivided by narrow *allées*, giving 24 beds of equal size.

While the garden was being rearranged, extensive planting was going on outside it. The 11,392 hawthorns bought in 1556 were probably for hedges made in the warren. In February 1557 Martin and two others were employed planting elms, hazel and other plants round the cabinets which were being made there. At the same time an avenue of elms was planted along the approach to the château. This was the main axis of a scheme to lay out the grounds on a much grander scale; and we may suspect the hand of Henri II's new architect in charge, Philibert de l'Orme, who was now directing work at Chenonceaux. It was he who in 1556/7 supervised the work on the bridge linking the château with the garden which was ultimately made on the far bank of the Cher; although these features were only completed later, to the order of Catherine de Médicis, and not to De l'Orme's designs.

The uniqueness of Chenonceaux lies in the way the site is used, building not along, but in the river. Jean Guillaume suggests that its originality goes beyond this.[40] At the time it was built, he says, the concept of a regular building, repeating the same measures or their multiples throughout, was only parallelled at Bury, then in the course of construction. The architect of Bury regularized the traditional courtyard plan; Chenonceaux was the compact type. The wide corridors which traverse the building are not really explained by the necessities of interior planning.

> The role of the corridors is to lead to the windows which give on the river. When one entered the château, after having enjoyed, to the right and left of the drawbridge, very fine views of the river and the woods which border it, one does not find oneself, as one does today, in a dark enclosed space but in open and bright surroundings. Through the window placed at its extremity one saw the other bank.

At Bury the axial approach reached its climax on the perron overlooking the parterre and the forest beyond the enclosing walls. The gradual revelation of the river was the true originality of Chenonceaux. It was De l'Orme's genius to recognize this, so that when he was required to link the château with the south bank of the Cher, he moved the axis slightly to one side, and placed the staircase to the right in order to preserve that interior space. His specification was for completing the bridge of Chenonceaux and building a gallery on it, as long as the bridge and about 6 metres wide.[41] At the end of the gallery there was to be 'a balcony to the right of the window to go out as onto a terrace to take the air'. When Du Cerceau made his drawings the gallery had 63
not been built; but he shows a garden on the south bank of the Cher consisting of two square areas separated by an *allée* which is an extension of the axis of the bridge. According to a register of the *chastellenie* of Chenonceaux drawn up in 1565, this garden was newly made. If this is correct then Du Cerceau must have made his drawings between 1559 and that date, for the inscription on his bird's-eye view says that it is 'a drawing of Chenonceaux as it is at present with the addition of two gardens which are being discussed'. On the plan he refers to 'two gardens which have been thought good to make'. The second garden is shown at the bottom of the view 65
and the plan, north of the park and west of the avenue. The 66
great elm avenue by which the château was approached from the north was thus part of an axial design which had the garden beyond the bridge as a climax; not by then a novel idea, but at Chenonceaux the axis was greatly extended, and sufficiently unusual to be noted by contemporary observers. A description of the entry of François II and Mary Stuart in 1560 says: 'The main avenue to the said château is a big road laid out as a fine *allée*, sanded, and about thirty paces wide and two thousand long, of which the verges are closed with big elms, evergreen oaks and other fine trees: . . . it is so level and so straight that if the doors of the château and the great bridge-room are open one sees through straight to the other bank. . . .' Because the passage to the bridge is not in line with the entrance, this is not quite true. Nevertheless, the axial intention is clear, and suggests an architect's overall conception. There are three whose names are associated with Chenonceaux: De l'Orme, Jean Bullant, and Du Cerceau himself. Blunt thinks that the grandiose scheme illustrated in Du Cerceau's drawings (B.M.93) was his own invention; but it owes something to De l'Orme's demonstration of how to create a balanced design from existing irregularity. The gallery on the bridge, as finally carried out, is attributed to Jean Bullant on stylistic grounds;[42] but this was certainly after his appointment as architect to Catherine de Médicis in 1570.[43] De l'Orme's presence at Chenonceaux is first recorded in 1555.[44] Although references are mostly to his work on the bridge, the nature of his office meant that he exercised general control; for instance, the fountainer, Valence, took orders from him.[45] The planting of the avenue coincided with his presence there; the bridge presupposed a garden, which suggests that the whole arrangement of avenue, bridge and garden along an extended axis was due to him.[46]

65, 66 Chenonceaux: Du Cerceau's plan (above) and aerial photograph (below). Note traces of the garden on further bank.

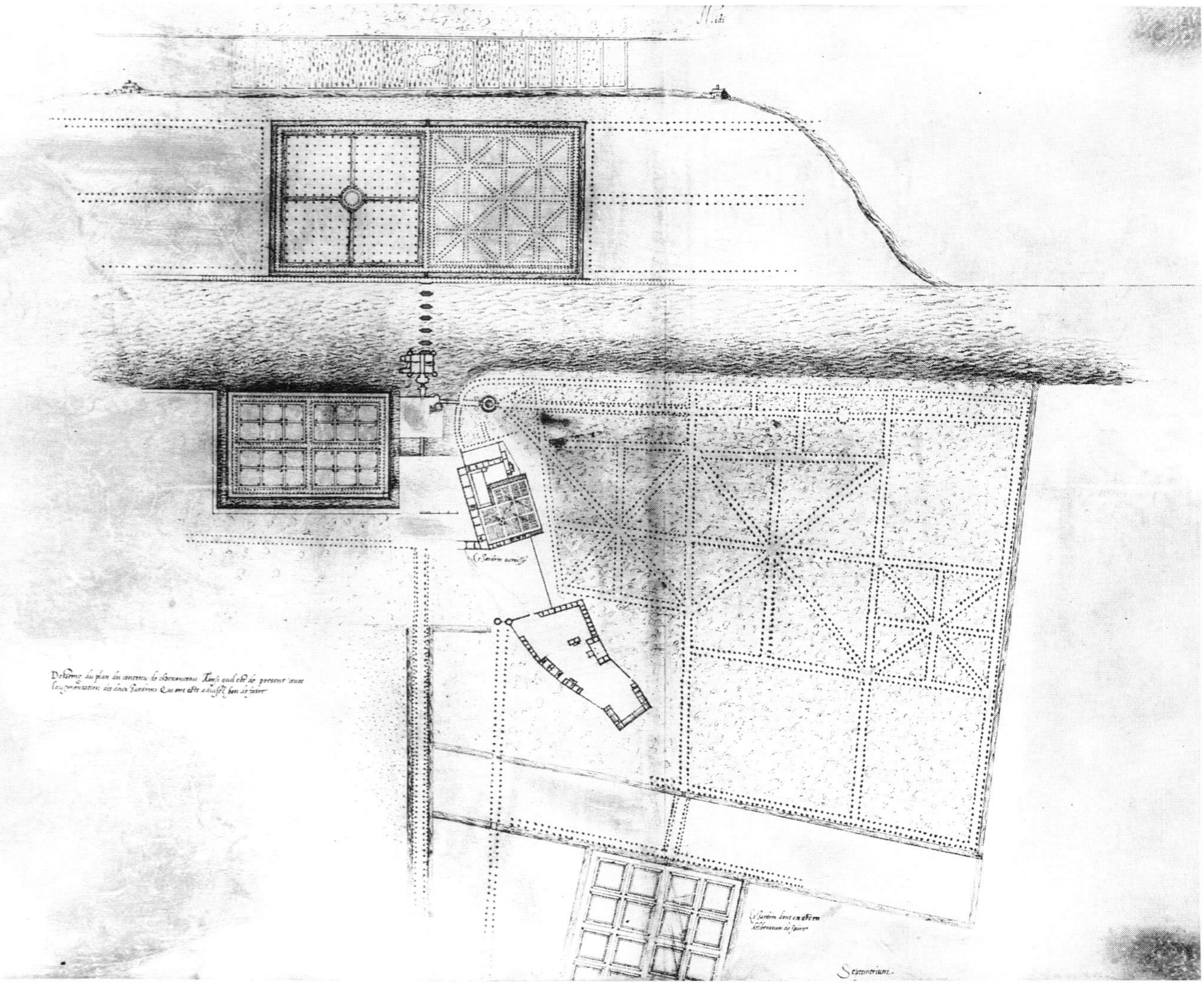
Midi

CHANTILLY

Chantilly came to the Montmorency in 1484, when Pierre d'Orgement, being without issue, left his possessions to his nephews, of whom Guillaume de Montmorency, Anne's father, was one. Guillaume followed Charles VIII and Louis XII to Italy. In 1522 he divided his property between his two sons: Anne, the elder of them, having Montmorency, Ecouen and Chantilly. Anne had immediate plans for enlarging and embellishing Chantilly, but little time to attend to it himself. The projects were therefore entrusted to his father. The château was an imposing fortress founded on a rock in the flat marshy valley of the little Nonette river. It was surrounded by large moats and fishponds, and adjoined on the south by a wooded park. In 1524 land was transformed into the large
67 square garden shown on Du Cerceau's plan (B.M.94). Although its function was evidently productive – with mulberry, plum, cherry and apricot trees brought from Normandy and Languedoc – a handsome gallery was built on the west side, with a bath house at the north end. After Pavia, work was suspended during the king's captivity. It was recommenced in 1527; and from 1528 to 1531 Pierre Chambiges, son of a well-known master mason, reconstructed the north and west sides of the château and completed the gallery and bath house. During these years Anne de Montmorency was occupied in negotiating the return of the royal hostages, in an embassy to London, and in governing Languedoc. In his absence, work at Chantilly was supervised by the Secretary of State, Villeroy, who wrote reporting the progress of the buildings. Those in the garden were almost finished: 'It is very good to see your gallery. I have seen your heronry which I have found very fine and well sited. There are about four dozen young herons; in a short time all the countryside will be populated by them.'[47] A description written in 1688 says: 'This gallery is so called
[Galerie des Cerfs] because it is decorated with many life-like 68
stags' heads, all bearing on their necks the arms of Montmorency and of the houses with which they were allied. It opens in an arcade on the parterre of orange trees. It is decorated with a fresco representing the story of Psyche.'[48] In May 1538 a contract was made with Jean Chocquet, master mason of Senlis, to construct the terrace between the château and the park. This was an important step towards regularity in an otherwise irregular design, and was later seized upon by Le Nôtre as the basis for his layout of the grounds. Five out of Du Cerceau's seven drawings of Chantilly are devoted to 'Le Petit Château', an independent complex of house and garden, surrounded by water and connected to the main *corps de logis* by a bridge. Although there is no record of its construction there is little doubt that it is by Jean Bullant, who worked for Montmorency at Ecouen
and Fère-en-Tardenois.[49] The design of 'Le Petit Château' 69
makes possible the enjoyment of its immediate surroundings. A narrow terrace runs along the water on the west side, to a portico or gallery communicating with a small garden on the north; a forerunner of island gardens like the Jardin de l'Etang at Fontainebleau. Besides adding to the amenities near the château, Anne de Montmorency acquired much of the land which was later used for the ornamental grounds, so that in the seventeenth and eighteenth centuries Chantilly rivalled the royal gardens in splendour and extent.

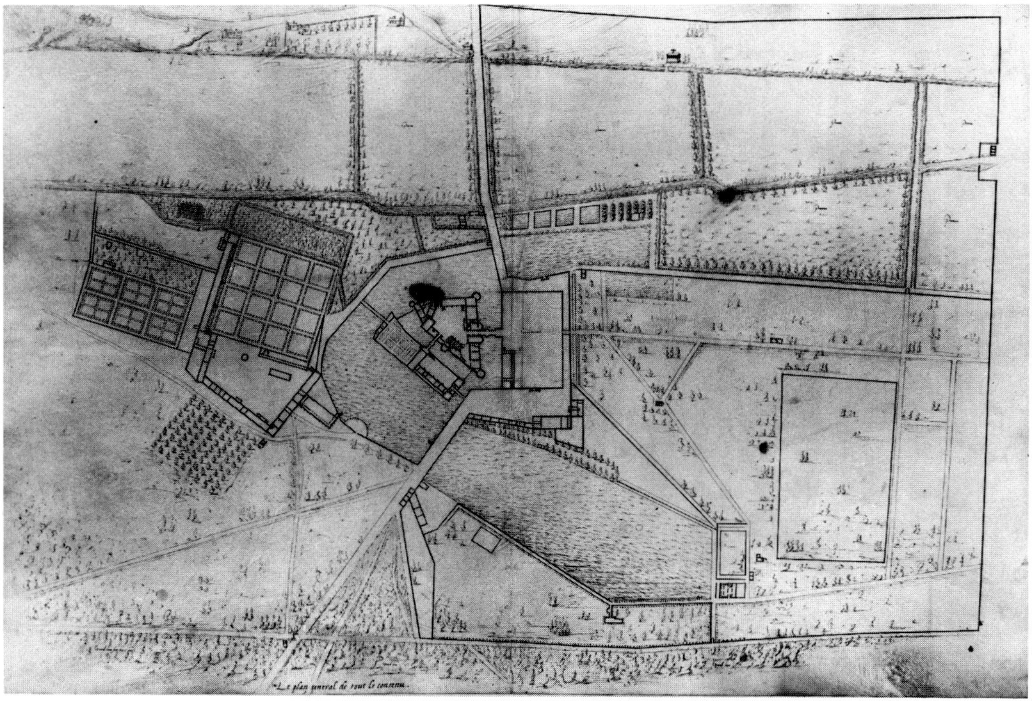

67 Chantilly: Du Cerceau's plan. The Galerie des Cerfs is on the side of the square garden furthest from the château on the extreme left.

68, 69 Chantilly: the Galerie des Cerfs (above) and a general view showing the Petit Château with the old château behind.

A
B

5

Gardens, politics and religion, 1560–98

Historical background: François II to Henri IV

IN THE ALMOST CONTINUOUS civil war in France during the last four decades of the sixteenth century, religion was the pretext; power the motive. The French Reformed Church was organized on a Calvinist basis; and by 1560 its members, known as Huguenots, represented a substantial minority; sufficient to constitute a political threat to the established Catholic order of the State. François II, who succeeded Henri II in 1559, married Mary Stuart, niece of the Guise, who thus gained control of the government. In 1560 a Huguenot conspiracy to overthrow them failed. François, who was only sixteen and in poor health, died the same year. During the minority of his brother Charles, Catherine de Médicis ruled as regent; and her influence continued until his death in 1574. Meanwhile the struggle between Huguenot and Catholic, led by the houses of Bourbon and Lorraine respectively, dominated French politics for forty years. Catherine, who favoured conciliation, remained uneasily balanced between the two. The marriage of her daughter Marguerite to Henri de Navarre, head of the house of Bourbon, brought Protestant and Catholic leaders together in Paris in 1572. The massacre of the Huguenots which followed on the Feast of Saint Bartholomew made rapprochement impossible. Charles IX died in May 1574. His brother succeeded him as Henri III. He was Catherine's favourite son, and the one she was least able to manage. Intelligent and well read, yet unable to give serious attention to affairs of state, he dismissed Catherine's trusted advisers, and surrounded himself with male favourites over whom he exercised little control. Religious mania alternated with periods of debauchery and addiction to trivial crazes, such as the game of cup and ball, or the collecting of fashionable small dogs. Henri's dislike of the Huguenots was equalled, if not surpassed, by his hatred of Henri, Duc de Guise. In December 1588 Guise was murdered in the château of Blois on Henri's orders, while Catherine lay ill in the room beneath. She died in January. Henri was assassinated eight months later. Thus ended the Valois dynasty in France. The heir to the throne was the leader of the Huguenots, Henri de Navarre, who, as Henri IV, became king in name. He finally enforced his claim by defeating the Catholic army in 1590 at Ivry, near Evreux, and by renouncing the Protestant faith in 1593. He entered Paris in 1594 as undisputed king of France, ending over thirty years of civil strife, and establishing the Bourbon dynasty which ruled France until the Revolution.

Catherine de Médicis' gardens

Catherine de Médicis' taste for building and elaborate theatrical display had little scope until Henri II's death in 1559, when as queen mother she assumed power on behalf of the young François II. One of her first acts was to suggest that all gifts prompted by the liberality of her late husband and his father should be returned to the State. Chenonceaux seemed to be in this category; but she accepted Diane de Poitiers' proposal to exchange it for another château. Catherine spent more time at Chenonceaux than her predecessor; and the gardens and park were the scene of some of her celebrated entertainments. Her major additions were the gallery on the bridge, and the garden beyond it on the south bank of the Cher. If we are to believe Du Cerceau, she had even more ambitious plans which she was unable to achieve.

In 1547 she began the château of Montceaux-en-Brie near Meaux which, although it was habitable by 1558, she was unable to finish. It is not certain who was Catherine's architect. In his *Nouvelles Inventions* De l'Orme refers to a roof he designed to cover the pall-mall alley: and he mentions this again in his *Instruction*, adding: 'là ou j'avais dressé de tant belles inventions'. In 1557, when he was still superintending the king's works, a contract was made for building a grotto and a garden pavilion to his design.[1] On Catherine's death in 1589 Montceaux was taken over by her creditors; and later bought by Henri IV for his mistress Gabrielle d'Estrées. The
château was finally completed by Salomon de Brosse[2] for 71
Marie de Médicis after 1601. But the gardens existed in 1600; and, because of the terracing required, they must have been planned some time before that. The wide platform on which the château was built, surrounded by a balustrade to give
uninterrupted views over the valley of the Marne to the east 72
and the gardens descending in two large terraces to the south, was contrived to delight the eye and expand the mind. It was Catherine who saw the possibilities of the site and acquired it in the first place.

70 Feast in a garden. From B. del Bene's *Civitas Veri*, published in 1609.

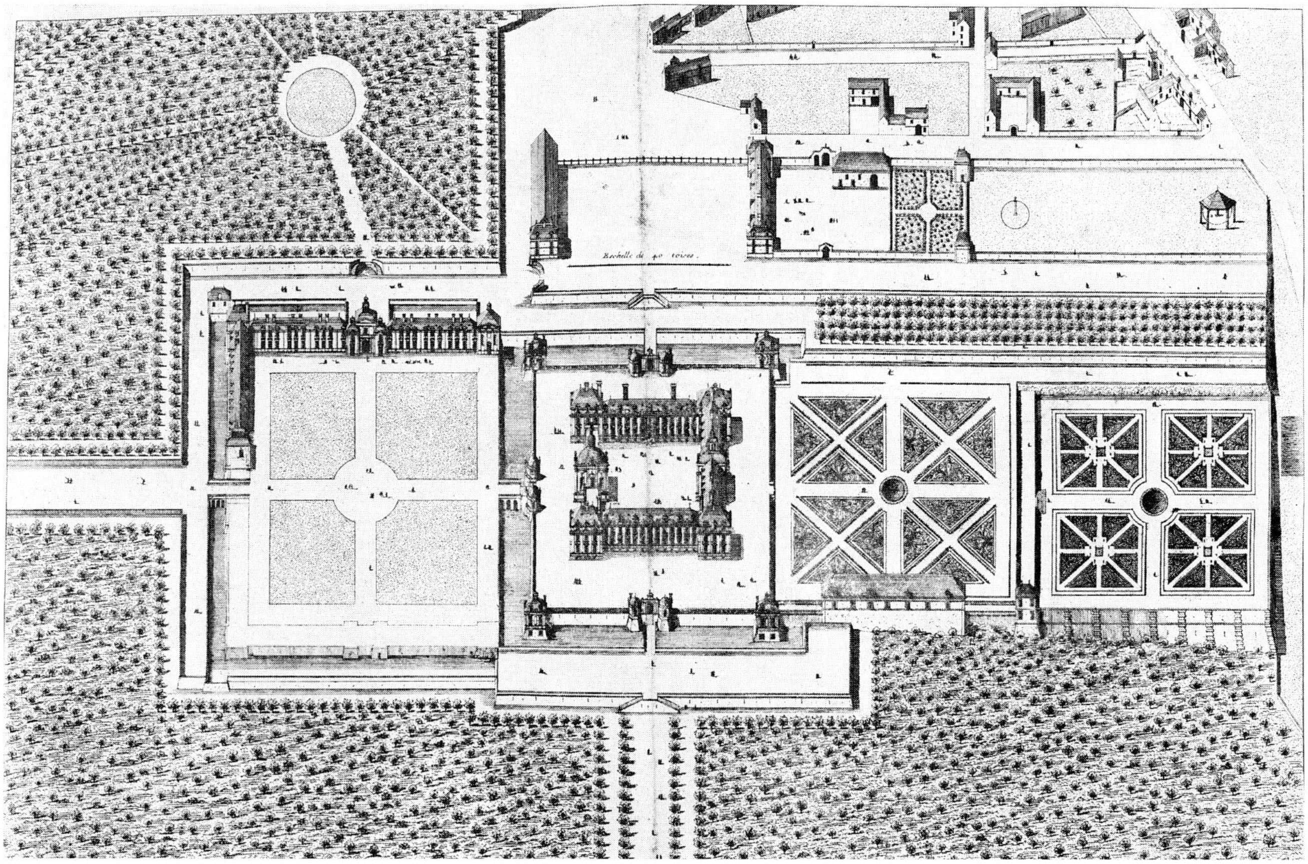

71, 72 Montceaux-en-Brie, plan (above) and general view (below) in 1673.

73 The garden of the Tuileries and the Porte de la Conference in the mid-seventeenth century.

Besides Chenonceaux and Montceaux she acquired Saint-Maur, east of Vincennes, from cardinal du Bellay's heir, Eustache du Bellay, in 1563, and commissioned Philibert de l'Orme to enlarge it. This work was also incomplete when she died. These were her private retreats. The main royal residences were the palaces of the Tournelles and the Louvre in Paris; the château of Madrid in the Bois de Boulogne; and, on the opposite side of the city, the old château of Vincennes which was essentially a stronghold. To the west of Paris, within easy reach by the river, was Saint-Germain-en-Laye. Fontainebleau to the south was the only palace to which she gave serious attention, and made the additions to the gardens which have already been described. Important festivals were held there in 1564. The next took place in her new garden of the Tuileries.

The site had been acquired by François I about 1519, because his mother, Louise de Savoie, found the palace of Tournelles, with its marshy situation close to open drains, unhealthy. Along the Seine to the west, just inside the city ramparts, was the old château of the Louvre, a prison rather than a residence. Beyond the walls stretched open fields and vineyards, small dwellings and an occasional house with a walled garden. Immediately outside the city boundary was property belonging to François' counsellor and financial secretary, Nicolas de Neufville. It comprised several houses with enclosed gardens, which adjoined land bordering the Seine used for the manufacture of bricks and tiles, from which it was called 'the Tuileries'. Plans for a vast palace with gardens extending to the west were made in Henri II's reign. After his death from a wound received while jousting at Tournelles, Catherine alienated that palace from the crown lands and it was sold in lots. In 1564 she began a new palace, on the site of the Tuileries, designed by De l'Orme. The 73
making of the garden was supervised by Catherine's favourite, Marie de Pierrevive. She was married to the Florentine banker, Antoine de Gondi, who had taken the name of Perron. Her son, Pierre de Gondi, bishop of Paris, headed the administration. The Gondi family were to play an important part in developing the sites of future royal gardens like Versailles and Saint-Cloud (*see* chapter 7). Although the gardeners at the Tuileries were French, they were subject to another Italian, Bernardo Carnesecchi.[3]

Catherine abandoned the building of the palace in 1572, for superstitious reasons it was said, since an astrologer had told her she would die near Saint-Germain, and the Tuileries were in the parish of Saint-Germain-l'Auxerrois. Most of her last years were spent at the Hôtel de Soissons, but she
continued to use the garden of the Tuileries regularly. 74
Charles IX ordered the town authorities to build walls to prevent it being overlooked by people walking on the ramparts. When Catherine died most of her houses were sequestered to pay her debts. The Tuileries belonged to the crown and therefore escaped this fate; but in the civil wars
which continued until 1593 the palace and gardens were 75
neglected. During Henri IV's siege of the city they were devastated.

74, 75 The Tuileries in 1570 (above) and in 1609 (below).

76 A rustic altar. Illustration to d'Urfé's *L'Astrée*.

Garden festivals

The use to which Catherine put her gardens was part of a tradition of spectacular display which influenced the course of garden design. At least three elaborate entertainments were held at Chenonceaux in 1560, 1563 and 1577. The various set pieces in the park on these occasions were the humble precursors of the *bosquets* of Versailles and the far greater extravagances of *Les Plaisirs de l'Isle Enchantée* in 1664. The festivities surrounding the entry of the young François II and his queen, Mary Stuart, in March 1560 (1559 OS) took place soon after Catherine had taken possession, and immediately after the court had witnessed the executions at Amboise following the first major Huguenot conspiracy. A contemporary record of the occasion was published in Tours.[4] A triumphal arch covered with ivy and with suitable inscriptions was erected between the avenue and the courtyard. The route was also marked by two fountains in the form of giant herms on rustic bases; two oak trees bearing torches which burned with different colours; and two obelisks draped in ivy and surmounted by a gilded oval ball. These features were arranged in the forecourt. The square terrace before the château is at a higher level, so that it was 'like being on a horse with a view over the gardens and parterres, even into the depths of the park'. The park was ornamented and varied with little theatres made of turf, tunnels, pavilions, green rooms, (*cabinets*), arbours (*berceaux*), walks, pall-mall *allées* and a big *jeu de balle* enclosed in box and fine fruit trees, all encircled by part of the River Cher. Certain places in the park were arranged for entertainment, especially in the shade of some great tree; an oak, for instance, which was reached by a winding path along the river bank.
Elsewhere, a green oratory made of turf had been set up in 76
the shade of an elm, away from the crowd and noise so that the silence of the place seemed to invite reverence and the thoughts of an all-powerful God who had brought together

such an illustrious and noble company there. Verses written on the tables in each of these spots aimed at inducing a suitable respect for the powers either of this or the celestial world. In the depths of a full-grown wood, under a great oak, the following inscription was written:

> Whither do you hasten princess? Pause! And see the simple blend in this great park, the flowers and arbours which surround me, along the bank of my neighbour the Cher. Before my Pallas, the mother of your king (may the great gods see that her love continues), took pleasure in this place, there was no living flower: but a wilderness of bushes was what I saw. The nymphs and gods who watched over these banks, disgusted by my wild brambles, had gone to hide their resentment in some corner. But when they learned that this great goddess had resolved to pass her time of mourning there, they gladly took Chenonceaux into their care again.[5]

Thus was the memory of Diane de Poitiers extinguished less than a year after her departure.

Celebrations for peace in 1563 included a firework display, a water fête, picnic and masque.[6] Catherine's most notorious entertainment celebrated the capture of La Charité from the Huguenots by her youngest son, François, Duc d'Anjou. The
77 scene was the Fontaine du Rocher in the park, surrounded by trees, west of the Marques tower. The trellis surrounding the fountain is shown in Du Cerceau's bird's-eye view as he describes it; 'on the right of the entrance there is a fountain in a rock, with several jets of water, and about this a basin of some 6 metres ['trois toises'] diameter, always full of water. Around this basin there was a path at ground level by way of a terrace; and above, another terrace about 3 metres high, going all round, covered with trellis, supported and enclosed by a wall enriched with niches, columns, figures and seats.'[7] Access was by a ramp from the terrace before the house, immediately south of the Marques tower.

Catherine's newly decorated Fontainebleau was the setting for festivals in February and March 1564, after the first civil war had ended inconclusively with the murder of François de Guise.[8] The theme of the occasion was the reconciliation of Huguenot and Catholic through the crown in the person of the young king, Charles IX. Banquets and entertainments were given alternately by leaders of the opposing parties. Catherine's own contribution was a display early one morning, when three sirens appeared swimming in the canals of the garden to greet the king with loyal songs composed by Ronsard and other court poets. In the opposite direction came Neptune, accompanied by music and drawn in a car by four sea-horses. Then a rock opened, disclosing a nymph who recited verses to the king. This little scene prophesied peace, and the return of woodland and water deities following the cease of civil strife. On the first of Lent Catherine entertained the king and the court at Mi-voye, vulgarly called 'La Vacherie'; and after that in the ballroom. The festivities concluded with the king's banquet, preceded

77 The site of the Fontaine du Rocher, Chenonceaux, where one of Catherine de Médicis' most lavish entertainments took place.

by a grand tournament, in which Catholic knights led by the dauphin, assaulted an enchanted island guarded by devils, a giant and a dwarf, and occupied by knights led by the prince of Condé, chief of the Huguenots. Catholic and Huguenot engaged in single combat for the favours of six nymphs, represented by some of Catherine's famous attendant beauties. This was the only time Catherine used the grounds of Fontainebleau for such an occasion. It is illustrated in the so-called Valois tapestries[9] in the Uffizi, for which Antoine Caron made the drawings. Also represented in this series is the entertainment in the Tuileries given to the Polish ambassadors when they came to offer the crown of Poland to Henri, Duc d'Anjou (the future Henri III), in 1573. An
78 artificial rock figured prominently, adorned with sixteen of Catherine's maids-in-waiting dressed to represent the provinces of France. After reciting verses in praise of France and the king of Poland composed by Ronsard, they descended to perform an elaborate ballet, concluding with a presentation of gold medallions to the king, queen mother and principal guests. Caron's drawing of the Tuileries festival shows it taking place in the garden, but in fact the ballet was performed in a specially constructed outdoor room, which is illustrated in Dorat's pamphlet.[10] It is probable that this theatre was in the same place as the one made early in 1571, when hedges and trees in the northwest corner were uprooted to make place for it.

The structures made for these theatrical occasions were becoming permanent features in gardens, where utility gave place to, or at times mingled with, symbolism and allegory. The artificial rock is a case in point. The Rocher de l'Hermitage, in Le Lydieu at Gaillon, was probably made in the 1560s under the cardinal de Bourbon. The most frequent reference was to Mount Parnassus, with Apollo and the
79 muses, as in the symbolic gardens illustrating B. del Bene's
70 *Civitas Veri* (1609), and reappearing in Salomon de Caus' *Les Raisons des Forces Mouvantes* (1615), where it is related to those artificial mounts having a practical function, being used either for storage or for providing suitable environments for tender or medicinal plants, as in Olivier de Serres' *Théâtre d'Agriculture* (1600). The proliferation of other free-standing architectural features (elaborate fountains, grottoes and cascades) at the beginning of the seventeenth century was stimulated by developments in Italy. They were preceded in France by the influence of the French edition of *Hypnerotomachia Poliphili*, with new illustrations by some artists of the Fontainebleau School; but in particular by the work of Bernard Palissy and Jacques Androuet du Cerceau, both Huguenots. Indeed Palissy, despite the protection of Catherine de Médicis and Anne de Montmorency while they were both alive, died for his beliefs in prison. Androuet du Cerceau enjoyed the protection of Renée de France, duchess of Ferrara, second daughter of Louis XII, an ardent convert to the Reformed religion and a friend of Calvin. During the religious wars she gave refuge to many Huguenots in her castle at Montargis, where Du Cerceau was her architect and almoner.

78, 79 Two examples of artificial rocks: from the Tuileries festival, 1573 with maids-in-waiting representing the provinces of France, and a garden symbolic of Parnassus with Apollo and the Muses.

The Mannerism of Bernard Palissy and Jacques Androuet du Cerceau

A broad definition of Mannerism used in this context would be 'the love of complexity rather than economy',[11] 'virtuosity for its own sake, and a taste for the ingenious and bizarre'.[12] Although Bernard Palissy was primarily a potter, and Androuet du Cerceau an architect, both have claims as garden designers, which rest on what they published rather than direct evidence of what they did.

BERNARD PALISSY

Palissy was a native of Saintonge (some say of Agen), born about 1510, and probably of bourgeois origin for he studied mathematics and geometry. His first trade was stained-glass making, which was going out of fashion. As a young man he travelled in the south and west, as far as the Pyrenees and up to Brittany, making observations on water, soil and other natural phenomena with a detachment unusual at the time. His skill in geometry and drawing was called upon in making plans for law suits; and in 1544 he was commissioned to survey the salt marshes of Saintonge for the administration of the salt tax. Looking for alternative employment when the work on the salt marshes came to an end, he turned potter. In his *Discours Admirables* (1580) he describes how he and his family were reduced to penury while he discovered for himself the secret of majolica glazes. Why he should have had to undertake random experiments is a mystery, as the art of glazed earthenware had long been known in France. Trade secrets were, of course, guarded; but in Palissy's case there was also an obstinate pride, going with his Calvinism, which led him to say, 'I do not wish in any way to imitate my predecessors, except in what they did according to the word of God'.

Palissy's reputation comes from his writings, the
80 originality of his observations, and the distinctive style of his pottery, encrusted with deeply modelled naturalistic
81 rendering of plants, reptiles and aquatic animals. It is mainly for *Le Dessein du Jardin Délectable* that he is remembered in the history of gardens.[13] In his dedication to Catherine, Palissy wrote: 'There are things written in this book which could greatly assist in the setting up of your garden of Chenonceaux; and when it pleases you to command me to be of service to you, I shall not fail to occupy myself there.' There is no evidence that Palissy worked at Chenonceaux; although there are parallels between his *jardin délectable* and the garden on the south bank of the Cher. But there are also important differences, particularly in the site, for Palissy's garden is overlooked by terraces cut into the hills on two sides, a situation which is more like that of Villandry. It is possible that he did work at La Fontaine du Rocher, a conjecture which is supported by the discovery of fragments of pottery on the site, and that he did something similar in connection with a grotto at the Tuileries.

Much of Palissy's description of his ideal garden concerns the making of ceramic grottoes, and green rooms of living trees. There are instructions for a flexible watering system, so that the water may be taken to any part of the garden; but there is little about plants and gardening as such, although he showed in other treatises that he made practical observations on soils, manures and the effects of cutting and pruning on the growth of trees. The site Palissy proposes for his garden is near a river, with springs coming from high ground which encloses the garden on two sides, and is cut into terraces, with rooms for storage and other purposes hollowed in the rock. He points out that such sites are common along the Loire, Gironde, Garonne, Lot, Tarn and other rivers; and that more than 4000 farms and noble houses could be found similarly situated in France. The form of the garden is rectangular, and divided into four parts by two intersecting walks. Enclosure by terraces on the north and west is completed by walls on the east and south. East of the garden lie orchards; to the south there is access to a meadow enclosed by hedges and tree-lined walks. Beside the walks which intersect the garden are streams which divide to form a circular island in the centre, in the manner shown by Du Cerceau in his drawings
of Chenonceaux, or in a drawing by Antoine Caron 82
illustrating the story of Artemesia.[14] A pavilion made from living poplars is the central feature of Palissy's garden. The trunks, planted in a circle, will form columns he says, upright as far as the cornice, then trained to form conical domes. Green rooms will similarly be made to close the paths on each side. These however will be square and made of elms. The idea of constructing rooms from living trees, even the choice of elm and poplar, comes from Crescenzi's *Rustican*; but Palissy describes precisely how he would make the base and capital of each column by cutting the bark to stimulate growth, how he would train the branches to form architrave, ribs and moulding, and how he will bend twigs to form inscriptions, all from the *Apocrypha*, on the frieze; for *Le Dessein du Jardin Délectable* is also a Protestant tract. Palissy justifies his constructions on moral and practical grounds. They are more natural and therefore superior to those built of stone. Quoting Vitruvius, he argues that the ancients took the model and the measure of their buildings from trees and human forms. The original is always to be preferred to the imitation, says Palissy; and the work of the sovereign builder is superior to that of human beings. Moreover, his green rooms would require less labour and expense of upkeep than is necessary in many fine gardens to maintain plants clipped into various shapes. Such creations only last a little time, whereas his rooms would endure more than a lifetime; and, when they are done with, the wood would still be useful to the owner.

It is evident that Palissy acquired many of his ideas from his reading. He mentions Serlio and Vitruvius, whose *De Architectura* was published in French by Jean Martin in 1547, the year following his French rendering of Colonna's *Hypnerotomachia*, which Palissy also mentions in order to say that he took nothing from it. Nevertheless, the device which turns in the wind and emits the sound of flutes at the apex of his central pavilion bears a strong relation to the winged figure forming the pinnacle of the bath house in the *Hypnerotomachia*, whose basin also contains representations of all kinds of aquatic animals. The idea of a garden with

80, 81 Dishes by Bernard Palissy, reflecting his interest in garden design and in the natural world. Above: La Belle Jardinière. Below: dish with reptiles, fishes and crustacea.

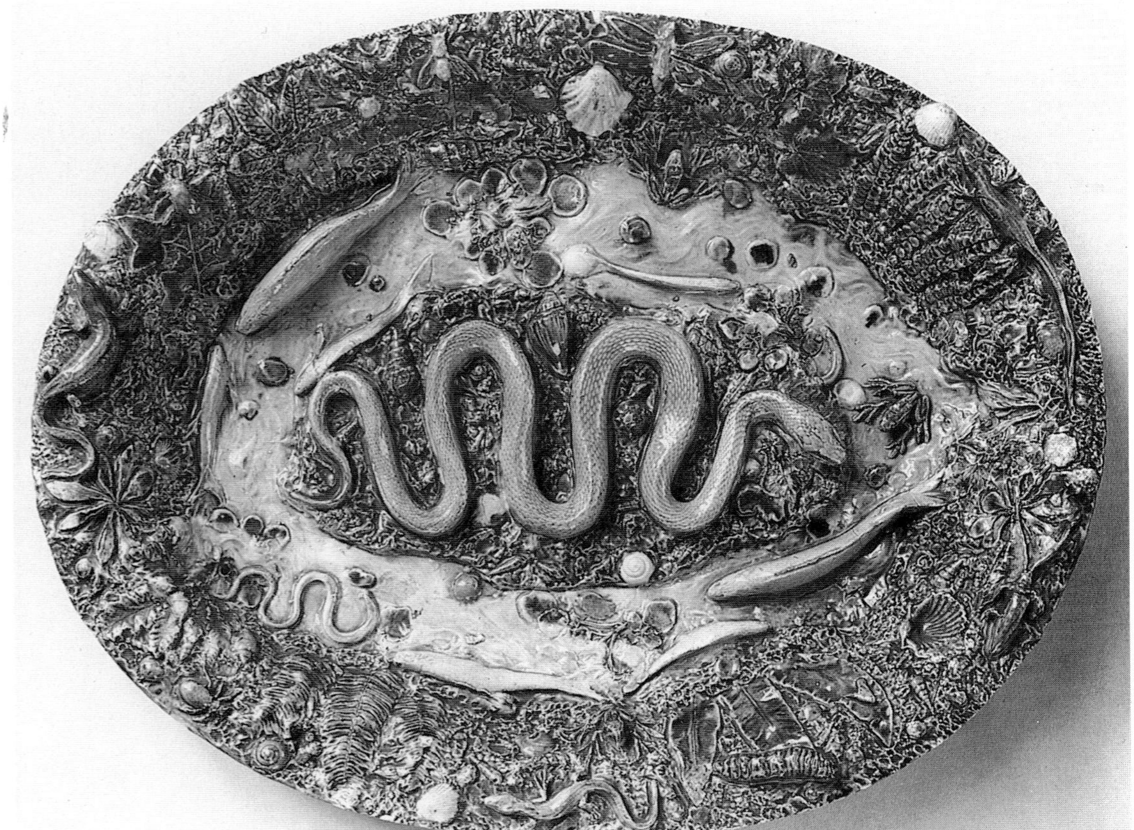

82 Drawing by A. Caron for a tapestry, showing a garden scene.

inscriptions of a didactic nature might also be said to derive from Colonna; Palissy's originality was to take these from biblical rather than from pagan sources. Despite his disapproval of fashionable tricks for soaking people, Palissy includes a statue which tips water over anyone who tries to read the scroll it is holding. A similar machine was recorded at Hesdin in the fifteenth century. Of course, the *jardin délectable* also derived from gardens Palissy knew, particularly those along rivers like the Loire with terraced cliffs and storage rooms hollowed in the rock. However, there is no evidence that Palissy ever made a garden except in his imagination. His picture represents a Renaissance ideal, like
82 the gardens in Caron's drawings which show green rooms such as Palissy describes. Indeed, it is not unlikely that Caron was influenced by Palissy in his ideas; both are somewhere between actuality and fantasy.

At each corner of his garden Palissy proposed rooms, with one side built into the wall of the garden made to look like rock. Each is treated differently; with white translucent pebbles, coral set in natural rock, or with stones which have been brought as ballast to Atlantic ports and cast on the sea shore. In the first, on the north side, the rock 'will be made of baked earth, crooked and lumpy, and enamelled with strange colours, like the one I made in the grotto of Monseigneur the Constable, but not arranged in that way because it is not a similar work.' The water issuing from the rock was to fall into a natural basin, in which there were to be realistic models of frogs, tortoises, crayfish, shells and branches of coral. In the holes and concavities of the wall, there were to be snakes and lizards; and higher still mosses and plants such as hart's-tongue and maidenhair, all modelled and glazed to imitate nature. Two of the grottoes were to be made 'as if a rock had been hammered out by great hammer blows' or having no appearance nor form of the art of carving, nor the work of the hand of man', the vaults being crooked and seeming to fall down because of several hanging 'lumps'. We have only to look at Caro's letter[15] describing the grotto of Giovanni Gaddi at Rome in 1538 to see that Palissy must have been familiar with such accounts. 'Some blocks', Caro writes, 'are set one above the other at random, or rather with a certain disordered order, which project in some parts and in others form hollows for planting grass. . . .' Caro also mentions the basin of a fountain in which there were fish and corals; also crabs, oysters and snails in holes of the rock, and hart's-tongue, maidenhair, moss and other sorts of water-loving plants on the margin. We may also note the realistic modelling of animals in the encrusted walls of the Grotticina di Madama in the Boboli gardens, begun in 1553 and completed the following year; and the grotto at Castello evidently by the same hand. Palissy had certainly heard of such places, although the ceramic grotto was apparently his invention. His idea was to construct it of brick, model the interior, cover it with raw glaze, light a fire inside and seal it up exactly as he would do with a kiln. The glazes would run and mingle, creating 'very pleasing forms and fancies'. When cool the joints would be covered, so that the room would appear as one piece. Palissy extols his grottoes as being a hundred times more durable than that of Meudon, because terracotta is harder than stone; and 'because, at Meudon, the enrichments within are slabs made of cement, brought in several pieces, which will be subject to being stolen when the place changes hands'.[16] There is no evidence that his method worked.

We have Palissy's word, however, that he made something of the kind for Anne de Montmorency at Ecouen. Without doubt he made a grotto for Catherine de Médicis at the Tuileries; but its whereabouts and appearance are uncertain. The *Devis d'une grotte pour la Royne du Roi* is more a description of how he would make a grotto if asked than a specification.[17] The drawing of a grotto inscribed 'la portraict de la grotte rustique . . . inventée par Madame la Grant', has also been declared to be a design for the grotto of the Tuileries.[18] This shows the section of a circular building with shell niches; and, in the wall above, a series of Roman busts surrounded by wreaths surmounted by eagles. This does not resemble what is commonly thought of as Palissy's style; nor does it agree with his *Devis*. An inventory made in 1589 after Catherine's death mentions 'the grotto of pottery . . . near the marble-mason's yard . . .', containing 'several earthen figures, fragile and of little value'.[19] Potters' kilns and moulds of the sixteenth century as described by Palissy, including some for figures made of shells, were found during excavations on the site of the Tuileries palace in 1865.[20] One thing is certain, that in 1570 'Bernard, Nicolas and Mathurin Palissis, sculteurs en terre', were paid for works of glazed terracotta, and for completing 'the four *pons* [bridges] round the inside of the grotto, begun by the queen in her palace near the Louvre'. Louis Dimier has proposed that the entry in the accounts should read *pans* ('sections').[21] 'The four sections round the inside of the grotto' then means nothing more than the four walls supporting the decoration; from which it follows that the grotto was not round but square. As to its position, there was no other place for it except attached to a building; the only building in the garden in Du Cerceau's plan was on the side near the river, six rooms of unequal size with a staircase in the middle. 'There, inevitably, were found the conciergerie and the depot of marble.'[22] Apart from these references there is no other mention of Palissy's grotto. A poem written by Guillaume de Peyrat in 1593, which lists the important features in the garden, does not refer to it. Renée de France visited the Tuileries in the summer of 1572, just before Saint Bartholomew's Day, and it is recorded that she gave 80 *sols* to the queen's gardener, and smaller sums to masons, architects and foremen who were working to finish the gardens; among whom was a poor workman, called Bernard, engaged in building a 'grotesque'. Dimier suggests that this was the fountain described by the Swiss ambassadors in 1575. It was in the form of a rock, with snakes, snails, tortoises, lizards, toads, frogs and other aquatic animals in terracotta, which they said was going to ruin. This certainly sounds like Palissy's work.

JACQUES ANDROUET DU CERCEAU

Du Cerceau's *Les Plus Excellents Bastiments de France* is an indispensable source of reference for the French Renaissance garden; but, as Rosalys Coope has said, Du Cerceau has suffered from being well known but too-little studied.[23] He published fifteen books of engravings between 1549 and 1584, but his life is thinly documented and he has been confused with his son, Jacques II Androuet du Cerceau.[24] The exact dates of his birth and death are not known, but are probably *c.*1515/20 to *c.*1584. Geymüller[25] attributes to him sheets in Munich from an Italian sketchbook datable from internal evidence to 1534–6.[26] A.-N. Dézallier d'Argenville states that Du Cerceau went to Italy to study antiquities under Georges d'Armagnac, who was ambassador in Rome from 1539 to 1544. Du Cerceau was granted a monopoly for the sale of his engravings by François I in 1545; and in 1546 he was appointed architect to François' sister, Marguerite d'Angoulême, queen of Navarre. His first known work, a collection of triumphal arches, was published at Orléans in 1549. He presided over fêtes in that city on the occasion of a visit by Henri II and Diane de Poitiers in 1552. Sometime between 1560 and 1566 he entered the service of Renée de France. In the dedication to Renée in 1566 of a book of *Grotesques*, Du Cerceau refers to the great losses suffered by himself and his family as a result of the troubles, which left him without the strength or the means to continue the drawings for his book on the most remarkable buildings of France. Some of the drawings for *Les Plus Excellents Bastiments* had thus been made before that time. Apart from supervising the rebuilding of the château of Montargis which was in bad repair, he served Renée in other capacities, as envoy and distributor of her charity. He is described in the registers of Montargis as 'almoner and architect'.[27] The Duc de Nevers, in his memoirs, calls him 'citizen of Montargis, who has been one of the greatest architects in France'. It is not known what happened to him after Renée's death in 1575; but he was employed at Verneuil-sur-Oise by her son-in-law, the Duc de Nemours, to whom he dedicated *Edifices Antiques Romains* in 1584. He is thought to have died shortly after its publication.

Du Cerceau's books of engravings had three main purposes: to spread the knowledge of antiquity, interpreted in a somewhat free and fanciful manner; to provide pattern books of all kinds, from grotesque decoration, ornament, furniture, fountains, pavilions and tombs to temples; and to provide designs for houses great and small. To these aims it

83, 84 Two engravings from early works by Jacques Androuet du Cerceau. Above: *Horti Caesaris* from *Monuments Antiques*, 1560. Below: garden from *Petites Habitations*.

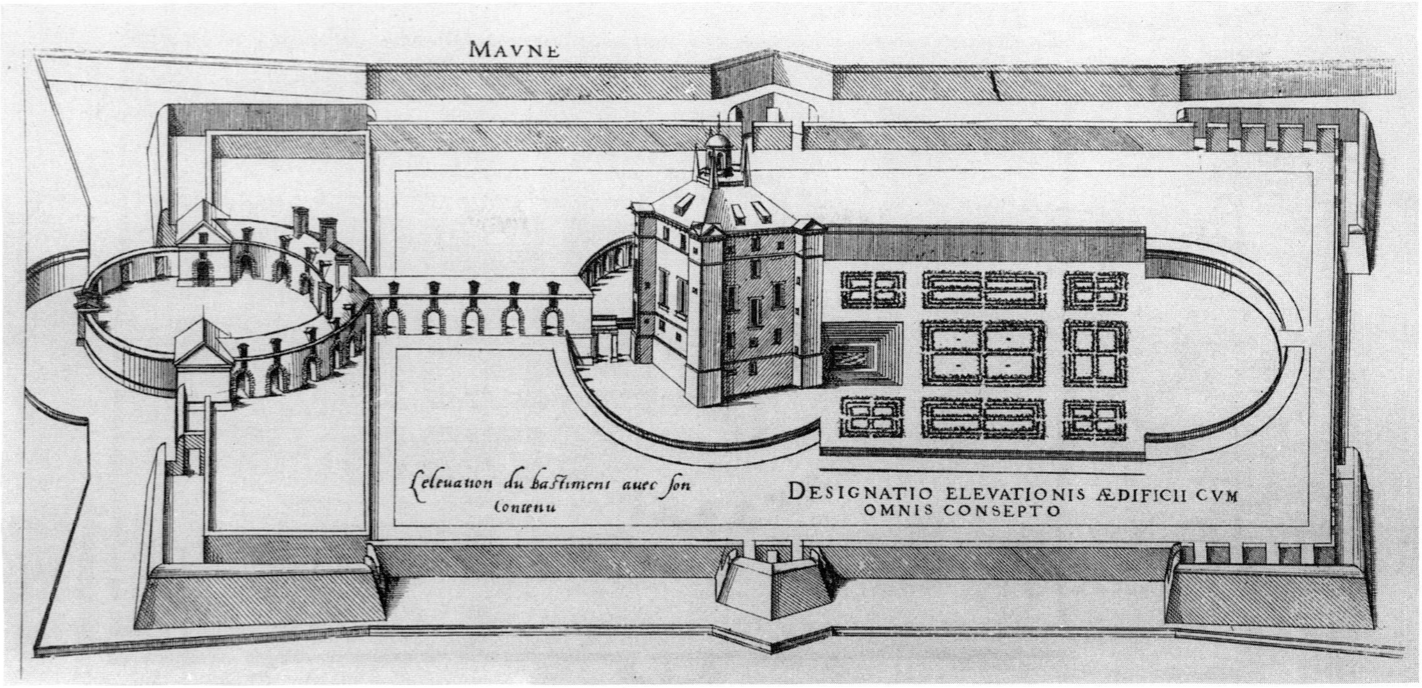

85 The château and garden of Maulnes, in Burgundy, one of the few plates in Du Cerceau's *Plus Excellents Bastiments* showing a site outside the Ile de France and the Loire.

could be added that his engraved work was a necessary expression of his fertile imagination, which was, in the full sense of the term, 'Mannerist'. It is overloaded with diffuse and often fantastic ornament, although there is more restraint in some later work. His *Livre d'Architecture* (1559) preceded Philibert de l'Orme's book by two years, and was thus the first printed practical architectural handbook by a Frenchman. There is little reference to gardens in it, but the *Second Livre d'Architecture* (1561) has designs for fountains and pavilions. Some of his *Monuments Antiques* (1560) show
83 gardens, such as the plate entitled *Horti Caesaris*. The severe architectural setting and the style are in marked contrast to
84 those of the *Petites Habitations* in the style of Vredeman de Vries.[28] His most important references to gardens are in the two volumes of *Les Plus Excellents Bastiments de France*, 1576 and 1579, which include the designs for Charleval and Verneuil.

As we have seen from the dedication of *Grotesques*, he had projected a book on 'les bastimens singuliers de France' before 1566, but had been prevented from pursuing his intention by the troubles which had come upon the kingdom. As he said, not only did such work involve much difficulty, but he had the problem of transporting himself to various places. In 1572 he appealed to Charles IX, who was staying with his aunt at Montargis, for help in visiting the important buildings which remained to be seen and engraved, saying that his age and indisposition were his excuse for asking. The drawings already done must have been made in times of relative peace between 1563 and 1566, and between 1570 and 1572. It has already been argued that the Chenonceaux drawings were made earlier than 1565.[29] Some of the *Grotesques*, he says, were taken from Fontainebleau and Montceaux, that is before 1566. The corrections, made in the engraved version, to the appearance of the Grotte des Pins at Fontainebleau, suggest a second visit. Differences of detail between drawings and engravings occur, to a greater or lesser degree, in most of the places illustrated; but although this may suggest that his record should be received with caution, it does not detract from the immensity of his enterprise, undertaken in extremely difficult circumstances and, in general, with remarkable accuracy.

Du Cerceau's engravings are supplemented by a text describing the buildings, sites and other features he feels require special mention. Some places receive more attention than others, both as regards written information and the number of drawings, which vary from two to eleven. The difference is mainly accounted for by his interest in the details of important contemporary buildings such as the Louvre, the châteaux of Madrid and Vallery, de l'Orme's work at Anet, and Jean Bullant's at Chantilly and Ecouen; as well as in places with which he was personally associated: Montargis, Charleval, Verneuil, and possibly Gaillon. *Les Plus Excellents Bastiments* is inevitably selective, in view of the nature of the work. The palaces and houses illustrated are mainly concentrated along the Seine and its tributaries in the region of the Ile de France, and in the Loire valley round Blois. Montargis is included for obvious reasons. The other
exceptions are Ancy-le-Franc and Maulnes in Burgundy: the 85
first because of its architectural importance, and probably

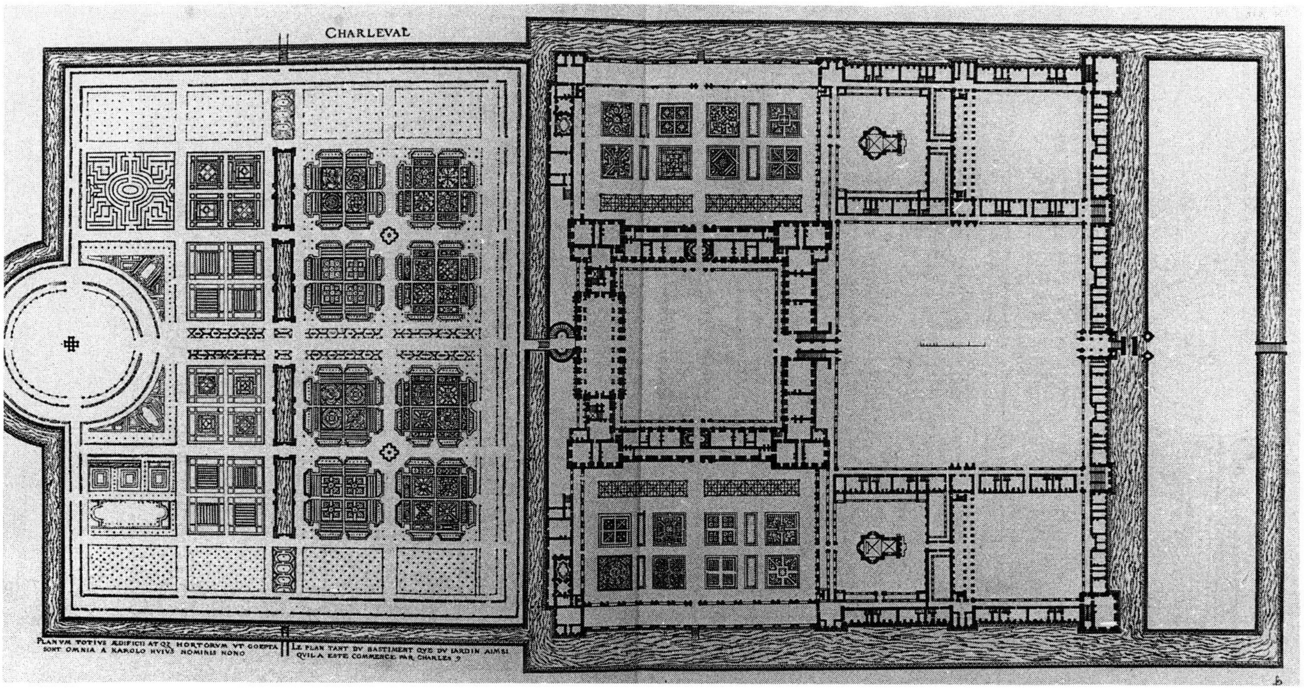

86 Design for the château and garden of Charleval.

(although Du Cerceau does not mention it) because it was the work of Serlio; the second for the originality of its design. Patronage, of course, was an essential consideration. Royal houses predominate in his selection; the most important are included. Montceaux is absent for some reason; possibly because it was incomplete. It has been suggested that Du Cerceau's choice of private houses is in some way influenced by the necessity to flatter.[30] But it is equally likely that Chantilly, Ecouen and Vallery are included for architectural reasons rather than because they belonged to the Montmorency or the childhood friend of Henri II. Du Cerceau, with his Huguenot associations, would have been less welcome in extreme Catholic circles. Of the Guise houses near Paris, Dampierre is included, but Meudon is not. As for Joinville-le-Grand-Jardin (Haute-Marne), the main Guise territory was a long way from Du Cerceau's area of working.

The plans for Charleval and Verneuil shown in Du Cerceau's drawings were never fully realized; and it has been questioned if he was the designer. Geymüller is convinced he was, and his argument has been accepted by historians such as Blunt. Despite doubts expressed by others, no plausible alternatives have been proposed.[31] Jal quotes the following entry from a list of the king's pensioners for 1577: 'Jacques Androuet dict Cerceau, architect 200 *l.* – Baptiste Androuet dict Cerceau à Charleval . . . 400 *l.*'[32] This is evidence that the Androuet du Cerceau were associated with Charleval, although Baptiste was the son of Jacques I, and not the father as Jal suggests; and the Jacques referred to is likely to have been Jacques II, Baptiste's brother. The plans for Charleval 86
integrate house and garden on a scale not previously seen in France. They would have rivalled Serlio's for the Louvre and De l'Orme's for the Tuileries; and as Blunt points out, this was probably Du Cerceau's intention. The site, in a valley south of Rouen, was flat with low hills on either side, but open towards the Seine some 12 kilometres to the west. The palace was designed round a cloistered courtyard, with gardens enclosed by porticos on either side. These buildings, together with offices and a huge forecourt, were contained in a square area surrounded by canals. Beyond this was another vast garden, larger than the whole palace complex, also surrounded and intersected by canals. At first sight the plan looks like a large and more elaborate garden in the tradition of Anet, but without the enclosing gallery. The area is divided into square parterres, those nearest the palace being more highly ornamented. They are framed on either side by rectangular *bosquets*; and, between the *bosquets* and the canal, a walk, lined with trees and hedges, which follows the entire periphery. The main walk, on the axis of the house, leads to a large oval space enclosed by a double row of trees. This is one of the most original features. According to Du Cerceau, Charles IX intended it to be the centre of the garden, which was to have been extended by an area corresponding to that shown on his plan. This would have made it 600 metres long and 360 wide. There is also an innovation in the shape of the parterres, which are not so much square as cruciform, with indentations at the points of the axes and diagonals, so that

they create further forms by their conjunction. This use of the oval, and the interplay of figure and ground, anticipates the complexity and ambiguity of Baroque plans; although in Du Cerceau's case the concept derives from tile decoration, and is related more to surfaces than architecture. Du Cerceau says the garden was laid out in Charles's lifetime, but very little of the palace was built when he died in 1574. As it is, the whole project may be regarded as intermediate to the integrated house-and-garden plan as realized at Anet, and the still larger and more comprehensive scheme for Richelieu in the following century.

If Charleval was the prototype of the French classical
87 garden on a flat or gently sloping site, Verneuil anticipates the terraces of Saint-Germain-en-Laye, at least as they were completed under Henri IV. The estate of Verneuil-sur-Oise had belonged to the Boulainvilliers family since 1415. Between 1558 and 1575 Philippe de Boulainvilliers began a new château, the plans of which were drawn and published by Du Cerceau.[33] The site was on high ground with valleys descending steeply on the south and east, where elaborate terraced gardens were projected. The house was to be built out of stone quarried round it; and contracts for masonry were drawn up in 1559 with Pierre des Illes, a master mason who had worked at Chantilly.[34] Unfortunately Boulainvilliers ran into financial difficulty with only the foundations and part of one of the wings completed. In 1575 he sold the property to the Duc and Duchesse de Nemours. Anne de Nemours was the daughter of Du Cerceau's protectress, Renée, and was therefore a d'Este. She had previously married François, Duc de Guise, whose assassination in 1563 confirmed her enmity for the Huguenot cause. Although this was a great grief for her mother, it did not alter their mutual affection, not did it extend to her architect who, though without doubt of Protestant persuasion, continued to work for the Nemours after Renée's death, which coincided with the purchase of Verneuil. The original designs were modified for the new owner. The building of the house continued between 1576 and 1585, when Nemours' death, and also that of Du Cerceau, brought the work to an end. It was recommenced between 1600 and 1616 by Du Cerceau's
grandson, Salomon de Brosse, for Henriette d'Entragues; but 89
the terraced gardens were never made.[35] Looking at the site

87 Projected design for the château and garden of Verneuil.

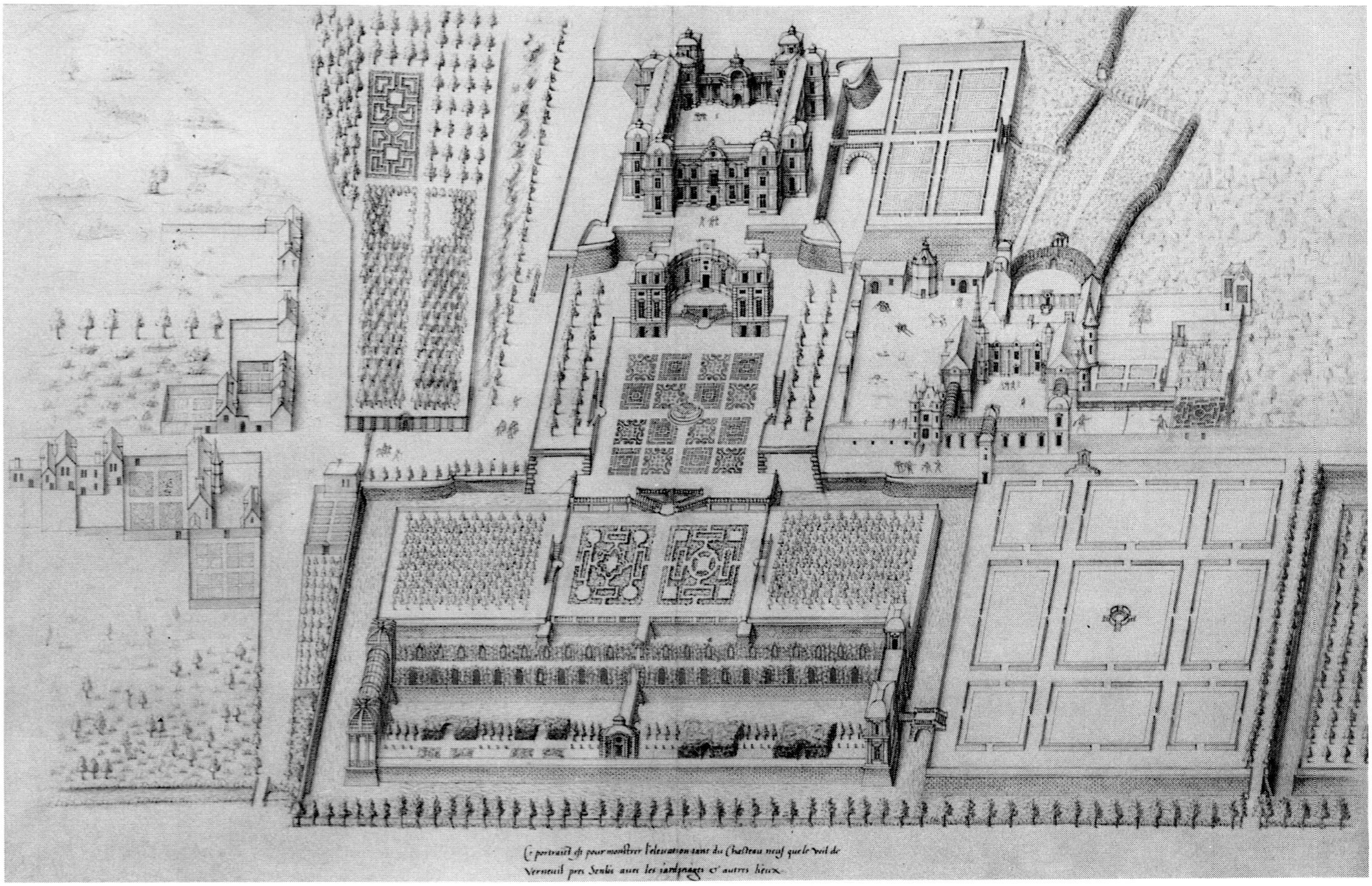

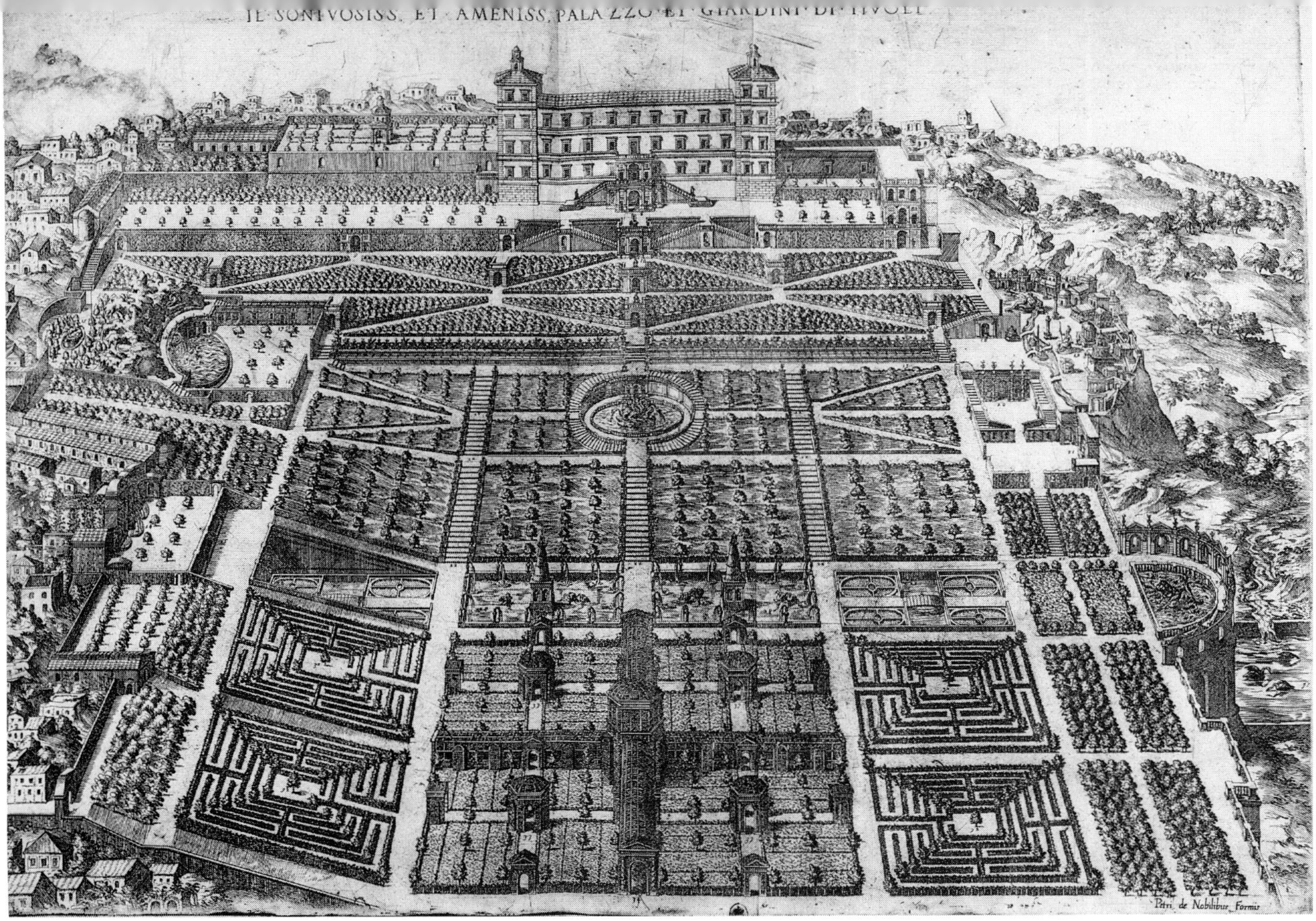

88 The Villa d'Este at Tivoli.

89 The château of Verneuil as built.

90 The gardens of the Villa Lante.

today, there is some doubt as to whether they could have been, and the highly original design must be considered hypothetical.

It is tempting to see the d'Este influence at Verneuil. Du
88 Perac's engraving of the villa at Tivoli was published in 1573; but Du Cerceau's drawn plan and bird's-eye view must have been made before 1575. It is possible that he knew De l'Orme's projected terrace gardens at Saint-Germain-en-Laye: or, less likely, those of the Villa Lante at Bagnaia made between 1568 and 1578. But all such comparisons are superficial, being no more than saying that the four gardens
90 are arranged in terraces on sloping sites. Lante is a perfectly proportioned garden, whose different parts, though distinct, merge most happily with one another. It is designed as a summer retreat, and not as the adjunct of a great house. Although the site is elevated, the changes in level are not abrupt; whereas at Tivoli they are precipitous, so that the terraces and ramps are numerous and narrow, but skilfully used to give transverse vistas at right angles to the main axis. This is assisted by the fact that the steep ground surrounds it on two sides, with abundant falling water to serve the various fountains and cascades.[36] A dramatic use of water, and a consciousness of the view of the *campagna* are the Villa d'Este's outstanding characteristics. There is no resemblance between these Italian sites and that of Verneuil, which overlooked a narrow valley whose small stream was to supply the canals in the lower gardens. The approach to the château was from the high ground, through the courtyard. The garden was intended as a climax. The door from the main *corps de logis* was to issue in a terrace which, taking advantage of the fall, was planned to cover a large room with a concave façade, flanked by two pavilions, and enclosing a second semicircular terrace called by Du Cerceau 'terrasse en théâtre'. The first design for this building is highly mannered, covered with fantastic ornament, the doorway dwarfed by four giant hanging figures, two on either side of it. In the
bird's-eye view (B.M.41) it is represented as much simpler, 87
the decoration consisting of rusticated pilasters reminiscent of Ammannati's courtyard of the Pitti palace. The steps leading to the parterre are also changed, from diverging to converging flights. The importance of this architectural arrangement is emphasized in Du Cerceau's text, where he refers to 'un vallon de grand plaisir', and continues, referring to the design for the Duc de Nemours:

91 The Maison Blanche, Gaillon. Drawing by Du Cerceau, who may have been the architect of the building.

92 The château, garden and gallery of Montargis.

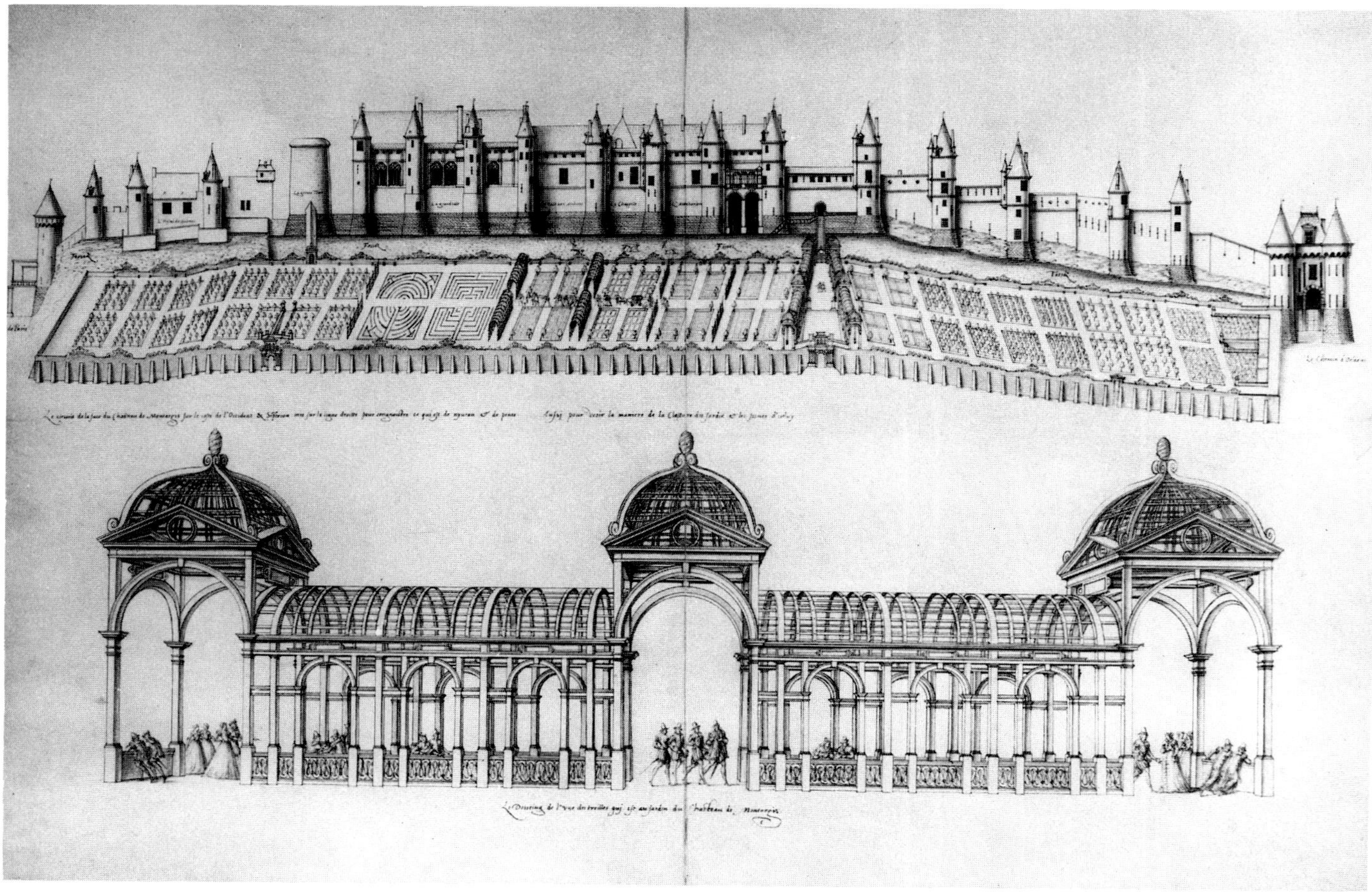

> His intention is to raise on the front, facing the valley, a hall 180 feet [30 *toises*] long, by 30 feet wide, and a room on each side, repeating [*revenantes*] the width of the hall, the whole covered as a terrace, and having the same outlook; so that one will emerge from the new house onto the terrace still looking towards the valley: which will offer great beauty, seeing that the small vale is made pleasant [*accommodé*] with gardens, canals, walks covered with alders, and all surrounded by these canals, with a pond between the gardens and the town.

Du Cerceau did nine engravings of Gaillon, showing the new embellishments added by Charles de Bourbon, archbishop of Rouen, between 1550 and 1590. They include
91 four details of the Lydieu and Maison Blanche, of which Geymüller thinks Du Cerceau may have been the architect. His evidence is purely stylistic, based on a comparison with pavilions in the fifty-eighth lesson of perspective, and composition 23 in the *Livre pour Bâtir aux Champs*. A further comparison might be made between the irregular cusped moat, and those in the drawing for a 'bâtiment à plaisir'
06 (B.M.120). So far as is known, there is nothing in sixteenth-century France like this little casino, with the canal and hermit's rock, concealed in the park away from the château and the main gardens. The nucleus of the Lydieu, however, was created by Georges d'Amboise between 1502 and 1504; and the Maison Blanche was built by 1566, since it was the scene of theatricals given for Charles IX and the queen mother, when it was called 'L'Isle Heureuse'. Later, in more sinister circumstances, it became 'Le Pavillon de la Ligue', when Charles de Bourbon was proclaimed king by the Catholic faction in opposition to Henri IV. Other additions, such as the gallery in the upper garden and the large garden below, were also made in the cardinal de Bourbon's time. Du Cerceau adds a long description of these works in his text, but nowhere does he claim to have been the architect of any building; not even at Montargis, with which he was so closely connected. Nor, surprisingly, does his text elaborate on the great semicircular terrace surrounding the precincts there, with gardens radiating from the walls and descending the slopes. He gives a detailed drawing of one of the large
92 wooden galleries, lining the way from the castle to the gate in the terrace wall, 'which are at present covered with ivy', the inscription reads. Du Cerceau praises the view all round as the finest and richest to be found anywhere; and his map of
93 Montargis (B.M.24) shows three avenues of elms radiating in a *patte d'oie* across the fields from the château gardens.

The ornamental planting of parterres shown in Du Cerceau's engravings is often taken as representing the appearance of a French Renaissance garden and, notably in the Jardin Potager at Villandry, used as a model for reconstruction. The laying out of beds in this manner was certainly practised from the early sixteenth century; but it is unlikely that it was as extensive as Du Cerceau suggests. Where such gardens did exist, they were not uniformly well kept. The passion for building and planning fine gardens outstripped the capacity to maintain them. Du Cerceau himself refers to the neglect in his day of Folembray, Villers-Cotterets and Fontainebleau. Practical considerations apart, the internal evidence of Du Cerceau's work shows that the ornamental layout of many of the gardens existed largely in his imagination. In places with which he was familiar, such as Montargis, there is correspondence between the drawn and the engraved version. In others, such as Bury, there are considerable differences. The style of decoration varies from mainly rectilinear patterns to elaborate curvilinear *broderie*.

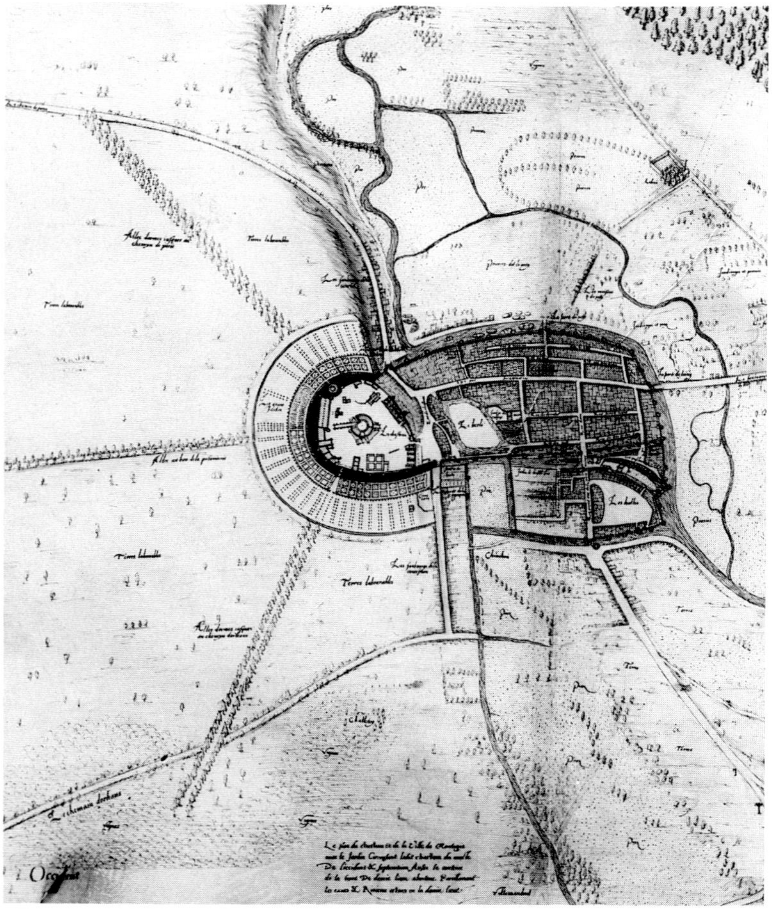

93 Detail of Du Cerceau's map of Montargis.

We may suspect that where his imagination was not controlled by a certain knowledge of the facts, his fancy wandered, filling the blank spaces to create a rich effect. By doing so he may well have influenced future developments in garden design. Du Perac, who is said by Claude Mollet to have introduced the *parterre de broderie* at Anet, did not do so until after 1582. He could therefore have got the idea from Du Cerceau. On the other hand it may have been the other way round; we have no means of knowing to what extent close contemporaries influenced one another. We do know that Jacques Androuet du Cerceau influenced a future generation of architects, not only through his books, but by establishing a dynasty, the most notable of whom was his grandson, Salomon de Brosse.

6

The vegetal component: French gardening in the sixteenth and early-seventeenth centuries

Gardening principles

French sixteenth-century gardening principles are contained in a few general treatises on agriculture and the management of estates, following the model of Pietro de Crescenzi's *Le Rustican* (see chapter 1) of which fourteen editions were printed between 1486 and 1540. The writings of Cato and Varro were available in printed editions from 1523. Three French editions of a translation of Columella's *De Re Rustica* were issued between 1551 and 1556. Agostino Gallo's *Le Dieci Giornati della Vera Agricultura* (1565), translated into French by François de Belleforest, was published as *Secrets de la Vraye Agriculture* in 1572. Much of what Gallo says on the garden is repeated by Elie Vinet[1] in a volume entitled *La Maison Champestre et Agriculture* (1607), which included a work on gardening by Antoine Mizauld.[2] The garden of Gallo and Vinet has the relatively simple form of a square divided into four equal parts by intersecting paths. In Italy these are tiled, but in France they are more usually of sand. The Italian custom is to surround the quarters of the garden by dwarf walls, ornamented with vases containing lemon trees, pinks, marjoram, basil or other bushy scented plants. As an alternative to walls Vinet recommends clipped borders of lavender, rosemary or box. He says that a garden is more beautiful if it is laid out in figures, such as coats of arms, wheels, rosettes, squares, triangles and so on; and abounding in sweet smelling herbs, lilies and violets.

Mizauld offers a scheme of eight plots (*positions*) divided into smaller squares; each plot given to plants for a specific use: green vegetables, edible roots, cooking herbs, gourds and herbaceous fruits, flowers, non-edible herbs, fruit trees, nuts, and trees such as bay and elder.

The most important of these sixteenth-century treatises was *L'Agriculture et Maison Rustique* by Charles Etienne and Jean Liébault. Etienne[3] came from a family of printers and scholars. He first studied medicine and was chosen by Lazare de Baïf as tutor to his son, Jean-Antoine, the poet. A number of Charles Etienne's writings on agriculture, horticulture and viticulture[4] were published by his brother Robert,[5] and collected in 1554 under the title *Praedium Rusticum*. It was translated into French by his son-in-law, Jean Liébault, and issued in 1564 as *L'Agriculture et Maison Rustique*. Other editions followed in 1570 and 1572 with additional material; and it was again revised in form and content in 1582. The separate chapters of the earlier editions were run together as paragraphs for longer chapters; the plant information was extended; and a whole chapter added on how to lay out herbs and flowers in compartments, with illustrations of various designs.

L'Agriculture et Maison Rustique is divided into seven books covering all aspects of life in a country house, from the general duties of the owner to venery, boar-hunting and falconry. It is not only a comprehensive manual for growing many kinds of plants, but also of their culinary and medicinal uses; and of baking, brewing and distilling. Books two and three, dealing with gardens and orchards, are as long as the rest put together, and are the parts to which Liébault added most. In Etienne and Liébault's work, aesthetics are closely linked with utility.

> The most pleasant and entertaining part of the small French farm is the flower garden. . . . It is a commendable and proper thing to look from one's windows on well-cultivated acres, meadows, ploughed fields or plantations of willow. . . . But it is also good to gaze on beautiful compartments, pretty arbours and rooms, pleasant borders of lavender, rosemary, box or suchlike things.
>
> (*Le Parterre ou Jardin à Fleurs.*[6])

Added to these, the songs of innumerable birds, the fragrance of the flowers, the dew sparkling in the rising sun, the sound of honey bees and the sight of scented herbs like thyme, lemon-balm, rosemary and marjoram cannot fail to give great satisfaction to everyone.

What Etienne and Liébault describe is a modest country 95
house, with forecourt, stables and offices on one side; gardens and orchard on the other. Just as in the grander houses we have described, the garden is the climax of an axial approach, which continues in a broad walk dividing *potager* from parterre, and thence through the orchard to a gate leading to the fields. It is a pattern which is still widely seen in France. Each part of the garden is enclosed by hedges, walls or *berceaux* made of trellis, according to the wealth and inclination of the owner. For hedges they recommend hazel, currant bushes, pepper plants, raspberry canes, brambles,

94 Nicolas Robert's portrait of Gaston d'Orléans, reflecting the latter's claims to eminence: war, learning – and flowers.

95 A modest country house and its gardens, early seventeenth century. (Compare the seat round the tree with ill. 6).

honeysuckle, viburnum, holly, elder mixed with thorn, wild apple, service, medlar and privet. Elm, wild plum and cherry planted in the hedge will strengthen it.

Both the parterre and the *potager* are surrounded by covered walks in the form of *berceaux* made of trellis, to support climbing plants such as jasmine and musk rose.[7] Other plants suitable for covering *berceaux* are ivy, traveller's joy, cucumber, hop, tomato and pea.[8] In its simplest form the frame was made of juniper or hazel, and willow. And of course, in important gardens, the covered walk was made by carpenters, as in the galleries of Blois, Gaillon or Anet. In the case of the *potager*, Liébault considers *berceaux* too costly, and recommends that it should be surrounded by a simple structure like an open shed or lean-to.

The parterre should be separated from the *potager* by a broad walk about 6 metres (18 *pieds*) wide, with a well or fountain situated half way between them. It should be divided into two equal parts; one for flowers for cutting, the other for plants grown mainly for their scent. In the first group, Liébault included violet, pink, marigold, pansy, daisy, stock or wallflower, lily of the valley, iris, columbine, lily; in the second, such herbs as southernwood, wormwood, rosemary, marjoram, mint, pennyroyal, costmary, hyssop, lavender, basil, sage, savory, rue, tansy, thyme, camomile, mugwort, catmint, lemon-balm, clary, dill and horehound. It will be observed that these divisions of the garden broadly correspond to the senses of taste, sight and smell, although some of the fragrant herbs in the last division would be used for flavouring. Whereas the squares in the *potager* are divided into strips[9] of different sizes according to the vegetable they are to contain, those in the parterre may be disposed in figures such as labyrinths or compartments of different shapes.

Liébault uses 'parterre' to mean the flower garden as a whole; 'compartiment', a single square treated as a design unit in the form of a knot (i.e. *entrelacs*); and 'carreau' (literally a 'tile'), parts of a design which are separate from one another. For example, 'un compartiment simple', is a 96
single square treated as a continuous knot; a 'parterre de carreaux rompus', is a design without knots composed of pieces separate from one another; and 'bordure de carreaux 97
rompus avec son milieu et cinq petits compartiments', a mixed design of five knots, combined with broken pieces.

Not all herbs and flowers are suitable for making compartments, says Liébault. He suggests pennyroyal, hyssop, wild thyme, rosemary, thyme, sage, marjoram, camomile, violet, daisy, basil; with borders of lavender or rosemary. Box may be used, but should be avoided if possible because of its unpleasant smell.[10] He refers to advances in designs of parterres made since the book was first published. We may take this to mean that the elaborate interlacing patterns which he illustrates came into fashion in the last part of the sixteenth century. In this connection he especially mentions 'M. Porcher, prior of Crécy-en-Brie, the most excellent in this art not only in France but in all Europe'.

L'Agriculture et Maison Rustique was influential not only in France but other European countries. An English version by Richard Surflet appeared in 1600; and the 'knot' designs were widely reproduced; for instance in the 1608 edition of
98 Thomas Hill's *The Gardener's Labyrinth*, where one of them replaces the original (1577) diagram of 'a proper knot'.

Le Théâtre d'Agriculture et Mesnages des Champs by Olivier de Serres was published in 1600, the most substantial work (over 1000 pages) on managing an estate to have been printed (perhaps anywhere). De Serres[11] was a native of Villeneuve-de-Berg in the Rhône Valley, where his father, Jacques de Serres, was a cloth merchant. The family were converts to the Reformed religion, and Olivier's brother, Jean, became a distinguished member of Calvin's circle. Olivier studied botany, medicine and law; and after travelling in Italy and Switzerland he returned to France and purchased the domain of Pradel in 1558. He left the farming of the estate to a tenant on the basis of half shares, while he himself lived at Villeneuve, visiting Pradel at weekends. During the wars of religion, when Villeneuve was successively controlled by Protestants and Catholics, De Serres was actively engaged. Although he and his family were installed at Pradel in 1578, it was not until peace was established at Villeneuve in 1589 that a settled agricultural life returned to an estate constantly threatened with devastation by opposing armies. Since 1571 he had bred silkworms; and in the course of compiling his work on agriculture had written a treatise on the subject. It was because of Henri IV's interest in the silk industry that De Serres came to the notice of his ministers. *La Cueillette de la Soye* was published in 1599; followed in 1600 by *Le Théâtre d'Agriculture et Mesnage des Champs*. De Serres, having rapidly become regarded as an expert on the white mulberry, was commissioned to provide trees for the royal parks. Of these, 20,000 were sent to Paris in 1601 and planted at Fontainebleau, Madrid and the Tuileries, where a school for the cultivation and preparation of silk was established in 1603. In May of that year, Olivier de Serres came to inspect the mulberry trees at the Tuileries and to speak with the king on agricultural matters. He thus became acquainted with Claude Mollet, the royal gardener. This explains how Mollet's designs for newly created parterres[12] at Fontainebleau, Saint-Germain-en-Laye and the Tuileries are illustrated in De Serres's book. Although embodying his own experience, De Serres obviously owed much to other texts. His list of herbs and flowers for making ornamental

96, 97, 98 Three diagrams from Etienne and Lièbault's *L'Agriculture et Maison Rustique*: 'compartiment simple', 'bordure de carreaux rompus,' and 'bordure avec son compartiment simple'.

compartments is similar to Liébault's: basil, camomile, daisy, hyssop, marjoram, pennyroyal, sage, thyme, wild thyme and violet, with the addition of sorrel and parsley. For borders and edging, myrtle is offered besides lavender and rosemary; and box is said to be in general use for the more delicate designs in the parterre. His instructions for making compartments are also more specific. The species should be kept distinct, and compartments made uniform in shape and colour on each side; for example, if the compartment is made of marjoram enriched with daisies on the right, so it must be on the left. Plants should be equidistant from one another, avoiding confusion and crowding. They should be kept low and free of weeds, so that the earth may be seen between the rows. A background of different coloured earths gives lustre to the parterre, making it like a picture; but only natural earths should be used, like broken slate for black.

De Serres sets down for the first time how the proportions may be adjusted to offset the effects of perspective; that is to say, where compartments are to be seen from a distance, the rows should be further apart. Or, the closer they are to be seen the nearer they should be together. The thickness of the rows must be proportioned to the size of the space occupied by the compartment. However, because rows overlap when seen from garden level, they are better viewed from above, as naturally happens at Saint-Germain-en-Laye because of the nature of the site; or from the terraces raised above the parterre, as in the avenue of mulberries at the Tuileries.

Claude Mollet's own book, *Le Théâtre des Plans et Jardinages*, was published posthumously in 1652; but had been in manuscript for some time previously. He was born about 1564,[13] and although he was not appointed royal gardener by Henri IV much before 1595, members of his family worked for Diane de Poitiers at Chenonceaux.[14] Claude Mollet repeatedly acknowledges his debt to his father, Jacques Mollet, who was gardener to Diane's grandson, the Duc d'Aumale, at Anet. *Le Théâtre des Plans et Jardinages* is over 400 pages long, essentially a gardener's treatise, with comprehensive lists of trees, flowers, vegetables, herbs, instructions on their uses, and when to plant them, particularly according to the phases of the moon. The importance of astrology for the conduct of life is emphasized. Mollet is not concerned with the architectural framework of the garden, or with its ornament, except in so far as these are vegetal. That is to say, he is explicit about the planting of *allées*, width in relation to length, and spacing; the laying out of *parterres de broderie* and *bosquets*, with examples by his sons André, Claude, Jacques and Noel; and the designing of *palissades* of beech or hornbeam in the forms of walls, arcades and porticos. The importance of his book is that it looks back over half a century of gardening practice with a wealth of detail and personal reminiscence.

Medicinal and botanic gardens

A great many plants had medicinal value. Doctors were prominent among those who wrote on gardening, or who established gardens, because an understanding of the medicinal properties of plants was essential to their profession. Olivier de Serres, in *Le Théâtre d'Agriculture*, devotes chapters 14 and 15 of his sixth book to medicinal gardens. He refers to those in Pisa, Padua and Genoa; and he gives diagrams and descriptions of two mounts, or artificial hills, for growing medicinal plants, with walled terraces forming micro-climates according to the direction they faced. The first is circular in plan, about 90 metres (270 *pieds*) in diameter, rising by a spiral ramp to a flat top of about 40 metres (120 *pieds*). The ramps are about 5 metres (15 *pieds*) wide, the beds being just over 1 metre (4 *pieds*), and the path
almost 4 metres (11 *pieds*). The second mount is in the form of 99
a pyramid with a flat top about 50 metres square, each face being about 100 metres at the base. Steps at each corner give access to the terraces. The interior is hollow, to store orange trees or other delicate plants in winter. There is a fountain in the middle of the flat area at the top, which may be planted (says De Serres) with pines, firs or other mountain trees.

A somewhat similar mount had recently been made to the
design of Richer de Belleval at Montpellier, except that it was 100
oblong, so that its terraces faced north and south. Montpellier was the first botanic garden in France, earlier than Paris. Belleval, a doctor, obtained support for his project from Henri IV, who created a chair for anatomy and the demonstrations of simples, or herbal drugs, at Montpellier and appointed Belleval to it. Hostility to Belleval on the part of the other professors was increased when he neglected his anatomy lectures in order to collect plants for his garden, which was for the instruction of his students. To assist in identification, the plants were arranged in six long troughs, with walks between, and with access from a promenade adjoining the master's house. Each section was approached through an arch labelled with the appropriate group, according to the habitat or use of the plants to be studied; those belonging to the rocks of the shore, sand, wood, copse, hillside or mountain, or for medicinal use. On one side of the troughs were reference numbers to identify the plants; on the other irrigation gutters. Medicine, botanic gardens and the search for plants were interrelated. Henri IV's instructions to Belleval, 'de rechercher les plantes de nostre royaume . . . et les faire porter dans nos jardins de Montpellier, Parys et Fontainebleau,' are a reminder of the encouragement he gave to gardeners.

99 Artificial mount, from Olivier de Serres's *Le Théâtre d'Agriculture*, 1600.

100 The mount in the Jardin des Plantes at Montpellier, designed by Richer de Belleval; remade after 1621.

IARDIN . DV . ROY . POVR . LA . CVLTVRE . DES . PLA
A la court de lentree
B la Court deuant la face du logis.
C le grand parterre diuise en quatre.
D quatre autres grands parterres.
E le bois
F le pre auec son eau Viue
G le Verger
H la Cerisee
I le pauillon en face de la grande allee des charmes
K la grande allee de la face de la maison.
L lallee de charmes quiua au bois
M Allee en terrasse au pied de laquelle est la Riuiere de biure
N la montaigne auec sa croupe esleuee de trois toises nommee belle Veue
O la petitte Croupe nommee beau seiour
P la maison
Q sa gallerie
R basse Court
S Iardin a tulipes
Federic Scalberge pict. sculp. et fe. Anno 1636

101 The royal 'Jardin des Plantes Médicinales', founded by Jean Héroard and Guy de la Brosse. The engraving (1636) is from La Brosse's *Description*.

Jean Robin (1550–1629), apothecary, established a garden in the west of the Île de la Cité (now Place Dauphine). Henri III gave him the direction of the gardens of the Louvre and the title of 'arboriste et simpliciste du Roi'; posts which were confirmed by Henri IV and Louis XIII. Robin's garden was famous for the number and variety of flowers, many of which were illustrated by Pierre Vallet in *Le Jardin du Roy très Chrétien Henri IV* (1608). Robin set the fashion for the tuberose (*polyanthes tuberosa*); and from seeds from Virginia he grew the first false acacia, named after him, *Robinia pseudo-acacia*. His son, Vespasien (1579–1662), who succeeded him as *arboriste du roi*, made expeditions to the south of France, the Alps, Spain and north Africa to collect plants; and naturalized others from eastern and north America.

When the idea was conceived in 1597 of establishing a medicinal garden in Paris, Jean Robin was invited to draw up the plan. However the project was not realized until 1626. Meanwhile Belleval's garden was destroyed in 1621 during the siege of Montpellier in Cardinal Richelieu's campaign to suppress the Huguenots in the south. Belleval remade it on a smaller scale, but its importance declined when Le Jardin
101 Royal des Plantes Médicinales was founded by Louis XIII's doctors, Jean Héroard and Guy de la Brosse.

La Brosse published a description[15] of the garden in 1636; at the same time disparaging Richer de Belleval's garden at Montpellier which, with its different walled enclosures, was 'more like a labyrinth than a spacious garden', he said. He thus stressed the importance of the aesthetic aspects of the design of the Paris garden: a large rectangular parterre, with a wide *allée* on the axis of the *logis*, intersected by transverse *allées*, with a circular basin and fountain at the centre. Along one side, an avenue of hornbeam and lime (about 320 metres long, 10 metres wide) stretched eastwards towards the Seine. North of this was an irregular area of wood, meadow and orchard, in the northwest corner of which a walled area, covering 5 acres, enclosed a mount with two ridges. The highest, over 18 metres (54 *pieds*) high, was surmounted by a spiral hillock from where there were views over Paris and the surrounding countryside for more than 25 kilometres. The mount was planted with rare varieties of vine; the valley round it with fruit trees and cypress; and the walks bordered by roses. At the foot of the mount, with its enclosure, was a crescent-shaped bed, facing south, with orange and lemon trees, myrtle, 'Acatia d'Egypte', palm, sugar-cane and other plants requiring warmth, which were covered by a wooden frame in winter. A terrace on the ridge facing the Seine had evergreens[16] on the east side, and plants from warm climates on the south.[17] Shade-loving plants were grown in the wooded area; water in the meadow provided suitable conditions for aquatic plants. In the parterres of the main garden the arrangement was according to family and species; the two nearest the *logis* contained evergreen and hardy flowering shrubs; two others were reserved for deciduous shrubs and hardy, half-hardy or annual plants. In fact it was a botanical garden going far beyond purely medicinal use (what plant did not have one?). According to La Brosse it covered 18 acres, compared with Montpellier's 6; and was not only a much larger garden, but drew its collection from wider fields. La Brosse's catalogue, the *Déscription du Jardin Royal* . . . (1636), lists some 2500 varieties and species, which, compared with the 1332 in Belleval's *Onomatologia* (1598), is some indication of the increase of plant-introduction into Europe.[18]

The flower garden and the parterre

A new interest in flower gardens was stimulated by advances in the science of botany, the consequent collection of new species and the cultivation of varieties, particularly Dutch tulips, by nurserymen. The number of kinds of ornamental plant increased from about 150 in 1550 to 800 in 1669, although this is partly accounted for in new varieties. Among new species introduced from the Near East in the latter part of the sixteenth century were the oriental hyacinth, crown imperial (*Fritillaria imperialis*), narcissus, ranunculus, anemone, iris and tulip. René Morin,[19] first of a dynasty of seventeenth-century nurserymen, was established in Paris by 1619. His catalogue of plants (the first organized trade list) included exotics from north America and elsewhere. He had a special interest in shrubs and woody plants, herbaceous perennials and, above all, bulbs. Evelyn, who visited Morin's gardens in April 1644, said it was 'of an exact oval figure, planted with cypress, cut flat and even as a wall: the tulips, anemones, ranunculuses, crocuses etc., are held to be of the rarest.'

Flowers were recorded by a series of botanical illustrators. Pierre Vallet's *Le Jardin du Roy très Chrétien Henri IV* (1608) has already been mentioned. Daniel Rabel (1578–1637), also known for his portraits, landscapes and designs for ballet, was an elegant flower painter. But for the most complete visual record of the mid-seventeenth-century French flower garden we must go to the paintings and engravings of Nicolas Robert (1614–85), which in brilliance and variety exceed all others. The first of these was a small volume of etchings, *Fiori Diversi*, published in Rome in 1640. His paintings for *Guirlande de Julie*, an album of flowers given to Julie d'Angennes,[20] were made shortly after, since they were
presented in 1641. This brought him to the notice of Gaston 94
d'Orléans, who employed him to record the flowers in his gardens of the Luxembourg and Blois. Two volumes of
etchings were published in 1665[21] and 1676,[22] containing 10
thirty-one and sixteen plates respectively, of elegantly composed groups of flowers. Flowers increasingly became subjects in their own right for painting and decoration; for
example, the panels in a room in the château of Ancy-le- 10
Franc. 10

102 Four etchings of flowers by Nicolas Robert from *Varie ac Multiformes Florum*: Corona Imperialis, Tulip and Mallow, Daisy and Lily, and Poppy.

Corona Imperialis
Couronne Imperiale
N. Robert del. fecil et ex. c.p.r.

Tulipe fond Jaune panachée de rouge
Tulipe panachée de blanc et violet
Mauue grisdelin

Bellis montana flore albo
Lilium purpureo Croceū maius
Lis Orangé

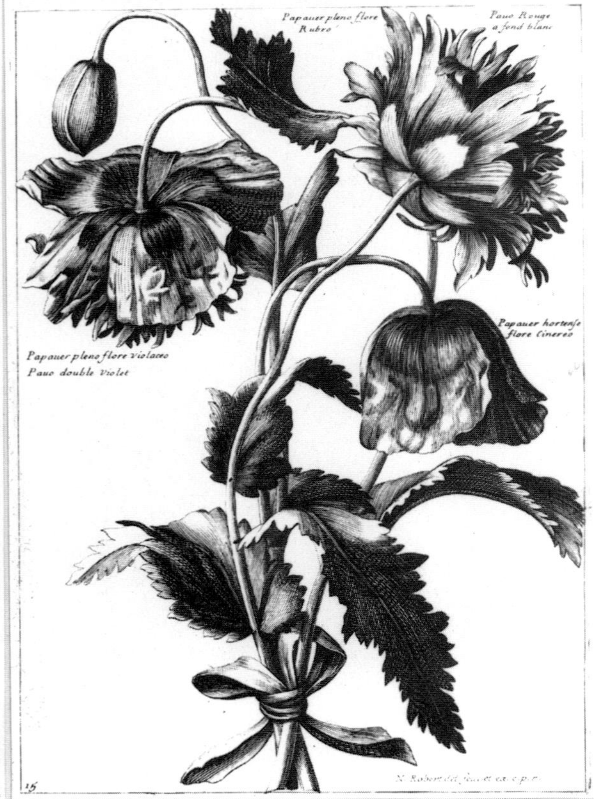
Papauer pleno flore Rubro
Pauo Rouge a fond blanc
Papauer pleno flore violaceo
Pauo double violet
Papauer hortense flore Cinereo

103, 104 Chambre des Fleurs, in the château of Ancy-le-Franc and (left) one of the panels.

Outside, flowers were either planted in the borders of the
105 parterre[23] or in a garden reserved for them, as at Liancourt. This was usually at one side of the château. From the early seventeenth century it was the fashion to lay out the area immediately facing the main rooms with trailing plant-like forms of box and cut turf, against backgrounds of coloured earth, known as *parterres de broderie*. The main purpose of this was as an ornament to the area immediately adjoining the château, kept level to reveal the architecture, and to accord with the general appearance of ordered regularity.

THE PARTERRE

The practice of laying out parts of gardens in various figures had very ancient precedents. Labyrinths and knots were symbolic in origin; and heraldic designs announcing the status of the owner were made at least by the beginning of the sixteenth century, as at Gaillon and Anet.[24] The earliest printed diagrams of figured beds with knot motifs (*entrelacs*) are in the *Hypnerotomachia Poliphili*, where they are said to resemble 'carpets'. In the French version (1546) the list of plants to be used for figure and ground does not correspond with the Italian, so may very well represent French practice at the time.[25] Liébault reproduces sixteen designs in the 1582 edition of *L'Agriculture et Maison Rustique*, and refers to the advances of this art made since the book was first published. In Du Cerceau's work there are considerable differences between drawn and engraved versions of the same place. The plans of the Tuileries, however, correspond in drawing and engraving, and we may feel assured that this late and important garden would reflect the most advanced taste of the time. Apart from one quarter of a square near the palace, laid out as a coat of arms, the designs are of a relatively simple geometric kind, which are more credible than those shown in the drawings of Dampierre and Saint-Maur which resemble majolica tiles.[26] While he did not anticipate treating the whole parterre as a single unit, his design for Verneuil, a

105 The flower garden at Liancourt (for other views of Liancourt see ills. 142–146).

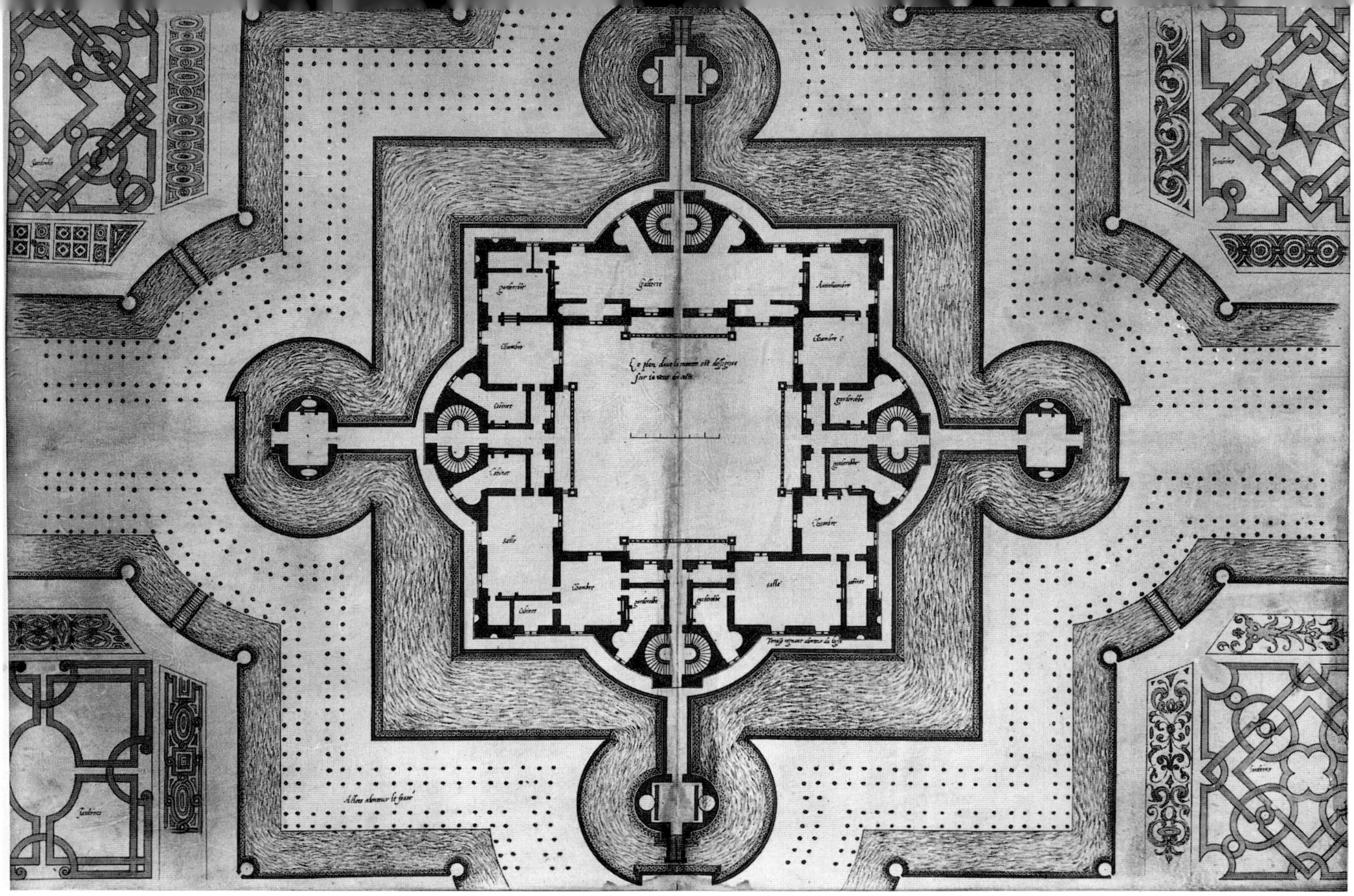

106 Design for a 'bâtiment à plaisir' by Jacques Androuet du Cerceau, showing gardens in the form of knots and embroidery.

repetition of two contrasting motifs, is a move towards unity and away from what was apparently the custom of treating each square differently. One of his fantasies for a 'bâtiment à
106 plaisir' (B.M.120) shows a garden in the four corners outside the moats, each consisting of an elaborate knot design[27] within a square with ornamental borders. Two strips in the bottom right-hand corner are derived from the plant-like forms of grotesque decoration or designs for embroidery, which foreshadow the *parterre de broderie* at Heidelberg illustrated by Salomon de Caus (*c.* 1576–1626) in his *Hortus Palatinus* (1620).

According to Claude Mollet, whereas it had been the custom to lay out the garden in squares of different designs, as in *L'Agriculture et Maison Rustique*,[28] Etienne du Perac, architect to the Duc d' Aumale, showed him how to make a garden in the form of a single compartment divided by large walks. This was at Anet after Du Perac's return from Italy in 1582. 'These were the first parterres and compartments *en broderie* which had been made in France,' he wrote, 'which is why I have always continued since to work on a large scale [faire des grands volumes] . . . so that I no longer stopped at making compartments in little squares, one of them one way and another in another.' He continued:

At the time I began to make the first *compartimens en broderie*, box was still rarely used, because very few people of rank wished to have box planted in their gardens, so that I planted my *compartimens en broderie* with several kinds of garden plant which gave a variety of green. But such plants cannot last long in this French climate, because of the extremes of heat and cold that we have. It was the great labour and expense of remaking and replanting the compartments every three years which led me to experiment with the box plant, so as not to have the trouble of remaking so often. Now because I needed a large quantity, I planted plenty in the nurseries, so as to have it when the need arose; so in a short time I raised very good box in such quantities as I might require. In 1595 the late king, Henry the Great, ordered me to plant the garden of Saint-Germain-en-Laye, and so I made it all of box, and also the garden at Montceaux, together with the little garden on the pond at Fontainebleau.

What Mollet is talking about can be seen in the Jardin de 108
l'Etang at Fontainebleau, an island about 68 metres square made in 1594 adjoining the Cour de la Fontaine and connected to it by a wooden bridge. A general idea of the
parterre is given by a plan of 1600;[29] a detail was among those 107
published in De Serres' book. It is clear that by 'broderie'

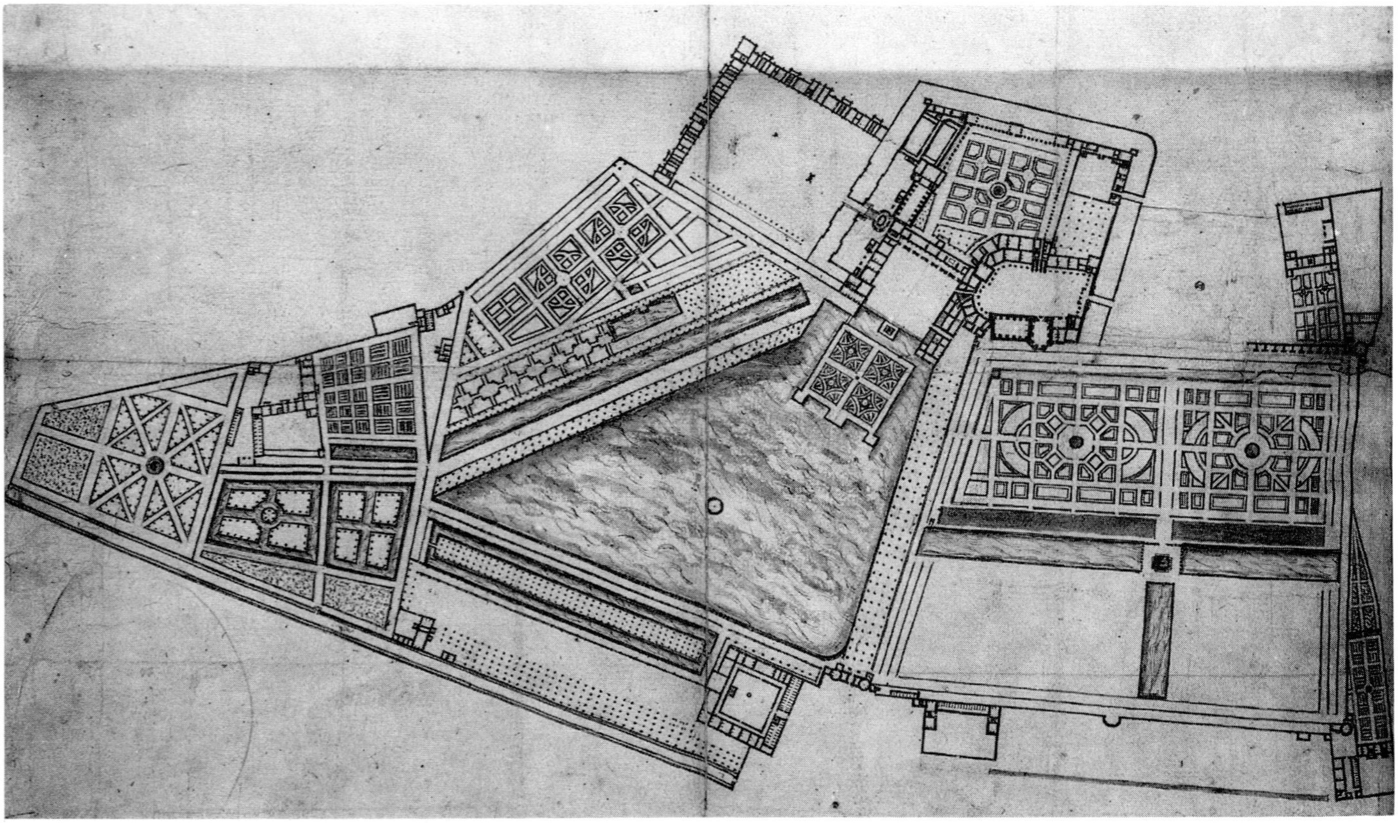

107, 108 Fontainebleau: plan of about 1600 showing the Jardin de l'Etang (below) built out into the lake from the Cour de la Fontaine.

109 Design for *parterre de broderie* in the style of Claude Mollet.

109 Mollet means treating the parterre as a unit, so that the
quarters combine to form a whole; he does not mean the style
110 of flowing plant-like forms of his sons André and Jacques II, with which his own book is illustrated. This style seems to have originated in France; and the earliest example appears to have been at Marie de Médicis' palace of the Luxembourg. She had a passion for flowers and took great pleasure in Jean Robin's garden. It was she who commissioned Pierre Vallet's drawings to serve as patterns for embroidery, in which she set a fashion for floral motifs. The Luxembourg *parterre de broderie*, surrounded by balustraded terraces,[30] was in direct relation to the palace. It has been attributed to Jacques Boyceau, because he was Intendant des Jardins du Roi at the time, and because the designs appeared in his posthumous
Traité du Jardinage (1638).[31] But it has been suggested that the 111
drawings in Boyceau's book were by Claude Mollet's son, Claude II.[32] Indeed this leads to the subject of the royal gardeners at the end of the sixteenth and beginning of the seventeenth centuries, and to the garden of the Tuileries with which the most important of them were associated.

110 Design for *parterre de broderie* in the style of Claude Mollet's son André; from Claude Mollet's *Théâtre des Plans et Jardinages*, 1642.

111 Design for *parterre de broderie* from Jacques Boyceau's *Traité du Jardinage*, 1638.

112 View of the Tuileries from the Seine, *c.* 1650.

113 View showing how the walled garden of the Tuileries, on the left, was separated from the palace by a public road.

The Tuileries: the garden and the gardeners

112 The Tuileries garden was begun in 1564 on a level site parallel
to the Seine. The boundary ran obliquely from the river,
with the longest side furthest from it, making a rhomboid
74 shape (see Du Cerceau's plan, B.M.79). The first concern was
to bring the whole of this area within the defensive walls of
the city. The water for the garden came from a spring at
Saint-Cloud noted for its purity; and according to De
l'Orme's plan it was brought about 2000 *pas* in underground
pipes and conduits.[33] In 1567 Catherine wrote asking that a
gate should be made from the river, so that she could pass
directly by boat into the canals of her garden. A channel was
114 cut entering the precincts east of the palace,[34] but her
intention to have canals in the Tuileries garden itself was not
fulfilled.

Planting began as early as 1566, with 500 fruit trees;[35] and crocuses were planted in 1568. But the main work was done in the spring of 1570 when a large number of trees were planted, including 100 pear, 50 almond, 150 cherry, 150 plum and 425 elms and limes. The garden was partly walled and partly hedged;[36] and over 1000 nut-wood poles were bought for making hedges round the parterres and pavilions. According to a deed of 1572 there were 6 parterres opposite the palace; 4 planted as garden and 2 with trees, particularly pine and cypress. Beyond that was a wood, with two fountains or basins. The garden was divided by *allées* in both directions; the two main ones, running east-west from the palace, were planted with sycamore, elm and fir, probably in that order, i.e. the central one with elm. Some of the squares adjoining the *allée des sapins* (fir) were planted with fruit trees. The parterres were surrounded by hedges supported on trellis made of nut-wood (hazel); the first four, facing the palace on either side of the central *allée*, had a pavilion or arbour at each end, probably made of willow and osier. Willow was also used for making the hedges of the labyrinth or dedalus.[37]

Contracts were drawn up, with various gardeners having charge of the different parts of the garden, in 1572. Among them was Pierre Le Nôtre, possibly the grandfather of the famous André.[38] His contract ran for three years from 1 January. He was responsible for cultivating the four parterres and the two squares planted with trees in the part of the garden nearest the palace; for clipping and replanting the borders; and for maintaining the pavilions and arbours, providing the necessary wood and osier himself. He had to care for the area of the grass (*préau*) in front of the queen's apartment. He was not only responsible for the walks in the parterres, but had to keep the main *allée* clean at all times, 'even under the large elms', replacing dead trees at his own expense. The fruit trees planted alongside the *allée des sapins* were also his charge, but he was not allowed to touch the fruit. About 70 metres (35 *toises*) of ground in the northeast corner of the garden were set aside for bedding (*couche*). For all this he was to receive 320 *livres tournois*[39] a year, paid quarterly, subject to the queen's approval of his work. This evidently met with her satisfaction for in 1599 he was a senior member of the corporation of gardeners of Paris and its suburbs. Important though Pierre Le Nôtre's position was, it was subject to that of Bernardo Carnesecchi, who had overall control of the garden. Carnesecchi was not strictly a gardener. He is described in an entry in the accounts of 1570 as 'Messire Carnassequi, gentilhomme servant de la dicte dame, mère du roi, intendant des plantes'.

Until its transformation by André Le Nôtre in the 1660s,
the garden was separated from the palace by a public road, 113
and walled on that side. Judging from Du Cerceau's plan, the rectangular areas into which it was divided were varied and irregularly placed. There was no marked emphasis on the central axis, such as Le Nôtre later gave it and as is shown in the engravings of Silvestre, but the main walks leading away

from the palace were each planted with a different kind of tree. Each square was fenced, according to long practice; those in the centre of the first two rows nearest the palace being laid out with flowers. Some of the squares in the two rows immediately west of the second transverse walk contained features like the labyrinth, made of bent osiers; with tables, seats and little beds formed of leafy boughs, and laid out with such skill that once entered it was very difficult to get out.[40]

After the devastation of the garden in the civil wars, Henri IV made it one of his first tasks to restore it. In June 1594 Pierre Le Nôtre was charged with remaking the parterres next to the palace, sowing them with grass and planting some flowers. At the same time André Tarquin was employed to plant and maintain trees (fruit trees, sycamores, pines and others); and he set up wooden fences, *palissades*, balustrades and arbours along the walks, round the fountains, in the squares for cherry trees and apricots, and in 'la salle des Polonais'.[41] Work was renewed in 1595 on one of the incomplete projects, a gallery, parallel to the river, linking the Louvre and the Tuileries. The garden to which we have hitherto referred was Catherine's garden on the west, separated from the palace by a wall and a public road, and known as Le Grand Jardin. Another garden, east of the Tuileries, was begun about 1600 and referred to as Le Jardin Neuf or Petit Parterre. It was bounded on one side by a canal, and is shown on a plan attributed to Jean de Fourcy.[42] This 114
garden, serving as an ornament to the Tuileries and the new gallery of the Louvre, was confided to Claude Mollet. He surrounded the squares with borders or *palissades* of cypress, made by his assistant Guillaume Moisy. A severe winter in 1608 killed them all. 'Therefore', wrote Mollet, 'I resolved never to plant *palissades* of cypress, but to use box; as I did when I began to represent works of architecture made only with the shears, without any dead wood or ties. But it needs patience; ten or twelve years for something fine of any height.' At the end of 1608 the parterres or squares were remade in the form of compartments of *broderie*, surrounded by *palissades* of juniper, with designs in box and rue drawn up by the king and Sully. They were arranged in two rows; and in 1609 a round basin was made in the middle, 12 to 14 metres diameter, at the centre of which was a fountain of white and red marble surrounded by five statues. A private garden, belonging to the royal apartments facing the river on the

114 Plan attributed to Jean de Fourcy, showing the two gardens of the Tuileries – Catherine's garden on the extreme right, and the so-called Jardin Neuf on the other side of the palace, bounded by a canal. On the left is the Louvre.

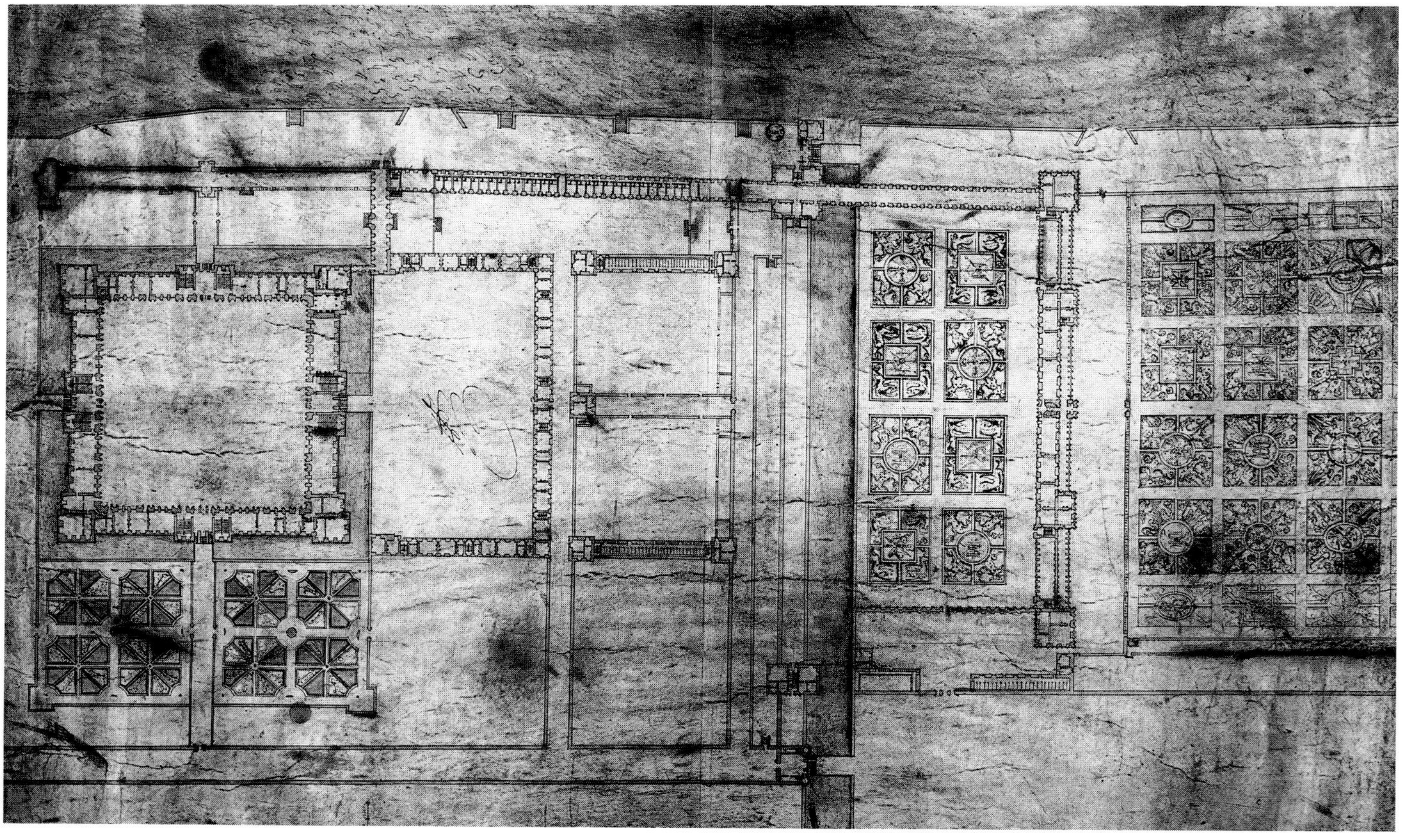

115 The Petit Jardin, planted by Henri IV on the south (river) side of the Louvre.

south side, was planted by Henri IV[43] and known as Le Petit
115 Jardin du Louvre to distinguish it from the old garden on the northeast side (shown in Merian's view) which was finally destroyed when Jacques Lemercier extended the buildings on the west side of the square court. It is *Le Petit Jardin* which is illustrated by Silvestre in his engraving made between 1650 and 1655 (some ten years after Louis' death), where the *parterre de broderie* is shown surrounded by shrubs or tall flowers within a low wall, and the central basin is encircled by cypresses.

The general arrangement of Catherine's original garden (Le Grand Jardin) remained unaltered, although within the rectangular divisions considerable changes took place. South of the central *allée* one of the compartments was converted into a basin, for which a bronze vase, almost 2 metres ($5\frac{1}{2}$ *pieds*) high, was delivered in 1609. A reservoir in Saint-Germain-l'Auxerrois, to which water was pumped from the Seine, supplied fountains in both gardens. In 1609 Henri ordered the *palissades* of box and old cypress to be taken out from the part of the garden nearest the palace, and a new parterre to be made, planted with dwarf box, privet and rue in compartments for which he himself drew up the design. The work was put to tender, and given to Jean Le Nôtre, father of André.

Henri IV's most lasting contribution to the Tuileries garden was the creation of the terrace along what is now the Rue de Rivoli, called La Terrasse des Feuillants because it adjoined property belonging to monks of that order.[44] It was lined with a double row of white mulberries. Large numbers of these trees were planted in royal gardens to stimulate the French silk industry. Some 15,000 to 20,000 were planted in the Tuileries;[45] and a building was set up in the west of the gardens for raising silkworms and processing silk in its early stages. A long line of ornamented compartments was made running the length of the garden below the Terrasse des
Feuillants, shown in Mathieu Merian's engraving of 1614/15. 116
A *berceau* of carpentry (600 metres long and $4\frac{1}{2}$ metres wide) ran parallel to the terrace and south of the parterre, with eight pavilions facing the transverse *allées*. In 1618 the parterre was surrounded by jasmine, quince, pomegranate and other shrubs; while a *palissade* of Judas trees was planted against the terrace wall.

Henri IV walked in the Tuileries gardens the morning of 14 May 1610, the day he was assassinated. Louis XIII was then a child of eight. Although there were some changes between that time and his death in 1643, they did not affect the main lines of the garden, which can be seen in Merian's plan and in Gomboust's of 1652. In the first, the topiary *palissades* referred to by Claude Mollet can be seen enclosing not only the individual compartments but the whole western end, in the middle part of which, terminating the central *allée*, is the projecting semicircular wall known as 'the Echo', because of the phenomenon it produced. Gomboust's plan shows a move towards broader effect, and simplification in the planting; compartments below the Terrasse des Feuillants combined into fewer units; less variety in the western half of

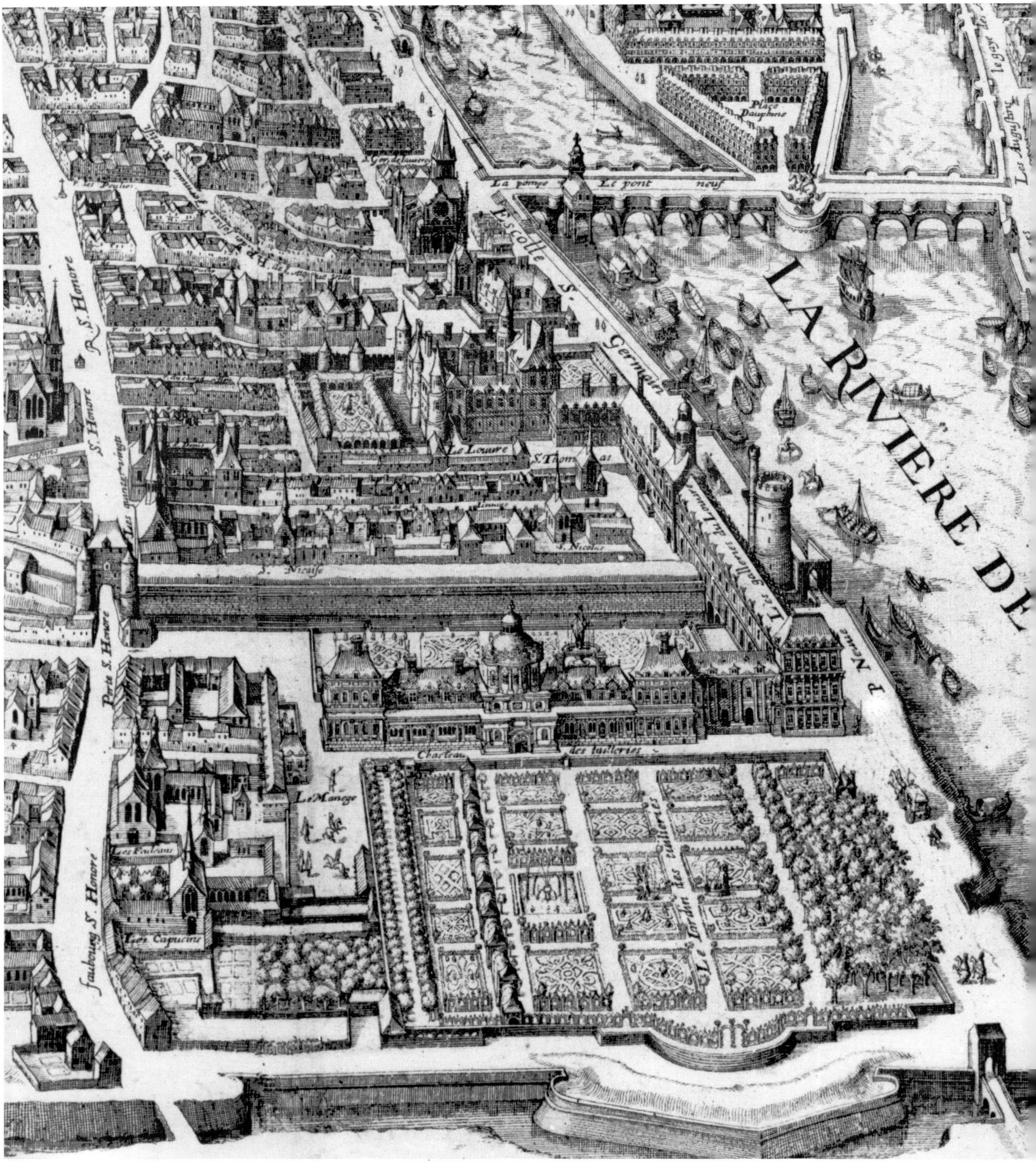
LA RIVIERE DE
Le pont neuf
Place Dauphine
Le Louvre
Chasteau des tuilleries
Le Jardin des tuilleries
Le Manege
Les Capucins
Les Feuillans
Porte S. Honore
faubourg S. Honore
S. Honore
Les quinze vingts
Escolle S. Germain
S. Nicolas
Les Augustins

116 Detail of Merian's plan of Paris, 1614–15, showing the Tuileries and the Louvre at the time of Louis XIII. The garden of the Tuileries is in the foreground, with the avenue known as the Terrasse des Feuillants forming its left-hand border. Behind the Tuileries is the canal and then the Louvre with the old garden on the left and the Petit Jardin on the right.

the garden, where most of the squares were planted with trees. The Grand Berceau was replaced by a new *allée* in 1624; but the irregularity of the slanting west boundary was not removed until 1666. In the northwest corner, outside the garden proper, was the Orangery. A rough piece of ground outside the boundary was acquired in 1630 and converted into a flower garden at the suggestion of Gilles Renard, who was employed in the king's household and described as 'commissaire ordinaire de ses guerres à la conduite et police du régiment de ses gardes.' It was cultivated and enjoyed by him in his lifetime, and known as Le Jardin de Renard (see the 117
engraving by Silvestre, 1658).

The large house with a garden, shown on Gomboust's plan adjoining the south side next to the river, was the dwelling of the *capitaine-concierge* in charge of the Tuileries;[46] in the 73
seventeenth century he was a member of the Congis family. Built into the wall were other smaller houses occupied by the gardeners.[47] Chief among these during the first half of the seventeenth century were the families of Mollet, Desgots and Le Nôtre. There does not seem to have been a question of seniority among them; each had charge of part of the garden, and of course had gardeners under him. Direction was the responsibility of the Intendant Général des Jardins du Roi. The intendants were not gardeners; but nor was it a purely nominal appointment. Jacques Boyceau[48] was the author of a considerable treatise on gardening; indeed his was the first devoted almost wholly to garden design. The most senior gardener in chronological terms was Pierre Le Nôtre who, as we have seen, was employed in the garden from its inception, and was charged with remaking the parterres in 1594. In 1618 Jean Le Nôtre, presumably his son, had charge of the new parterres in the Grand Jardin. He was paid 1020 *livres* a year for this work and as a retainer to work on the design of parterres generally in the royal gardens. André Le Nôtre was first engaged in January 1637, to serve the king in the absence of his father; but Jean was still responsible for the parterres in front of the palace in 1638, at an annual salary of 1500 *livres*, and presumably continued until André was appointed in 1643 as Dessinateur des Plants et Parterres of all royal gardens, and gardener in charge of the two big parterres at the Tuileries, with a salary of 1000 *livres* a year.

117 The Jardin de Renard, outside the boundaries of the Tuileries garden, 1658.

Claude Mollet was employed, from the time he left the Duc d'Aumale at Anet in 1595, to design parterres in all royal gardens. His responsibility at the Tuileries was particularly for the new garden east of the palace, for which he received 1500 *livres* a year in 1618, nearly a third more than Jean Le Nôtre was earning at that time. In addition he had charge of the avenue of mulberries in the Grand Jardin, together with the *palissades* of pomegranates there, the *palissades* below, and those made of Judas trees at each end. This work was divided between his sons in 1630 and 1634; reversion of responsibility for the new garden being given to Claude II, the younger, and for the Grand Jardin to the eldest, Pierre. Claude II's post was confirmed in 1643 by the new king, Louis XIV, in terms similar to those appointing André Le Nôtre; that is to say Dessinateur des Plants, Parcs et Jardins and Dessinateur des Plants et Parterres respectively. Mollet had charge of the parterres in the new garden of the Tuileries; Le Nôtre of those in the Grand Jardin.

Jean Desgots, who in 1618 was responsible for the upkeep of the *allées* and *palissades* of the Tuileries, was replaced in 1624 by his brother Pierre, who married Jean Le Nôtre's daughter, Elizabeth, in 1616. Their son Claude became André Le Nôtre's close collaborator. Jean Le Nôtre's second daughter, Françoise, married Simon Bouchard who succeeded his father, Yves, as keeper of the Orangerie. The succession of the various posts was jealously sought within the family.[49] The Tuileries of Henri IV and Louis XIII was the nursery of great French gardeners.

PART III

The Classical Tradition

7

Between Mannerism and Classicism

Historical background

Henri IV was materially assisted to the throne of France by Ferdinando de' Medici who, when he succeeded his brother, Francesco, as Grand Duke of Tuscany in 1587, put his resources and influence behind Henri's struggle with the Catholic League, and eventually smoothed the way with the pope for his conversion to Catholicism. At the same time Ferdinando arranged the marriage of his niece Marie de Médicis[1] to Henri, after his former marriage to Marguerite de Valois had been dissolved. The Medici, in the persons of the Grand Dukes of Tuscany, were at the height of power at this time; and their gardens were among the most celebrated in Europe, certainly the most publicized. Cosimo I, created Grand Duke by the pope in 1569, had made the gardens of Castello; and in 1549 had acquired the Boboli estate and Pitti palace at Florence. Marie de Médicis spent her childhood there, and was inspired by the memory when she later built the Luxembourg palace in Paris.

Henri IV was a prodigious builder, but unlike other French monarchs with a similar bent, not purely extravagant; for, aided by able ministers, the chief of whom was Maximilien de Béthune, Baron de Rosny, Duc de Sully, his patronage was aimed at restoring a country devastated by civil war. The consequences of his assassination in the prime of life are imponderable. The immediate result was to leave the country in the ineffectual hands of his widow, Marie de Médicis, as regent for the child Louis XIII. Louis was nominally king in 1610; he was effectively so from 1617 to 1643. As a child he witnessed the making of great gardens; and from the age of five he had his own at Fontainebleau. 'I know how to make fine gardens,' he wrote to his father in 1606, 'I have made one in this beautiful house, and you will see it the day you come here. I have also made a fine little fountain; I began a little house, but I have not been able to finish it because my man Birat left my hammer and chisel at Saint-Germain.' Jean Héroard[2], his physician, gives many instances of this childhood interest:

> 9 February 1607: He draws out a square garden in an *allée*, trenches and arranges it, and plants it with cabbage. . .
>
> 10 February: Taken to the Jardin des Pins he amuses himself shifting earth and wood to make a garden and a bridge. After supper the Sieur Outrehan, a king's singer, comes to bring the news that the king would arrive tomorrow. The dauphin blushes and jumps for joy and for fear on account of the garden he had made. 'We must go and take it away,' he says, 'in case Papa is cross.' He soon willingly went to remove it.
>
> 29 March 1608: He goes to find the king in the Jardin du Tibre, making M. Birat run after him right across the parterre. Dines with the king . . . he goes to the Jardin de l'Etang; amuses himself with gardening and planting peas. He cannot be dragged away from it.
>
> 6 May: He goes to his little garden; amuses himself by digging; hands out tools to others saying: 'Work, or I will beat you'.

The impression made on Louis by his father's personality extended to his work. He did not seek to emulate Henri in making new palaces and gardens, but remained attached to the places he had seen created as a child, particularly Saint-Germain-en-Laye where he mainly lived. A small hunting lodge on the estate of Henri de Gondi at Versailles was one of his few building projects to have momentous consequences. The estate had been bought in 1575 by Albert de Gondi, eldest son of the Florentine banker Antoine de Gondi and Marie de Pierrevive, Catherine de Médicis' favourite. Albert's son, Jean-François de Gondi, archbishop of Paris, owned Saint-Cloud. As Alfred Marie has observed,[3] Gondi's perceptiveness seems to have guided the Bourbons to the sites of their finest châteaux, parks and gardens.

The first royal house at Versailles was ready for occupation in 1624; a simple redbrick building, 24 metres long by 6 metres wide, with white stone quoins and a slate roof. Louis did not own the estate until 1632. The previous year Philibert le Roy[4], who had been responsible for the earlier building, was employed to enlarge it. Other land was acquired, and by 1636 walls enclosed a park corresponding roughly in area to the Petit Parc.

This was divided by *allées* into a regular grid, which has remained the basis of all subsequent modifications of the design. The château was on rising ground, near the site of the old Gondi residence. The principal (west) façade overlooked a *parterre de broderie* whose design is given in Boyceau's *Traité du Jardinage* (1638). Jacques de Menours, Boyceau's nephew,

118 The Grotte d'Orphée by Thomas Francini, one of the mechanical marvels of Saint-Germain-en-Laye.

119, 120 Italian influence in French garden design: avenue of fountains at Pratolino (above) and cascade at Caprarola (below).

121 A late seventeenth-century cascade at Le Brun's château of Montmorency. Compare with Caprarola.

was in charge of the work, having succeeded his uncle as Intendant des Jardins du Roi; but it is by no means certain that the parterre is by him. There were fountains in the garden, the water for which was brought, by means of a pump and a horse-driven mill, from the large pond at Clagny to a reservoir.

From the time he joined the king's council in 1624, Cardinal Richelieu dominated French politics. His great administrative gifts were devoted to the aggrandizement of France, the triumph of Catholicism and the consolidation of the autocratic powers of the monarchy. His rise to power was bitterly opposed by Marie, whose support for the intrigues of her younger son, Gaston d'Orléans, twice resulted in civil war. Forced to choose between his mother and his minister, Louis chose the latter on the so-called 'Journée des Dupes', 11 November 1630. The following year Marie de Médicis went into permanent exile first in Flanders, and ultimately Cologne.

Water

The most important development in garden design during the late sixteenth and early seventeenth centuries was in the ornamental use of water in canals, fountains and cascades, and the accompanying architectural adornments, stimulated by
Italian gardens such as Pratolino, the Villa d'Este at Tivoli, 119
the Villa Lante at Bagnaia, the Villa Farnese at Caprarola; 120
and, in the early part of the seventeenth century, the villas at
Frascati (Aldobrandini and Torlonia). These gardens were on 121
steep or elevated sites; French sites dictated their own 122
conditions. The most favoured form of cascade for relatively level sites was a row of fountains falling into bowls, arranged side by side as at Liancourt (and later Vaux), or stepped in monumental set pieces, as in Cardinal Richelieu's garden at Rueil (and later at Saint-Cloud). On the other hand, sites with marshy ground provided sheets of water serving both ornament and use.

Whereas the architectural cascade is essentially Italian in origin, large garden canals are characteristically French; and the defensive moats of many medieval castles were later turned to ornamental use. As Philibert de l'Orme had said, in draining marshy ground the architect has to use imagination, and turn practical necessity to other uses. The area round Fontainebleau was a case in point. The earliest monumental canal seems to have been at Fleury, west of Fontainebleau. It was 800 metres long and 20 metres wide; and according to Père Dan[5] it inspired Henri IV to make the Grand Canal at

122 Cascade at the Villa Torlonia, Frascati.

123 Fontainebleau (1200 metres long, 40 metres wide), clad with stone, and stretching eastward into the park. The canal was begun in 1607 and was full of water by October 1609, when the young Louis went in a galley with his father and took the helm. At the head it was separated from the garden (as it has always been) by a public road leading from the town to the forest. It was lined on either side by avenues of elm (*ypréaux*).[6] Some time before 1600 the Grand Jardin of the Valois was remade. It was divided by two canals running east-west, on either side of which were ornamental compartments, two to the north and two to the south. In the centre the statue of Tiber, cast by Vignola for François I,
124 surmounted a rock-work fountain in a rectangular basin surrounded by a balustrade. This, and four other fountains in the compartments, were the work of the Francini.

THE FRANCINI

The hydraulics engineer, Tommaso (Thomas) Francini,[7] arrived in France about 1598, doubtless sent by the Grand Duke Ferdinando de' Medici. He was followed by three other relatives, the most important of whom was his brother Alessandro (Alexandre). Thomas was given privileges of residence and ownership of property in 1600; and, having bought a house and garden at Saint-Germain in 1604, he married Louise de Porcher, daughter of one of the king's *valets de chambre*. Alexandre spent most of his life at Fontainebleau, where he died about 1648. When he was appointed Intendant Général des Eaux et Fontaines de France, Thomas was given authority over all workmen concerned with the ornament of fountains and grottoes, subject only to the Duc de Sully, Surintendant des Bâtiments. Houdard[8] maintains that the Francini were not only hydraulics engineers, but artists who designed the grottoes and fountains. There is no doubt that the Francini were invited to France in the first place to create the grottoes and automata at the Château-Neuf of Saint-Germain-en-Laye, in emulation of those at the Villa Medici of Pratolino. Engravings of the grotto by Abraham Bosse in 1624 are

123 Fontainebleau: the Grand Canal.

124 Fontainebleau: the Fontaine du Tibre.

125, 126, 127 Garden architecture by Alexandre Francini: triumphal arches (left and right) and gateway (below), both from his *Livre d'Architecture*, 1631. Bottom right: Grotte du Luxembourg, engraving by Jean Marot.

inscribed 'T. de Francini inven.' Alexandre Francini published a book of architecture in 1631 with designs for
125 doorways and entrances in a Mannerist style which, in view
126 of the Francini's responsibility for the waterworks in Marie de Médicis' gardens of the Luxembourg, suggests that Alexandre was the designer of the famous so-called Grotte du
127 Luxembourg.[9] Similarly the design of the architectural
128 grotto at Wideville, built between 1630 and 1636 for Claude de Bullion,[10] may be attributed to him.[11]

In 1612 plans were approved for an aqueduct to bring
129 water from springs at Rungis, near Arcueil, to the Luxembourg quarter of Paris. Thomas Francini was the engineer, though not necessarily the designer. Its size was out of all proportion to its requirements.[12] Water, about half of which was allocated to the Luxembourg palace and its gardens, reached a reservoir in the Rue d'Enfer in 1623. The upkeep of the aqueduct remained the responsibility of the Francini family until 1780.[13] Thomas's descendants dropped the Italian form of their name and called themselves 'Francine'. On Thomas's death his son, François Francine, took over his post and later, as Intendant de la Conduite et Mouvements des Eaux et Fontaines played a major part in the creation of Versailles.

128 The Grotte de Wideville, perhaps by Alexandre Francini.

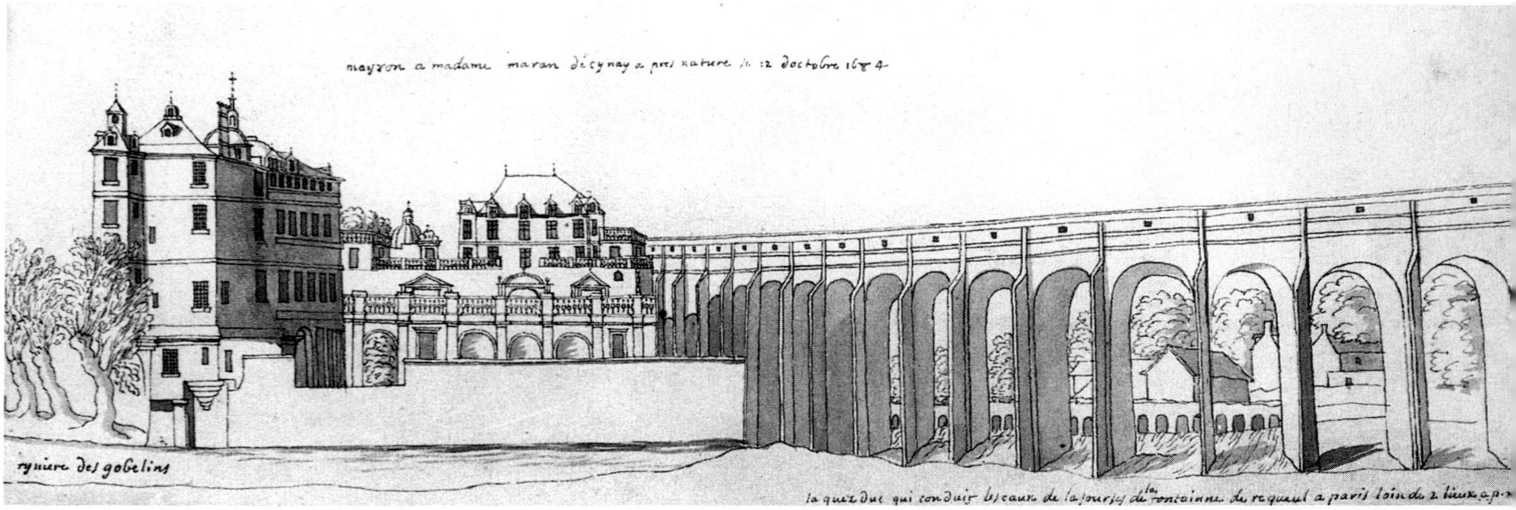

129 Aqueduct at Rungis, possibly by Thomas Francini.

HYDRAULICS: SALOMON DE CAUS

The principles on which the hydraulic achievements of the Francini were based (although of ancient origin) were expounded by Salomon de Caus (*c.*1576–1626) in his *Les Raisons des Forces Mouvantes* (1615). A Frenchman and a Huguenot born in the Dieppe region, he passed much of his working life abroad, travelling in Italy some time before 1601, in which year he entered the service of the Archduke Albert of Brussels, to whom he was appointed engineer in 1605. About 1607 he went to England at the invitation of James I, working for Anne of Denmark at Somerset House and Greenwich.[14] He taught drawing to Princess Elizabeth and Henry, Prince of Wales, to whose household he became attached as engineer in 1610. He advised the prince on waterworks at Richmond, and set up a Neptune statue in marble for Robert Cecil at Hatfield House. After Prince Henry's death in 1612, De Caus followed Princess Elizabeth to Heidelberg when she married the Elector Palatine, Frederick V, in 1613.

Les Raisons des Forces Mouvantes, dedicated to Louis XIII, was written in Heidelberg and published in Frankfurt. It is divided into three books. The first concerns the theory and practice of hydraulics. Eighteen theorems set out the
principles which govern syphoning, the expansion of water 130
under heat, the effect of air pressure, and mechanical principles used in the construction of pumps and other devices for moving water. There follow twenty-four problems in which the theory is applied to various situations; including waterclocks, fountains and automata, such as whistling birds and a set piece of 'Galatea drawn by dolphins', as at Pratolino. He deals briefly in the first book with the construction of water organs, to which the whole of the third book is devoted. Hydraulic machines were of ancient origin. They are the subject of Vitruvius's tenth book, of which chapter thirteen concerns water organs. Jean Martin published a French translation in 1547. The water organ at the Villa d'Este, Tivoli, admired and described in some detail by Montaigne in 1581, had been set up by two French fountainers, L. Le Clerc and C. Venard, in 1568.[15] De Caus's book therefore formulated existing practice rather than fostered innovation. Indeed, by 1615 the fashion for
automata and similar toys was declining, giving way to a 131
more sophisticated and elaborate use of ornamental water in fountains and cascades. At the time it was published, *Les Raisons des Forces Mouvantes* was backward-looking in other respects. The fanciful designs for grottoes and fountains in book two belong in spirit to the end of the sixteenth century, and not to the incipient classicism of the second decade of the seventeenth. The sources of inspiration for most of them are evident: Giambologna's Neptune fountain at Bologna (plate V), and his giant figures of Apennine at Pratolino and

130, 131 Two diagrams from Salomon de Caus's *Les Raisons des Forces Mouvantes*, 1615. Top: water heated by the sun's rays shining through lenses expands and provides the pressure for a fountain. Bottom: a moving figure of Neptune and nymphs powered by a water-wheel.

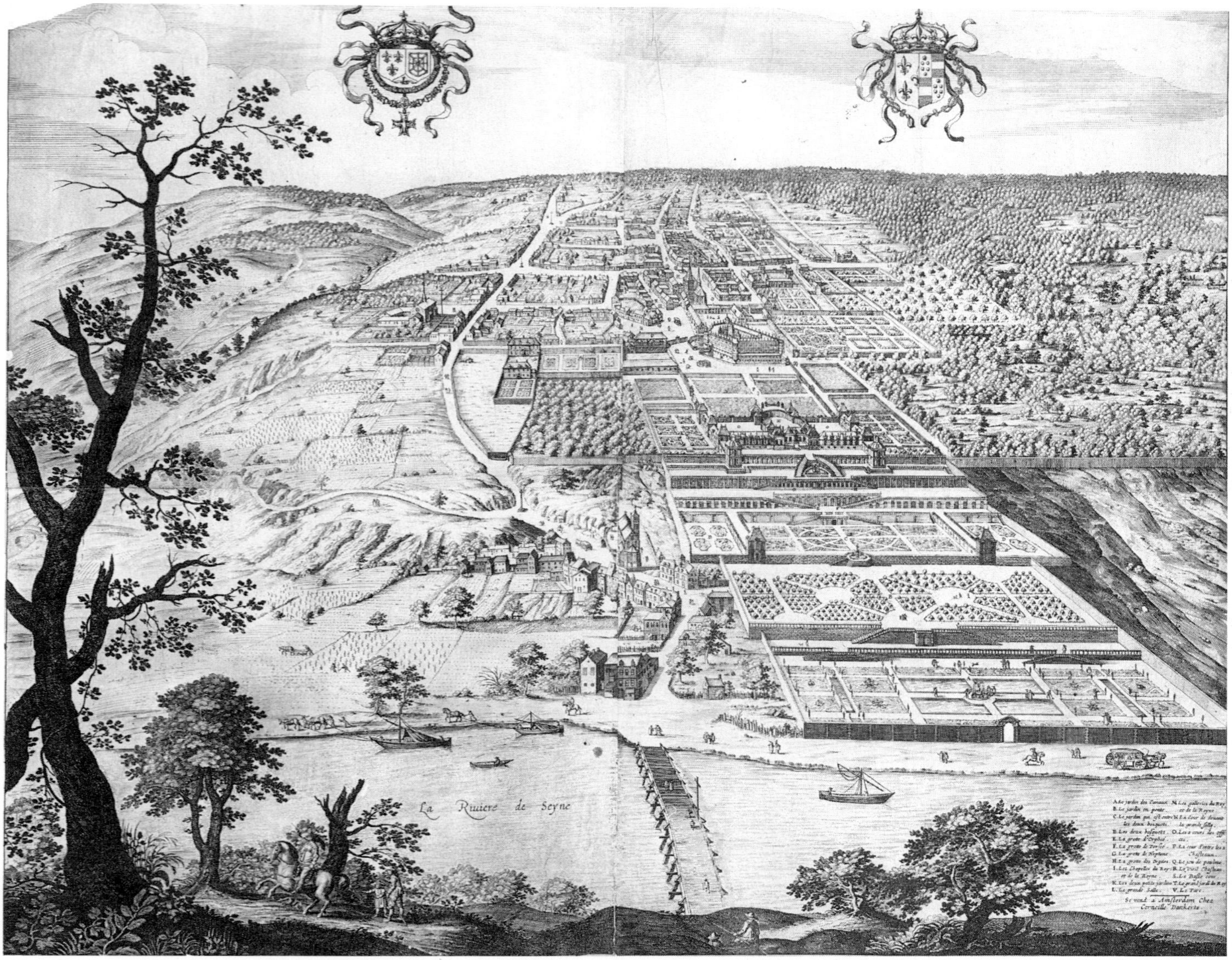

132 Bird's-eye view of the terraced gardens at Saint-Germain-en-Laye, showing a projected water-garden at the lowest level.

Castello (plate XVI); the grotto with the mask (the mouth of hell) at Bomarzo (plate X); Francini's fountains at Fontainebleau (plate VI), and the grottoes of Orpheus and The Lady playing the organ at Saint-Germain-en-Laye (plates XVII and XVIII); the Mount Parnassus of Catherine de Médicis' Festival of the Polish Ambassadors (plate XIII). The terraced gardens and grottoes recall those he designed for Frederick and Elizabeth at Heidelberg,[16] illustrated in his *Hortus Palatinus* (1620).

The Château-Neuf of Saint-Germain-en-Laye

The construction of the terraces at Saint-Germain-en-Laye was an enormous undertaking. We do not know how much of De l'Orme's scheme[17] existed; but there must have been a substantial substructure to support the terrace shown on Du Cerceau's plan. Etienne du Perac, who was appointed Architecte du Roi in 1595, may be assumed to have supervised the building. He was familiar with the Villa d'Este at Tivoli, of which he had published an engraving in 1573.[18] 88
Tourasse,[19] although he gives 1594 for earlier work on the château, says that the gardens, terraces and grottoes were begun about 1599; but in which case, to what garden does Claude Mollet refer when he says he planted the parterre with box in 1595? Moreover, as sixteen barrels of shells, mother-of-pearl, conglomerates and other sea-stones were delivered for the decoration of the grottoes in June 1599, it may be assumed that the vaults were ready to receive them, and a team of craftsmen assembled to carry out the work. There is also some confusion about what was, or was not, ultimately done. Abraham Bosse's engraved bird's-eye view 132
after a drawing by Alexandre Francini (1614) shows eight terraces descending to the river. The lowest one, called Le Jardin des Canaux, is an elaborate water garden, with a rustic fountain, engraved by Bosse after Thomas Francini. There is

133, 134 A pre-1660 view of Saint-Germain-en-Laye and a plan, which show no trace of the water-garden appearing in Francini's view (132).

no mention of the garden in seventeenth-century descriptions, where this part of the grounds is said to be a
133 meadow. An engraving by Silvestre in 1655 shows no trace;
134 and it seems probable that the whole ambitious scheme stopped short of completion. Bosse's engraving of the Château-Neuf (1614), and I. Lauro's plan of the Villa Lante in *Antiquae Urbis Splendor* (1612), both figure the water parterre prominently in the foreground. By ignoring all the dissimilarities between the two sites, this has been taken to indicate that the French design derived from the Italian one.[20] It seems probable that simply in order to render his idealized view complete, Francini consulted the earlier engravings.

The ground on which the Château-Neuf was built had been rendered unstable by quarrying. Huge retaining walls and ramps, too massive merely for descent, were necessary for buttressing the hillside. Old excavations between the terraces were turned into galleries, and grottoes were furnished with automata worked by water. At the highest level a promenade, roughly 142 metres long and 72 wide, lay between projecting pavilions known as the king's chapel (north) and the queen's oratory (south). A garden along the south side of the château was reserved for the queen's use; while a corresponding area on the north was planted with white mulberries (replaced after Henri's death by a garden for Anne of Austria). A horseshoe flight of steps led to a 135
second terrace. As at Pratolino, water had to be brought in conduits from springs some distance away; and these converged in La Fontaine de Mercure, enfolded in the arms 136
of the stairway, where the height of 55 metres above the Seine provided great pressure, giving lively action to the automata and lower fountains. Ramps descended to the third and fourth terraces. From the Doric terrace, a portico of fifteen arches, there was access to the grottoes of Neptune, the Dragon, and the Lady playing the organ. The grottoes of Orpheus, Hercules and Perseus were beneath the Doric terrace, with access from the Tuscan terrace, which had a portico of thirteen rusticated arches faced with marble. The garden on the fifth level was enclosed on the north and south 137
by galleries whose roofs, with the Tuscan terrace, formed a continuous promenade round three sides, looking down on an ornamental parterre known as Le Jardin en Dentelles. There were eight compartments planted with box, showing Henri IV's monogram surrounded by an ornamental border. There were bosquets on either side of the parterre – that is on the other side of the galleries – which terminated in two pavilions: on the north side, Le Pavillon du Peintre; on the

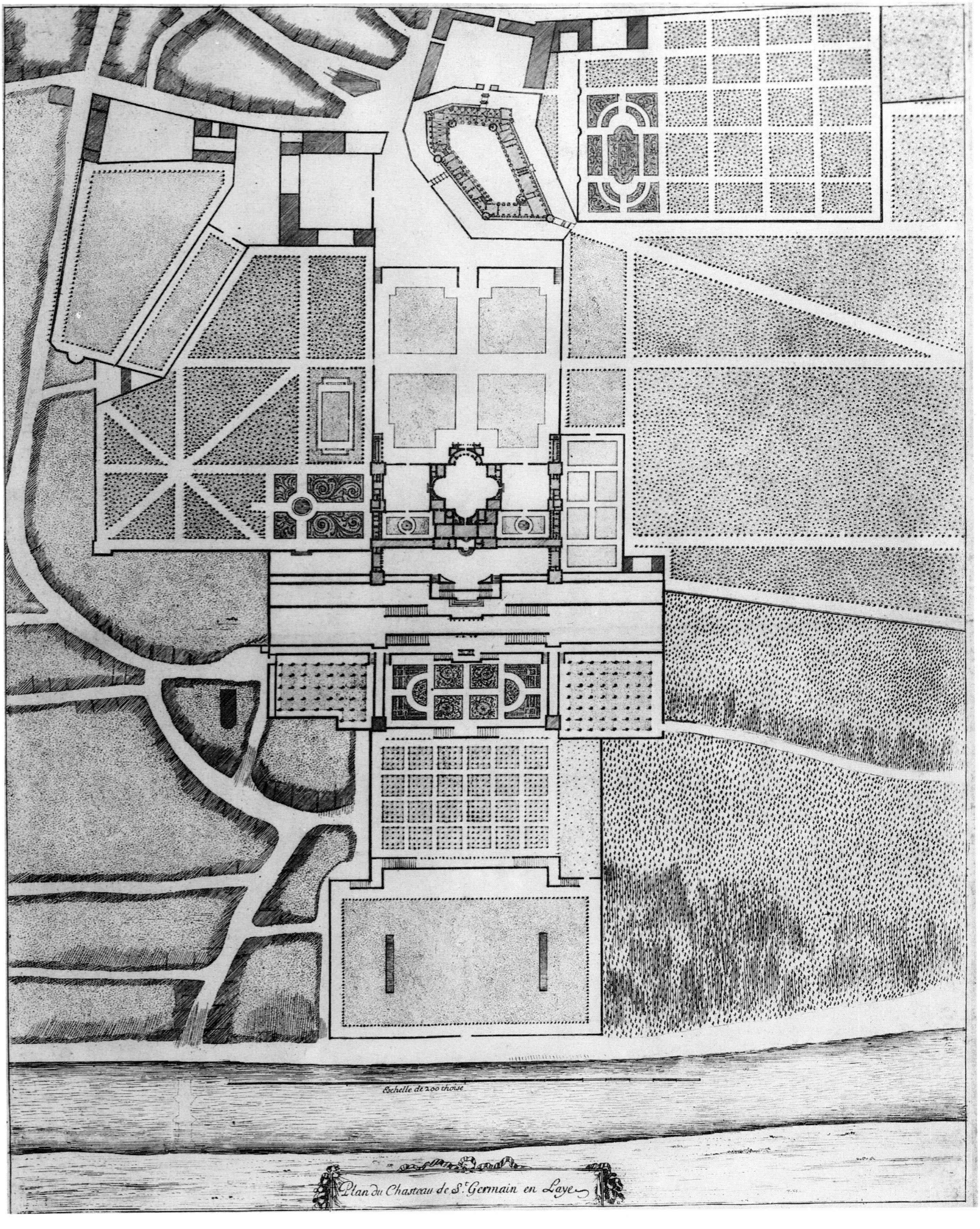
Eschelle de 200 thoise
Plan du Chasteau de S.t Germain en Laye

135 The upper terrace of the Château-Neuf, Saint-Germain-en-Laye, with one arm of the curved steps leading to the château.

136 The Fontaine de Mercure, between the two arms of the staircase, by Thomas Francini.

137 (facing page) Saint-Germain-en-Laye: the garden of the fifth terrace (Jardin en Dentelles), with the upper terraces as rebuilt after 1660.

south, Le Pavillon du Jardinier.[21] Immediately below Le Jardin en Dentelles the ground sloped, levelling towards the river. The whole of this area was walled and divided by a terrace across the middle. The upper (sloping) part was planted with fruit trees; the lower, whatever was intended, seems never to have been more than a meadow.

The Château-Neuf is an architectural ensemble where the whole question of 'the garden' is in question. Planted or not, the various terraces were outdoor spaces; the grottoes were part of these, inaccessible from inside the house.[22] The automata in the grottoes were in many cases quite elaborate. They were made of bronze or brass. In the life-size figure of
118 Orpheus there were movements of the head and arms as he appeared to play several tunes on his lyre, while animals issued from caves on either side and passed before him. The figures in the grotto of Perseus and Andromeda were more complex. Perseus, larger than life, descended from the vault, striking the head of a dragon which then disappeared below the water. At the same time the chains binding the figure of Andromeda to a rock fell apart. In the same grotto water fell from a cup, held by a figure of Bacchus seated on a rock, and set in motion figurines of craftsmen (a smith, a weaver, a carpenter) engaged in their trades. The fashionable trick of soaking the spectators with surprise jets was not lacking. This kind of joke, and even the marvels of automatic movement, must quickly have become stale. Their importance lies in the mechanical ingenuity which gave rise to this rather crude display; and in the settings which were masterpieces of the grotto-maker's art.

The most vivid account of the Château-Neuf at the time of Henri IV comes from the journal recording the childhood of Louis XIII, by his physician, Jean Héroard. He describes the little dauphin amusing himself by turning on the stopcocks; and being frightened by the figure of Orpheus, so that he will not enter the grotto until it is covered and the key handed to him so that he may be sure it will not play. Indeed the figure haunted him, for over a year later, on 20 July 1606, Héroard wrote: 'Put to bed, he talks of the Orpheus of the fountain, who plays the lyre. I ask him what the strings are made of. He replies, "Of brass", which was true. I begin to tell him who Orpheus was, and how well he played the lyre which he taught to men. I draw him the shape of the antique lyre, and say that after his death, his lyre was put in the sky with the others stars. He asks, "Were there no violins?"' At that time there were doubts about the stability of the building. On 18 January 1606, Héroard's entry reads: 'I tell him he should go and see his papa in the new building. He replies: "Ho! Ho! I don't want to go to the new building, it's all tumbling down; when the frost comes it will all fall down." He had heard us talking about it among ourselves.' The great terraces did collapse, but not for another fifty-five years; and from being undermined by a neglected water system rather than from faulty building. The child who enjoyed playing with the taps, for whom Francini made little models of the fountains and who, at the age of seven, understood how they moved and worked, saw to it that the Château-Neuf was cared for. It was where, as king, he preferred to live, and where he died. Louis XIV was born there. But even by 1618 the grottoes were in sad need of repair. In 1622 the masonry of the grotto of Orpheus was dilapidated, the accessories rotted, and the pipes stolen. All had to be renewed. In 1656 most of the grottoes were decayed beyond repair. Louis XIV rebuilt the terraces after 1660, but the clanking gods and heroes were gone for ever.

The gardens of the Luxembourg Palace

Marie de Médicis conceived the idea of building a palace for herself shortly after Henri IV's death. In 1611 she bought the *hôtel* belonging to François de Luxembourg in the Rue de Vaugirard; and she wrote to her aunt, Christine de Lorraine,[23] saying she wished to build a house on the model of the Pitti palace where she had passed her childhood, and whose architecture she had always admired. She therefore proposed sending Louis Métézeau, one of the king's architects, to bring her detailed information of the building and its decoration both within and without. The Hôtel Luxembourg had a park extending for some 800 metres from east to west, but was limited on the south by grounds of the Carthusian monastery, and further restricted by properties on either side along the Rue de Vaugirard, and in the southeast corner by the farm of the Hôtel Dieu. These she began to acquire, starting in 1613 with the farm and the Hôtel Champrenard immediately adjoining the Hôtel Luxembourg on the east. The Carthusians were unwilling to part with any ground; it was only in 1626 that they ceded 6½ acres on condition that no building was erected within 12 metres of their wall. A further 16½ acres on their north boundary was exchanged for an enlargement of their bounds on the east in 1627. This limitation precluded expansion of the garden on the axis of the proposed palace, as Marie would have wished. The creation of a strong lateral axis at right angles to the parterre resulted more from the original shape of the area, and the inability to do otherwise, than from a desire to emulate the Boboli gardens, as has been suggested.[24] Nor in the event did Salomon de Brosse's Luxembourg owe much to the Pitti palace, the only echo of which was the parterre in the shape of the Boboli amphitheatre, a sunken square with a rounded end, 166 metres long, separated from the walk surrounding it by sloping banks surmounted by a marble balustrade.

The first stone of the palace was laid in 1615; but from the moment of possession Marie concerned herself with planting *allées* in the park, 2000 elms (*ypréaux*) being ordered in 1612 and planted by Nicolas Deschamps, 'jardinier ordinaire des jardins et parterres de sa maison et Hostel de Luxembourg'. It is not clear where these *allées* were. A plan by François
138 Quesnel and Claude Vellefaux, bearing the date 1615,[25] shows a walled garden behind the Hôtel Luxembourg divided into rectangular areas by walks, according to the traditional sixteenth-century practice. There is also a row of trees in the eastern strip of park towards the Rue d'Enfer. The properties along the Rue de Vaugirard, which were acquired for the building of the palace, are shown intact; but there is a rough indication of a *bosquet* in the southeast corner, with circular *allées* intersected by others radiating from the centre, corresponding to a similar feature on Gomboust's map of 1652. This is evidently the development in the vicinity of the windmill of the Hôtel Dieu where Guillaume Boutin, 'jardinier de l'Hostel de Luxembourg', planted seventy-eight elms, dug a ditch and set up a *palissade* as early as 1615. It has not been estimated exactly when the Luxembourg gardens reached the stage of completion shown on Gomboust's plan, nor who was responsible for their design. Three men were certainly concerned: Salomon de Brosse, the designer of the palace; and the Francini brothers, Thomas and Alexandre, who were responsible for the waterworks and for terraces on either side of the parterre. Besides these there were Jacques Boyceau, Intendant des Jardins du Roi, and the gardeners Guillaume and Claude Boutin, although the last two were probably not in any way concerned with the conception. Lastly, the queen mother had ideas of her own as to what she wanted. The period of her closest association with the new Luxembourg was between 1623 and 1631. Louis XIII exiled her to Blois on taking power in 1617; and she was in open conflict with her son until 1620.

The most notable innovation in the new gardens was the
parterre de broderie surrounded by balustraded terraces and in 139
direct relation to the palace. This has been attributed to Jacques Boyceau[26] because he was Intendant at the time, and because a design for the parterre was included in his posthumous *Traité du Jardinage* (1638). But a plan drawn
before the boundary with the Carthusians was altered (that is, 141
before 1627) shows that the design was not carried out as originally intended. The *parterre de broderie* was made; Evelyn described it in 1644:

> The parterre is indeed of box, but so rarely designed and accurately kept cut, that the embroidery makes a wonderful effect to the lodgings which front it. 'Tis divided into four squares, and as many circular knots, having in the centre a noble basin of marble near thirty feet diameter (as I remember), in which a Triton of brass holds a dolphin, that casts a girandola of water near thirty feet high, playing perpetually, the water being conveyed from Arcueil by an aqueduct of stone built after the old Roman magnificence. About this ample parterre, the spacious walks and all included, runs a border of freestone, adorned with pedestals for pots and statues, and part of it near the steps of the terrace, with a rail and baluster of pure white marble.

We know that Thomas Francini was responsible for the waterworks, and also for the terraces and balustrades on either side of the parterre, one of which carried a distribution channel.[27] An estimate for work in the gardens presented to the Conseil du Roi in 1635 includes placing five bronze figures by Guillaume Berthelot in the central fountain, and making an artificial rock; completing the fountain of the 'demogorgon'[28] at the head of the *grande allée*; and making the flight of steps and large mask of white marble above the fountain at the head of the *grand jardin*[29] according to the design determined by the queen. Indeed, there is more evidence for the Francinis' involvement in the design of the gardens than for anyone, for Alexandre Francini, together with Salomon de Brosse, advised Marin de la Vallée in June 1626, after he had replaced De Brosse as contractor for the building work.[30] And this leads to the most important architectural feature of the gardens, the so-called Grotte du Luxembourg or Fontaine Médicis.

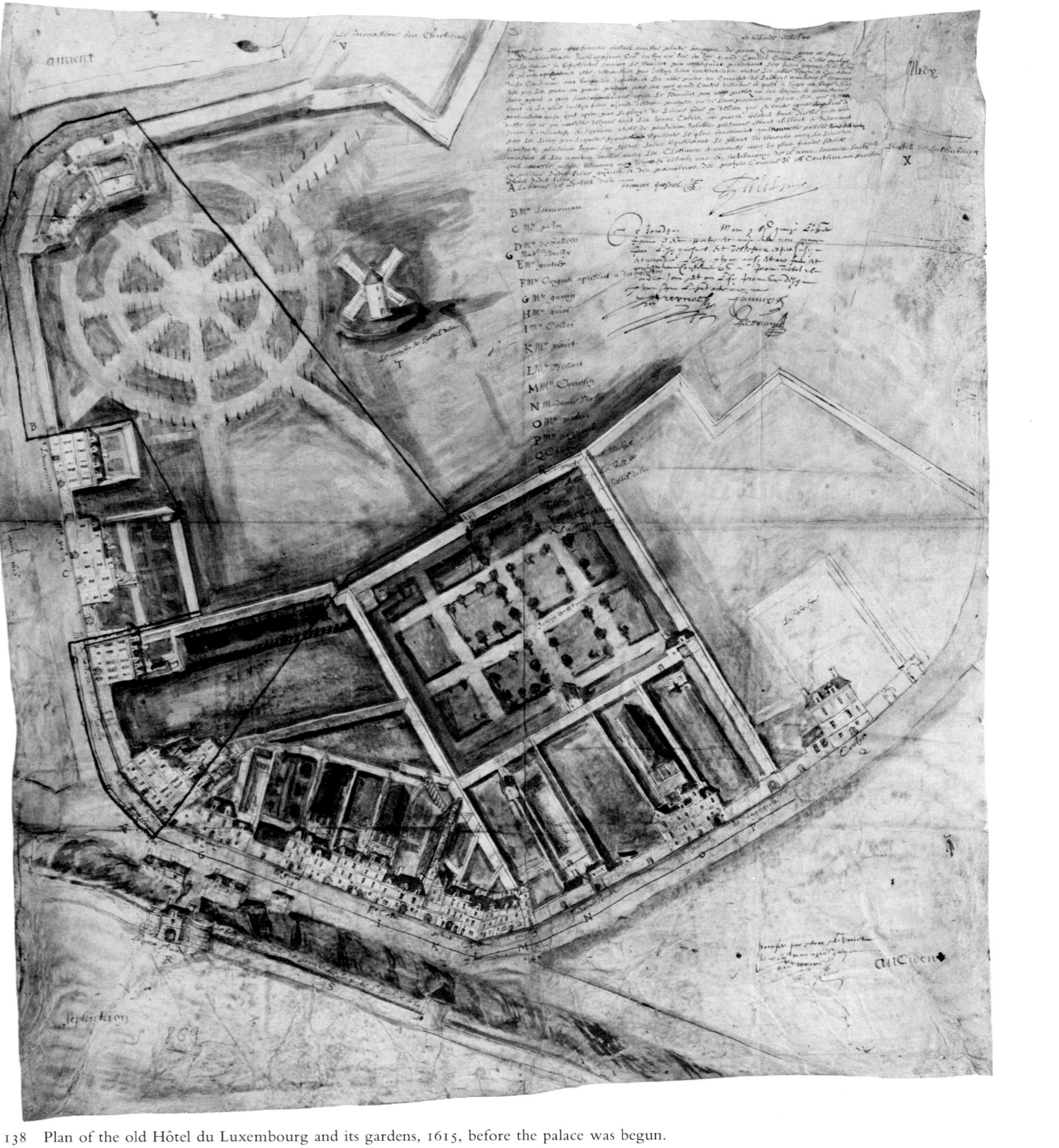

138 Plan of the old Hôtel du Luxembourg and its gardens, 1615, before the palace was begun.

139 The Luxembourg: *parterre de broderie*, with the new palace in the background.

140 The *allée* between the palace of the Luxembourg and the *parterre*, with the Grotte in its original position in the distance. (See also ill. 127.) It has since been moved and is known as the Fontaine Médicis.

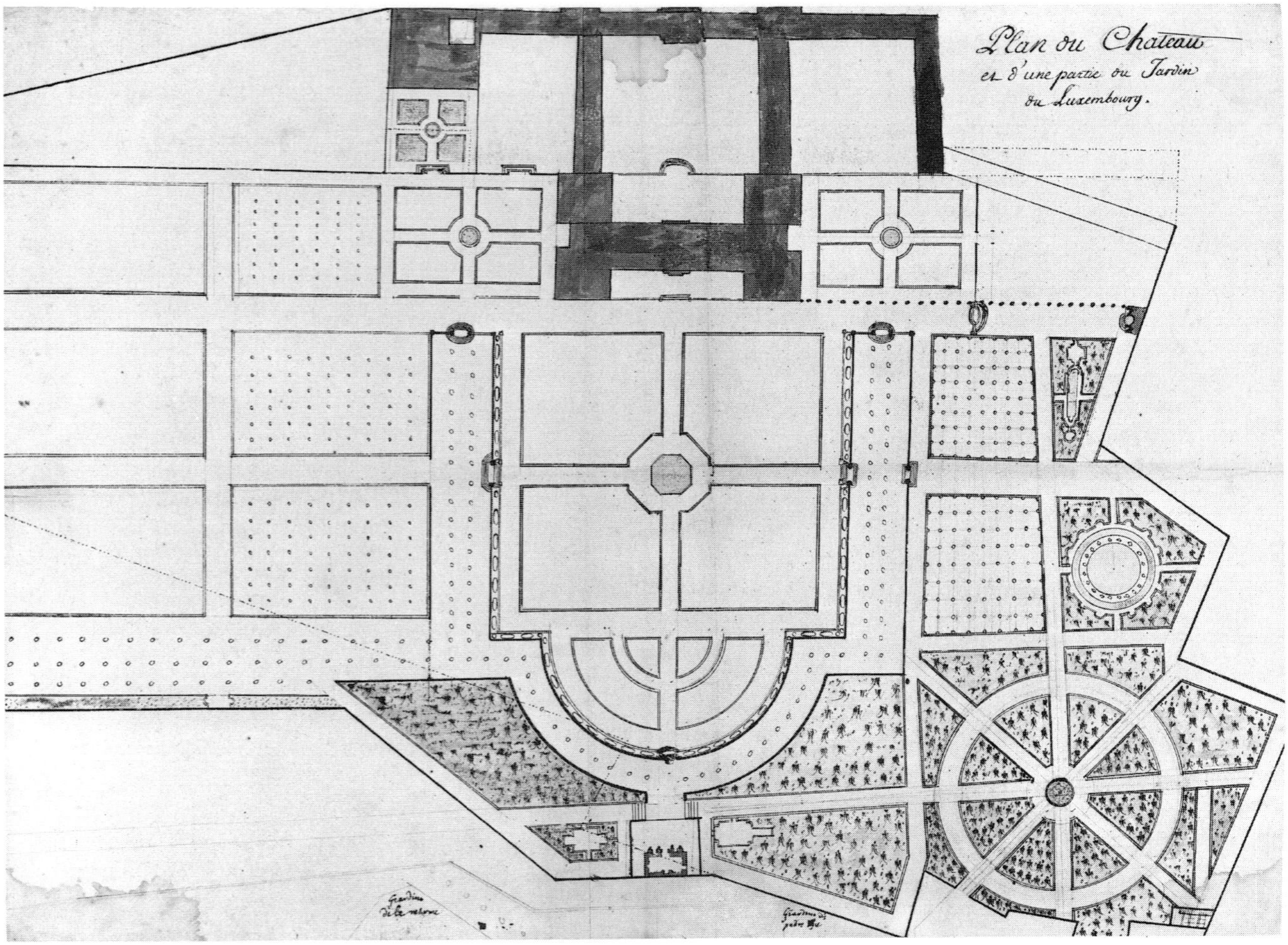

141 Plan of the Luxembourg made before 1627, showing an intended building closing the central axis, probably a grotto as at Wideville.

From the first, Marie de Médicis saw to it that her palace and gardens were well supplied with water. Plans were approved in 1612 for the aqueduct to bring water from springs at Rungis (see page 127). It is clear from Francini's estimates that the fountains were not completed until after Marie de Médicis' final departure in 1631. The probable reason was the collapse of part of the aqueduct due to the subsidence in the park between 1625 and 1634.

127 It was evidently intended to close the vista along the axis of the parterre, against the Carthusians' wall; for this is the
141 apparent interpretation of the building shown there on the pre-1627 plan. It would have been an architectural grotto,
128 having a similar function to the one at Wideville[31]. The Grotte du Luxembourg was built between 1623 and 1630 to
140 terminate the east end of the *allée*, passing between the parterre and the palace, and as a screen against houses in the Rue d'Enfer. Although called the Fontaine Médicis,[32] it was not supplied with water until the nineteenth century, and the basin shown in Marot's engraving remained dry. The Grotte had three niches in the form of a triumphal arch, with an upper storey containing a panel with the arms of Marie de Médicis, and crowned with a curved pediment and three vases. The panel was supported by two reclining statues by Pierre Biard, representing the Rhône and the Seine. The panels, niches and attached columns supporting the entablature were covered with stalactite-like decoration. The author of the design has not been established; but the nearest parallels are to be found among the designs for monumental 125
doorways in Alexandre Francini's *Livre d'Architecture*, 126
published in 1631, the year after Biard was paid for the sculpture. Admittedly the ornament of the Luxembourg is more restrained, but Francini's plate VI shows a similar decoration, and his plates X and XXXIV have likenesses to other aspects of the design. Buontalenti's grotto in the Boboli gardens is an obvious precedent, but the Francini model is much nearer.

Marie de Médicis did not see the Luxembourg after 1631; but she continued to direct work on her palace from a distance. In 1634 she dismissed Thomas Francini from his post as Intendant (possibly because 46 metres of the aqueduct collapsed as a result of a landslip between 1625 and 1634), but this was ignored by Louis. In 1635, as we have seen, Francini was estimating for the completion of the fountains and other work, including the fountain and its marble border in front of the Petit Luxembourg (as the old *hôtel* was now called). Marie died in poverty in 1642.

It has been assumed by Hustin that the gardens were then neglected until 1646, when Louis XIV agreed that Gaston should have the Luxembourg. Gaston had taken possession previously however, for when Evelyn visited the palace in 1644 he found the gardens in 'exquisite order', even though he saw no gardeners at work, for all was done early in the morning 'without the least confusion'. Was this due to the management of André Le Nôtre, who was described in 1635 as 'premier jardinier de Monsieur, frère du roi'?[33]

Gomboust's plan of the Luxembourg gardens in 1632 may be compared with Evelyn's account. Following the description of the parterre he continues:

> The walks are exactly fair, long and variously descending, and so justly planted with limes, elms and other trees, that nothing can be more delicious, especially that of the hornbeam hedge, which being high and stately, buts full on the fountain.
>
> Towards the farther end is an excavation intended for a vast fishpool but never finished, and near to it is an inclosure for a garden of simples, well kept; and here the Duke keeps tortoises in great number, who use the pool of water on one side of the garden. Here is also a conservatory for snow. At the upper part, towards the palace, is a grove of tall elms cut into a star, every ray being a walk, whose centre is a large fountain.
>
> The rest of the ground is made into several inclosures (all hedge-work or rows of trees) of whole fields, meadows, bocages, some of them containing divers acres.
>
> Next the street side, and more contiguous to the house, are knots in trail, or grass-work, where likewise runs a fountain. Towards the grotto and stables, within a wall, is a garden of choice flowers, in which the Duke spends many thousand pistoles. In sum, nothing is wanted to render this palace and gardens perfectly beautiful and magnificent; nor is it one of the least diversions to see the number of persons of quality, citizens and strangers, who frequent it, and to whom all access is freely permitted, so that you shall see some walks and retirements full of gallants and ladies; in others melancholy friars; in others, studious scholars; in others jolly citizens, some sitting or lying on the grass, others running and jumping; some playing at bowls and ball, others dancing and singing; and all this without the least disturbance, by reason of the largeness of the place.

142 Bird's-eye view of the château and gardens of Liancourt, 1654.

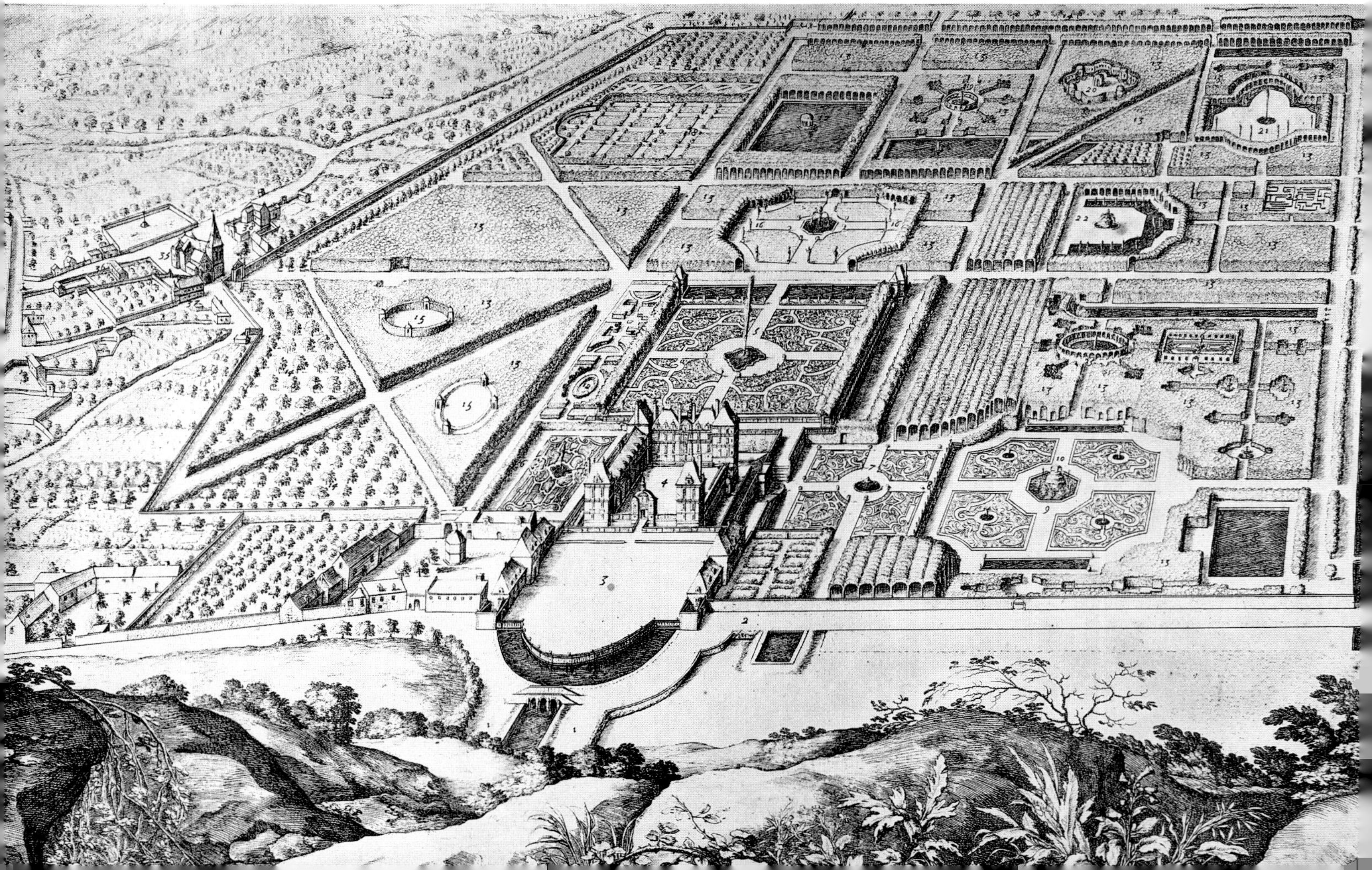

143 Liancourt: the Nappe d'eau, centre right in the previous picture.

Liancourt

The French garden most admired for its water in the early part of the seventeenth century was Liancourt. The earliest description is by Denis II Godefroy in 1637;[34] information before that date is at present scanty. The estate belonged to the Du Plessys family from 1463. Guillaume du Plessys (1491–1550) was ambassador to Switzerland under Henri II. His son, François, was murdered on Saint Bartholomew's Day, 1572, and may therefore be presumed to have been a Huguenot. Charles du Plessys (*c.*1540–1620) was married to Antoinette de Pons, daughter of Antoine de Pons, an adherent of the Reform and protector of Bernard Palissy. It was with his rebuilding of the château of Liancourt in the
142 1580s that the history of the gardens began. Mauperché's plan (1654) and Silvestre's views (1655) show the gardens as enlarged by Roger du Plessys,[35] who inherited Liancourt on his father's death in 1620. The same year he married Jeanne de Schomberg de Nanteuil-le-Haudouin (1600–1674), who became a fervent Jansenist. Tallemant des Réaux[36] said that it was her taste and imagination which inspired new embellishments in 1630, and that each year she added some new beauty.

The site at the foot of the hills on the west side of the valley of the Brèche, between Clermont and Creil (Oise), had abundant water. The Brèche and the smaller Beronelle were evidently canalized at the end of the sixteenth century. According to Godefroy the gardens covered over 200 acres and were being enlarged daily. The wooded park, divided chequerwise, gave a regular framework to the *bosquets* which enclosed various set pieces in a way foreshadowing the Petit Parc at Versailles. There were at least twelve, the majority
incorporating fountains, canals or *pièces d'eau*. Some dozen 143
fountains are marked on Mauperché's plan: a few of the 146
overflowing bowl type, but mainly jets. Water was thrown
to a height of about 15 metres in the *grand parterre* 144
immediately south of the château. This was the largest parterre, overlooked by the principal rooms, laid out in four compartments of *broderie*, and planted with fastigiate trees, probably cypress. It was bounded on the west by a very fine *jeu de paume longue*; on the south by a broad canal; and on the
east by an *allée* of great extent. Next to the gallery on the east 105
of the château was the *parterre à fleurs*, according to Silvestre's view planted in beds of varying shape (circular, crescent, rectangular) or in the border surrounding the whole, with

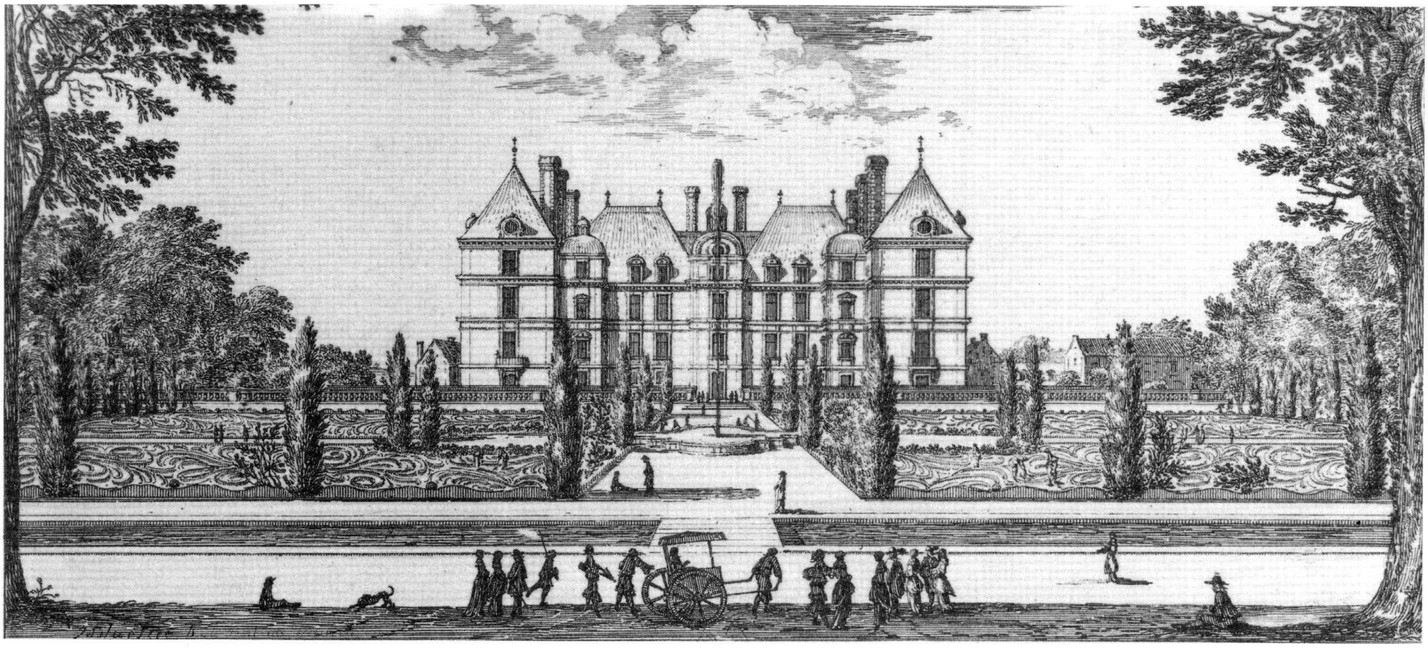

144 Liancourt: the *grand parterre* – top centre, on axis of château, in ill. 142.

145 Liancourt: cascades, centre right of the château in ill. 142.

146 Liancourt: *le grand quarré d'eau*, top centre in ill. 142.

green arbours (a slightly old-fashioned touch) in each corner. South of this, and east of the *grand parterre*, was a garden described by Mauperché as 'Petit cabinet d'arbres toujours verts'. This may correspond with a garden seen by Godefroy from the east wing of the château, called the *parterre d'hiver* because it was planted with evergreen trees and shrubs (pine, cypress, fir, bay, box, rosemary and others). The most elaborate new adornments were on the west of the house, where the parterres were overlooked by galleries supporting a terrace on that side of the courtyard. The parterres descended in two stages; the upper of *broderie* with a bowl-type fountain, the lower of cut turf with a fountain of five
145 bowls set in an octagonal basin at the centre, and smaller jets in each quarter. Between the two parterres was a cascade which Godefroy described as 'most unusual', the style and form deriving from 'the finest pleasure gardens of Italy'.[37] It consisted of twenty-two jets falling into shell bowls of rose-grey marble,[38] the intervening bank being of turf. Godefroy implies that this form of cascade was a novelty in France.

The Swedish architect, Nicodemus Tessin the younger, visited Liancourt in 1687[39] and found the gardens not very well kept. Despite their great extent there were only four boys and no head gardener. The woods and *palissades* were very high; but the beauty was that the fountains played day and night. The great wheel supplying water for the *gerbe* (a fountain in the form of a powerful jet falling as spray) and another big jet, had worked without ceasing for nearly eight years. Of the original 140 buckets, 40 had been removed to allow it to turn more easily. The sculptures (presumably the shell bowls) of the twenty-two cascades had deteriorated; and the jets had been lowered. Tessin was given details of the water system by the fountainer. There was an inspection chamber under the terrace near the house, from which a conduit of tile and cement, about 14 to 15 *pouces* in diameter, led to the first jet; thence at right angles to the twenty-two fountains, each fed by a lead pipe (reducing from 3 *pouces* to $1\frac{1}{2}$) running from the conduit. Liancourt retained its essential character until after the Revolution, when the then Duc de Liancourt, returning from exile, transformed it into a modern estate *à l'anglaise*, with a pottery and textile mill.

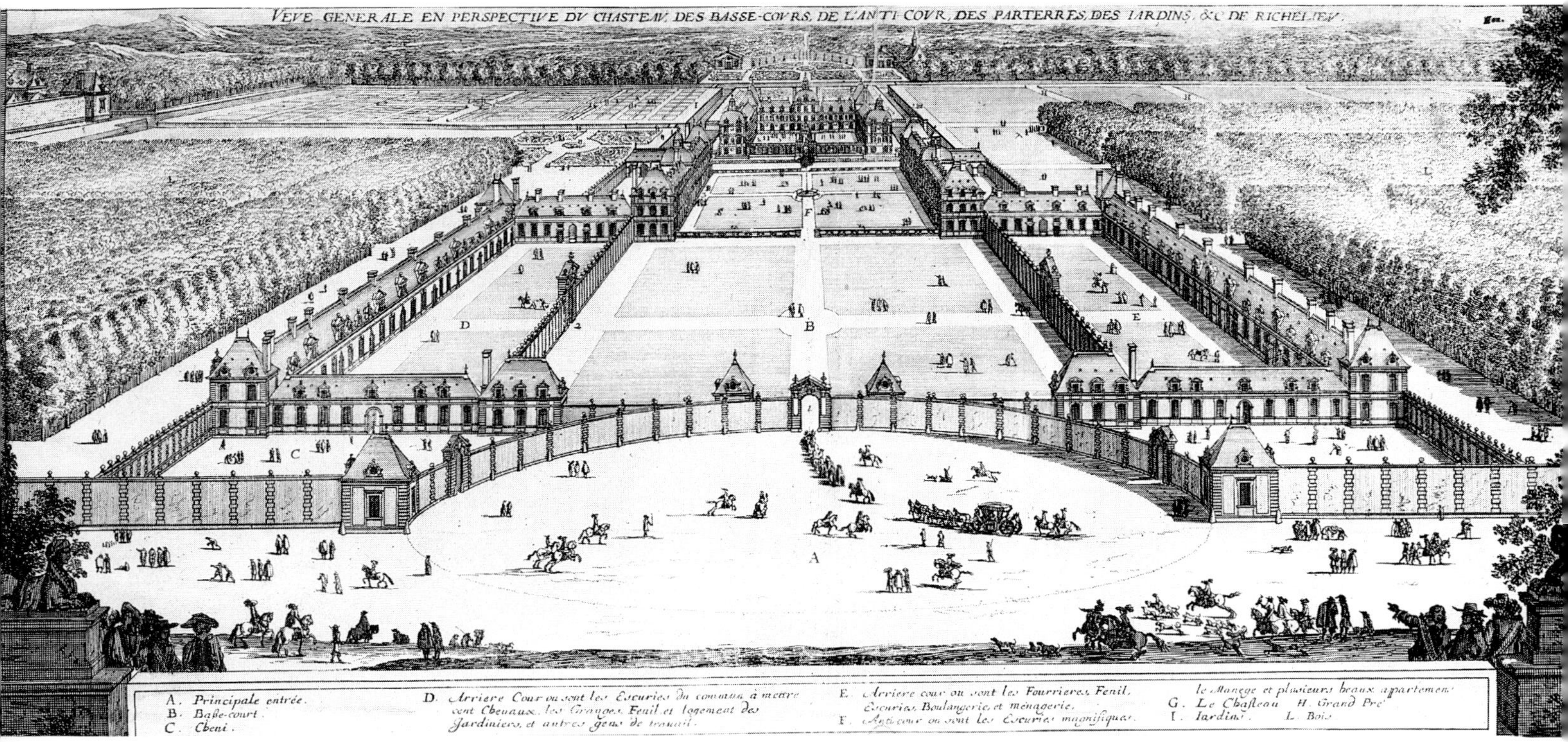

147, 148 Above: Richelieu's gardens, a general view of the château and gardens of Richelieu. Below: the alternative tradition, a picturesque interpretation of the old grotto at Rueil, 1661.

8

Richelieu's gardens and the alternative tradition

'Formal' is often used as a synonym for 'regular' or 'architectural', but here the implication is the same as in 'formal occasion'; that is, one in which conventional behaviour predominates, and above all where marks of social status are in evidence. The extended approach through huge forecourts is a preliminary intended to impress and overawe. The *parterres de broderie*, requiring much labour to maintain, but whose function is purely ornamental; vistas and canals of great length suggesting a limitless domain, all demonstrate the power and status of the occupant, his wealth and the extent of his possessions.

Supreme power had advantages for Richelieu's personal fortune. In 1617, at the outset of his political career, his revenue was 25,000 *livres*; in 1634 it was over 500,000 *livres*; and in the following years exceeded 3,000,000 *livres*, half deriving from church benefices.[1] His gardens set a standard of magnificence greater than any previously seen. The Hôtel de Richelieu, (called the Palais Cardinal, and subsequently the
149 Palais Royal) north of the Tuileries and the Louvre, was begun in 1633. The courtyard was closed on the north side by an arcade supporting a terrace which overlooked the rectangular garden, the largest in Paris after the Luxembourg and the Tuileries. At the far end was a circular pond about 170 metres (84 *toises*) in circumference, 'surrounded by a broad walk, and a little wood where the silence is only broken by the gentle murmur of the fountain at the centre of the basin'.[2] Evelyn referred briefly in 1644 to the 'large garden in which is an ample fountain, grove and mall'; and in 1650 he wrote: 'The fabric of the place is not magnificent, being of but two stories; but the garden is so spacious as to contain a noble basin and fountain continually playing, and there is a mall with an elbow or turning to protract it.' There is no visual record of the garden in Richelieu's time; it was completely redesigned by Le Nôtre *c.*1673.[3]

Richelieu

Jacques Lemercier[4] was Richelieu's architect for all his projects. The most important domestic commission he received was to transform the cardinal's modest family home
150 in Touraine, with gardens and park on an unprecedented
151 scale, combined with a new town of perfect regularity. The sole reason for this project was the satisfaction of Richelieu's sense of family pride. The manor and village from which his title derived were in the flat marshy valley of the little River Mable. Half-way between Tours and Poitiers, remote from any centre of importance, the area was unsuitable for a palace; and there was no economic necessity for a town, in which it proved always difficult to find occupants for the houses. As Blondel reported to the Marquis de Marigny in 1760,[5] the ground was so waterlogged that it was not possible to make cellars, and the ground floor, almost level with the garden, was hardly habitable.

Royal assent to the building of a new town was given in May 1631. By that time Jacques Lemercier's plans had been made, and the work on the château begun, managed by Lemercier's brother, Pierre. Richelieu's brother, Henri d'Escloubeau de Sourdis, archbishop of Bordeaux, who frequently supervised the cardinal's projects, wrote in August 1633: 'We will be out of your château this year . . . provided the plague does not prevent us. . . . There will be only two thirds of it done.'[6] And shortly after: 'The *allées* in your park are being planted; I hope next year you will have the pleasure of your house and that you will be able to receive the king there.'[7] The main part of the château and park was finished by 1639.

Lemercier's general plan consisted of an axial approach through the forecourts to the house, with the garden as a climax, but on a much larger scale than hitherto. Three avenues of elms converged on a circle, 100 metres in diameter, before the entrance. The distance from there to the *grille* separating the gardens from the park was some 700
metres. The approach to the *corps de logis*, through the 147
courtyard with the offices, and the forecourt with stables for 100 horses, extended for some 450 metres. The château was built round three sides of a courtyard, closed on the fourth by a terrace with a monumental domed entrance of two storeys. The main rooms overlooked a parterre of four compartments, planted with flowers, round a central basin and a fountain with Neptune and a sea-horse in bronze. It was known as the Parterre des Romains because of the antique statues placed there. Both château and parterre were surrounded by moats from the canalized River Mable, which

149 Palace and garden of the Palais Royal, Paris, formerly the Palais Cardinal.

formed a secondary axis at right angles to the main one, a precedent used to great effect by Le Nôtre. Beyond the canal
152 there was another large circular *parterre de broderie* of four compartments round a central basin, with a fountain in which jets of water issued from sea monsters. This parterre was closed against the park by a crescent-shaped hedge of *phillyrea*, cut into niches containing statues. A *grille* in the central part of the crescent allowed an extended vista into the
153 park. The hedge was flanked by two pavilions (*grottes*) in a plain rusticated style with a triangular frontispiece, the only ornament being a grotesque mask over the central doorway. This arrangement, instead of closing the central axis with a building, as at Wideville for instance, left it open. The parterres forming the immediate framework of the château were extended by gardens and lawns on either side; orchards planted in quincunx adjoined the canalized Mable; and parallel to it stretched a *mail*, almost a kilometre long, lined with elms. The chapel of Saint Nicolas, built by Richelieu's ancestors, was preserved in the trees near the right-hand (south) *grotte*. In another *grotte* elsewhere in the park, Saint Antony sat, bell in hand, surrounded by animals spouting water from nostrils, mouths and ears; while a satyr, holding a shell of mother-of-pearl constantly filled with water, appeared to cast an envious eye on a cask of wine, designed for the refreshment of the gardeners, cunningly concealed near a little window in the grotto's recess. From above the rock, spring water poured in silver threads and random cascades into a vast tank, and thence into the moats of the town. Solitude could be found in the complex windings of a shady labyrinth, or on an island where the silence was only broken by the lapping of water and the twittering of birds.

The quantity of sculpture at Richelieu, largely antique or after antique models, was unprecedented. River gods flanked the bridge across the moats. In the central arch over the gateway to the main courtyard was a statue of Louis XIII; above him, crowning the dome, Fame by Guillaume Berthelot. In niches on either side of the entrance were Hercules and Mars; left and right of them statues emblematic of Charity, Justice, Religion, Piety, Abundance, Labour, History. This was the nearest approach to an iconographic

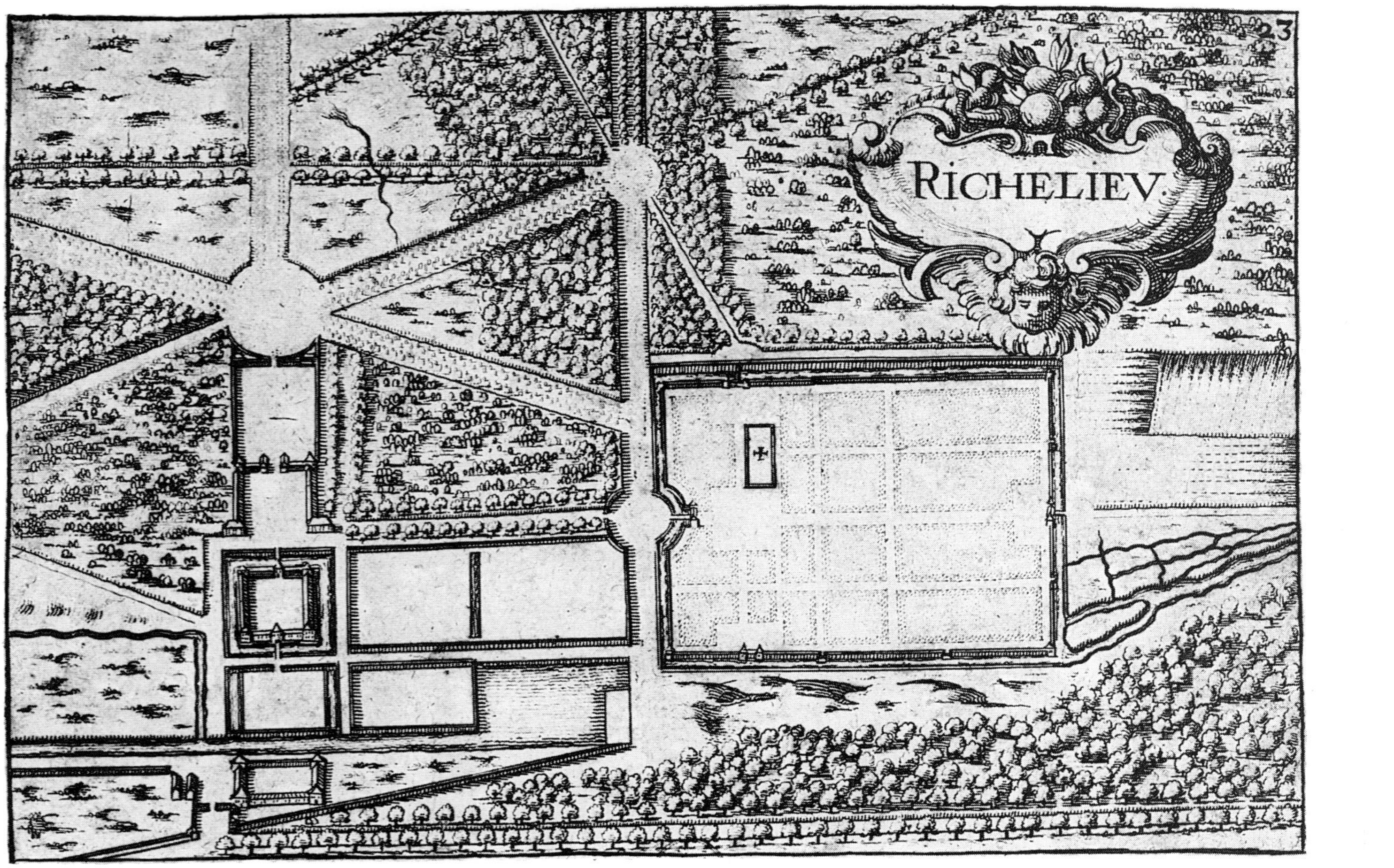

150, 151 The château, park, garden and new town of Richelieu, a seventeenth-century plan and (below) an aerial photograph. The château has been demolished.

B
C

programme. Two Slaves, by Michelangelo, originally intended for the tomb of Julius II, were placed at balcony level in the central pavilion of the main *corps de logis*. In the spaces between other windows and between the windows of the wings, were some eighty antique busts and statues, principally of Roman emperors and their wives, the subject being evidently determined by availability rather than systematic choice. In the Parterre des Romains, Albinus and Venus stood at the extremities near the château; Bacchus and Pertinax in corresponding corners near the river; elsewhere, antique marbles included Venus, Mars, Flora, Vertumnus, and Ceres and Isis as children. Terms with the heads of Morpheus and Homer stood at either end of the crescent-shaped hedge, whose niches held a mixed sequence of gods, goddesses, emperors and other figures.[8] The heads of the pillars supporting the *grille* at the entrance to the park were busts of Augustus, Claudius, Otho, Titus and Drusus.

Despite the regularity and order manifest in the grid-like arrangement of the parts, in one respect at least the cardinal showed a concern for the natural state. In 1638 he wrote to his friend and neighbour, the bishop of Chartres,[9] 'I am delighted you do not wish to make a star in my park, as I do not at all like having the wood cut.'[10] Neither in the choice of ground, nor in the design of areas with clear boundaries added to one another and related but not integrated into a whole, did Lemercier's Richelieu show much imagination. It departed from precedent in its enormous scale, and in the open-ended axis implying indefinite extension. In this sense it can be said to be a prototype for the great landscape compositions of Le Nôtre. Richelieu's other garden, at Rueil, was not only a different kind of site and more confined; it also had a different purpose.

152 Château de Richelieu, Grand Parterre de la Demi-Lune.

153 Richelieu: one of the two pavilions (*grottes*) flanking the ends of the semi-circular hedge.

Saint-Cloud and Rueil

It is often assumed that the regularity of the classic French garden was an ideal to which all aspired; and that irregularity in a site was something to be avoided or removed. But the need to escape from the formality of polite society into the imagined simplicity of Arcadia is a constant theme in Western culture. Fashion in garden design, as in the other arts, fluctuates between the extremes of licence and of control, seeking a balance between 'art' and 'nature'. Montaigne while in Rome in 1581 remarked how hilly irregular sites had been transformed by art into pleasure gardens of uncommon beauty, taking advantage of diversity to give a charm impossible to imitate on the level sites of France.[11] The high ground west of Paris offered such varied situations; and it is not surprising that it should have been an Italian, Jérôme de Gondi, a nephew of Albert, first Duc de Retz, who, at the end of the sixteenth century, should have chosen Saint-Cloud[12] to build a small pleasure house, with terraced gardens overlooking the Seine. Jérôme died in 1604
154 and La Maison de Gondi (as it was called) passed to Jean-Baptiste de Gondi (1598–1664, third son of Alexandre de Gondi), who sold it in 1618. In 1625 Jean-François de Gondi became the first archbishop of Paris, with suzerainty over Saint-Cloud, of which he was awarded the purchase by decree on 25 May 1620. This extravagant and licentious prelate, emulating the style of living of his Italian counterparts, added much by way of ornament to the garden. The waterworks were almost certainly designed by Thomas Francini; statues included copies of the Belvedere Cleopatra and Laocoon. Among the numerous visitors were Elie Brackenhoffer and John Evelyn, who wrote in 1644:

> By the way, we alighted at St. Cloud, where, on an eminence near the river, the Archbishop of Paris has a garden (for the house is not very considerable) rarely watered and furnished with fountains, statues and groves; the walks are very fair; the fountain of Laocoon is in a large square pool, throwing water near forty feet high, and having about it a multitude of statues and basins, and is a surprising object. But nothing is more esteemed than the
> 155 cascade falling from the great steps into the lowest and longest walk from the Mount Parnassus, which consists of a grotto, or shell-house, on the summit of the hill, wherein are divers waterworks and contrivances to wet the spectators; this is covered with a fair cupola, the walls painted with the Muses, and statues placed thick about it, whereof some are antique and good. In the upper walks are two perspectives, seeming to enlarge the alleys, and in this garden are many other ingenious contrivances.

On the same day (27 February), fourteen months after Cardinal Richelieu's death, Evelyn visited Rueil and noted:

> The house is small, but fairly built, in form of a castle, moated round. The offices are towards the road, and over against it are large vineyards, walled in. But, though the house is not of the greatest, the gardens about it are so magnificent, that I doubt whether Italy has any exceeding it for all rarities of pleasure.

The site was a shallow valley sloping from south to north, with high ground on the west: part of the area south of the Seine from Meudon to Saint-Germain whose varied levels attracted so much royal building. Louis XIII had been familiar with Rueil since childhood,[13] when he had been taken there with other members of the royal family to be entertained by Jean Moisset,[14] known as Montaubon, who had bought the château of the Val de Ruel (*sic*), with a park of 16 acres in 1606, together with another property of 20 acres more. He spent large sums of money on the house and on embellishing the grounds, where he entertained lavishly. On his death in 1620, Rueil passed to his principal heir, Pierre Payen (Deslandes-Payen). Marie de Médicis certainly occupied Rueil, for Héroard says that her son Louis visited her there in 1624. Peter Heylyn, an English traveller who visited Rueil in 1625, says she bought it. Whatever the case, Marie went into exile in 1631, never to return. Payen was evidently involved in the opposition to Richelieu, who appropriated the château and park for his own use; finally bought it in 1633;[15] and in 1639 acquired additional land.[16] He lived at Rueil when the court was at Saint-Germain; but it was also his favourite residence, where he not only entertained and gave theatrical performances, but conducted important affairs of state. Father Joseph, the 'Eminence Grise', Richelieu's spiritual and political adviser, lived in a lodge where he died in 1638.

The boundaries of Moisset's garden are uncertain, but since the house was near the Saint-Cloud road, it may be assumed that the grounds lay round about it. It was an oblong, fairly level area, sloping gently from south to north; beyond it to the west the ground was more steep and irregular. It would thus have included three pieces of water which still exist, and, as we know, it contained grottoes and waterworks which delighted the young Louis XIII.[17] Heylyn described 'two fountains of admirable workmanship. In the first the portraitures of Cerberus, the Boar of Calidon, the Naemean Lyon, and in the navel of it Hercules killing the Hydra. In the other only a crocodile full of wild and unruly tricks, sending from his throat a music not far distant from organs.' This is the trick fountain later described by Brackenhoffer[18] as the Fontaine du Dragon, and by Evelyn as 'a basilisk of copper which, managed by the fountainer, casts water near sixty feet high, and will of itself move round so swiftly, that one can hardly escape wetting'.

'The variety of ground . . . and walks of great length', which Evelyn found so admirable in 1644, had also struck Heylyn in 1625.

> And now we are come into the Grove, a place so full of retired walks, so sweetly and delicately contrived, that they would even entice a man to melancholy; because in them even melancholy would seem delightful. . . . It seemed a grove, an orchard, and a vineyard, so variously enterwoven and mixed together, as if it had been the purpose of the artist to make a man fall in love with confusion. In the middle of the wilderness was seated the house, environed round about with a moat of running water; the house pretty and therefore little, built rather for a banquet than a feast.

154, 155 The Maison de Gondi, Saint-Cloud: a view in the park (above) and the *grotte* (below).

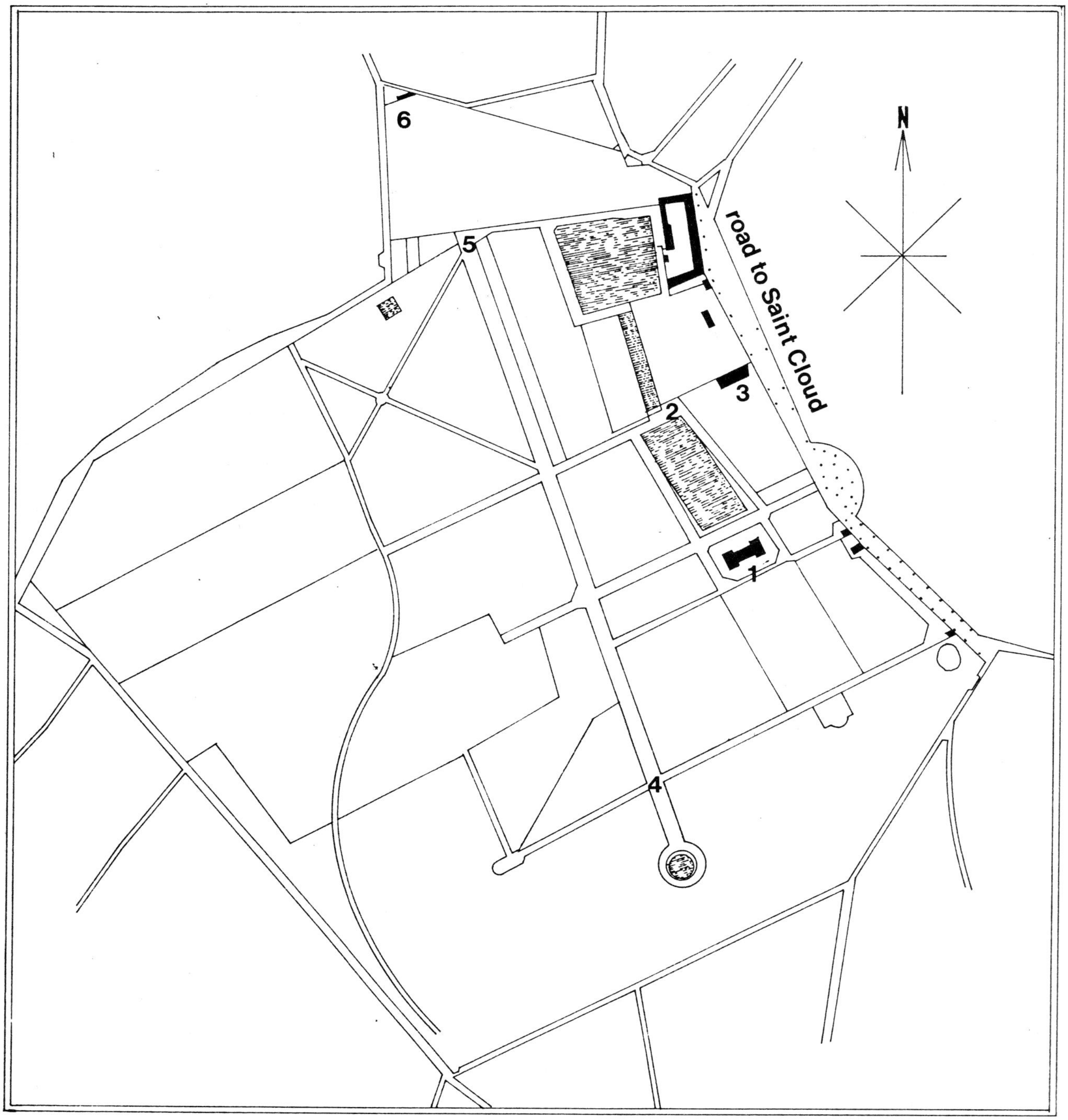

156 Reconstructed plan of Rueil, after an original of 1818. 1. The château; 2. Grotte; 3. Orangerie; 4. Grande Cascade; 5. Grand Escalier; 6. Grotte de Rocaille.

157 Rueil: Grande Cascade.

Already in 1632[19] the cardinal's architect, Jacques Lemercier, had plans for alterations to the house; and one of the Francinis (probably Thomas) was advising on new waterworks and ornaments for the garden. According to the contract with his mason, Jean Thiriot, the main work of building was not begun until 1636; nevertheless much preparation had to precede it. Water for the reservoir above the Grande Cascade had to be brought from springs a couple of kilometres away,[20] which with the conduits, compensation to landowners, inspection chambers and the construction of the reservoir itself, cost more than 60,000 *livres*; which may be compared with the original purchase price of 147,000 *livres*.

Dr Launay's reconstructed plan of the gardens[21] may be
accepted with certain reservations. The cadastral plan of
156 Rueil in 1818 establishes the position of the Grand Réservoir
and the Grotte de Rocaille, the château, the Orangerie and
the offices. The ponds and canals still exist, and there are
vestiges of the Grande Grotte. An aerial photograph shows
the extent to which the modern street plan reflects the
structure of the *allées* in the park. Evelyn noted 'walks of vast
length'. The chief of these was the Grande Allée, over 800
metres long, running the length of the estate from south to
north and marked by Richelieu's most substantial ornaments.
157 At the upper end was the Grande Cascade, the first of those
French architectural cascades emulating the Italian pro-
158 totypes at Frascati; lower down, the Grand Escalier, 'twenty-
159 four steps, with fine stone ramps on either side', leading to 'a
small grove of cypresses beside a little orchard', and a grotto
161 in the form of 'a big grimacing face' closing the *allée* at the
north end. This version of the 'mouth of hell', after Italian 160
prototypes,[22] is apparently unique in French garden
architecture, and probably due to Thomas Francini; at least it
is quite alien to the classical canon of Lemercier. 'The head
was of fine stone', says Brackenhoffer, 'with a great open
mouth three or four times the height of a man, with big ears
and a powerful throat, frightening from a distance. The
inside was fashioned like a rock, with shells and snails, and
contained a fountain.'

The Grande Allée divided the higher more irregular parts
of the park from the older gardens, confined on the east by
the Saint-Cloud road. These were more irregular than Dr
Launay's plan suggests; the two ponds and the canal north of
the château were neither rectangular, nor placed in the same
axis. And indeed this is evident in Adam Perelle's engraving
of the upper pond near the north side of the house, where the
balustraded platform forming the roof of the grotto is shown
at an oblique angle to the basin. Stairs at one side descended to
the grotto and canal at the lower level. The outside of the 162
grotto is clearly illustrated in Adam Perelle's engraving; the
inside is fully described by Brackenhoffer.

> It is octagonal, very prettily vaulted with dressed stone, well built and everywhere artistically furnished with fine sculptures and figures, flowers, snails, agates, mirrors, coagulations and other materials. In four of the angles there are satyrs, in the other four nymphs, all lifesize prettily formed of sea shells and snails; each character makes a strange gesture with the hand, sometimes putting a finger on the thigh, sometimes on the mouth, while the

158, 159 Rueil: Grand Escalier (above), and a view looking in the opposite direction (below), from the top of the staircase to the Grande Allée, with the Grotte de Rocaille at the end.

160 Garden portal of the Palazzo Zuccari, *c.* 1590, one of the Italian prototypes for the Grotte de Rocaille.

161 Rueil: the Grotte de Rocaille.

162 Rueil: the grotto in the garden (No. 2 on the plan), with part of the canal. The roof of the grotto forms a balustraded terrace level with the upper pond.

> other hand directs the *membrum virile* in the air and water spurts from it; all that is treated with great realism. On four of the sides there are fountains with fine oval basins; near each stand three marble figures also discharging water from their genitals. On the four other sides there are benches, to which one is careful to retire when all the jets of the Grotto are playing. In the middle stands an octagonal marble table on which one could do all kinds of amusing things, in that by pressing the instrument or tube coming from the centre, one made all kinds of figures with the water, for example lilies, cups, flowers, glasses, moons, stars, parasols. When the whole grotto plays, water spouts from all parts (above, below, from the side) . . . as if a heavy shower was falling and the wind blowing from all sides, mingling the jets, so that whoever does not immediately get to the benches does not escape a soaking. But, in particular, the jets are directed towards the exit, so that people who seek to slip out that way are just those who get most wetted. Near the door are two monkeys who squirt water; and in front of the grotto, on each side, two bronze men with arquebuses, hidden behind a fine green hedge, aim together at the fugitives and fire at them with their muskets.

These aggressive water games were a positive encitement to disorder. Louis Huygens wrote[23] that people were obliged to leave their swords at the entrance, because of the disturbances arising from those who were annoyed at being wetted.

The canal flowed into another large pond, where there was an island planted with bushes and lofty trees; and a rock on it with caves and holes giving shelter to numerous duck and geese. As Evelyn put it, 'In this rupellary nidary do the fowls lay eggs and breed.' He said it was 'built of vast pieces of rock, near fifty feet high.' In the upper pond there was also 'une petite maisonette dans laquelle les cygnes et les canards se retirent la nuit.'[24]

Parallel with the lower pond, against the road, where the modern buildings of the Sandoz group now stand, were the offices. North of it, returning towards the house, was the Orangerie, filled with 'many exotic plants, pomegranates, lemon and orange trees'. Near it was the famous *trompe-l'oeil*
triumphal arch painted on a wall about 1638 by Jean Lemaire, 163
collaborator and friend of Nicolas Poussin. If the position on Dr Launay's plan is correct (and it seems reasonable, since an Orangerie is marked there on the cadastral plan of 1818), the painted wall was on the boundary, and its purpose was to serve as a barrier against the road, and to give an illusion of depth in a restricted space.[25] When Louis Huygens visited Rueil in 1655, the arch was viewed from a distance of fifty or sixty paces through an iron *grille* which closed the Orangerie.

The main rooms of the château opened onto a balcony

163 Rueil: Orangerie and *trompe-l'oeil* arch.

overlooking the Grand Parterre on the south side. This was raised about 1 metre (3 *pieds*) and levelled by Richelieu at a cost of 10,000 *livres*; and there were other gardens. A contract for the general upkeep with the gardener, Jean Magnon, in 1638, refers to 'les parterres, le jardin de fleurs, le petit jardin de la terrasse, le tapis vert'; also care of the bushes and the *allée* of almond trees. Plants were supplied by Pierre Desgots[26] from the Tuileries. Among the flowers, tulips were particularly favoured; the cardinal gave the name 'chancelière' to a rare violet-and-white variety. Richelieu gave particular attention to his plantations, and was known for his love of fine trees. An *allée* at Rueil was planted with horse-chestnuts, some of the first in France. These trees also surrounded the upper pond, where they were known as 'les cardinaux'.

These are the main parts of Richelieu's gardens for which the evidence is clear; but others have gone without a record. For instance, Brackenhoffer describes a circular island surrounded by a moat, suggestive of the Boboli Isolotto. It was entered by a little drawbridge, says Brackenhoffer; in the middle was a fountain, and all round thickly planted trees so that it was a pleasant shady retreat in the summer.

Although in no way as notable as that in the Touraine garden, sculpture was important at Rueil; in fact it was one of Richelieu's first considerations when he wrote to his brother in 1632, concerning a marble statue for a fountain Francini was proposing, saying that, as for other statues, it depends on what he should chance to come across. Bronze statues commissioned through M. des Roches at Florence included a Jupiter with the face of Henri IV; Anne of Austria as Juno; and a Hercules pierced so that water issued from his club held in the air. He also wanted a statue of the god Terminus, about 3 metres (9 *pieds*) high, to stand on a column in the middle of the garden. Des Roches criticized the thought of putting Terminus on a column; and whereas water could be made to come from the jaws of Samson's ass, he found the idea of it issuing from a club unfortunate. Evelyn refers to 'divers noble brass statues,' in the parterre, 'perpetually spouting water into an ample basin, with other figures of the same metal.' These are not shown in Silvestre's engraving of 1661, although he does show statues on pedestals at the foot of the Grande Cascade and on the Grand Escalier.

While descriptions of Rueil by Evelyn and Brackenhoffer were written only two years after Richelieu's death, the visual record by Israel Silvestre and Gabriel Perelle (1604–77) his sons (Nicolas, 1631–*c.*1695; and Adam, *b.*1640) present an image of the garden some fifteen years later, after changes made by Richelieu's niece and heiress, the Duchesse d'

Picturesque images of the garden.

164 (facing page) Italian palace in a park, by Paul Bril. A prototype for French seventeenth-century engravers.

165 (facing page) Imaginary landscape with château and *parterre* by Adam Perelle.

166 The Grotte de Meudon in an imaginary setting by Gabriel Perelle.

167 The Isle of Cythera, engraving by Larmesin after Watteau.

Aiguillon. According to the *Mémoire des dépenses*[27] she constructed basins and fountains, and brought water to them in new conduits. She remade the Grande Cascade, which would account for the difference between Silvestre's and Nicolas Perelle's versions; and she also made the lower cascade, the *parterre d'eau* and the grotto.[28]

The picturesque image

If regularity was the architect's ideal, the image of the garden presented by engravers, under the influence of the Italian school of landscape deriving from Paul Bril (1554–1626), was
164 quite another matter. Bril's mixture of topographic realism, idealized nature and a nostalgia for the past represented by the cult of ruins, is reflected in the work of Israel Silvestre (1621–91) and Gabriel Perelle. Perelle introduced Gothic ruins as well as Classical into his inventions, and combined
166 fact and fantasy; as in his picture of the Grotte de Meudon in an imaginary setting. It is hardly surprising that gardens like Rueil inspired 'picturesque' interpretations; some purely fanciful, as in the *View of the Old Grotto* by Gabriel's son, 148
Nicolas. But so essential were the irregular and the natural to the conception of what a picture should be, that few views of regular architectural garden scenes were without a broken foreground of figures, rocks, or old contorted trees.

In one of Adam Perelle's[29] imaginary provincial 165
landscapes, scenes from peasant life are the foreground to an elegant parterre which is open to the countryside. In the immensely popular romances such as Honoré d'Urfé's *L'Astrée* (published in three parts, 1607, 1610 and 1619) Arcadia and courtly life are never far apart. Lésigny,[30] as interpreted in Adam Perelle's engraving after Silvestre, 168
might almost be the setting for Watteau's Isle of Cythera. 167
Meanwhile the role of painting in the design of gardens was not yet recognized. The architect's influence remained paramount.

168 Israel Silvestre's picturesque image of the garden at Lésigny.

Namur Pinx.
Edelinck Sculp C P R.
Francois Mansart
Architecte du Roy.

9

The gardens of the new financial elite

The financiers

SOME OF THE MOST notable contributions to garden design, culminating in the creation of Vaux-le-Vicomte for Nicolas Fouquet, were made under the patronage of financiers, who were among the most wealthy and powerful men in France, especially after the civil wars which ruined many of the older nobility. The class included not only bankers, but those who administered the country's finances in one way or another. The royal practice of selling hereditary offices laid the foundations of many a family fortune. Of a different kind were the Intendants or king's commissioners, who were appointed to exercise control over the affairs of a region, and were directly responsible to the king, or rather to his chief minister, such as Richelieu. Called, for example, Intendant de Justice, Intendant de Police, or Intendant des Finances, the appointments were of limited duration, but were nevertheless profitable, especially where the collection of taxes was concerned.

The government's main sources of revenue were the *tailles* (direct taxes on land), the *aides* (indirect taxes on merchandise) and the *gabelle* (salt tax). There was also a tax for the maintenance of troops during a campaign, to avoid them living directly on the population. There were many exemptions from taxation, the burden falling on the common people. For purposes of tax collection France was divided into districts (*généralités*), subdivided into smaller units such as parishes. An Intendant appointed to a district was responsible for apportioning the tax between the various parishes. The task of collecting was farmed out to individuals who employed clerks to do the actual collection, which was enforced with the help of companies of soldiers. The money was then sent to the treasurer of the *généralité* (Trésorier Général) and eventually to the royal treasury. But the government was only concerned in receiving what had been budgeted; there was no fixed relation between this and the tax collected, which included cuts taken by the various intermediaries. The overall director of these operations was the Surintendant, who was answerable only to the king, without being obliged to give an account.

169 François Mansart, a decisive influence on classical French garden design.

MONTJEU

Under Henri IV and Sully reserves had been accumulated; but these were dissipated when Marie de Médicis became regent. It was not easy to find men fitted for the post of Surintendant; integrity and ability were rarely combined. After Henri's death, Pierre Jeannin, president of the parliament at Dijon, was appointed. Son of a tanner who sent him to be educated in Paris, Jeannin sided with the League against Henri IV, and served Henri de Lorraine, Duc de Mayenne, governor of Burgundy. When peace was made (says Tallemant des Réaux) he retired to Burgundy to live in a house he had acquired there in a very wild place. Henri IV sought him out saying that if he had served a petty prince so well he would serve a great king better. He held the post of Surintendant on two occasions. When he was replaced by Henri de Schomberg in 1619 he again retired to Burgundy where, says Tallemant, 'He amused himself by building. The good man built and rebuilt his houses I don't know how many times; however, they are not badly conceived [*entendues*] for the time.'

The 'very wild place' is probably Montjeu where, on a mountain site surrounded by acres of wild park south of Autun, Jeannin created one of the most remarkable garden settings of the early seventeenth century. The sloping ground is terraced both on the axis of the château and on either side. The main approach is at right angles to the entrance façade, in front of which the terrace fans out to take advantage of spectacular forest and mountain views. This arrangement has been attributed by Ganay[1] to Le Nôtre; but a bird's-eye view 170
of the early seventeenth century[2] shows that the whole framework of terraces belongs to an earlier period, and was therefore part of Jeannin's scheme.[3] It appears that the gardens were laid out on the terraces above the fan-shaped area, which was open and supported by a massive concave wall forming a theatre, with a large fountain at a lower level. The main parterre was behind the château, laid out with radiating paths, and with fountains in the centre and at the corners. Modifications were subsequently made; especially in the fan-shaped terrace, to which a *parterre de broderie* and a

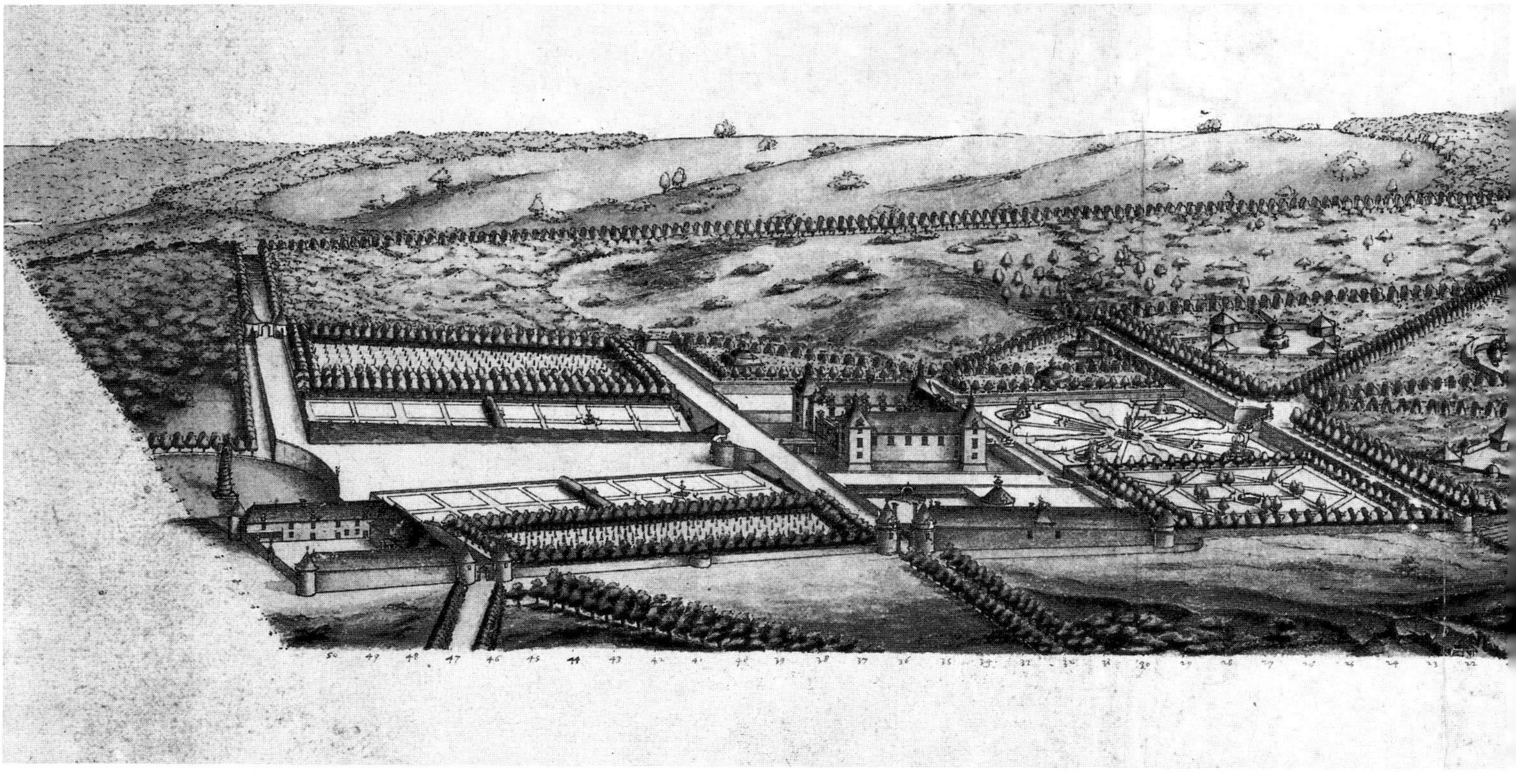

170 Montjeu: bird's-eye view of the château and park, early seventeenth century.

circular basin were added, the designs for which could have been given by Le Nôtre. The whole of this splendid framework has survived intact.

WIDEVILLE

Claude de Bullion, who was appointed Surintendant des Finances by Richelieu in 1632, jointly with Claude Bouthillier, came from a family of lawyers and had been employed in diplomatic missions both by Henri IV and Louis XIII. He was one of those responsible for establishing the Jardin des Plantes in Paris. Between 1630 and 1636 he built the château of Wideville 'in a lonely valley, amid thick woodland and far from all which could intrude upon the unsociable moods of his royal master. His trouble and work were rewarded; Louis XIII came frequently to rest, and even sleep.'[4] The garden included the interesting architectural
128 grotto closing the axis of the parterre. The façade resembles the Grotte du Luxembourg, except that the arched openings are closed by *grilles*, elaborately wrought with motifs of tulips and lilies, behind which is a room decorated with polychrome shell-work and a painted ceiling. The grotto overlooked a basin, and was extended by wings in the form of a wall with statues. These have disappeared; but the grotto still stands facing the château on the axis of the parterre, the finest example of an early architectural grotto in France. As at the Luxembourg, Thomas Francini was responsible for the waterworks. The grotte was Bullion's only extravagance. Tallemant says that he pulled down the manors on land he acquired rather than pay for their upkeep. He quadrupled his fortune by economy before he died of apoplexy in 1640.

TANLAY

It was with Particelli d'Emery that the Surintendants earned a reputation for luxurious living. He came from a family of Italian merchants settled in Lyon. Richelieu appointed him Intendant de l'Armée in the war over the succession to Mantua in 1628. In 1631 he was Intendant des Finances in Languedoc, with a secret commission to watch the intrigues of the governor, the Duc de Montmorency. Particelli was subsequently sent as ambassador to Turin from 1636 to 1639. After Louis XIII's death, when the Comte d'Avaux and the president de Bailleul took over the Surintendance from Bouthillier, the real power was exercised by Particelli as Contrôleur Général. This was an office created by Mazarin to keep a register of all the finances and to examine the receipts. Particelli was without scruple. If a village was slow to pay its taxes he imprisoned one of its inhabitants and seized his goods. There were said to be 23,000 prisoners of this kind at one time, many of whom died in captivity. He was appointed Surintendant in 1646; but was dismissed by

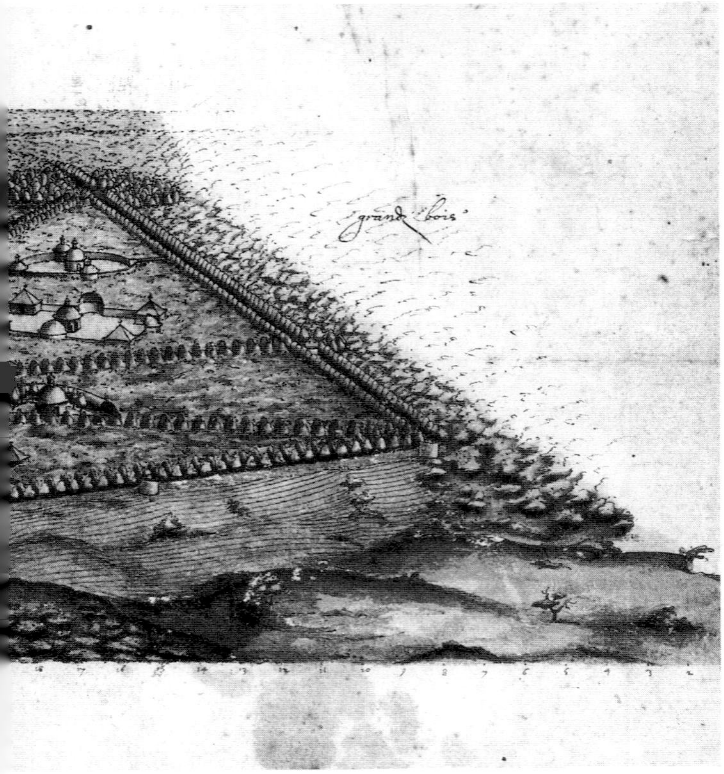

Mazarin as a scapegoat in the conflict with the parliament of Paris in 1648. Recalled for a few months in 1649, he died the following year.

Particelli had a house near Saint-Denis, La Chevrette, celebrated for the beauty of its gardens. In 1642 he bought Tanlay, a château east of Auxerre belonging to the Chatillon-Coligny family, which had descended through the female line to the then owner, Claude Vignier de Saint-Liébault et de Villemont, first president of the parliament of Metz. It was thus at the end of his life, between 1643 and 1648, that Particelli invited the architect Pierre Le Muet[5] to produce plans for unifying the old buildings, which belonged to several periods, and to add to them. Le Muet's scheme was illustrated in the second edition of his book, *Manière de Bien Bâtir Pour Toutes Sortes de Personnes* (1647); and included the design for the *grotte*, or *château d'eau*, which stands at the head
of a monumental canal, 526 metres long and some 23 metres 171
wide, conducting the water to the moats. While being ornamental, the building also served as a screen to disguise
the pond in which the water was collected. Its form, a centre- 172
piece with a large arched niche, surmounted by an oval panel 173
for a coat-of-arms and flanked by reclining figures, belongs to the same family as the *grottes* of the Luxembourg and Wideville; and like these it had wings with arched recesses. The plain, heavily rusticated style is however quite new. The centre-piece has coupled columns of the Doric order on either side of the central niche; while the curving wings, with

171 Tanlay: park, grounds and *grotte*; the new gardens are parallel to the canal, which is lined with trees newly planted above the bank.

172, 173 Tanlay: the *grotte* at the end of the canal in a seventeenth-century engraving and (right) as it is today.

arched niches, are topped by a balustrade and statue. In front of the screen, a balustraded terrace with steps on either side faced down the canal towards the château. A series of engravings by Israel Silvestre, made probably in the early 1650s shortly after the grotto was built, shows the water cascading from five lion-like masks below the platform.[6] There are gardens with *broderies* on either side of the canal, framed in newly planted trees continuing a line of mature trees left from some earlier plantation. As the canal was dug in slightly sloping ground, the resulting bank develops from ground-level, increasing in size towards the *grotte*; the trees planted on top of the bank thus being farther from the canal as they recede.[7] This gives the effect of a *perspective ralentie*, but it seems likely that this was the inevitable result of planting above the bank, in relation to the parterre, rather than a deliberate optical effect, as some have claimed.[8] The
174 circumstances which caused the canal to be placed obliquely to the château were probably related to its function in conducting water to the moats by the most direct route. Its aesthetic interest is largely due to the focus Le Muet's building gives it.

174 Aerial photograph of Tanlay. The canal is the horizontal line at the bottom.

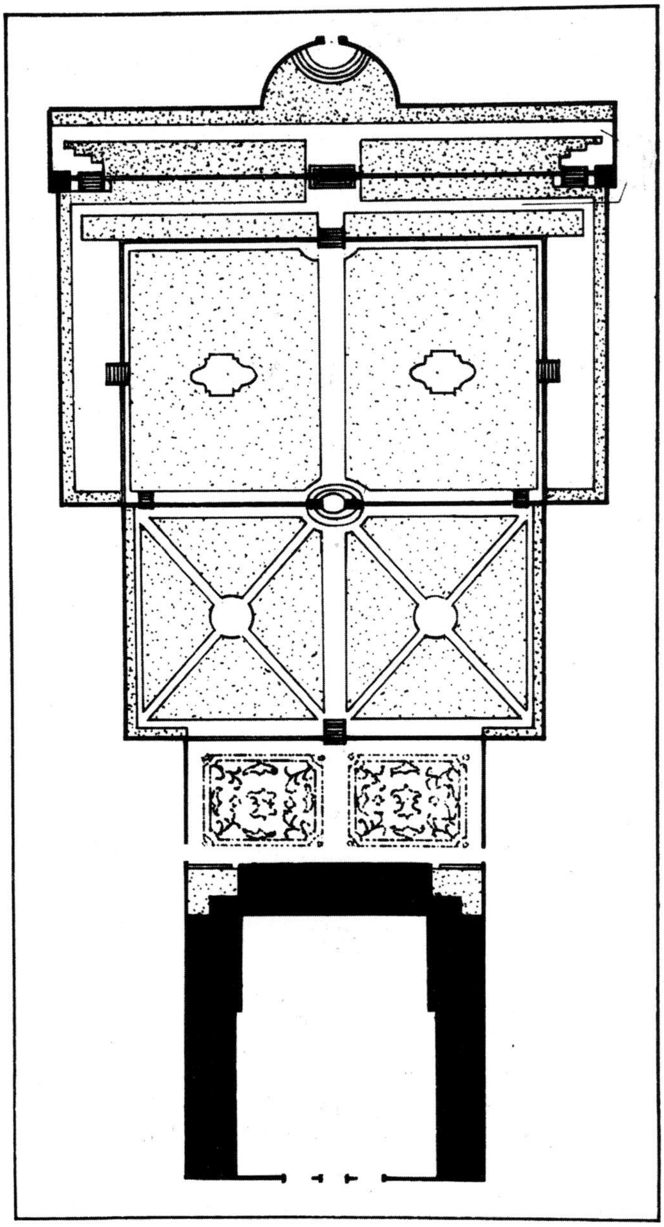

175 Plan of Brécy in Calvados.

BRÉCY

A remarkably sophisticated arrangement of terraces from the first part of the seventeenth century survives at Brécy, near Bayeux. Little is known about its origin, except that the house was built for Jacques le Bas, Seigneur de Cambe, who was a relative of Jean de Choisy for whom François Mansart built Balleroy. Brécy is little more than a modest manor house to which a monumental entrance gate and a handsome architectural garden were added. Reginald Blomfield[9] suggested that the garden was intended for a more grandiose scheme which was not completed; but as Marcus Binney has observed,[10] the width of the lowest terrace is accommodated to the existing house; the others, which mount the hill behind in five stages, expand as they recede. The second and third comprise a square area, with oval steps at the centre giving access between the levels. The upper area is surrounded by a raised terrace on three sides, forming the fourth level. The fifth terrace is long and narrow like the fourth. This framework is symmetrical about the axis, which ends in a double pair of gate piers; the first at the head of the steps from the fourth terrace, the second supporting the elegant iron *grille* leading to the park, and preceded by a curved flight of steps. The sculptured urns with protruding bunches of fruit and flowers, and some of the ornament over the doorways on either side of the first terrace, are closely related to late Mannerist ornament as represented in Alexandre Francini's *Livre d'Architecture* (1631); and this would support Blomfield's suggested date of 1630. There is no evidence, however, to confirm his attribution to François Mansart, except the sophistication of the plan, and the fact that the owner was related to Jean de Choisy.[11]

175 176

François Mansart

François Mansart has for long been recognized as the leading and most original architect among those who created the French Classical style. It is only comparatively recently that his importance as a garden designer has been noted,[12] especially in his attention to siting the château in relation to its grounds. This is not just a continuation of the tradition which we have traced from the theory of Alberti, through the work of the unknown designer of Bury, Philibert de l'Orme, Jacques I Androuet du Cerceau to Jacques Lemercier, but a refinement which was an essential prelude to the work of Le Nôtre. As M. Jean-Pierre Babelon has put it: 169

> The special attention given to this surrounding space is a second characteristic of Mansart's art which is of prime importance. The building does not exist without the air around it; it is placed within the field of successive lines of sight which, in a certain way, resolve it into as many different objects. . . . Not a château without an immense axial vista through villages or forests; simple and direct axes as at Balleroy; axes which intersect in the mature works, and which permit an indirect approach, a sequence of revelations to the visitor's aroused curiosity. Standing aloof on the horizon, adjoined – but at a respectful distance – by the outbuildings and offices . . . the château takes on a quasi-sacred character . . . the goal of a pilgrimage

176 Brécy: the first terrace with sculptured vases and doorway in the late Mannerist style of A. Francini.

glimpsed at a distance and of which each skilfully contrived articulation of the road will offer some surprising new aspect, the elements of the façades becoming gradually differentiated from the general mass at first seen as a whole. One then understands the importance given by Mansart to gardens with a vista, and the decisive influence he could have on the genius of Le Nôtre.[13]

Mansart was born in 1598, the son of a carpenter in the king's service, who died when François was a child. Little is known about his early life. He received training from his uncle, Marcel Le Roy, who was an engineer. His brother-in-law, Germain Gaultier, was a royal architect who worked with Salomon de Brosse on the Palais du Parlement at Rennes. Mansart may also have worked under De Brosse at the château of Coulommiers, which he completed in 1631 after De Brosse's death. By that time he had a sufficient reputation to be appointed architect by Gaston d'Orléans, to remodel the château of Blois. While a perfectionist in his art, Mansart had a reputation for being obstinate, arrogant and unscrupulous in his business dealings, infuriating clients by his extravagance in not hesitating to pull down and rebuild parts he found unsatisfactory. This was the case at the château of Maisons, built between 1642 and 1651 for René de Longueil, who was nevertheless wealthy enough to tolerate it in order to have the house he wanted. Maisons was one of the few of Mansart's major domestic projects to be completed. His grandiose scheme for rebuilding Blois was not finished. Other major schemes incorporating gardens were the château of Berny (1623–4), Balleroy (*c.*1626–36), Fresnes (*c.*1644–50), Petit Bourg (late 1640s–1660s) and Gesvres (1650s and 1660s). Of these only Balleroy and Maisons still exist.

177, 178 Berny: a view from the entrance side (above) and the *parterre* (below).

BERNY

The château of Berny,[14] the site of which is now covered by urban development and main roads between Fresnes and Sceaux, south of Paris, was acquired in 1615 by Nicolas Brulart (1544–1624), chevalier de Sillery, when he was chancellor of France. Even before his death his son Pierre, Vicomte de Puisieux, was styled chevalier de Berny; and it was with him that Mansart contracted to reconstruct the château in 1623. Mansart was then only twenty-five, and virtually unknown. The contract specified the demolition and replacement of an existing central wing, thus the relation of Berny to its setting cannot be said to have been due to the new architect. The important characteristics of Mansart's mature style – the siting of the main building in relation to its approaches, and his use of a greatly extended axis in the design of grounds – are as yet undeveloped. Nevertheless there was at Berny an openness of aspect which points in this direction. The relatively short approach was at right angles to the main axis of the house, running parallel to the canalized River Bièvre which divided the grounds of the château from the fields into which the entrance front of the house looked.
177 An engraving by Marot and Della Bella after Silvestre, published in 1651,[15] shows the main courtyard enclosed by a low balustrade beside the canal, beyond which the cattle graze in park-like meadow with clumps and belts of trees.[16] Denis II Godefroy gave a detailed account of his visit in March 1636;[17] and about eight years later Brackenhoffer also wrote down his observations.[18] The main rooms looked onto
a square flower garden with four compartments laid out in 178
broderie of box round a fountain, beyond which, placed in a semicircle, were statues of Bacchus, Flora, Hercules, Mercury and Diana. The parterre was enclosed on the right by an *allée de mail* 9 to 10 paces wide, bordered by a double row of trees on each side stretching for about 500 paces. It was separated from the kitchen garden by a partition of high iron *grilles*, painted green and with gilded flower motifs. Godefroy remarked on the variety of the ornaments (fountains, quadrants, sundials, statues); and on a pond edged with dressed stone in which there was an island planted with broom and other 'woodland shrubs', the home of numerous tortoises. Hidden in the park on the side opposite to the *mail* and the *potager* was a round basin, some 320 paces in circumference, quite overshadowed by tall trees. In the centre was a statue of Neptune – seated on four 'serpents' says Brackenhoffer – from whose heads water was shot into the air. Life-size marble statues emblematic of the Virtues and

179 Berny: detail of a bird's-eye view of 1684.

180 Balleroy, showing Mansart's forecourts and the long street extending the axis of the château.

their corresponding Vices were paired on either side of the four entrances in the high elm hedge surrounding the basin. Each had an inscription pointing to the moral. Thus,

> *Pleasure of the senses*
> Sensual pleasures
> bring the great to shipwreck.
>
> *Temperance*
> He whose plans are moderate
> does not fear the storm.

And so on for Prudence and Fortune, Envy and Patience, Calumny and Truth. The personification of the Vices and Virtues was an old theme, and had been represented by Mantegna in a painting with a garden setting;[19] and yet its use 20
in the iconography at Berny appears to have been unusual, and may have been inspired by Ripa's *Iconologia* which, as Alfred Marie has shown,[20] was later used by Charles Le Brun as the basis for the original sculpture programme at Versailles. The main features in the disposition of the grounds at Berny are clearly seen in a plan of the estate dated 1684;[21] 179
although the stream 'terminating in a bubbling spring' and a 'dry grotto', as well as the many 'labyrinthine woodland paths', are not apparent. Nor probably do these details have much to do with Mansart, whose characteristic manner first appears in the approaches to Balleroy.

181 The château of Balleroy, seen from the village.

BALLEROY

The château was built in the late 1620s for Jean de Choisy,[22] who was Surintendant des Finances, Secrétaire du Roi et des Finances (1600), and Secrétaire Général des Finances de Caen (1603). The whole emphasis is on displaying the architecture of the house to greatest advantage, particularly on approaching it from the front, for from the side its proportions are too meagre. It was sited on one side of the valley which is the line of the old village street. A new village
180 street, laid out at right angles, enabled the approaches to be greatly extended, and to be sited across the valley so that
181 descending from the higher ground the building appeared to rise up before one. According to precedent, the parterre was overlooked by the principal rooms, the climax of the axial approach; but far greater attention was given to the elaboration of the forecourts of the château, standing up on a platform surrounded by dry moats. The new layout was probably begun in 1634;[23] the majority of the houses were not built until 1650–70, and do not show Mansart's influence. But although the orientation of the approaches cannot be definitely assigned to him, the arrangement is so similar to what he did elsewhere that it is almost certainly his idea. Balleroy is the only existing example of Mansart's domestic architectural ensembles, except for Maisons. The *parterre de broderie* at present laid out in the forecourt was not, of course, part of the original scheme.

182 Aerial photograph of Maisons Lafitte showing the great avenue of the château on the diagonal, and the roads following the lines of the original *allées* in the park.

183 Maisons: the château seen from the garden.

MAISONS

Maisons, on the Seine to the north of Saint-Germain-en-Laye, was the most complete expression of Mansart's idea of a country house; a far more satisfactory object than Balleroy, to be contemplated from every point of view. The patron, René de Longueil, came from a long line of lawyers who, for nearly three centuries, had served the parliament of Paris. He himself had done so from an early age, first as Conseiller au Grand Conseil in 1618, and Président à la Cour des Aides[24] in 1620. When he commissioned Maisons in 1642 he was President à Mortier of the Paris parliament, a post he relinquished in 1653 after he had been appointed Capitaine des Chasses. In 1651 he was Surintendant des Finances. The following year his house was ready to receive the young Louis XIV and the queen mother, an occasion for a sumptuous entertainment; but not long after he was deprived of his post. Huygens,[25] who visited Maisons in 1655, reported that the courtyard of the offices was not finished because of the disgrace of the master 'for having refused to consent to the return of certain exiled councillors'. After a discreet retirement of a few years he returned to royal favour; and in 1638 Maisons was raised to a marquisate. De Longueil died in 1677.

From all accounts Mansart received a free hand in the building of Maisons, for which no expense was spared. Every aspect is open. The entrance from the village is on one side, so that the approach is at right angles to the main axis of the château, which is marked to the northwest by an enormous
182 avenue, $1\frac{1}{2}$ kilometres long, leading into the forest of Saint-Germain. It is closed by a large circular excavation in the form of a *saut de loup* leaving the central vista open, access to the avenue being by gates and pavilions on either side. The château is raised on a platform, surrounded by dry moats and
a terrace overlooking gardens on three sides. The main rooms 183
faced the *grand parterre*, with the Seine beyond and the axis continued in an avenue *à perte de vue* on the far side of the river. This, together with the way in which the surroundings are designed to display the château which is raised above them, makes it a true precursor of Vaux-le-Vicomte. Maisons was allowed to fall into disrepair during the eighteenth century, until it was bought in 1777 by the Comte d' Artois (the future Charles X), who filled in the moats and transformed the gardens into a park *à l'anglaise*.[26] In 1818 it was bought by the banker, Jacques Laffitte, who sold off most of the park in lots. The general lines of the *allées*, including the great avenue, with the *saut de loup* against the forest, were preserved in the subsequent development. After the château was acquired by the state in 1911, the parterre was restored, so some idea of Mansart's original conception has survived. This is not the case with his remaining schemes. The terraced garden he proposed overlooking the Loire at Blois was never made. His other important garden layouts were at Petit-Bourg, Fresnes, and Gesvres, all between the mid-1640s and 1660.

GESVRES

Gesvres, northeast of Meaux, was the old château of Tresmes remodelled by Mansart and renamed after the then owner, René Potier, first Duc de Gesvres. According to a bird's-eye view dated 1711,[27] château and gardens were contained in

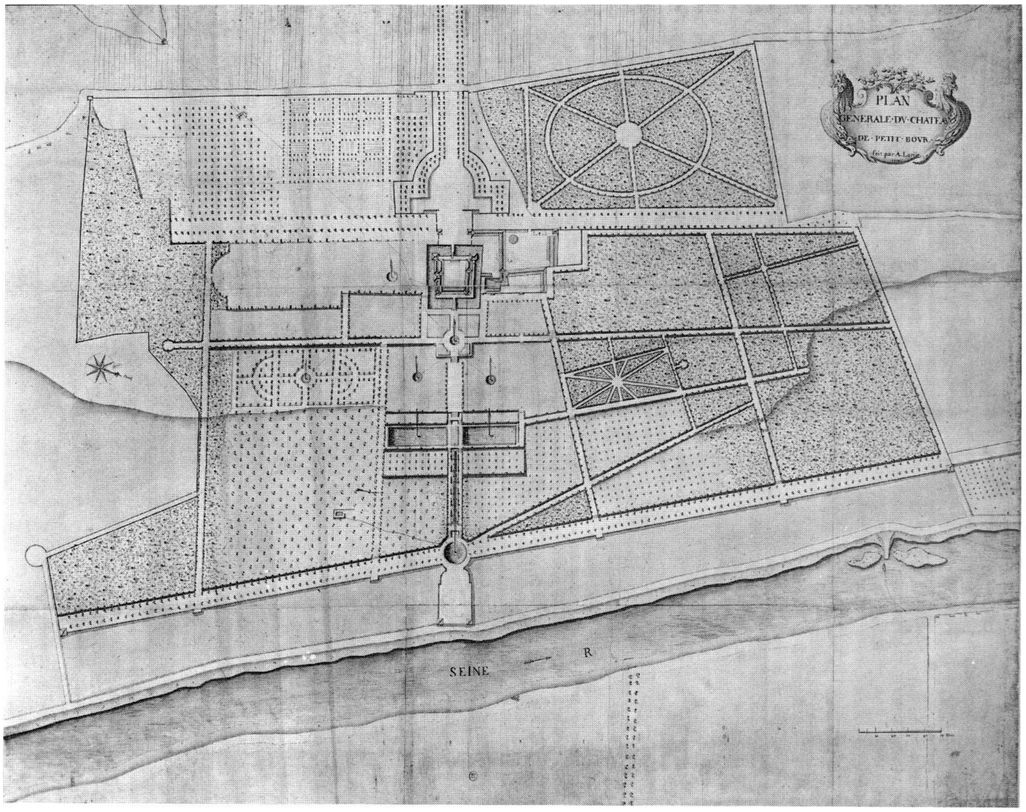

184 Maisons: the château seen from the side, with a *parterre de broderie* in the foreground and Mansart's service wing, since demolished, on the left.

185 Plan of the château and garden of Petit Bourg, 1696.

moats formed by canalizing the streams adjoining the River Ourc. A grand avenue from Crouy led to the forecourt entrance, separated by walls pierced with *grilles* from stables and offices on one side and a garden on the other. The house was arranged around three sides of a courtyard closed on the fourth by an iron *grille*. A parterre beyond the main wing looked onto the moat which was enlarged to form a rectangular basin framed by two pavilions. Filling the space between these central areas and the canal were other gardens of similar proportions, but of varied form (*bosquet*, basin, parterre, ornamented with fountains).

FRESNES

Fresnes-sur-Marne,[28] south of the main road from Paris to Meaux, was bought in 1641 by Henri de Guénégaud[29], who immediately started spending large sums of money in additions to the buildings and in laying out the grounds. The Guénégauds were among Mansart's most faithful patrons. Henri was the son of Gabriel de Guénégaud, Seigneur de Plessis-Belleville, Trésorier de l'Epargne, to which post he had succeeded on his father's death in 1638. His cultivated and beautiful wife, Elizabeth de Choiseul-Praslin, was an ardent Jansenist, and a friend of Madame de Sévigné and Mademoiselle de Scudéry, in whose novel *Clélie* she appears as Amaltée. At the Hôtel de Nevers[30] she held literary salons; while Fresnes was the scene of even more exclusive gatherings associated with *préciosité*, concerning which Antoine Adam[31] has this to say:

> It designates certain attitudes and forms of language that were fashionable at the end of the period of unrest [the Fronde] within the new society whose characteristics were very different from those it replaced . . . A study of *préciosité* is necessarily a study of an aspect of social life. . . . In those days of increasing and unashamed pleasure-seeking, the *précieuses* showed no sympathy for vulgar licentiousness. But they did put the search for personal happiness above all other moral values. . . . The *précieuses* were at one in wanting to rid society of the impurity of words as well as of things and raise conversation to a higher plane.

In pursuit of this aim they used affected language which brought them into disrepute. 'The *précieuses* and high society as it was after the Fronde were not quite the same thing. But the *précieuses* differed from it only because they took to extremes the tendencies that were clearly present in that society: the desire for refined elegance, a very keen sense of the autonomy of the individual which should emancipate him from social pressures as well as from the demands of the instincts, the need for lucidity and freedom.' It was such people who appreciated and encouraged Mansart; and who formed the circle to which Nicolas Fouquet belonged.[32]

There are few detailed records of Fresnes before the eighteenth century.[33] Mademoiselle de Scudéry described it in *Clélie*; Huygens,[34] who visited it in 1655, said this of the grounds:

> At the house, on the left of the *bassecour*, an iron *grille* leads into the park where at first you enter an *allée* 60 feet wide, with a view of very fine country at the end of it. At the side of this big *allée* are several others, cut in the thickness of the wood, and bounded between the trees on each side (as is also the large one I have just spoken of and almost all those I have seen of the same kind) by an *espalier* rising to 20 or 30 feet, which makes a very pleasant tapestry on one side and the other. There are several of these *allées* in the form of a star; and here and there *cabinets* of cypress and fir at which they are still working every day. Behind the house are two big parterres one after the other, and a round basin in the last, in which a fountain is soon to be made. The moat of the house is at least 60 feet wide, entirely edged with dressed stone.

PETIT-BOURG

Petit-Bourg, on the west bank of the Seine near Corbeil, has now entirely disappeared, and the site is occupied by a block of flats. It was bought in 1646 by Louis Barbier, abbé de la Rivière, an intimate of Gaston d'Orléans, who later allied himself with Mazarin, and became bishop of Langres in 1655. Huygens, who visited Petit-Bourg that year, admired the gardens as much as any he had seen. They descended by four
or five stages, terminating in a crescent-shaped platform[35] 185
with a balustrade overlooking the Seine. 'But what surpasses all,' wrote Huygens, 'is a very beautiful cascade which
descends from the first garden to the second by large shells 186
with twenty or thirty jets of water on either side.' The jet at the lower level, against the crescent, was the loftiest he had yet seen in France. Mansart worked for Barbier in the early 1650s; and if the garden is rightly attributed to him, it may be regarded as his most original design.

It seems probable, as Braham and Smith have said, that Mansart's example strongly influenced the development of garden design in the latter half of the seventeenth century, particularly the type of plan centred on a broad open vista of great extent. He also had a direct influence upon his successors. According to an anonymous manuscript,[36] François Mansart's great-nephew, Jules Hardouin-Mansart, worked under his uncle at Maisons, where, among other things, he was given responsibility for 'les entrées et pavillons aux avenues'. The account continues, 'from there, his uncle took him to Fresnes, near Lagny, where he did many works for him in the forecourt, as well as all the gardens with many terraces, avenues, canals, planting a great number of *bosquets* in a very large park. Finally, M. Mansart, finding that his nephew had an individual style in these sorts of things, employed him much in all those places where he was working, especially at Gesvres for all the gardens and *pièces d'eau*.' As Jules Hardouin-Mansart was only twenty when his uncle died in 1666, his part is either very much exaggerated or else the work was carried out very late in Mansart's career. More plausible is the statement that André Le Nôtre worked under Mansart, and that it was in this situation that the long association between Louis XIV's gardener and architect began. Mansart, says the manuscript, gave Le Nôtre openings with pleasure, in that he found in him a subject worthy to

186 View of the château and garden of Petit Bourg, 1727.

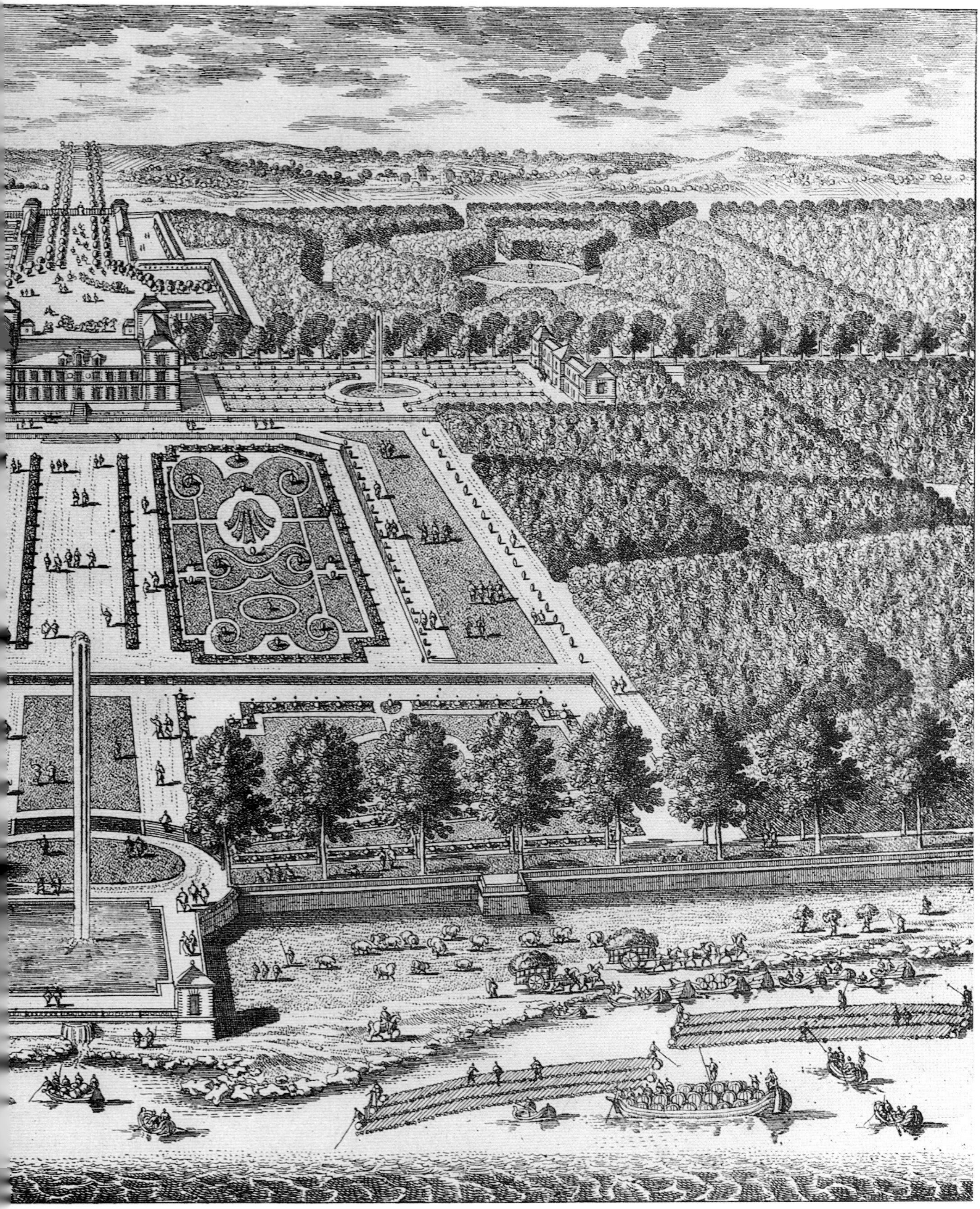

profit by it. Louis II Le Vau, creator of Vaux-le-Vicomte and Versailles, also profited by his example. Some of Mansart's important patrons belonged to Nicolas Fouquet's circle; two (Macé II Bertrand, Seigneur de la Bazinière, and Claude Boislève) were implicated in the Surintendant's later downfall and were imprisoned. Mansart himself survived this event by five years.

Le Jardin de Plaisir: Jacques Boyceau and André Mollet

With these advances in garden design, more attention was given to the ornament of the pleasure garden in gardening treatises. Reference has already been made (Chapter 7) to Jacques Boyceau's *Traité du Jardinage*, published posthumously in 1638 by his nephew, Jacques de Menours. Boyceau was born of a noble Protestant family in Saintonge. He entered the service of Henri IV as Gentilhomme Ordinaire de la Chambre du Roi about 1602, but very little is known about his life, or what he actually contributed to garden design,[37] beyond the fact that he was regarded as a sufficient authority to be consulted by the Duc de la Force about the design of his garden at Perigord in 1610. Fabri de Peiresc also asked his advice on Beaugentier, and corresponded with him over plants. At that time Boyceau was 'Intendant des Jardins de Sa Majesté à Paris aux Tuileries'. He is thought to have died about 1633.

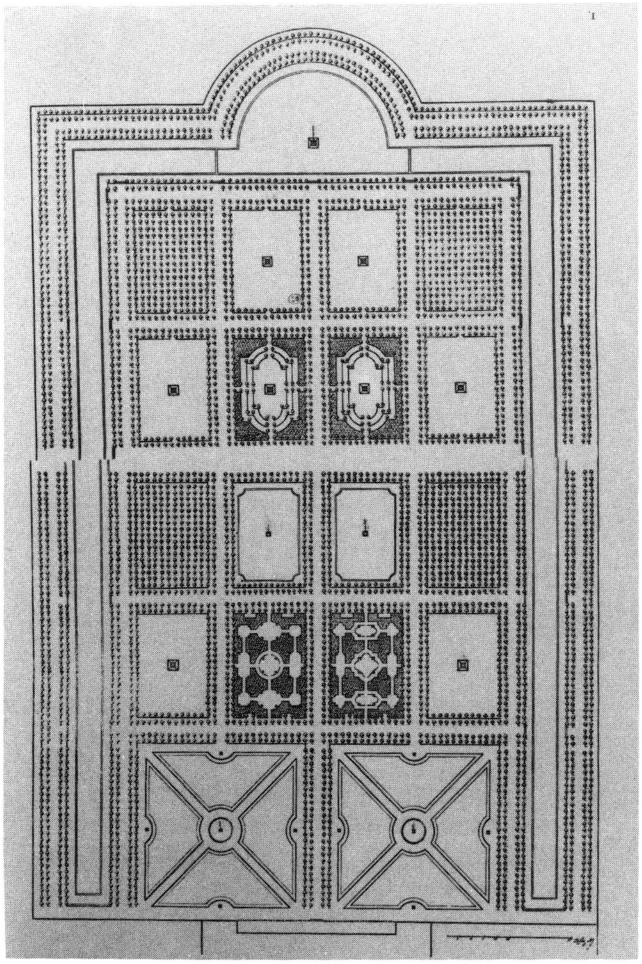

187 The classic French concept of the garden, from André Mollet's *Le Jardin de Plaisir*, 1651.

His is the first book to give particular attention to the pleasure garden and its ornament, besides dealing with the essentials of gardening (soil, situation and plants). The text consists of a mere eighty-seven pages, followed by sixty pages of designs, mainly for *parterres de broderie*, including some for specific gardens (Louvre, Luxembourg, Saint-Germain-en-Laye, Tuileries, Versailles). A chapter of only fifteen lines is given to this part of the garden. Parterres, he writes, are made of several kinds of dwarf shrub fashioned in different ways.[38] Beds of the parterre may include medicinal plants and herbs as well as flowers to form a coloured carpet; the taller flowering plants being put in borders. Similarly with trees, he discourses in general terms on their nature and problems in growing, reproduction from cuttings and by layering, but with next to no information about particular species and varieties. On the proportions of avenues and walks he is more exact, noting that a covered *allée* appears wider than one which is open to the sky; and that the longer the *allée* is, the wider it should be. 'Of those which are very long,' he writes, 'the widest I have seen have seemed to me the most beautiful, as can be seen in the elm *allée* at the Tuileries, which is thirty feet wide, and is much finer than the two of plane trees on either side which are only twenty wide against 600 yards (*trois cens toises*) long. . . . Even the elm *allée* appears better proportioned when seen at a certain distance along, than when it is seen in its entire length.' This is a point that Le Nôtre was to observe when he redesigned the Tuileries some forty years later.

Boyceau criticizes the common practice of laying out gardens in a rectilinear fashion, stressing the importance of variety: rounded forms as well as straight, paths placed obliquely, dividing the parterre into triangular quarters, or combinations of these to give hexagons or octagons. Sites with differences of level have the advantage of giving a view of the parterre as a whole. Seeing the whole and being able to appreciate the good relation between the parts gives more pleasure than perceiving it piecemeal, as it appears when on a level where the vertical elements get in the way.

His short chapter on *Relief* (the raised parts of the garden such as *allées*, *berceaux* and architectural features like pavilions), on the use of water for canals and fountains, on grottoes and aviaries, apply in general to important gardens of the first decade of the century. He refers to the importance of providing space for outdoor games, such as a pall-mall *allée*. And in writing of the vegetable garden, he says that this too will not go unembellished. The *allées* will be lined with fruit trees, hedges, espaliers, or covered with walks of vines on vaulted trellis. He is the only one of these writers to suggest that the colour and form of plants in the vegetable garden may be used in a decorative manner; artichokes, for instance, forming a border to smaller plants, like little strawberries, arranged in chequer fashion, or as labyrinths.

The most advanced parts of Boyceau's book are the designs for parterres. The text has a slightly old-fashioned flavour, and most of what he says can be related to the great gardens of the first two decades of the century. This suggests that the illustrations may have been added by the publisher. It must be noted, however, that Jacques de Menours does say in his dedication that he has included several designs of parterres, *bosquets* and other ornaments 'de son invention', meaning his uncle's.

Claude Mollet's *Le Théâtre des Plans et Jardinages*, 1652, is not concerned with the architectural framework of the garden, nor with its ornament, except in so far as these are vegetal. His son, André, published *Le Jardin de Plaisir* in Stockholm in 1651, when he was in the service of Queen Christina. Apart from Sweden, he spent much time in foreign courts, Holland and particularly England,[39] introducing the French style of gardening into those countries. The book is very short – just over forty pages of text– but handsomely produced and including many designs for parterres and *bosquets*. His *broderies* are less intricate and more open than those of Boyceau, or the earlier examples of his own work shown in his father's book. As the title suggests, more space is given to flowers and flowering shrubs than to the kitchen garden. He mentions that whortleberry may be used as a substitute for the more tender box in the parterres of Sweden. His reference to other garden ornament is cursory; but alone among these writers he gives two plans for the
187 laying out of grounds and sets out the classic French concept of the design of the garden as a whole:

> First we should say that the royal house must be sited to best advantage, in order to ornament it with all things necessary to its embellishment; of which the first is to be able to plant a big avenue with a double or triple row of female elms, or lime trees (which are the two species of tree which we esteem most suited to this effect) which must be placed in line at right angles to the front of the château. . . . Then, facing the rear of the house must be constructed the *parterres en broderie*, near to it so as to be easily seen from the windows, and gazed upon without obstacles such as trees, *palissades* or any other elevated thing which can prevent the eye from embracing its full extent.
>
> Following the said *parterres en broderie* will be placed the parterres or compartments of turf, as well as the *bosquets*, *allées* and high and low *palissades* in their proper place; made in such a way that most of the said *allées* lead to something and always terminate in a statue or the centre of a fountain; and at the extremities of these *allées* put fine perspectives of painted canvas, so as to be able to remove them from damage by weather when one wishes to. And to perfect the work, statues should be placed on pedestals, and grottoes built in the most suitable places. Then raise terrace walks according to the convenience of the place, without forgetting aviaries, fountains, water jets, canals, and such ornaments which, duly being carried out, each in their place, form the perfect pleasure garden.

Louis XIV attained his legal majority in 1651.[40] For three years a section of nobility led by Louis de Bourbon, Prince de Condé, in alliance with a rebellious Paris parliament, had challenged the authority of the crown; or more correctly the alliance of the queen mother with Mazarin. In 1652 the young Louis triumphantly re-entered Paris. André Le Nôtre was thirty-nine. Vaux-le-Vicomte was only four years away; and it is to the creation of that masterpiece, the culmination of the process we have been tracing, that we must now turn.

Nicolas Foucquet
de Vaux, Conseiller du
d'Estat, surintendant des
de sa Mayeste
Roy
finances et Procureur General
R. Nanteuil ad viuum ping. et sculpebat

10

Vaux-le-Vicomte

The background

After the death of Cardinal Richelieu at the end of 1642, French politics were dominated by the personality of the chief minister, Cardinal Mazarin.[1] When the royal government came into conflict with the parliament of Paris, essentially over its right to vote or refuse taxes, hostility focused on Mazarin rather than the queen. In the civil war which followed, known as La Fronde,[2] Mazarin was forced into exile in Germany from where, through his agents, he continued to direct the policies of the queen and the young king. He returned to France in 1652 as principal adviser to the king, who had reached his legal majority the previous year. He continued to conduct the affairs of France until his death in 1661; and through his choice of assistants, notably Jean Colbert, he laid the foundations for the administration of France during the most important part of Louis XIV's reign.

By 1648, what with the war against the empire and Spain, and the unstable internal situation, the revenues had been consumed for several years ahead. A declaration of bankruptcy, defaulting on the payment of interest to those who had lent money to the state, precipitated a further crisis and made the financiers extremely reluctant to lend. A series of Surintendants failed to deal with the situation. Particelli d'Emery's successor was La Meilleraye, 'grand master of artillery, a mediocre warrior and no financier'.[3] In July 1648 the government announced that it was postponing repayment of treasury bills against which it had been accustomed to borrow money. Dealings in money stopped suddenly. The Trésorier de l'Epargne, Nicolas Jeannin de Castille,[4] had difficulty in raising 25,000 *livres* on his own credit and those of his relatives.[5] La Meilleraye was dismissed; Particelli d'Emery was recalled, but unfortunately died the following year. René de Longueil, known as the Président de Maisons, who had long had ambitions for the post, was given his chance. He proved incapable; and in desperation Mazarin appointed the Marquis de la Vieuville, who had been a not unsuccessful Surintendant twenty-three years previously, but had been disgraced and imprisoned by Richelieu on suspicion of creating divisions between Gaston d'Orléans and Marie de Médicis. La Vieuville was then seventy-one; he died two years later. It was in these circumstances that Abel Servien and Nicolas Fouquet were appointed joint Surintendants des Finances in 1653.

Servien was over sixty, Fouquet's senior by more than twenty years. His father had been rewarded by Henri IV with the post of Conseiller Honoraire to the parliament of Grenoble, where Abel Servien began his professional career. On being made Conseiller d'Etat he settled in Paris, acquired a post as Maître des Requêtes in 1624, and in 1630 became Secrétaire d'Etat. He displeased Richelieu by quarrelling with the Abbé Bois-Robert; and was obliged to give up his post and retire to his estate in Anjou. After Richelieu's death he returned to affairs of state, taking part in negotiations for the Treaty of Westphalia which ended the Thirty Years War. He was appointed as a minister in 1649, but was out of power during Mazarin's exile.

MEUDON

In 1654 Servien bought Meudon, to the southwest of Paris, from the Guise. The château was again in disrepair having been pillaged by Condé's troops during the Fronde. Servien employed Louis II Le Vau to remodel and restore the grotto and to create a framework of terraces linking one to the other. The village of Meudon was removed to make a huge wall of cliff-like proportions along the side of the valley
looking towards Paris, setting the château on a huge platform 189
and allowing for a fine approach avenue. The gardens were in three stages: a parterre on the level of the château; a parterre at a lower level to the right in front of the grotto; and still lower down the massive arcaded entrance to the orangery beneath the terrace opened onto a third parterre. This was a prototype for Versailles. In order to extend the vista into the distance, Servien acquired the woods of Clamart and Trivaux; and he made the two ponds in the
valley, which are shown in Silvestre's drawings of Le Nôtre's 190
arrangement of the central vista in the time of the Marquis de Louvois, later in the century. In 1656 he had permission to enlarge and enclose the park on the high ground behind the grotto, whose terrace walls were extended giving views over the valley of the Seine. To the great natural beauties of the setting were added a scheme of immense grandeur in which

188 Nicolas Fouquet, the builder of Vaux-le-Vicomte. Engraving by R. Nanteuil.

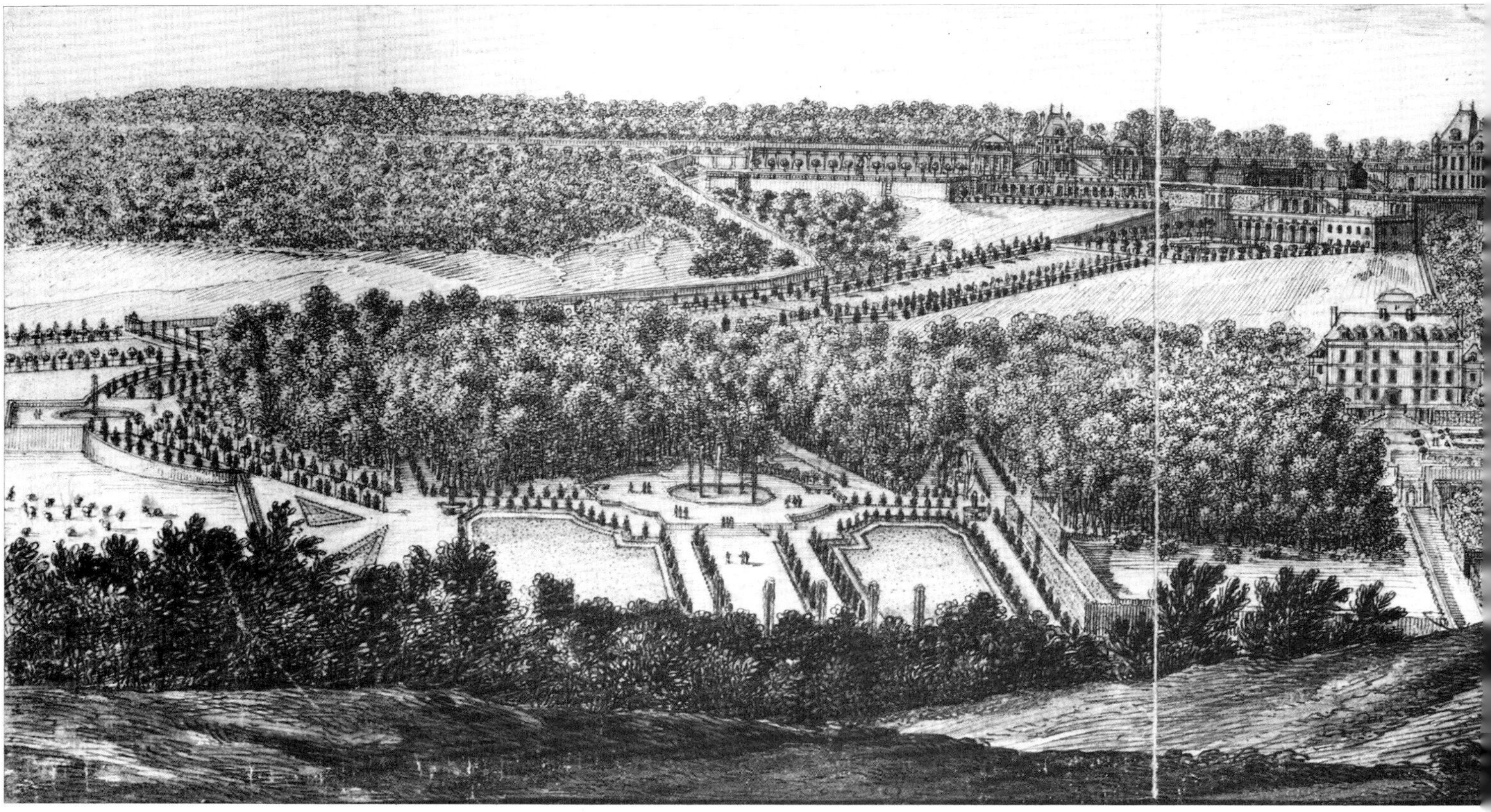

189 Meudon: general view in the time of Louvois showing the terraces and extensive lower gardens.

45 the character of Charles de Guise's grotto (Chapter 4) was lost. As Comte Paul Biver has put it, 'the more the château is shown to advantage by its terrace and parterres, the more the grotto, a delicate masterpiece, loses its charm amid this pompous regularity.'[6] Suspicions that Servien might have milked public funds to meet this great expense are apparently ill-founded. He conducted the financial affairs of the state with a fair degree of integrity, spending his personal fortune on the extravagance of Meudon, as his heir was soon to discover.

Nicolas Fouquet

Compared with the natural advantages of Meudon, Vaux-le-Vicomte had little to offer in the first place; but its owner was exceptionally endowed with taste, imagination, energy and ambition. Servien's co-Surintendant was born in 1615, second son of François III Fouquet, Conseiller at the parliament of Paris. Four other sons also arrived at positions of influence. François IV, the eldest, became successively bishop of Bayonne, of Agde and archbishop of Narbonne; Basile (abbé de Barbeaux et Rigny, and then abbé de Noailles) was Mazarin's agent; Louis was also a bishop of
188 Agde. Nicolas was educated by the Jesuits, and was also destined for the Church when, in 1633, his father obtained for him the post of Conseiller to the parliament of Metz newly established by Richelieu. His advancement was rapid and easy: Procureur Général to the Metz parliament (1639); and Intendant de Police, Justice et Finances to the army defending the southern frontier (1642). As Intendant to the Dauphiné he was suspected of leniency in dealing with a rebellious situation; but in fact moderation, and an ability to persuade people to cooperate rather than to impose his will on them, were characteristics which enabled him to succeed. In 1648 he was appointed Intendant of the *généralité* of Paris, a particularly delicate and unenviable post at that time. And in 1650 he bought the office of Procureur Général, placing him in a commanding position as intermediary between the king and parliament during the civil war in which, while serving Mazarin's interests, his efforts were conciliatory. He retained this post when he became Surintendant des Finances. The situation he inherited could not have been more difficult, Mazarin had only recently returned to Paris, and his requirements for meeting the expenses of the continuing war with Spain were enormous; while at the same time the bankruptcy of 1648 had made financiers reluctant to lend. Recognizing Fouquet's powers of persuasion, and the wealth of his family connections, Mazarin entrusted him with the task of finding the money; the older, more cautious, rather negative Servien was given the responsibility of the distribution. Fouquet set out his policy of establishing confidence: never to go back on one's word or threaten to default; to offer favourable terms instead of quibbling about interest and profit; in a few words, to gain consent by gentle persuasion and by appearing to be generous. Generosity and

optimism, a ready smile, cultivated taste, a lively mind, these were qualities which brought other rewards and disadvantages. He understood artists and spared no expense to enable them to give their best. He attracted the company of lively and interesting women: Suzanne de Bruc, Marquise du Plessis-Bellière, Madame de Sévigné and Mademoiselle de Scudéry, in whose novel, *Clélie*, he appears as Cleonime, 'a man who makes nothing but what is great, and whose mind by its vast range cannot conceive little designs'. Mazarin's opinion, expressed to the king, was that if they could get women and building out of his head, great things might be done with him.

SAINT-MANDÉ

Fouquet owned various Paris houses from time to time. His father's house was in the Rue de Jouy between the Rue Saint-Antoine and the river. From there he moved to a house surrounded by large gardens belonging to his second wife, Marie-Madeleine de Castille, in the Rue Vieille du Temple. About 1658, his elder brother, the archbishop of Narbonne, sold him a house in the Rue Saint-Honoré; but Mazarin, wishing to have Fouquet near him, persuaded him to buy the Hôtel d'Emery, Rue Croix-des-Petits-Champs, with fairly large gardens covering a third of the present Place des Victoires. He lived mainly at Saint-Mandé however, adjoining the park of Vincennes. To the modest house he

190 Meudon: view from the Orangerie, showing Le Nôtre's later arrangement of the central vista.

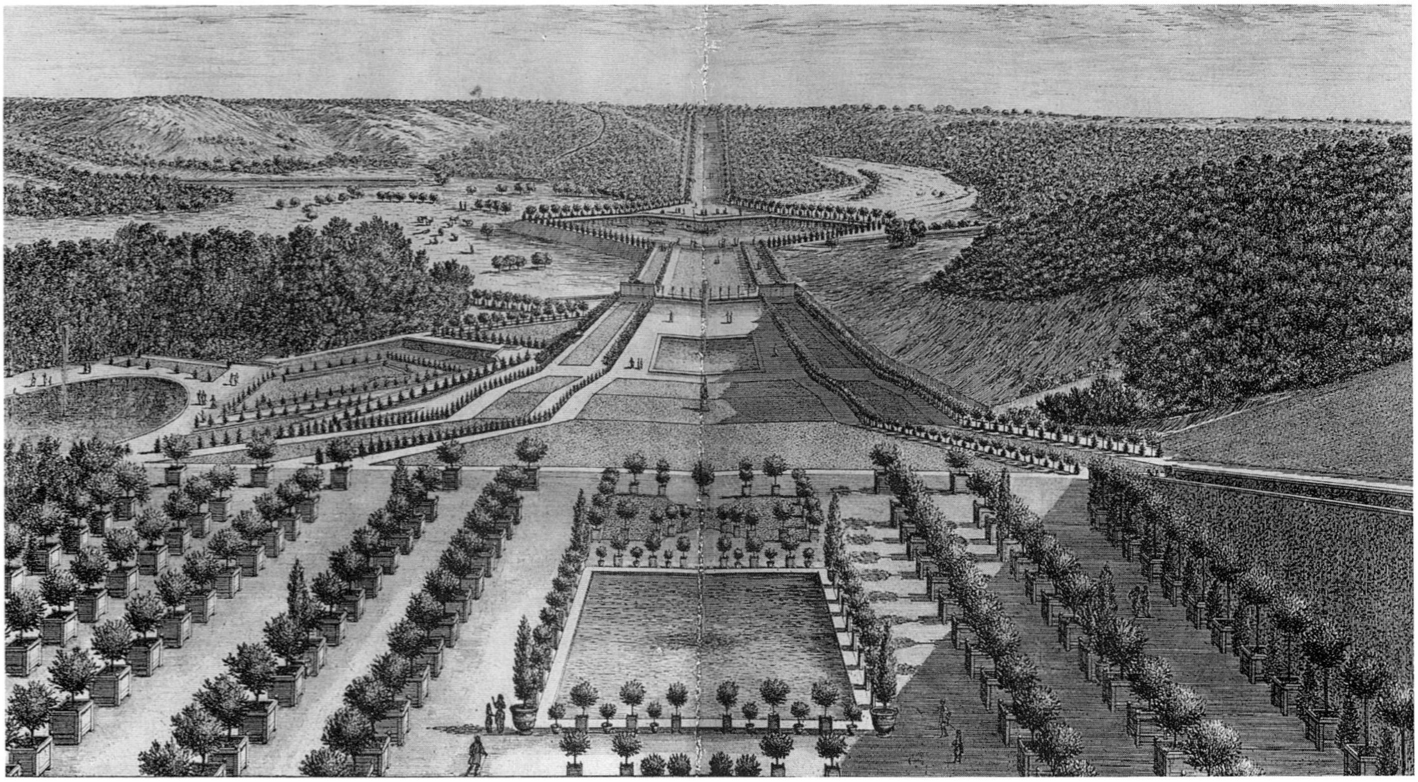

191 Saint-Mandé: plan of the château and garden in 1663.

added galleries to contain his collection of sculpture and his library of 27,000 books. In contrast to Vaux, Saint-Mandé was a private place, frequented by scholars and poets; and where (the abbé de Choisy wrote), while the world thought he was shut in his study devoting himself to the work of the state, 'by a secret staircase he descended to a little garden . . . where nymphs came to keep him company for weight of gold'.

191 The garden was the most notable aspect of Saint-Mandé, covering some 30 acres, and disposed in the classical manner formulated by André Mollet, except that the axis, instead of following that of the house, lay to one side of it. The main entrance led directly to the garden, which was separated from the forecourt by a *grille*. The main garden was about 100 metres square, the central part laid out in the prescribed sequence: *parterre de broderie*, lawns, *bosquets*. On the right an *allée* of cypress separated these from the *potager*. The corresponding part on the left-hand side, facing the orangery, was planted with trees, probably fruit trees. The central *allée* extended a further 100 metres or so to a balustraded terrace adjoining the Paris road. One boundary turned to follow this; the other was made to correspond in plan, forming a pentagon. Adjoining the house, galleries opened onto two smaller *parterres* of *pièces coupés* with round basins in the middle. This much can be learned from the plan of 1663. The two small *parterres* were ornamented with antique herms representing two adolescents, one with drapery on his head, the other dressed as a senator. In the area containing a fountain in a circular basin, between the big *parterre de broderie* and the lawns, stood a goddess Flora and a Roman lady copied from the antique. A small garden to the left of this enclosed a *berceau* containing a statue of Atalanta; while in the crescent at the extreme left of the central *allée* stood a Roman emperor. The chief ornaments of the garden were plants, a rare collection of exotic flowers and shrubs in charge of a German gardener called Besseman. There were 200 orange trees, which were later among the spoils from Fouquet's gardens that ultimately went to enrich Versailles. Saint-Mandé was an outstanding garden, and in all probability the one from which Fouquet derived most enjoyment. As it is, it has been eclipsed by the splendours of Vaux, the ultimate achievement of French classical garden design.

Louis II Le Vau and André Le Nôtre

Although the gardens of Vaux are always regarded as the work of André Le Nôtre, there is no precise information as to the part played by gardener and architect. Nor perhaps does it matter; it suffices to say that a close collaboration must be assumed. Louis II Le Vau was a year older than Le Nôtre. His father was Inspecteur Général des Bâtiments; Louis II worked with him, and in 1638 held the post of Architecte du Roi. By 1654 he had a considerable reputation as an architect of town and country houses. The earliest of these was possibly the château of Sucy-en-Brie; his authorship is not established, but he worked on the Paris hôtel of the owner, J.-B. Lambert. There is no question, however, that he designed Le Raincy for Jacques Bordier, Intendant des Finances, where, tradition has it, the extensive gardens were laid out by Le Nôtre. That would not only have been their first collaboration, and Le Nôtre's first great garden, but it would provide the precedent without which it is hard to account for the sudden appearance of a masterpiece such as Vaux. The original seventeenth-century layout at Le Raincy was destroyed to make a *parc à l'anglaise* for Louis-Philippe-Joseph, Duc d' Orléans (Philippe Egalité), in the 1770s; and this in turn has been covered by the suburban development of Paris. A plan of 1663 and engravings

192 Le Raincy: axis parallel to the château, with steps leading to the wooded park.

by Silvestre and Gabriel Perelle, which preserve the appearance, suggest that it had at least some of the characteristics of Vaux-le-Vicomte: the sequence of fore-courts, château and elongated parterre on the main axis, which was extended at each end to the limits of the estate; the rising ground on the left, to the southeast, descending in terraces to the northwest; the secondary transverse axis parallel to the
192 garden front of the château, with steps ascending into the wooded park on one side and leading down to further gardens on the other. Since Le Vau's work at Meudon began in 1654 and continued until 1659, Meudon and Vaux continued side by side.

André Le Nôtre was born in 1613, in a house near the Tuileries where his father was one of the chief gardeners, with responsibility for the *parterre* of the Grand Jardin, which at that time was a walled area separated from the palace by a road. As a very young man André studied painting in the studio of Simon Vouet, where Charles Le Brun was a fellow student. All his life he bought paintings, and had some notable works in his collection, including pictures by Nicolas Poussin and Claude Lorraine. More significantly, he worked under François Mansart; and the lessons that he could have learnt there in the choice of ground and the siting of features cannot be underestimated. It is unlikely that Le Nôtre thought of becoming a painter or an architect in the full sense, but he certainly saw the importance of these disciplines in advancing himself in his profession. Although one of his life-long charges was to see that the flower garden at the Tuileries was stocked with flowers, 'even in the winter' as the contract says, yet his main concern and talent was in controlling the various parts of huge compositions, which we may properly call 'landscape gardens'. Exactly how he arrived at this expertise is not recorded. By 1635 he was head gardener to Gaston d'Orléans at the Luxembourg; and in 1637 he was given the succession to his father at the Tuileries, finally taking over the post in 1649. He was appointed Dessinateur des Parterres de tous les Jardins du Roi in December 1643. Apart from his hypothetical connection with Le Raincy, he had designed a new *parterre* in the Jardin de la Reine at Fontainebleau in 1645–6. But the post of Contrôleur Général des Bâtiments du Roi, to which he was appointed in 1657, gave him much wider powers. Henceforth he was classed among the king's architects.

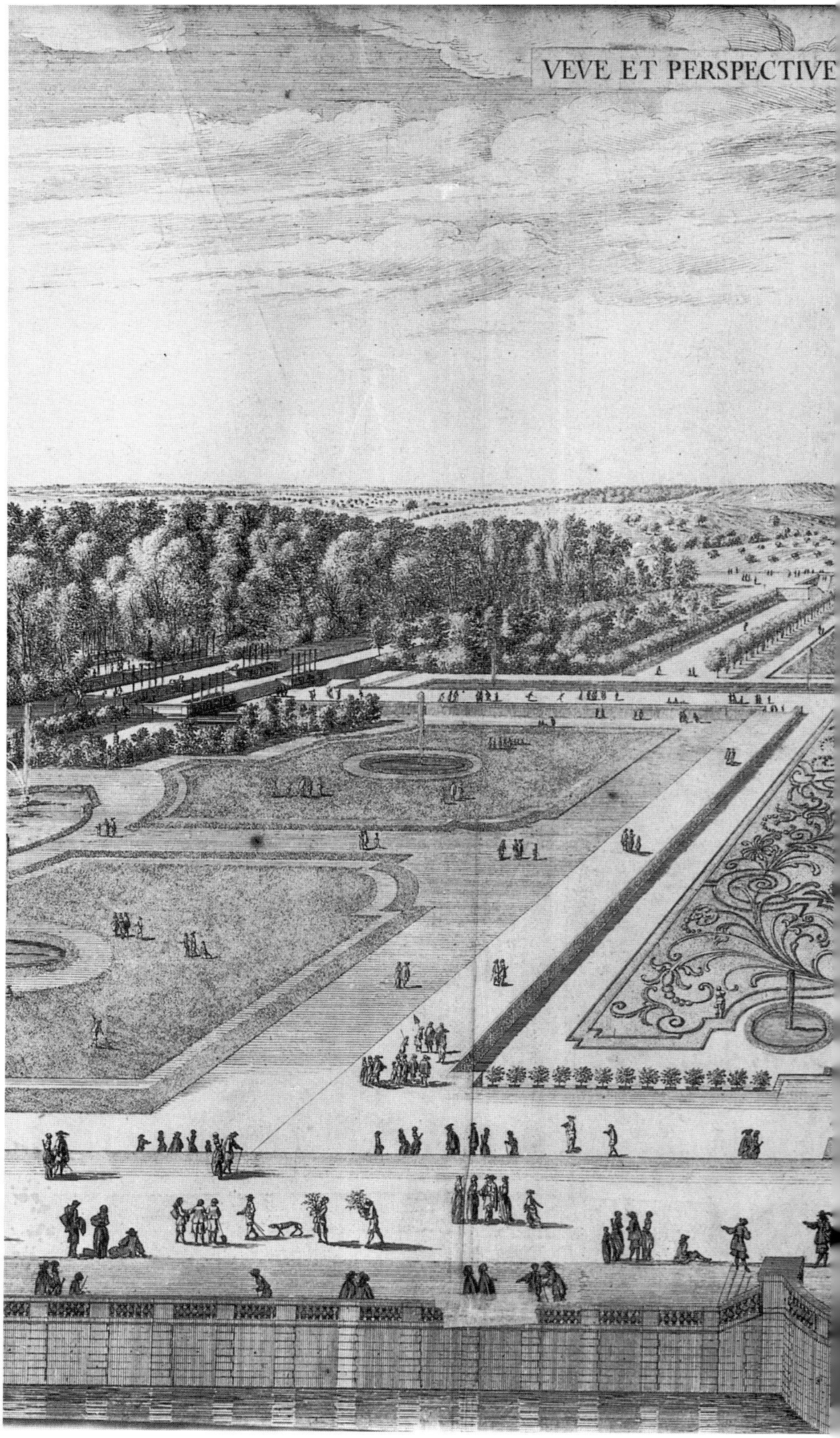

193 Vaux-le-Vicomte: the central vista looking away from the château.

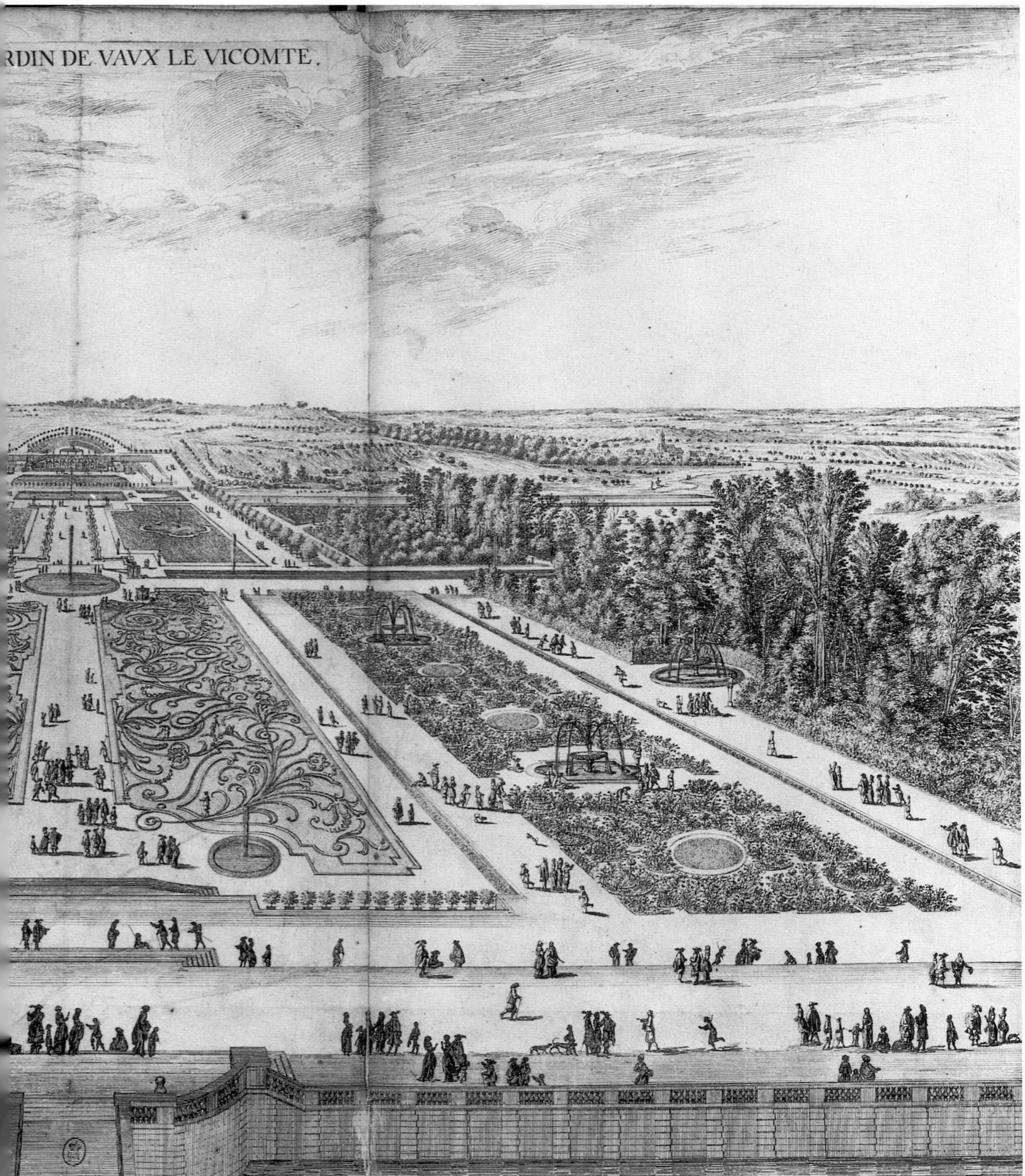
RDIN DE VAUX LE VICOMTE.

194 Vaux-le-Vicomte: the restored central vista as it is today.

195, 196 Views to the right and left of the central vista, looking away from the château: the flower garden (top) and the Fontaine de la Couronne.

Vaux-le-Vicomte

Vaux was a small estate inherited by Fouquet from his father in 1640, with no natural advantages, but bringing a title with it. He said in his *Défenses*[7] that he regarded it as his principal establishment and wished to make it a place worthy of his position. The earliest document is a plan annotated by Fouquet and signed by the architect, Le Vau, on 2 August 1656. An agreement between Le Vau and the contractor Villedo[8] was dated eight days later. In the dedication to Fouquet of Claude Mollet's *Théâtre de Plans et Jardinages* (1652) the publisher refers to the 'superb gardens of Vaux-le-Vicomte where you set Art to fight with Nature, and add each day new beauties and enrichments.' This means that work on the garden had begun previously; inevitably much levelling had taken place to create the levels and the platform on which the château was to be set. The archetypal French garden plan, as formulated by André Mollet, was a rectangle divided by *allées* into a regular grid, with a hierarchy of parts (*parterre de broderie*, *parterre de gazon*, *bosquet*) arranged symmetrically about the central axis; an idealized Tuileries. Even the Petit Parc at Versailles retains this form deriving from its origins. Variety occurred in the planting and arrangement of the individual rectangles, which nevertheless remained distinct from one another. Just as in older gardens of great extent, like Richelieu, the effect was additive; one garden added to another. Modifications of the ideal resulted from the emphasis on the central axis, and its extension beyond the bounds of the garden; and the emphasis of secondary axes at right angles to the main ones.

The originality of Vaux does not lie in any of the above characteristics, but in the way they are integrated into a unified design, perceived in every dimension and from every point of view. Plans and aerial views of Vaux do little to advance our understanding; like all Le Nôtre's compositions it has to be seen on the ground. And it takes time; it cannot be seen at a glance; it grows in the mind. Unlike Servien's Meudon, it owed nothing to the site, which was rough and uneven. The village of Vaux-le-Vicomte, and the hamlets of Jumeau and Maison Rouge had to be removed before levelling could begin to create an enormous platform, sloping from north to south towards the valley of the little River Anqueil, which was enlarged to make a monumental canal nearly a kilometre long at right angles to the main axis. The ground also sloped gently from west to east across the main axis. The differences in level
are small and the transitions between the various areas so 193
skilfully managed that the boundaries between them are hardly noticeable; one moves easily from one to the other, so much so that the revelation of the cascades and the canal is all the more dramatic. From the château the vista appears continuous; the architectural grotto forming the base of a terrace on the far side of the canal seems to sit on the edge of a rectangular basin immediately above the invisible cascades, while beyond, the ground rises behind a grass amphitheatre to a colossal statue of Hercules silhouetted against the horizon.
Conversely, from the amphitheatre, the cascades fall into place 197
as the foreground of a vista which has as its climax the château raised upon a platform, twenty steps above its surroundings. The *parterre de broderie*, immediately below the windows of the château, is the central part of three levels descending from the
flower garden on the right to the sunken water garden with 195
the Fontaine de la Couronne on the left, implying a transverse 196
axis.

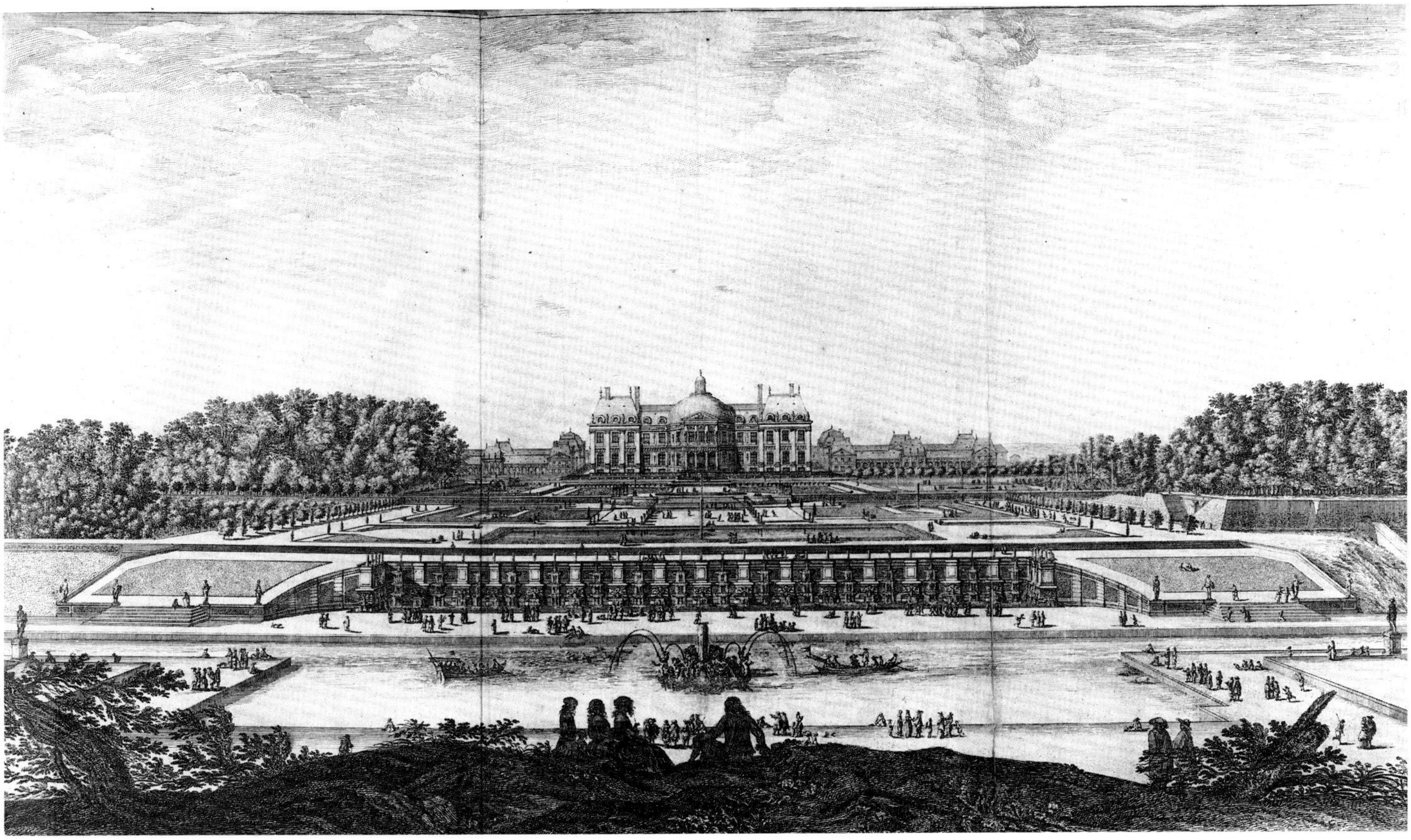

197, 198, 199 Vaux-le-Vicomte: a view looking towards the château (above), showing the cascades; the Grille d'Eau (above right); and the view from the Grille d'Eau towards the *potager* (below right).

Architectural features in the rising ground on the left also
198 mark secondary axes. The most important is the Grille d'Eau, monumental steps facing down the *allée* below the parterre
199 and leading to the gates of the *potager*; the Confessional, lower down, a grotto with a three-arched opening supporting a terrace, implies another less strongly marked axis. Thus, although the main emphasis is on the principal vista along the axis of the house, there are invitations to contemplate the garden from every direction; and the width of its area ensures that the château is always in view. It is also one of Le Nôtre's qualities that the parts are proportional to the whole; the generous approaches are a necessary introduction to the scale of what follows; the size of the basins and the width of the walks are such as to give the right effect when seen from the château; the water is so placed as to catch the light or the
203 reflection for the best effect. The huge size of the cascades and the grotto, and the steps and ramps round them, are in proportion to their distance from the château; in fact one of the skills in designing such features is to know how to make them read at a distance.

The sculptural programme was directed by Charles Le Brun, six years younger than Le Nôtre, but already with an established reputation. He had collaborated with Le Vau at the Hôtel Lambert; and as soon as the building of Vaux was far enough advanced Fouquet installed him in the château to supervise the decoration. The work in the garden was carried out by the sculptors Michel Anguier and Lespagnandel, the most important part being in the grotto, where two enormous river gods by Lespagnandel were placed in niches beneath the steps on either side. Most of the statues that decorated the garden were soon to be removed, leaving the carving that was an integral part of the architecture: the huge herms between
the niches of the grotto; the masks and bowls of the Grille 200
d'Eau and Cascades; the giant Janus-faced pillars supporting 201
the forecourt *grille*. Some of the intended sculpture, such as the Galatea and Cyclops mentioned by Mademoiselle de Scudéry,[9] was never put in place. The series of herms designed by Nicolas Poussin,[10] bought and transported to Versailles in 1684, were commissioned in 1655 by Nicolas Fouquet's brother, the Abbé Louis Fouquet. According to the inventory made in 1665, ten were in the 'grand parterre' and two 'à côté de la gerbe au dessus de la grande cascade'. So far as can be seen in Silvestre's drawings, two stood against the hedge at the corners of the little semicircular recess on the right of the flower garden, four against the semicircular hedge behind the Fontaine de la Couronne on the left, and six were grouped round the circular basin and the steps at the bottom of the *parterre de broderie*. The subjects (Pan, Faunus, Hercules,

200, 201 Vaux-le-Vicomte: the canal and *grotte* (above) and Grille d'Eau (below).

Pomona, Minerva, Bacchus, Ceres, Flora) are those associated in Classical times with gardens, horticulture or fertility generally, and were inspired, says Blunt, by the famous series of antique herms in the gardens of the Villa Ludovisi in Rome.

The fountains, under Claude Robillard, were integrated with the architecture to a degree not seen before: enlivening the static framework with their sound and movement; spraying out from the centre to fall into a basin as in the Fontaine de la Couronne; in rows of single jets, as in the Grille d'Eau; or lining the central walk, 'like a crystal balustrade' as Mademoiselle de Scudéry described it. The volume of sound increased with the scale of the architecture, reaching a climax 202
at the Cascades, the water pouring over the rocks on the 203
opposite side of the canal, and the 'jet of water fifteen feet high, of a width so prodigious and extraordinary that it seemed like a glass column', rising from the circular basin above the grotto.

Vaux epitomizes the spirit in which the great gardens of the seventeenth century were made. It is the culmination of those tendencies which we have observed towards the garden as a pure work of art, from which the useful side of horticulture has been removed. At the same time, while the workmanship compels admiration, the talent and resources devoted to its achievement are disproportionate to the end. As a place of private enjoyment it is almost entirely useless, compared with Lante, for instance, the Italian masterpiece in which the architectural ideal of the relation of the parts to the whole is most nearly realized. As Alberti had maintained, proportion-

202 Vaux-le-Vicomte: the Cascades today.

must be observed in the social as well as in the physical dimensions. The well-known sequel to the making of Vaux shows that there is a limit to which a demonstration of wealth and power is tolerated in individuals. Fouquet himself understood this too late. Anyone in his position was a subject of envy and suspicion. Even though he may not have used public funds to his own advantage to a greater degree than others of his contemporaries (Mazarin for instance), the fact that he was evidently engaged in extravagant building suggested that he did. As he said in his *Défenses*, he enjoyed a large income from various sources, including his wife's estates; but when he started to build, the plans were bigger than he intended, and the expense far exceeded the estimate. Among his enemies was Jean-Baptiste Colbert, assistant to Mazarin, extremely able, and ambitious to succeed to Fouquet's post. When Servien died in 1559, he fully expected to be appointed; but the cardinal, having first thought of appointing himself, left Fouquet in sole control. Two years later, when Mazarin himself lay dying, Colbert persuaded him to denounce Fouquet to the king. Louis had personal reasons for animosity towards the Surintendant. He was twenty-three and was in love with Louise de la Vallière, an intrigue which had begun as a cover for his flirtations with his sister-in-law, Henriette d'Angleterre, but which had developed into the first serious attachment of his life. Louise, who was a simple girl without money or any great position, returned his affections without reserve. Fouquet, paying court to a person whom he sensed might be of some influence, sought to advise her, and put large sums of money at her disposal. Outraged at what she regarded as an invasion of her deepest private feelings, Louise complained to the king, whose resentment at Fouquet's presumption knew no bounds. When Fouquet entertained the Court at Vaux on 17 August 1661, his downfall was already planned; and it was only because of the intervention of Anne of Austria, the queen mother, that he was not arrested in his own garden at the moment of his apparent triumph.

It was his intention, having displayed his creation in all its magnificence, to offer it to his king; that is to say to offer to sell it. The scene on that occasion has amply been described.[11] The air was filled with the sound of a thousand fountains falling into marvellously fashioned basins, 'as if it were the throne of Neptune', as a contemporary put it. Louis advanced down the central walk towards the canal between walls of water from a hundred jets. He looked at the garden from every point of view. After a sumptuous supper, Molière's *Les Facheux* was performed on the steps of the Grille d'Eau. Molière appeared in his everyday clothes affecting to be taken by surprise, saying that he had no actors and no time to prepare the entertainment that was apparently expected, unless some unforseen help was forthcoming. He begged the king to order the spectacle to begin. Thereupon a shell opened, revealing a Naiad who delivered a prologue; trees came to life, statues walked and the spectacle proceeded. When night had fallen lanterns placed along the cornices of the château made it seem ablaze. The grotto was lit up; and suddenly from the grass amphitheatre beyond, a display of rockets shot into the air, forming figures of fleurs-de-lys and other devices above the heads of the spectators; while a whale advanced down the canal, discharging fireworks to the accompaniment of drums and trumpets, as if a furious battle were being fought. When all was apparently over, and the king was returning to the château, more rockets, fired from the dome, covered the whole of the garden with a vault of fire. Ten days later Fouquet followed the king to Nantes, where he had gone for the assembly of the Etats de Bretagne. Fouquet had received warnings of the danger he was in, but, eternal optimist, hoped that he was about to succeed to the post of Premier Ministre. Louis did not discourage the belief, while planning the arrest with Colbert. On the 5 September, Fouquet arrived at the château with the members of the Conseil, unaware that his disgrace was imminent. He was arrested as he left, outside the castle precincts, by D'Artagnan, an officer of La Compagnie des Mousquetaires.

During the three years it took to collect and assess the evidence against him, the balance of sympathy shifted in his favour. His defense was skilful and vigorous, more than a match for those who cross-examined him. The charges were high treason and embezzlement. Nine members of the Cour de Justice voted for the death penalty; thirteen for banishment and confiscation of his property. This was acquittal on the major charges; he would virtually go free. Louis intervened; Fouquet was sentenced to imprisonment for life in the fortress of Pignerol, where he died of a stroke in 1680.

The sale of the contents of Vaux and Saint-Mandé began in 1665 and continued until September 1666. Thousands of shrubs and trees in the nurseries went to the royal gardens. Madame Fouquet retained possession of Vaux, which was occupied by her eldest son Louis-Nicolas Fouquet, Comte de Vaux, an officer in the king's army. Without resources to maintain them the gardens fell into disrepair; the statues and even the lead from the fountains were sold. The Comte de Vaux died prematurely in 1705, aged forty-eight. His mother, who was still living, sold Vaux to Marshal Villars, recently created hereditary duke by Louis in recognition of his services in the Dutch wars.[12] Under the administration of Colbert the talents of Le Vau, Le Brun and Le Nôtre were exploited to the full. It was against Colbert's advice that Louis made his father's hunting lodge into his principal residence, and eventually the seat of government. It was in the public image that the largeness of Le Nôtre's ideas matched those of his master, so that Versailles became a symbol of French absolutism and, at the same time, the embodiment of the national genius. Versailles, however, stimulated many talents; and unlike Vaux, the final form was the result of modifications to the original concept over at least twenty years. That being so, it is perhaps appropriate to consider its development, apart from its place in the sequence of Le Nôtre's work as a whole.

203 Vaux-le-Vicomte: the Cascades in the seventeenth century.

Robert
R.B.D.B.

11

Versailles

After Fouquet's disgrace Colbert took control of the finances, although he was not officially appointed Contrôleur Général until 1665. He set out to build the sound manufacturing and trading base on which he saw prosperity must rest. The corollary was the defeat of rivals in these areas, particularly the Dutch, and the securing and expansion of French frontiers to the north and east. Notable military success followed under the generalship of those two old rivals of the Civil War, Louis II de Bourbon, Prince de Condé, and Henri, Vicomte de Turenne. The decline in Louis XIV's fortunes was due partly to his own mistaken policies, partly to circumstances outside his control. The revocation of the Edict of Nantes of 1598, by which the Protestant religion had been recognized in France, resulted in the emigration of Huguenots and a decline in trade. The fall of the Stuarts in England and the extinction of the Spanish Hapsburg line changed the balance of power in Europe. Louis' implacable enemy, William of Orange, became king of England in 1688. In the wars which followed, an alliance was formed against which Louis exhausted French resources. The building of Versailles corresponded with the period of Louis' rise to a position of unprecedented power in Europe, and incidentally with Colbert's good management of the state finances. After his death in 1683, Michel Le Tellier, Marquis de Louvois, a minister much devoted to war, took his place. The late 1670s and early 1680s were also critical in the king's personal life. His youthful passion for Louise de la Vallière had faded by 1667, giving way to the more sophisticated charms of Françoise-Athénaïs de Rochechouart, the Marquise de Montespan. By the time of the queen's death in 1683, Louis was already involved with the pious Madame de Maintenon, whom he secretly married a few months later.

Louis XIV's increasing attachment to his father's little hunting lodge led to its progressive enlargement, first as a place of entertainment, a setting for elaborate spectacles inspired by those he had seen at Vaux-le-Vicomte; then, as his visits became more frequent, the château was enlarged, finally being transformed into a palace, the Court's principal residence and seat of government. As Versailles became a place where Louis lived in public, so he made private retreats, first at Trianon, and later at Marly. The palace now formed the focus of a new town, a veritable garden city which embraced not only the 205
gardens of the palace itself (the Petit Parc and the Potager du Roi) but those of Trianon and the château of Clagny, built for Madame de Montespan (1674–6). We are so familiar with the famous view to the west, the grand canal leading to the two poplar trees on the horizon, that it may come as a surprise to learn that this was not part of the original concept, and that the main vista until 1668 was to the south, over the Orangerie. This was due partly to the nature of the site, and partly to an unusual arrangement of the apartments in the first enlargement of the château by Louis Le Vau.

The structure of Versailles: 1661–8

Louis XIII's small château and park were surrounded by marshy land on which water accumulated in huge standing ponds. The house was shut in on three sides by the woods of the park, sloping away on the south, east and west. Louis XIV's first extensive work at Versailles was done between 1661 and 1664, shortly after his marriage to the Infanta Marie-Thérèse. The team he employed was the same that had made Vaux-le-Vicomte: Louis Le Vau, Charles Le Brun, and André
Le Nôtre, but controlled by Jean-Baptiste Colbert. While the 204
interior of the château was being modified to accommodate the king and queen, major work was undertaken to establish a platform on which further additions to the building would
depend. Le Vau's Orangerie and the terrace above it were 206
made in 1662–3, and were reminiscent of his work at Meudon. Marie-Thérèse's apartments in the south wing looked over the so-called Parterre de l'Amour, laid out by Le Nôtre in 1662,[1] to the hills of Satory. A plan of about 1664–5[2] shows a
projected hexagonal lake on the site of the future Pièce d'Eau 207
des Suisses. The king's apartments in the north wing overlooked a parterre divided into four by walks, and extended beyond the central axis in a tapering cascade ending
in a circular basin. The width of this parterre was doubled in *Frontis*
1663, and laid out in an original manner by Le Nôtre, with two symmetrical parts, each of five pieces composed of turf, surrounded by box-edged borders containing flowers and cut yews. Attention has recently been drawn to the political significance of the king's apartments being in the north wing, and the queen's apartments being given equal

204 Jean-Baptiste Colbert, Louis XIV's finance minister during the creation of Versailles, and the builder of Sceaux, a painting by Nicolas Robert.

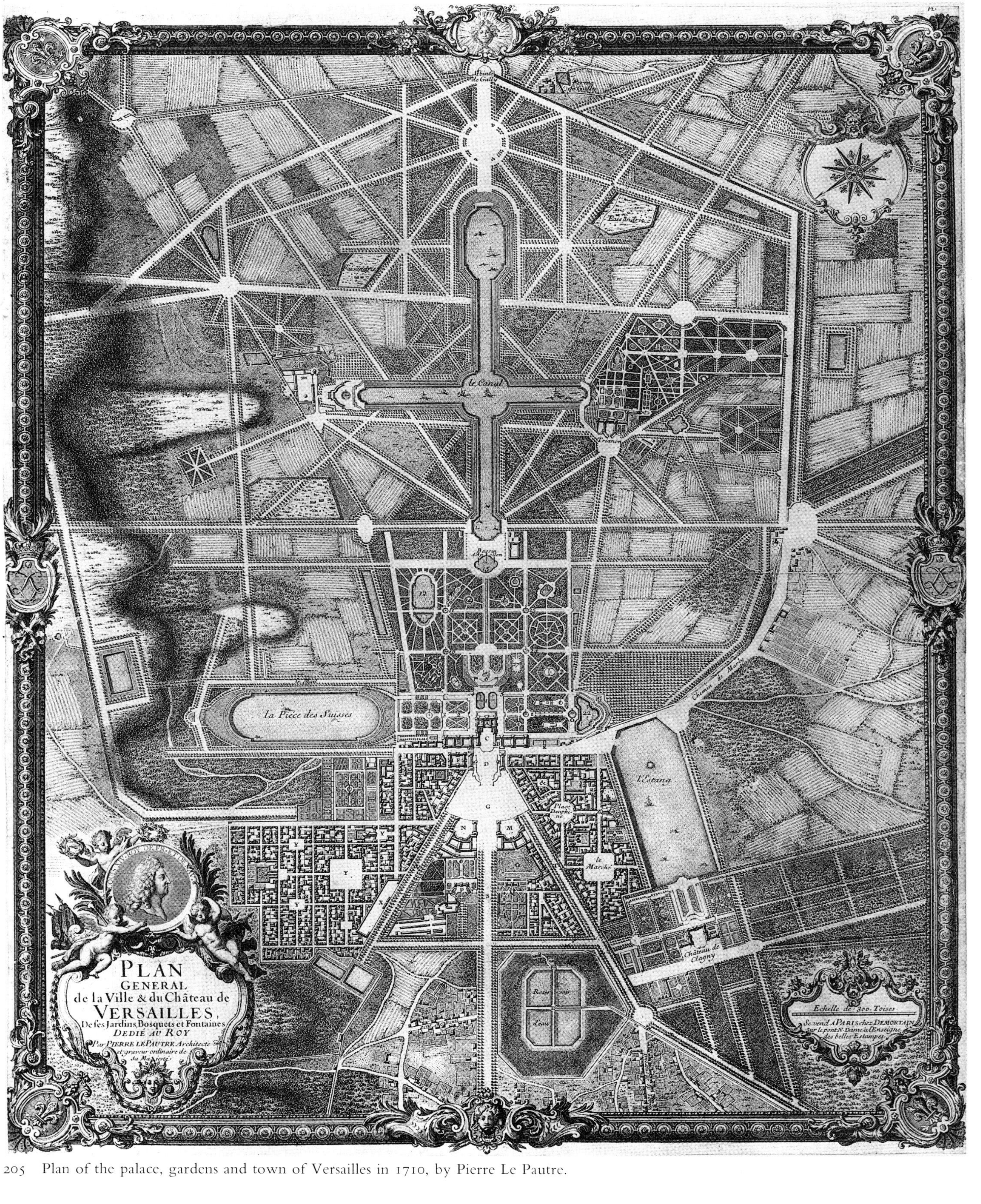

205 Plan of the palace, gardens and town of Versailles in 1710, by Pierre Le Pautre.

206, 207 Versailles in 1664: view from the south (above) and plan (right), showing a projected hexagonal lake.

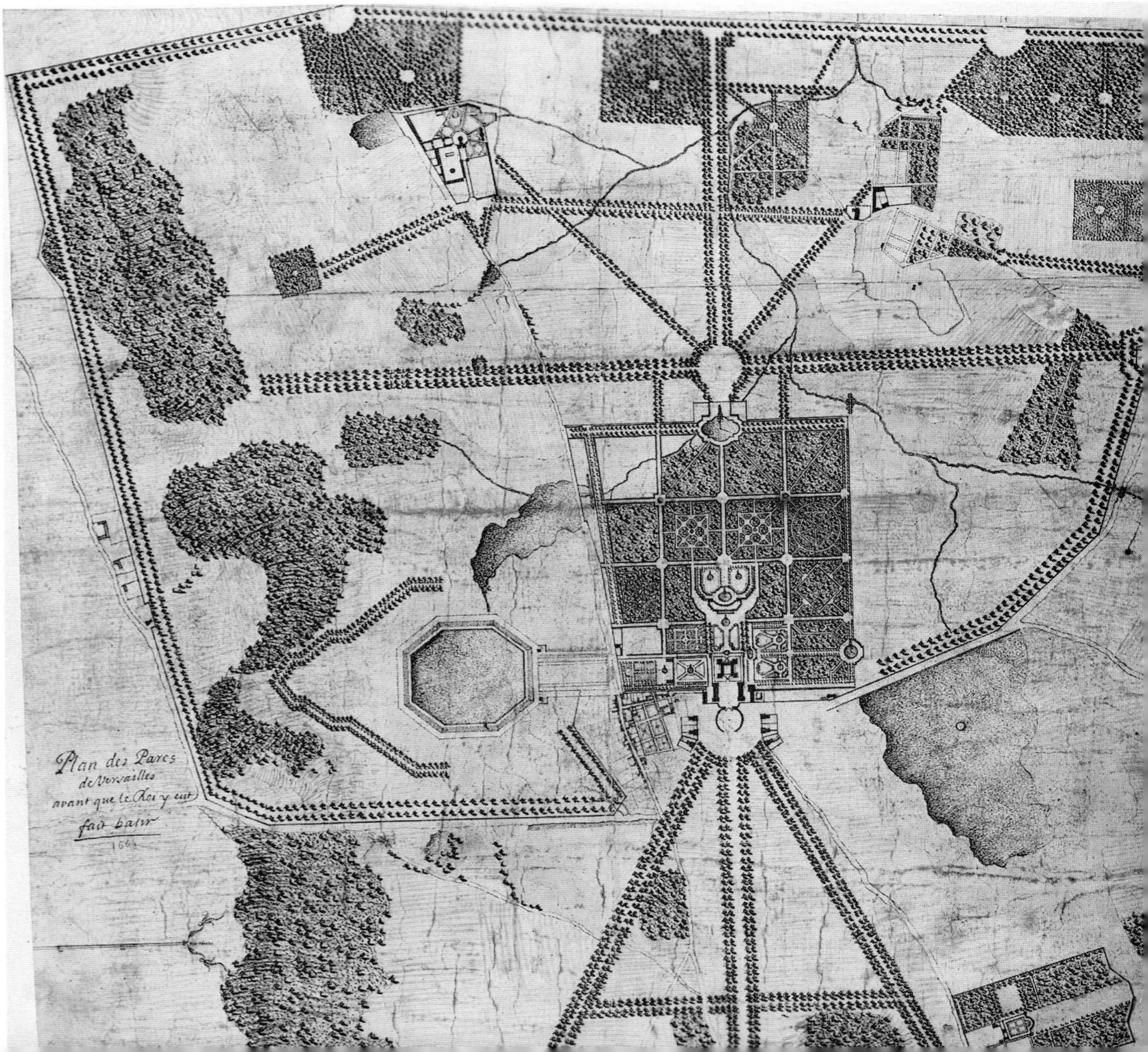

status – a recognition that Marie-Thérèse was a queen in her own right.[3] This arrangement, without precedent in the planning of a royal residence, was continued in Le Vau's new château of 1668–71; and it was only after the queen's death in 1683 that the king's apartment was moved to its customary position in the centre block.

Meanwhile, until 1667, the central *allée* (Allée Royale) on the axis of the château remained relatively narrow, ending in the so-called Bassin des Cygnes (later the Bassin d'Apollon) which had existed since the park was first made by Louis XIII. A plan of about 1663 shows the addition of a semicircular terrace to the west parterre, and the widening of the central *allée* as far as its intersection with the second transverse *allée*. On the occasion of *Les Plaisirs de l'Isle Enchantée*, five days of festivities given in May 1664, a stage was set up in this spot for
208 the first two spectacles. A drawing of this scene[4] shows the view towards the château, with the *allée* of trees, before it was cut down to make the Parterre de Latone and Bassin de Latone. The third day's spectacle took place on an island in the Bassin des Cygnes. At this time the canal did not exist. The Ménagerie, southwest of the Bassin des Cygnes, had just been completed at what was to be the end of the canal's southern arm. At a corresponding point to the northwest, the village and manor house of Trianon were being demolished, with some idea of making a garden; but the Trianon de Porcelaine had not yet been conceived.

Le Nôtre's most important contributions to the general concept were the opening of the areas immediately west and north of the château, and the Parterre du Nord (1663–4) with its extension in the Allée d'Eau (1666), and the Parterre de Latone (1664–5). The plan of about 1664–5, referred to above, shows these new additions. The Parterre de Latone, with Le Nôtre's characteristic architectural device of a horseshoe terrace to accommodate different levels and with ramps to facilitate descent on either side, was the first step towards a dominant axial development on the west. Although the canal was not begun until 1668, it must be assumed that it was conceived sometime earlier as part of Le Nôtre's scheme; but

208 *Les Plaisirs de l'Isle Enchantée*, the first day of the festivities held at Versailles in May 1664, showing the *allée* of trees leading towards the palace, later cut down to form the *tapis vert*.

209 Grotte de Thetis, built between 1667 and 1669 near the north wing of the palace of Versailles.

the fact that it was sited towards the setting sun was a happy circumstance from which symbolic interpretations followed. A step in this direction was the transformation of the Bassin des Cygnes into the Bassin d'Apollon, with Baptiste Tuby's group of Apollo and his horses (the rising sun), begun in 1668 and installed in 1670, a symbolic gesture which was not complete until the king's apartment was moved from the north wing to command the view from the centre of the château in 1683. The
209 Apollo theme had already been established in the Grotte de Thetis (1661–9), at the southeast corner of the north parterre, near the north wing of the château. This architectural grotto was nearly the last, and certainly the finest, of its kind: the walls and vaults richly decorated with designs of shell and rockwork, stones, crystals, corals, mother of pearl. From a large reservoir in the roof, hidden jets could issue as sprays or sheets of water falling over the walls. A water organ was installed in 1666, which among its effects produced the sounds of birds represented in shellwork in various niches. The iconography was suggested by Charles Perrault and the design carried out by his brother Claude. Apollo retires to sleep with the nereid Thetis, having made the circuit of the earth, just as the king retires to Versailles having worked for the good of all the world. The façade facing the gardens, with three large arched openings, was decorated with sculptured reliefs of Apollo in his chariot going down into the sea, flanked by groups of sirens and tritons. The wrought iron *grilles* closing the openings repeated the sun theme. Inside, opposite the entrance, the central niche contained a magnificent group (Les 225
Bains d'Apollon) by Girardon and Regnaudin, showing Apollo being bathed by the nymphs of Thetis; while in niches on either side, groups by the brothers Marsy and by Guérin, represented Apollo's horses groomed by tritons. The sculpture was installed in 1675.

It would be inappropriate in a general history to attempt to follow every detail of the changes which occurred in the gardens of Versailles; these have been recorded in Alfred Marie's monumental work;[5] but the main steps towards a final structural framework have to be understood.

The structure of Versailles 1669–78

The circumstances of Le Vau's second enlarging of the château are given in three undated memoranda by Colbert.[6] Colbert

210 Palace of Versailles from the side of the Parterre d'Eau before 1678.

had been opposed to Louis' ambitions for Versailles both because of the site and the expense. He favoured spending money on the Louvre, and in an earlier, now famous, letter had written that, 'failing brilliant feats of arms in war, nothing shows the greatness and mind of princes more than their buildings. . . . Oh! What a pity that the greatest and most virtuous king should be measured by the yardstick of Versailles!' The impossibility of acquiring property between the Louvre and the Tuileries, or land on the opposite bank of the Seine, now led to the conclusion that, with sufficient manpower, the marshy ground at Versailles could be made into a splendid garden with an unspoilt vista stretching into the forest on the horizon. One of the main problems was whether to pull down the old château or to preserve it, which was what the king wished to do. Colbert's first memorandum discusses the pros and cons of this issue, while repeating his observations on the disadvantage of the site for making anything more than a small *maison de plaisance*. He notes to begin with that 'All fine houses must be elevated, the more the better. The [house] at Versailles is almost hidden from the basin below by the amphitheatre parterre.' Sometime before 1669, Colbert set out instructions for what the king required. Various architects[7] submitted plans, those of Le Vau being ultimately selected. The old château was to be preserved, enclosed in an envelope consisting of two new north and south wings, linked by a terrace which left the old west front exposed. This is the château shown in the big bird's-eye-view painting of Patel and various engravings by Israel Silvestre in 1674.

The south apartments overlooked a parterre divided diagonally into four triangular compartments, with a circular basin in the centre, and enclosed by an iron *grille*. Steps on either side led to the Orangerie. Beyond the Saint-Cyr road a marshy piece of land extended to the hills of Satory closing the horizon.

The west apartments of the old château, not yet occupied by the king, opened onto a terrace between the newly built south and north wings. The features along the west axis were already established in their essentials. A water parterre replaced the earlier parterres of *broderie* and turf, a departure from the traditional ordering of the garden formulated by André 210

211 Versailles: the Bassin de Latone in 1678.

Mollet. The importance of this innovation in relieving the heaviness of the building by a foreground which reflects the sky can best be appreciated on the site. The complex form of the basins in 1674, was replaced after 1683 by two large ones roughly rectangular in shape. A broad flight of steps in the centre of Le Nôtre's horseshoe terrace led to the Parterre de
211 Latone, so-called because of the fountain (1668–70) represent-
213 ing Latona (Leto) with the infant Apollo and Diana, surrounded by six shepherds and frogs spouting water.[8] The reference is to an episode in the myth of Leto. When fleeing with her children, Apollo and Diana, from the wrath of Hera, she stops at a pool to drink, and is prevented by shepherds who stir the water to muddy it. Leto turns them into frogs. The symbolic association is with the childhood of Louis, when he and his mother were forced to fly from the Paris mob – circumstances which were of great importance in leading him to prefer Versailles.

The central *allée* (Allée Royale) was enlarged in 1667; and the lawn, (the *tapis vert*) was sown in 1680. Between the lawn
212 and the canal was the Bassin d'Apollon, with Tuby's group (1668–71) continuing the solar myth. The canal, $1\frac{1}{2}$ kilometres long and 62 metres wide, with branches to Trianon (400 metres) and the Ménagerie (600 metres), was completed between 1668 and 1672.

Unlike the extensive view over the Orangerie to the south, the vista on the north side has always remained relatively closed. At the end of the central *allée* of Le Nôtre's north
parterre (1663) stood Girardon's Fontaine de la Pyramide 214
(1670). Two ramps on either side led to the Allée d'Eau (1666), two rows of fountains falling into bowls supported by sculptured groups of children. At the bottom of the slope was a circular basin (1664), called the Bassin du Dragon from a sculpture which it received in 1667. Beyond, the wall of the park curved out in a crescent bay round the north of the basin, with a *grille* in the centre, according to a design given by Le Nôtre in 1664. Between 1679 and 1682 this bay was greatly extended to accommodate a much larger piece of water, first called the Pièce d'Eau des Sapins, and later (1684) the Bassin de Neptune.

212, 213, 214 Three Versailles fountains and their sculpture. Opposite above: Apollo and his horses, by Tuby, in the Bassin d'Apollon. Opposite below: the Bassin de Latone, as remade in 1689. Above: the Fontaine de la Pyramide by Girardon.

215 The Orangerie of Versailles, enlarged by Jules Hardouin-Mansart, 1682–88.

1678–88: THE ORANGERIE AND THE PIÈCE D'EAU DES SUISSES

Despite many modifications, especially in the sculptural ornament, the only major alteration of the main structure as it has been outlined above was in the south, when the château was enlarged for the third time by Jules Hardouin-Mansart.[9] Le Vau's Orangerie and the south parterre designed to complement the south front of Le Vau's château, were no longer proportional to the huge south wing which arose between 1679 and 1683. Le Nôtre, as we have seen, had already made a north parterre double the size of the original; it was logical, therefore, to make a south parterre of equal width, by cutting down the old *bosquet* known as the Bois Vert.[10] It
215 followed that the Orangerie also had to be enlarged; and this was done to Hardouin-Mansart's design between 1682 and 1688. It was not only twice as wide, but twice as high, since the ground of the old Orangerie had followed the natural slope to the Saint-Cyr road. This was now excavated to make a level parterre, designed by Le Nôtre with six compartments of cut turf and a round basin. Meanwhile, a huge rectangular lake[11] (approximately 670 metres by 220 metres) was being made to the south of the Saint-Cyr road. Called the Pièce d'Eau des Suisses because regiments of Swiss soldiers were employed in its excavation, it was begun in 1679 and finished in 1688. The earth was transported to raise the level of the new Potager du Roi which adjoined it on the east, and was being made simultaneously. Madame de Sévigné reported that bodies of dead workmen, killed by the marsh gas released by the digging, were carried away by the cartload every night.

The structural framework only existed by virtue of the control of vistas opened in the body of the Petit Parc which, as we have seen, originally enclosed the château on three sides. The site contained few natural advantages at all, and Le Nôtre's great achievement was to make a virtue of necessity in using those which did exist. Thus, the elevation of the château above the surrounding country suggested the extension of the main vista in the canal, which also served to drain the marsh. Such canals already existed at Vaux, Chantilly, Fontainebleau and elsewhere; but none were contrived to be seen with such favourable effect. The woods themselves, out of which this formal framework was contrived, were cut at right angles by secondary *allées*, and in the resulting areas of woodland a variety of *bosquets* were made with fountains and set pieces.

In contrast to the permanent framework, these were constantly changing so that their history is complex and confusing.

The Bosquets of Versailles 1664 to 1713

	DATE	ORIGINAL BOSQUETS	SUBSEQUENT CHANGES
1	1664	North bosquet	1669 Bosquet du Dauphin
2	1664	South bosquet	1669 Bosquet de la Girandole
3	1664–77	Le Labyrinthe	
4	1670–4	Le Marais	1704 Bains d'Apollon (2nd site)
5	1671	Le Berceau d'Eau	1677–8 Les Trois Fontaines
6	1671–2	Le Pavillon d'Eau	1677–8 L'Arc de Triomphe
7	1671–2	L'Etoile (La Montagne d'Eau)	
8	1671–4	L'Isle Royale	
9	1671–4	Le Miroir	
10	1671–4	Le Théâtre d'Eau	
11	1671–4	La Salle des Festins (du Conseil)	1706 L'Obélisque
(a)	1672	Bassin de Ceres	
(b)	1672	Bassin de Flore	
(c)	1673	Bassin de Bacchus	
(d)	1674	Bassin de Saturne	
12	1675–6	L'Encelade	
13	1675–8	La Renommé	1684–6 Bains d'Apollon (1st site) 1699–1704 Les Domes
14	1679–82	Bosquet des Sources	1685–7 La Colonnade
15	1680–3	La Salle des Antiques or Galerie d'Eau	1704 Salle des Marronniers
16	1681–3	La Salle de Bal	changed 1690–1. Restored 1712
17	1713	Le Bosquet de Diane (unfinished)	

216 Plan of the Bosquets of Versailles, made about 1680.

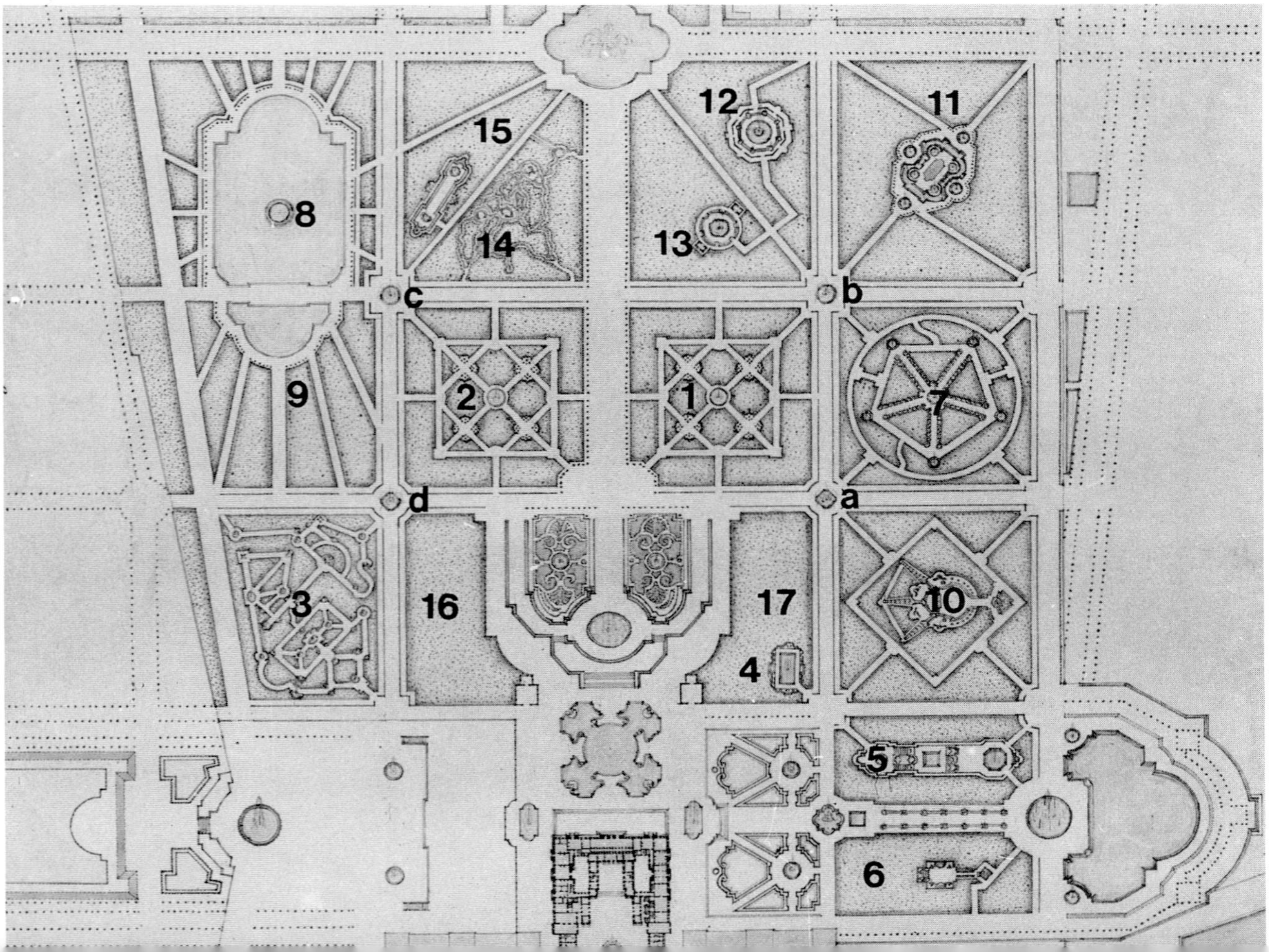

217, 218 Versailles: banquet at the Fontaine de l'Etoile (above) and the Bassin de Flore (below).

219 Versailles: Le Marais, a rectangular basin surrounded by reeds with a tree in the middle, all made of metal concealing jets of water.

The bosquets

Alfred Marie[12] describes the making of the *bosquets* and their
216 various transformations in detail. Only a summary can be attempted here, according to the main periods of their construction. Before 1664 they were few and fairly simple, consisting of walks laid out regularly (square or diagonal) and opening into green rooms at their intersection or in the centre. Such was the Bois Vert which was cut down when the south parterre was enlarged to correspond to Hardouin-Mansart's Orangerie. West of the Parterre de Latone were two symmetrical *bosquets* [1, 2], the north and south *bosquets*, called after 1669 du Dauphin and de la Girandole, on account of the fountains which were placed in the centres. The Labyrinthe [3], designed by Le Nôtre, was laid out between 1664 and 1667. After 1669 it was modified, and the whole assumed a didactic character by the addition of thirty-nine fountains and statues representing Aesop's *Fables*.[13] North of these was the
217 Bosquet de l'Etoile [7], consisting of a circular walk enclosing a pentagon, with paths radiating from the centre. This must have been in existence by 1668, because it was the setting for a banquet during the festivities which took place that year. On that occasion, the central basin was disguised, leaving a single jet shooting up from a rock. Round it were five large tables supported on gilded caryatids, loaded with different delicacies: a mountain concealing cold meats in its hollow, a palace made of marzipan and other sweetmeats, tiers of vases filled with liqueurs. After the king and ladies had eaten, the tables were abandoned to the followers, and the destruction of these beautiful arrangements provided further amusement to the court.[14]

As in the fêtes of 1664, elaborate settings were erected at the crossings of the *allées*: a theatre, a banquet hall and a ballroom. Although of a temporary nature, these were veritable works of architecture, which later gave the idea of more permanent constructions in the various *bosquets*. These served not only for collations and concerts but as showpieces in themselves. In 1672–3 permanent basins and fountains were set up at crossings, north and south of the central Allée Royale, representing the seasons. Between 1674 and 1677 these were
given statues of Ceres, Flora, Bacchus and Saturn.[15] 218

During the period between 1668 and 1682 Louis' visits to Versailles became more frequent, but it was still a private retreat and not the official residence of the court and the seat of government. It was the time when the Marquise de Montespan took precedence as royal mistress. It was she,
according to Charles Perrault (*Mémoires*), who suggested Le 219
Marais [4], a rectangular basin with a tree in the centre and surrounded by reeds, all composed of metal, and containing innumerable jets of water. The *buffets d'eau* set in rectangular niches on either side were a further innovation. André Félibien left the following description:

220 View of Versailles from the north after 1688, by J. B. Martin, showing the Bosquets of the Arc de Triomphe and the Trois Fontaines, made in 1677.

221 The Théâtre d'Eau, one of the most ingenious of the Versailles water-spectacles, in a painting by Jean Cotelle.

[Le Marais] is a little wood with a big rectangular piece of water, longer than it is wide, in the middle of which is a big tree so ingeniously made that it appears natural. From the tips of its branches spring many jets of water which cover the Marais. Besides these, a great many others spurt from the reeds which fringe the borders of the basin. At the two ends and in the thickness of the *palissades* are two green recesses like small rooms into which you go up by two turf steps. In each recess there is a big white marble table, and on each table is a basket of gilded bronze full of life-like flowers from which rises a big jet of water which falls back and is lost without wetting the table. There are similar recesses in the middle of the sides of the rectangle where, raised on grass steps, are long tables of white and red marble with tiers of shelves arranged as *buffets*. From these shelves water flows, which by various adjustments forms ewers, goblets, decanters and other kinds of vase, which seem to be made of rock crystal decorated with red and gold.[16]

Four other fountain displays of varying complexity were begun in 1671 in the *bosquets* on the north side of the Petit Parc; the Pavillon d'Eau and the Berceau d'Eau, respectively east and west of the Allée d'Eau, were replaced in 1677 by the Arc
220 de Triomphe [6] and the Trois Fontaines [5].

West of these (i.e. north of the Marais in line with the
Parterre de Latone) was the Théâtre d'Eau [10], perhaps the 221
most ingenious of the set pieces which the combined talents of Le Nôtre and François Francine contrived. Félibien describes it as a big round space, about 52 metres in diameter, divided into two; one part being an amphitheatre with three tiers of turf seats, the other a stage, just over a metre higher. Three *allées* converged on the stage, each with a canal falling in cascades whose water flowed ultimately into basins surrounding the stage. On either side of the canals, round about the stage and in niches in the hedge surrounding the auditorium, were a multitude of fountains, whose jets could be changed in five different ways: straight upward; curving to make *berceaux*, inwards or outwards; or circles, in front or behind. Rock and shell-work, sculptured vases and the bowls into which the water fell, added to the decorations. The theme of the sculpture was infancy; and naked infants singly or in groups were represented mounted on a dolphin, playing with a swan or some other object with aquatic associations; while the fountain at the end of the three *allées* showed the gods Jupiter, Pluto and Mars in infancy. The sculptors Desjardins, Houzeau, Le Gros, Masson and Tuby worked under the direction of Charles Le Brun. Lines of tapering yew, clipped hornbeam

222, 223 Two of the features added to the Versailles gardens in the 1680s, the Colonnade (above) and the Salle de Bal (below).

hedges, climbing plants and porcelain pots filled with a changing variety of flowers, created a polychrome effect, the taste for which (as Marie points out) disappeared in the eighteenth century. We have dwelt on this *bosquet* at some length as representative of its kind; a theatre composed mainly of water and plants. Inevitably these *bosquets* decayed and
223 disappeared, while their architectural successors (Salle de Bal
222 [16] and the Colonnade [14]) have survived. The Salle des Festins (or Salle du Conseil [11]) in the northwest corner of the Petit Parc, was designed by Le Nôtre at the same time as the Théâtre d'Eau in 1671.

The southwest corner of the Petit Parc was very marshy. Before the canal was made, a large pond on the south side of the Saint-Cyr road drained across it into the Bassin des Cygnes (d'Apollon). Between 1671 and 1673 a large rectangular basin was excavated here, with an island in the middle (the Ile Royale [8]); and adjoining it, across the transverse *allée* to the east, another semicircular basin (the Miroir [9]). Work on consolidating, planting and furnishing these ponds, went on until 1680. Meanwhile, in the *bosquet* north of the Ile Royale, Le Nôtre, departing entirely from principles of regularity, created a place of meandering streams and islands (the Bosquet des Sources [14]), an essay which he perfected at Trianon in 1687–8. Proceeding north, on the other side of the Allée Royale, were the *bosquets* of La Renommée [12] and
224 L'Encelade [13], created in 1675. L'Encelade,[17] a large circular basin in the centre of which an enormous giant engulfed by rocks (the figure by Gaspard Marsy) shoots a massive column of water into the air, is the only one of these pre-1680 *bosquets* to survive today. By their nature many are subject to decay, even when they were not destroyed to satisfy Louis' whims for something new. Thus, the Trois Fontaines, said to have been conceived by the king himself, replaced the Berceau d'Eau [5] in 1677; at the same time as the Arc de Triomphe replaced the Pavillon d'Eau [6]. The Salle des Antiques [15] was the last of the elaborate set pieces to be commenced before Hardouin-Mansart's influence began to be felt. In 1704, when Louis began to tire of these elaborate compositions, it was replaced by a simple lawn surrounded by chestnut trees (the Salle des Marronniers).

When Versailles became the official residence of the court, the gardens lost any privacy they may have had, and became an instrument of propaganda demonstrating to all Europe the superiority of French gardening. Louis himself wrote instructions on how tours should be conducted.[18] By 1689 (the date of the first of these manuscripts) important new additions to the *bosquets* had been made. Their essentially architectural character showed how the influence of the king's architect was replacing that of his gardener[19] in these matters. The Salle de Bal (1680–3) was the least so, being an oval bowl-shaped theatre, enclosed at the highest level with chestnut trellis. The sides rose steeply in nine turf steps. These faced five cascades, also arranged in steps, lined with exotic shells loosely attached with brass wire so that they trembled and rang as the water flowed over them. This sound mingled with the music of the instruments when concerts were given here. The musicians were seated on an island in the arena surrounded by the canal into which the water from the fountains and cascades flowed. This island was later suppressed, the arena levelled in 1690–1, and flowers were introduced: 100 double stocks (*giroflées*), 2150 sweet rocket (*juliennes blanches*), 250 veronica and 300 roots of pink. The Salle de Bal was designed in a previously unused *bosquet* between the Parterre de Latone and the Labyrinthe.

In June 1684 the king ordered La Colonnade to be built of marble on the site of the Bosquet des Sources [14]. This is the most purely architectural of the *bosquets* at Versailles, a circular arcade of thirty-two arches supported on coupled Ionic pillars and within each a single jet of water falling in a bowl. Thirteen sculptors were employed to make the reliefs decorating the spandrels; while Girardon's group of the Rape of Proserpine by Pluto, commissioned in 1675, was eventually put in the centre in 1699. Attention has already been drawn (Chapter 2) to parallels between the Colonnade and Colonna's peristyle in the Island of Cythera.

On the opposite side of the Allée Royale, the Bosquet de la
Renommé [13] was renamed Les Bains d'Apollon (Apollo 225
bathed by nymphs) in 1684, when the sculpture from the Grotte de Thétis was moved there. A new *bosquet* was created for it in 1704, adjoining the Parterre de Latone on the north, part of which had been occupied by Le Marais [4]. In 1778 a rock setting was designed by Hubert Robert, which is how the groups of Apollo bathed by nymphs and Apollo's horses appear today.

224 L'Encelade, created in 1675.

225 An engraving by J. Rigaud (1730) of the second *bosquet* (1704) created to receive the groups of Apollo bathed by nymphs originally made for the Grotte de Thétis.

Sculpture

The sculpture programme at Versailles surpassed any other in Europe, both in the number of statues and their quality. Charles Le Brun determined the subjects and made the drawings from which a team of between forty and fifty sculptors worked. The chief of these had others working under them, so that despite the numbers of people involved, there is a unity of style which makes it hard to distinguish the work of one from another. Plaster models were set in place on wooden

plinths to ensure beforehand that the statue was of the right proportion.

Before 1668 the statues were relatively few, representing established garden-sculpture themes such as nymphs and satyrs; and also the theme of love, represented in groups of naked infants. The earliest of these were infants with the
296 Sphinx (1668–70) placed on either side of the steps leading to the Bassin de Latone. The theme of infancy, coupled with dolphins (these *dauphins* were an obvious reference to the royal heir) predominated in Le Brun's designs for the fountain of the
Pyramide; and groups of infants supported the bowls of the 214
fountains in the Allée d'Eau.

The principal theme was of course the analogy between
Louis XIV and Apollo, aspects of whose myths are represented 213
in the Bassin de Latone (see above), the Bassin d'Apollon 212
(1670–1, see above); and Les Bains d'Apollon (1666–75). The sculpture in the Labyrinthe, added between 1672 and 1677, followed a theme related to Aesop's *Fables*. It was the work of

about a dozen sculptors.[20] The number of statues greatly increased after 1674, with commissions for the decoration of the Parterre d'Eau. As Emile Magne was the first to note, Le Brun took his themes from Cesare Ripa's *Iconologia* which was translated into French in 1644. They were emblematic.[21] Five groups of four were commissioned representing the times of
226 day, the seasons, the elements, the temperaments, the modes of
227 poetry and the four parts of the world (the continents without
228 Australia). In addition to these there were to be four large groups representing the rapes of Proserpine, Orethyia, Cybele and Coronis. Only three were carried out; and none were placed in the Parterre d'Eau, which had meanwhile been given a new form. The groups of Saturn carrying off Cybele by Thomas Regnaudin, and Boreas and Orethyia by Gaspar Marsy and Anselme Flamen were first put in Hardouin-Mansart's Orangerie, and moved to the Tuileries after 1716. François Girardon's work, the Rape of Proserpine by Pluto, became the centrepiece of the Colonnade. Statues were always being moved about as the ornament of the *bosquets* changed; apart from that, one of their main situations was lining the Allée Royale and the outside of the *bosquets* framing the parterre. After 1683 the theme of France Triumphant emerges. A major piece with that title was placed in the *bosquet* of the Arc de Triomphe [6]; while a marble statue by the Italian Domenico Guidi, showing Fame writing the history of Louis le Grand, upheld by Time and treading Envy under foot, was placed in the Orangerie in 1686.[22] Bernini's equestrian statue of Louis, which arrived at the same time, was so disliked by the king that it was eventually relegated to the far end of the Pièce
d'Eau des Suisses. Two large marble vases by Antoine 229

Coysevox, with reliefs symbolic of war and peace, were placed on the terrace below the west front of the château in 1684; while between 1686 and 1690 the Parterre d'Eau itself received its final decoration of eight huge bronzes of gods and
230 goddesses representing the rivers of France, together with
231 other bronze statues of nymphs and cupids. An extended catalogue of all the sculpture at Versailles is beyond the scope of this brief outline. They included copies after famous antique
232 models, such as the Ariadne from the Vatican, first cast for François I at Fontainebleau, four groups of fighting animals on the north and south side of the terrace above the Parterre de Latone, innumerable vases, and of course the fountains in the various *bosquets* and the four main intersections of the *allées* north and south of the Allée Royale.

226, 227, 228 (facing page) Three statues at Versailles: Winter (from the Four Seasons, by Girardon); Earth (from the Four Elements, by Masson); and America (from the Four Continents, by Guérin).

229 Marble vase with emblems of the sun by Drouilly, Versailles.

230, 231 Two of the rivers of France: the Garonne, by Coysevox (above) and the Loiret, by Regnaudin (below).

232 Replica of the Vatican Sleeping Ariadne by Corneille van Clève.

Water

The outstanding feature of Versailles was its water, especially the elaborate fountain displays in which Louis XIV took a particular pride. Their architect was François Francine, Intendant de la Conduite et Mouvements des Eaux et Fontaines. Under him was the chief fountainer at Versailles. Until 1668 this was Denis Joly, who was taken ill while supervising the installation of the organ in the Grotte de Thétis. He was succeeded by Claude Denis, who in 1671 received a salary of 6000 *livres* for the upkeep of the pumps and fountains of Versailles, increased to 10,000 *livres* in 1673. This was a very large sum, equal to what François Francine was earning[23] from his various appointments; but out of this Denis had to pay his expenses, including the wages of his assistants. Colbert's *Règlement pour les fontaines de Versailles*, 9 November 1672 is instructive:

> The master-fontainer Denis must always have three assistant plumbers and six boys as is specified in his contract. They will all lodge in the pump building according to the allocation which will be made. None of the said assistants may lodge elsewhere on pain of dismissal from the service. None of them shall be taken off duty without giving us notice.
>
> The Sieur Denis will be obliged to give each their fixed post, with instructions as to what each must do when the king orders the fountains to be played.
>
> He will give them keys for the taps and fittings, ladders, whalebone rods [*baguettes de baleine*], and all other kinds of tool necessary to remedy faults in the fountains.
>
> Every time an assistant or boy is not found at his post when the order is given, the said Denis will be docked an *écu* for each assistant, and 30 *sols* for each boy, except that it is up to him to make the same cut.
>
> When one of them lacks one of the above mentioned tools in the presence of the king, the same reduction will be made. When any of them absents himself, the said Denis will be docked 6 *livres* for an assistant, and 3 *livres* for a boy for each day's absence.
>
> In the case of his not having the full number, 3 *livres* a day will be deducted for an assistant missing, and 30 *sols* a boy until they are replaced.
>
> The said Denis will be obliged to produce the said assistants and boys to the Contrôleur Général des Bâtiments serving in this place, or such another as we will entrust, and will not be paid by the treasurer except on the certificate of the said Contrôleur or another, declaring that he is satisfied with the contract and the present regulation.

Providing enough water, and above all pressure, to make the fountains work was always a problem in a site without much fall; and it increased as more fountains were created. The
233 fountain of the Encelade [12], for instance, had a very thick central jet rising to 23 metres, for which the water came 200 metres. It was never possible to have the fountains playing all at once. A highly organized routine was operated, involving boys with whistles, so that whenever the king or another important visitor was in the gardens, the fountain should be playing until he was out of sight. One of the main functions of the Intendant was to devise pumps and other means by which water could be raised and circulated. Until after 1680 the source of all the water was the pond at Clagny, northeast of the palace, from where it was raised by six pumps and four windmills into four reservoirs, one of which was on top of the Grotte de Thétis. Water, and the means of bringing it to Versailles, was a constant preoccupation; the cost of doing so reaching huge proportions. A sum of 40,000 *livres* was set aside in 1676 for Nicolas le Jongleur to search for new sources. A scheme for collecting water in artificial lakes and bringing it by means of aqueducts and underground conduits into the reservoirs of Versailles was devised by the astronomer Picard and completed in 1678. A similar and more ambitious scheme by the engineer Gobert was unfinished at Colbert's death in 1683. Meanwhile, a spectacular project for raising water from the Seine to the height of 162 metres had been devised by a Belgian, Baron Arnold de Ville. Known as the Machine de 234
Marly, it consisted of 14 huge waterwheels, 12 metres (36 *pieds*) in diameter, which powered a series of 221 pumps working at intervals up the hill, conveying water to reservoirs at Louveciennes and Le Trou d'Enfer, and thence to the royal gardens of Marly, Versailles or Trianon as required. The project cost over 3 million *livres* between 1682 and 1688; and the annual maintenance charge after that averaged between 50,000 and 60,000 *livres*.

But a still more extravagant plan was now afoot to satisfy the insatiable demands of the fountains of Versailles. In 1684 the possibility of diverting the waters of the River Eure was explored and found feasible. The great military engineer, Sebastien le Prestre, Seigneur de Vauban, was allotted 30,000 soldiers to build an embankment 20 metres (60 *pieds*) high, and an aqueduct over 5 kilometres long. Well over 8 million *livres* had been expended before events overtook the scheme. When Louis' determined enemy, William of Orange, became king of England in 1688 and set about creating an alliance, the soldiers were required for other duties and the aqueduct of the Eure was abandoned short of completion. The remains of this
monumental folly can still be seen today. At the château of 278

233 L'Encelade in the seventeenth century (compare ill. 224).

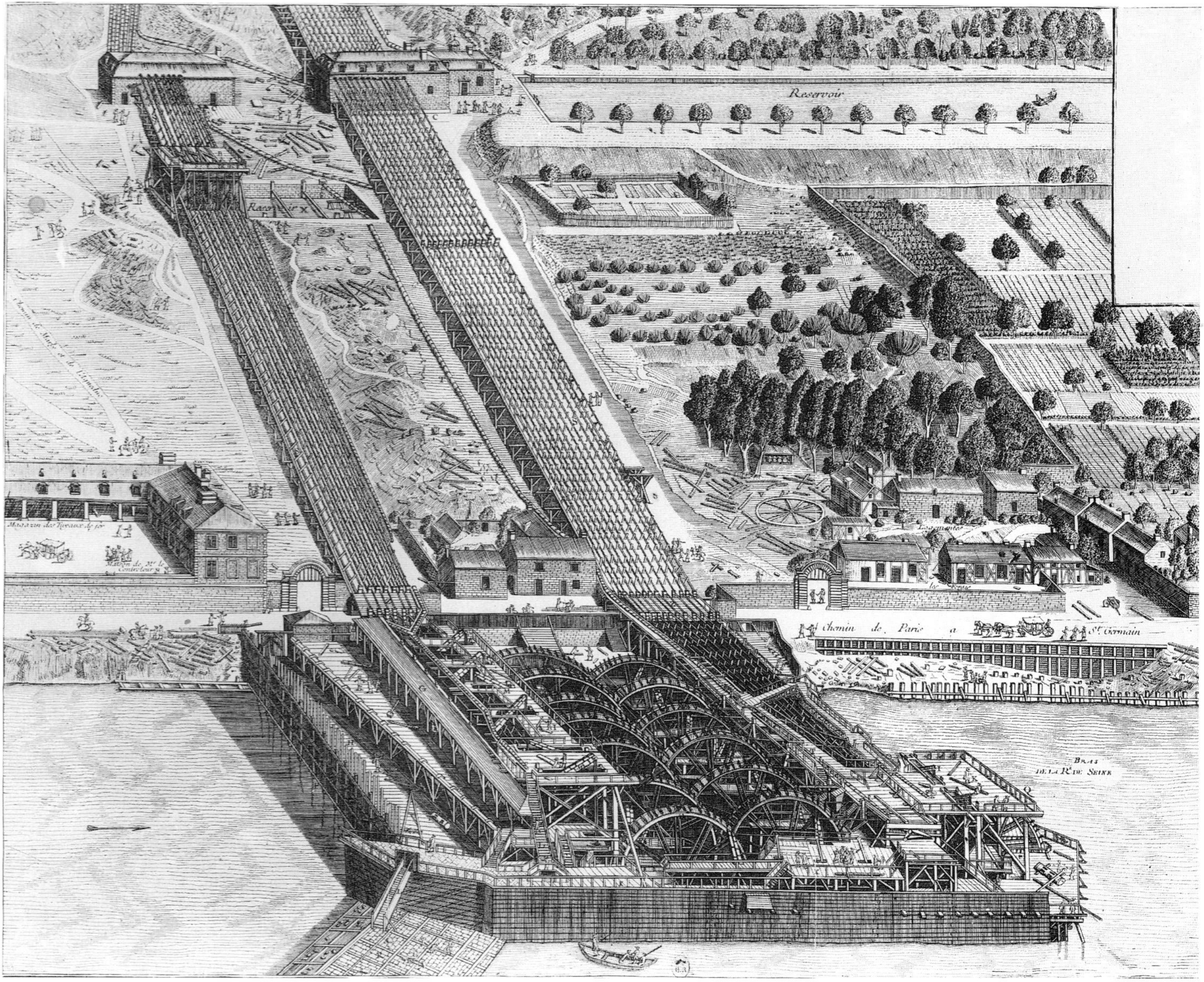

234 The Machine de Marly, fourteen huge water-wheels to raise water from the Seine for the fountains of Marly and Versailles.

Maintenon, from where Louis viewed its progress in 1686, it forms a melancholy, if impressive, termination to Le Nôtre's grand canal.

The Potager du Roi

The practical functions of the garden in providing fruit and vegetables for the court was not Le Nôtre's concern. From 1670 this was the responsibility of Jean-Baptiste de la Quintinye (1626–88), who had forsaken the profession of the law to study the physiology of plants, and in 1665 obtained the posts of gardener to the king, and to the Prince de Condé at Chantilly. In 1670 Louis appointed him Intendant pour les Soins des Jardins Fruitiers et Potager; and in 1673 Jardinier en Chef. The old *potager* was inadequate to supply the needs of the greatly extended palace as the seat of government. In 1677 Quintinye began to construct a new one, on a marshy site with a large pond, southeast of the château. He set about raising the level of the ground with the sand excavated from the Pièce d'Eau des Suisses, covering it with top soil from the nearby
hills of Satory. It was complete in 1683, a rectangular area 235
covering about 20 acres, with twenty-nine walled enclosures providing suitable conditions for growing all kinds of fruit and vegetable, including exotics such as sago-palm. The large central area was sunken and was divided into sixteen raised beds, with a round basin and a fountain in the centre. The terrace surrounding it was sufficiently high for vines to be grown against the walls.

235 The Potager du Roi, Versailles, the royal fruit and vegetable garden laid out by Jean-Baptiste de la Quintinye between 1677 and 1683. The key is given on the right.

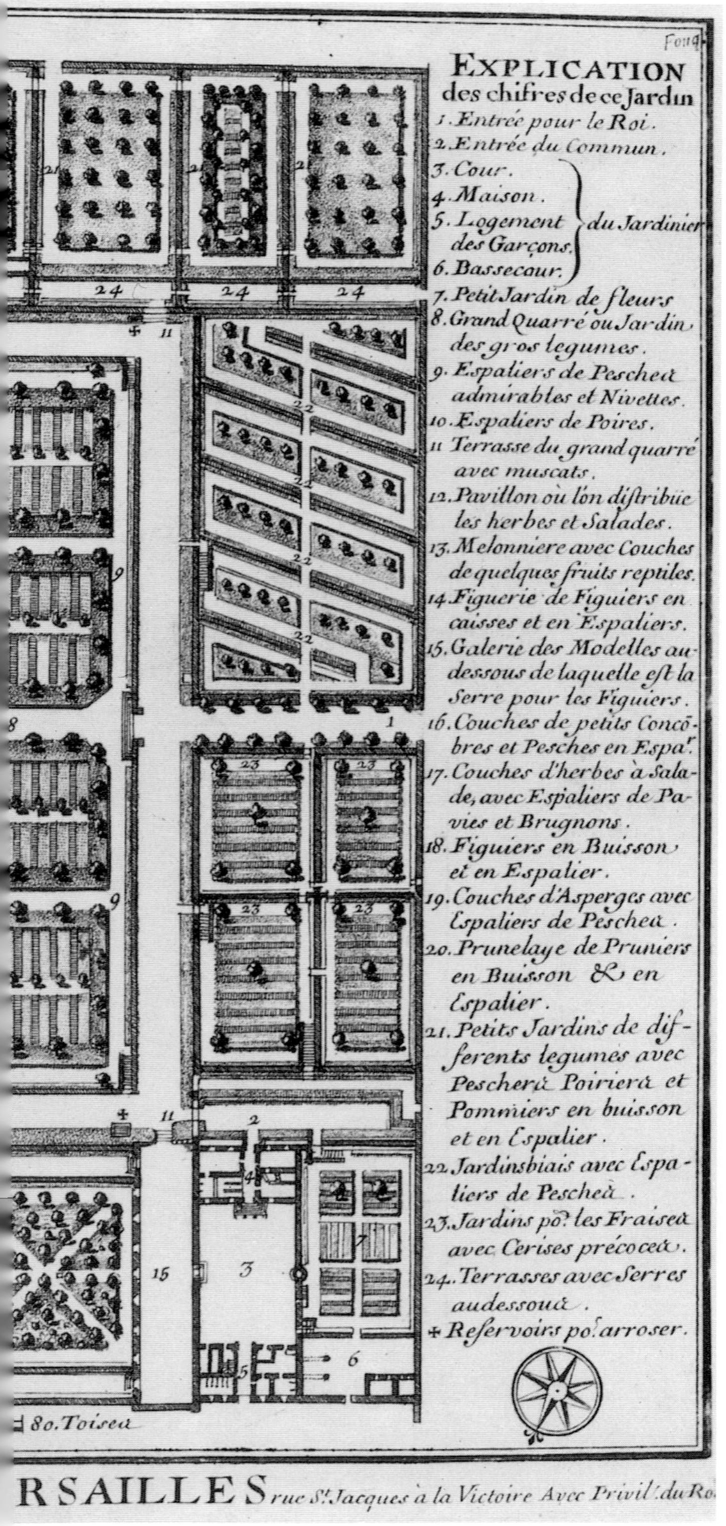

Versailles in perspective

Versailles has assumed an importance in the history of French gardening proportional to the political significance which attached to it as a symbol of the French monarchy. The gardens have become synonymous with the style of Le Nôtre; and certainly few gardeners have ever had the power and resources which he had. Descartes was of the opinion 'that often there is less perfection in works composed of several pieces and made by different masters than in those at which only one person has worked. So it is that one sees that buildings undertaken and completed by a single architect are usually more beautiful and better ordered than those that several architects have tried to put into shape.'[24] By these criteria Versailles falls short of the Cartesian ideal. Perhaps it reached the highest peak of perfection when it was still essentially the work of the team which created Vaux-le-Vicomte.

There were criticisms of Versailles, and these can be summed up by those of Abbé Marc-Antoine Laugier in his *Essai sur l'architecture*. Whereas some see the virtue of Versailles in what was achieved in overcoming natural disadvantages, the site was ill-chosen and lacking a pleasant outlook on a landscape adorned with rural charms. In such a situation it is difficult to avoid monotony; or, as he calls it, 'les fadeurs de la symmétrie'. The solid mass of trees, which is necessary to the structure of the garden, at the same time shuts one in. The straight *allées* with their high walls of hornbeam are like very boring streets. This monotony is reinforced by lack of variety and freshness in the planting; only box and coloured earth in the parterres, with some mediocre flowers, and uniformity in the *bosquets*. This aspect of his criticism, at least in the parterres, would not necessarily be true at other times; although it does remind us that colour and variety were dependent on the constant changes provided by the gardeners in bedding out, and a far more limited range of plants than we have today.

Finally he deplored the lack of water in a garden which depended on fountains for its liveliness: 'What has not been spent to bring water to Versailles? . . . After devoting innumerable sums to this work, all is reduced to being in working order two or three times a year, to produce . . . water which miraculously shoots into the air for a few minutes. . . . The remainder of the time one sees not a drop of running water; one meets only dry fountains, and half-filled basins, stagnant and ill-smelling.'[25]

Nevertheless, Versailles remains one of the most spectacular gardens of the world, in which, despite its great size, detail is exactly proportioned to the scale of the design; a unity due as much to the control exercised by Louis and his minister, Colbert, as to Le Nôtre. In the words of Victor Tapié, 'The gardens outside the palace form another composition to which the word "architecture" is also fitting, to such an extent does the order of the *miroirs d'eau*, the terraces, the elegant caprice in the design of the parterres, the canal wide as a river, seem necessary there; in short, the logical progression which leads from the setting of stone to the open countryside. This clear intelligence, which allowed varied teams, with very different technical skills, to share in a general work and to give it perfect unity, without doubt constitutes the superiority of Versailles and its highest classic quality.'[26]

12

The Royal Gardens under Louis XIV

Organization

BESIDES VERSAILLES and its dependencies (Trianon, Clagny, the Ménagerie) there were of course parks and gardens attached to other royal houses. First the Louvre and the Tuileries; then the old palaces and castles of Saint-Germain-en-Laye, Fontainebleau, Vincennes. Marly, whose construction began in 1679, assumed importance as a favoured retreat. Meudon, bought from Servien by Michel Le Tellier, Marquis de Louvois, in 1679, became a royal house and residence of the Dauphin in 1695. Among other royal gardens which had to be maintained were those of the Palais Royal and the Jardin Royal (Jardin des Plantes); the nurseries of the Roule (established 1671); and the Luxembourg, left to the crown by Gaston d'Orléans' daughter Louise, Duchesse de Montpensier, on her death in 1693. Royal properties in the provinces included the châteaux of Saint-Léger, Limours, Montceaux, Compiègne, Amboise and Marimont. Chambord (which had fallen into ruin since it was abandoned by François I) was partly restored
237 by Gaston d'Orléans. Louis XIV's project to create gardens by canalizing the Cosson to drain the site, was begun in 1683, but abandoned soon after 1685.[1]

To maintain all these places an army of gardeners and other specialists was required, in addition to huge numbers of other tradesmen (masons, terracers, carters) engaged in major work of construction. The accounts for the years between 1664 and 1680 name 305 gardeners, which is a far larger number than those in other trades; and they would include only those who received wages or payments directly from the Treasury, out of which the wages of assistants and other expenses had to be paid. Michel Le Bouteux, for instance, who was in charge of the gardens of Trianon (and indeed was their designer) received 18,000 *livres* a year between 1672 and 1681. A sum of 500 *livres* was for the upkeep of the fountains; and the larger proportion of the rest for expenses in providing plants or paying his assistants. It was Colbert's constant preoccupation to see that the gardeners and fountainers were not receiving money for wages which were not in fact paid.[2] At Versailles there were distinct areas involving different skills and duties: the Orangerie and the flower garden (the parterres); the Petit Parc (*bosquets*); and Grand Parc; the Potager. Although individual gardeneners had a main responsibility for one of these areas, they did work elsewhere as circumstances demanded. Marin Trumel[3] and Henry Dupuis were jointly responsible for laying out the gardens of Versailles in 1664. It was Trumel who supervised the moving of shrubs from Vaux in 1665. From 1666 Trumel received wages for the upkeep of the Orangerie and flower garden; while Dupuis had no special responsibility. Dupuis supervised work at the Louvre, the Tuileries, Saint-Germain and the Palais Royal until he took over Trumel's responsibilities on the latter's death in 1676. These appointments did not exclude other work in the Petit Parc. For instance, it was Trumel and Dupuis who were responsible for excavating the *pièce d'eau* of the Ile Royale, and for making the Salle des Festins between 1671 and 1673. The large sums of money they received (29,000 *livres* in 1671) was for the cost of earthmoving. The largest gardener's wage was for the upkeep of the Petit Parc which called for skill in trelliswork in the various *bosquets*. Jean Colinot, who succeeded Macé (or Massé) Fourché in 1672, was an expert in this craft. In 1674 he was receiving 8800 *livres* as an annual wage, compared with 3000 *livres* paid to Trumel and to Vaultier who had charge of the Potager.[4] In 1681 (after Jean Colinot's death) Henry Dupuis took over the management of the Petit Parc and of the *allées* round the canal, receiving altogether 18,400 *livres*.

Obviously a large part of the work in the Petit Parc was
concerned with planting trees; and as fashions changed from 238
time to time, these were taken out and replaced by others. Thus in Colbert's *Ordres et Règlements* (24 October 1674) we read, 'Take out all the firs which are along the Allée de la Pyramide, and that of the cascade, and put spruce there. . . . Finish the *allées* between Apollo and the canal. . . . Finish all the *allées* round the canal according to the contract made with Marin. . . . As soon as the time for planting comes, urge Ballon[5] to do them, all following the specifications of Sieur Le Nôtre. . . . Make the cross-walk from the fountain of Saturn to the lime walk, and plant maple there. . . . Refurnish with maple all the cross-walks where they are lacking. . . . Make trenches and fill them with good earth in the *allée* between the wall and the Ile Royale, to plant lime trees in place of those which are dead.' The constant changes made in the *bosquets* and Louis's impatience to see immediate results meant that quantities of well-grown saplings were transported from all over France,

236 The Grand Trianon, or Trianon de Marbre at Versailles, showing the *parterres*. Painting by Jean Cotelle. For a key to the planting see p. 231.

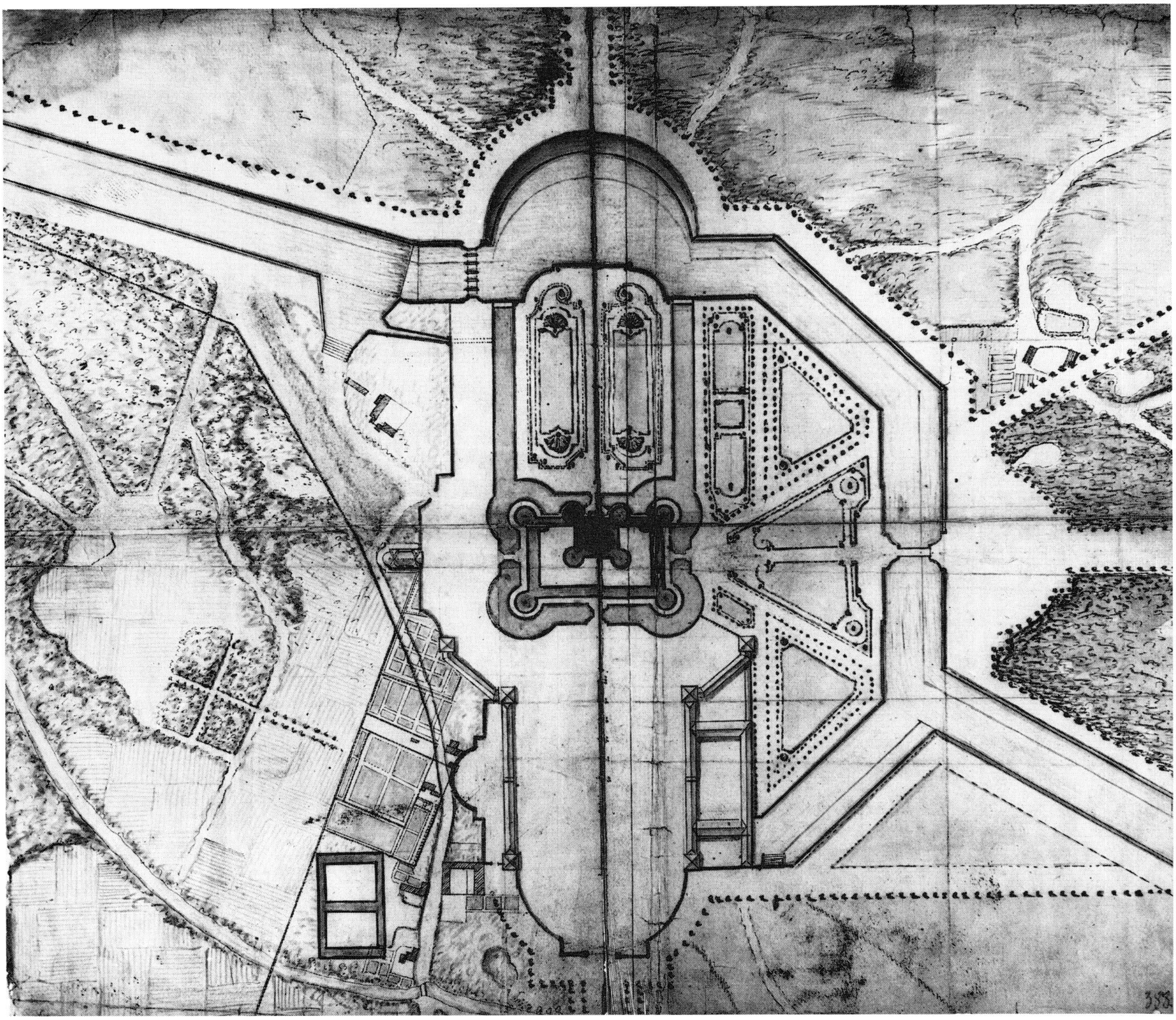

237 Plan of Chambord, showing the garden layout attributed to Jules Hardouin-Mansart, later modified.

many of which must inevitably have died. Sometimes large trees were transplanted. A spruce 8 metres high was lifted and brought to Versailles by Louis Germain in 1682. Octavien Henry was employed between 1671 and 1680 almost entirely to search for and transport plants. Thus in 1671 he brought holly and juniper from the forest of Fontainebleau; spruce from Grenoble; yews from Normandy. And in 1672 he took up 7000 spruce in the mountains of Dauphiné.[6] The estimates for planting and replanting in the parks of Versailles during 1681 and 1682 were 30,000 and 40,000 *livres* respectively. Elms were used in avenues, many of which came from Flanders where a large leaved species (*ypréau*) came from Ypres. An increasing number of horse-chestnut was planted from 1668; but by far the largest and most constant item in the tree bill was for hornbeam (*charmille*) to form the hedges lining the *allées* of the park and the *bosquets*.[7] These were clipped to form the *palissades* enclosing the woods. The practice of lining the *allées* with trees of a single species (spruce, fir, beech, lime, evergreen oak) gave way to planting rows of cut yew and box in front of the hornbeam. From 1674 trellis, covered with some climbing plant (jasmine, honeysuckle, rose), replaced hedges, particularly in the *bosquets*. Runs of trellis were made of sweet chestnut painted green; but the more elaborate architectural pieces were made of iron. For the trelliswork in the *bosquet* of l'Encelade (1675–6) Colbert's estimate[8] set aside 5000 *livres* for 'le treillage de fer', and 4000 *livres* for 'le treillage de bois, y compris la peinture'. These were fairly large individual items, although far exceeded by the cost of the conduits; 34,350 *livres*.

Flowers had their place in the parterres of Versailles; and temporarily on special occasions in the *bosquets*.[9] As with trees, a constant search was made to supply the royal gardens. 'You know that for ornamenting the gardens of the royal houses it is necessary to have a large number of flowers', wrote Colbert (5 September 1670) to M. Arnoul, Intendant of the galleys at Marseilles. 'As several species are met with in Provence I beg you to buy all the daffodils and tuberoses you can find, and in general all the other curious flowers you think could contribute to this ornament, and send them punctually, so that they may be planted for next spring.'

And in 1672 the director of la Compagnie des Indes Occidentales was ordered to search for 'fine shells, rare plants, evergreen shrubs and extraordinary flowers'. Of course some of these were tender; on the other hand even seasonal or half-hardy plants were cultivated in pots under glass so that the king could have flowers in his garden all the year round. It was thus that bedding out became the French mode of flower gardening *par excellence*; and the place where that was developed to a high degree was Trianon.

238 Gardeners at work carrying plants at Versailles, a detail of ill. 210.

TRIANON

239 The Trianon de Porcelaine (so-called because of the ceramic tiles with which the roof was decorated) was no more than an elegant pavilion set in a flower garden. Its genesis in 1671 corresponded with the rise of Madame de Montespan as royal mistress; and its final destruction in 1687, to make way for the Trianon de Marbre (Grand Trianon), marked her decline. As we have seen (Chapter 11), in 1667 a garden had preceded the
240 building of the pavilion. What relation this had to Le Vau's buildings is not known. Michel Le Bouteux's garden, laid out in 1670, consisted of an upper garden of cut box onto which the pavilion opened; and a lower garden of four compartments of cut box enclosed on the north and south by trellis *berceaux*, and planted with orange trees, jasmine and other scented shrubs. Here for the first time orange trees were planted in the open, and protected in the winter by a covered wooden frame.[10] The axis of these gardens was continued through the woods to a parterre of cut turf (*boulingrin*) and a large circular basin. In the woods to the north of this there was a *bosquet* with an octagonal walk surrounding a circular grove with another round basin. In 1671 sixty horse-chestnuts were bought and planted in rows at the end of the lower garden, between the two *berceaux*, apparently the first time these trees had been planted in the royal gardens.[11] When the north branch of the canal was finished in 1675, Trianon could be reached by boat, and a grand entrance, with a balustraded terrace and horseshoe flights of stairs surrounding a basin, was made at that point. It was completed in 1679. One's arrival was greeted by the scent of flowers arranged in tiers of beds in the sloping ground on either side. Of course this effect was achieved by massive bedding-out operations, the extent of which is shown by the purchase of flowers and flower pots. Among scented flowers planted in large quantities[12] the largest purchases were of tuberose (*Polianthes tuberosa*) a half-hardy bulbous plant, native of Mexico and introduced in 1629, its white, very fragrant flowers in long terminal racemes sometimes more than a metre high. These came from the south of France.[13] The generous provision Le Bouteux received, corresponded to his responsibility to satisfy the king's expectations. In 1670 Colbert wrote, 'Le Bouteux is inconveniencing me still more; for he has given me no plan of what he wants to do. Today he has only asked me for 300 orange trees.' And in September 1673 Louis wrote to Colbert, 'I expect to find a lot of flowers, late or early, for my brother has told me that the garden is not so full of them as usual and that Le Bouteux has some in reserve; I believe that is the reason. Look into it.' Lefèvre had instructions to see that Le Bouteux had flowers for the king during the whole of the winter, and to send a weekly account of the flowers he had.[14] Le Bouteux was relieved of his charge in 1682 and sent to the garden of the Orangerie at Fontainebleau,[15] a post he held until his death in 1689. His immediate successor was Antoine Trumel, formerly flower gardener at Vaux, and since 1670 in charge of establishing the royal nurseries at Le Roule.[16] He was joined in 1684 by Laurens Trumel who was responsible for the upkeep with an annual allowance of 9000 *livres* until 1686, when his post was taken over by Olivier Fleurant, who had been in charge of the garden at Clagny. Laurens Trumel ceases to appear in the accounts; but Antoine received a pension of 1500 *livres* a year.

239 The Trianon de Porcelaine, which lasted barely sixteen years, 167

ore being replaced by the Trianon de Marbre. On the horizon: Clagny (centre) and Versailles (right).

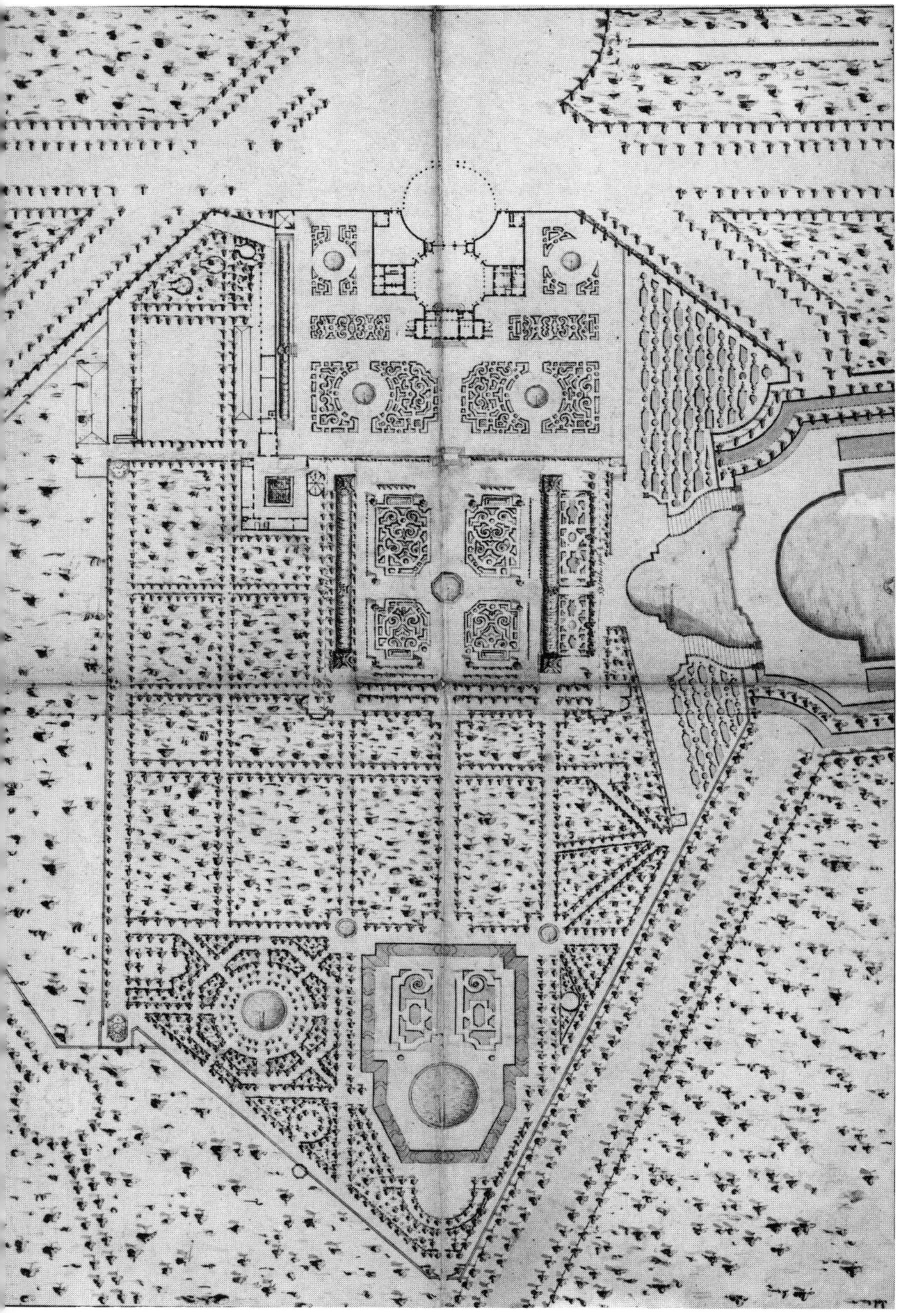

240 Plan of the Trianon de Porcelaine.

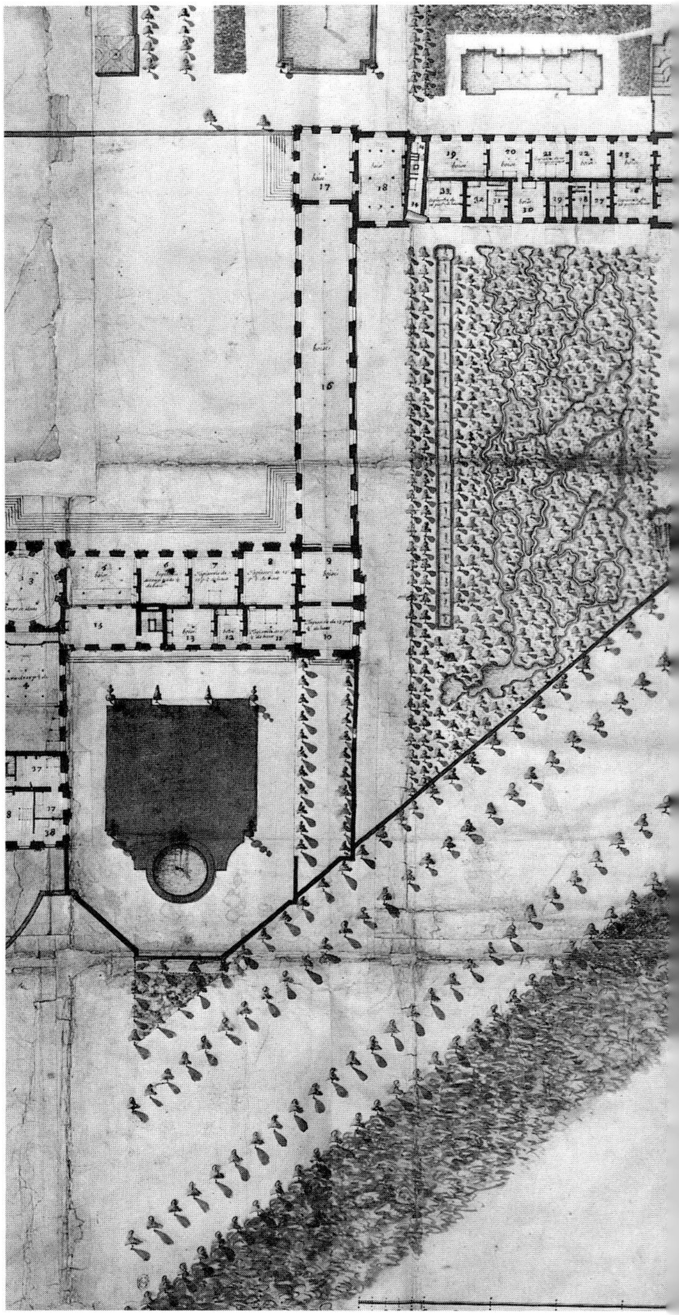

241 The Trianon de Marbre, Versailles, a detail showing Le Nôtre's Bosquet des Sources.

A large nursery was established northwest of the park in 1686, and enormous numbers of flowers were bought, together with the unprecedented order for a quarter of a million flower pots in
236 1686 and 1687. With the building of Grand Trianon (Trianon de Marbre) a gallery was made along the north side of the parterre, linking the main building with another suite of rooms, Trianon-sous-Bois. In the part of the garden enclosed by these
241 additions, Le Nôtre created an unusual garden, the Bosquet des Sources (1687–8), a network of meandering streams, small enough to step across, with islands of turf large enough for a gaming table and seats. Old trees were preserved, and the whole irregular composition contained by two straight canals. The essential structure of Le Bouteux's gardens was preserved, although the details were remade. But after 1691 Louis began using Trianon as an occasional residence, and at the same time to extend the pleasure grounds by taking in part of the nursery. Between 1693 and 1695 a new garden was made to the north, corresponding with the transverse axis of the lower garden. It was on two levels, with grass lawns surrounded by beds and flowering shrubs, and lined by a double row of horse chestnuts (backed by elms) which gave it the name of the Jardin des Marronniers.[17] Le Nôtre died in 1700 and Louis' detailed orders to Hardouin-Mansart between 1699 and 1702 are a demonstration of the close personal attention the king gave to the management of the gardens.[18] Very precise instructions were given about the planting of trees, and included requests for changes in the parterres; for instance, 'de défaire le parterre de son petit jardin à Trianon[19] pour en faire un autre avec des allées et des pièces de broderie au lieu de pièces découpées'; and, two weeks later, 'de changer la broderie du parterre de son petit

Method of planting parterres at Trianon

Box hedge

ABACABABACABABACABABACABABACABABACABABACABABACABABA

F G H I K L M N F G

ABACABABACABABACABABACABABACABABACABABACABABACABABA

F G H I K L M N F G

ABACABABACABABACABABACABABACABABACABABACABABACABABA

O P Q R S O P Q R S

ABACABABACABABACABABACABABACABABACABABACABABACABABA

F G H I K L M N F G

ABACABABACABABACABABACABABACABABACABABACABABACABABA

F G H I K L M N F G

ABACABABACABABACABABACABABACABABACABABACABABACABABA

Bulbs

A	Tulippes	40500
B	Narcisses blanches (printannieres ou doubles)	27000
C	Hiacinthes	13500

Perennial Flowers

F	Juliennes doubles	1500
G	Veroniques (grande)	1500
H	Oeillets de Poete	1500
I	Hiacinthes orangeres	1500
K	Iacess	1500
L	Coqueloürdes doubles	1500
M	Oeillets d'Espagne	1500
N	Violettes de Mer	1500

Large Perennial Flowers

O	Matriquaires	600
P	Campanelles	600
Q	Giroflée (grande)	600
R	Lis Blanc	600
S	Valeriennes Grecques	600

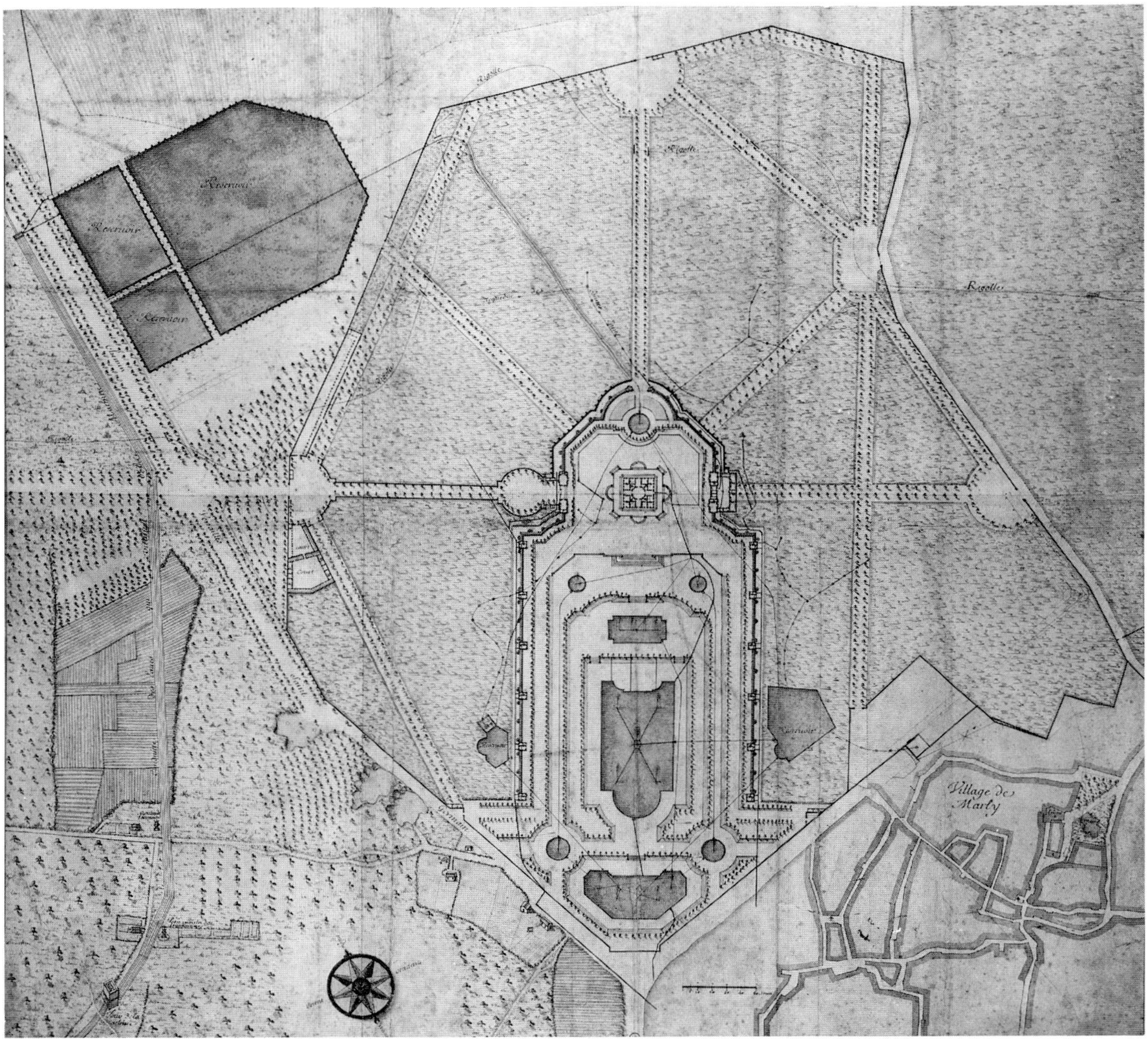

242 Plan of the château and garden of Marly, in 1685.

jardin, d'en faire les fleurons et enroulements plus grands pour pouvoir mettre des fleurs dans ladite broderie.' At the same time he decided that the planks surrounding the flower beds should be replaced by box. He ordered a Jeu de Mail to be made, 640 metres (320 *toises*) long, in one of the principal *allées* of the park; and 'des fossez revêtus' (ha-has) at the end of the *allées* instead of grilles. A new cascade (or *buffet d'eau*) was designed by Hardouin-Mansart to close the *allée* which divided the old garden from the Jardin des Marronniers (formerly part of the nursery). By 1715 the whole of the nursery had become part of the park. On 11 July 1691, Louis embarked from Versailles with the exiled English king. To the sound of music they sailed up the canal to Trianon, brightly lit for the occasion. The ladies followed in gondolas and chaloupes. It was the prototype of many such 'Embarkations for Cythera', later immortalized by Watteau. Meanwhile, Trianon had been supplanted by Marly as the last and most extravagant of Louis' exclusive retreats.

MARLY

In 1678 Louis' popularity and reputation was at its height. Under his personal command his armies had been victorious in the north; and peace had been concluded, with the annexation of Franche-Comté and parts of Flanders. The second Versailles, the Trianon de Porcelaine, and Clagny were completed; he had refashioned Saint-Germain to his taste, and, it seemed, had all the places he could require for public and private satisfaction. At this point, if we are to believe Saint-Simon, he reacted against all this, and desired only some small secluded place where he could escape from all the grandeur and ceremony which he had created. He chose for this retreat a valley almost entirely shut in with steep hills; 'a muddy hollow, a stinking bog, avoided by the inhabitants of the neighbouring village, a "nest of serpents" where only a few daring poachers ventured'. What it did have was a view over the silver windings of the Seine to the château of Saint-Germain in the distance. Needless to say Louis'

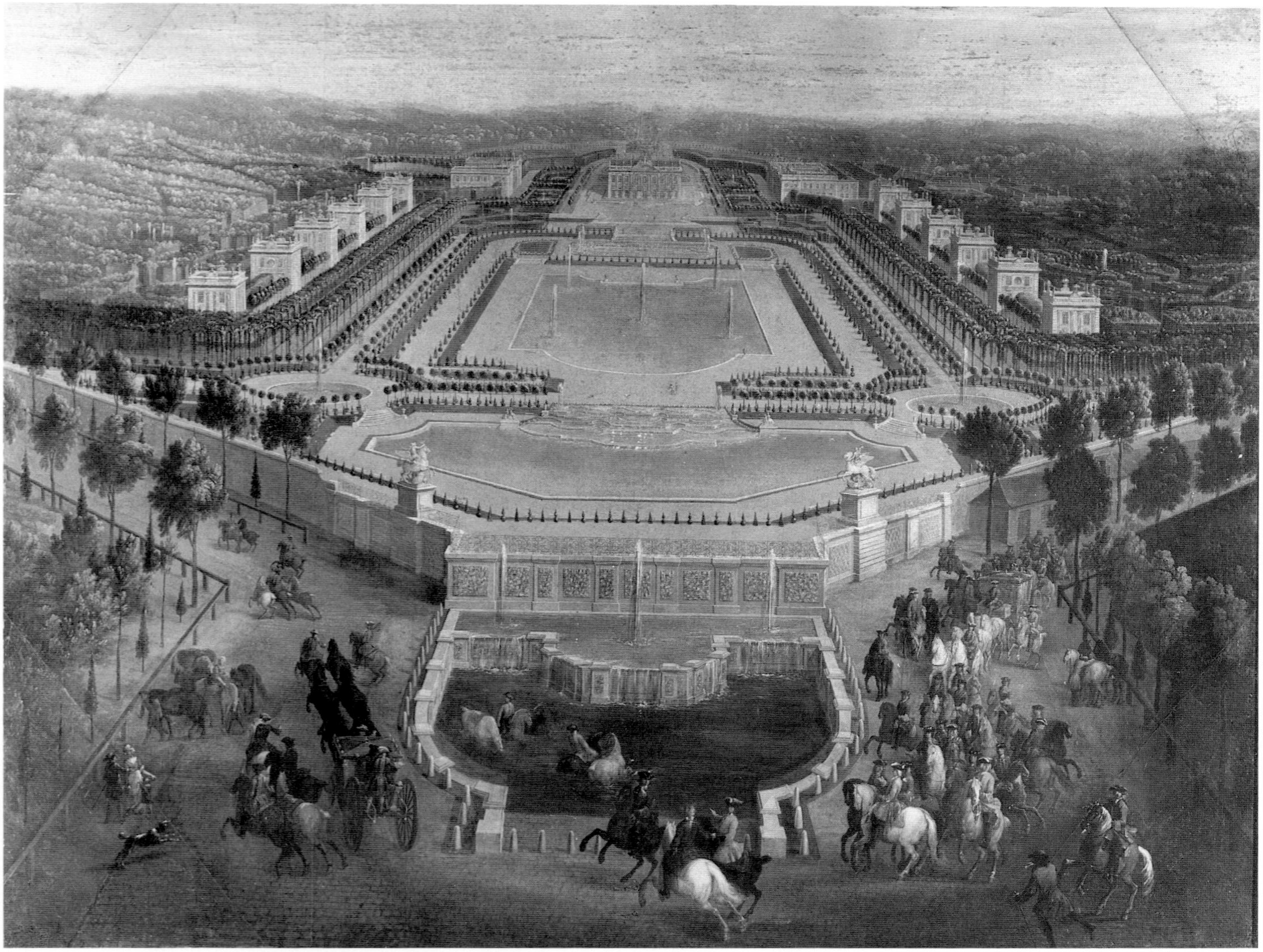

243 Marly, a general view of the terraces by J. B. Martin.

conception of a hermitage soon turned out to be something considerably more extravagant, especially when he employed Hardouin-Mansart as his architect. Apart from Versailles, Marly[20] cost more than any of his other projects; but even this was exceeded by the expense of the enormous machine erected to bring the water from the river to the ponds and fountains, and ultimately to Versailles.

Louis' Conseil des Bâtiments consisted of Colbert, Hardouin-Mansart, Le Brun, Le Nôtre and François Francine; but the design of Marly, it appears, was entirely due to Hardouin-
242 Mansart. The valley was to be shaped in a series of four
243 horseshoe terraces overlooking a great central basin. The château was placed on a platform at the head of the horseshoe, tucked into the hill and facing down the valley. His guests were to be accommodated in small pavilions: ten on either side of the château, twelve on the upper terraces to left and right of the central axis. In the event the first ten were not built; so the king's privacy was ensured. Hardouin-Mansart implied an extension of the solar symbolism; the pavilions representing the twelve months of the year, or twelve signs of the zodiac. The approach was down the steep hill from the direction of Saint-Germain in the west. Since this proved inconvenient for carriages coming from Versailles, it was changed to an almost equally steep approach from the east. In other respects the essentials of Hardouin-Mansart's original conception remained in a modified and elaborated form. In the first years of construction, from 1679 to 1683, Louis only occasionally visited the site. The first entertainment was given in November 1683, shortly after Queen Marie-Thérèse's death, and his marriage to Madame de Maintenon. It took place on a building site hurriedly disguised. The château lacked outer doors, staircases or furniture. The simulated architectural ornament, with which by way of economy the various faces of the building were to be painted, was not done. The fountains did not work, as the Machine de

Marly was not yet complete. Colbert died that year, and in 1684 Louis took over the supervision of his buildings in person. During the summer months of 1685 Marly was used intermittently for evening entertainments (music, dance, theatre or just a walk in the grounds with supper). On a freezing day in January 1686 he dragged a party which included Mesdames de Maintenon and de Montespan, his son, his brother and their wives, to walk in the gardens, shivering in furs; and afterwards to gamble, returning to Versailles after supper. He did not sleep there until September.

Louis succeeded in making Marly private and exclusive. Only select guests were admitted; formality was relaxed. Indeed Louis, by extending and withholding invitations, used Marly as an instrument of power. Official visitors were barred, although the exiled James II and his family, who were established nearby at the château of Saint-Germain from 1689, frequently took part in the hunts, promenades, picnics, nocturnal fêtes, concerts and gambling, which were the usual distractions of what came to be called 'les Marlys', arranged at intervals and lasting four days. Marly was the chief occupation of the king's leisure for the rest of his life. And it was there, after 1686, when he had suffered from a fistula in the anus and was unable to go on horseback, that he indulged his passion for gardening. Madame de Maintenon detested the place, disapproved of gambling, disliked the walks, the water and the fountains. She remained shut in her room. She was indifferent to the gardens, and if constrained to go there went in her chaise with the windows closed.

Hardouin-Mansart's original design was a purely architectural concept, without parterres or *bosquets*. But as Louis' passion for the place grew, so were increasing quantities of flowers bought, approaching in number even those for Trianon. In 1690–3 these included 209 bushels of tulip bulbs, 84½ bushels and 149,080 bulbs of narcissus or daffodil, together with smaller quantities of other flowers.[21] Flower-beds were laid out along the two lower longitudinal terraces before 1689. They were subsequently enclosed in box borders, that were clipped by the
244 gardener, Charles Amelot, into balls, acorns, mushrooms, trefoils and cups. The upper terrace, below the pavilions, remained bare until 1689, when they were furnished with two arcades of elm trained over iron frames. Amelot was employed at Marly from 1686 under Louis Le Rusé, who was Contrôleur des Bâtiments. Indeed Le Rusé, in the absence of other evidence, has been credited with the design of the gardens. He was relieved of his post in 1699, when Hardouin-Mansart was appointed Surintendant des Bâtiments, delegating Marly to his brother-in-law, Robert de Cotte. Amelot was appointed to superintend the gardens in 1700,[22] although he had in fact been responsible for planting the trees in the *allées*, making the
245 *berceaux* and flower-beds, and constructing the *bosquets*. In 1693–4 he provided in excess of 20,000 hornbeam for the hedges (*palissades*), besides large numbers of elm, oak and sweet chestnut. As at Trianon, Louis demanded that his garden should be always full of flowers; and he had ambitions to establish all kinds of exotic species sent by his agents overseas. In 1700 he appointed the Sieur Loitron to organize 'un petit jardin de fleurs rares' in a warm corner where the seeds would be grown. But the climate of Marly did not favour horticulture of this kind. Cold, and above all wet, the soil was unstable. Springs which never dried up caused ravines, necessitating heavy expense in walls to stop the water invading the walks, and gutters to carry it away. These circumstances favoured the creation of ornamental water-gardens; and in 1700 Louis' passion turned from flowers to carp, of which he collected varicoloured specimens. These were designated royal fish, and christened 'La Royale', 'La Dauphine', 'La Bourgogne', and other fancy names.[23] Four new basins were made on either side of the château; and meanwhile cascades, fountains and other waterworks multiplied along the long axis of the garden, and in the ornamental *bosquets*[24] which were made in the woods east and west of it. In 1697–9 Louis realized the project of building an enormous water stairway (La Rivière) on the hill behind the château. This may have been the result of Le Nôtre's visit to Italy in 1679. Le Nôtre made a proposal for a *grande cascade* at Marly which is preserved at Stockholm,[25] together with his nephew Claude Desgots' sketch of an unexecuted project for the lower end of La Rivière (THC 7810). These may well have been made by 1685, when Louis first mentioned the idea to Dangeau. Unfortunately, as cascades and fountains multiplied, the Machine de Marly, whose cumbersome clanking machinery laboured to supply them, failed to do so. As a result some fountains were suppressed, and the others, on which the liveliness of the gardens depended, were limited to a few hours a day, instead of twelve. With the extension of the axis in La Rivière at the upper end, Louis conceived an enlargement of the central vista below. Sixteen hundred soldiers were employed to remove a hill which interfered with the proposed avenue. Meanwhile, every part of the gardens was furnished with statues and vases in marble and bronze; some antique or copies of the antique, others representing groups of children and hunting scenes. Coysevox was commissioned to make two large statues to frame either side of the vista on the walk above the Abreuvoir.[26] He proposed Mercury and Fame on horseback. The work was delayed while blocks of marble were brought from Italy. As Madame de Maintenon wrote, 'Marly sera bientôt un petit Versailles'.

The older royal gardens

Among the older royal gardens the Tuileries was always important because of its position in relation to Paris and the Louvre; moreover, it was the one with which André Le Nôtre and his relatives were most intimately connected. Nevertheless it had no personal appeal for Louis; and was very much a public garden. Fontainebleau always retained its popularity as a residence because of its proximity to the forest for hunting. Saint-Germain-en-Laye received quite a lot of attention. The terraces of the Château-Neuf collapsed in 1660 and were rebuilt; after which it became the house of Henriette d'Angleterre, daughter of Charles I and wife of Louis XIV's brother Philippe, Duc d'Orléans. Following her early death in 1670 it became the home of the exiled Stuarts in 1688. Before 1680, under the direction of Le Nôtre, all these gardens underwent major transformations.

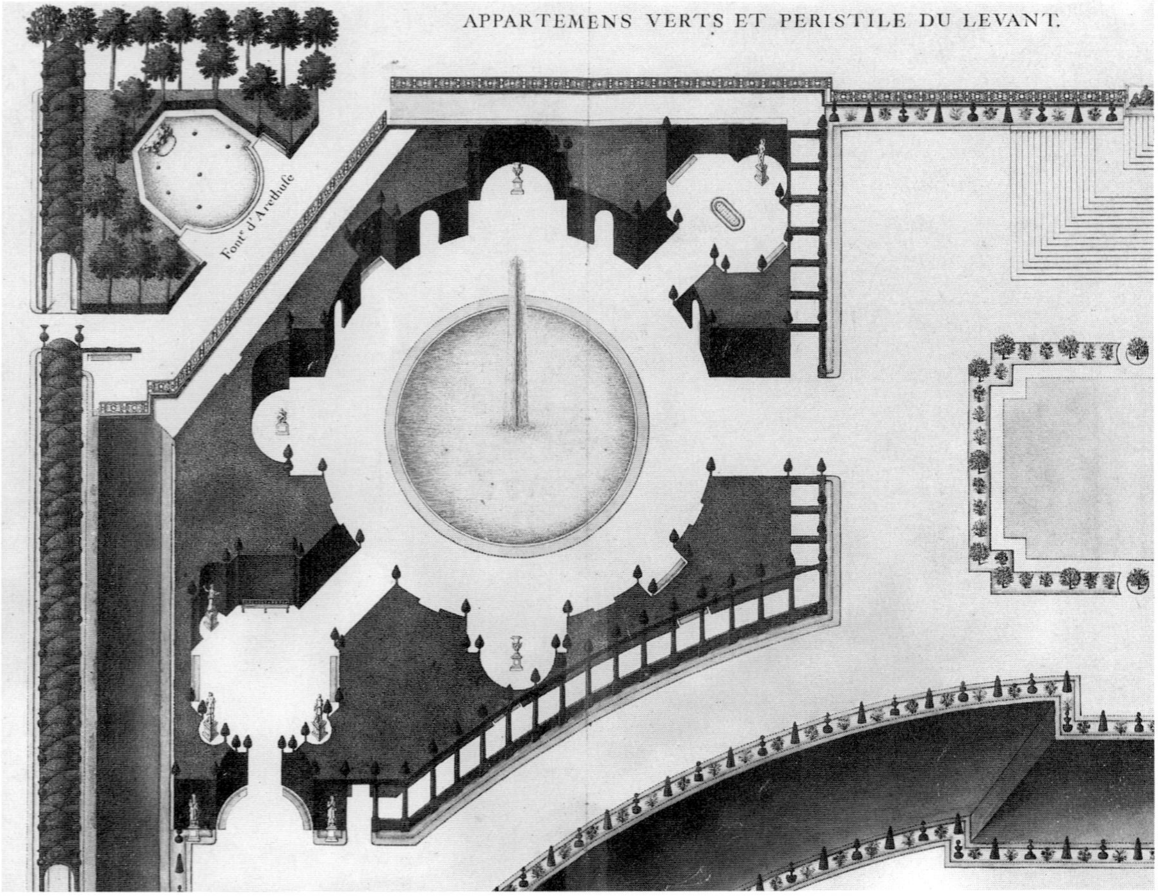

244, 245 Two details of the garden of Marly. Above: 'Green rooms and the eastern peristyle', at the head of the terraces on the right of the château in Martin's painting.
Below: the Bosquet de Louveciennes, *c.* 1700, west of the terraces.

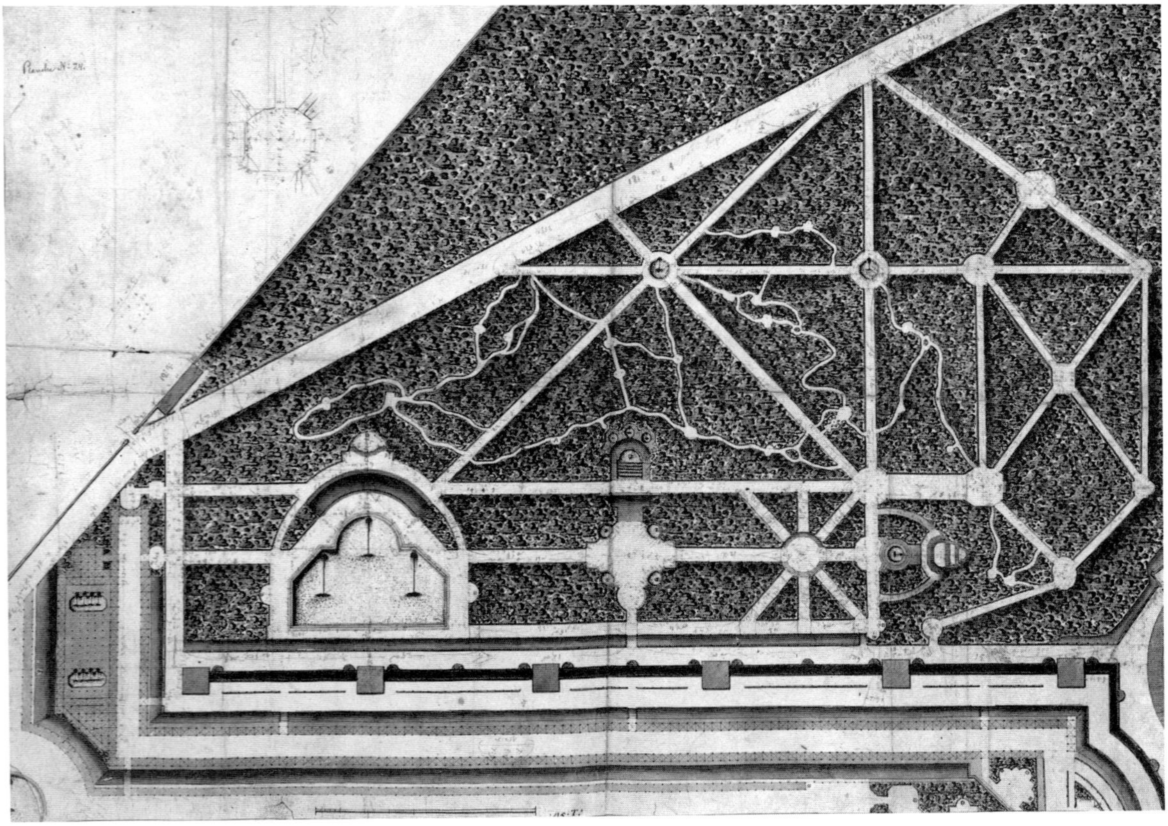

246 Fontainebleau: the Orangerie designed by Le Mercier and the Jardin de la Reine as remade by Le Nôtre in 1645–47. A version of the sleeping Ariadne is in the foreground.

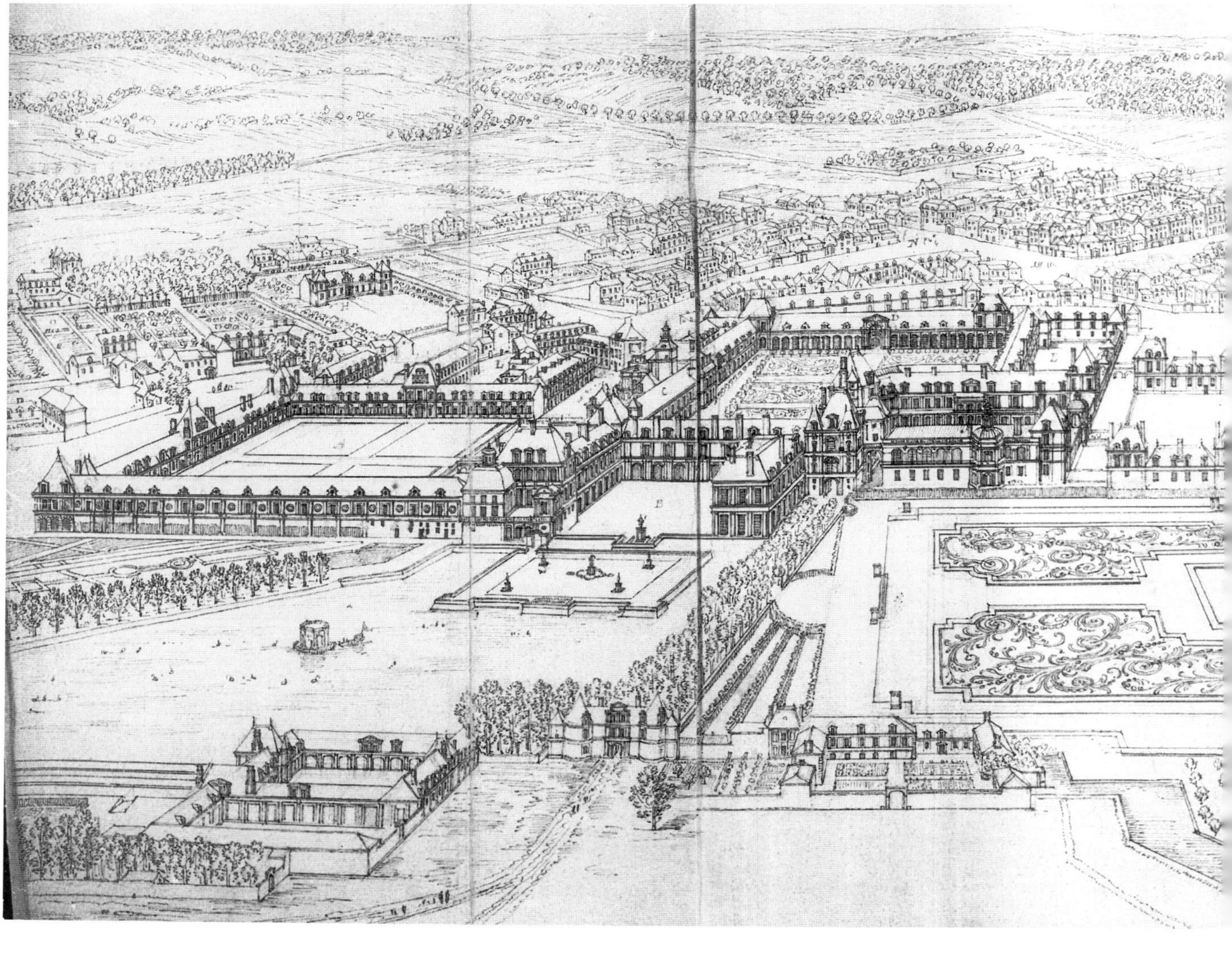

FONTAINEBLEAU

Fontainebleau was the oldest, a collection of gardens which had grown up round the palace since 1528. On the north side was the Jardin de la Reine, a private garden with access from the royal apartments. This was redesigned in 1645–7.[27] The purpose
246 was to make an orangery, which was built to the design of Le Mercier on the site of the former aviary, enclosing a roughly square area north of the *corps de logis*. This was divided into quarters round a circular basin, and ornamented with *broderie* designed by Le Nôtre, his first recorded commission after his appointment in 1643 as Dessinateur des Parterres et de tous les Jardins du Roi. Besides the statue of Diana, with which Henri IV had ornamented the central fountain, the garden was adorned with bronze casts after the antique (Laocoon, Apollo Belvedere, the Sleeping Ariadne) commissioned by François I, and others. The garden was evidently redesigned by Charles Mollet in 1671.[28] The final form is shown in an engraving by Silvestre dated 1679.

Le Nôtre's first big undertaking after Vaux was to reorganize
247 the Parterre du Tibre, east of the big pond and the causeway. Here, from 1661 to 1664, he made one of his largest parterres;[29] four large compartments round a square central basin, surrounded by a raised terrace and rows of clipped trees which disguised the irregularity of the area and the unsymmetrical line of buildings to the north. On the south side a large circular basin was made, projecting into the forest, from which it was separated by a moat, leaving the view unobstructed. The flat site of Fontainebleau was not one which gave much scope for Le Nôtre's talents. The Grand Canal had none of the dramatic possibilities of Vaux or Versailles; but its lack of connection with the Grand Parterre was to some extent remedied by the brothers Francine[30] who designed an architectural cascade against the east
side of the Grand Parterre and at the head of the canal, with rows 248
of jets and falls round a rectangular basin. Between the raised terraces on either side, ramps closed by wrought-iron *grilles* gave access to the road.

West of the pond was the old Jardin des Pins; and, in the southwest corner, fruit and vegetable gardens, and the so-called Bois de Canaux. South of the big pond was the Jardin du Chenil in which Henri IV had planted mulberry trees surrounded by a canal; and parallel to this a Jeu de Mail bounding the whole area. In 1713, after Le Nôtre's death, these parts were replaced by a

247 Fontainebleau: general view showing Le Nôtre's new Parterre du Tibre (Grand Parterre).

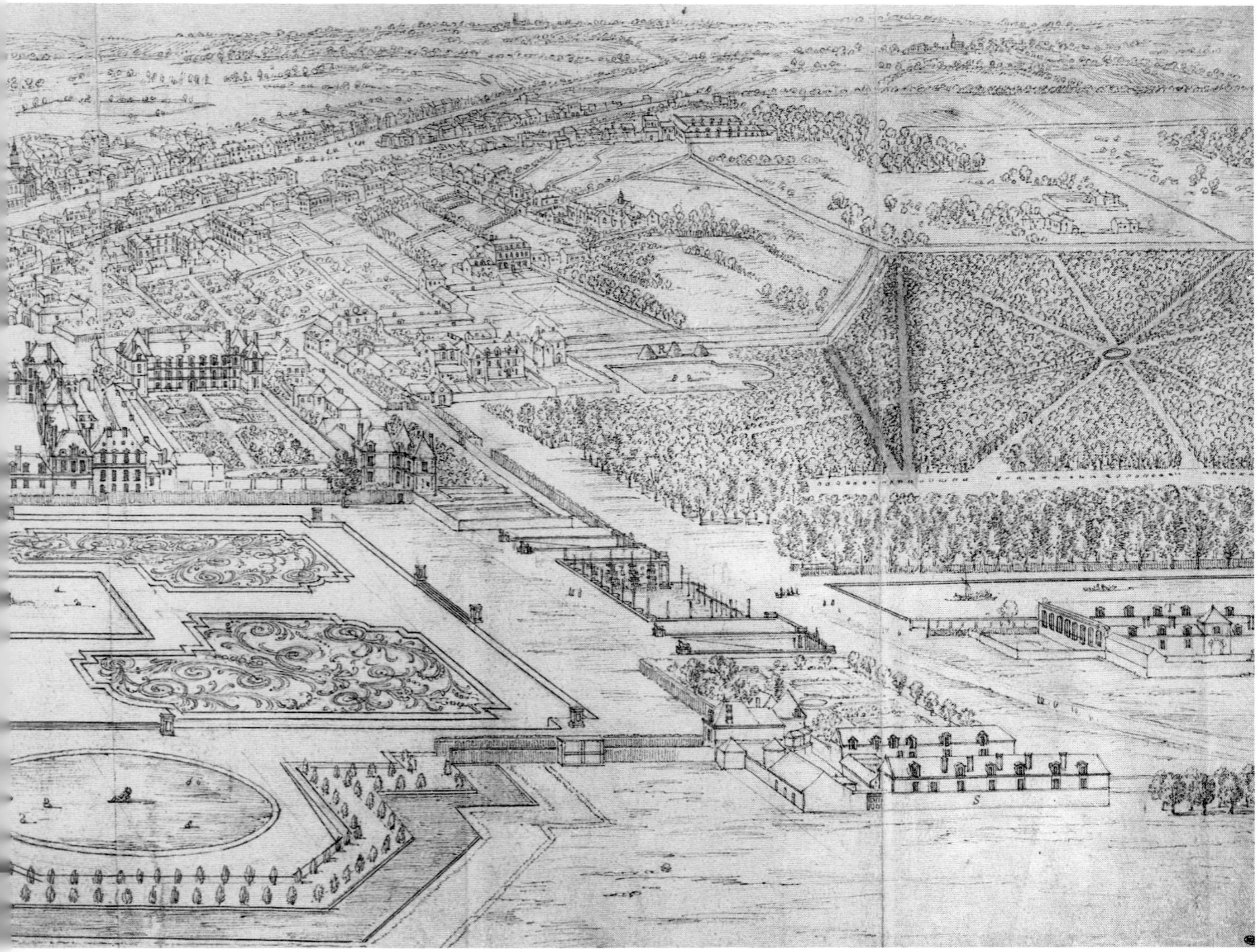

unified plan of *allées* radiating from a huge circular walk at the southwest corner of the pond. At the same time the Jardin de l'Etang, which stood in the water adjoining the Cour de la Fontaine, was abolished.

The upkeep of all these gardens was in the hands of families of gardeners, who intermarried and passed on the posts to their widows and children. Thus, Anne de Bray divided the responsibility for the Parterre du Tibre with Nicolas Poiret. In 1672 she is described as 'la veuve de Bray' and was paid 900 *livres* for 'the upkeep of half the king's Grand Parterre, formerly called *le Tibre*, recently remade and planted anew; for clipping the box of the two squares of this on the side of the causeway, cleaning the said squares, all the walks and terraces, steps and hedges planted and to be planted, and the extension of the round pond, walks and parterres about it.' On her death in 1688 the post was taken by Julien de Bray and subsequently by his widow. Similarly Nicolas Poiret's duties with regard to the other half of the parterre and its extension in the round basin (*rondeau*) were taken over by his widow; and then her daughters Madeleine and Anne. On Madeleine's marriage the post was taken over by her husband, Gaspard Quinteau de Richemont, in 1689. Jean Desbouts had charge of the Jardin de l'Etang. Louis Desbouts was responsible for the 'palissades, plattes-bandes, tapis du parc et allées entre les cascades et canal'; that is to say, while Jean looked after the gardens east of the Grand Parterre, Louis was concerned with those on the west. The gardener in charge of the Orangerie until 1670 was Claude-Charles Buis. After 1670 he was replaced by Jacques-Philippe Boiseau Chastillon, who received 1000 *livres* a year for the upkeep.[31] When Michel Le Bouteux ceased to be responsible for the gardens of Trianon after 1682, he received a pension of 3000 *livres*, and the duty of caring for the orange trees at Fontainebleau; while Chastillon continued to draw 1000 *livres* for the upkeep of the garden. Although these were the most important posts, worth an annual wage of up to 1000 *livres*, there were altogether nine gardeners having posts of responsibility in any one year.[32]

248 Fontainebleau: the cascades and Grand Parterre from the head of the canal, 1678.

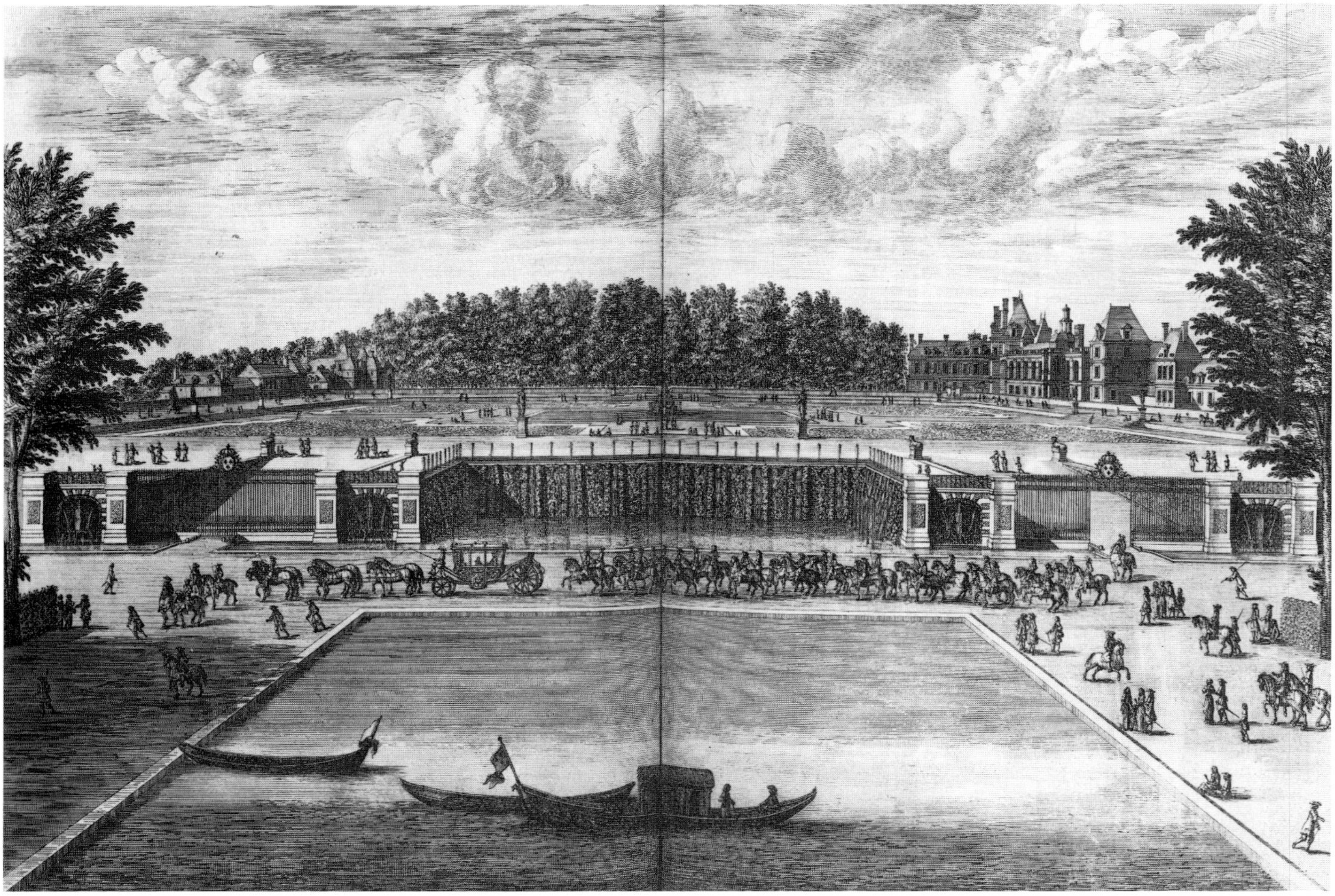

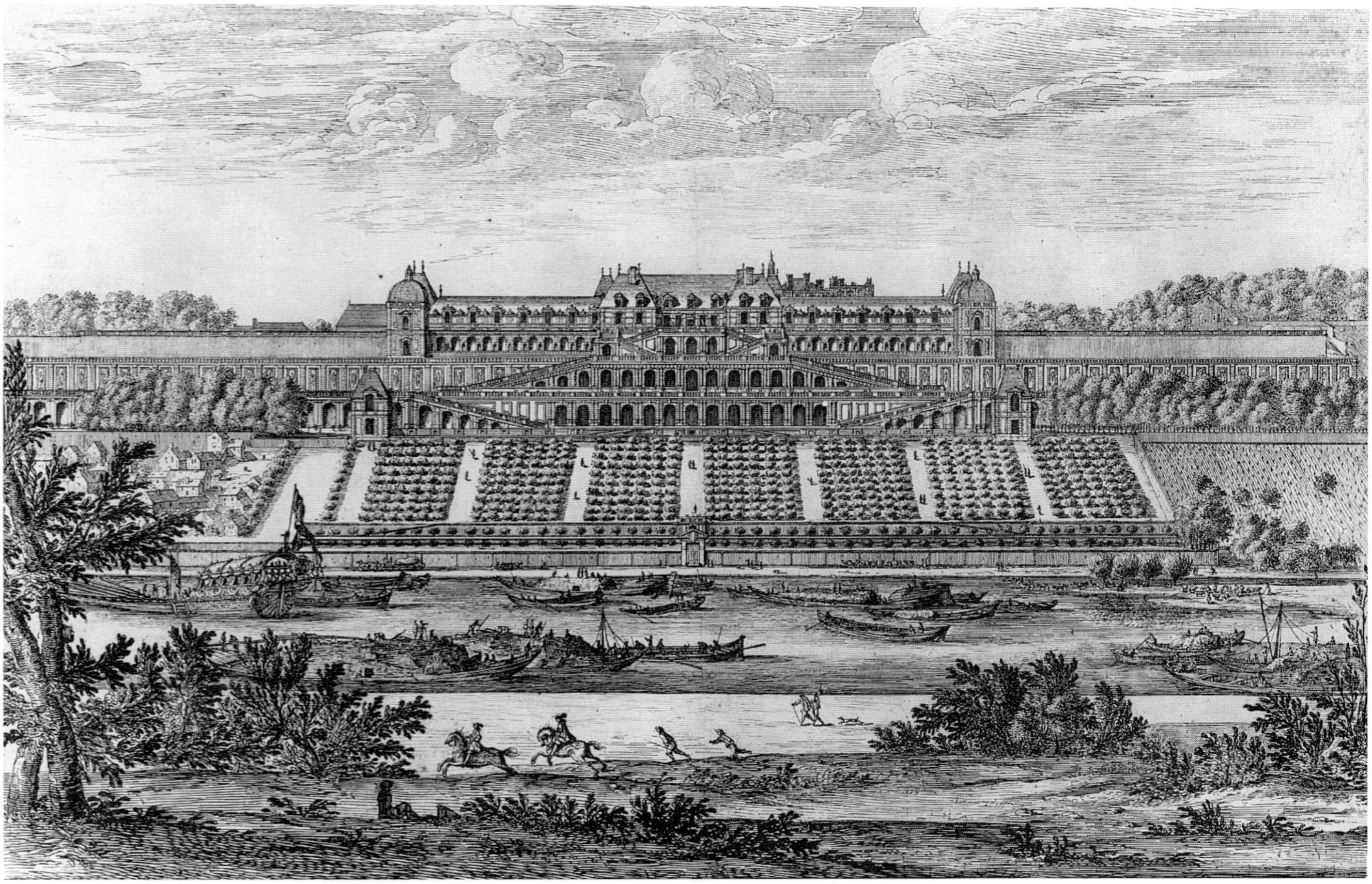

249 Saint-Germain-en-Laye: the Château-Neuf and the terraces in 1665, rebuilt following a collapse about 1660.

SAINT-GERMAIN-EN-LAYE

There were four distinct areas of garden at Saint-Germain-en-Laye; one to the north of the old château; two on either side of the Château-Neuf; and the terraced gardens descending to the river on the east. The grottoes forming the foundations of the upper terraces had collapsed in about 1660, carrying with them the horseshoe steps leading from the first to the second terrace.
249 These were rebuilt in 1662 and 1665 in the form shown in Israel Silvestre's engraving of 1666. The automata were beyond repair, and François Francine's salary for their maintenance was reduced from 1200 *livres* to 400 *livres* 'in view of the destruction of most of the grottoes'. The parterre below the grottoes, formerly referred to as Le Jardin en Dentelles, remained unaffected, and was tended first by François Bellier, and then by his son-in-law, François Lavechef, who doubtless lived in the Pavillon du Jardinier which flanked it on the south side (see Chapter 7). Although an engraving by one of the Perelle family shows the parterre extended towards the river with steps and a horseshoe ramp enclosing a basin, similar to the arrangement of the Bassin de Latone at Versailles, it is evident from the topography of the site and subsequent engravings that this is a fantasy which was never realized.[33] Another engraving shows the parterre laid out in the style of Boyceau rather than Le Nôtre.

When Henriette d'Angleterre[34] went to live at the Château-Neuf in 1661, she had a garden made south of her apartments on the upper level, and called 'Le Boulingrin'. According to Antoine l'Aîné,[35] a former valet de chambre of Louis XIII:

> It was so named by the late Mme Henriette d'Angleterre . . . and she gave the design when she was first in this place; this garden was planted in front with a pretty parterre of cut pieces with flower-beds round furnished with shrubs and flowers of all kinds and seasons, and behind with a sort of amphitheatre, with, round about it, several porticos of honeysuckle, cross walks of cypress and arbours at the four corners suitable for taking cover. The terrace, which contained the whole frontage of this garden, added to the beauty and made it a very pleasant walk.

Changes were made later. 'It has been planted', wrote Antoine

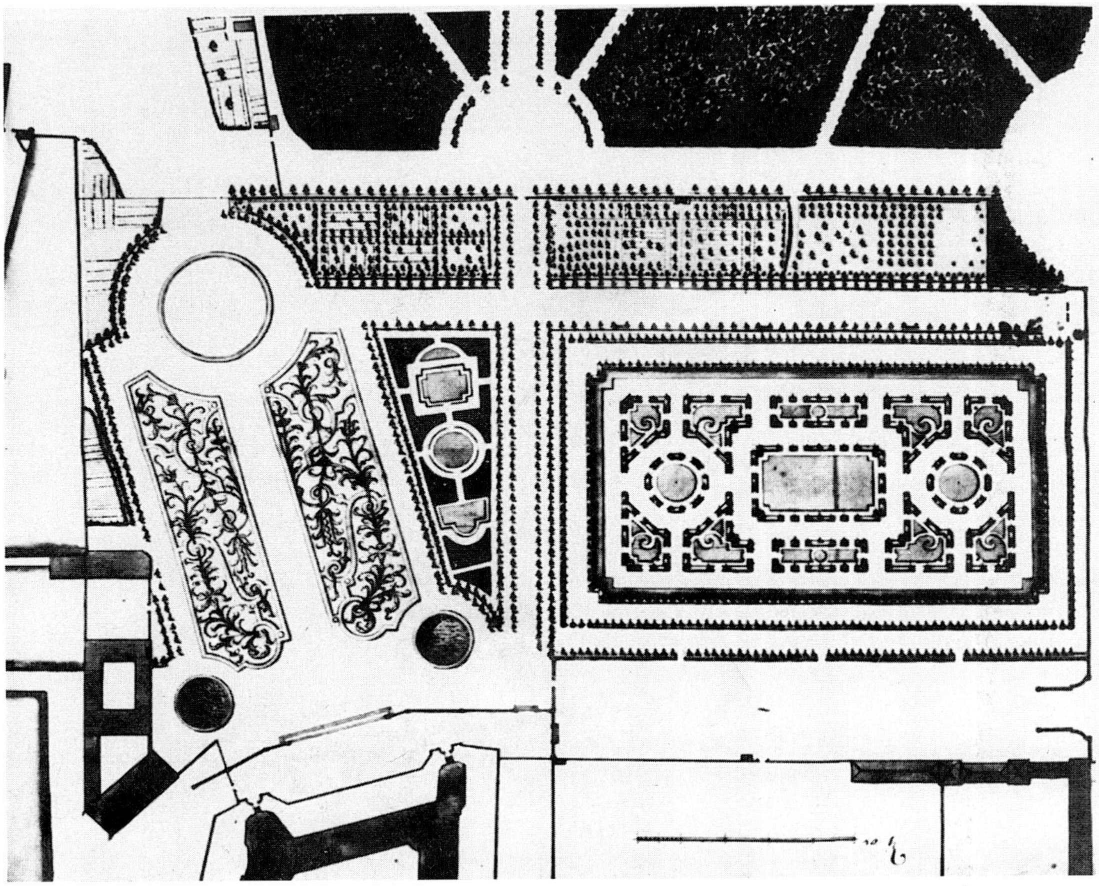

250 Detail of a plan of Saint-Germain-en-Laye in 1696 showing Le Nôtre's Jardin de la Dauphine on the right, north of the Château-Neuf, and the *parterre* of the old château on the left. The Grande Terrasse extended north from the top right-hand corner.

l'Ainé, 'as a parterre with a sort of meadow or lawn, surrounded by evergreen shrubs, together with a *bosquet*, planted with *palissades* of hornbeam and elm, where there are several fine *allées* to walk in the shade.'

In 1679 a large rectangular garden was made to the north of
250 the Château-Neuf, adjoining the terrace overlooking Paris to the west. It was known as Le Jardin de la Dauphine,[36] who arrived in France at that time. According to Antoine l'Ainé, it was laid out with compartments of turf surrounded by a quantity of yews clipped into different shapes with cross walks of spruce. This formed part of Le Nôtre's scheme for creating an orderly plan linking the Grand Parterre north of the château
251 with the Grand Terrasse. The Grand Terrasse was conceived in 1679, a huge promenade along the escarpment above the Seine, linking the Château de Saint-Germain with the Château de Val in the forest to the north. It was planned by Louis Le Vau and Le Nôtre in consultation with Colbert; but since Le Vau died in 1670, the building of the terrace walls was supervised by Hardouin-Mansart. The terrace is the subject of one of the rare surviving drawings from Le Nôtre's own hand.[37] Le Vau favoured a line standing back from the edge of the escarpment and changing direction slightly at a *rond-point* part of the way along. This cautious solution would probably have avoided the building of so massive a retaining wall. In the event, Le Nôtre's advice prevailed, and the terrace stretches in an unbroken line for almost 2½ kilometres, dipping slightly towards the centre, so that the apparent length seems rather less. From the crescent belvedere at its southern end, two broad *allées*, planted with elms, parallel to the Jardin de le Dauphine, linked it to the circular basin at the end of Le Nôtre's Grand Parterre placed in relation to the axis of the old irregular château's north front. According to Antoine l'Ainé, the parterre was made in 1674, 'planted in two big pieces of box *broderie*, separated in the middle by a fine *allée* 60 feet [*dix toises*] wide, surrounded by beds of flowers of all seasons, with cross walks of spruce and horse-chestnut, having three big basins of water in various places . . .'. Characteristically, the axis of the parterre was extended by an avenue into the forest.

251 The Grande Terrasse of Saint-Germain-en-Laye.

252 View looking from the Tuileries gardens to the palace, after the road that originally separated them had been removed.

THE TUILERIES

The Tuileries was the garden with which Le Nôtre was most closely associated throughout his life, near which he was born, and the only one for whose maintenance he was directly responsible. Since Catherine de Médicis' day it had remained separated from the palace by a wall and a public road. Because of this, and of its site on the fringe of the city, it had become used as a public garden. The private garden, or Petit Jardin, of the Tuileries, between the palace and the Louvre, was maintained by the Mollet family. On Gomboust's map of Paris (1652) it is called the Parterre de Mademoiselle, because Gaston d'Orléans's daughter, Mademoiselle de Montpensier, had lived there until Louis ordered her to leave in 1652. The garden was suppressed in 1662, shortly before Le Nôtre began the transformation of the Grand Jardin between 1665 and 1672. The Tuileries was the model for André Mollet's archetypal garden: a rectangular area, subdivided by *allées* into a regular grid-like plan, hierarchically arranged in relation to the house or palace, with *parterre de broderie*, *bosquets*, symmetrically placed about a central axis. Few sites are so free of restricting circumstances as to permit the realization of this ideal. The Tuileries was no exception. The first requirement was easy enough; the removal of the wall and the suppression of the road so that for the first time the palace
252 was directly connected with the garden. At the western end the boundary sloped in towards the river, and beyond was the
garden of Monsieur Renard, which was now destroyed in order 117
to correct the irregularity and make a balanced plan. All along the north side ran the Terrasse des Feuillants planted with mulberry trees. On the south side there was no such corresponding feature; the wall ran along the quay to the Port
de la Conference, with the houses of various people concerned 112
with supervising the gardens adjoining it. These were destroyed to make a terrace along the river; and since the site sloped, it was made higher to correspond with the terrace on the north. This was not a matter of logic, so much as a sensibility to optical effect, which was again demonstrated in the treatment of the central axis. Boyceau, it will be remembered (Chapter 9), had criticized the main *allée* of the Tuileries as being too narrow for
its length. Le Nôtre remembered this, and made it double the 253
width of those on either side. In designing the parterre to be seen from the raised terrace on which the palace was now set, the sides of the compartments furthest away were longer, and the paths surrounding the central basin wider on the far side, so that optically it would seem centrally placed. Similarly, the octagonal basin at the western extremity of the central *allée* was very much larger than those nearer to the eye. A further innovation was the inclusion of two parterres of cut turf *à l'anglaise* on either side of the triangular compartments of

253 View from the west end of the Grande Allée of the Tuileries.

broderie round the basin of the Grand Parterre. Le Nôtre created an open-ended vista leaving a gap in the terrace closed by a *grille*, with an avenue beyond stretching to the horizon; and he surrounded the opening by one of his horseshoe ramps, in order that the promenade should be continuous. The *bosquets* were varied, but more regular than those of Versailles. As an engraving published by Langlois shows, the *bosquet* near the river was planted with horse-chestnuts, spruce and yew; as was the theatre in the northwest corner. Horse-chestnut replaced the old mulberries in the Terrasse des Feuillants; while the avenue parallel to it below was planted with limes, replacing elms in 1672. Yew, fir trees and shrubs were brought from Saint-Mandé in 1667. Antoine Trumel supervised the transplanting of evergreen shrubs from Vaux in 1668, possibly holly and box, which was required in large quantities. Other trees referred to in the accounts are cypress, maple, sycamore and acacia.

From 1673, in addition to his salaries as Contrôleur Général des Bâtiments du Roi (1657) and as Dessinateur des Parterres et de tous les Jardins du Roi, Le Nôtre received 8000 *livres* a year specifically for the upkeep of parts of the Tuileries, namely: the *parterre de broderie*, which he himself had designed immediately adjoining the palace, together with the parterres of turf and the *palissades* of the crescent planted with fir, yew and cypress, as far as the first horse chestnut tree of the great central walk. His duties included weeding, smoothing and raking the walks; clipping and manuring the box; and stocking the borders with flowers in season at his own expense. For this he received 5000 *livres*; and in addition he was paid 1500 *livres* for a flower-garden between the Grand Parterre and the Terrasse des Feuillants, which he had always to keep full of flowers, particularly during the winter; and 1500 *livres* for the espalier of *jasmin d'Espagne* along the wall of the terrace.

Le Nôtre's brother-in-law, Pierre Desgots, was in charge of the rest of the park; his nieces, daughters of Simon Bouchard and Françoise Le Nôtre, were responsible for the orangery and the 'parterre à fleurs et autres jardins à fleurs derrière, près la Garenne' (that is, near the site of Renard's garden). The *allée* of white mulberries, *palissades*, Judas trees, and the box of the transverse *allées*, had been maintained by Claude Carbonet after Pierre Mollet's death. In 1670 his widow succeeded to the post. The only other gardeners receiving a regular salary were Guillaume Masson and his sisters-in-law Claude and Elizabeth Le Juge, who were employed to trim the box in the Grand Parterre and other *palissades* of jasmine, quince, pomegranate and Judas trees.

The general appearance of the garden newly planted is clearly 254
shown in a drawing by Israel Silvestre.[38] The Grand Parterre in the foreground is the main area for which Le Nôtre was

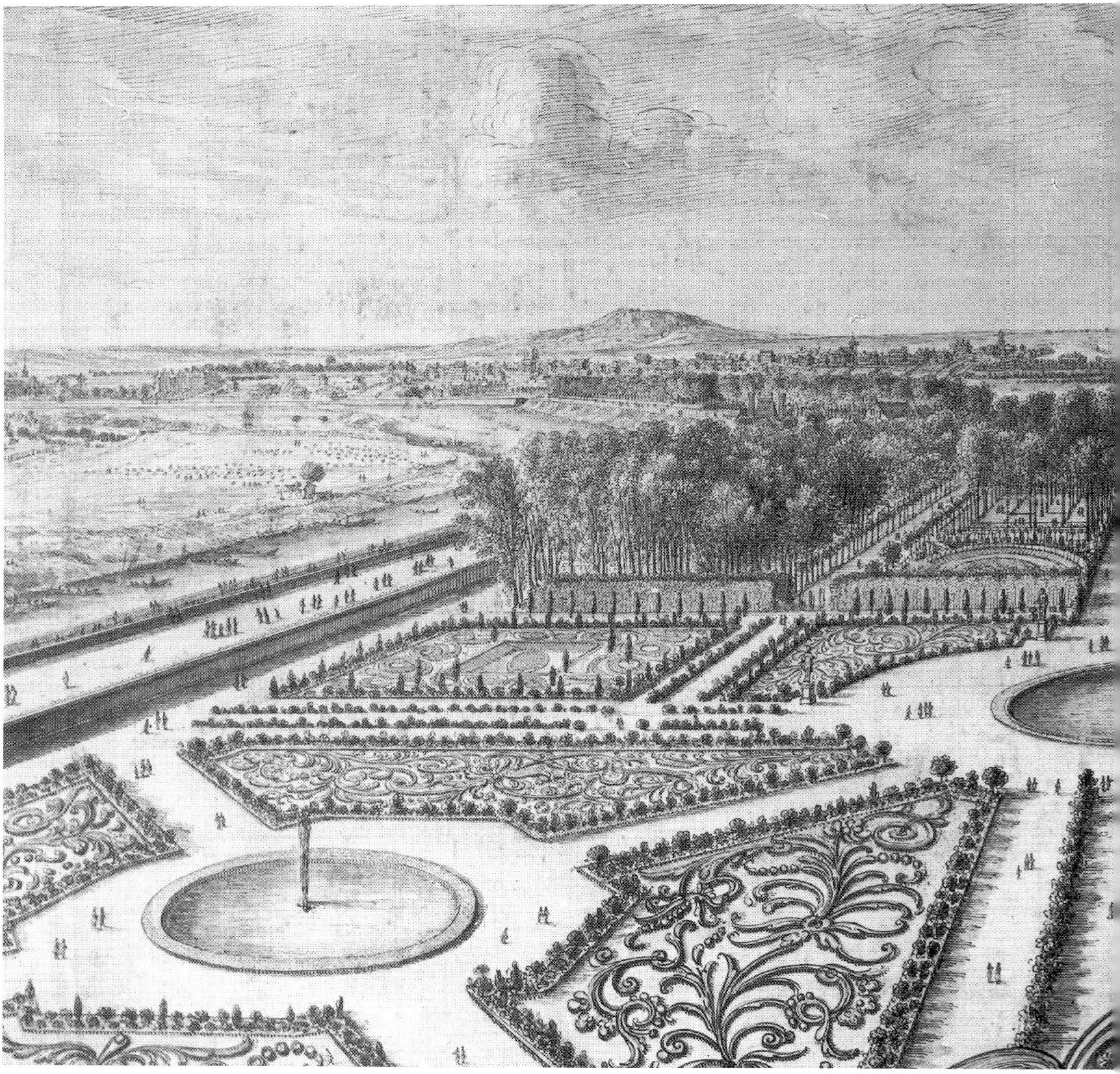

254 The Tuileries gardens, newly planted, looking west to the future route of the Champs Elysées.

responsible; with the row of cypress separating it from the rest of the park. The central *allée* extends in a virtually unbroken line to the avenue which is the future Champs Elysées. On the right is the *allée* of lime trees, hiding the Terrasse des Feuillants; on the left is the new terrace and, as Germain Brice wrote in 1713[39], 'the Seine forming a wide canal along the Cours de la Reine; and beyond, a countryside dotted with villages as far as the hills of Meudon and Saint-Cloud'. According to Charles Perrault, when the garden was newly planted Colbert wished to close it to the public. '"Come," M. Colbert said to me, ... "this garden must be kept for the king and not allowed to be ruined by

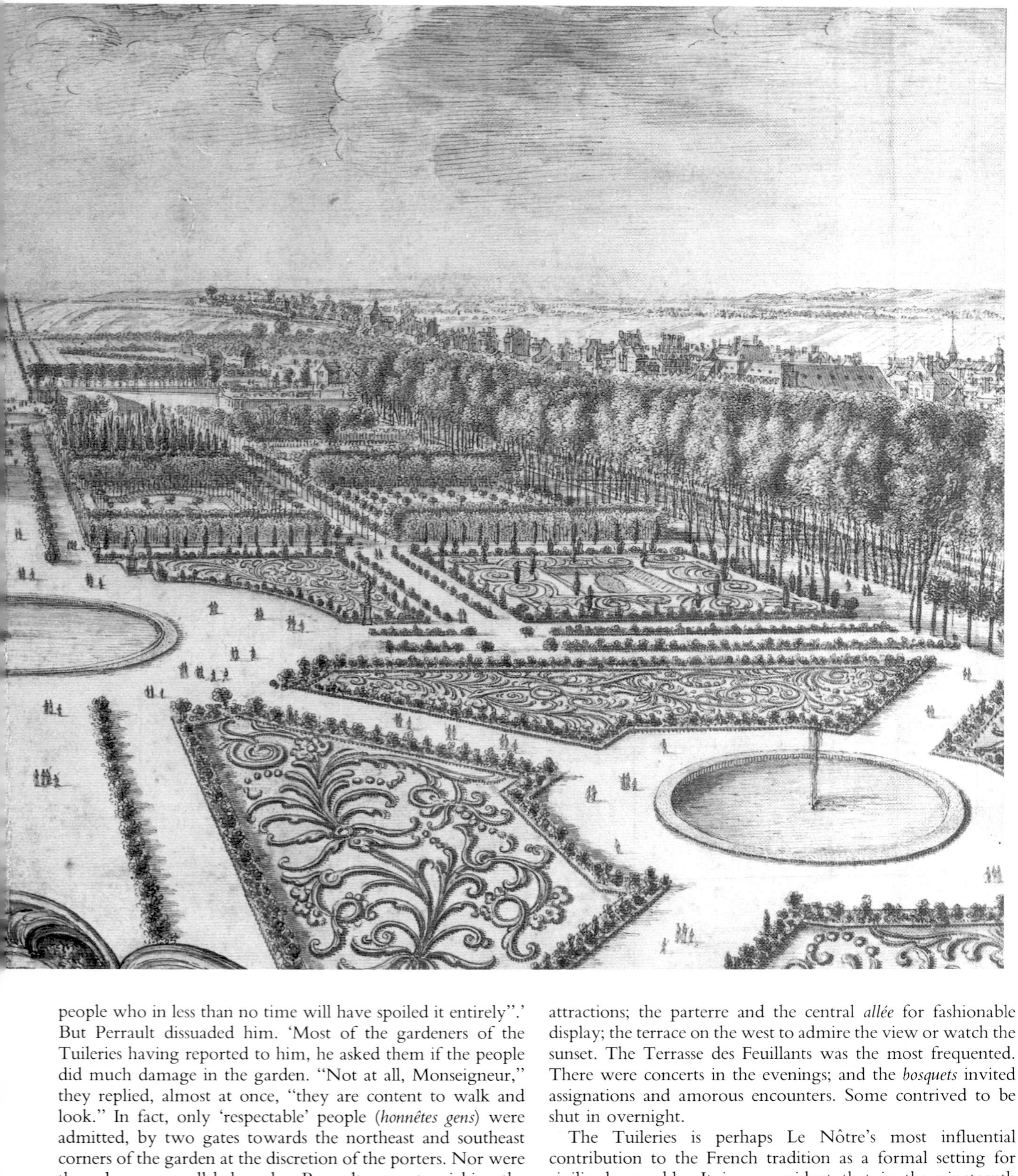

people who in less than no time will have spoiled it entirely".' But Perrault dissuaded him. 'Most of the gardeners of the Tuileries having reported to him, he asked them if the people did much damage in the garden. "Not at all, Monseigneur," they replied, almost at once, "they are content to walk and look." In fact, only 'respectable' people (*honnêtes gens*) were admitted, by two gates towards the northeast and southeast corners of the garden at the discretion of the porters. Nor were they always as well behaved as Perrault suggests, picking the flowers in the parterres, breaking through the hedges, defacing the trees with carved initials. All parts of the garden had their attractions; the parterre and the central *allée* for fashionable display; the terrace on the west to admire the view or watch the sunset. The Terrasse des Feuillants was the most frequented. There were concerts in the evenings; and the *bosquets* invited assignations and amorous encounters. Some contrived to be shut in overnight.

The Tuileries is perhaps Le Nôtre's most influential contribution to the French tradition as a formal setting for civilized assembly. It is no accident that in the nineteenth century the great lines of his garden formed the basis for Haussmann's plan for Paris.

13

Le Nôtre and the Genius of the Place

LE NÔTRE HARDLY EVER worked on a virgin site; Vaux and
256 Clagny are the only ones that come to mind. Nor were
257 conditions often favourable for creating regular gardens in the classical tradition. In fact those of any size rarely do conform to the ideal, and the talents of the landscape gardener have to be applied to a variety of situations between the extremes of flat, irregular and steep. While the gardener may prefer flat ground, differences of level offer more opportunities to the landscape gardener; and there is no doubt that that is where Le Nôtre's talent lay. His formula was a broad straight vista sweeping to the horizon, preferably sited across a shallow valley, with a great canal at right angles to it. Ideally the main lines of the composition were on the axis of the house, as at Vaux; but often circumstances prevented this.

CHANTILLY

After Anne de Montmorency's death in 1567, Chantilly had passed to his son, Henri, Constable of France under Henri IV; and eventually to his grandson Henri II de Montmorency, who was executed at Toulouse in 1632 for taking part in Gaston d'Orléans' rebellion against Richelieu. His estates were confiscated, but returned by Anne d'Autriche to his sister Charlotte, who had married Henri de Bourbon, Prince de Condé. Their son, Louis II de Bourbon, known as 'Le Grand Condé', led the army of the anti-Mazarin faction during the Fronde. In 1652 he fled to the Low Countries, and his properties were confiscated. The young Louis XIV had need of Condé's talent as a military commander; and his estates and offices were restored in 1659. Between 1667 and 1675 he was responsible for notable military successes against the Spaniards in the Franche-Comté and the Dutch in Flanders. Conquered by gout in 1675, he retired to Chantilly and devoted his restless energy to directing the work on his estates until his death in 1685.

The park and gardens of Chantilly had remained more or less as they are shown on Jacques Androuet du Cerceau's plan of the 1570s. That is to say, that the old château of the Montmorency and the Petit Château stood in huge pond-like moats. West of these was a large square garden with the Galerie des Cerfs; and beyond that an orchard and vegetable garden. East of the château was the constable's terrace and the park. The approach was from the southwest, by a causeway across the moats and the so-called Étang de Sylvie, with direct access to the Petit Château, or through the park to the terrace opposite the main entrance of the old château.

In 1662 Condé employed Le Nôtre, who had recently completed Vaux-le-Vicomte, to redesign his grounds. Montmorency's park covered roughly 250 acres (*arpents*); but Condé's plans embraced an area ten times as great, involving several villages and tracts of forest acquired mainly from the Church. Le Nôtre's scheme imposed regularity by means of a giant axial arrangement, with the Constable's terrace as its centre. The approach from the southwest had not given direct access for carriages to the old château, which was entered from
the terrace. Carriages could reach this by an avenue through the 258
park on the east leading straight to the main entrance. This direct approach could have been opened up, but to little purpose. A formal approach on the level from that direction would have been an anticlimax, since there was no possibility of creating a grand parterre on the same axis to the west. It is characteristic of Le Nôtre that he should have sited his new approach at right-angles to the main façade and across a valley, to give differences of level which could be used to great effect. This can only be appreciated on the ground. From the south a
grand esplanade slopes up to the terrace, beyond which is 259
concealed the transformation of the marshy valley of the Nonette, with the biggest garden canal ever made. A branch of this marks the continuation of the axis to the north, and separates two identical water parterres with basins and fountains. On the far side of the canal, a crescent-shaped bay and a grass theatre lined with busts of the twelve Caesars closed the vista; although at either end of the axis avenues stretched into the forest.

The work at Chantilly is exceptionally well recorded, both by a series of plans and by documents, many of which are quoted by Gustave Maçon in his *Les Arts dans la Maison de Condé* (1903). Le Nôtre was assisted by his brother-in-law and his nephew, Pierre and Claude Desgots; the hydraulics engineer, Jacques de Manse; and Daniel Gittard, the architect. La Quintinye, who was appointed Jardinier du Roi in 1665, also served Condé.[1] The Grand Parterre was laid out by December 1666, when Condé wrote to his secretary: 'Dites à M. Le Nostre que je le prie de venir ici. Nous avons essayé La Gerbe[2] mais cela

255 André Le Nôtre: marble bust by Antoine Coysevox

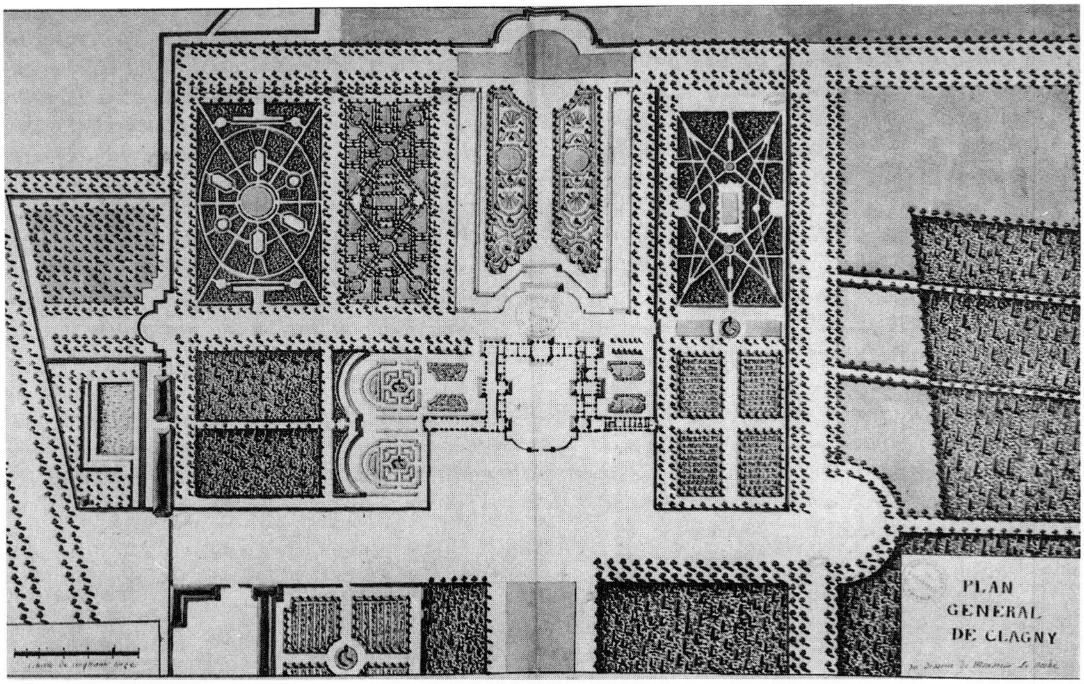

256, 257 Clagny: plan of the château and garden as designed by Le Nôtre (garden at the top), and a view from the garden side in 1679, which does not conform to Le Nôtre's plan.

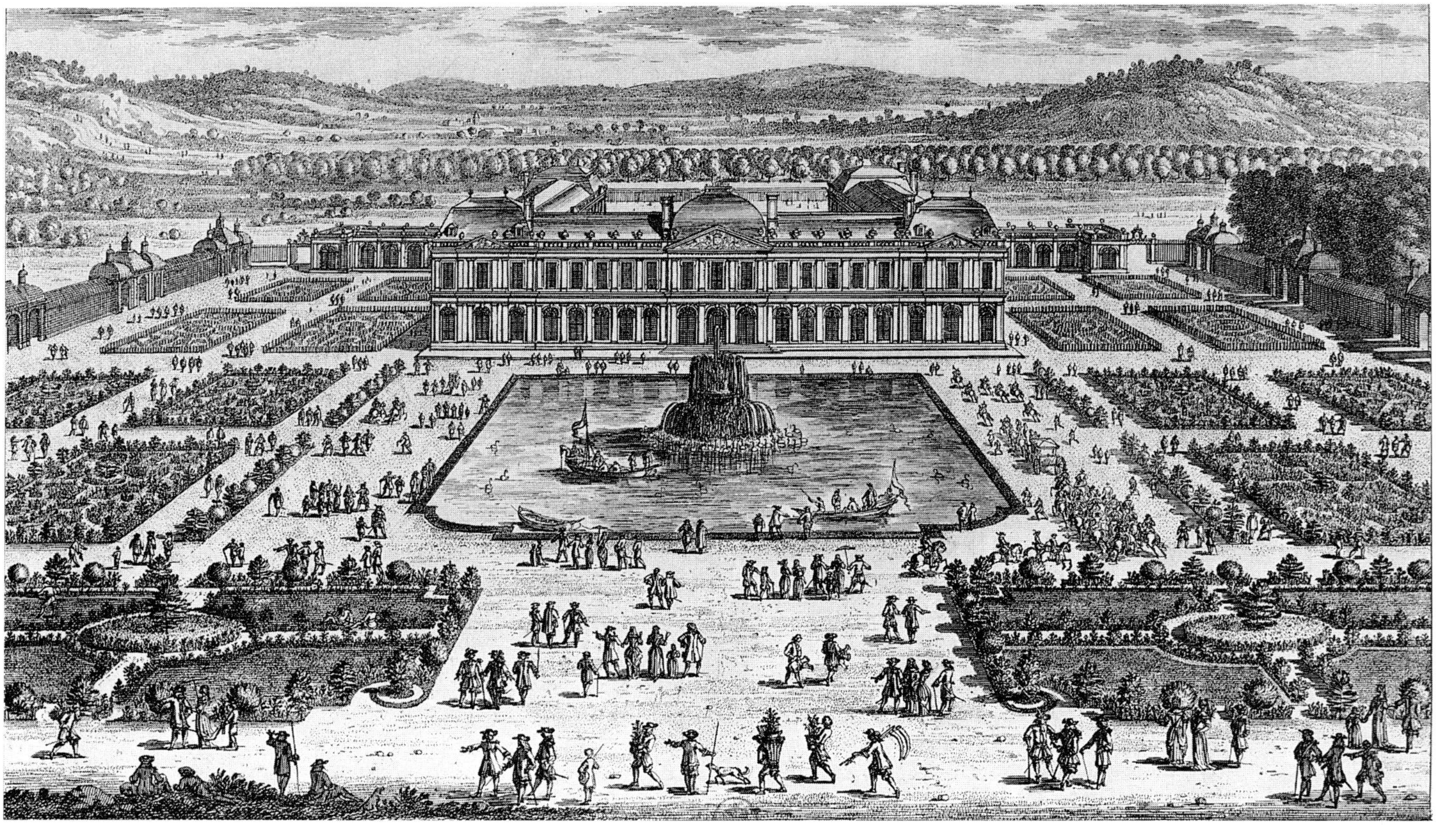

ne fait pas tout l'effet que j'avais espéré; il faut son avis pour la raccommoder.' The monumental steps (Le Grand Degré), designed by Gittard, leading from the terrace to the parterre, were not completed until 1684, when the sculptor Jean Hardy finished the statues of the giant River Gods, in niches on either side.

The Grand Canal was excavated in 1671/2; but the stone cladding took ten more years and was still not finished in 1681.
260 Pierre Desgots' plan of 1673 shows the whole of Le Nôtre's scheme. That same year Condé himself, in the presence of Le Nôtre, staked out in the ponds the limits of the great esplanade forming the approach to the terrace from the south. This is but one example of the part he took in directing the work at Chantilly, even while campaigning in Flanders; indeed enemy skills served his gardens, for he employed Dutch craftsmen for the trellis porticos and pavilions, observing that 'les Hollandais sont les plus habiles gens du monde pour ces sortes de cabinets'. These were in the area west of the moats, where the old gardens of the Montmorency were transformed between 1663 and 1680. The redesigning of the square garden with the Galerie des Cerfs was in fact that first work Le Nôtre undertook at Chantilly. An orangery, designed by Hardouin-Mansart, was built on the south side and at right angles to the Galerie, between 1683 and 1686, after which it became known as the Parterre de l'Orangerie. West of this there stretched an irregular collection of pleasure gardens, kitchen and fruit gardens and *bosquets*.

Immediately to the north, between the parterre and the water meadows, was a long rectangular island entered through a
portico of trelliswork. The end of the walk was lined with 261
fountains falling into bowls, and the canals on either side merged in a cascade. Immediately behind the Galerie des Cerfs
was a straight walk, with a long parterre of turf (Le Boulingrin) 262
on the right (north) side. On the left side were the so-called Cascades de Beauvais. The *Mercure Galant* described them in 1688,[3] on the occasion of a week of fêtes given in honour of the Grand Dauphin by Condé's son, as having water issuing from bronze masks falling into as many shells, and eventually into a basin. By 1680 the pleasure ground west of the moats stretched for over a kilometre. Concealed in the *bosquets* at the far end was
the Grand Cascade, an elaborate architectural set-piece of 264
fountains, steps and basins, the water from which eventually passed underground into one of the canals. This cascade is also described in detail in the *Mercure Galant*.

The source of the water was far away to the east, where the little Nonette fell into two great circular and hexagonal basins at the head of the canal. In order to feed all these cascades and

258 Chantilly: the pre-Le Nôtre carriage approach to the main entrance from the east. Jules Hardouin-Mansart's Orangerie can be seen on the left.

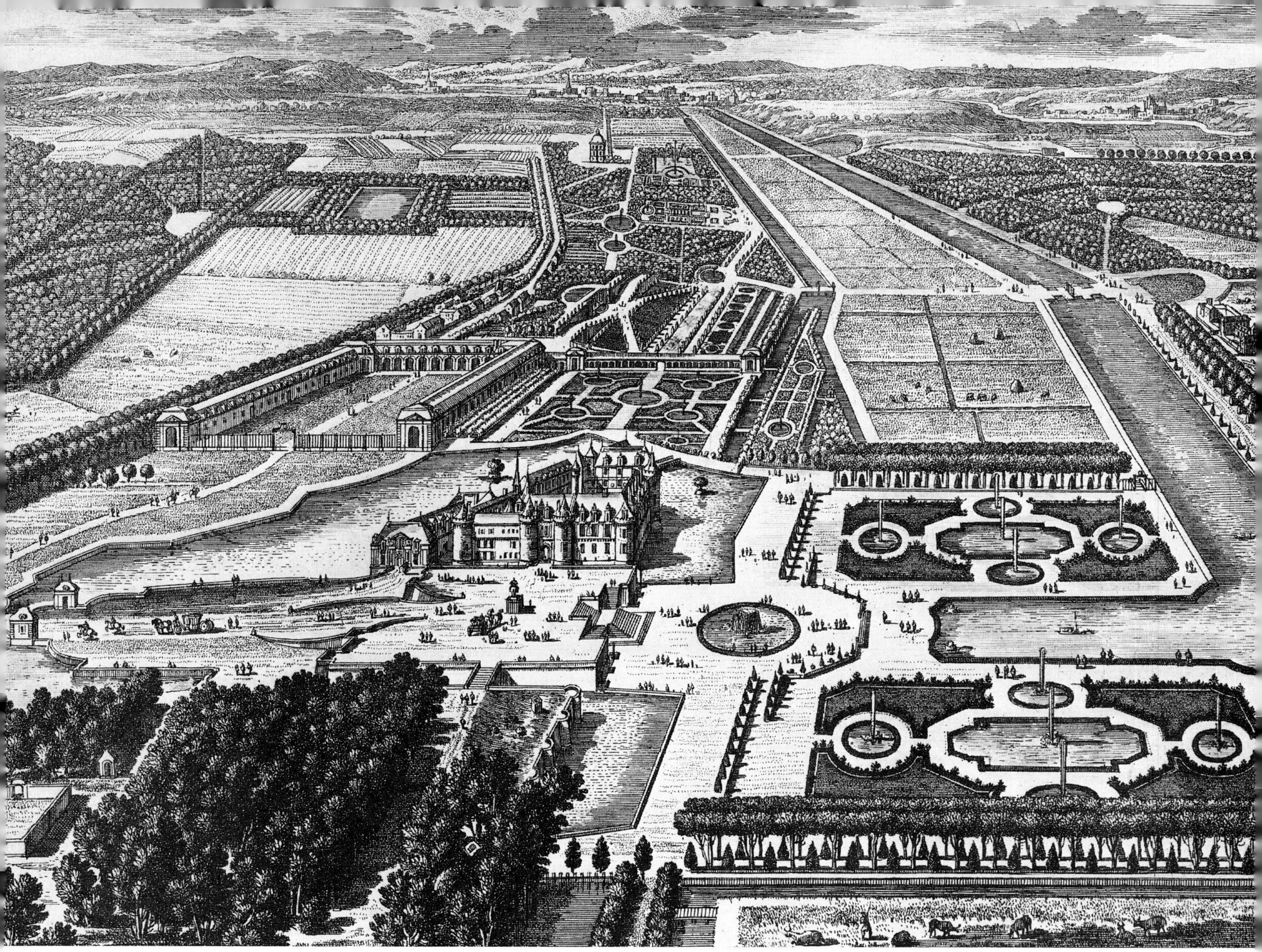

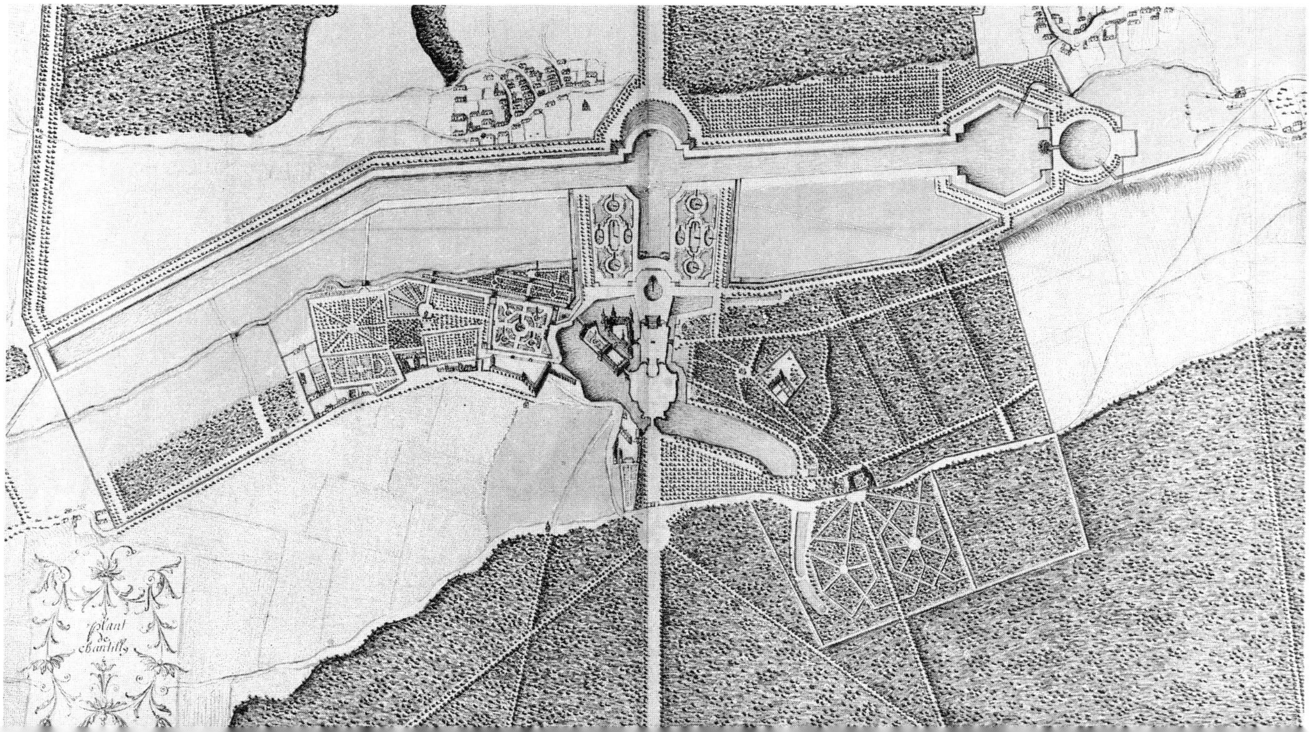
Plant
de
Chantilly

259 Chantilly: general view from the east, showing the Grand Canal excavated in 1671–2 on the right. Beyond the château, the Parterre de l'Orangerie and gardens stretching for over a kilometre to the west.

260 Pierre Desgots's plan of 1673 (south at bottom) showing Le Nôtre's scheme based on a new approach at right-angles to the façade.

261, 262 Chantilly, the Cascades du Petit Bois north of the Grande Parterre (top); the Boulingrin and the Cascades de Beauvais (centre).

263 Chantilly: esplanade from the south, showing the dramatic use of the slope up to the terrace.

264, 265 Chantilly: the Grande Cascade (above) and the Pavillon de Manse.

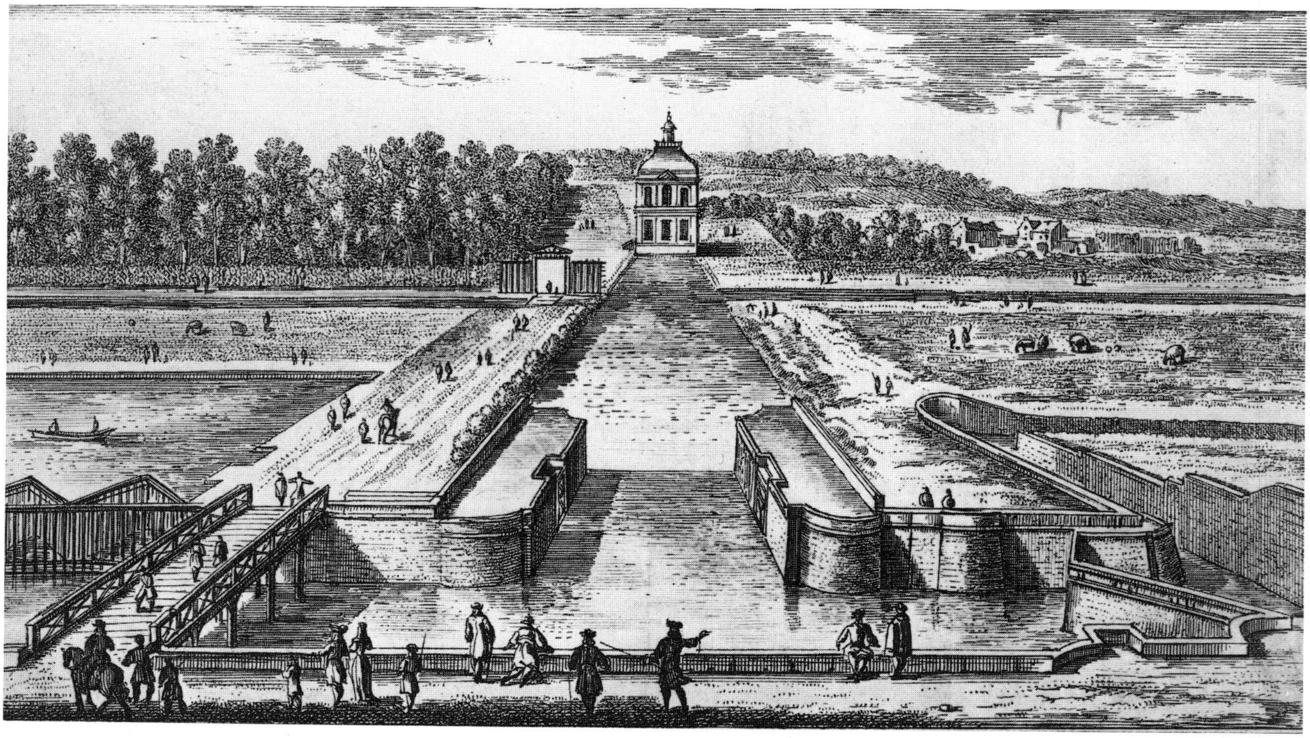

265 fountains in an absolutely flat site, the engineer de Manse devised an elaborate hydraulic machine in the southwest corner of the park to pump the water into a reservoir. On 26 April 1679, Claude Richard, concierge at Chantilly wrote to Condé: 'Your Highness's blacksmith yesterday brought part of the pipes and pumps of the machine of the pavilion; the carpenters promise that the wheel will be put in place at the end of this week. M. de Manse can make his arrangements on that assumption.' By the end of the year it was functioning satisfactorily. Claude Desgots laid out a huge labyrinth in the
266 park east of the château, and the so-called Maison de Sylvie[4] was also rebuilt about 1670, with a small garden of three triangular compartments enclosed in *berceaux* of trelliswork. Chantilly was a great complex, all the details of which are beyond the scope of this book. Le Nôtre received from Condé an annual salary of 2200 *livres*, for what he regarded as one of his most important works. As he wrote to William III's ambassador, the duke of Portland, after a visit to France in 1698, 'Souvenez-vous de tout ce que vous avez vu de jardins en France, Versailles, Fontainebleau, Vaux-le-Vicomte et les Tuileries et surtout Chantilly.'

DAMPIERRE

The formula Le Nôtre inherited for laying out the grounds of great houses was an architect's concept, designed to display the house as a symbol of the status of the owner, and is properly called 'formal' in the sense of 'ceremonial'. The hierarchical arrangement of the axial approach, through imposing forecourts with the garden as a splendid climax, is not a necessary part of the ideal deriving from the Vitruvian concept of beauty, bringing all parts into harmonious relation with one another. These were the general principles on which Le Nôtre worked. On the other hand, he sought to give variety by departing from a strictly symmetrical arrangement of the parts, by creating secondary axes, and by the element of surprise. Although he did not originate the extended axis, he exploited this feature to greater effect than anyone had done before him. Characteristic of his style are open-ended vistas dominating the landscape. But the art of Le Nôtre lies in the way in which the principles are adapted to a great variety of situations, which impose their own conditions by their topography; for it can be said that no site exactly resembles any other. Most of the sites where Le Nôtre worked had old gardens. In some cases, as at Chantilly, he was not able to incorporate the old château in his
plan. But at Dampierre (Yvelines) the old house of the Lorraine 44
was rebuilt by Hardouin-Mansart for the Duc de Chevreuse[5] between 1675 and 1686, with an approach through a hierarchy
of courtyards. This enabled Le Nôtre to orientate his design of 267
parterres, basins and cascades on the axis, across the valley, extending it in vistas through the park at either end. Thus, while retaining the framework of the earlier causeway and canals, he changed the emphasis.

266 Chantilly: the Maison de Sylvie with its garden.

267 Air view of Dampierre showing Le Nôtre's reworking of the earlier garden (see ill. 44).

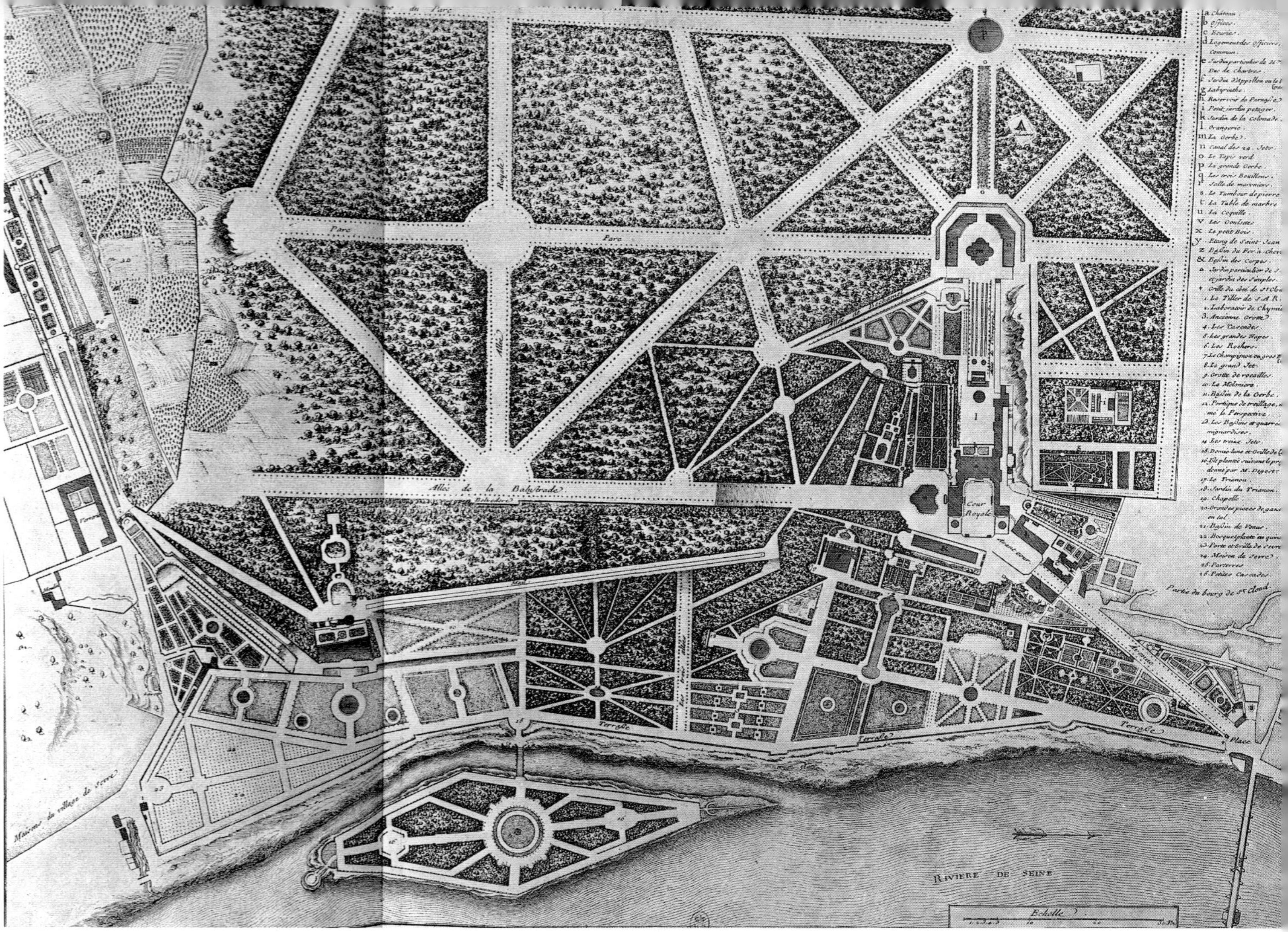

268 Plan of the château and garden of Saint-Cloud, redesigned by Le Nôtre after 1665.

SAINT-CLOUD

268 A far more complex situation existed at Saint-Cloud.[6] The already magnificent garden of Jean-François de Gondi (see Chapter 8) was sold after his death in 1654 to Barthélemy d'Hévart, Intendant des Finances, a Protestant of German origin who had been of great service to Mazarin and the king. He restored the grounds, which during the Fronde had been the scene of a battle between Condé and Turenne, and enlarged them by the purchase of hundreds of acres of adjoining land. He also acquired rights to springs in the region to fill his reservoirs and increase the water supply for new hydraulic creations. Huygens[7] wrote in 1665:

> The same evening we again went to Saint-Cloud to see Gondi, the garden which formerly belonged to the archbishop of Paris, cardinal de Retz, but is now sold for 24 thousand *ecus* to Monsieur Intendant des Finances, who has more than 200 people working in the gardens daily. As he chanced to be there with several ladies, he gave us permission to enter; the house is mediocre, but much decorated on the outside with fresco paintings which have however suffered from exposure to the weather. The garden is no bigger than our Hofwyck, but wonderfully beautiful and pleasant.
>
> The trees are tall, the *allées* dark, the parterres well kept, the fountains natural, the grotto well fashioned, the cascade delightful, although not so abounding in water as the one at Rueil . . . On entering the gardens there is a marvellous view of Paris over the parterres . . . There are several other fine gardens to see here at St. Cloud, but we did not have the time.

In 1658 Saint-Cloud was bought by Louis XIV's younger brother, Philippe de Bourbon, Duc d'Anjou, who became Duc d'Orléans on the death of his uncle, Gaston. The same year (1660) he appointed Antoine Le Pautre[8] as his Contrôleur Général des Bâtiments. Among Le Pautre's works was the great 269
architectural cascade in the garden, finished in 1667 and enlarged 270
after 1675 by Hardouin-Mansart.

According to Piganiol de la Force,[9] Le Nôtre was employed to redesign the gardens in 1665. The approach to the château was by an avenue running diagonally from the bridge across the

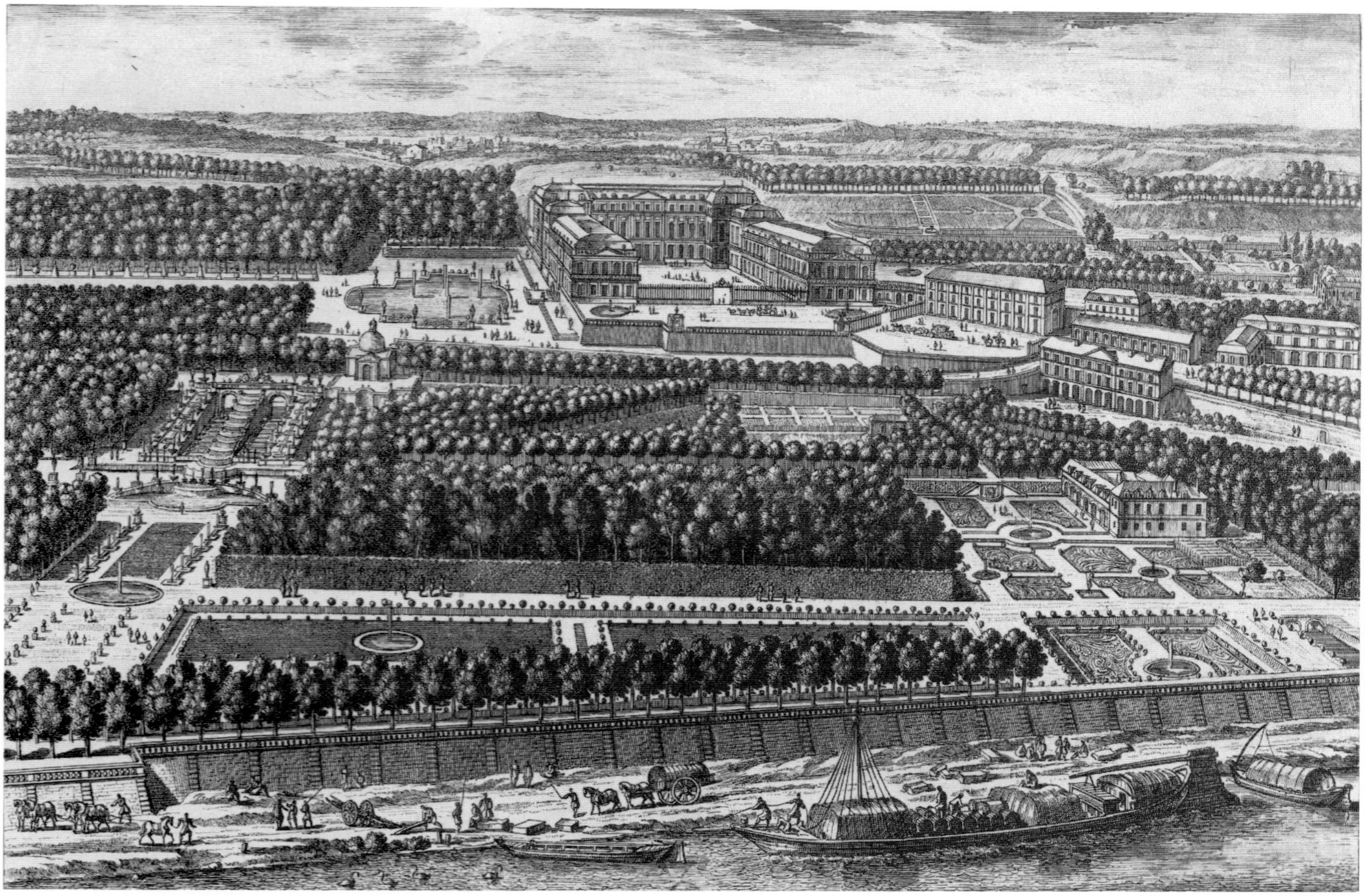

◁ 269, 270 The Cascade at Saint-Cloud as designed by Antoine Le Pautre (opposite above) and as enlarged after 1675 by Jules Hardouin-Mansart (opposite below).

271 Saint-Cloud: general view of the château and gardens from the east. Hardouin-Mansart's Cascade is centre left. Right of it is the old *grotte*. See ill. 155.

Seine to the main courtyard on the east. On the west a wide vista 271
was opened up, with the Orangerie in the foreground, sloping up to a water parterre with a quatrefoil basin and a horseshoe canal. Beyond this the axis was prolonged into the park, to where eight great *allées* met in a star with a circular basin in the centre. East of the château, where the ground fell away steeply to the river, it was Le Nôtre's idea to continue the axis. In one of his rare surviving drawings (National Museum, Stockholm, THC 7939) he shows monumental stairs imposed on the old irregular gardens, leaving Le Pautre's cascade on the left. This scheme was not carried out. The Duc d'Orléans had his apartments in the wing facing south, also designed by Le Pautre, overlooking what was formerly the old garden of the Gondi.
Opposite this, Le Nôtre made a broad *allée* which descended 272
and then rose up the opposing hill[10] to a platform with 273
magnificent views over Paris on one side, and, on the other, a semicircular clearing from which three other *allées* diverged in a huge *patte d'oie*. If we look at the plan of Saint-Cloud we can see that this *allée* formed the basis of le Nôtre's geometry.

274 The château of Sceaux from the approaches. The *allée* leading to the cascade (276) is on the left beyond the château

SCEAUX

At Sceaux abrupt differences of level were used to even greater effect. The barony was acquired in 1670 by Colbert, who rebuilt the château and employed Le Nôtre to lay out the grounds. The house and the adjoining gardens were placed on a level platform, approached by the usual avenue and courtyards. A 274
plan of the original scheme[11] shows the site to be restricted to the south and terraced in three stages, with a *parterre de broderie* and a rectangular basin. The only room for an extended axis was on the east; and here, where the ground fell steeply, Le Nôtre made a magnificent cascade or water-stairway, falling into a large 275
octagonal basin. Later the grounds were enlarged so that the vista was extended beyond the basin and up the opposing hill. 276
Between 1695 and 1700 a huge canal was made in the bottom, also in a west-east direction; and at the same time, on the axis of the house, the vista extended into a great lawn sloping to the south.

272, 273 Saint-Cloud: the south front in an eighteenth-century drawing (opposite above), and the south vista looking from the former château (opposite below), showing Le Nôtre's broad *allée*.

277 Meudon: Le Nôtre's *parterre* below the *grotte* in 1705.

275, 276 Opposite: the octagonal basin and cascade at Sceaux in the seventeenth century (top) and the view today looking in the opposite direction. The original cascade was destroyed; this is a modern reconstruction.

MEUDON

One of the most spectacular sites was at Meudon, where Servien's estate was acquired by the Marquis de Louvois[12] in 1679; and in 1695, after his death, became the residence of the Grand Dauphin. Le Nôtre cannot be said to have designed Meudon, whose great natural advantages had been recognized and exploited by Servien. The château and the grotto tucked into the hillside, to face south and east respectively, commanded views towards wooded hills on either side. The south aspect was chosen for the making of a great vista through fields and woods
to the horizon. Silvestre's panoramic drawings convey the 189
splendour and variety of the situation better than any 190
descriptions. Le Nôtre's originality is shown in his treatment of the parterre below the grotto, a single design of *broderie* and cut
turf round a square basin, adapted to be seen from the terraces 277
on any side.

278 Maintenon: the garden canal with the abandoned aqueduct intended to bring the waters of the Eure to Versailles.

279 Anet: an air-view today.

MAINTENON

We have already seen how Le Nôtre exploited the canal as a feature in flat marshy sites. In 1676, when he redesigned the grounds of the old château of Maintenon,[13] he canalized the River Eure, extending the moats to form an island parterre and continuing the axis in a canal. Closing the vista was the
278 abandoned aqueduct intended to bring the waters of the river to
Versailles, a perpetual reminder of the extravagance the marquise so much deplored.

ANET

A similar scheme was planned for Anet when Louis-Joseph de Vendôme employed Le Nôtre (or more probably Claude Desgots) to redesign the grounds on a scale which dwarfed the Renaissance garden. A canal at right angles to the château collected the waters of a small tributary of the Eure to feed the moats surrounding a huge parterre. A plan of the original
scheme (National Museum, Stockholm, THC 7934) shows the 280
intention to extend this in a canal on the axis of the château (as at
Maintenon) to join the canalized Eure itself in a great T. This 279
part of the scheme was not carried out.

CASTRIES

Of many other smaller gardens designed by or attributed to him, one of the most interesting is at Castries (Hérault). Here, for René Gaspard de la Croix, Marquis de Castries, gardens

280 Anet: the scheme of 1681–88. The huge canalization of the Eure in the form of a T was never carried out.

281 View from the terrace of Castries, with circular basin and vista in false perspective.

were laid out in 1666 which have the marks of his style in miniature: the double axis, the use of water, the element of surprise. The main parterre with two circular basins and fountains is laid out on the foundations of a demolished wing.
281 On the far side of this, when the balustrade is reached, a large circular basin is revealed, with an avenue in false perspective continuing the axis beyond. To the left of the terrace is a small *parterre de broderie*, framed in ramps on either side. The most extravagant part of the scheme is a great aqueduct 7 kilometres long, designed by the engineer Riquet and built between 1670 and 1676 to bring water to the château, and ending in an unusual dripping grotto.

Conclusion

Le Nôtre spent the last years of his life living comfortably in his house near the Tuileries, with his collections of pictures, tapestries, bronzes, silver, gems, medals and porcelain. He had a garden of his own, two gardeners and a coachman. He died in 1700. He had had the good fortune to serve a prince who placed at his disposal the resources of the wealthiest and most powerful state in Europe. Gardens were designed on a commensurate scale; and Le Nôtre's talent was to coordinate these vast compositions in a variety of situations, so that the parts were related within a rational plan; what one author calls 'les jardins d'intelligence'.[14] Despite this, he seems to have been a relatively simple man. Even Saint-Simon (not noted for the generosity of his comments) wrote of his integrity and straightforwardness. The stories of his warmth and spontaneity are too consistent to be anything but true. Louis XIV gave him wealth and honours; but he also gave him his affection.

PART IV

The Legacy of Le Nôtre

The general Disposition of a Garden whose Slope is in Front of ye Building.

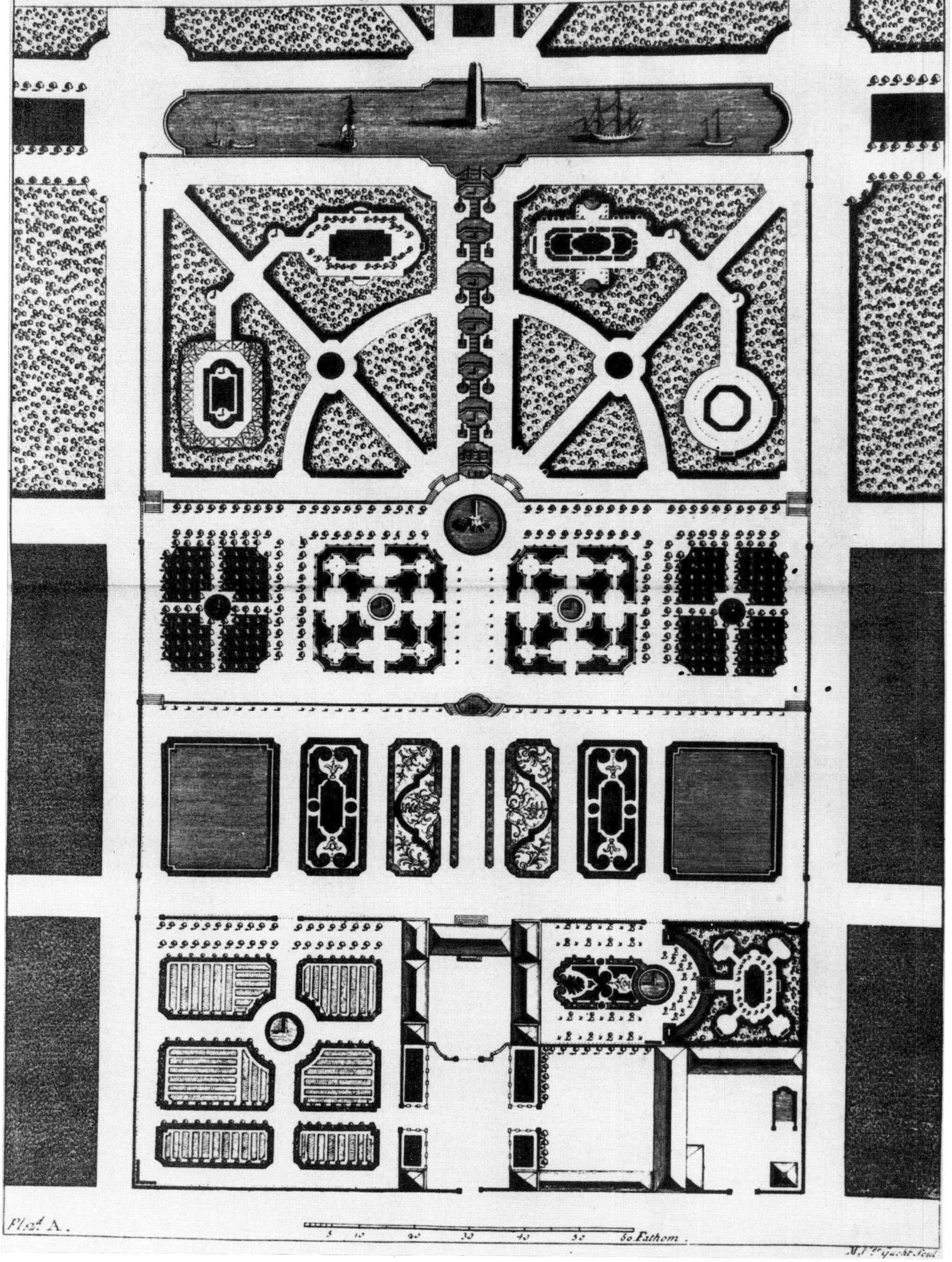

Pl. 2d. A.

M. J. Vr Gucht Sculp.

14

The theory and practice of gardening

Le Nôtre codified

THE FRENCH FORMAL STYLE received its fullest expression under Louis XIV. Subsequent modifications added little to the basic concept. This book would not be complete however without a survey of developments which led to the revolution of taste in the eighteenth century, and the reaction resulting in restorations of classical French gardens in the late-nineteenth and early-twentieth centuries.

The tradition of Le Nôtre was continued by his nephew, Claude Desgots, who succeeded him as Contrôleur des Bâtiments du Roi. Claude's father, Pierre Desgots, was an expert draughtsman who assisted his brother-in-law in
260 interpreting his schemes, as at Chantilly. Claude also worked with his uncle, taking responsibility for major work. Among important gardens designed by or attributed to him are: Anet for Louis-Joseph, Duc de Vendôme; Bagnolet for the Duchesse d' Orléans; Bizy[1] for the Maréchal de Belle-Isle; Champs[2] for the financier Paul Poisson, called Bourvalais. He was sent to England in 1698 in connection with plans for Windsor and Greenwich; and in 1713 he provided designs for parterres in the gardens at Cliveden, Buckinghamshire.[3]

The French grand manner was imitated by all the princes of Europe. A knowledge of French practice was widely diffused in *La Théorie et la Pratique du Jardinage*, by A.-J. Dézallier d'Argenville[4] published anonymously in 1709, the definitive manual of the style. Jean-Baptiste de la Quintinye's *Instruction pour les Jardins Fruitiers et Potagers* had been published posthumously in 1690; but there had been no book solely on pleasure gardens since André Mollet's *Le Jardin de Plaisir* (1651). 'There is even room for surprise,' wrote Dézallier, 'that of all those who have written about gardens of fruit trees and vegetables, none have spoken thoroughly of formal gardens,[5] which are unquestionably the most beautiful and noble of all, whatever a modern author [La Quintinye] may say of them, who tries to give preference to fruit and vegetable gardens.' Such authors 'even believe that, because they know how to prune a fruit tree and plan the bed of a vegetable garden, they have a perfect understanding of formal gardens, the laying out and cultivation of which are a very different matter.'

Dézallier speaks for Le Nôtre; and we can perhaps detect overtones of an old rivalry between the king's chief gardeners; or between the professions of architecture and gardening. *La Théorie et la Pratique du Jardinage* certainly marks the ultimate separation of the *utile* from the *agréable*. 'All these kitchen gardens, all these fruit trees, however fine they may be, are always put in places apart, separated from other gardens; an obvious proof that they are deemed more necessary and useful for a house than to add to its beauty and magnificence.' The gardens to which Dézallier refers (Versailles, Saint-Cloud, Meudon, Sceaux, Chantilly, Marly) are far removed from René d'Anjou's 'Verger' at Aix; or even Richelieu's gardens at Rueil, with their mixture of 'vineyards, cornfields, meadows . . . and walks of great length.'

So Dézallier's book deals with the ordering of a garden according to André Mollet's classic formulation; a hierarchy of parterres, and *bosquets* arranged symmetrically about a central walk, an extension of the axis of the house. It is in fact an extension of the living space, 'thrown into those figures that are most commended in the platform of a house', as Alberti put it. But if the plan of a house gives a poor idea (at least to a layman) of the spatial reality, even less does a plan convey the experience of a garden, not only of its relief, but of the relation to its surroundings.

In fact Dézallier's plans are schematic generalizations of Le Nôtre's style; which itself was a development from the Vitruvian concept of beauty as regularity and balance. Such principles could only be applied in gardens of limited extent; irregular sites impose their own logic and, as Montaigne had observed of the gardens of Italy in 1580, these could be turned to good advantage. Indeed, as we have seen, such sites were deliberately chosen.

In the revised, 1713 edition of Dézallier's book (Part I, Chapter 3) we read: 'Four fundamental maxims may be distinguished for laying out a garden well: the first is to make art give way to nature. . . . Second, not to over-enclose [*offusquer*]; third, not to reveal too much; fourth, always to make it appear larger than it is.'

282 Plate from A.-J. Dézallier d'Argenville's *La Théorie et la Pratique du Jardinage*, 1709, showing a house (at the bottom) with a garden sloping down to a canal.

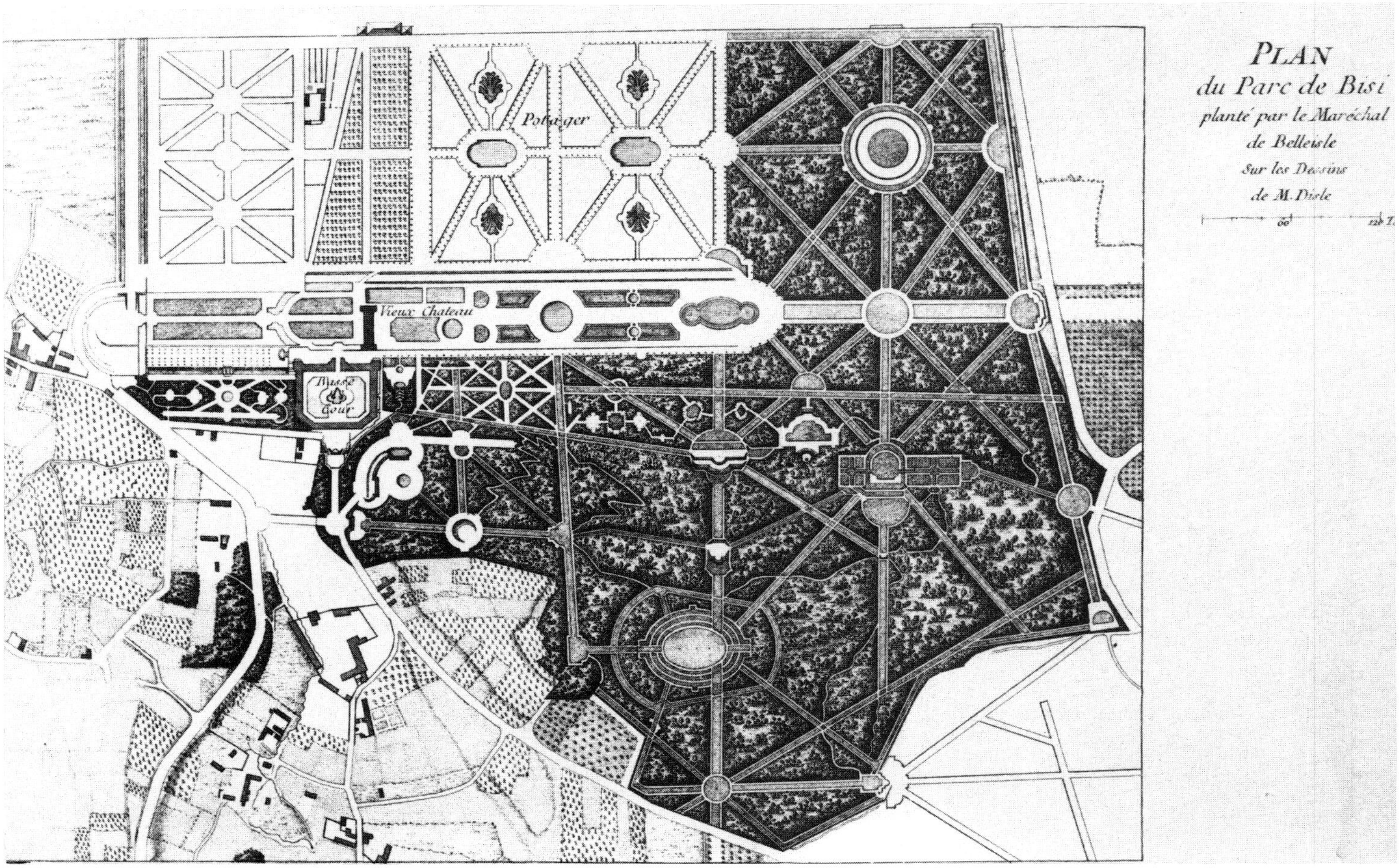

Pope almost paraphrases Dézallier:

> In all, let Nature never be forgot.
> But treat the Goddess like a modest fair,
> Nor overdress, nor leave her wholly bare;
> Let not each beauty ev'rywhere be spy'd,
> Where half the skill is decently to hide.
> He gains all points, who pleasingly confounds,
> Surprises, varies, and conceals the bounds.[6]

When Dézallier writes, 'a garden should owe more to nature than to art, which must only be used to show it to best
284 advantage', he is talking about 'the noble simplicity of steps,
285 banks and ramps of turf, natural arbours, simple hedges without trellis', as opposed to extravagant architectural ornament, stone terraces, overdecorated fountains, too many trellis porticos decorated with statues and vases. The more 'natural' gardens to which he refers are Chantilly, Saint-Cloud and Sceaux, as opposed to Meudon. The garden is intermediate between the architecture of the house and the open countryside or, as at Fontainebleau, the forest. 'There is nothing more entertaining, nor more pleasant in a garden, than a fine view, and the sight of a beautiful country. The pleasure of revealing from a terrace many villages, woods, rivers, wooded hills, meadows richly stocked with animals and watered by a stream, and a thousand other things which go to make up a fine landscape, surpasses all that can here be said. It is something which has to be seen for its beauty to be judged.' (Dézallier, I, 2.)

283 Plan of the gardens at Bizy, probably laid out by Le Nôtre's nephew, Claude Desgots.

284, 285 Opposite: two illustrations from Dézallier d'Argenville's *La Théorie et la Pratique du Jardinage*. Above: Palissades at Trianon and Versailles. Below: turf steps and ramps.

Palissade de Trianon.
fig. 4e.
Palissade du Théatre d'eau á Versailles.
fig. 6e.
Escalier meslé de Rampes et de Pailliers.
fig. 5e.

286, 287 Two mid-eighteenth century gardens designed for Madame de Pompadour: the château of Menars, with simple terraces overlooking the Loire (above); and Bellevue near Meudon, an elevated site with extensive views (below).

Parterres, being flat, need to be set off and given relief by 'elevated features like groves and *palissades*. But, before planting, regard should be had to the situation. If there is a fine view, beware of blocking it with groves, unless they are planted in quincunx, open, with low hedges, which do not impede the eye from wandering among the trunks of the trees and discovering the fine prospect on all sides.' (I, 3.)

Dézallier's model plans resemble one another in their hierarchical grid-like arrangement. It is only by reading carefully the accompanying text that the true nature of his
282 intention is revealed. Thus his second plan represents a house and garden of 25 acres, situated in the countryside on a slope, with terraces descending from the house. The lines of the walks are assumed to continue through the woods and fields. From the house 'you go down the steps into the gardens, which present you first of all with a great terrace, quite open for the sake of the prospect. The second terrace has groves, two of which are open in compartments, two planted in quincunx, which do not interrupt the view.' The cross walk below the second terrace is planted with horse chestnut. In the centre is a large circular basin at the head of a cascade which descends between woods of forest trees to a canal separating the garden from the park. The effect which this suggests is not one of openness, but rather like the
276 view from the head of the cascade at Sceaux.

Economic reasons alone made greater simplicity desirable. Practical necessity was justified by theory. Nevertheless, regularity and extended vistas on the main axis of the house continued to dominate French theory and practice for the first two thirds of the eighteenth century. *La Théorie et la Pratique du Jardinage* remained the principal source book for garden design. The fourth edition, published in Paris in 1747, comprised 466 pages, compared with the original 218 (in the English edition), with new material on the flower garden and hydraulics.

J.-F. Blondel

Jacques-François Blondel, after Dézallier d'Argenville, was the most important eighteenth-century theorist of the French
288 regular style. The garden plans in his *De la Distribution des Maisons*
289 *de Plaisance* (1737) differ from those of Dézallier in variety; some very simple, others more complex. In his *Cours d'Architecture*,[7] Blondel noted that the French style of laying out gardens was criticized by the English for its too great a love of symmetry and its inability to seize on the enchanting variety of circumstances offered by nature; for ignoring 'the genius of the place'.

> They tell us that the form of our walks is boring, our *palissades* are too monotonous and contrived; in short that our gardens are overdressed, stiff and subject to the rules of art. This criticism is not entirely without foundation; but it is nonetheless true that prodigious talents were needed to produce Versailles, Marly, Trianon – perhaps the only gardens in our country which affect a too scrupulous correctness. . . . At Versailles, the Orangerie, the Grand Canal, the Pièce de Neptune, the Pièce des Suisses, and the Parterre d'Eau, are of a size and magnificence which have no, or few, rivals in Europe; that at Marly the arrangement of the château and the twelve pavilions, surrounded by the accompanying artificial *berceaux*, are a happy invention, and

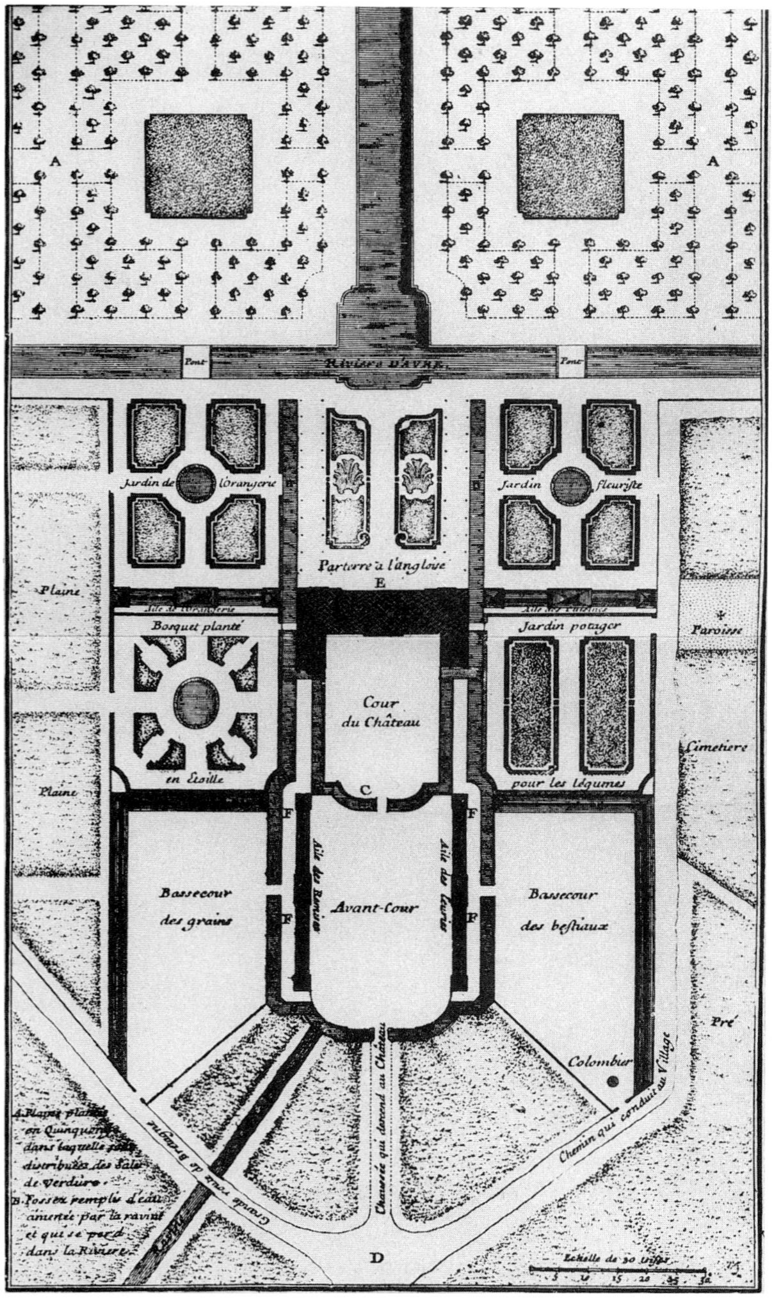

288 Garden plan from Jean-François Blondel's *De la Distribution des Maisons de Plaisance*, 1737; the château of St-Remi.

289 Design for trellis work in the Rococo style by Blondel, 1737.

treated in the best manner; that finally the same may be said of the gardens and buildings of Trianon . . . The gardens of Meudon, Sceaux and Chantilly offer other beauties; certainly nature appears there with more brilliance; and these three works are a visible proof that Le Nôtre, as a man of genius, knew how to profit from the lie of the land. . . .[8]

It is not that we would wish to be understood to mean that Nature, in her various aspects, is not good to imitate; only we believe that she should not always be followed strictly (*la saisir à la rigeur*). For example, at the end of a big garden, as a relief from too affected a symmetry which is often essential in the open parts, one offers the view of a countryside with little cultivation; or after a long closed *allée* one allows the beauties surrounding the site to appear. Such surroundings, by their picturesque negligence, tend to set off to advantage the regular arrangement of the garden within. Certainly then, this mixture of nature and art produces a sublime effect, and can only serve to reveal the ability of the artist, as has already been noted at Marly, and still more at Sceaux.

But . . . is it really imitating nature to seek to introduce in a garden of small extent, under pretext of variety, hillocks, tortuous walks, zigzag paths, ponds of irregular form, caves, mounds, finally clumps of trees unrelated to one another and of different species, all intermixed with kiosks, pavilions, obelisks, colonnades and tombs scattered here and there?[9]

Le Jardin Anglais and the 'style paysager' (1770–1880)

In England the development of a 'natural' style proceeded more rapidly in the 1730s and 1740s, although geometric principles and axial symmetry were by no means abandoned. The winding paths in the wooded areas of Lord Burlington's Chiswick Villa were, like the Bosquet de Louveciennes at Marly, contained within a framework of regular walks. Le Nôtre himself had departed from geometric principles in the two Bosquets des Sources at Versailles and Trianon. Lancelot 'Capability' Brown's landscaped parks, with wide irregular sweeps of grass broken by clumps and surrounded by belts of trees, only became general after 1760. Gardening styles became polarized, and a matter of national pride. In 1770, Horace Walpole could write: 'We have discovered the point of perfection. We have given the true model of gardening to the world'.[10] For the French, even those with anglophile tendencies, the style of Le Nôtre was paramount. 'He has never had an equal', wrote the Chevalier de Jaucourt in the article on 'Gardens' in the *Encyclopédie* (1765). At the same time he went on to deplore the decline of the art of garden design in his day: 'We no longer know how to do those things in which he excelled.'

The French version of Whately's *Observations on Modern Gardening*, to which Blondel refers, contains a detailed description of Stowe by the translator. It is gardens such as this, where architecture is used to create character by association,[11] which Blondel has in mind. And, like most Frenchmen at the time, his experience was secondhand,[12] due partly to the state of war which existed between the two countries throughout much of the eighteenth century. It is true that liberal-minded Frenchmen looked to England for inspiration; and that English agriculture was much admired by the physiocrats or *économistes*, who maintained that land was the only source of wealth and that property in land was the basis of the social order. Such a man was Louis-René Girardin, who visited England in 1763 and was much impressed by William Shenstone's *ferme ornée* at the Leasowes near Halesowen. Girardin's estate at Ermenonville was landscaped in a wholly irregular style between 1766 and 1776.[13] But the more usual type of *jardin anglais* in the 1770s and 1780s was one of relatively small dimensions attached to a French-style regular layout arranged on the axis of the house, as in the garden of M. Boutin, Rue de Clichy, one of 290
the numerous big gardens in what were then the suburbs of Paris. More famous were the Parc Monceau (1773), made for the Duc de Chartres,[14] a convinced anglophile; Bagatelle (1777), designed by the architect F.-J. Bélanger and the Scottish gardener Thomas Blaikie for the Comte d' Artois;[15] and the Folie Saint-James made for the Treasurer of the Admiralty, Baudard de Saint-James. These were the gardens Blondel criticized, miniature landscapes with artificial rivers, 291
rocks, cascades, and buildings in all styles. They were fantasy worlds created by the wealthy who could afford such pastimes.

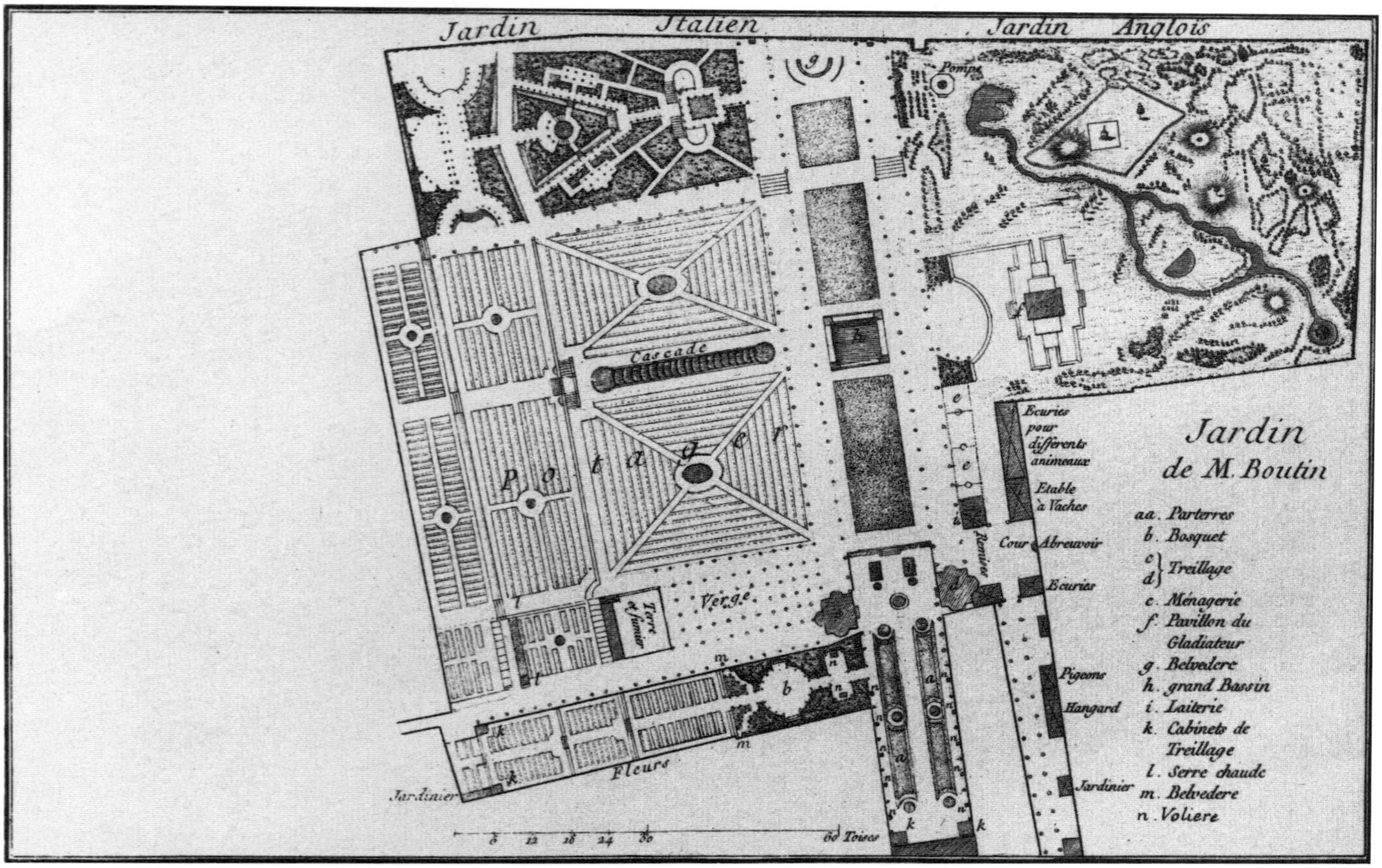

290, 291 The early *jardins anglais* were miniature landscapes forming part of larger formal layouts: 'Jardin de Monsieur Boutin' in the suburbs of Paris (above) and project for a Jardin Anglo-Chinois (below).

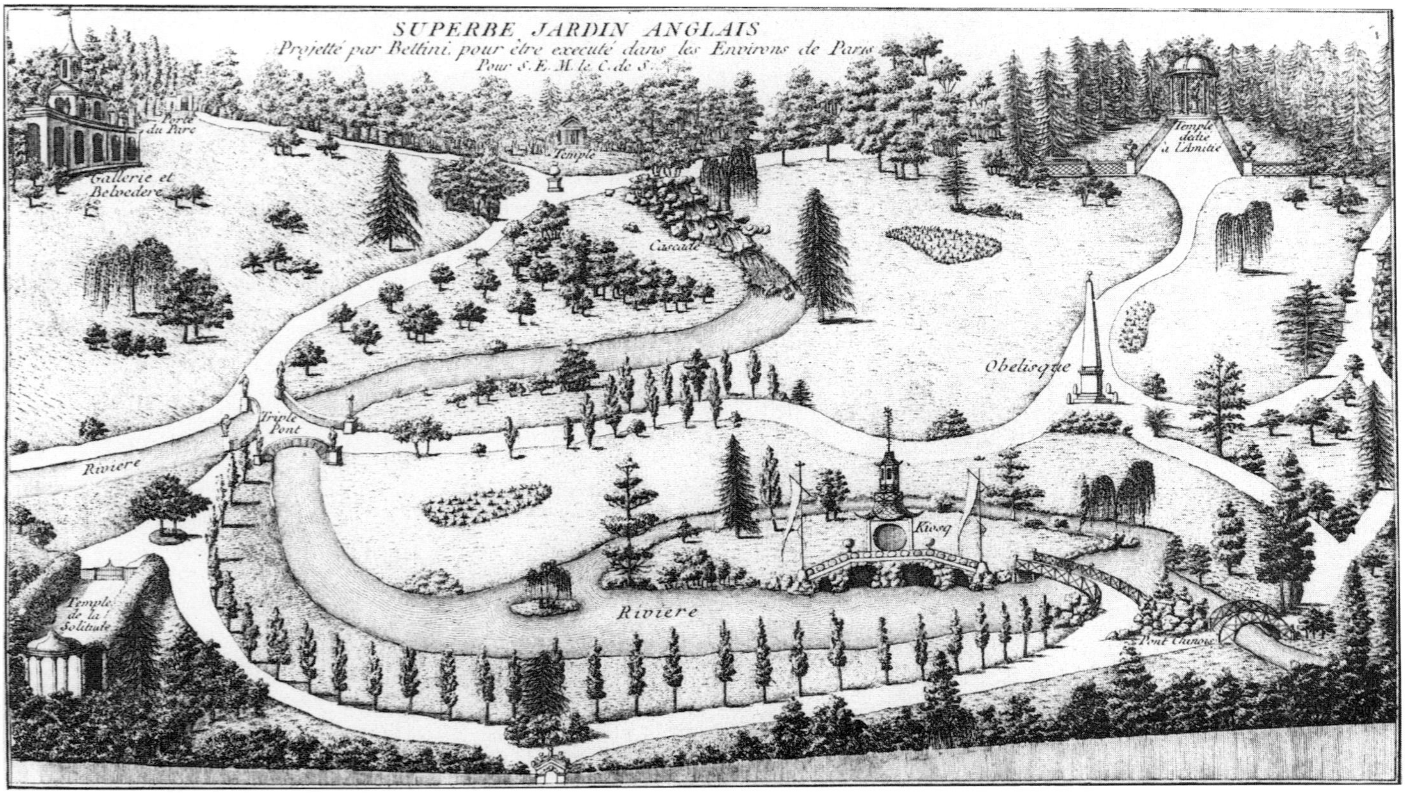

292 Salon and dining room disguised as rustic cottages, designed for the mock hamlet at Chantilly in 1773.

293 A view of the temple in the park at Méréville, an example of *fabriques*, fanciful buildings, for ornamenting parks and gardens.

Closely associated with the fashion of the *jardin anglais*[16] was the cult of rural life, expressed in mock rustic buildings, as in Marie Antoinette's hamlet at Trianon (1785), and her dairy at Rambouillet which was attached to an experimental farm where the king raised merino sheep. The group of half-
292 timbered Norman cottages in the hamlet at Chantilly (1773) was no more than a theatrical disguise. Within were a sophisticated salon and a dining-room painted to represent a wood. Parks on an altogether larger scale, like Ermenonville,
293 Méréville, Morfontaine, Betz, the Désert de Retz, also contained buildings of a fanciful nature, but combined with an economic function.

The reasons for this change of fashion were complex. It is all too simple to say that they originated in contrasting political attitudes: geometric formality representing autocracy, and the more natural irregular garden representing the freedoms of democracy. In so far as all artefacts emanate from the human psyche, they partake of its nature. An excess of rationality provokes a reaction in favour of its opposite. From the social point of view constraints upon behaviour by the observance of a too-artificial code of manners imposes strains which have to be relieved. As we have seen, the concept of Arcady, a land where nymphs and shepherds live in 'natural' simplicity, is a perennial theme in European culture. Jean-Jacques Rousseau's philosophy, that man is by nature virtuous and happy, but is corrupted by society, is an extension of the Arcadian idea with political overtones. Rousseau, who was protected and befriended by Girardin, was buried at Ermenonville. Thus the 'natural' or irregular style of landscaping later became associated with revolution and social disorder.

Jean-Marie Morel, who assisted Girardin at Ermenonville, attacked the application of geometric principles to the design of gardens,[17] at least when these were situated in the countryside. Architecture was a science before being an art, based on calculation, geometry, mechanics. It was more than likely that the symmetrical distribution of forms in a building derived from the application by the architect of these sciences, which taught him that when one part creates a bias to a certain side, it must be matched by an equal resistance on the other to achieve equilibrium. A concept of beauty deriving from architectural principles had been applied to

294 The park of Le Raincy was transformed in the English style in the early nineteenth century. Compare this view of 1808 with ill. 192.

gardens, where nature's forms, free from the shackles of method, know no rules but those of feeling, and no principle but taste.

Nevertheless, he continues, there are situations where symmetry and architectural ornament are appropriate, namely in the gardens of palaces and town houses. Public gardens too are only open spaces in towns to which citizens might resort not to enjoy the spectacle of nature but for exercise, to display their wealth and to satisfy their curiosity. It is there that the layout should be such that people of either sex, whose aim is to be seen, should see all at a glance and appear to best advantage, because they are at the same time both the spectators and the spectacle. The greatest ornament of formal gardens consists in the crowds.

The Revolution completed what fashion had begun. Not only were the gardens of Le Nôtre associated with the *ancien régime*, but the *émigrés* returning to their neglected estates found it more convenient to restore them in the English manner. Alexandre de Laborde, son of the creator of Méréville, recorded the gardens of the First Empire in his *Déscription des Nouveaux Jardins de la France* (1808), which
294 shows country houses, illustrated by Constant Bourgeois, in park-like settings reminiscent of Brown and Repton. Like Blondel, Laborde rejects what he calls *le genre Chinois*, which consists in producing different scenes in a very small space, torturing the ground in a thousand bizarre ways, with many little hillocks, winding paths, trickles of water issuing from an immense rock twice a week, by means of a pump, and a so-called cascade feeding a stone-built river which a child could jump across with feet together. No less ridiculous was a new-found and exaggerated enthusiasm for all aspects of the countryside, which produced in people so affected a puerile ecstasy, and caused them to find in nature a thousand things which did not exist. He continues:

> The true art of gardens seems to me to be the science of creating in any place whatever the most pleasing appearance that the site is capable of representing. Once established, this rule restrains both creative ambition and destructive mania; it obliges one to follow what nature indicates by the shape of the ground, the situation, the extent of the site; it permits the conservation of the greater part of the old forms, old works, when they are not in conflict with the new plan, and thus greatly reduces expense, time and difficulty.

These precepts illustrate the essentially conservative nature of picturesque landscaping; the preservation and improvement of the rural scene as it exists; 'unity of design and character with regard to the whole,' as John Loudon put it.[18] Laborde's method was probably inspired by Humphry Repton,[19] at least in so far as in the section of his book concerned with the theory of gardens there is a series of engravings showing the effect before and after improvement.

The majority of the parks illustrated in *Nouveaux jardins de la France* were designed by, or under the influence of, the owners; landscape gardens each with their own individual style. In 1820 Gabriel Thouin, who called himself a garden

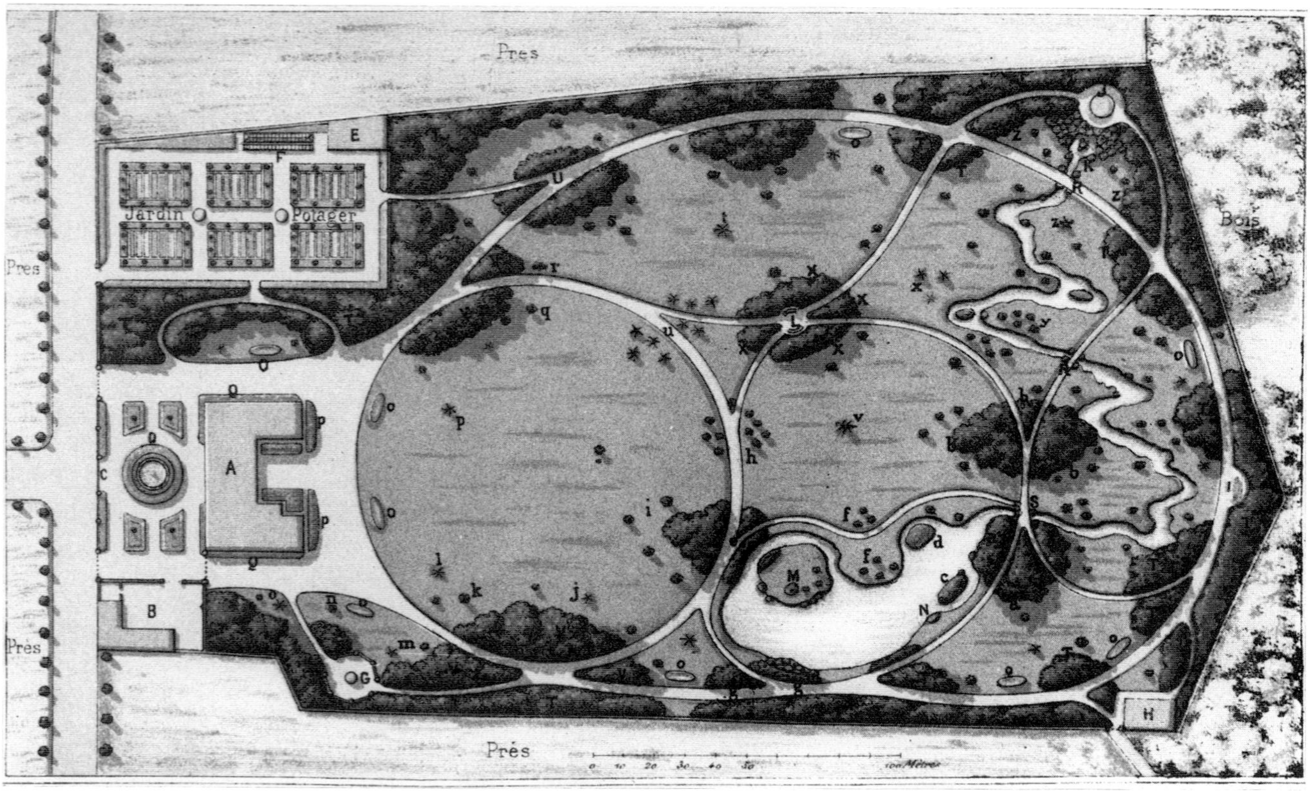

295 The *Style Paysager*: a design by Edouard André published in 1879.

architect,[20] published *Plans Raisonés de toutes éspèces de Jardins*, which established the *style paysager* as a method which dominated professional practice throughout the nineteenth century. It consisted of a framework of paths laid out in regular curves round lawns punctuated by clumps of vegetation (trees, shrubs and flowerbeds), and linked to a great circular walk. The absence of straight lines is in complete contrast to the advice given by Blondel[21] to avoid circular forms in the parts of the garden unless the main framework is rectilinear. The *style paysager* had the greatest influence during the Second Empire (1851–71), especially in the design of public parks: Bois de Boulogne, Montsouris, Buttes-Chaumont in Paris; and in the work of the brothers Bühler, for example the park of the Tête d'Or in Lyon, and the Jardin Thabor at Rennes. The style even extended to England in the design of Sefton Park, Liverpool (1867–72), by Edward André and L. Hornblower.

But, as Repton observed in 1795,[22] 'mankind are apt to fly from one extreme to the other; thus because straight lines and highly finished and correspondent parts prevailed in the ancient style, some modern improvers . . . call every species of regularity formal, and, with the hackneyed assertion that "nature abhors a straight line", they fatigue the eye with continual curvatures. There appears to be in the human mind a natural love of order and symmetry.' Repton reinstated architectural principles in the design of gardens; and justified the practice by reference to historic precedents. But ornamental planting was greatly enriched by the vastly increased range of exotic flowers and hybrids available after about 1820. 'Carpet bedding', flower gardening by bedding out of annual plants in geometric patterns, or using plants with variegated foliage ('mosaiculture'),[23] became increasingly popular in the middle of the nineteenth century, and is still practised with skill by French municipal gardeners.

André, who was closely associated with Jean-Charles Adolphe Alphand in the creation of the Paris parks, wrote the definitive treatise on French nineteenth-century gardening theory and practice. In *L'Art des Jardins* (1879) he recognized three styles: the *style géometrique*, *régulier*, or *symétrique*; the *style paysager*; and *style composite* or *mixte*, a judicious combination of the two. He saw the future of garden design as belonging to the latter; the regular garden as an extension of the house – a *péristyle champêtre* – intermediate between it and the landscape. He recommended landscape architects of the future to direct their energies to 'the surroundings of palaces, châteaux, and historic buildings, treated according to the laws of architecture and geometry, merging gradually with wild nature in the remote parts of the park'. 'Unfortunately,' he added, 'as soon as it is a question of composing a formal garden, the ruler and compass of the architect surrender to capricious layouts and plans which have no relation to historic truth and the architectural period of the building they should accompany. None of them seems to think of opening a book to learn from the models which have been handed down to us; in short, to apply the reliable method of archaeological research to the art of gardens.' 295

296, 297 The restoration of Versailles. Above: the North Parterre, with bronze Venus by the brothers Keller, after Coysevox. See frontispiece. Below: the South Parterre, with one of the two sphinxes by Lerambert which originally stood by the steps leading to the Bassin de Latone.

15

The Classical Revival 1875–1935

André's appeal did not go unnoticed. The study of the records by French scholars had already laid the foundations.[1] One of the first of Le Nôtre's great gardens to be restored was Vaux-le-Vicomte, by the architect Henri Duchêne and his son Achille, after drawings by Israel Silvestre, for the industrialist Alfred Sommier. Under the curatorship of Pierre Nohlac the palace and gardens of Versailles were gradually returned as far as possible to their original state. Le Nôtre's reputation had been sustained through the centuries when his gardens had been neglected. Now he became a culture hero; and his gardens a symbol for the greatness of the French nation, the superiority of French culture. The revival had nationalistic, political and social overtones. Lucien Corpechot was its mouthpiece.

> Our gardeners, like the Greek architects, have brought to perfection within the grasp of all an art entirely fed by national qualities.
>
> The French have been the only people in the world to understand this art of gardens, as Le Nôtre understood it. . . . They [the gardens of a Mollet, a Boyceau, a Le Nôtre] no longer only rejoice the heart, but satisfy the reason. They are intelligible nature as the tragedies of Corneille or Racine are intelligible life. They are gardens of intelligence. (*Parcs et Jardins de France*: *Les Jardins de l'Intelligence* 1911, 1937 ed., pp. 7–8.)
>
> The garden of Le Nôtre no longer has anything in common with what other peoples of the world call a garden and which is made for the delight of the senses. It is a construction of the mind. . . . All the little ends which humanity had in view in cultivating its first orchards have disappeared . . . [the gardens of Le Nôtre] answer no material need, and thus they escape mortal vicissitudes, for what is useful changes ceaselessly . . . Le Nôtre is not concerned with our peace of mind or our appetites. Order alone concerns him. His gardens are pure *jeux d'esprit*. Everything there is opposed to instinct, indifferent to the senses, exalts reason. And it is in this that they are so French! (pp. 160–1).

Henri and Achille Duchêne

During the first two decades of the twentieth century Achille Duchêne established himself as the leading professional exponent of the traditional French classical style, not only in the matter of restorations like Vaux-le-Vicomte but in creating new gardens. The part played by his patrons in this revival should not be underestimated.

VOISINS

The Comte de Fels, who bought the estate of Voisins, near Rambouillet, from the banker Joubert in 1892, was one of the first. In his memoirs[2] he describes in detail how the château and gardens were created. The original 'feudal' house had been rejuvenated by A.-J. Gabriel in the eighteenth century, altered in the nineteenth century and thrown quite off balance by the addition of an immense hall '*à l'anglaise*' stuck onto the east front. De Fels was an admirer of Gabriel's buildings, 'the *chefs d'oeuvre* of a period which marks the high point in French art, that of Louis XV'. There was nothing he could do with the old house but pull it down and build a new one. He found that Gabriel's work was little studied in the architectural schools;[3] he therefore undertook his own research of Gabriel's buildings and unpublished designs, and picked up the ideas to inspire his collaborators. First among these were the architect Samson for the château and Henri Duchêne for the gardens. The idea was to build on a spur of the park dominating a view of the valley and sloping gently to the River Guéville. At the same time De Fels envisaged an architectural framework in the pure French tradition: approach avenue planted with two or four rows of trees, forecourt enclosed by railings flanked by two pavilions, main courtyard (*cour d'honneur*), *parterres de broderie* and turf and so on, all in proportion to the importance of the building. There was difficulty in making the approach avenue because a local road prevented it. This was solved by negotiation with the parish of Saint-Hilarion. The major problem was how to relate a large formal garden to its natural setting, a series of hilly valleys crowned with forest trees and strewn with great sandstone rocks like those in the forest of Fontainebleau.

The solution is shown in Duchêne's drawing of a bird's-eye view. In De Fels' words: 298

> Our general conception was to improve – it could even be said create or at least complete – the natural site which must serve as a view. To this end a lake was dug within sight of the principal façade of the château. One descends to the water's edge by three successive terraces and four great flights of stone steps, crossing the parterre laid out by

> M. Duchêne with his faultless understanding of French art. I myself gave him the most important idea for these parterres, that for the third terrace which resembles a huge *tapis de la Savonnerie* thrown on the ground of an outside salon. I found this idea in Gabriel's plan for the gardens of Compiègne in 1755.

South of the château was a low-lying marshy meadow. The water here was canalized; and in the ground forming the lowest of three terraces on the south, it was made into an ornamental feature surrounding a rectangular island before flowing into a pond by a weir. The parterres of the south terraces were of turf laid out *à la française* and not 'stupidly cut into serpentine or rounded shapes which are painful to eyes accustomed to Classic art'.

The construction of the gardens, begun in 1903, was not complete until 1925. A detailed description would here be out of place. The immediate purpose is to give the circumstances in which Duchêne worked, the essential concepts of the design, the important part played by the owner and the attitudes which determined his ideas. Voisins was a different exercise from one which involved the restoration of the French classical layout according to existing plans, as at Champs,[4] for instance, where the eighteenth-century gardens had been entirely replaced by an immense *parc à l'anglaise*.

COURANCES

Courances is one of Achille Duchêne's most sympathetic restorations, due perhaps to the character of the place, which depends on an abundance of clear water from springs and the River Ecole, which is canalized for a stretch of 500 metres in
the woods. The traditional axial arrangement was established 299
by the mid-seventeenth century and modified in the 300
eighteenth century. After a period of neglect following the Revolution, Courances was bought in 1872 by the Baron de Haber who laid out the gardens in the fashionable irregular or picturesque style. On his death Courances passed by his daughter to the de Ganay family; and in the years just before the 1914 war the then Marquise de Ganay employed Duchêne to restore the park and gardens in the French
classical taste. The result is a restrained version of the French 301
grand manner, depending for its effect on a happy combination of fine trees, grass, and water arranged in a series of basins and canals which enliven what might be a rather dull scene[5] with a recurring series of mirror images. The

298 Project by Achille Duchêne for the restoration of Voisins, about 1900.

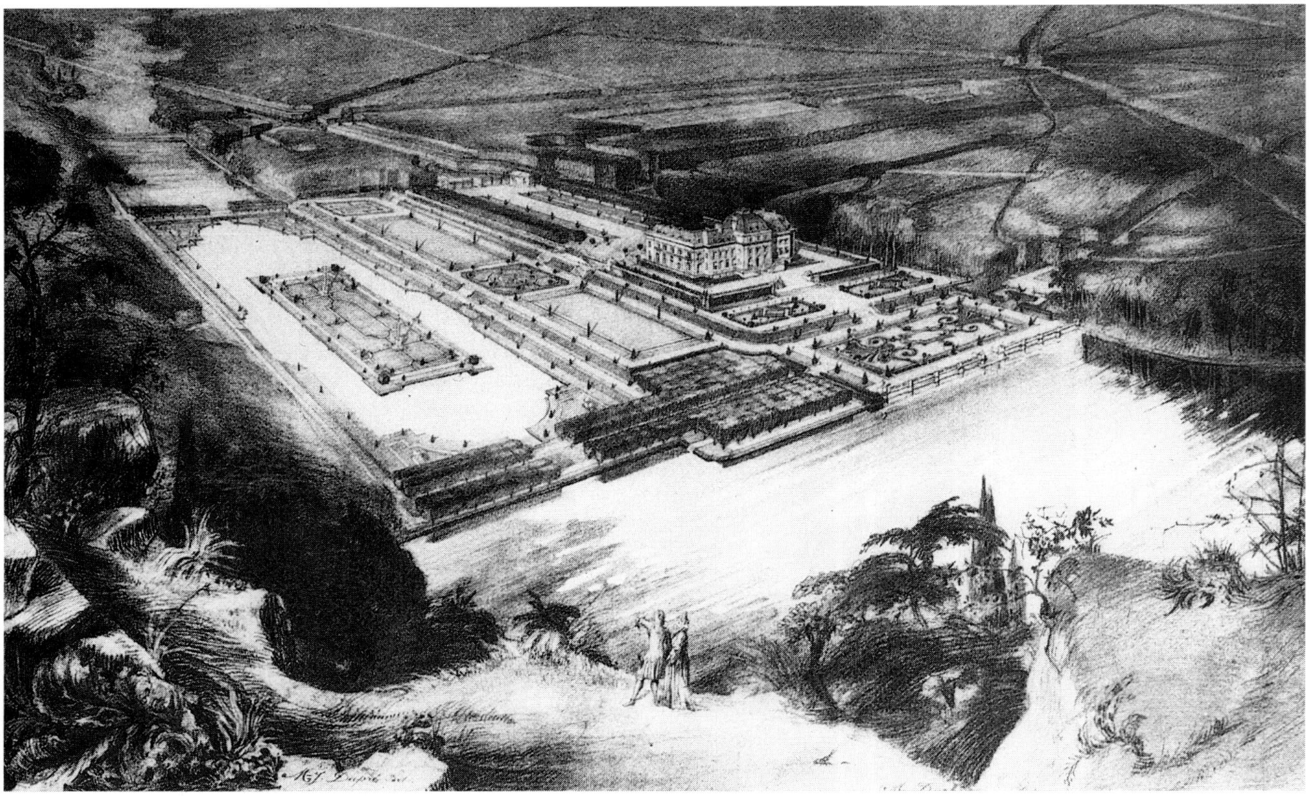

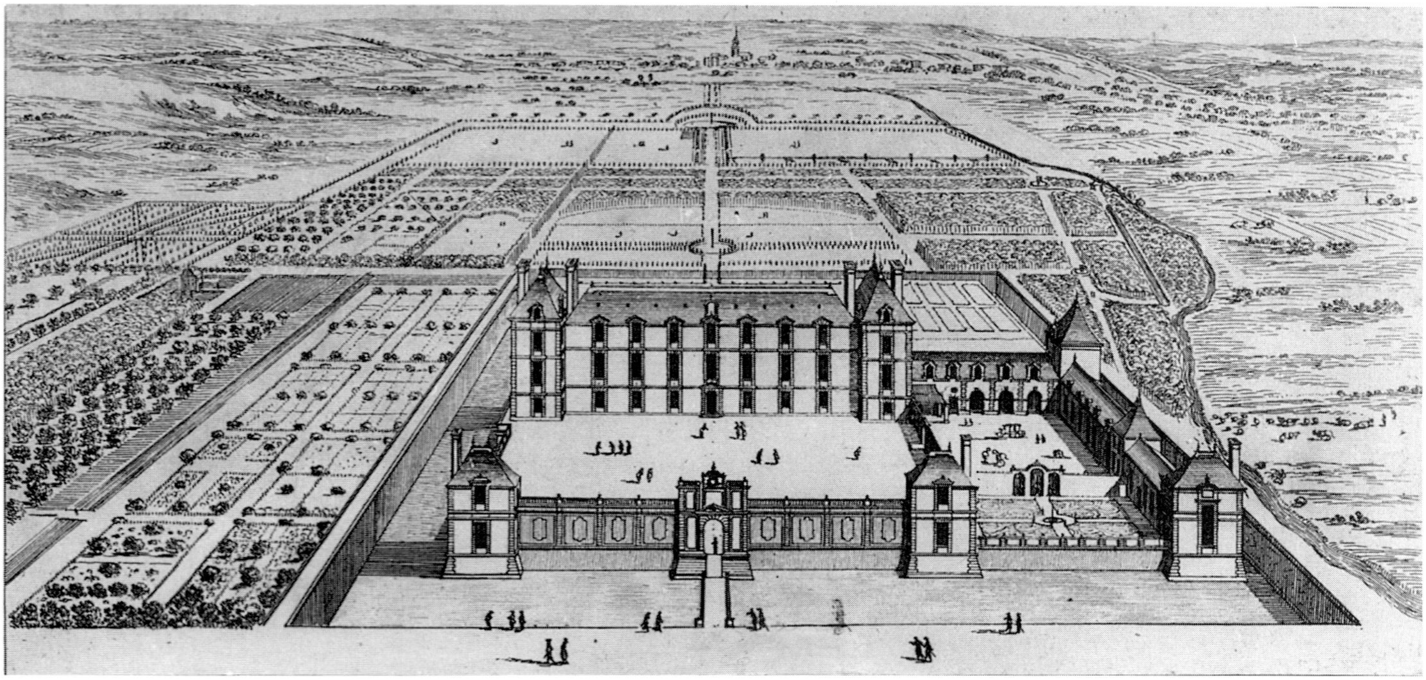

299, 300 Courances in the seventeenth century: General view from the north (above); South front with parterre (below).

301, 302 In the nineteenth century the neglected park and gardens of Courances were laid out in the fashionable 'natural' style. They were restored in a restrained version of the grand manner by Achille Duchêne. Above: the château from the east. Below: *parterre* and central vista looking south.

303 Project for part of the park of M. Carolan in California, by Achille Duchêne.

302 *parterre de broderie* adjoining the château is of modest size, sufficient to mediate between the house and the park without being dominant. In the same way the simplicity of the carefully proportioned basin beyond introduces the vista, and joins art to nature by the trees and sky reflected in its surface.

DUCHÊNE IN CALIFORNIA

Duchêne also received commissions from abroad. He worked at Blenheim in England and Nordkirchen in Germany; but perhaps he found the greatest scope for designing in the grand manner in the United States,[6] where
303 the house and park he was called upon to design for Mr Carolan-Pulmann was on a scale as great as any of Le Nôtre's creations, but in a landscape very different from any in France. In no other place, he wrote, had he found a clearer demonstration of the intimate connection between architecture and landscape.

His analysis of the problems is also a statement of the principles of French classical garden design established by Le Nôtre and Le Vau at Vaux-le-Vicomte:

1 to site the approach and entrance on the side of least interest for its view and orientation;

2 to arrange the building so that the principal reception rooms should have the most favourable aspect for the time of day they are to be used; and the view of greatest interest and grandeur, while taking into account the extent of the ground and its topography, in order to create a garden architecture in scale with the building, and of a nobility to dominate the themes relating to the other façades;

3 to place the offices so that they are unobtrusive;

4 to establish the level of the ground floor so as to allow the line of sight to embrace a view of the gardens sufficient in its extent to match the scale of the buildings, and so that no obstacle, such as a balustrade or top of an embankment, cuts awkwardly into the view of the gardens immediately beyond those in the foreground;

5 to fix the style or character of the building so as to harmonize with the landscape; in other words, so that the movements of the façades, the silhouette of the roofs, and the relief of the mouldings are such that the house is seen to best advantage from all the principal viewpoints in the park, taking account of their distance and elevation in relation to the building.

304 Gardens of La Roche-Courbon, a design by Ferdinand Duprat, between 1925 and 1935; view from above the architectural grotto.

Ferdinand Duprat and La Roche-Courbon

The conceptions of Duchêne's younger contemporary, Ferdinand Duprat, were less rigid and more eclectic. His
304 great architectural garden at La Roche-Courbon, in Charente-Maritime, is due to a romantic notion of the novelist, Julien Viaud, or Pierre Loti as he called himself. As a student, Loti used to spend his holidays with his married sister at Saint-Porchaire; and while there, his imagination was captured by the château of La Roche-Courbon, deserted by its owner since 1856, fast becoming derelict and its neglected gardens reverting to a wilderness. He called it the 'château de la belle au bois dormant' (Sleeping Beauty). During his life as a sailor he continued to return to the forest of La Roche-Courbon; and when the estate was put up for sale in 1908 he wrote an impassioned appeal to save it from destruction. The conditions of sale were then altered to stipulate, as far as possible, the preservation of the château and the forest.

It was eventually bought in 1920 by Loti's friend, the industrialist Paul Chénereau. The seventeenth-century gardens had virtually disappeared. The valley of the River Bruant was a swamp. Duprat's 'restoration', carried out between 1925 and 1935, and loosely based on a seventeenth-century painting by Hackaert, has as its main feature a fine regular lake or *miroir d'eau* and a monumental architectural grotto or fountain facing the château on the south. Gardens in a regular style are laid out along the water on a balustraded terrace parallel to the south front. The result is unlike a traditional French garden, although the use of water as a reflecting surface serving both ornament and use, as Philibert de l'Orme had recommended, is characteristically French.

VILLETTE (VAL D'OISE)

Duprat also produced designs for restoring the gardens of the elegant small château of Villette, designed *c.*1663 by François Mansart and completed by Hardouin-Mansart. In 1824 the gardens had been redesigned in the 'picturesque' style by J. Lalos. Duprat's design was not used. The present owner, M. Gerard, has restored them *à la française* with a magnifi- 305
cent water-stairway and *buffet d'eau* on the axis of the house. 306

305, 306 Villette: the cascade, based on substructures discovered during excavation, and restored by M. Robert Gerard after 1945 (above); and the *buffet d'eau* (left).

307, 308 Villandry: the château and garden restored (above) and as it looked at the beginning of the century (below).

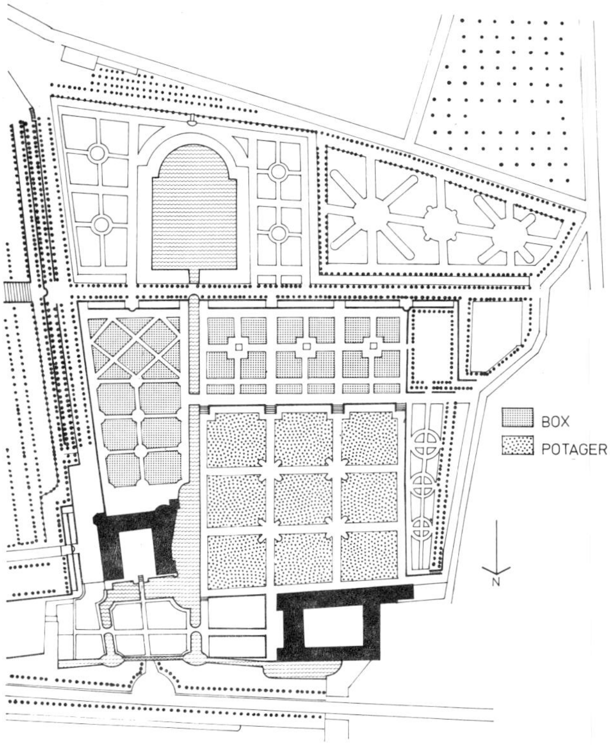

309 The garden of Villandry, as restored by Dr Joachim Carvallo after 1906.

VILLANDRY

One of the most interesting restorations was at Villandry, a château of twelfth-century origin enlarged in the Renaissance style and covered with eighteenth-century accretions. The structural lines of the garden (terraces, basins and canals) had been laid down about 1762.[7] In the nineteenth century there were lawns with beds of unorthodox design south of the house; but the larger part of the gardens was converted to a *parc à l'anglaise*. In 1906 the owners were intending to divide it into lots and demolish the château, when it was bought by Dr Joachim Carvallo[8] and his American wife. They intended
307 to restore it and give the gardens their sixteenth-century character. There were no plans to show what this might have
309 been, so the concept evolved according to Carvallo's own ideas.

The first stage, completed before 1914, involved clearing the moats, which had been filled in, to reflect the lines of the building; and opening up the view of the château from the village ('I ask you,' he said, 'what use is architecture in the middle of a jumble of trees?'). On the axis of the house, and beneath the south façade, the nineteenth-century garden was
replaced by an ornamental parterre of clipped box, with 311
figures symbolizing the different moods of love: *l'amour volage, l'amour tendre, l'amour tragique, l'amour folie*. This has no evident precedents in French tradition, except for the tendency of the sixteenth-century mentality to express itself in emblematic form; and in gardens to outline figures in some plant like lavender, rosemary or box, filling in the background with flowers or herbs. The formal aspects of this parterre are extremely interesting. Whether by accident or design, the area is of trapezoidal shape, 100 metres long, 42 metres wide at the north end, 56 at the south. This reduces the effect of perspective seen from the first floor windows of the house, and makes the area appear rectangular. Despite an apparent regularity, hardly any part is regular. Particularly skilful is the change of direction of the paths from rectangular in the northern part to diagonal at the southern end. This not only distracts one from the irregularity, but relates the garden to the eighteenth-century ramps which close the vista, of which the diagonal paths form an inverted image. The terrace of the ornamental parterre is extended at right angles below an avenue of pleached lime separating it from another garden at a higher level.

310, 311 Villandry: the ornamental *potager* designed in the sixteenth century manner (above), and the box *parterre* to the south of the château, with figures symbolizing the moods of love in the foreground (below).

At a lower level, in the angle formed by the two box
310 terraces, an ornamental kitchen garden was made between 1914 and 1918, consisting of nine squares laid out in geometric figures after illustrations of sixteenth-century gardens in Du Cerceau's *Les Plus Excellents Bastiments de France*. The *potager*, and indeed the whole garden, was expressive of Carvallo's social and religious beliefs.

> Our ancestors had a different conception of life from ours. Their house was built to answer all family needs, and to live in. Around the château, on a lower level, were the outbuildings. The château itself was a closed courtyard; and behind the château the terraced gardens were arranged in tiers. The various elements of domestic order thus each had its place, closely related and without any possible confusion. The animals were lower than the servants, and the servants were not on a level with the masters. . . . This order began to disappear towards the middle of the eighteenth century. . . . The nineteenth century, contrary to nature and good sense, destroys all its hierarchies, and brings man back to the level of the beasts. Whether one wishes it or not philosophy informs all our acts and our life is but the expression of our ideas.
>
> (J. Carvallo, preface to Prosper Péan's *Jardins de France*, 1924.)

This postulated hierarchy had been observed in the arrangement of the gardens; but the stages which separated the various courts had been suppressed, so that, as he put it, 'men and their belongings slid imperceptibly towards the stables, while the animals, without the least difficulty, could come into the drawing room'. Carvallo could not reverse the social order, but he could destroy the symbol of what he so much disliked. He did so with dynamite. When a peasant said, 'We have trees a hundred years old and you massacre them!' Carvallo replied, 'Maybe it breaks your heart; but what matters is intelligence not sensibility'.

The principle at Villandry is the one used by Le Nôtre, balance about a controlling axis where, given the space, the design could theoretically expand indefinitely from the centre. The renaissance ideal was symmetry and closure. Villandry is not the model of a sixteenth-century garden; but this does not detract from the magnitude of Dr Carvallo's achievement.

The revival reassessed

In 1932 the *Comité de l'Art des Jardins de le Soc. Nat. d'Horticulture* met to consider the state of modern garden design.[9] In an introductory paper Prosper Péan claimed that the proper name of *jardin régulier*, as opposed to *jardin irrégulier* (called English, Chinese or Landscape), should be *jardin français*, because it was in their country that this type was born due to the genius of the illustrious Le Nôtre. It has been the purpose of this book to trace the development of the French formal style. Has Péan's claim been shown to be justified? The earliest precedents for the architectural garden, at least in the period we have covered, were Italian. But Italian ideas interpreted in the social and environmental conditions in France were transformed into something recognizably different. Whereas Italian gardens like Lante were private retreats where the house was of secondary importance, the French style developed in association with the principal residence as a setting for the architecture of the house. It is a style properly called 'formal' in the sense that it proclaims the status of the owner. As formulated by André Mollet, it is a hierarchical arrangement of the parts about the main axis: approach avenue, forecourts, *cour d'honneur*, principal *corps de logis*, *parterres de broderie*, *parterres de gazon*, *bosquets*. Certain garden features such as *parterres de broderie*, sanded walks, groves planted in quincunx, the idea of the *bosquet* as at Versailles, monumental garden canals, if not strictly French in origin, were at least developed in a specifically French way.

The classical revival was not however purely a matter of restoring great gardens or making new ones in an old style; it was one of those swings of taste between freedom and control which occur in the arts. The principle of regularity was no longer upheld by metaphysical belief. The human need for order and authority reappeared as an appeal to
tradition applied to small gardens in a modern manner. As 312
André Vera put it: 'We will make no pastiches. From Le 313
Nôtre's masterpieces we will extract, as it suits us, new things and old things. . . . Our romantic ancestors have procured us an abundance of flowers and plants with coloured foliage . . . We will readily retain all the introductions and acquisitions of our immediate forbears . . . [but] we will study the discipline in which Le Nôtre's contemporaries were formed. We refuse to be overwhelmed by the beauties of nature. . . . Our garden will not be an accumulation of pleasant plants, as was the *jardin paysager*.'[10]

The spirit of French gardening is reflected in the orderly plantations of poplars in the landscape, and the erect lines of trees along the roads; but, above all, the tradition of Le Nôtre lives in the boulevards of Haussmann's Paris. The great axis, extending from the Louvre along the Champs Elysées to the Arc de Triomphe, has its origins in the Tuileries, the archetypal French garden, conceived in the Renaissance, perfected under Louis XIV, and associated throughout the world with all that is quintessentially French.

From another point of view the story told in this book may be read as the rise of the profession of landscape architect. This originated when the architectural emphasis became predominant in the design of gardens. As these became larger, incorporating the park, and even large areas of the countryside, skills were needed which were beyond the competence of either gardener or architect. It might be said that Le Nôtre was the first to combine both, exercising control over a wide range of specialized skills in creating huge unified schemes which are among the most remarkable achievements of garden art. The great French gardens of the seventeenth century are the first properly so-called 'landscape gardens'.[11] These were only possible, however, in the social conditions which then prevailed.

In 1935, Achille Duchêne,[12] looking back over his career, expressed sadness in seeing the tradition he admired, and had striven to uphold, become outdated. 'What seems to me to

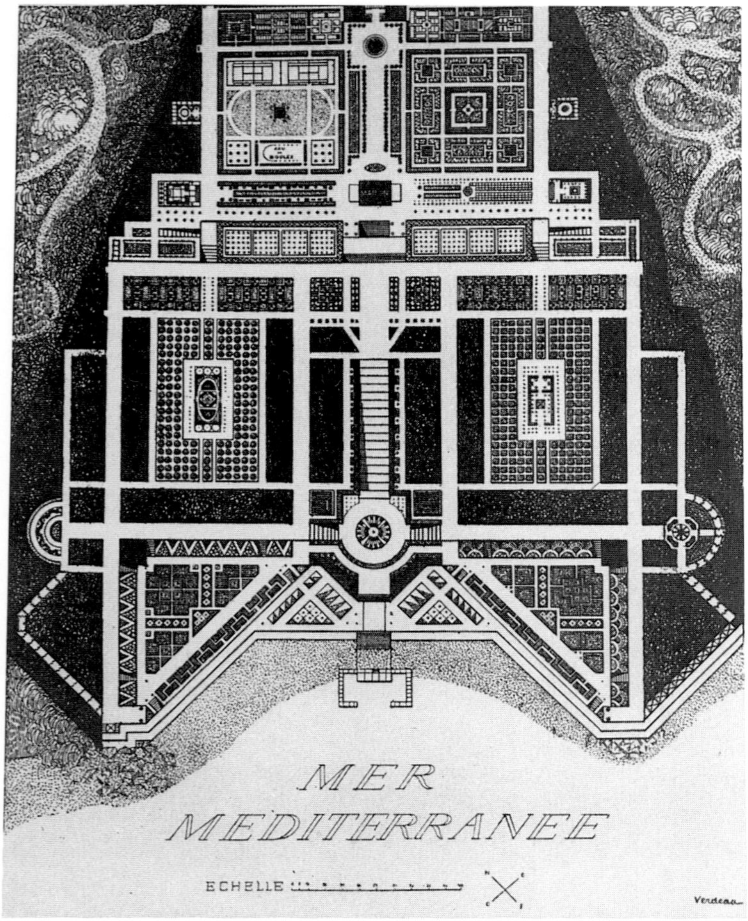

312, 313 The classical principle in the early twentieth century: two drawings by the thirties designer André Vera: plan of a Jardin du Soleil on the shores of the Mediterranean (right) and the central vista towards the house.

314, 315 Two restorations of traditional designs. Above: box *parterre* in the form of a labyrinth at the château of La Gaude, Provence. Below: Le Nôtre's garden of the former bishop's palace at Castres.

dominate the conditions of artistic production today is the progressive lessening of great private wealth, the collective organization of artistic "consumption" founded on tastes less individualized and more uniform than formerly.' He saw the future of the profession in the public sphere. 'Looking at the art of gardens from the social angle, we will create a new formula which will give birth to an art of great power put in the service of the community. Here luxury will cease to have an end in itself; a certain useful value will be added to it, since instead of expressing the sophisticated taste of a few privileged beings, it must satisfy the aesthetic aspirations of the masses.'

But, as he himself wrote, 'The object of an art, in essence, is to communicate feeling for and understanding of those things which cannot be conveyed by intellectual argument.' How far collective taste is responsive to this lofty aim, and how far the professional landscape-architect is capable of fulfilling it, is questionable. For surely the history of gardens reveals that great examples of the art arise from the controlling influence of an individual. The work of art is a human artefact which is basically symbolic in intention; that is to say it has meaning that lies beyond its material usefulness, and beyond its decorative appeal. At the same time the garden is a universal and potent image because it is so fundamental to civilization. What François Carvallo[13] has to say about Villandry is applicable to the whole art of garden-making whatever the scale or style. Writing of the ornamental *potager* he says:

> In the winter the pattern of the beds forms a clear contrast with the paths. The sand of the Loire appears to change: grey in winter, shimmering like mother-of-pearl in spring, almost white in summer, and pink in the autumn light. The planting of the vegetables in the parterres, whose raison d'être is ornamental, must be rigorously controlled. The colours must be clearly distinguished from one another while harmonizing among themselves. A whole square must be planted at the same time; and the vegetables gathered evenly from each part of the pattern to preserve the balance. Nor is the pattern static. The green tomato becomes a brilliant yellow, then bright red, shining and satiny like a piece of porcelain. The cabbage turns from grey-green to bluish, then to a sumptuous Veronese-crimson. Celery has surprising shades of empire-green. The light-green leek darkens with age and finishes like an old tapestry woven with silver thread. The humble beetroot goes from sea-green to the red of Bordeaux wine sprinkled with ochre and earth-brown. To achieve all this requires a considerable intellectual effort. Choosing vegetables is not only a matter of colour but of understanding how they mature and balancing their rate of growth. Moreover they must be changed every year or two in order not to exhaust the soil. A garden obliges its owner to cultivate the qualities of patience and imagination, and the virtue of love. It is, as it were, an image of the soul, which is also a garden to be well ordered and carefully maintained. The influence the external world has on ourselves is boundless and mysterious.[14]

Villandry demonstrated the principles of regularity, balance and proportion which have long been the theoretical basis of the French tradition. By combining this with the life-sustaining function of gardens Carvallo returned us to their origins, and the symbolic overtones embodied in the act of gardening itself which go far deeper than what Anthony Ashley Cooper, third Earl of Shaftesbury, called 'the formal mockery of princely gardens.'

Notes to the text

AB Art Bulletin
BSAT Bulletin de la Societé Archéologique de Touraine
BSHAF Bulletin de la Societé de l'Historie de l'Art Français
GBA Gazette des Beaux Arts
GIAJ Gazette Illustrée des Amateurs des Jardins
JWCI Journal of the Warburg and Courtauld Institutes

Introduction pages 9–10

1 Marguerite Charageat, *L'Art des Jardins* (1962), p. 102, referring to René of Anjou's garden at Chanzé.
2 Pietro de Crescenzi, *Ruralium Commodorum Liber*; printed French edition (1540), *Le Bon Mesnaiger*.

Chapter 1 pages 13–21

1 Reference is to the edition in modern French, translated by André Lanly, Paris, 1971–3. See bibliography.
2 Reference is to the printed French edition of 1540 entitled *Le Bon Mesnaiger*. There are textual differences between this and French manuscripts such as *Livre des prouffits champestre et ruraulx*. British Library Ms. Roy. 14 E VI.
3 Hélène Nais, 'Le Rustican. Notes sur la traduction française du traité d'agriculture de Pierre Crescens', *Bibliothèque d'Humanisme et Renaissance*. Travaux et documents, XIX, 1957.
4 *L'Agriculture et Maison Rustique*, 1570.
5 *Théâtre d'Agriculture*, 1600.
6 'Dessein du Jardin Délectable', *Oeuvres de Bernard Palissy*, ed. B. Fillon, 1868.
7 Charles Diehl, *Palerme et Syracuse*, 1907.
8 Marguerite Charageat, 'Le parc d'Hesdin, création monumentale du XIIIe siècle', *BSHAF*, 1950.
9 L.E.S.J. de Laborde, *Les Ducs de Bourgogne*, 1849–52.
10 For these and other references to features in the park at Hesdin see C. C. A. Dehaisnes, *Documents. . . concernant l'Histoire de l'Art dans la Flandre, l'Artois et le Hainault*, 1886.
11 Quoted in Michel Brunet, 'Le Parc d'Attractions des Ducs de Bourgogne à Hesdin', *GBA*, December, 1971.
12 See *op. cit.* note 8, and M. Charageat, *L'Art des Jardins*, 1962.
13 Brussels, Bib. Roy. Albert Ier, Ms. 9392.
14 British Library, Ms. Roy. 14 E IV.
15 Henri Sauval, *Histoire et Recherches des Antiquités de la Ville de Paris*, 1724. Vol. II p. 283.
16 Bib. Nat. Paris. Ms. Fr. 143.
17 Bib. l'Arsenal, Paris. Ms.5104.
18 The standard biography is still A. Lecoy de la Marche, *Le Roi René*, 1875. Reference has also been made to *Le Bon Roi René*, Jacques Levron, 1972.
19 A. Lecoy de la Marche, *Extraits des comptes . . . et mémoriaux du Roi René*, 1873 (Archives Nationales). L'Abbé G. Arnaud d'Agnel, *Les comptes du Roi René. . . . Archives des Bouches-du-Rhone*, 1908.
20 Arnaud d'Agnel, item 9, 21 juin 1451 refers to 'quatre maczons qui ont carrelé la gallerie du petit jardin, la où est le carreau verd'.
21 Lecoy de la Marche, *Le Roi René*, Vol. II, p. 9.
22 Lecoy de la Marche, *Comptes*, items 268–9. Otherwise information is from Lecoy de la Marche, *Le Roi René*.
23 J. Plattard, *La vie de François Rabelais*, 1928.
24 Lecoy de la Marche, *Comptes*, items 15 ff.
25 Lecoy de la Marche, *Comptes*, item 230, 8 avril 1454.
26 Ibid, item 231, 26 mars 1459.
27 Ibid, item 166, 17 mars 1459.
28 Ibid, item 253.
29 Arnaud d'Agnel, items 25 ff.
30 Lecoy de la Marche, *Le Roi René*, Vol. II, pp. 50–1.
31 Charageat (1962), p. 103, and M. Chaillan, *Le Roi René à son Château de Gardanne*, 1909.
32 Arnaud d'Agnel, item 3310.
33 Ibid. item 3308.
34 Brussels, Bib. Roy. Ms. 10308.
35 Vienna, National Library, Ms. 2597.

Chapter 2 pages 23–36

1 Colonna's words in this passage are 'La area ancora tutta era strata di rotundatione vitrinule & altre convenientissime figuratione, ad suprema gratia . . .' The French translation of 1546 reads: 'Le plan et parterre du jardin estoit faict a compartimens composez d'*entrelaz* et autres figures de belle grace. . . .' 'Entrelaz' can be interpreted as 'knot' in the sense of a complex pattern of interweaving bands or loops. As with the labyrinth, this form almost certainly has a symbolic origin (see Marcel Brion, 'Le thème de entrelacs et du labyrinthe dans l'oeuvre de Leonardo de Vinci', *Revue d'Esthétique*, v, 1, Jan.–Mar., 1952 and 'Les Noeuds de Leonardo de Vinci et leurs significations', *Etudes d'Art*, 8–10, 1953–4). Although Colonna described such patterns in connection with the gardens of Cythera, '*rotundatione virtinule*' can hardly be interpreted as 'entrelac'. A free English translation of 1592 gives 'the ground was here and there covered with great round balls of glass'.
2 Compare the monster in the circuit at Bomarzo over whose mouth is the inscription, 'Lasciate ogni pensiero voi ch'entrate' (Abandon thought all you who enter here).
3 Jean Martin, who is named as editor, did no more than revise a text given him by his friend Jacques Gohorry, who at first intended to do it himself. For those who might complain that he had not restored the book according to the Italian version, Martin offers the excuse that he only undertook the revision to oblige his friend (Gohorry), and has done no more than correct the spelling and rewrite some passages which did not seem well expressed. He explains, in his address to the reader, that the original is such a confused mixture of Italian, Greek and Latin that even Italians, unless they were particularly learned, could make little sense of it. *Hypnerotomachie ou Discours du Songe de Poliphile*, published in 1546, is more a paraphrase than a translation, with the passages rearranged, left out and occasionally inserted. The many qualifying adjectives and similes with which the original is embroidered are omitted, so that the French version is considerably shorter. Thus, in describing the outer circle of plantations in the island of Cythera, 162 lines of Colonna's text are reduced to 30. For example: 'Mirai & uno altro nemorulo nelquale cum aequabile locatione era uno perratissimo querceto di tenelle fronde. Et quivi vidi latifolia & querno & roburi & hemeris pducente il medicinale Canchry, & halipheos salsicortex, cum assai & aesculi & cerri, & suberi, & fagi, & ilice, overo smilace, overo aqfolia, qui cum non casure fronde fogliosi, culto dalle qrquetulane nymphe', becomes, 'en la première ce sont Chesnes de toutes les espèces'.
4 Anthony Blunt, 'The *Hypnerotomachia Poliphili* in Seventeenth Century France', *JWCI*, I, 1937.
5 Luigi Dami, *Il Giardino Italiano*, 1924.
6 In what follows I am indebted to Mrs Joan Gadol's *Leon Battista Alberti*, Chicago, 1969; Professor Anthony Blunt's *Artistic Theory in Italy*, Oxford, 1962; and, of course, to Alberti himself in Leoni's English translation of *De re aedificatoria*, 1726 (1755 edition).
7 *Ennead* I: 6, 3. Quoted by Gadol, p. 101.
8 F. M. Cornford's *Plato's Cosmology*, II, 59 ff., quoted by Otto von Simson, *The Gothic Cathedral*, 1956, p. 29.
9 A. Caro to Monsignor Guidiccione, 13 July 1538, in A. Caro, *Lettere familiare*, ed. A. Greco, Florence, 1957, pp. 105–9. This garden was well known to men such as Philibert de l'Orme, and

will be discussed in the context of early French Renaissance grottoes.

10 First French translation by Jean Martin, 1546.

11 *Journal de Voyage en Italie*, March 1581.

12 The various references by modern writers to this garden are confusing. Luigi Dami (*op. cit.*) calls it the garden of Bernardo Rucellai at Quaracchi; which is clearly the garden described by the writer of *Lo Zibaldone* which Lise Bek ('Le ville de Plinio e il concetto del giardino nel rinascimento', *Analecta Romana Instituti Danici*, VII, 1974), says was called *Lo Specchio*, and was on the road from Florence to Pistoia. André Chastel (*Art et Humanisme à Florence au temps de Laurent le Magnifique*, 1959), referring to Poggio a Caiano, also situated on the Pistoia road, says that Lorenzo bought it from Rucellai about 1479. It is clearly not the garden in which Bernardo Rucellai held his famous philosophical discussions between 1502 and 1506, for which he acquired the land between Florence's second and third wall; see 'Bernardo Rucellai and the Orti Oricellari: a study on the origin of modern political thought', *JWCI*, XII, 1949, pp. 101–31.

13 George L. Hersey, *Alfonso II and the Artistic Renewal of Naples 1485–1495*, New York and London, 1969.

Chapter 3 pages 39–49

1 Quoted by H-F. Delaborde, *L'Expedition de Charles VIII en Italie*, 1888, p. 245.

2 J. de la Pilorgerie, *Campagne et Bulletins de la Grande Armée d'Italie . . . 1494–1495*, 1866, p. 152.

3 Pilorgerie, *op. cit.*, p. 196.

4 François Gebelin (*Les Châteaux de la Renaissance*, 1927) has pointed out that they were few in number.

5 He figures in the royal accounts of 1498 as 'Frère Jehan Jocundus, religieux de l'ordre Saint-Francoys, deviseur de bastimens'. B.N. Ms.fr.11350, published by A. de Montaiglon, Archives de l'Art Fr.

6 Pierre Lesueur, 'Fra Giocondo en France', *BSHAF*, 1913, pt I, p. 115 ff.

7 It had originally been commissioned by Maréchal de Gié. After his disgrace it was finished by another artist, and despatched to Robertet on the recommendation of the Florentine ambassador.

8 P. Lesueur (*Les Jardins du Château de Blois*, 1904–6) attaches little importance to the terms 'Jardin du Roi' & 'Jardin de la Reine', which he says are interchanged.

9 *Op. cit.*

10 Bib. Nat. Paris, Ms. Lat. 9474.

11 In the sense of 'formal dress', appropriate for public occasions and the display of status.

12 Joseph de Croy, *Nouveaux documents pour l'histoire de la création des Résidences Royales des bords de la Loire*, 1894.

13 Dom Antonio de Beatis, *Voyage du Cardinal d'Aragon en Allemagne, Hollande, Belgique, France et Italie 1517–1518*, translated from an Italian manuscript in the library at Naples by Madeleine Harvard de la Montagne, 1913. Beatis was secretary to Louis d'Aragon, grandson of Ferrante I of Naples. He was related to the d'Este of Ferrara and was made a cardinal by Alexander VI about 1495.

14 See Pierre Lesueur, 'Pacello de Mercogliano, et les jardins d'Amboise, de Blois et de Gaillon', *BSHAF*, 1935, pp. 90–117.

15 Lesueur, *Les Jardins du Château de Blois*, 1905.

16 Du Cerceau's engraved plan shows it slightly southwest of centre, so that the gardens on one side of the axis are rectangular, while on the other they are square.

17 When it collapsed in 1665 the weight of timber broke the marble fountain; see A. Félibien, *Memoires pour servir à l'histoire des Maisons Royales*, Paris, 1681.

18 Lesueur (1905) and Ganay (1949) say that the orange trees were housed in the gallery above Le Jardin de Bretonnerie, and the gardens below it. This conflicts with what Beatis says; but from Du Cerceau's plan it is difficult to see where else the Orangerie could be.

19 It was also referred to as 'Le Jardin cis prés Saint Nicolas'.

20 The historical outline depends largely on E. Chirol, *Le Château de Gaillon*, 1952.

21 B.M. MS Lansdowne, 772, f. 23 r, published by Roberto Weiss, 'The Castle of Gaillon in 1509–10', *JWCI* XVI, 1953.

22 A. Deville, *Documents inédits sur l'histoire de France*, 1850. Lesueur, 'Pacello de Mercoliano'.

23 'Fra Giocondo en France', *BSHAF.*, 1931.

24 There is some confusion about the two fountains. The conclusion as to which was which is Chirol's. The basin of one is now at the Château of La Rochefoucauld in Charente.

25 At the end of his life he was invited to advise on hydraulics at Saint-Germain-en-Laye.

26 Quoted G. Port, *Dictionnaire historique de Maine et Loire.*

27 Martine Garczynska (Madame Tissier de Mallerais', *Le Château de Bury*, thesis presented for Le Diplôme d'Étude Supérieure d'Histoire de l'Art, 1963/4. I am greatly indebted to Madame Tissier de Mallerais for the opportunity to read her thesis, and for her help generally in the history of Bury.

28 Gebelin, *op. cit.*

Chapter 4 pages 51–74

1 Ludwig H. Heydenreich, 'Leonardo da Vinci, architect to Francis I', *Burl. Mag.* 595, Vol. XCIV,Oct. 1952.

2 J. Martin-Démezil, 'Chambord, étude des abords du château', *Mem. de la Soc. des Sciences et Lettres de Loir-et-Cher*, Juin 1971.

3 F. Lesueur and J. Martin-Démezil, 'Deux plans des abords du château de Chambord', *Mem. de la Soc. des Sciences et Lettres de Loir-et-Cher*, 1946; Georges Penet, 'Les travaux de J. Hardouin-Mansart à Chambord', ibid. Vol. XXXIV, 1963.

4 The projected terrace roof was modified in 1556 on the orders of Philibert de l'Orme, who constructed a roof with a promenade on the crest as shown by Du Cerceau.

5 By the Seine in the Bois de Boulogne.

6 'Francesco Primaticcio', *The lives of the painters, sculptors and architects*, Vol. VIII.

7 Du Cerceau, *Les Plus Excellents Bastiments de France*, Vol II.

8 See L. E. S. J. de Laborde, *Les comptes des bâtiments du roi, 1528–1571*, for this and the following references.

9 Jean Guillaume and Catherine Grodecki, 'Le Jardin des Pins à Fontainebleau', *BSHAF*, 1978.

10 Ibid. p. 45. They were sown from seed, but eventually they disappeared, as they could not survive the northern winter.

11 The other gardener referred to by name in the accounts was Robert Saguière.

12 'Apuyes' or 'appuis', railings enclosing the squares.

13 Guillaume and Grodecki, pp. 49–50.

14 L. E. S. J. de Laborde, *Comptes* I, 252.

15 François had completely rebuilt the old castle of Villers-Cotterets east of Senlis. Although not particularly new in style, it was regular in plan, with grounds arranged in a series of rectangular areas on three sides. According to the accounts the garden was laid out by 'Guillaume le Moyne, gardener to Madame de Vendôme' (mother of Antoine de Bourbon who married Jean d'Albret) who was sent from Chantilly to Villers-Cotterets in 1538 to choose and mark out the most convenient place for it. Villers-Cotterets had better soil than Fontainebleau, and was probably the more important garden from the productive point of view.

16 *Comptes* I, 112. Dimier (1925) says that perhaps the plaque was never installed.

17 Anthony Blunt, *Art and Architecture in France, 1500–1700*, Harmondsworth, 1953.

18 A. Caro to Monsignor Guidiccione, *Lettere familiare*, ed. A. Greco, Florence, 1957.

19 L. Dimier, *Le Primatice*, 1928.

20 *Le Trésor des merveilles de la maison royale de Fontainebleau* (1642).

21 Active at Fontainebleau 1537 to 1550. Cat. *L'Ecole de Fontainebleau*, 1972, entry 315.

22 *Ecole de Fontainebleau*, Cat. 370.

23 The gardener's daily wage was 4 *sols* (one fifth of a *livre*).

24 Although the first to be published it was the fourth of a series of eight projected books.

25 The third book.

26 W. B. Dinsmoor, 'The literary remains of Sebastiano Serlio', *AB*, 1942.

27 Jean Guillaume, 'Serlio est-il architecte d'Ancy-le-Franc?', *Revue de l'Art*, V, 1969.

28 Hersey, 1969.

29 Rosalys Coope, Salomon de Brosse, 1972, p. 22, note 14, says that fig. XXVI of Du Cerceau's *First Book of Architecture* is derived from Serlio's unpublished projects for a sixth book, the manuscripts of which are now at Munich and Columbia. See note 26.

30 'Instruction de M. d'Ivry, dict De l'Orme, Abbé de Saint-Sierge', a defence against charges of corruption made after his disgrace in 1560, the manuscript of which was discovered and published in the nineteenth century. The text is given in A. Blunt, *Philibert de l'Orme*, 1958, Appendix C.

31 Pierre Heliot, 'Documents inédits sur le

château d'Anet', *Mem. de la Soc. Nationale des Antiquaires de France*, LXXXII, 1951.

32 A precedent existed for this at Fontainebleau, where the *Cour de la Fontaine* was created overlooking the lake as a new focus for the palace. A notable subsequent use of the principle was Le Nôtre's very strong symmetrical layout about a colossal extended axis at Chantilly, which dominated the irregularity of the old buildings.

33 From J. Rigaud's engraving it seems that only one was made.

34 *Le château d'Anet*, 1877.

35 Designed by Raphael *c.*1516, but not completed according to his intention due to the sack of Rome in 1527.

36 E.g. Gaillon and the Tuileries.

37 'Sur ce lozange ainsi trassé
Qu'un beau cordon entrelassé
Faict à plusieurs noedz environné
Est une ducal coronne,
Semée de petites fleurs,
Toutes de divers couleurs.'

38 They were thus made between 1582 and 1595, the year Charles d'Aumale left France to escape being put to death for high treason.

39 Chevalier, *Archives Royales de Chenonceau, Comptes*, 1864.

40 Jean Guillaume, 'Chenonceaux avant la construction de la galerie', *GBA*, 1969, LXXIII.

41 'Devys des travaulx du pont et du la gallerie de Chenonceau, par Philibert de l'Orme, 1557', Chevalier, *Archives Royales de Chenonceau*, III, 1864.

42 A. Blunt, *Philibert de l'Orme*, 1958.

43 Bullant had previously designed a gallery on a bridge at Fère-en-Tardenois for the constable, Anne de Montmorency. This has been dated between 1555 and 1560 (François-Charles James, 'Les travaux de Jean Bullant pour le connétable de Montmorency', thesis, Ecole des Chartes; quoted by O. Choppin de Janvry, *Le Château de Fère-en-Tardenois*, undated, *c.*1975) which is just the time that De l'Orme was working for Diane de Poitiers at Chenonceaux. De l'Orme's design for the gallery was already made by then. It is now almost impossible to say with whom the idea originated; except to point out the marked similarity between Bullant's bridge and gallery at Fère-en-Tardenois and Filarete's drawings for a bridge and gallery by which the garden of the temple at Sforzinda was to be entered.

44 An order to pay Pierre Hurlu, the mason, for attendance there, Chevalier, 1864.

45 'Pour mectre des thuaulx et conduire la fontaine du parc jusqu'au droict de l'allée dudict pont'. Chevalier, 1864.

46 A. Braham and P. Smith (*François Mansart*, 1973) have claimed that Mansart originated the extended axis. But it was the use of the extended axis on complementary slopes, as in the approach to Balleroy, that was Mansart's innovation; a device learned from him and successfully exploited by Le Nôtre.

47 Quoted by Gustave Macon, *Chantilly et le musée Condé*, 1910.

48 Ibid. An account of the fêtes in honour of the dauphin in 1688.

49 There is little of importance at either of these places for the history of garden design. The work at Ecouen was done between 1540 and 1550, partly to Bullant's design. Du Cerceau shows a walled garden at the right of the entrance, but says that it was not finished at the time he made his drawing. The grotto Palissy says he made for the constable was presumably here, but there is no record of it. Bullant's bridge with gallery at Fère-en-Tardenois, replacing the old drawbridge, was built between 1555 and 1560. It was thus contemporary with, even slightly anterior to, De l'Orme's design for Chenonceaux. At Fère it was the entrance to the castle, not part of the approach to a garden.

Chapter 5 pages 77–95

1 The grotto with a semi-circular façade beneath one of the terraces was apparently not built. The pavilions were two circular *tempietti*, recorded and sketched by Scamozzi in 1600. Rosalys Coope, *Salomon de Brosse*, 1972, p. 22.

2 Nicolas Lemercier and Jacques II Androuet du Cerceau, de Brosse's uncle, had also worked on it. Coope, *op. cit.* pp. 231–2.

3 P.-M. Bondois, 'Bernardo Carnesecchi, jardinier de Catherine de Médicis', *Revue du XVIe siècle*, 1930. The Carnesecchi were a noble Florentine family, whose most celebrated member was a poet Pietro Carnesecchi, a leading adherent of the reformed religion, who had taken refuge with Catherine from the Inquisition in 1557. It is possible that Bernardo was also a Protestant.

4 *Les Triomphes faict à l'entrée de François II et de Marie Stuart au chasteau de Chenonceau, dernier jour de mars MDLIX/1560 n.s./* par le Plessis. . . . réédité par M. le Prince Auguste Galitzin, Paris, 1857.

5 Le Plessis, ed. Galitzin, p. 16, translation by the author (original in verse).

6 Roy Strong, *Splendour at Court*, London, 1973.

7 *Les Plus Excellents Bastiments*, II, p. 5.

8 Leader of the Catholics (see Chap. 4), assassinated by a Huguenot at the siege of Orléans.

9 Frances Yates, *The Valois Tapestries*, London, 1959.

10 Jean Dorat, *Magnificentissimi spectaculi a regina regem matri in hortis suburbanis editi . . .* 1573.

11 John Shearman, *Mannerism*, London, 1967, p. 22.

12 'Mannerist style', J. Fleming and H. Honour, *The Penguin Dictionary of Decorative Arts*, 1977.

13 Published as part of *Recepte véritable par laquelle tous les hommes de la France pourront apprendre à multiplier leurs thrésors*, 1564.

14 Louvre, Cabinet de Dessins, RF 29728 bis. 4.

15 Chapter 4, note 18.

16 *Devis d'une grotte pour la Royne du Roy*, a manuscript discovered by B. Fillon at La Rochelle, and attributed by him to Palissy. Published by A. Berty in *Topographie . . . du Vieux Paris*, 1866. It is in the same style as *Dessein du Jardin Délectable*.

17 See footnote 16.

18 In *Archives de l'Art Français*, VII.

19 Marcel Poëte, *Au Jardin des Tuileries*, 1924, p. 74.

20 A. Berty (1866), pp. 46 ff.

21 Louis Dimier, 'Bernard Palissy, Rocailleur, Fonteneur et Décorateur des Jardins', *GBA*, XII, 2e trimestre, 1934.

22 Dimier, *op. cit.*

23 Rosalys Coope, *Salomon de Brosse*, 1972.

24 A. Jal, for instance, in *Dictionnaire Critique de Biographie et d'Histoire*, 1867.

25 H. von Geymüller, *Les Du Cerceau*, 1887.

26 Blunt (*Philibert de l'Orme*, 1958, p. 15) does not agree that they are by Du Cerceau and points out that the dates of the Munich drawings coincide with De l'Orme's presence in Rome.

27 E. Rodocanachi, *Renée de France*, 1895, p. 477.

28 The influence may have been the other way. In his *Architecture* (1577), de Vries places Du Cerceau with Serlio and Vitruvius.

29 Chap. 4.

30 Françoise Boudin et Hélène Couzy, 'Les plus excellents Bâtiments de France: une anthologie de châteaux à la fin du XVIième siècle', *Informations d'Histoire de l'Art*, Nos 1 and 3, 1974.

31 Blomfield, *A History of French Architecture*, accepts the evidence of the entry quoted below, that Baptiste was the architect of Charleval. For Verneuil he suggests Du Cerceau's son-in-law, Jehan de Brosse, described as 'maître architecteur', and resident in Verneuil in 1568.

32 Jal, *Dictionnaire Critique*, 1867.

33 D. A. Thomson, *Jacques Androuet du Cerceau the Elder*, unpublished thesis, London University, Courtauld Institute, suggests that it was the result of collaboration between Boulainvilliers and Du Cerceau, replacing an earlier plan, now in the Vatican Library. *Burl. Mag.* XLVIII, 1956, pp. 153–7.

34 Thomson, *op. cit.*

35 This is clear from later maps, e.g. Carte de la Forêt d'Halate, Archives Nationales, N III, Oise, 179.

36 It is in fact conveyed in ducts through the mountain.

Chapter 6 pages 97–118

1 1509–87, professor (1539) and principal (1562) of the College of Guyenne.

2 *c.*1529–78, a doctor and astrologer much sought after at the French court, where he was admitted to the confidence of Catherine's daughter, Marguerite de Valois.

3 1504–64.

4 *De re hortensi libellus* (1535); *Vinetum* (1537); *Arbustum*; *fonticulus*; *spinetum* (1538); *Sylva*; *frutetum*; *collis fruticum herbarum, piscium & avium liber*, (1545).

5 1503–59; printer to François I and later to Calvin in Geneva.

6 This use of 'parterre' as synonymous with 'flower garden' should be noted.

7 Also '*s(c)eau* nostre-dame'; probably black bryony.

8 And *coquerelle* called variously strawberry,

tomato, winter cherry, bladder herb. It is also the name of clusters of hazelnuts in their green cases.

9 *Planches*, i.e. an area considerably longer than wide.

10 Claude Mollet, in his *Théâtre des plans et jardinages*, 1652, also says that box was not much used in the sixteenth century for this reason. It came into general use with the *parterre de broderie*, when it became necessary to have plants which did not need replacing every three years.

11 *c.*1538/9–1619.

12 Mollet was commissioned to lay out the gardens on the terraces of Saint-Germain-en-Laye in 1595. Fontainebleau and the Tuileries were later.

13 See Sten Karling, 'André Mollet and his family', *The French Formal Garden*, 1974, p. 8, note 6.

14 An André Mollet was employed to mend trellis in the garden in 1550; and there is reference in the Chenonceaux accounts to Pierre and Claude Mollet, joiners.

15 *Description du jardin royal des plantes médicinales établi par le roi Louis le Juste à Paris, contenant le catalogue des plantes qui y sont de present cultivées, ensemble de plan du jardin*, Paris, 1636; reprinted 1641, 1665.

16 Pine, fir, yew, holly, evergreen oak, cork oak (*lièges*), juniper, phillyrea, pyracantha and others.

17 *Sabines, baxiferes, lantisques, thérébintes, citisus, cistus ledon* (C. Ladanifer? 'Gum Cistus'), *stecas, labdanes, rosmarins, sauges, thin, t(im?)bra* and others.

18 Abel Brunyer, who established the botanical collection for Louis XIII's brother, Gaston d'Orléans, at Blois, lists from 2200 to 2300 varieties and over 500 species in his catalogue, *Hortus Regius Blesensis* (1655).

19 Marjorie F. Warner, 'The Morins', *National Horticultural Magazine*, July 1954.

20 Daughter of Catherine de Vivonne, Marquise de Rambouillet (1588–1665).

21 *Variae ac Multiformes Florum Specie. . . . Rome*, J. de Rubeis.

22 *Plusieurs Espèces de Fleurs*, Paris, G. Audran.

23 C. Mollet, chapter XXX: 'After squaring the garden which you want to make in the form of compartments (either *en broderie* or otherwise) it is necessary to make a border six feet wide [en forme de voyale] all round your square so that the gardener can plant all the tall flowers there, making a belt spaced in an orderly way all round the four squares. Also it is necessary to intermix them, so that when one flower is over, the place will not be left empty, and that one may always be able to see there all sorts of colours of flowers on one side of the compartment as much as the other; by this means the tall flowers will add greatly to the ornament of the compartments.' (*Haut* would seem to be a relative term; that is, tall in relation to the low plants which go to make up the patterns in the compartments.)

24 Chap. 3, and Chap. 4.

25 See Appendix B for plant names. *Edging plants*, for framing or delineating the design; basil, costmary or balsamint, lavender, lemon balm, marjoram, pennyroyal, rue, southernwood, thyme;
plants for background or solid pattern; asarabacca, bugle, camomile, house-leek, lily of the valley, marigold, mint, orache, pansy, periwinkle, stocks or wallflower, tarragon, violet;
plants as single upstanding features: hollyhock or mallow, balls of hyssop, juniper, rosemary.

26 See his engravings for the Château of Madrid.

27 There are a series of engraved knot designs by Du Cerceau (B.N.Est:Ed.2d) some of which correspond with those in B.M.120.

28 He says forty or fifty years ago, which would suggest he is writing in the first two decades of the seventeenth century.

29 National Museum, Stockholm. THC 23.

30 The form of a theatre or circus is related to the Boboli gardens where Marie de Médicis spent her childhood.

31 See F. H. Hazlehurst, *Jacques Boyceau and the French Formal Garden*, 1966.

32 Sten Karling, 'The importance of André Mollet and his family for the development of the French formal garden', *The French Formal Garden*, Dumbarton Oaks, 1974.

33 In his discourse, 'Des eaux et fontaines', in *Discours Admirables*, Bernard Palissy wrote disparagingly of this idea, claiming that the water would have been better brought overground in aqueducts.

34 See a plan of 1624 attributed to Jean de Fourcy, B.N.Est: Ve 53h.

35 'Fruitiers à noyaux', probably plum and cherry.

36 A. Berty. *Topographie . . . du vieux Paris*, 1866, p. 49.

37 Laborde, *Comptes*, II, Feb.–May, 1570.

38 Records of 1571 mention a René Le Nôtre; also Bastien Tarquin, Jean Paillart, Jehan Espallard, Girard Auglard. See P.-M. Bondois, 'Bernardo Carnesecchi, jardinier de Catherine de 'Medicis', *Revue du XVI siècle*, 1930, p. 31.

39 The *livre* was the equivalent of a pound of silver and was sub-divided into twenty *sous* (*sols*) each *sou* consisting of 12 *deniers*. The *livre tournois* was the *livre* of Tours. and was a standard.

40 A. Berty, *Topographie . . . du vieux Paris* Vol. II, 1866. See also Laborde, *Comptes*, 'quatre cents perches de saulx pour faire le dedalus'.

41 Presumably the place made for the entertainment of the Polish ambassadors (see Chap. 5).

42 See note 34.

43 Sauval, VII, p. 13.

44 A branch of the Cistercians.

45 It has to be remembered that for purposes of silk production they were not allowed to grow big.

46 Silvestre, 'Veue et perspective du Jardin des Tuileries et de la Porte de la Conference', 1645.

47 Gabriel Perelle after Silvestre, 'Veue et Perspective du Jardin et Pont des Thuileries', 1650/55. They were demolished to make room for a new terrace in 1664.

48 *Nouvelles archives de l'Art Français*, 1872, 'Listes des artistes et artisans employés à l'embellissement et à l'entretien des châteaux royaux etc. 1605 à 1656'.

49 Often passing to the widow. Françoise succeeded her husband in 1638, assisted by her daughters, Françoise and Anne, whose position was confirmed by royal warrant in 1662.

Chapter 7 pages 121–141

1 Daughter of Francesco de'Medici, but brought up by Ferdinand after his brother's death.

2 Jean Héroard was Louis XIII's physician. *Journal sur l'Enfance de la Jeunesse de Louis XIII* was published in 1865.

3 Alfred Marie, *Naissance de Versailles*, 1968, Vol. I, p. 7. Pierre de Gondi was succeeded as bishop of Paris by Albert de Gondi's second son, Henri. On his death in 1622, the bishopric passed to his younger brother, Jean-François, and in the same year was raised to be an archbishopric.

4 Described as 'ingénieur et architecte de sa Majesté; came from a family of master masons at Montpellier. He had been engineer to the bishop of Angoulême; and was architect to Gaston d'Orléans in 1625; 'Architecte du Roy' in 1627.

5 *Le Trésor des Merveilles de la Maison Royale de Fontainebleau*, 1642.

6 *Ypréaux*, a broadleaved variety from round Ypres.

7 A Florentine family. A. Mousset, *Les Francine*.

8 Georges Houdard, *Les Châteaux royaux de Saint-Germain-en-Laye*, 1909.

9 The author of the design has not been identified.

10 Surintendant des Finances under Richelieu.

11 Marguerite Charageat, 'La Nymphée de Wideville et la Grotte du Luxembourg', *BSHAF*, 1934.

12 Mousset notes that a comparable Roman aqueduct conveyed 1000 cu metres a day compared with the Rungis average of 360 cu metres.

13 The last Francine to hold the title of 'Gouverneur des eaux et Château d'Eau d'Arcueil' died a minor in 1784.

14 See Roy Strong, *The Renaissance Garden in England*, 1979.

15 David R. Coffin, *The Villa d'Este at Tivoli*, Princeton, 1960.

16 Richard Patterson, 'The "Hortus Palatinus" at Heidelberg and the Reformation of the World', *Journal of Garden History*, I, Nos 1 and 2, 1981.

17 See Chap. 4.

18 It may have been drawn before its completion as it shows features never made.

19 L. de la Tourasse, *Le Château-Neuf de Saint-Germain-en-Laye*, 1924.

20 Karling (1974), Hazlehurst (1966).

21 This exists as a private residence and is known as *Le Pavillon de Sully*.

22 Unlike Pratolino, where the grottoes were connected by a stairway to the ground floor of the villa.

23 Widow of Ferdinand I, died 1609.
24 F. H. Hazlehurst, *Jacques Boyceau and the French Formal Garden*, 1966.
25 Earlier, according to Hustin (*Le Luxembourg*, 1910).
26 Hazlehurst, *op. cit.*
27 Hustin, 'La création du jardin du Luxembourg par Marie de Médicis', *Archives de l'Art Français*, VIII.
28 Hustin defines 'demogorgon' as symbolizing the spirit of the earth in the form of an old man covered with moss. The statue, of which there is no other record, was to be over life-size, reminiscent of Giambologna's figures of Appenine at Castello and Pratolino. Hustin says it was intended for a second basin in the axis of the parterre, where the semicircle began, and corresponding to the transverse axis which was to end in a great circular basin to the west. Silvestre's engraving of the parterre in 1652 shows a circular bed without a statue.
29 Hazlehurst interprets this as meaning the western extension of the park, and thinks the note refers to steps and a mask beyond the projected round basin there. This is unlikely because there was no rise to account for steps; and there was no question of a fountain.
30 De Brosse resigned in 1624 after complaints of mismanagement, bad technical advice and delays in the building programme. He died in 1626.
31 Marguerite Charageat, 'La Nymphée de Wideville et la Grotte du Luxembourg', *BSHAF*, 1934.
32 It was moved when the rue de Médicis was made in 1862, and is now a free-standing feature at the head of a canal north of its original site. At the same time the statues of the rivers were replaced, and others added to the niches, with the big group of *Polyphemus discovering Acis and Galatea* by Ottin in the centre.
33 E. de Ganay, *André le Nôtre*, 1962. Claude Boutin contracted for upkeep and works in the garden in 1631, assisted by Toussaint Lemaire and Jean le Breton. In 1637 he is described as 'jardinier ordinaire du Palais du Luxembourg'; and in 1648 he received an annual salary of 1840 *livres* from Gaston d'Orléans. By 1664 he was 'Surintendant et Contrôleur des Bâtiments et Jardins du Roi' (Hustin, 1916).
34 Bibliothèque de l'Institut de France, Ms. Godefroy 218, p. 98. See Jean Tremblet, 'Liancourt (Oise) en 1637', *BSHAF*, 1918–19.
35 1598–1674; created Duc de la Roche-Guyon, 1643, Marquis de Liancourt, 1673.
36 *Historiettes*, II. Pléiade edition, 1970.
37 The prototype was the Hundred Fountains at Tivoli.
38 Tremblet's footnote says that one exists at Ratigny, Oise.
39 See *BSHAF*, 1932.

Chapter 8 pages 143–158

1 Mariéjol, *Histoire de France*, VI, 2, p. 435, quoted by R. Blomfield, *A History of French Architecture*, II, 1911.
2 Henri Sauval, *Histoire et Recherches des Antiquités de la Ville de Paris*, II, p. 172.
3 See J. J. Guiffrey, *Comptes des Bâtiments du Roi sous Louis XIV*, (1673–4).
4 Lived *c.*1583–1654. Born into a family of master masons from Pontoise, he was the oldest of the generation of architects who followed Baptiste and Jacques II Androuet du Cerceau and Salomon de Brosse in establishing the French classical style.
5 Introduction to 'Plan du Château royal de Blois', Institute de France, Ms. 1046.
6 *Lettres, etc. du Cardinal Richelieu*, ed. M. Avenel, 1853–77, IV, pp. 476–77.
7 *Lettres*, IV, p. 477.
8 Old woman, Hermaphrodite, Greek lady, Rhea, Julian the Apostate, Roman lady, Vitellius, Pallas, Marcus Aurelius, Flora, Mars, Roman lady, Apollo, Diana, Brutus.
9 Leonor d'Estampes Valencay.
10 *Lettres*, VI, p. 5.
11 'Journal de Voyage en Italie', *Oeuvres complètes*, Pléiade, 1962, pp. 1234–5.
12 The nucleus of the estate was the Hôtel d'Aulnay, given by Catherine de Médicis to Jérôme de Gondi, Baron de Codrun in 1578.
13 See Héroard's *Journal*: 6 août 1605; 11 sept. 1608; 10 août, 20 sept., 3 nov., 2 dec. 1610; 1 fev. 1611; 15 août 1612; 4 juin 1614; 1 juin 1617; 26 juillet, 27 août 1624.
14 A former tailor to Henri IV. In 1604 he got the post of Receveur de la ville de Paris; and was later Fermier Général des Rentes, Aides et Gabelles. He died in 1620.
15 Payment in 1635.
16 A *Mémoire des dépenses* drawn up by Richelieu's niece, Madame d'Aiguillon, for Colbert reads: 'Monsieur le Cardinal a aggrandi le parc de Ruel de beaucoup plus de la moitié par l'acquisition qu'il a fait de plusieurs terres . . . [qui] lui ont cousté au moins 80,000 livres. Et comme c'étaient de bonnes terres labourables, des prés et des vignes et que c'est un terroir haut et bas, il a fallu les aplanir avec bien des travaux pour les reduire en état d'y planter de grandes allées ce qui a cousté avec le plan des allées plus de 40,000 livres.' A. Cramail, *Le Château de Ruel et ses Jardins*, 1888, pièces justicatives.
17 Héroard, 'ler juin 1617, jeudi. A. Ruel dine, il va s'asseoir à table avec la compagnie, y mange peu, va aux Grottes, y mouille, y est mouillé.'
18 '[The Fontaine du Dragon] was no other than a dragon with a pipe in its mouth which could be turned at will; a square wooden balustrade, about a man's height, went twice round, and was closed by a gate which the fountainer hastened to shut behind him once strangers were inside; then he directed the pipe towards them, so that all were wetted and no one could escape even by withdrawing to the other passage, because they were reached through the fence. . . . The contrivance consists in this, that when the dragon plays it turns unceasingly, throwing the water round it to the height of a house in a spiral jet which was beautiful to see.' Elie Brackenhoffer, *Voyage de Paris en Italie, 1644–46*, trans. Henry Lehr, Paris, 1927. The English translation from the French is by the author.
19 Letter to his brother, archbishop of Bordeaux. See Chap. 4.
20 Brackenhoffer says, 'La source est au dam de bois à un mille'; the *Mémoire des dépenses* says, 'plus de demie lieue' (about 2 kilometres).
21 That is, Cramail, *op. cit.* after Dr Launay.
22 The nearest is Frederico Zuccari's garden portal, Palazzo Zuccari, Rome. The most famous example is in the Sacro Bosco of Bomarzo (1550–70). John Shearman (*Mannerism*, pl.65) claims that the earliest is a fireplace in Palladio's Palazzo Thiene at Vicenza, *c.*1553.
23 H. L. Brugmans, 'Châteaux et Jardins de l'Ile de France d'après un Journal de Voyage de 1655', *GBA* XVIII, 1937.
24 Brackenhoffer, *op. cit.*
25 A painted arch was later made at the Hôtel d'Aumont in Paris; and there were painted perspectives closing vistas at Saint-Cloud.
26 Gardener at the Tuileries; he replaced his brother Jean in 1624.
27 See note 16.
28 It is not entirely clear what this means. Both grottoes were seen by Brackenhoffer; they could hardly have been made between the cardinal's death and 1644. On the other hand Huygens wrote in 1655: 'Au bout d'une longue allée on a fait encore une grotte qui n'est pas tout à fait achevée.'
29 1640–95; son of Gabriel.
30 Lésigny-en-Brie belonged to Louis XIII's favourite, Charles d'Albert, Duc de Luynes.

Chapter 9 pages 161–179

1 E. de Ganay, *André Le Nôtre*, 1962.
2 Archives Nationales NIII, Saône et Loire 32, *Catalogue Général des Cartes, Plans et Dessins d'Architecture*, III.
3 According to Ganay, by the Jesuit architect, Père Martelange.
4 Marquis de Galard, *Wideville, histoire et description*, 1874.
5 *b.* Dijon, 1591; *d.* 1669.
6 These are no longer there; nor are the balustrade on the terrace or the statues. Otherwise the structure is well preserved.
7 A rise of 2.40 metres, and a difference of width of 6.75 metres: Marguerite Charageat, 'Le Grand Canal de Tanlay par Pierre Le Muet', *BSHAF*, 1956 (1955).
8 Charageat, *op. cit.*
9 *A History of French Architecture, 1494–1661*, II, p. 112.
10 'Château de Brécy, Normandy', *Country Life*, CLIX, June 17 1976.
11 See Allan Braham and Peter Smith, *François Mansart*, 1973, p. 272.
12 Braham and Smith, *op. cit.*
13 'François Mansart, dieu de l'Architecture', *Bulletin Monumental*, 133, IV, 1975.
14 Part of a façade is incorporated in a house at 34 Chemin du Moulin.
15 L. E. Faucheux, *Catalogue raisonné de toutes les estampes qui forment l'oeuvre d'Israel Silvestre*, 1875, No. 62, item 8.
16 Buildings on the left of the forecourt have been omitted to reveal the view; a fictitious pavilion has been added to the château to make the design appear symmetrical.
17 Institut de France, Ms. Godefroy 219, pp. 47–54.

18 Brackenhoffer, *op. cit.*
19 *Wisdom overcoming the vices*, Paris, Louvre.
20 *Naissance de Versailles*, 1968, Vol. I, p. 147.
21 By Jean Millet and Claude Revel, Archives Nationales, NI Seine 32.
22 The probability that he was the patron, rather than his son, Jean II, who was chancellor to Gaston d'Orléans, is argued in Braham and Smith, *op. cit.*
23 Braham and Smith, *op. cit.*
24 Concerned with suits arising out of the collection and farming of taxes.
25 Brugmans, *op. cit.*
26 Under the direction of F.-J. Bélanger. See *Diary of a Scotch Gardener* (Thomas Blaikie), ed. Francis Birrell, 1931.
27 Gaignières collection, Bib. Nat. Est. Va. 342 IV.
28 Not the suburb of Fresnes south of Paris.
29 1609–76, Marquis de Plancy et de Guicherville, Comte de Montbrison, Vicomte de Semoine, Baron de St-Just, Seigneur du Plessis et de Fresnes.
30 Also altered by Mansart.
31 *Grandeur and Illusion*, trans. Herbert Tint, 1972.
32 See U. V. Chatelain, *Le Surintendant Nicolas Fouquet, protecteur des lettres, des arts et des sciences*, 1905.
33 Braham and Smith cite descriptions by Piganiol de la Force, *Nouvelle description de la France*, 1718; and A. N. Dézallier d'Argenville, *Voyage Pittoresque des Environs de Paris*, 1762 edition; layout plans, Arch Nat. F^{14} 10152; Archives Seine et Marne, C 41, 1793.
34 Brugmans, *op. cit.*
35 A plan made in 1696 shows it as rectangular.
36 Bib. Nat. N.A.fr. 22936.
37 See Hazelhurst, *op. cit.*
38 Compartimens, feuillages, passements, moresques, arabesques, guillochis, rosettes, gloires, targes, escussons d'armes, chiffres, devises.
39 He was in the service of Prince Frederick Henry of Orange between 1633 and 1635, when he designed the gardens at Buren and Honselaersdijk near the Hague. He was in England *c.*1630, and again in 1642, redesigning the gardens of Wimbledon House for Henrietta Maria. At the end of his life he was gardener-in-chief at St James's Palace. See Sten Karling, 'André Mollet and his family', *The French Formal Garden*, Dumbarton Oaks, 1974, and Roy Strong, *The Renaissance Garden in England*, 1979.
40 At the age of 13.

Chapter 10 pages 181–194

1 Giulio Mazarini, 1602–61, was born in the Abruzzi, son of a Sicilian nobleman. He was educated in Rome; and studied law in Spain while in the service of Abbé (later Cardinal) Girolamo Colonna. About 1625 he entered the papal army and was employed by the pope in diplomatic missions. His skill in negotiating peace between French and Spaniards in Italy was noted by Cardinal Richelieu, who invited him to France and used his influence to have Mazarin made cardinal in 1641. Before his death in 1643, Louis XIII appointed Mazarin to the Regency Council which was to govern France during Louis XIV's minority. The queen mother, Anne of Austria, made him her chief minister.
2 Literally a means for throwing stones.
3 J. A. Lair, *Nicolas Foucquet*, 1890. This account of the *surintendance* is taken mainly from Lair's book, Vol. I, Part 4, chapter 1: 'Organisation financière avant 1654'.
4 Baron de Montjeu and grandson of President Jeannin.
5 Of whom one was Nicolas Fouquet, through his second wife, Marie-Madeleine de Castille.
6 *Histoire du château de Meudon*, 1923.
7 *Défenses de M. Foucquet*, 1661.
8 Anatole France and Jean Cordey in *Le Château de Vaux-le-Victomte*, 1933.
9 In *Clélie*, 1660, Fouquet appears as Cléonime, and Vaux as Valterre. The description of the château and gardens is one of the most detailed contemporary accounts; and as it was written before completion, it includes some features which were not executed. Among these were 'two pyramids in imitation of those which are near Memphis', intended to house two Egyptian sarcophagi which had arrived in France in 1652 and were bought by Fouquet about 1659.
10 Anthony Blunt, *The Paintings of Nicolas Poussin: a critical catalogue*, 1966, p. 148 ff. That is to say, Poussin gave the designs to be carried out by a sculptor or sculptors who have not been identified. Thirteen are referred to in Simon Thomassin's *Recueil des Figures etc. . . . dans le Château et parc de Versailles.* He omits a *Ceres*. Piganiol de la Force, *Nouvelle description . . . de Versailles et de Marly*, 1701, mentions fourteen.
11 'Relation anonyme de la fête de Vaux', in Jean Cordey, *Vaux-le-Vicomte*.
12 Marshal Villar's son sold Vaux to the Duc de Choiseul-Praslin in 1764. His descendants lived there until 1847, when the fifth duke, having murdered his wife, committed suicide in prison. Vaux was abandoned for twenty-five years, and bought in 1870 by the industrialist, Alfred Sommier. He and his son, Edmé Sommier, restored the gardens with the help of the landscape architect, Henri Duchêne.

Chapter 11 pages 197–223

1 A design for this parterre at Stockholm (Tessin Collection, 7774) is inscribed, 'Executé à Versailles par Monsr. Le Nostre, le 6 mars, l'an 1662'.
2 B. N. Est: Va 448f. This plan has been dated 1664–5, but could be later. The Petit Parc follows the arrangement in a plan drawn by La Pointe and dated 1664, which shows the Parterre de Latone (not begun until after the fête of 1664) and the paths of the Labyrinthe, finished in 1667. For reproduction and discussion of the various plans of Versailles, see F. H. Hazelhurst, *Gardens of Illusion*, 1980.
3 K. O. Johnson, 'Il n'y a plus de Pyrénées: the iconography of the first Versailles of Louis XIV', *GBA* Dec. 1980.
4 Archives Nationales, O^1 3242.
5 *Naissance de Versailles*, 1968; *Mansart à Versailles*, 1972; *Versailles au temps de Louis XIV*, 1976.
6 These have been dated by Fiske Kimball, May 1669, before June 1669 and June–July 1669, on the basis of a letter from Charles Perrault describing the project put forward by various architects for the new château. These dates have been adopted as more reasonable than those put forward by Alfred Marie (*Naissance de Versailles*, I, ch. 4; see K. O. Johnson, *op. cit.*). Colbert's memoranda are published in *Lettres, etc. de Colbert*, ed. P. Clément, 1868, Vol. V. nos 23, 38, 39 and are reproduced by Marie.
7 Louis Le Vau, Claude Perrault, Antoine Le Pautre, A.-J. Gabriel, Carlo Vigarini, Thomas Gobert.
8 The present fountain with four oval steps of white and pink marble, crowned by the statue of Latona and her children with peasants and frogs arranged on the steps, dates from 1689.
9 Hardouin-Mansart was the great-nephew of François Mansart, under whom he had begun his apprenticeship. Early in his career he was associated with Le Nôtre, thirty-three years his senior. They had worked together at Saint-Germain-en-Laye (1669–73), and at Dampierre (1675) for Colbert's son-in-law, the Duc de Chevreuse. That year they also collaborated in designing the château and grounds of Clagny for Madame de Montespan, near the northeast approaches to Versailles. Hardouin-Mansart rose rapidly in the king's favour, becoming chief architect in 1685, and Surintendant des Bâtiments in 1699. His success was due not only to his competence as an architect, but to his ability to interpret the king's wishes, notably at the *Grand Trianon* (1687) and Marly (1679–86).
10 See plan of 1664–5, B.N.Est. Va 448f.
11 See Colbert, *Lettres*, Vol. V, p. 382: 'M. Le Nostre fait faire un modèle de la nouvelle pièce pour y travailler incessement.'
12 *Naissance de Versailles*, 1968, and *Versailles au temps de Louis XIV*, 1976.
13 Jean de la Fontaine's *Fables* after Aesop were published at intervals from 1668, when the first six books appeared, dedicated to the Dauphin. Charles Perrault's *Le Labyrinthe de Versailles*, with engravings of the fountains by Sebastien Le Clerc and explanatory verses by Isaac de Benserade, was published in 1677. Two of the fables were Benserade's invention; one La Fontaine's.
14 See Marie, *Naissance de Versailles*, II, p. 329, and engraving by Pierre Le Pautre (1678).
15 By T. Regnaudin, J.-B. Tuby, G. Marsy, and F. Girardon respectively.
16 *Divertissement de Versailles*, 1674.
17 Estimate (Recette 1675) for the fountain of Encelade: 'De luy (Sr du Metz) 54752L 10s pour employer au payement des ouvrages de la Fontaine d'Encelade dans le petit parc du chasteau de Versailles, . . . et 452L 10s pour les taxations.
Pour la conduitte d'un pied, de cent toises de longeur 15000

Pour une autre de huit pouces, de pareille longeur	7200
Pour les trois robinets qui se mettrent sur cette conduitte de huit pouces chacun	1650
Pour une autre conduitte d'un pied depuis lad. fontaine d'Encelade jusqu'à celle d'Apollon	12150
Pour les deux robinets de cette conduitte, de huit pouces chacun	1100
Pour la coupe du bois, le défrichage et le régallement du tour du bassin et des allées qui y conduisent y compris la fouille dud. bassin	1500
Pour le conroy idem	1200
Pour les ouvrages de pavé	800
Pour l'aqueduc servant de décharge	1200
Pour le treillage de fer	5000
Pour le treillage de bois, y compris la peinture	4000
Pour le group d'Encelade avec le rocher	2000
Pour les deux portes de fer avec la closture de perches de lad. pièce	1500
Total	54300

M. Jules Guiffrey
Comptes des Bâtiments du Roi, I, 1664–80, p. 814.

18 *Manière de Montrer les jardins de Versailles*; six manuscript versions from 1689-1705. The first is very brief; the longest is the second, *c.*1699. B.N.Est. Va 362, Vol. I. See also Christopher Thacker, *Garden History*, I, 1 September 1972.

19 Le Nôtre was really a gardener, despite being classed as an architect.

20 E. and J. Blanchard, M. Desjardins, J. Houzeau, Le Hongre, Le Gros, B. Massou, P. Mazeline, J. Raon, T. Regnaudin, Sybrayque, J.-B. Tuby.

21 In the sense of being personifications of abstract concepts; and not, as sometimes used at present, to denote sculpture with any symbolic or associative attribution, as in the Apollo theme.

22 It was later put in the Bassin de Neptune.

23 François Francine received 2250 *livres* annually for his post as Intendant; 7000 *livres* for the upkeep of the 'fontaines de Rungis, Luxembourg, Croix-de-Tiroir et du Louvre'; and 400 *livres* for the upkeep of the fountains and grottoes at Saint-Germain-en-Laye, reduced from 1200 in view of their deterioration. In 1675 he received 12000 *livres* as a gratuity 'en considération du soin particulier qu'il rend des fontaines de Versailles'. *Comptes*, I 813.

24 *Discourse on Method*, 2, trans. F. E. Sutcliffe, Harmondsworth, 1968.

25 M.-A. Laugier, *Essai sur l'architecture*, 1755, pp. 248–9.

26 Victor L. Tapie, *Baroque et Classicisme*, 1972.

Chapter 12 pages 225–245

1 The work was renewed under Louis XV in 1730. See Georges Penet, 'Les Travaux de J. Hardouin-Mansart à Chambord', *Mem. de la Soc. des Sciences et Lettres de Loir-et-Cher*, XXXIV, 1963.

2 'Compter les garçons de Colinot; voir qu'il en ayt toujours le nombre porté par son marché, et m'envoyer son certificat tous les mois.'

'Voir que Le Bouteux ayt des fleurs pour le Roy pendant tout l'hyver qu'il ayt le nombre de garçons auquel il est obligé.' Instruction to Lefèvre, *Contrôleur des Bâtiments*, 24 Oct. 1674.

3 Spelt thus in the accounts. Antoine Trumel was flower gardener at Vaux, and was subsequently in charge of the Pépinière du Roule. He succeeded Le Bouteux at Trianon in 1682.

4 This was before the new potager was made in 1682; but La Quintinye, although he received 18,000 *livres* for upkeep, only got an official salary of 2000 *livres*. This, as in the case of others, was sometimes supplemented by gratuitous payments in recognition of services. Men like Le Nôtre also held several posts from which they derived a considerable income.

5 Giles Ballon directed the planting of trees in the avenues of all the royal houses, mainly elm or lime. He received an annual salary of 1800 *livres*. Part of his job was to find the trees; for instance in 1664 he was sent to Flanders to choose and bring back elms and limes. But as Colbert's note indicates, he carried out instructions from Le Nôtre. He also received payments for keeping and feeding swans on the Oise and the Seine. When he died or retired in 1694 he was succeeded by his son.

6 The district round Grenoble.

7 As an example of the quantity involved, Louis Germain was paid for 2,870,000 'plans de charmille' from the forest of Lyons for Versailles in 1685.

8 See Chap. 11, note 17.

9 '1668, 6 aoust: à Le Bouteux, jardinier, pour les festons, bouquets et ornemens de fleurs qu'il a fourni pour la décoration des salles du festin, du bal et de la collation . . . 900 *l.*' *Comptes* I, 305.

Also, '1671, 24 juillet, à Michel Dubois, jardinier, pour des oeillets et chèvrefeuilles qu'il a fournis au jardin de Versailles, 165 *l.*' À Louis Barbier jardinier, pour 370 chèvrefeuilles qu'il a fournis à la pièce de l'Estoile du petit parc, 277 *l.*'

'31 juillet, à Antoine Deslauriers, jardinier, pour plusieurs plantes et fleurs qu'il a fournies pour les allées de l'Estoile dans le petit parc, 786 *l.*'

10 Derived, according to Marie, *Naissance de Versailles*, II, p. 200, from a prototype at the Villa Aldobrandini, Frascati.

11 Richelieu had them at Rueil, and they had been planted at Vaux (see note 17).

12 Honeysuckle, jasmine, rose, jonquil, hyacinth, carnation.

13 10,000 from Avignon in 1672, 5000 in 1674, 7000 in 1675.

14 'Ordres et Règlements', 24 Oct. 1674, Colbert, *Lettres*, p. 368.

15 Michel Le Bouteux has been confused with his son, Jean-Michel Le Bouteux, e.g. Colbert, *Lettres*, p. 296, note 2. Jean-Michel was appointed to the Orangerie at the Tuileries. Designs by him and his father were published by Langlois, *Plans et Desseins Nouveaux de Jardinage du Sieur Le Bouteux*, *c.*1690.

16 The Pépinière du Roule was situated northwest of the Tuileries in the area round the present Place Saint-Augustin. The first purchase of land was in 1669.

17 Ten large horse chestnut trees were brought from Vaux. Altogether 2500 of these trees were bought that year.

18 Marie, *Versailles au temps de Louis XIV*, pp. 160–70.

19 On the east side of the north wing.

20 For Marly see Emile Magne, *Le Château de Marly*, 1934; and Gerald Weber, 'Der Garten von Marly', 1975.

21 Jacinthe, julienne, oculus christi, matrequaire, oeillet d'Espagne, oeillet de poète, véronique, coquelourde, campanelle, ancolie, soleil vivasse, mufle de lion, pivoine, iris, pensée, lys, marguerite, giroflée jaune.

22 14,666 *livres* for the year 1700–1.

23 L'Aurore, la Passetoute, le Soleil d'or, la Gris de lin, la Damasquinée, la Perle, la Topaze, la Mille-fleurs, la Fradée, le Tulipe, la Brocatelle, la Chrysolithe, l'Aventurine, le Beau-miroir.

24 Cascades Champêtres at the entrance to the Bosquet de Louveciennes (1693); Fontaine des Coquilles, Fontaine de Diane, Fontaine des Sénateurs (1695).

25 Tessin-Harleman Collection 7811; Runar Strandberg, 'André Le Nôtre et son école. Dessins inédits ou peu connus dans la collection Tessin-Harleman au Musée National de Stockholm', *BSHAF*, 1960.

26 A watering place for horses, outside the boundary walk below the lower pond.

27 Jean Pierre Samoyault, 'Le Nôtre et le Jardin de la Reine de Fontainebleau en 1645–1646', *BSHAF*, 1974 (1973).

28 *Comptes* I, 536/7, 'pour avoir levé le plan du jardin de l'Orangerie de Fontainebleau et en avoir fait des desseins. . . . 75 *l.*'

29 It is first referred to as the Grand Parterre in 1672.

30 Thomas's two sons. While François was appointed to succeed his father as Surintendant de la Conduite et Mouvement des Eaux and the upkeep of the fountains and grottoes at Saint-Germain, Pierre succeeded his uncle Alexandre at Fontainebleau.

31 'Tondre les buis, nettoyer les quatre carrez dud. jardin, les allées et terrasses d'iceluy, ensemble d'entretenir les palissades de buis qui sont tant contre lesd. terrasses que contre les murs dud. chasteau, filerias, cyprès, et les salettes de gazon, ovalles et quarrez, comme aussy de fournir les charbons nécessaires pour l'orangerie, faire raccommoder les caisses desd. orangers, rafraischir les terres, toutes et quantes fois que besoin en sera, faire sortir au printemps lesd. orangers dans le jardin et les faire rentrer dans lad. orangerie, et générallement faire et fournir tout ce qui sera nécessaire pour led. jardin . . . 1200 *l.*'

32 I.e. in 1695:

Julien de Bray, Grand Parterre	1000
Gaspard Quinteau de Richement	1000
Gabriel Desbouts, Jardin de l'Etang, Jardin des Pins	700

J. P. B. Chastillon, Jardin de la Reine, Orangerie	1600	
Gabriel Dorchemer, Conciergerie	44	20
Jacques Besnard, Hôtel d'Albret	100	
Zabulon Nivelon, Jeu de Mail	108	10
Nicolas Varin, parc	972	60
Louis Desbouts, parc et canal	2100	
La Veuve Vieuxpoint, potager, jardin fruitier	180	

33 F. H. Hazlehurst, *Gardens of Illusion*, plate 163, shows an unexecuted project (National Museum, Stockholm, THC 7955) for redesigning the gardens and extending the park beyond the river, which he dates 'from about 1663'.
34 Daughter of Charles I and Henrietta Maria; married Louis' brother, Philippe, Duc d'Orléans, and died in 1670.
35 Ms. Journal. Quoted in L. de la Tourasse, *Le Château-Neuf de Saint-Germain-en-Laye*, 1924.
36 Victoire, Princess of Bavaria.
37 Bibliothèque de l'Institute, Ms. 1307, No 74; Alfred Marie, 'Sur quelques dessins d'André le Nostre', *BSHAF*, 1947–8; Marguerite Charageat, 'André Le Notre et ses Dessins', *GIAJ*, 1953.
38 Louvre, Cabinet des Dessins, 3.3012.
39 *Description de la Ville de Paris*, 1713.

Chapter 13 pages 247–264

1 After the retirement of Antoine Le Gendre, Curé d'Hénouville, who had worked at Richelieu for the cardinal (*Lettres etc. de Cardinal Richelieu*, ed. Avenel, IV, pp. 476–7). Le Gendre was the author of *La Manière de cultiver les arbres fruitiers*, 1652; English translation by John Evelyn, 1655 (J. D. Hill, 'A French horticulturalist of the seventeenth century', *Garden History*, IV, 1, 1976.
2 The fountain in the big circular basin below the terrace.
3 Two years after Condé's death.
4 The name originated when Théophile de Viau, condemned in 1623 for the licentiousness of his poems, was given protection by Henri II de Montmorency. In his verse he addressed the young duchess as 'Sylvie'.
5 Charles-Honoré d'Albert, grandson of Louis XIV's favourite, the Duc de Luynes; married Colbert's daughter, Jeanne-Marie.
6 The various transformations of the site are exhaustively discussed by F. H. Hazlehurst, *Gardens of Illusion*, 1980.
7 Brugmans, *op. cit.*
8 1621–91; already designated 'architecte du roi'.
9 *Description de Paris, de Versailles, de Marly, de Meudon, de Saint-Cloud, de Fontainebleau etc*, Paris, 1742.
10 A drawing at Stockholm for an extended cascade (THC 2104) is thought by Hazlehurst to be a proposed scheme for this area.
11 National Museum, Stockholm, THC 7946.
12 Michel Le Tellier, Marquis de Louvois, succeeded Colbert as chief minister after 1683.
13 Madame Scarron took the title of Marquise de Maintenon after Louis bought her the estate.
14 L. Corpechot, *Parcs et Jardins de France: Les Jardins de l'Intelligence*, 1912; republished 1937.

Chapter 14 pages 267–277

1 In Le Rouge, IX, pl. 3 it is attributed to Garnier d'Isle. (See n. 2).
2 Ernest de Ganay, 'Le Château et les Jardins de Champs', *GIAJ*, 1933–4, attributes the original design to him, although Dézallier d'Argenville says that the larger part of the gardens was designed by Desgots' pupil and son-in-law, Jean-Charles Garnier d'Isle.
3 For Lord Orkney. The drawings are in an album belonging to the National Trust, on loan to the RIBA Drawings Collection, 21 Portman Square, London. See Gervase Jackson-Stops, 'Formal Garden Designs for Cliveden', *National Trust Yearbook*, 1977–8.
4 It owed much to the plates of Jean-Baptiste Alexandre Le Blond, engraver and architect, who had produced designs for parterres published by Pierre Mariette. Although Mariette gave Le Blond as the author of the book in some later editions, the text was undoubtedly by Dézallier, whose mother was Marie Mariette, one of the publishing family. He later called himself Dézallier d'Argenville, after buying a property of that name.
5 'Jardins de propreté', translated in John James's English edition, 1712, as 'pleasure gardens', but strictly meaning gardens made in a correct and precise manner.
6 *Epistle to Lord Burlington* (1731), lines 50–56.
7 Vol. IV, 1773, published shortly after the French translation of Thomas Whately's *Observations on Modern Gardening* (*L'Art de former les Jardins Modernes ou – L'Art des Jardins Anglais*), translated by François de Paule Latapie.
8 Blondel, *op. cit.* pp. 4, 5. Translation by author.
9 Ibid. pp. 5, 6.
10 *The History of the Modern Taste in Gardening*; manuscript dated 2 August 1770; printed in *Anecdotes of painting in England*, 1771.
11 Kenneth Woodbridge, 'Iconographic Variations', *Lotus International* 30, 1981.
12 For French opinion of English gardens see Dora Wiebenson, *The Picturesque Garden in France*, 1978; and Kenneth Woodbridge, 'Bélanger en Angleterre', *Architectural History*, 25, 1982.
13 The date of J.-M. Morel's description of Ermenonville in *Théorie des Jardins*.
14 Brother of Louis XVI, later Duc d'Orléans. At the Revolution he took the name of Philippe Egalité and voted for the death of the king his brother. Despite his professed revolutionary sympathies, he was guillotined.
15 Younger brother of Louis XVI and Louis XVIII, later Charles X.
16 Called by G. L. Le Rouge 'Jardins Anglo-Chinois', because, he wrote, 'everyone knows that English gardens are only an imitation of those of China'. *Jardins à la Mode et Jardins Anglo-Chinois*, Book XV, 1786.
17 *Théorie des Jardins*, 1776.
18 *A Treatise on Country Residences*, Vol. II, p. 358.
19 Repton's *Sketches and Hints on Landscape Gardening* was published in 1795, and his *Observations on the Theory and Practice of Landscape Gardening* in 1803.
20 He was the son of a gardener at the Jardin des Plantes, Paris. His brother André was a distinguished nurseryman, and a specialist in plant physiology.
21 *Cours d'Architecture*, Vol. IV, 1773, p. 12.
22 *Sketches and Hints on Landscape Gardening*, 1840, p. 86.
23 Brent Elliott, 'Mosaiculture: its origins and significance', *Garden History*, IX, 1, 1981.

Chapter 15 pages 279–291

1 L. E. Faucheux's *Catalogue Raisoné* of the work of Israel Silvestre (1857); the Abbé C. Chevalier's *Archives Royales de Chenonceau* (1864); the marquis Léon de Laborde's *Les Comptes des Bâtiments du Roi, 1528–71, (1877–80);* H. de Geymüller's *Les Du Cerceau* (1887); Jules Guiffrey's monumental *Comptes des Bâtiments du Roi sous Louis XIV* (1881–1901), and others.
2 Extract published in *La Gazette des Amateurs des Jardins*, 1929.
3 Ecole des Beaux Arts.
4 Seine-et-Marne; château built 1701–07; gardens laid out before 1727 in the manner of Le Nôtre.
5 A.-N. Dézallier d'Argenville, *Voyage Pittoresque des Environs de Paris*, 1742, remarked that all Courances lacked was a view.
6 See R. de Passilé, 'Les Jardins français aux Etats Unis', *GIAJ*, 1923.
7 Plan in the Archives Departementales d'Indre-et-Loire, Tours.
8 Joachim Carvallo, born 1869 at San Benito near the Portuguese border; studied medicine in Madrid and Paris, where he met Ann Colman, a fellow medical student, and daughter of an American mine owner. They were married in 1899, and on her parents' death they gave up medicine and retired to the country. For a detailed study of Villandry see K. Woodbridge, 'Dr Carvallo and the absolute,' *Garden History*, VI, 2, 1978.
9 *Jardins d'aujourdhui*, Paris, 1932.
10 Freely adapted from André Vera's *Les Jardins*, 1919. André and Paul Vera belonged to a cubist generation; but their older contemporaries, Jacques Greber and J. C. N. Forestier, also created gardens in a modern regular style, besides working in the classical French tradition.
11 The term 'landscape-gardening' was first used, so far as I am aware, by William Shenstone, 'Unconnected thoughts on gardening', 1764. 'Gardening may be divided into three species – kitchen-gardening – parterre-gardening – and landskip, or picturesque gardening.'
12 *Les Jardins de l'Avenir*, 1935.
13 Son of Dr Joachim Carvallo, note 8.
14 This is not an exact translation, but is adapted from 'Le Jardin Potager d'Ornement de Villandry', *GIAJ*, 1955–6.

Appendix A

A list of plants used for ornamental purposes

A comprehensive list of plants grown in the sixteenth and seventeenth centuries is beyond the scope of this book. The following list is provided to give some guidance in interpreting the names of plants referred to in a formal or ornamental context in the main French gardening manuals of the period, namely: Charles Etienne and Jean Liébault's *L'Agriculture et La Maison Rustique*, 1564 (abbreviated as **MR**); Olivier de Serres's *Le Théâtre d'Agriculture et Mesnages des Champs*, 1600 (abbreviated as **OS**); Claude Mollet's *Le Théâtre des Plans et Jardinages*, 1652 (abbreviated as **CM**). The chapter on plants in A.-J. Dézallier d'Argenville's *La Théorie et la Pratique du Jardinage* was only added in the later edition of 1747 (abbreviated as **DA**). Plants in these manuals are mentioned in general terms, usually by their common name. Variations in spelling, printers' errors and the fact that the same names are sometimes used for different flowers make identification difficult. There is little attempt to distinguish species. Mollet, for instance, refers to twenty kinds of *oeillet*. *Marguerite* and *pasquerette* are used as alternative names for daisy-like flowers, although *pasquerette* is more usually applied to small daisies (*Bellis*). The modern classification has only been included where it assists in identifying a plant.

The most useful book of reference for interpreting the French is P. Tournefort's *Eléméns de Botanique*, 1694 (3 vols), which contains an index of French names and good illustrations. Where the French name can be linked with the latin pre-Linnaean classification, John Gerard's *The Herball or Historie of Plants* (1633), is helpful, as is John Parkinson's *Paradisi in Sole* (1629). Gerard gives many French equivalents. Other books consulted include; *The Garden Book of Sir Thomas Hanmer*, published in 1933 from a manuscript of 1659; J. Harvey, *Early English Gardening Catalogues*, 1972; *Hillier's Manual of Trees and Shrubs* (undated); *The Dictionary of Gardening*, the Royal Horticultural Society 1951 (1965); and *Early Floral Engravings*, Emmanuel Sweerts, pub. 1976 from the 1612 'Florilegium'.

French	English	MR	OS	CM	DA	Notes
absi(y)nthe	wormwood			★		*Artemisia absinthium*
acacia	false acacia				★	*Robinia*
aconit d'hiver	winter aconite				★	
aconit tue-loup	wolf's-bane/monkshood				★	
agnus castus	chaste tree	★		★		*Vitex agnus castus*
alaterne	alaterna				★	'Species of Phylleria also used for making *palissades*.' DA
alisier	service tree	★			★	*Sorbus domestica*
alleluya	wood sorrel			★		*Oxalis*, 'has little white flowers'
althea frutex (Guimauve royale)	shrubbed mallow				★	see Gerard, p. 933
alvine	wormwood	★				*Artemisia absinthium*
amarante	amaranthus				★	called by Parkinson, 'The Flower Gentle'
ambrette (charbon bénit)	hibiscus seed				★	'Herbe á la poudre de Chypre.' *Littré*
amomum/solanum	Jerusalem cherry				★	*Solanum pseudocapsicum*
anc(h)olie	columbine	★		★	★	
anemone	anemone		★	★	★	
anet	dill	★				'Fragrant herb for the parterre'
anthirinum (muffle de lion)	snapdragon/*Antirrhinum*				★	
arbre de Judée	Judas tree			★	★	
armérie	sweet william			★		*Armerius/Armeria*. See also *Oeillet de Poete*
armoise	mugwort	★				*Artemisia vulgaris*
aspic	great lavender/spike			★		*Lavendula spica*
au(l)ne (verne)	alder	★	★		★	'For making water pipes.' DA
aurosne	southernwood	★				*Artemisia abrotanum*
azerolier	thorn				★	*Crataegus azarolus*
baguenaudier	bladder senna	★			★	'Yellow flowers.' DA Hanmer, pp. 119–20
balsamine panaché	balsam				★	*Impatiens Balsamina*. 'Panaché' = variegated
barbe de bouc	goat's beard	★				*Tragopogon*

French	English	MR	OS	CM	DA	Notes
basilic	basil	★			★	
bassinet (bouton d'or)	globe flower			★	★	
baume (mélisse)	lemon balm	★				
belle de nuit	marvel of Peru				★	*Mirabilis*
belvedere	summer cypress/broom toad flax		★			See Harvey, p. 118, re Belvidere (*Kochia scoparia*), *and Gerard, pp. 554–5.*
bouleau	birch	★	★		★	'Wood only suitable for brooms and sabots.' DA
brusc (housson)	butcher's broom (knee holly)	★				
buisson ardent (piracanta)	firethorn/*Pyracantha*				★	
buys/bouis/buis	box	★	★		★	
camomille/camamine	camomile			★	★	
campanelle/clochette	campanula/bell flower				★	
campanula/volubilis major	see *Volubilis*					
cap(p)rier	caper	★				*Capparis spinosa*
capucine/cresson d'Inde	nasturtium				★	
carrouge (carroubier?)	carob tree?	★				*Ceratonia siliqua. Silique* or *Carrobe.*
cèdre	cedar	★		★		
cerisier	cherry		★			
charme	hornbeam	★		★	★	'Walks, *palissades* and woods. Especially *palissades* and *charmilles*.' DA
cha(s)taignier	sweet chestnut (Spanish)	★	★	★	★	'More for woods than walks. Profitable. For making vats, hoops, barrels and vine props.' DA
chesne	oak	★	★	★	★	'More for woods and forests than to form straight walks.' DA
chesne vert (yeuse)	ilex	★	★	★	★	'Good for forming *allées*.' DA
chèvrefeuille	honeysuckle		★	★	★	
ciclamen (pain de pourceau)	cyclamen				★	
citisus (cytisus)	broom			★	★	'Only for the parterre.' DA (Trifolium)
citronnier	lemon tree	★				
colutea	bladder senna				★	'Purple flowers.' DA See Hanmer, pp. 119–20
concombre	cucumber	★				Used as a climbing plant
coq	costmary	★				
coquelico(t)	wild red poppy				★	
coquelourde	pasque flower	★			★	Anemone pulsatilla. Also applied to *Lychnis coronaria*
coquerelle (coqueret[te])	bladder/winter cherry	★				*Physalis alkekengi*
cormier	see *Alisier*					
cornouiller	cornel/dogwood				★	
coudrier (noisetier)	hazel		★		★	
couleuvrée	bryony	★				From 'couleuvre', grass snake
courge	gourd	★				'For *berceaux*'
couronne impériale	crown imperial		★	★	★	*Fritilleria imperialis*
Crocus (saf[f]ran)	crocus				★	
croix de Jérusalem/de Malte	*Lychnis chalcedonica*				★	
crustrion	unidentified			★		Dwarf plant with small blue flower
crysantemon/grande paquerette	large daisy				★	Possibly *Chrysanthemum hosmariesne*
cypres(z)	cypress	★	★	★	★	'Suitable for *allées* and *palissades*.' DA
digitale	foxglove				★	
Emerus (syturidaca)	bladder senna				★	'Yellow flowers, leaf like common jasmine.' DA. *Colutea scorpioides*, see Miller, 1735 edition
épine blanche/aubépin(e)	whitethorn/hawthorn				★	'For quick-set hedges.' DA
épine-vinette	berberis/barbary				★	
érable	maple	★	★	★	★	'To fill up woods and plant *palissades*.' DA. '*Herable*.' CM
éternelle	everlasting flower				★	see *immortelle*
espargout(r)e	spur(r)ey	★				A species of the genus *Spergula*. 'A fragrant herb for the parterre.'

French	English	MR	OS	CM	DA	Notes
figuier	fig tree	★			★	
flambe	iris/gladiolus	★				
fleur de la Passion (grenadille)	passion flower				★	
fou(s)teau, see hestre						
framboisier	raspberry cane		★			
frêsne	ash	★			★	'Seldom used in gardens except in *bosquets*.' DA
fraxinelle (dictame)	bastard dittany				★	
fre(i)tillaire/frittilaire	fritillary			★	★	
fusin (fusain)	spindle tree				★	
garde-rob(b)e	santolina	★				see Tournefort, p. 365
garrobier	unidentified		★			
genest/genêt	broom	★	★	★	★	usually called G. d'Espagne. See *Citisus*
genèvre/genève/genièvre	juniper	★			★	see also *Savinier/Sabine*
geranium couronné	unidentified				★	
geranium triste	sweet cranesbill				★	see Hanmer, p. 70
giroflée	wallflower (*cheiranthus*) stock gillyflower, carnation	★		★	★	The Royal Horticultural Society dictionary definition of gillyflower reads 'From the French *giroflée*. Originally given in Italy to flowers of the pink tribe, especially to the carnation . . . but later in England to stocks and wallflowers (*cheiranthus*). . . .'
girotier à rozes (griottier)			★			Robert says of griottier, 'Seizième siecle, rare, Cerisier qui produit les griottes'. See also Parkinson, p. 574.
grenadier	pomegranate	★	★		★	
groseillier/vinetier	gooseberry		★			'For barriers and *palissades*.' Also called *espine bénoite*.
glaieul/glayeul	gladiolus		★	★		
hémérocale	day lily				★	
hépatique (épatique)	noble liverwort				★	see Gerard, p. 1203 (*Anemone hepatica*)
herbe aux chats	catmint	★				*Cataria nepeta* (also applied to *valerian*)
herbe de la nuict	marvel of Peru		★			see *belle de nuit*
herbe au soleil (heliotrophon/ vire soli)	heliotrope		★			see *tourne-sol*
Herbe à Suisse	unidentified			★		'Tall flower'
hestre/haistre/hêtre	beech	★	★	★	★	'Walks, *palissades*, woods.' DA. Also called *fou(s)teau* CM and MR
houblon	hop	★	★			
houx	holly		★		★	'Used for making rods or switches.' DA
hyacinthe	hyacinth	★				
if	yew	★		★	★	'For *palissades* and ornamenting borders or parterres.' DA
immortelle/elichrysum	everlasting flower				★	or xeranthemum, see *éternelle*
immortelle d'Italie	everlasting flower				★	see *éternelle*
iris	iris			★	★	
isope vert/hyssoppe	hyssop	★		★		
jacinthe/jacinte	hyacinth			★	★	
jasmin/josmin/jessemin	jasmine	★	★	★	★	
jassé des Indes	cornflower				★	Jacée (Robert)
jonquille	jonquil (narcissus)				★	
julienne	rocket (sweet rocket)				★	Sometimes called Dame's Violet
laurier	bay	★	★	★	★	
laurier-rose	oleander			★	★	
laurier-raige	unidentified			★		
laurier-cerise	common or cherry laurel				★	
laurier-thim	laurustinus				★	*Viburnum tinus*

French	English	MR	OS	CM	DA	Notes
laurier d'Alexandrie	Alexandrian laurel				★	*Danae racemosa*
laurier Saint-Antoine	a species of willow herb				★	possibly the French willow or Rose bay
lavande	lavender	★		★		
lentisque	mastic tree	★			★	*Pistachia Lentiscus*
leonurus	lion's ear				★	*Leonitus Leonorus*
liège	cork oak	★				
lierre	ivy	★	★	★		
lilas(c)	lilac			★	★	
limonnier	sour lime	★				
liseron	morning glory			★		*liseron bleu* is Morning Glory
lys/lis	lily	★	★	★	★	
lys d'estang	water-lily	★				
marguerite/pa(s)querette	daisy	★	★	★	★	Large or small
mariolaine/marjolaine	marjoram	★		★	★	
maroutte	camomile				★	*camomille puaute*
marronier d'Inde	horse chestnut				★	'For making walks, but not in squares of wood.' DA
marrubium	*horehound*	★				
marsaut	see *saule*					
martagon de Levant/ de Constantinople	martagon lily		★	★	★	
masticq	see *lentisque*					
matricaire	feverfew				★	
menthe	mint	★				
merisier	wild cherry				★	
meserion	daphne mezereon?			★		
m(e)urier blanc et noir	mulberry		★	★	★	
mignardise/éfilé	pink				★	*Dianthus plumaris*
mirabolanier	plum (mirabelle)				★	
monon	unidentified		★			Small shrub with small red berries
muguet (grand)	lily of the valley	★	★		★	
muscipula (attrape-mouche)	catch fly (lobels)				★	see Parkinson, p. 254/5
myrte/meurte/murte	myrtle	★	★	★	★	
myrtil	whortleberry	★				
narcisse	narcissus	★			★	
oculus christi/aster atticus	inula				★	see Sweerts, II.29
oeil de boeuf/bustalmon	ox-eye				★	see Parkinson, p. 293. (*bupthalmum*)
oeil de chat/patte d'araignée	love-in-a-mist				★	
oeillet	pink	★	★	★	★	
oeillet d'Inde	French marigold	★	★	★	★	also called 'de Turquie' (OS), and 'Rose d'Inde' (DA)
oeillet/jacinte des poëtes (compagnons)	sweet william				★	
olivier	olive tree	★	★			
oranger	orange tree	★			★	
oreille d'ours	bear's ear/*auricula*				★	
orme	elm	★	★	★	★	'Esteemed for planting walks and groves.' DA
ornythogalon(um)	star of Bethlehem				★	
ortogalon				★		*Possibly Ornythogalon*
osier	water-willow		★	★	★	
palma Christi/ricinus	satyrion/finger orchis/castor oil plant				★	
palmier	palm	★				
passe-fleur	pasque flower	★				*Anemone pulsatilla*. See *coquelourde*
pa(s)querette	daisy		★	★	★	see *marguerite*
passe-rose	hollyhock		★	★		see *rose trémière*
passe-velours/queue de renard	amaranthus	★	★		★	'The small purple Flower-gentle.' Parkinson, p. 371

French	English	MR	OS	CM	DA	Notes
pavot	poppy			⋆	⋆	
pensée (menue)	pansy	⋆	⋆		⋆	
perce-neige (leucoyon)	snowdrop/snowflake				⋆	In the seventeenth century snowdrops and snowflakes were both classified as *Leucojum bulbosa*
persicaire	knotweed				⋆	
peuplier	poplar	⋆	⋆		⋆	
phaseole/pois des Indes	scarlet bean				⋆	*Phaseolus Americanus* (see Hanmer, p. 99)
phileria/phyllyria/filaria	phillyrea				⋆	'Sought after for *palissades*. Variegated variety is grown in tubs'
picea (épicéa)	Norway spruce				⋆	'Woods and great double walks, planted between detached trees, but not now used in parterres because it grows too tall'
pied d'alouette/cornette	larkspur			⋆	⋆	
pin	pine	⋆	⋆	⋆	⋆	
pion/pivoine/peaulne	paeony			⋆	⋆	
pistache(ier)	pistachio	⋆				*pistacia vera*? (not introduced into England until 1770)
plane		⋆		⋆	⋆	Distinct from *platane*, bears a leaf similar to sycamore
platane	plane			⋆	⋆	
pois de merveille	everlasting (sweet) pea	⋆				
pomme d'amour	aubergine		⋆			
pomme dorée	tomato		⋆			
pomme de merveille	cucumber	⋆	⋆			
poncille		⋆				Possibly a corruption of 'Poncire', 'a variety of citronnier from Media' *Littré*; *Citrus medica*
potiron	pumpkin		⋆			
pouliot	pennyroyal	⋆				
primevers/prime vere/paralyse	cowslip/primrose			⋆	⋆	
printanière	'Spring flowers'		⋆	⋆		CM calls them 'bulbous'
reine Marguerite	aster		⋆		⋆	
renoncule	ranunculus				⋆	
rododendron (Rosago)	rhododendron		⋆			
Rosier	rose tree	⋆	⋆	⋆	⋆	
rosier de gueldre	guelder rose			⋆	⋆	*Opulus sterile*
rose d'Inde	French marigold				⋆	see *oeillet d'Inde*
rose trémière	hollyhock				⋆	see *passe-rose*
rosmarin/romarin	rosemary	⋆	⋆	⋆	⋆	
rue	rue	⋆		⋆		
sain-foin d'Espagne	sainfoin				⋆	
sandalida cretensis	'The crimson blossom'd or square codded pease'		⋆			*Sandalida cretica*, Parkinson, p. 340
sanguine					⋆	Possibly *sanguinelle*, dogwood.
sapin	fir			⋆	⋆	'Suitable for woods and forests, especially for elevated places'. DA
sariette	savory	⋆				
savinier (sabine)	juniper	⋆	⋆		⋆	
saule (saulx)	willow	⋆	⋆		⋆	General name for species, see Marsaut.
sauge	sage	⋆		⋆		
scabieuse	scabious				⋆	
seringat(l)	syringa			⋆	⋆	
serpolet	wild thyme			⋆		
sicomore/sycomore	sycamore			⋆	⋆	'Little or no use.' DA
souci/soucy/solfiz	marigold	⋆	⋆		⋆	
statissée	sea lavender				⋆	Probably a misspelling of 'Statice'
stramonium/pomme épineuse	thorn apple				⋆	*Datura*
sureau/suzeau	elder	⋆	⋆		⋆	

French	English	MR	OS	CM	DA	Notes
talaspic annuel/talaspic vicace					★	Possibly candytuft, see Parkinson, p. 390, or thlaspi (tufts), Hanmer, p. 85
tamarin(d)	tamarind tree			★		
tamaris(c)	tamarisk tree	★	★			
tenaisie	tansy	★				
térébinthe	turpentine tree	★				*Pistacia terebinthus*
tilleul/tillet/teillot	lime	★		★	★	'Most sought after for *allées* and groves. Dutch lime, large leaves.' DA
tin/thym	thyme	★		★		
tourne-soleil/tournesol or *heliotrope*	turnsole/heliotrope			★	★	Name given to plants of which the flowers or leaves turn so as to follow the sun. In early times applied to sunflower, marigold etc. (O.E.D.)
toute-bonne	clary	★				
tremble	aspen		★		★	'Fine walks about canals and ponds.' DA
troesne	privet	★	★		★	OS calls it *Ligustrum*
tubereuse	tuberose				★	
tulippe/tulipan	tulip		★	★	★	
tricolour blanc et noir					★	Possibly a viola, or any multicoloured flower, e.g. Amaranthus.
vege	unidentified		★			'Suitable for wet sites'. Coupled with *tamaris*
valerienne	valerian				★	
véronique (Greque)	speedwell				★	
vigne (sauvage)	wild vine		★			Name for a few climbing plants
violette	violet			★		
violette de Damas	sweet or Queen's rocket	★				*Hesperis matronalis* (see *julienne*)
violette de Mars	spring violet	★	★		★	
violette de Marie	Coventry (Canterbury) bell	★				
violier (musquez)	stock	★	★	★		*Matthiola*. 'Giroflées, white, yellow and red.'
volubilis/grand liseron	see *liseron*				★	

Appendix B

Four designs for figured gardens from the French version of *Hypnerotomachia Poliphili*.

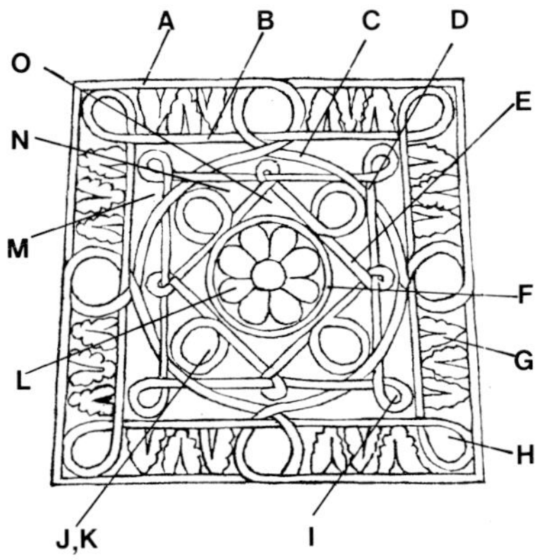

A marjoram
B thyme
C southernwood
D lemon balm
E hyssop
F costmary
G figured acanthus leaves alternately reversed, one of pennyroyal, the other of rue

The Italian version also lists 15 species

H big ball of hyssop, a foot and a half high
I mallow (*maulve de jardin*) three cubits high
J camomile
K one plant of rosemary
L red stocks
M marigolds (*solsiz fleurez*)
N pansies (*menues pensees*)
O spring violets

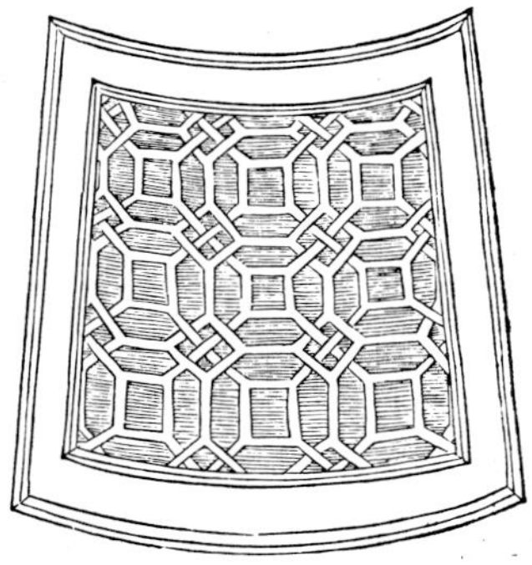

Bands of white marble	Lavender
In the band round the square	Lavender
In the nine squares	Marjoram
In the octagons	Tarragon

The voids were filled with flowers of marigolds

The Italian planting is richer and includes 13 species

The bands forming squares and the big circle	Thick rue
The eagle	Asarabacca (cabaret)
The letters	Senicle (orache)
The four circles in the corners between the two squares	Bugle
Background	Lily of the valley covered with white flowers
In each of the four little circles	A ball of myrtle on a stem two feet high

The Italian version lists 8 species

The square and the circle filled with	Basil
The birds	Mint
The letters	Camomile, with white flowers
The four little circles	Houseleek (*Joubarbe*)
The background	Periwinkle with blue flowers
In the middle of the little circles an evergreen plant about three feet high	two juniper (savine) two juniper (genevre)

The Italian version lists 14 species

Appendix C

Kings and Queens of France 1422–1715	**French gardens, begun**	**Italian gardens, begun**
Charles VII 1422–1461	René of Anjou's gardens at Aix and Provence	
Louis XI 1461–1483		
Charles VIII 1483–1498	Amboise	
Louis XII 1498–1515	Blois (1499) Gaillon (1502) Montargis (1510) Bury (1511)	Cortile del Belvedere (1505)
François I 1515–1547	Chantilly (1522) Fontainebleau (1528) Villers Cotterets (1539) Saint-Maur (1541) Ancy-le-Franc (1545) Anet (1546)	Villa Madama (1516) Pallazo del Tè (1525) Castello (1540) Giusti (1545)
Henri II 1547–1559	Valléry (1550) Chenonceaux (1552)	Boboli gardens (1549) Villa Papa Giulio (1551)
François II 1559–1560	Saint-Germain-en-Laye (1560)	Villa Pia (1559) Caprarola (1559)
Charles IX 1560–1574 Catherine de Médicis Regent, 1560–64	Verneuil (1565) The Tuileries (1566)	Villa d'Este (1565) Villa Lante (1566) Pratolino (1568)
Henri III 1574–1589		Villa Medici (1580) (Rome)
Henri IV 1589–1610	Saint-Germain-en-Laye	Aldobrandini (1598)
Louis XIII 1610–1643 Marie de Médicis Regent 1610–1617	Luxembourg (1612) Brécy (1623) Balleroy (1625) Wideville (1630) Richelieu (1632) Rueil (1636) Liancourt (1637) Petit Bourg (1640) Maisons (1642) Tanlay (1643) Montjeu (before 1640)	Ludovisi (1623) Isola Bella (1630)
Louis XIV 1643–1715 Anne of Austria Regent 1643–1651	Vaux-le-Vicomte (1656) Versailles, first enlargement (1661) Fontainebleau, grand parterre (1662) Chantilly (1662) The Tuileries transformed (1665) Versailles, second enlargement (1669) Sceaux (1670) Trianon de Porcelaine (1671) Versailles, third enlargement (1679) Saint-Germain-en-Laye, Grand Terrasse (1679) Marly (1679) Trianon de Marbre (Grand Trianon) (1687)	

Glossary

Some French terms do not have an exact English equivalent or are ambiguous.

Accoudoir
balustrade or railing of a height to rest arms on.

Allée
the sanded walks forming the framework of the garden *à la française*, or the tree lined walks or rides in the park, usually of turf; as opposed to an avenue, a tree lined road or drive approaching a house or town.

Berceau
a vaulted arbour of trellis-work covered with foliage, or trees trained as an arbour without trellis.

Bosquet
an ornamental grove, thicket or shrubbery pierced by walks – called in England a '*wilderness*'.

Boulingrin
an ornamental sunken lawn or turf parterre, corruption of 'bowling green'.

Buffet d'eau
a stone or marble garden fountain in the form of a stepped table with water gushing out of it and falling into basins.

Corps de logis
the main residential part of a château.

Entrelacs
a design of interlacing bands. Applied to ornamental gardens, a knot garden.

Étang
a large pond or small lake.

Eau, Miroir d'
a formal basin designed as a reflecting surface.

Eau, Pièce d'
a formal pond or basin, usually of stone construction.

Galerie
an arcade or covered walk overlooking a garden; a peristyle. Also applied to the big free-standing carpentry arcades, as at Montargis and Fontainebleau.

Gerbe
a fountain in the form of a powerful jet descending as spray all round.

Mail
a game where a boxwood ball was propelled by a mallet through a suspended hoop with the minimum number of strokes. Hence the tree-lined *allée* made for the purpose.

Nappe
in gardens; a sheet of water below a fall, or a fall in the form of a sheet.

Palissade
a hedge of any height clipped into a smooth wall.

Parterre
a flower garden laid out in an ornamental manner, particularly the flat area adjoining the house.

Parterre de broderie
flowing plant-like designs of box against a background of coloured earth. Sometimes with bands of turf.

Parterre à l'anglaise
of cut turf.

Parterre de pièces coupées
a design where the individual pieces are flower beds edged with box.

Préau
a grass enclosure or courtyard within a castle or monastery.

Tonnelle
an elongated form of arbour.

Bibliography

Abbreviations

AB	Art Bulletin
BSAT	Bulletin de la Societé Archéologique de Touraine
BSHAF	Bulletin de la Societé de l'Historie de l'Art Français
GBA	Gazette des Beaux Arts
GIAJ	Gazette Illustrée des Amateurs des Jardins
JWCI	Journal of the Warburg and Courtauld Institutes

Adam, Antoine, *Grandeur and Illusion*, trans. Herbert Tint, 1972

Adams, W. H., *The French Garden, 1500–1800*, 1979

Adhémar, J., 'Aretino: Artistic adviser to Francis I', *JWCI*, XVII, 1954

Ady, Cecilia, M., *Pius II*, 1913

Alberti, L. B., *Ten Books on Architecture*, trans. James Leoni, 1755 edition

André, Edouard, *L'Art des Jardins. Traité Général de la Composition des Parcs et Jardins*, 1879

Androuet du Cerceau, J., *Les Plus Excellents Bastiments de France*, Vol.I, 1576; Vol. II, 1607 edition; Gregg reprint, 1972

Arnaud d'Agnel, G., *Les comptes du Roi René . . .* Archives des Bouches-du-Rhone, 1908

Audiat, L., *Bernard Palissy, Etude Sur Sa Vie et Ses Travaux*, 1868

Babelon, Jean-Pierre, 'François Mansart, dieu de l'architecture', *Bulletin Monumental*, 133, IV, 1975

Batiffol, Louis, *La Vie Intime d'une Reine de France, Marie de Médicis, au XVIIe siècle*, 1906

Beatis, Dom Antonio de, *Voyage du Cardinal d'Aragon en Allemagne, Hollande, Belgique, France et Italie, 1517–1518*, trans. Madeleine Harvard de la Montaigne, 1913

Bek, Lise, 'Le ville di Plinio e il concetto del giardino nel rinascimento', *Analecta Romana Instituti Danici*, VII, 1974

Bellaigue, R. de, *Le Potager du Roy, 1678–1793*, (1982)

Bene, Bartolommeo Del, *Civitas Veri*, 1609

Berty, A., *Topographie historique du vieux Paris*, 1866–97

Binney, Marcus, 'Château de Brécy', *Country Life*, CLIX, 1976

Biver, Comte Paul, *Histoire du Château de Meudon*, 1923

Blomfield, R., *A History of French Architecture, 1494–1661*, 1911

Blomfield, R. and Thomas, F. Inigo, *The Formal Garden in England*, 1892

Blondel, Jacques-François, *De la Distribution des Maisons de Plaisance*, 1737

— *Cours d'Architecture*, 1771–7

Blunt, A., *Artistic Theory in Italy 1450–1600*, 1940

— *Art and Architecture in France 1500–1700*, 1953

— *Philibert de l'Orme*, 1958

— *The paintings of Nicolas Poussin, a Critical Catalogue*, 1966

— 'The Précieux and French Art', *Memorial Essays to Fritz Saxl*, ed. D. J. Gordon (n.d.)

— 'The Hypnerotomachia Poliphili in seventeenth century France', *JWCI*, I, 1937

Blunt, Wilfred, *The Art of Botanical Illustration*, 1950

Boccaccio, Giovanni, *The Decameron*, trans. J. M. Rigg (n.d.)

Bondois, P. -M., 'Bernardo Carnesecchi, jardinier de Catherine de Médicis', *Revue du XVIième siècle*, 1930–1

Boudon, Françoise and Couzy, Hélène, 'Les plus excellents bâtiments de France: une anthologie de châteaux à la fin du XVIe siècle', *Informations d'histoire de l'art*, 1974

Bourdeille, Pierre de, Seigneur de Brantome, *Oeuvres*, ed. Prosper Mérimée et Louis Lacour, 1859–95

Bourdigné, J. de, *Chroniques d'Anjou et du Maine . . .*, 1529. Ed. T. de Quatrebarbes, 1842

Bourgeois, A., *Le Château d'Anet*, 1877

Bourilly, V. -L., 'Le Cardinal Jean du Bellay en Italie, juin 1535–mars 1536', *Revue des études Rabelaisiennes*, V, 1907

Boyceau de la Barauderie, Jacques, *Traité du Jardinage*, 1638

Brackenhoffer, E., *Voyage de Paris en Italie, 1644–46*, trans. Henry Lehr, 1927

Braham, Allan and Smith, Peter, *François Mansart*, 1973

Brion, Marcel, 'Les Noeuds de Leonardo de Vinci et leurs significations', *Études d'Art*, 1953–4

— 'Le thème d'entrelacs et du labyrinthe dans l'oeuvre de Leonardo de Vinci', *Revue d'Esthétique*, V.1, 1952

Brugmans, Henri, L., 'Châteaux et jardins de l'Ile de France d'après un journal de voyage de 1655', *GBA*, XVIII, 1937

Brunet, Michel, 'Le parc d'attractions des Ducs de Bourgogne à Hesdin', *GBA*, 1971

Brunyer, Abel, *Hortus Regius Blesensis*, 1655 (2nd edition)

Cahen-Salvador, Georges, *Un Grand Humaniste, Peiresc, 1580–1637*, 1951

Caisse Nationale des Monuments Historiques, *Jardins en France, 1760–1820*, exhibition Catalogue, 1977

Campbell, P. G. C., *L'Épitre d'Othéa*, 1924

Caro, A., *Lettere Familiare*, ed. A. Greco, 1957

Carvallo, François, 'Le Jardin Potager d'Ornament de Villandry', *GIAJ*, 1955–6

Caus, Salomon de, *La Perspective Avec la Raison des Ombres et Miroirs*, 1612

— *Les Raisons des Forces Mouvantes*, 1615

— *Hortus Palatinus*, 1620

— 'Lettres inédites. . . . conservées dans les archives de la ville de Rouen', *Revue des Societés Savantes*, XXIX

Cenac-Moncaut, M., 'Les jardins du Roman de la Rose comparés avec ceux des Romains et ceux du Moyen Age', extract from *L'Investigateur*, 1869

Chaillan, M., *Le Roi René à son château de Gardanne*, 1909

Chaillou des Barres, *Les Châteaux d'Ancy-le-Franc, de Saint-Fargeau, de Chastellux et de Tanlay*, 1845

Champigneulle, Bernard, *Promenades dans Fontainebleau*, 1965

Charageat, Marguerite, *L'Art des Jardins*, 1930

— *L'Art des Jardins*, 1962

— 'La Nymphée de Wideville et la grotte du Luxembourg', *BSHAF*, 1934

— 'Le parc d'Hesdin, création monumentale du XIIIe siècle', *BSHAF*, 1950

— 'Le grand canal de Tanlay', *BSHAF*, 1956

— 'André Le Nôtre et ses dessins', *GIAJ*, 1953

Charvet, E. L. G., *Sebastien Serlio, 1475–1554*, 1869

Chastellain, G., *Chroniques des ducs de Bourgogne*, 1827

Chatelain, U. V., *Le Surintendant Nicolas Foucquet, protecteur des lettres, des arts et des sciences*, 1905

Chatfield, Judith, *see* Gurrieri and Chatfield

Chevalier, C., *Archives royales de Chenonceau . . . Debtes et créanciers de . . . Catherine de Médicis 1589–1606*, 1862

— *Archives royales de Chenonceau. Pièces historiques . . . sous Louis XII, François I, et Henri II, Diane de Poitiers et Catherine de Médicis*, 1864

— *Archives royales de Chenonceau. Lettres et devis de Philibert de l'Orme et autre pièces relatives à la construction*, 1864

— *Archives royales de Chenonceau. Comptes des receptes et despences faites . . . par Diane de Poitiers*, 1864

— *Archives royales de Chenonceau. Diane de Poitiers au conseil du Roi, 1535–1556*, 1866

— *Les jardins de Catherine de Médicis*, 1868

— *Histoire de Chenonceau*, 1868

Chirol, E., *Le château de Gaillon*, 1952

Cimber, M. L. (ed.), *Archives curieuses de l'histoire de France*, 1834–40

Ciprut, E. S., 'Nouveaux documents sur Etienne Dupérac', *BSHAF*, 1960

Clouzot, H., 'Saint-Maur', *Revue des études Rabelaisiennes*, 1909
— *Philibert de l'Orme*, 1910
Coffin, David, R., *The Villa d'Este at Tivoli*, 1960
Colbert, J. B., *Lettres, instructions et mémoires*, ed. Pierre Clément, Vol. V, 1868
Colonna, Francesco, *Hypnerotomachie ou Discours du Songe de Poliphile*, trans. Jacques Gohorry and Jean Martin, 1554
— *Hypnerotomachia Poliphili*, 1499, Gregg facsimile, 1969
Coope, Rosalys, *Salomon de Brosse*, 1972
— 'The château of Montceaux-en-Brie', *JWCI*, XXII, 1959
Corpechot, Lucien, *Parcs et Jardins de France: Les Jardins de l'Intelligence*, 1912, republished 1937
Courcelle, Genevieve; Guillemot, Roger; and Perceval, Alain, *Le domaine de Vaux-le-Vicomte* (n.d.)
Couzy, Hélène, *see* Boudon
Coville, A. A., *La vie intellectuelle dans les domaines d'Anjou-Provence de 1380–1435*, 1941
Cramail, A., *Le château de Ruel et ses jardins*, 1888
Crescentiis, Petrus de (also called Pietro Crescenzi and Pierre Crescens), *Le Livre des prouffitz champestres et ruraulx*, British Library Ms. Roy: 14 E VI
— *Le Bon Mesnaiger*, 1540
Croy, J. de, *Nouveaux documents pour l'histoire de la création des résidences royales des bords de la Loire*, 1894
— 'Documents sur le château d'Amboise', *BSAT*, XIX, 1913/14

Dami, Luigi, *Il Giardino italiano*, 1924
Dan, Pierre, *Le Trésor des merveilles de la maison royale de Fontainebleau*, 1642
Decrue de Stoutz, Francis, *Anne de Montmorency, grand maître et connétable de France à la cour, aux armées et au conseil du roi François Ier*, 1885
— *Anne, duc de Montmorency, connétable et pair de France, sous les rois Henri II, François II et Charles IX*, 1889
Dehaisnes, C. C. A., *Documents . . . concernant l'histoire de l'art dans la Flandre, l'Artois et le Hainault*, 1886
Delaborde, H. F., *L'Expédition de Charles VIII en Italie*, 1888
Demieul-Cormier, Anne, *The Renaissance in France, 1488–1559*, trans. Anne and Charles Freemantle, 1969
Des Garets, M. -L. de G., *Un Artisan de la renaissance française au XVième siècle. Le roi René, 1409–1480*, 1946
Dézallier d'Argenville, Antoine-Joseph, *La Théorie et la Pratique du Jardinage*, 1709; revised editions 1713 and 1747
Dezallier d'Argenville, Antoine-Nicolas, *Voyage pittoresque des environs de Paris*, 1762
Diehl, Charles, *Palerme et Syracuse*, 1907
Dimer, L., *Fontainebleau*, 1925
— *Le Primatice*, 1928
— 'Bernard Palissy, rocailleur, fonteneur, et décorateur des jardins', *GBA*, XII, 1934
Dinsmoor, W. B., 'The literary remains of Sebastiano Serlio', *AB*, 1942

Dorez, Léon, 'Des origines et la diffusion du Songe de Poliphile', *Revue des Bibliothèques*, 1895
Duchêne, Achille, *Les Jardins de l'avenir*, 1935
Dulieu, Louis, 'Pierre Richer de Belleval', *Monspeliensis Hippocrates*, 1968
Dunlop, Ian, *Versailles*, 1956

Elliott, Brent, 'Mosaiculture', *Garden History*, 9.1.1981
Ephrussi, Charles, *Etude sur le Songe de Poliphile*, 1888
Estienne, Charles, *Praedium Rusticum*, 1554
— *L'Agriculture et Maison Rustique*, 1570, trans. J. Liébault. Augmented and revised J. Liébault 1586, 1598
— *Maison Rustique or the Countrie Farme*, trans. Richard Surflet, 1600
Evelyn, John, *Diary*, ed. William Bray, 1862

Faucheux, L. E. *Catalogue raisonné de toutes les estampes . . . d'Israel Silvestre*, 1857
Félibien, A., *Mémoires pour servir à l'histoire des maisons royales*, edited after Ms. of 1681, 1874.
Fels, le Comte de, 'Le château de Voisins', *GIAJ*, 1929
Ferrière, Hector de la, *Lettres de Catherine de Médicis*, 1880–1909
Fleming, John V., *The Roman de la Rose*, 1969
France, Anatole and Cordey, Jean, *Le château de Vaux-le-Vicomte*, 1933
Friedman, Alice, T., *Bernard Palissy; sixteenth-century garden art and design*, unpublished dissertation, University of London, 1974

Gadol, Joan, *Leon Battista Alberti*, 1969
Galard, Marquis de, *Wideville*, 1874
Galitzin (Golitsuin), le Prince Auguste de (ed.), *Les Triomphes faict à l'entrée de François II et de Marie Stuart au chasteau de Chenonceau, dernier jour de mars, MDLIX*, 1857
Gallo, Agostino, *Secrets de la vraye Agriculture*, trans. F. de Belleforest, 1572
Ganay, Ernest de, '*Le* château et les jardins de Champs', *GIAJ*, 1933–4
— *Les Jardins à la française en France au XVIIIième siècle*, 1843
— *Les Jardins de France et leur decor*, 1949
— *André Le Nôtre*, 1962
— 'Courances', *GIAJ*, 1951–2
Garczynska, Martine (Madame Tissier de Mallerais), *Le château de Bury*, unpublished thesis for le Diplome d'Etude Supérieur l'Historie de l'Art, 1963–4
Gaspar, C. and Lyna, F., *Les Principaux manuscrits et peintures de la Bibliothèque Royale de Belgique*, 1937
Gebelin, F., *Les châteaux de la Renaissance*, 1927
Geymüller, H., *Les Du Cerceau, leur vie et leur oeuvre*, 1887
Gilbert, Felix, 'Bernardo Rucellai and the Orti Oricellari; a study of the origin of political thought', *JWCI*, XII, 1949
Giradin, R. -L. de, *De la composition des paysages*, 1777
Godefroy, Denis II, 'Description du beau lieu de Berny . . . ', Institut de France, Ms. Godefroy, 219

Golson, Lucille, M., 'Rosso et Primatice au Pavillon de Pomone', *Actes du colloque internationale sur l'art de Fontainebleau*, 1975
— 'Serlio, Primaticcio and the Architectural Grotto', *GBA*, 1971
Goubert, Pierre, *Louis XIV et vingt millions de Français*, 1966
Grandmaison, Louis de, *Compte de la construction du Château Royal d'Amboise, (1495–96)*, 1912
Gromort, Georges, *L'Art des jardins*, 2nd edition, 1969
Guiffrey, G. (ed.), *Lettres inédites de Dianne de Poytiers*, 1866
Guiffrey, J. J., *Comptes des Bâtiments du Roi sous Louis XIV*, 1881–1901
— *André Le Nôtre*, 1912
Guilbert, P., *Description historique . . . de Fontainebleau*, 1731
Guillaume, Jean, 'Chenonceaux avant la construction de la galerie', *GBA*, LXXIII, 1969
— 'Serlio est il l'architecte d'Ancy-le-Franc?' *Revue de l'art*, V, 1969
Guillaume, Jean and Grodecki, Catherine, 'Le Jardin des Pins à Fontainebleau', *BSHAF*, 1978
Guirand, L., 'Création et restauration du jardin du roi à Montpellier par Richer de Belleval, 1593–1632', *Archives de la ville de Montpellier*, IV, 1920
Gundersheimer, W. L., *Ferrara. The style of a Renaissance*, 1973
Gurrieri, Francesco and Chatfield, Judith, *Boboli gardens*, 1972

Hautecoeur, Louis, *Histoire de l'Architecture classique en France*, II, 1948
Hazlehurst, F. H., *Jacques Boyceau and the French Formal Garden*, 1966
— *Gardens of Illusion: the genius of André Le Nostre*, 1980
Heliot, Pierre, 'Documents inédits sur le château d'Anet', *Mem. de la Soc. Nat. des Antiquaires de France*, LXXXII, 1951
Herlinson, H., *Artistes Orléannais*, 1863
Héroard, Jean, *Journal sur l'enfance et de la jeunesse de Louis XIII, 1601–1628*, ed. E. Soulié and E. de Barthelemy, 1865
Hersey, George, L., *Alfonso II and the artistic renewal of Naples, 1485–1495*, 1969
Heydenreich, Ludwig., 'Leonardo da Vinci, architect of Francis I', *Burlington Magazine*, XCIV, 1952
Heydenreich, Ludwig and Lotz, Wolfgang, *Architecture in Italy, 1400–1600*, 1974
Heylyn, Peter, *The Voyage of France*, 1673 edition
Hill, Thomas (Didymus Mountain), *The Gardener's Labyrinth*, 1577
Houdard, Georges, *Les Châteaux Royaux de Saint-Germain-en-Laye, 1124–1789*, 1909
Hustin, A., *Le Luxembourg*, 1910
— 'La création du jardin du Luxembourg par Marie de Médicis', *Archives de l'Art Français*, VIII, 1916

Jackson-Stops, Gervase, 'Formal Garden Design for Cliveden', *National Trust Year Book*, 1977–8

Jal. A., *Dictionnaire critique de Biographie et d'Histoire*, 1867
Jarry, Daniel, M., 'Le premier jardin de Richer de Belleval', *Monspeliensis Hippocrates*, 1970
Jaucourt, Chevalier de, 'Jardins' in *Encyclopédie*, 1765
Johnson, Kevin Orlin, 'Il n'y a plus de Pyrénées: the iconography of the first Versailles of Louis XIV', *GBA*, 1980

Karling, Sten, 'The importance of André Mollet and his family in the development of the French formal garden', *The French Formal Garden*, Dumbarton Oaks Colloquium on the History of Landscape Architecture, III, 1974

Labande, L. H., *Avignon au XVe siècle*, 1920
Laborde, Alexandre L. J. de, *Descriptions des nouveaux jardins de la France*, 1808
Laborde, L. E. S. J. de, *Les Comptes des Bâtiments du roi, 1528–1571*, 1877
— *Les Ducs de Bourgogne*, 1849–52
La Brosse, Guy de, *Description du Jardin Royal des Plantes Médicinales*, 1636
Lair, J. A., *Nicolas Foucquet*, 1890
Langlois, Ernest, *Origines et sources du Roman de la Rose*, 1891
Langlois, Rose-Marie, *Le château de Maisons* (n.d.)
La Pilorgerie, Jules de, *Campagne et Bulletins de la Grande Armée d'Italie commandée par Charles VIII*, 1866
Laugier, M. -A., *Essai sur l'architecture*, 1755
Lecoy de la Marche, R. A., *Le Roi René*, 1875
— *Extraits des Comptes . . . et Mémoriaux du Roi René*, 1873
Le Muet, Pierre, *Manière de Bien Bastir Pour Toutes Sortes de Personnes*, 1647
Lequenne, Fernand, *La vie d'Olivier de Serres*, 1942
Le Rouge, Georges Louis, *Détails des nouveaux jardins à la mode: Jardins Anglo-Chinois*, 1776–87
Lesueur, F. and Martin-Demezil, J., 'Deux plans des abords du château de Chambord', *Mem. de la Soc. des Sciences et Lettres de Loir-et-Cher*, 1946
Lesueur, P., 'Fra Giocondo en France', *BSHAF*, 1931
— 'Pacello Mercogliano et les jardins d'Amboise, de Blois et de Gaillon', *BSHAF*, 1935
— *Dominique de Cortone dit Le Boccador*, 1929
— *Les Jardins du Château de Blois et leurs dépendances*, 1904–06
Levron, Jacques, *Le bon Roi René*, 1972
Lister, Martin, *A journey to Paris in the year 1698*, edited R. P. Stearns, 1976
Loris, D., *Le Thrésor des Parterres de l'Univers*, 1629
L'Orme, Philibert de, *Nouvelles Inventions Pour Bien Bastir . . .*, 1561
— *Le Premier Tome de l'Architecture*, 1568
Lorris, Guillaume de, and Meun, Jean de, *Le Roman de la Rose*, traduction en français moderne par André Lanly, 1971–2
Lotz, Wolfgang, *see* Heydenreich

Macon, Gustave, *Les Arts dans la Maison de Condé*, 1903
— *Chantilly et le Musée Condé*, 1910
Magne, Emile, *Le château de Saint-Cloud*, 1932
— *Le chateau de Marly*, 1934
Magny, Olivier de, *Les Odes*, ed. E. Courbet, 1876
Marcel, Pierre, *Jean Martin*, 1927
Marie, Alfred, 'Sur quelques dessins d'André Le Nôtre', *BSHAF*, 1947–8
— *Jardins Français classiques des XVIIe & XVIIIe siècles*, 1949
— *Jardins Français créés à la Renaissance*, 1955
— *Naissance de Versailles*, 1968
Marie, Alfred and Jeanne, *Mansart à Versailles*, 1972
— *Versailles au temps de Louis XIV*, 1976
Mariéjol, J. H., *Catherine de Médicis, 1519–1589*, 1920
Martin-Demezil, J., 'Chambord. Etude des abords du château', *Mem. de la Soc. des Sciences et Lettres de Loir-et-Cher*, 1971
Masson, Georgina, *Italian gardens*, 1961
Matthews, W. H., *Mazes and Labyrinths*, 1922; Dover edition, 1970
Maulde-la-Clavière, M. A. R., *Louise de Savoie et François Ier, trente ans de jeunesse, 1485–1515*, 1895
Mayer, Marcel, *Le château d'Anet*, 1961
Miller, Naomi, *French Renaissance Fountains*, 1977
Mitchell, Charles, 'Archaeology and Romance in Renaissance Italy', *Italian Renaissance Studies*, ed. E. F. Jacob, 1960
Mitford, Nancy, *The Sun King*, 1966
Mizauld, Antoine, *see* Vinet and Mizauld
Mollet, André, *Le Jardin de Plaisir*, 1651
Mollet, Claude, *Théâtre des Plans et Jardinages*, 1652
Montaiglon, A. Courde de (ed), *Archives de l'art français*, 1851–66
Montaigne, M. de, 'Journal de voyage en Italie', *Oeuvres complètes*, 1962
Morel, J. -M., *Théorie des jardins*, 1776
Mousset, Albert, *Les Francine. . . . 1623 à 1784*, 1930
Muntz, M., *La Renaissance en Italie et en France à l'époque de Charles VIII*
Musées Nationaux, *L'Ecole de Fontainebleau*, 1972 (Exhibition catalogue)

Nais, Hélène, 'Le Rustican. Notes sur la traduction française du traité d'agriculture de Pierre Crescens', *Bibliothèque d'Humanisme et Renaissance, Travaux et documents*, XIX, 1957
Nohlac, Pierre de, *Versailles, les jardins*, 1905
Nys, E., *Christine de Pisan*, 1914

Ogg, David, *Louis XIV*, 1933 (1973 edition)
Orléans, H. E. P. L. duc d'Aumale, *Histoire des princes de Condé pendant les XVIe et XVIIe siècles*, 1863, etc.
Orliac, Jehanne d', *Diane de Poitiers*, 1930

Pacht, Otto, 'René d'Anjou et les Van Eyck', *Cahiers de l'association internationale des études françaises*, 1956
Patterson, Richard, 'The 'Hortus Palatinus' at Heidelburg and the Reformation of the World', *Journal of Garden History*, I, 1981
Péan, Prosper, *Jardins de France*, 1924
Péchère, René, 'La Roche-Courbon', *GIAJ*, 1969
Penet, Georges, 'Les travaux de J. Hardouin-Mansart à Chambord', *Mem. de la Soc. des Sciences et Lettres de Loir-et-Cher*, XXXIV, 1963
Pericaud, Marc Antoine, *Notice sur Hippolyte d'Este*, 1865
Perrault, Charles, *Le Labyrinthe de Versailles*, 1677
Philip, Lotte Brand, *The Ghent Altarpiece and the Art of Jan Van Eyck*, 1971
Piganiol de la Force, J. A., *Nouvelle description de la France*, 1718
— *Description de Paris, de Versailles, de Marly, de Meudon, de Saint-Cloud, de Fontainebleau et de toutes les autres belles maisons et chateaux des environs de Paris*, 1742
Pisan, Christine de, *Oeuvres poétiques*, 1886
Plattard, J., *La vie de François Rabelais*, 1928
Poëte, M., *Au Jardin des Tuileries*, 1924
Port, C., *Dictionnaire historique de Maine-et-Loire*, 1878
Pozzi, Giovanni and Ciapponi, Lucia, A., 'La cultura figurativa di Francesco Colonna e l'arte Veneta', *Lettere Italiane*, XIV, 1962

Quatrebarbes, T, de, *Oeuvres du Roi René*, 1845

Raynal, Marcel, 'Le Manuscrit de C. Denis, Fontainier de Louis XIV à Versailles', *Versailles*, Nos 36–7 (1969) and Nos 42–4 (1971)
Réau, Louis, *La Miniature. Histoire de la peinture au moyen-age*, 1946
René, duc d'Anjou, *Livre du Cueur d'Amour espris*, eds. O. Smital and E. Winkler, 1927
Repton, Humphry, *Works*, ed. J. Loudon, 1840
Richelieu, A. J. du Plessis de, Cardinal, *Lettres, etc.*, ed. M. Avenel, 1853–77
Robb, N. A., *Neoplatonism of the Italian Renaissance*, 1935
Robertson, D. W., 'The doctrines of charity in medieval literary gardens', *Speculum*, XXVI, 1951
Robineau, E. M. D., *Christine de Pisan*, 1882
Robinson, William, *The Parks, Promenades and Gardens of Paris*, 1869
Rodocanachi, E., *Une protectrice de la réforme, Renée de France*, 1896
Rosaco, Betsy, 'The Sculptures of Marly and the Programme of Versailles', *Journal of Garden History*, III, No.4, Oct.–Dec. 1983
Roussel, Pierre Desire, *Histoire du château d'Anet*, 1875

Samoyault, Jean Pierre, 'Le Nôtre et le jardin de la reine de Fontainebleau en 1645–1646', *BSHAF*, 1974 (1973)
Santarcangeli, Paolo, *Le Livre des Labyrinthes* (Il libro dei Labirinti), trans. Monique Lacau, 1974
Sauval, H., *Histoire et Recherches des Antiquités de la Ville de Paris*, 1724

Savine, Albert and Bournand, François, *Nicolas Fouquet*, 1908
Scudéry, Madeleine de (George de), *Clélie*, 1660–62
Séjourné, l'Abbé, *Les anciens jardins de Blois*, 1891
Serlio, Sebastiano, *The Book of Architecture* (English edition 1611, Bloom reprint, 1970)
Serres, Olivier de, *Théâtre d'Agriculture et Mesnage des Champs*, 1600
Shearman, J., *Mannerism*, 1967
Simson, Otto von, *The Gothic Cathedral*, 1956
Smith, Webster, 'Pratolino', *Journal of the Society of Architectural Historians*, XX, 1961
Société Nationale d'Horticulture de France, *Jardins d'Aujourd'hui*, 1932
Spencer, John, R. (ed.), *A. V. Filarete's* Treatise on Architecture (1965)
Spont, A., 'Documents relatifs à la construction du château d'Amboise, 1495–1498', *Correspondence historique et archéologique*, 1894
Strandberg, Runar, 'André Le Nôtre et son école: Dessins inédits ou peu connus', *BSHAF*, 1960
— 'The French Formal Garden after Le Nôtre', *The French Formal Garden*, Dumbarton Oaks, 1974
Straub, A., *Hortus Deliciarum*, 1901
Strong, Roy, *The Renaissance Garden in England*, 1979
— *Splendour at Court*, 1973

Tallemant des Réaux, *Historiettes* (annotated by Antoine Adam), 1967
Tapié, Victor, L., *Baroque et classicisme*, 1972
— *France in the age of Louis XIII and Richelieu*, trans. D. Mc. N. Lockie, 1974
Theurillat, Jacqueline, *Les Mystères de Bomarzo et de jardins symboliques de la Renaissance*, 1973
Thomassin, S., *Recueil des figures etc . . . dans le château et parc de Versailles*
Thomson, D. A., 'Jacques Androuet du Cerceau the Elder', unpublished thesis, Courtauld Institute of Art, London University
Thou, J. A. de, *Histoire universelle*, Vol. 7, 1734
Tonnellier, Chanoine, *La Roche-Courbon*, 1961
Tourasse, L. de la, *Le Château-neuf de Saint-Germain-en-Laye*, 1924
Tremblet, Jean, 'Liancourt (Oise) en 1637', *BSHAF*, 1918–19

Vallet, Pierre, *Le Jardin du Roy très chrétien Henri IV*, 1608
Van de Kemp, Gerald and Lemoine, Pierre, *Versailles et Trianon*, 1979
Van Dyke, Paul, *Catherine de Médicis*, 1923
Varennes, Claude de, *Le Voyage de France*, 1639
Vasari, Giorgio, *Lives of the Painters, Sculptors and Architects*, trans. A. B. Hinds (n.d.)
Vaughan, Richard, *Philip the Good*, 1970
Vera, André, *Les Jardins*, 1919
Villeneuve-Bargemont, L. F. de, *Histoire de René d'Anjou*, 1825
Vinet, Elie, and Mizauld, Antoine, *La maison champestre et agriculture*, 1607

Warner, Marjorie, F., 'The Morins', *National Horticultural Magazine*, 1954
Watelet, C. -H., *Essai sur les jardins*, 1774
Weber, Gerold, 'Der Garten von Marly, (1697–1715)', *Wiener Jahrbuch für Kunstgeschichte*, 1975
Weiss, R., 'The castle of Gaillon in 1509–1510', *JWCI*, XVI, 1953
Welch, A. K., *Of Six Medieval Women*, 1913
Whately, Thomas, *Observations on Modern Gardening, (L'Art de former les jardins modernes)*, trans. with an introduction by François-de-Paule Latapie, 1771
Wiebenson, Dora, *The Picturesque Garden in France*, 1978
Wolkan, R. (ed.), *Der Briefwechsel des Eneas Silvius Piccolomini*, 1905
Woodbridge, Kenneth, 'Bélanger en Angleterre; son carnet de voyage', *Architectural History*, XXV, 1982
— 'Dr. Carvallo and the Absolute', *Garden History*, VI, 1978
— 'Richelieu's Gardens at Rueil', *Garden History*, Vol. 9, No. 1. Spring 1981

Yates, Frances, A., *The French Academies of the sixteenth century*, 1947
— *Giordiano Bruno and the Hermetic tradition*, 1964
— *The Rosicrucian Enlightenment*, 1972 (1975)
— *The Valois Tapestries*, 1959
Young, G. F., *The Medici* (1928 edition)

Zerner, Henri, 'Observations on Dupérac and the *Disegni delle Ruine di Roma e come anticamente erono*', *AB*, XLVII, 1965

Sources of illustrations

Abbreviations

Bib. Nat.	Bibliothèque Nationale, Paris (Est = Cabinet des Estampes)
B.L.	British Library, London
B.M.	British Museum, London
C.I.	Courtauld Institute, London
I.G.N.	Institut Géographique National, Paris

Frontispiece, Allegrain, *Un des jardins de Versailles*, Château de Versailles. Photo Giraudon. **1, 2.** Bib. Nat. Ms. fr. 143. **3.** Bib. Nat. Ms. fr. 145. **4.** Bibliothèque Royale, Brussels. Ms. IV III. **5.** B.L. Ms. Harley 4425. **6, 7.** Bibliothèque Royale, Brussels. Ms. 9392. **8.** Paris, Bibliothèque de l'Arsenal. Ms. 5072–5075. **9.** Paris, Bibliothèque de l'Arsenal. Ms. 5104. **10.** Author's photo. **11.** Bib. Nat. Est. **12.** Bibliothèque Royale, Brussels. Ms 10308. **13.** Uffizi, Florence. Photo Soprintendenza alle Gallerie, Florence. **14.** Bib. Nat. Ms. fr. 22552. **20.** Louvre. Photo Giraudon. **23.** Musée de Versailles. **24.** Author's photo. **25.** Museo Storico di Firenze. Photo Soprintendanze alle Gallerie, Florence. **27.** Bib. Nat. Ms. fr. 1537. **28.** Drawing by A. Félibien. Château de Cheverny. **29, 30.** Bib. Nat. Ms. lat. 9474. **32, 33.** Drawing by J. A. Du Cerceau. B.M. Photo C.I. **34, 35.** Engraving by Israel Silvestre. Bib. Nat. Est. **36–38.** Drawing by J. A. Du Cerceau. B.M. Photo C.I. **39.** Bib. Nat. Est. **40.** Drawing by J. A. Du Cerceau. B.M. Photo C.I. **41.** Author's photo. **42–44.** Drawing by J. A. Du Cerceau. B.M. Photo C.I. **45.** Engraving by Israel Silvestre. Bib. Nat. Est. **46.** Author's photo. **47.** Drawing by J. A. Du Cerceau. B.M. Photo C.I. **48, 49.** Author's photo. **50.** Drawing by J. A. Du Cerceau. B.M. Photo C.I. **51.** Engraving by Israel Silvestre. Bib. Nat. Est. **52.** Ecole des Beaux Arts, Paris. **53.** Engraving by Israel Silvestre. Bib. Nat. Est. **54.** Drawing Bib. Nat. **55.** Photo I.G.N. **56.** Drawing by J. A. Du Cerceau. B.M. Photo C.I. **57.** Museo Storico di Firenze, Florence. Photo Soprintendenza alle Gallerie, Florence. **58.** Drawing by J. A. Du Cerceau. B.M. Photo C.I. **59.** Louvre, Cabinet des Dessins. **60, 61.** Author's photo. **62.** Engraving by J. A. Du Cerceau. **63.** Drawing by J. A. Du Cerceau. Photo R. B. Fleming. **64.** Author's photo. **65.** Drawing by J. A. Du Cerceau. **66.** Photo I.G.N. **67.** Drawing by J. A. Du Cerceau. B.M. Photo C.I. **68.** Engraving by A. Perelle. Bib. Nat. Est. **69.** Engraving by Israel Silvestre. Bib. Nat. Est. **71.** Engraving by Israel Silvestre. Bib. Nat. Est. **72.** Drawing by Israel Silvestre. Louvre, Cabinet des Dessins. **73.** Engraving by Israel Silvestre. Bib. Nat. Est. **74.** Drawing by J. A. Du Cerceau. B.M. Photo C.I. **75.** Detail of plan of Paris by François Quesnel. Bib. Nat. **76.** Engraving by D. Rabel for H. d'Urfé's *L'Astrée*. **77.** Author's photo. **78.** Engraving from Jean Dorat's *Magnificentissimi Spectaculi*. **79.** Engraving from B. del Bene's *Civitas Veri*, 1609. **80, 81.** Louvre. **82.** Louvre, Cabinet des Dessins. **83, 84.** Bib. Nat. Est. **85.** Engraving by J. A. Du Cerceau, *Les Plus Excellents Bastiments de France*. **86, 87.** Drawing by J. A. Du Cerceau. B.M. Photo C.I. **88.** Engraving by E. du Perac. Bib. Nat. Est. **89.** Engraving by Israel Silvestre. Bib. Nat. Est. **90.** Author's photo. **91–93.** Drawing by J. A. Du Cerceau. B.M. Photo C.I. **94.** Paris, Museum d'Histoire Naturelle, Bibliothèque. Photo Giraudon. **95.** Bib. Nat. Est. **100.** Author's photo. **101.** Bodleian Library, Oxford. **103, 104.** Photo B. Sonnet, Dijon. **105.** Engraving by Israel Silvestre. Bib. Nat. Est. **106.** Drawing by J. A. Du Cerceau. B.M. Photo C.I. **107.** Nationalmuseum Stockholm. **108.** Engraving by G. Perelle after Silvestre. Bib. Nat. Est. **109.** Engraving from Olivier de Serre's *Le Théâtre d'Agriculture*, 1600. **112, 113.** Engraving by Israel Silvestre. Bib. Nat. Est. **114.** Bib. Nat. Est. **115.** Engraving by Israel Silvestre. Bib. Nat. Est. **116.** Photo Archives Nationales. **117.** Engraving by Israel Silvestre. Bib. Nat. Est. **118.** Engraving by A. Bosse. Bib. Nat. Est. **119.** Engraving by Stefano della Bella. Photo C.I. **120.** Author's photo. **121.** Drawing by Silvestre. Louvre. **122.** Engraving by G. B. Falda. **123.** Engraving by Gabriel Perelle. Bib. Nat. Est. **124.** Engraving by Israel Silvestre. Bib. Nat. Est. **127.** Bib. Nat. Est. **128.** Photo E. de Ganay. **129.** Drawing by Gasselin. Chatsworth. Photo C.I. **132.** Engraving after A. Bosse. Bib. Nat. Est. **133–135.** Engraving by Israel Silvestre. Bib. Nat. Est. **136.** Engraving by A. Bosse. Bib. Nat. Est. **137.** Engraving by Perelle. Bib. Nat. Est. **138.** Archives Nationales. **139, 140.** Engraving by Israel Silvestre. Bib. Nat. Est. **141.** Anonymous drawing. Bib. Nat. Est. **142.** Engraving by Henri Mauperché. Bib. Nat. Est. **143–146.** Engraving by Israel Silvestre. Bib. Nat. Est. **147.** Engraving by Jean Marot. Bib. Nat. Est. **148.** Engraving by Perelle after Silvestre. Bib. Nat. Est. **149.** Engraving by Perelle. Bib. Nat. Est. **150.** Bib. Nat. Est. **151.** Photo I.G.N. **152.** Engraving by Perelle. Bib. Nat. Est. **153.** Author's photo. **154.** Engraving by Israel Silvestre. Bib. Nat. Est. **155.** Engraving by Perelle after Silvestre. Bib. Nat. Est. **156.** After cadastral plan of 1818, A. Cramail, *Le Château de Rueil*, 1888. **157.** Engraving by Israel Silvestre. Bib. Nat. Est. **158, 159.** Engraving by Perelle after Silvestre. Bib. Nat. Est. **160.** Detail of photo by Fototeca Unione, Rome. **161, 162.** Engraving by Perelle after Silvestre. Bib. Nat. Est. **163.** Engraving by Perelle. Bib. Nat. Est. **164.** Louvre, Cabinet des Dessins. **165.** Engraving by Adam Perelle. Bib. Nat. Est. **166.** Engraving by Gabriel Perelle. Bib. Nat. Est. **167.** Engraving by Larmesin after Watteau. Bib. Nat. Est. **168.** Engraving by Perelle after Silvestre. Bib. Nat. Est. **169.** Engraving by Edelinck after Namur. From Charles Perrault, *Les Hommes illustres qui ont paru en France pendant ce siècle*, 1696–1700 **170.** Archives Nationales, Paris. **171, 172.** Engraving by Israel Silvestre. Bib. Nat. Est. **173.** Author's photo. **174.** Photo I.G.N. **176.** Author's photo. **177.** Engraving after Silvestre. Bib. Nat. Est. **178.** Engraving by Perelle. Bib. Nat. Est. **179.** Plan by Jean Millet and Claude Revel. Archives Nationales, Paris. **180, 181.** Author's photo. **182.** Photo I.G.N. **183.** Engraving by Israel Silvestre. Bib. Nat. Est. **184.** Drawing by Adam Perelle. Musée de l'Ile de France, Sceaux. Photo Giraudon. **185.** Plan by A. Larue. Bib. Nat. Est. **186.** Engraving. Bib. Nat. Est. **189.** Drawing by Israel Silvestre. Louvre, Cabinet des Dessins. **190.** Engraving by Israel Silvestre. Bib. Nat. Est. **191.** Nationalmuseum, Stockholm. **192.** Engraving by Perelle. Bib. Nat. Est. **193.** Engraving by Israel Silvestre. Bib. Nat. Est. **194.** Author's photo. **195, 196.** Drawing by Israel Silvestre. Louvre, Cabinet des Dessins. **197.** Engraving by Israel Silvestre. Bib. Nat. Est. **198, 199.** Drawing by Israel Silvestre. Louvre, Cabinet des Dessins. **200.** Author's photo. **201, 202.** Author's photo. **203.** Engraving by Israel Silvestre. Bib. Nat. Est. **204.** Paris, Museum de Histoire Naturelle, Bibliothèque. Photo Giraudon. **205.** Plan by

Pierre Le Pautre, 1710. Bib. Nat. Est. **206.** Engraving by Israel Silvestre. Bib. Nat. Est. **207.** Plan of Versailles. Bib. Nat. Est. **208.** Drawing by Israel Silvestre. Archives Nationales. **209, 210.** Engraving by Perelle. Bib. Nat. Est. **211.** Engraving by Le Pautre. Bib. Nat. Est. **212–215.** Author's photo. **216.** Drawing by Israel Silvestre. Louvre, Cabinet des Dessins. **217.** Engraving by Perelle. Bib. Nat. Est. **218.** Engraving by J. Le Pautre. Bib. Nat. Est. **219.** Engraving by Perelle. Bib. Nat. Est. **220.** J. B. Martin, *Bassin de Neptune*. Château de Versailles. Photo Giraudon. **221.** J. Cotelle, *Le Théâtre d'eau*. Château de Versailles. Photo Documentation photographique. **222, 223.** Engraving by Perelle. Bib. Nat. Est. **224.** Author's photo. **225.** Engraving by J. Rigaud. Bib. Nat. Est. **226–232.** Author's photo. **233.** Engraving by Perelle. Bib. Nat. Est. **234.** Detail of engraving by Gaspard de Baillieul. Bib. Nat. Est. **235.** Engraving by Perelle. Bib. Nat. **236.** Jean Cotelle. *Parterre de Trianon*. Château de Versailles. Photo Giraudon. **237.** Drawing attrib. Jules Hardouin-Mansart. Archives départmentales, Loire et Cher. **239.** Engraving by Perelle Bib. Nat. Est. **240–242.** Bib. Nat. **243.** J. B. Martin, *Château de Marly*. Château de Versailles. Photo Giraudon. **244.** Archives Nationales. **245.** Nationalmuseum Stockholm. **246.** Engraving by Israel Silvestre. **247.** Drawing by Israel Silvestre. Louvre, Cabinet des Dessins. **248.** Engraving by Silvestre. Bib. Nat. Est. **249.** Engraving by Israel Silvestre. Bib. Nat. Est. **250.** Bib. Nat. Est. **251.** Author's photo. **252.** Drawing by Perelle. Musée Carnevalet, Paris. Photo Bulloz. **253.** Engraving by Perelle. Bib. Nat. Est. **254.** Drawing by Israel Silvestre. Louvre, Cabinet des Dessins. **255.** Church of St. Roch, Paris. Photo Archives Photographiques. **256.** Bib. Nat. Est. **257.** Engraving by Perelle. Bib. Nat. Est. **258.** Engraving by A. Perelle. Bib. Nat. Est. **259.** Bib. Nat. Est. **260.** Musée Condé, Chantilly. Photo Giraudon. **261, 262.** Engraving by A.Perelle. Bib. Nat. Est. **263.** Author's photo. **264.** Engraving by A. Perelle. Bib. Nat. Est. **265.** Engraving by Perelle. Bib. Nat. Est. **266.** Engraving by A. Perelle. Bib. Nat. Est. **267.** Photo I.G.N. **268.** Bib. Nat. Est. **269.** Louvre, Cabinet des Dessins. **270.** Author's photo. **271.** Bib. Nat. Est. **272.** Louvre, Cabinet des Dessins. **273.** Author's photo. **274, 275.** Engraving by A. Perelle. Bib. Nat. Est. **276.** Author's photo. **277.** Engraving by Israel Silvestre. Bib. Nat. **278.** Photo Country Life. **279.** Photo I.G.N. **280.** Nationalmuseum Stockholm. **281.** Author. **283.** Le Rouge. **286.** Perignon, *Château de Menars*. Louvre, Cabinet des Dessins. **287.** Engraving by J. B. Rigaud, Bib. Nat. Est. **290, 291.** From Le Rouge, *Details des nouveaux jardins à la mode*, 1776–87. **292.** Salon and salle à manger by N. Lallemant. Musée Condé, Chantilly. Photo Giraudon. **293, 294.** From A. de Laborde, *Descriptions des nouveaux jardins de la France*, 1808. **295.** From E. André, *L'art des jardins*, 1879. **296, 297.** Author's photo. **298.** From *Les jardins d'aujourd'hui*, 1932. **299.** Bib. Nat. Est. **300.** Engraving by Israel Silvestre. **301, 302.** Author's photo. **303.** Gazette des Amateurs des Jardins. **304–307.** Author's photo. **309.** R. Holden, after plan of *c.*1924. **310, 311.** Author's photo. **312, 313.** A. Véra, *Les jardins*, 1919. **314, 315.** Author.

Index

Numbers in bold type refer to the plates and their captions

Abbate, Niccolò dell' 61
Adam, Antoine 175
aesthetic theory, (classical, Renaissance) 30–33; see also Vitruvius; garden design
Agnel, Abbé G. Arnaud d' 21
Aiguillon, Marie-Madeleine de Vignerot, duchesse d' 155–6, 296n
Aix-en-Provence (Bastide d'Aix) 20–21
Alberti, Leone Battista 23, 30–33, 34, 42, 66, 166, 193, 267
Albon, Jacques d', see Saint-André
Albon, Jean d' 54
Aldobrandini, villa 123
Alexander VI, Pope, (Rodrigo Borgia) 39
Alfonso II, King of Naples 35, 39
allées (walks); principles of design, Boyceau 178; Mollet, 179
allées de mail (pall-mall) at Berny 169; Chenonceaux, 81; Fontainebleau 237; Montceaux-en-Brie, 77; Richelieu, 144
Alphand, Jean-Charles Adolphe 277
Amboise, château and garden 42, 52; **31**
Amboise, Georges d', Cardinal Archbishop of Rouen 41, 45, 47, 49, 95
Amelot, Charles, gardener at Marly 234
Ammannati, Bartolomeo 93
Ancy-le-Franc, château and garden 61, 63–64, 89, 104; **53, 54, 55, 56, 103, 104**
André, E 277; **295**
Anet, château and garden 10; De l'Orme at, 52; rebuilt by Diane de Poitiers, 65; De L'Orme's plans for, 66–68; heraldic planting at, 68; decay of, 69; parterre de broderie originated at, 95, 108; grounds redesigned by Claude Desgots, 263, 267; **58, 59, 60, 61, 62, 279, 280**
Angennes, Julie d' 104
Angers 18–20; **10**
Angoulême, Charles de Valois, comte d' 51
Angoulême, Marguerite d' 51, 61, 87
Anguier, Michel, sculptor 190
Anjou, François, duc d' 82
Anne of Austria, Queen of France, mother of Louis XIV 130, 173, 179, 181, 193, 247
Anne de Bretagne, Queen of France, 34, 39, 41, 42, 44, 51
Anne of Denmark, Queen of England 128
Apollo, theme of at Versailles 201, 213, 215; **209, 213**
aqueducts (see also conduits) at Castries, 264; Eure, 220–221, 263; Rungis, 127, 134, 137, 295n; **129**
Arcadia 33, 148, 158, 275
architecture, principles of 31–32; and garden design 33, 42, 275. *See also* garden design
Armagnac, Georges d' 87
Artois, comte d' (see also Charles X) 272
L'Astrée 33, 158; **76**
Atri, Jacopo d' 44, 45, 46
Auglard, Girard, gardener at the Tuileries 295n
Augustine, Saint 31
Aumale, Charles de Lorraine, duc d' 68, 69, 100, 108, 118
automata 9, 16, 86, 124, 128, 130, 133, 148, 239; **118, 131**
aviaries 16; at Anet, 69; Gaillon, 45; Ponts-de-Cé, 20

Babelon, Jean-Pierre 166
Bagatelle, garden (Paris) 272
Bagnolet, garden 267
Baïf, Jean-Antoine de 97
Baïf, Lazare de 97
Balleroy, château and garden 166, 167, 170; **180, 181**
Ballon, Gilles 225, 298n
Barbier, Louis, Abbé de la Rivière 175
Barbier, Louis, gardener at Versailles 298n
Bastie d'Urfé 55; **46**
Baugé, castle and garden 20
Beatis, Dom Antonio de 42, 44, 45, 293n
bedding out (*see also* flower growing) 227, 228, 277
Bedford, John duke of 17
Bélanger, F.-J. 272
Belleforest, François de 97
Belle-Isle, Maréchal de 267
Belleval, Richer de 100
Bellevue **287**
Bellier, François, gardener at Saint-Germain-en-Laye 239
Belriguardo (Ferrara) 34, 51
Bene, B. del 83; **70, 79**
Benserade, Isaac de 297n
berceaux (arbours) see also tonnelles; at Chantilly, 253; Chenonceaux, 81; Fontainebleau, 57; Saint-Mandé, 184; the Tuileries, 115; **76, 82**
Bernini, Gian Lorenzo 216
Berny, château and garden 167, 169–70; **177, 178, 179**
Berry, Jean duc de 17
Berthelot, Guillaume, sculptor 134, 144
Bertrand, Macé II, Seigneur de la Bazinière 178
Besseman, gardener at Saint-Mandé 189
Betz, park 275
Biard, Pierre, sculptor 137
Biver, Paul, comte 182
Bizy, château and garden 267; **283**
Blaikie, Thomas 272
Blanchard, E. and J. sculptors 298n
Blois, château and garden 40; under Louis XII, 41, 42–45; 46, 51, 68, 77, 98, 104, 134, 167, 295n; **28, 32**
Blomfield, R. 9, 166
Blondel, Jacques-François 143, 271, 272, 277; **288, 289**
Blunt, Anthony 29, 59, 68, 72, 90, 192
Boboli gardens (Florence) 87, 134, 137
Bohier, Antoine 70
Bohier, Thomas 70
Bois de Boulogne (Paris) 277
Boislève, Claude 178
Bois-Robert, Abbé 181
Bomarzo, garden 129, 292n, 296n
Borgia, Cesare 41
bosquets at Ancy-le-Franc 63, 64; the Luxembourg, 134; the Tuileries, 243; Versailles, 206–213
Bosse, Abraham 124, 129, 130; **118**
Bouchard, Françoise, gardener at the Tuileries 118, 243
Bouchard, Simon, gardener at the Tuileries 118, 243
Bouchard, Yves, gardener at the Tuileries 118
Boulainvilliers, Philippe de 91, 294n
boulingrin 228, 239, 308
Bourbon, Cardinal, Charles de 47, 68, 83, 95
Bourbon, Monseigneur de 39, 40
Bourdichon, Jean, miniaturist 41; **29, 30**
Bourdigné, J. de 19
Bourgeois, A. 68
Bourgeois, C. 276
Bourvalais, Paul Poisson 267
Bouthillier, Claude 162
Boutin, Claude and Guillaume, gardeners at the Luxembourg 134
box, use of **295n**
Boyceau, Jacques, Seigneur de la Barauderie 110, 117, 121, 134, 178–179, 239, 242; **111**
Brackenhoffer, Elie 148, 151, 155, 169
Braham, Allan 175
Bramante, Donato 41, 61, 66
Bray, Anne de and Julien de, gardeners at Fontainebleau 238
Brécy, château and garden 166; **175, 176**
Brézé, Jacques de 65
Brézé, Louis de 52, 65, 66
Brice, Germain 244
Briconnet, Guillaume 39
Bril, Paul 158; **164**
Brodier, Jacques 184
Brosse, Jehan de 294n
Brosse, Salomon de 77, 91, 95, 134, 167
Brown, Lancelot ('Capability') 271, 276
Bruc, Suzanne de 183
Brulart, Nicolas, chevalier de Sillery 169
Brulart, Pierre, vicomte de Puisieux 169
Brunelleschi, Filippo 31
Brunyer, Abel 295n
Bühler brothers 277
Buis, Claude-Charles, gardener at Fontainebleau 238
Bullant, Jean 72, 74, 89
Bullion, Claude de 127, 162
Buontalenti, Bernardo 137
Burchard, Jean 35
Buren, designed by A. Mollet 297n
Burgundy, dukes of 13, 16
Burgundian gardens 16–18
Burlington, third earl of 272
Bury, château and garden 41, 48–49, 65, 66, 72, 95; **40**
Buttes-Chaumont (Paris) 277

California, park of Mr. Carolan **303**
canals, typically French 123; at Anet, 68, 263; Berny, 169; Chambord, 225; Chantilly, 247, 249; Courances, 280; Fleury, 123; Fontainebleau, 123–124; Maintenon, 263; Sceaux, 259; Tanlay, 163–164; Vaux-le-Vicomte, 188; Versailles, 197, 200–201, 203, 206; Voisins, 280
Caprarola, cascade and casino **120**
Carbonet, Claude, gardener at the Tuileries 243
Carnesechi, Bernardo 79, 113, 294n

Caro, Annibale 86
Caron, Antoine 83, 84, 86; **82**
Carvallo, François 291
Carvallo, Dr. Joachim 286–288, 299n
cascades, architectural; Italian prototypes 123; Pratolino, **119**, Caprarola, **120**; Torlonia, **122**; types favoured in France, 123; Chantilly, 249; **261, 264**; Fontainebleau, 237; **248**; Liancourt, 141; **145**; Marly, 234; Montmorency **121**; Petit-Bourg, 175; Rueil, 151, 158; **157**; Saint-Cloud, 148, 255; **269, 270**; Sceaux, 259; **275, 276**; Vaux-le-Vicomte, 188, 190, 192; **197, 202, 203**; Versailles, 197, Villette, **305**
casinos (*see also* pavilions) 46, 95, at Gaillon, **91**; at Meudon, 55; **45**
Castello, villa and garden 64, 87, 121, 129; **57**
Castres **315**
Castries, château and garden, 263–264; **281**
Castries, René Gaspard de la Croix, marquis de 263
Catherine de Médicis 52, 55, 57, 59, 61, 70, 71, 72, 77–79, 81, 82, 83, 84, 87, 95, 112, 113, 114, 115, 129
Cato, Marcus Porcius 40, 97
Caus, Salomon de 83, 108, 128–129; **130, 131**
Cecil, Robert, 1st Earl of Salisbury 128
Cellini, Benvenuto 51
Chambord, château and park, 51–52, 225; **237**
Champs, château and garden 267, 299n
Champs Elysées (Paris) 244, 288
Chantilly, château and park 54, 74, 89, 90, 206, 221, 272; Le Nôtre at, 247–253; **67, 68, 69, 258, 259, 260, 261, 262, 263, 264, 265, 266**
Chantilly, the hamlet 275; **292**
Chanzé (La Baumette) 19; **11**
Charles V, King of France, 16
Charles VII, King of France, 18
Charles VIII, King of France 34, 35, 36, 39–41, 42, 65, 74
Charles IX, King of France 77, 79, 82, 89, 90, 91, 95
Charles X, King of France 173
Charles V, Holy Roman Emperor 52, 53
Charles II of Anjou 16
Charles le Téméraire, duke of Burgundy 18
Charleval, château 89, 90–91; **86**
Chartres, duc de (*see also*, Orléans, Louis-Philippe-Joseph) 272
Chastel, André 293n
Chastellain, Georges 16
Chastillon, Jacques-Philippe Boiseau, gardener at Fontainebleau 238
Chénereau, Paul, 284
Chenonceaux, château and garden 53, 70–72, 77, 81, 82, 84, 89, 100; **63, 64, 65, 66, 77**
Chevalier, Abbé Casimir 70
Chevreuse, Charles-Honoré d'Albert, duc de 253
Chirol, E. 47
Chiswick villa 271
Choiseul-Praslin, Elizabeth 175
Choiseul-Praslin, duc de 297n
Choisy, Jean de 166, 170
Christina, Queen of Sweden 179
Christine de Pisan 16
Clagny, château and garden 197, 225, 228, 247; **256, 257**
Claude de France 51
Claude Lorrain 185
Clélie 175, 183, 297n
Cliveden (Bucks) 267
Colbert, Jean-Baptiste 181, 193, 194, 197, 201–202, 219, 220, 223, 225, 227, 228, 233, 234, 240, 244–245, 259; **204**
Colinot, Jean, gardener at Versailles 275
Colonna, Francesco (see also *Hypnerotomachia Poliphili*) 23–29, 63, 84, 86, 213, 292n
Columella, Lucius Junius Moderatus 40, 97
Compiègne, château and park 225
Condé, Henri I de Bourbon, Prince de 83, 247
Condé, Louis II de Bourbon, Prince de 179, 197, 221; and Chantilly, 247–253
conduits, *see also* aqueducts; at Liancourt, 141; Rueil, 151; the Tuileries, 112; Versailles, 220, 227
Congis, family 117
Contarini, Venetian envoy 39
Coope, Rosalys 87
Corpechot, Lucien 279
Cotte, Robert de 234
Coulommiers, château 167
Courances, château and garden 280–283; **299, 300, 301, 302**
Coysevox, Antoine, sculptor 217, 234; **230, 255, 297**
Credi, Lorenzo di **13**
Creil, Claude, gardener at Fontainebleau 57
Crescenzi, Pietro de 9, 13, 16, 27, 84, 97
Cythera, Island of, in *Hypnerotomachia Poliphili* 23, 27; Watteau's paintings, 158, 232, 292n; **167**

Dami, Luigi 29
Dampierre, château and garden, 55, 90, 107, 253; **44, 267**
Dan, Pierre 61, 123
Dangeau, Philippe, marquis de 234
Decameron, garden in 29
Dagault, Lois, gardener at Chenonceaux 71
Della Bella, S.; **119**
Denis, Claude, fountainer, 219
Desbouts, Jean and Louis, gardeners at Fontainebleau 238
Descartes, René 223
Deschamps, Nicolas, gardener at the Luxembourg 134
Désert de Retz 275
Desgots, J. 118
Desgots, Pierre 118, 155, 243, 247, 249; **260**
Desgots, Claude 69, 118, 234, 247, 253, 263, 267
Desgots, family 117
Desjardins, M. sculptor 211
Deslauriers, Antoine, gardener, Versailles 298n
Dézallier d'Argenville, A.-J. 267–271; **282, 284, 285**
Dézallier d'Argenville, A.-N. 87
Diane de Poitiers 52, 53, 65, 68, 69, 70, 71, 77, 82, 87, 100
Dimier, Louis 59, 87
Domenico del Barbiere 55
Donatello 41, 49
Dorat, Jean 83; **78**
Drouilly, sculptor **229**
Du Bellay, Eustache 79
Du Bellay, Cardinal Jean 51, 52, 79
Dubois, Michel, gardener, Versailles 298n
Du Cerceau, Baptiste Androuet 90
Du Cerceau, Jacques Androuet I 29, 72, 77, 83, 84, 87–95; drawings/engravings referred to, 42–49 *passim*, 52–74 *passim*, 82, 107, 112, 113, 129, 247, 288; **31, 32, 33, 36, 37, 38, 40, 42, 43, 44, 47, 50, 56, 58, 62, 63, 65, 67, 74, 83, 84, 85, 86, 87, 91, 92, 93, 106**
Du Cerceau, Jacques II Androuet 87, 90
Duchêne, Henri 279
Duchêne, Achille 279–283 *passim*, 288, 291; **298, 303**
Du Pérac, Étienne 68, 93, 95, 108, 129; **88**
Du Plessys, family 139
Duprat, Ferdinand 284
Dupuis, Henri, gardener at Versailles 225
Dutertre, Jacques, gardener at Chenonceaux 71
Duval, Jean 55

Écouen, château 54, 74, 87, 89, 90, 294n
Elizabeth, Queen of Bohemia 128, 129
English influence in the eighteenth century 272; after the Revolution, 276. See also *jardin anglais*
Entragues, Henriette d' 91
Ermenonville, château and park 272, 275
Escloubeau de Sourdis, Henri d' 143
Espallard, Jehan, gardener at the Tuileries 295n
Este, Ercole d' 34
Este, Ippolito d' 51, 52, 53
Este, villa d', Tivoli 51, 93, 123, 128, 129, 296n
Estrées, Gabrielle d' 77
Étienne, Charles 16, 97
Étienne, Robert 97
Evelyn, John 104, 134, 138, 143, 148, 151, 154, 155
exotic flowers 104, 184, 228, 234, 277

Fabriques **292, 293**
Fancelli, Luca 35
Fantuzzi, Antonio, engraver 61
Félibien, André 44, 209, 211
Fels, comte de 279–280
Fère-en-Tardenois, castle 74, 294n
festivals, *see* garden festivals
figured beds, introduced by Italians 10, 44; in Colonna 23, 306; at Anet 68; at Blois 44; at Bury 49; at Gaillon 46; designs for in Serlio 61; in Du Cerceau 95. *See also* knots, labyrinths, parterres
Filarete, A. 23, 34, 294n
Flamen, A. sculptor 216
Fleurant, O. gardener at Clagny 228
Fleury, canal at 123
flower garden, 104–107; in *La Maison Rustique* (Etienne and Liébault) 98; at Liancourt 107; **105**; at the Tuileries 117; at Vaux-le-Vicomte 188, 190. *See also* parterre
flower growing, in *La Maison Rustique* (Etienne and Liébault) 97–99; by René of Anjou 21; at Trianon 228–232, 298n; at Marly 234, 298n; at Versailles 227. *See also* exotic flowers and bedding out
flower painting 41, 104; **29, 30, 102, 103, 104**
flowers, see plants and planting
Folembray, château 95
Fontainebleau, château and garden. The forest 33, 52, 234; favoured by François I, 52; his creation of château and garden, 56–59; Italians at, 59, 61; Grotte des Pins, 59; additions by Catherine de Médicis, 61, 79; festivals at, 82–83 sculpture at, 61, 217; neglect of, 95; Claude Mollet's designs for parterres, 99, 108, 295n; Louis XIII as child at, 121; canals at 123, 124, 206; the Francini at, 129; Le Nôtre at, 185, 237–8; Michel Le Bouteaux at, 228, 238, 295n; **47, 48, 49, 50, 51, 107, 108, 123, 124, 246, 247, 248**
fountains, in *Le Roman de la Rose* 13; Du Cerceau's designs for 89; in *Hypnerotomachia Poliphili*, 23; **15**; in the *Decameron*, 29; in De Caus, 128; **130**; in miniatures, **7, 14**; at Amboise, 42, 71; at Anet 68; **58, 61, 62**; at Blois, 42; at Chenonceaux, 71, 81, 82; at Fontainebleau, 56, 124; **124**; Gaillon, 46; **36**; Hesdin, 16; Liancourt, 139, 141; Hôtel de Richelieu, 143; Rueil, 148, 158,

296n; Saint-Cloud, 148; Saint-Germain-en-Laye, 129, 130; **136**; Saint-Pol, 17; the Tuileries, 87, 114; Vaux-le-Vicomte, 188, 192; **196, 198**; Versailles, 123, 203, 209, 211, 219, 220, 223, 297n; **211, 212, 213, 214, 218, 221, 224, 233**
Fouquet, family 182
Fouquet, Nicolas 175, 178, 181–184, 188–194; **188**
Fouquet, Louis-Nicolas, comte de Vaux 194
Fourché, Macé (Massé), gardener at Versailles 225
Francini/Francine, family 124, 127
Francini, Alexandre 124–127, 129, 134, 137, 166; **125, 126**
Francini, Thomas, 124–127, 129, 134, 137, 138, 148, 151, 162; **118, 136**
Francine, François 127, 211, 219, 233, 239
Francine, François and Pierre 237, 298n
François I, King of France 33, 39, 48, 51, 52, 53, 54, 56, 61, 79, 87, 124, 217, 225, 237
François II, King of France 55, 72, 77, 81
Frascati, *see* Aldobrandini and Torlonia
Frederick II, Emperor 16
Frederick V, King of Bohemia 128, 129
Frederick of Orange, Prince 297n
Fresnes, château and garden 167, 175
Fronde, La 181
fruit growing (including fruit trees and shrubs) at Blois, 42, 44; Chantilly, 74; Chenonceaux, 71–72; Fontainebleau, 57; Gaillon, 45; the Tuileries, 112, 113; Versailles, 221; Dézallier d'Argenville on, 267. *See also* orangeries

Gabriel, A.-J. 279, 280
Gaddi, Giovanni, Cardinal 33, 59, 86
Gaillon, château and garden 41, 42, 44, 45–47, 48, 68, 83, 89, 95, 98, 107; **33–38**
galleries at Aix, 21; Amboise, 42; Blois, 42; Gaillon, 45; Fontainebleau, 56, 59, 61; Anet, 68; Chantilly, 74; Liancourt, 141; **52, 92**
Gallo, Agostino 97
Ganay, E. de 161
Ganay, family 280
Gardanne 21
Garden architecture, integral to formal gardens 10. *See also* casinos, fabriques, galleries, grottoes, pavilions, temples, trellis-work
garden, concept of 9; function of (useful, ornamental, symbolic) 9, 13, 17, 44, 46, 97–99, 192–193, 267. *See also* flower garden, *hortus conclusus*, *hortus deliciarum*, island gardens, *jardin de plaisir*, medicinal and botanic gardens, *parterres* and *potager*.
garden design, a composite art, 9; sources in architectural principles, 33, 42, 275; natural 32, 267, 268, 271, 275, 276; integrated house and garden plan, at Bury, 48; Ancy-le-Franc, 63; Anet, 65; Charleval, 90; axial approach, precedents for, 48, 65–66, 72; extended axis at Richelieu, 144, 147; Mansart's use of, 170, 173, 175; in Le Nôtre, 243, 247, 253, 257, 261; styles of garden design, formal, regular or geometric, defined 9, 42, 143, 277, *style paysager* 277, 288; *style mixte* (composite) 277; *anglo-chinois*, see *jardin anglais*; national styles, 10; French style formulated by Mollet, 179; by Dézallier d'Argenville, 267–271; Le Nôtre's formula 247, 253; revival 279–291; principles summarised 283
garden festivals, at Chenonceaux, 81–82; Fontainebleau, 82–83, the Tuileries, 200; Vaux-le-Vicomte, 193–194; Versailles (1664), 200; **208**; (1668) 209.
gardens in literature, *Decameron*, 29; *Civitas Veri*, 83; *Clélie*, 175. *See also*, *Roman de la Rose*, *Hypnerotomachia Poliphili*
garden treatises, Crescenzi, 13–16; Étienne and Liébault, Gallo, Vinet and Mizauld, 97–99; de Serres 99–100; Claude Mollet, 100; Boyceau, 178–179; André Mollet, 179; eighteenth century French and English, 267–277
gardeners of Louis XIV, 225–245 *passim*
gardening, at Chenonceaux, 71, 72; Versailles, 225–232 *passim*
Garnier d'Isle, 299n
Gébelin, François 41, 55
Gerard, Robert 284
Gesvres, château and garden 167, 173–175
Geymüller, H. von 87, 90, 95
Giambologna, sculptor 128, 296n
Gié, Pierre de Rohan, Maréchal de 41, 48, 49, 51
Gienot, Nicolas, gardener at Aix 21
Giocondo, Fra 35, 40
Girardin, Louis-René 272, 275
Girardon, François 201, 203, 213, 216; **214, 226**
Gittard, Daniel, 247, 249
Giulio Romano 33, 59
Gobert, Thomas 220
Godefroy, Denis II 139, 141, 169
Gohorry, Jacques 292n
Gomboust, Jean 115, 117, 134, 138, 242
Gondi, family 79, 121, 148, 295n
Gondi, Henri de 121
Gondi, Jean-François de, Archbishop of Paris, 121, 148, 255, 295n
Gondi, Jérôme de 148
green rooms/*cabinets de verdure*, at Ancy-le-Franc, 63; Chenonceaux, 81; how to make (Palissy) 84; Fresnes, 175; Versailles, 209, 211; **244**
Greenwich 128, 267
grottoes 10; in Alberti, 33; created by the Francini, 124; in Mollet, 179; designed and executed by Palissy, 84, 86–87; at Bastie d'Urfé, 55; Castries, 264; Ecouen, 87; Fontainebleau, 59; **49, 51**; La Roche-Courbon, 284; the Luxembourg, 127, 134; **127, 140**; Meudon, 55, 181–182; **45**; Pratolino, 295n; Richelieu, 144; **153**; Rueil, 151, 154; **148, 161, 162**; Saint-Cloud, 148; **155**; Saint-Germain-en-Laye, 130, 133, 237; **118**; Tanlay, 163–164; **171, 172, 173**; Vaux-le-Vicomte, 188, 190; **200**; Versailles, 201; **209**; Wideville, **128**
Guarini, Battista 33
Guenégaud, Gabriel de 175
Guenégaud, Henri de 175
Guérin, Charlot, gardener at Chenonceaux 71
Guérin, G. sculptor 201; **228**
Guidi, Domenico 216
Guillaume, Jean 57, 63, 72
Guise, Charles de, Cardinal de Lorraine 55, 182
Guise, Claude de Lorraine, duc de 54
Guise, François de Lorraine, duc de 54
Guise, Henri I, duc de 77

Haber, baron de 280
Hardouin-Mansart, Jules 29, 51, 175, 206, 213, 230, 232, 233, 234, 240, 249, 253, 255, 284, 297n
Hardy, Jean, sculptor 249
Haussmann, Georges, baron 245, 288
Hazlehurst, F.H. 296n, 299n
Heidelberg 108, 128, 129
Henri II, King of France 52, 53, 54, 55, 59, 65, 70, 72, 77, 79, 87, 139
Henri III, King of France 77, 83, 104
Henri IV, King of France, 77, 79, 91, 99, 100, 104, 108, 114, 115, 121, 123, 161, 162, 237
Henriette d'Angleterre, duchesse d'Orléans, 193, 234, 239
Henrietta Maria, Queen of England 297n
heronries, at Anet, 69; Chantilly, 74
Henry, Prince of Wales 128
Henry, Octavien, trees for Versailles 226
herbs, *see* plants and planting
Héroard, Jean 104, 121, 133, 148
Heron of Alexandria 16
Hersey, George 35, 64
Hesdin, castle 16, 86
Hévart, Barthélemy d' 255
Heydenreich, Ludwig H. 51
Heylyn, Peter 148
Hill, Thomas 99
Honselaersdijk, designed by A. Mollet 297n
Hornblower, L. 277
Hortus conclusus 13; **1, 3, 8, 12, 16, 17, 27**
Hortus deliciarum 13; **4, 5, 17**
Houdard, Georges 124
Houzeau, J. sculptor 211
Huguenots 77
Hustin, A. 138
Huygens, Louis 154, 173, 175, 255
hydraulics, principles of, 128–129; hydraulic machines, 128, 220, 233–234, 253
Hypnerotomachia Poliphili 23–29, 33, 42, 63, 83, 84, 107, 292n; **15, 16**. See also, *Songe de Poliphile*

Island gardens, at Chantilly, 74; Fontainebleau, 108; **108**; at Richelieu, 143–44
Italian gardens 33–36; compared with French, 10, 33–34, 64, 65, 97; influence on French gardens 39–42, 46–47, 51–65 *passim*, 79, 83, 93, 123, 128–129, 141, 151, 192

Jal, A. 90
James I, King of England 128
James II, King of England 232, 234
jardin anglais, challenge to French formal style, 10; Maisons transformed, 173; Le Raincy transformed, 184; **294**; development in eighteenth century, 272; **290, 291**; Blondel's criticisms of, 272
jardin de plaisir 178–179
Jardin Royale des Plantes Medicinales (Paris) 104, 225; **101**
Jardin Thabor, Rennes 277
Jaucourt, Chevalier de 272
Jeannin de Castille, Nicolas 181
Jeannin, Pierre 161
Jerôme de Naples 45
jeu de mail 232, 237
Joinville-le-Grand-Jardin 54, 90
Joly, Denis, fountainer 219
Julius II (Giuliano della Rovere), Pope, 23, 39, 41

Keller brothers, bronze founders; **297**
Kimball, Fiske 297n
knots/entrelacs, symbolic in origin 107; in *Hypnerotomachia Poliphili*, 23, 107, 306, 292n; introduction of, 44; in *La Maison Rustique* (Etienne and Liébault), 98–99; sixteenth century designs for, 107–108; **96–98, 106**

LABORDE, ALEXANDRE DE 276; **293, 294**
La Brosse, Guy de 104; **101**
labyrinths, symbolic in origin, 107; medieval, 17; in the *Hypnerotomachia Poliphili* 23; **18**; in Filarete, 23; in Serlio, 61; at Chantilly, 253; Chenonceaux, 72; Gaillon, 46; the Tuileries, 112, 114; **74**; Versailles, 207, 209, 297n
Laffitte, Jacques 173
La Fontaine, Jean de 297n
La Gaude **314**
Lalos, J. 284
Lambert, J.-B. 184
La Meilleraye, Charles, duc de 180
landscape garden, term defined 9; applied to Le Nôtre's designs 185, 288. See also *style paysager*
Lante, villa and garden, Bagnaia, 10, 61, 93, 123, 130, 192; **90**
La Quintinye, Jean-Baptiste de 221, 247, 267, 298n
La Tourasse, L. de 129
Laugier, Marc-Antoine 223
Launay, Dr. 151, 154
Lauro, I. 130
La Vallée, Marin de, contractor for the Luxembourg 134
La Vallière, Louise de 193, 197
Lavechef, François, gardener at Saint-Germain-en-Laye 239
La Vieuville, marquis de 181
Leasowes, ferme ornée 272
Le Bas, Jacques 166
Le Blond, Jean-Baptiste Alexandre 299n
Le Bouteux, Jean-Michel 298n
Le Bouteux, Michel 225, 228, 230, 238, 298n
Le Breton, Gilles 56, 57
Le Breton, Jean, gardener at the Luxembourg 296n
Lebrun, Charles 170, 185, 188, 194, 197, 211, 214, 216, 233
Le Clerc, Sebastien 297n
Lecoy de la Marche, A. 19
Lefèvre, *contrôleur des bâtiments* 228
Le Gendre, Antoine 299n
Le Gros, Pierre, sculptor 211
Le Hongre, sculptor 298n
Le Jongleur, Nicolas 220
Le Juge, Claude and Elizabeth, gardeners at the Tuileries 243
Le Lydieu, Gaillon, 46–47
Lemaire, Jean 154
Lemaire, Toussaint, gardener at the Luxembourg 296n
Lemercier, Jacques 115, 143–147, 151, 237
Lemercier, Nicolas 294n
Lemercier, Pierre 143
Le Moyne, Guillaume, gardener at Villers-Cotterets 293n
Le Muet, Pierre 163, 164
Le Nôtre, André 10, 69, 144, 161, 162, 166, 179, 194, 239, 247–264, 267, 272, 276; **255**; biographical details, 185, 230; his character, 264; as cultural hero, 279; as landscape architect, 288; and Mansart, 175; at Castries, 263–264; at Chantilly, 74, 247–253; at Clagny, 247; at Fontainebleau, 237; at Dampierre, 253; at Maintenon, 263; at Marly, 233, 234; at Meudon, 181, 261; at the Palais Royal, 143; at Saint-Cloud, 255–257; at Saint-Germain-en-Laye, 240; at Sceaux, 259; at the Tuileries, 113, 117, 118, 178, 185, 234, 242–245; at Vaux-le-Vicomte, 184, 199; at Versailles, 192, 200, 203, 206, 209, 211, 213, 221, 223, 225
Le Nôtre, Jean 115, 117, 118
Le Nôtre, Pierre, 113, 114, 117
Le Nôtre, René 295n
Le Nôtre, Françoise (see Bouchard) 118
Le Nôtre, Elizabeth 118
Leo X (Giovanni de' Medici) Pope 48, 52
Leonardo da Vinci, at Amboise, 51; designs for Romorantin, 51
Le Pautre, Antoine 255, 257; **269**
Le Pautre, Jean; **218**
Le Pautre, Pierre **205, 211**
Le Raincy, château and garden 184–185; **192, 294**
Lerambert, sculptor 296
Le Rouge, G.L. **283, 290, 291**
Le Roy, Philibert 121
Le Rusé, Louis 234
Les Baux, Provence **41**
Lésigny-en-Brie 158, 296n; **168** (Lusigny)
Lespagnandel, sculptor 190
Lesueur, Pierre 42, 46
Le Vau, Louis II 178, 181, 184, 185, 188, 190, 240; at Versailles 197, 200, 201, 202, 206
Le Verger, château 41, 48; **39**
Liancourt, château and garden 107, 123, 139–141; **105, 142, 143, 144, 145, 146**
Liancourt, duc de 141
Liébault, Jean 97–99, 107
Liédet, Loyset, miniaturist 16
Limours, château 225
Loitron, Sieur, gardener at Marly 234
Longueil, René de 167, 173, 181
L'Orme, Philibert de, biographical details, 52–53, 59, 61; at Anet, 65–66, 68; at Chenonceaux, 70, 72; at Montceaux, 77; at the Tuileries, 79, 112; 123, 129
Lorraine, René II, duc de 54
Lorris, Guillaume de 13, 23
Loti, Pierre 284
Loudon, John 276
Louis IX, Saint Louis 56
Louis XI, King of France 16, 39
Louis XII, King of France 41, 42, 48, 51, 74, 83
Louis XIII, King of France, his childhood 121, 133; 104, 115, 124, 128, 134, 138, 148, 162
Louis XIV, King of France 118, 133, 138, 173, 179, 181; and Fouquet, 193, 194; 225, 247, 264; and Versailles, 197–223 *passim* 225; and Trianon, 230, 232; and Marly, 232–234
Louis XV, King of France 298n
Louise de Savoie 41, 51, 79
Louvois, Michel le Tellier, marquis de 181, 197, 225, 261
Louvre, palace 63, 79, 89, 114, 202, 225; Petit Jardin **115**; Merian's plan **116**
Ludovisi, villa (Rome) 192
Luynes, Charles d'Albert, duc de 296n
Luxembourg, palace 104, parterre, 110; 121; water for, 127; creation of gardens, 134–138, 143; Le Nôtre at, 185, 225; **138, 139, 141**
Luxembourg, grotte de (Fontaine de Médicis) 127, 134, 137, 162, 163; **127, 140**

MACHINE de Marly 220, 233–234; **234**
Maçon, Gustave 247
Madama, villa (Rome) 68
Madeleine de la Tour d'Auvergne (mother of Catherine de Médicis) 52
Madrid, château 52, 79, 89, 99
Magnon, J. gardener at Rueil 155
Magny, Olivier de 68
Maiano, Giuliano da 35
Maintenon, Françoise d'Aubigné, marquise de 197, 233, 234, 263
Maintenon, canal and aqueduct 221, 263; **278**
Maisons, château and garden 167, 173; **182, 183, 184**
Mannerism, defined 84; 84–95 *passim*
Mansart, François 166–178, 185; at Balleroy, 170; Berny, 169–170; Blois, 167; Maisons, 173; Fresnes, 175; Gesvres, 173–175; Petit-Bourg, 175; Villette, 264; **169**
Manse, Jacques de 247, 253
Mantegna, Andrea 27, 170; **20**
Marcellus II (Marcello Cervini), Pope 52
Marguerite de Valois 77, 121
Marie, wife of James V of Scotland 55
Marie, Alfred 121, 170, 201, 209, 213
Marie Antoinette, Queen of France 33, 275
Marie de Médicis, Queen of France 77, 110, 121, 123, 127, 148, 161; at the Luxembourg 134–138
Marie-Thérèse, Queen of France 197, 200, 234
Mariette, Pierre 299n
Marimont-en-Hainaut, château 29, 225
Marly, château and garden 197, 220, 225, 232–234, 272; **242, 243, 244, 245**
Marot, Jean 137; **127**
Marques, Jean II 70
Marsy, Balthazar and Gaspard, sculptors 201
Marsy, Gaspard, sculptor 213, 216
Martin, Jean 29, 33, 63, 84, 128, 293n
Martin, Guillaume, gardener at Chenonceaux 71, 72
Mary, Queen of Scots (Mary Stuart) 55, 72, 77, 81
Marzano, Leonore de 40
Masson, B., sculptor 211; **227**
Masson, Guillaume, gardener at the Tuileries 243
Maulnes, château 89; **85**
Mauperché, H. 139, 141; **142**
Mayenne, Henri de Lorraine, duc de 161
Mazarin, Giulio Mazarini, Cardinal 162, 175, 179, 181, 182, 183, 193, 297n
maze, *see* labyrinth
Mazeline, sculptor 298n
Medici family 54
Medici, Cosimo I 64, 121
Medici, Ferdinando de' 121, 124
Medici, Giovanni de' see Leo X
Medici, Lorenzo de' (the Magnificent) 35
Medici, Lorenzo II de' 52
Medici, Pietro de' 39
Medici, villa (Pratolino) 124
Médicis, Marie and Catherine de, *see under* Marie and Catherine
medicinal and botanic gardens 100–104
menageries, at Fontainebleau, 61; Saint-Germain-en-Laye, 52; Versailles, 200, 203
Menars **286**
Menours, Jacques de 121–123, 178, 179
Mercogliano, Pacello de 40, 42, 44–45, 46
Méréville, château and park 275; **293**
Merian, Mathieu 115
Métézeau, Louis 134
Meudon, château and garden 55, 87, 90, 181, 185, 225, 261, 272; **45, 189, 190, 277**
Meun, Jean de 13
Michelangelo Buonarroti 54, 56, 144
Michiel, Marcantonio 35, 64
Miélot, Jean **6, 7**
miniatures, gardens in 13, 17, 19; **1, 3, 4, 5, 8, 9, 12, 27**
Mizauld, Antoine 97
Moisset, Jean (Montaubon) 148
Moisy, Guillaume, gardener at the Tuileries 114
Molière, Jean-Baptiste 193
Mollet, André 100, 110, 179, 184, 188, 203, 242, 267, 288, 295n; **187**
Mollet, Charles, at Fontainebleu 237
Mollet, Claude 68, 95, 99, 100, 108–110, 114, 115, 118, 129, 179, 188, 294n, 295n; **109**
Mollet, Claude II 100, 110, 118
Mollet family 117, 242

Mollet, Jacques 68, 100
Mollet, Jacques II 110
Mollet, Pierre 118, 243
Montaigne, Michel de 34, 128, 148, 267
Montargis, château and garden 61, 83, 87, 89, 95; **92, 93**
Montceaux-en-Brie, château and garden 77, 89, 90, 108, 225; **71, 72**
Montespan, Françoise-Athénaïs de Roche-Chouart, marquise de 197, 209, 228, 234
Montjeu, château and garden 161–162; **170**
Montmorency, cascade at **121**
Montmorency, Anne de 53–54, 74, 83, 87, 247
Montmorency, Guillaume de 74
Montmorency, Henri I de 247
Montmorency, Henri II de 247
Montpellier, botanical garden at 100, 104; **100**
Montpensier, Louise, duchesse de 225, 242
Montsouris, park 277
Morel, Jean-Marie 275–276
Morfontaine, park 275
Morin, René 104
mounts (artificial hills) 83, 100, 104; **99, 100**

NANTES, Revocation of Edict of 197
nature, concept of 10, 33, 84, 148, 267–8, 272, 275
Nemours, duc de 87, 91, 93
Nemours, Anne, duchesse de 91
Neufville, Nicolas de 79
Nevers, duc de 87
Nicholas V (Tommaso Parentucelli), Pope 34
Nohlac, Pierre 279

ORANGERIES, at Anet, 69; Blois, 42–44; Chantilly, 249; Fontainebleau, 57–58, 237, 238; **246**; Meudon, 181; Rueil, 151, 154; **163**; Saint-Cloud, 257; Trianon, 228; the Tuileries, 117; Versailles, 197, 202, 206, 209; **215**
Orgement, Pierre d' 74
Orkney, Lord 295n
Orléans, Gaston, duc d' 104, 123, 138, 167, 185, 225; **94**
Orléans, Louis-Philippe-Joseph, duc d' (Philippe Egalité) 184. *See also* Chartres, duc de
Orléans, Philippe de Bourbon, duc d' 234, 255, 257

PAILLART, JEAN, gardener at the Tuileries 295n
painted perspectives (*trompe l'oeil*), at Fontainebleau, 61; Hôtel d'Aumont, 296n; Rueil, 154; Saint-Cloud, 296n
Palais Royal, Paris 143, 225; **149**
Palermo, gardens at 16
Palissy, Bernard 16, 29, 83, 84–87, 139, 295n; **80, 81**
Palissy, Mathurin 87
Palissy, Nicolas 87
Palladius 40
Papa Giulio, villa 10, 61, 65
Parc Monceau, Paris 272
parks, for animals, 9, 16, 39, 48; **2**; as type of garden, see *jardin anglais*, landscape garden
parks, public 277
parterre 107, 108, 110; in *Hypnerotomachia Poliphili* 23, 27; in Étienne and Liébault 97–99. *See also* water parterre, flower garden
parterre à l'anglaise (cut turf) 308; in Mollet, 179, at Saint-Germain-en-Laye, 240, at the Tuileries, 242, 243; at Voisins, 279. *See also* boulingrin
parterre de pièces coupées, 308; at Saint-Mandé, 184; at Saint-Germain-en-Laye, 240; at Trianon, 230; at Villandry, 286
parterre de broderie, defined 107, 308; introduction of, 68, 95, 108–110; designs for in Boyceau and Mollet, 178–179; **109–111**; at Berny, 169; Castries, 264; Courances, 283; **302**; Fontainebleau, 237; Liancourt, 139–141; **144**; the Luxembourg, 134; **139**; Meudon, 261; **277**; Montjeu, 161, Richelieu, 143–144; **152**; Saint-Germain-en-Laye, 238; **250**; Saint-Mandé, 184; **191**; Sceaux, 259; Trianon, 230, 232; the Tuileries, 243; **254**; Vaux-le-Vicomte, 188; **193, 194**; Versailles, 121, 197, 200, 202, 203
Particelli d'Émery 162, 181
Patel, the elder 61, 202
pavilions at Amboise, 42; Anet 66, 68; Blois, 41, 42; **28**; Fontainebleau, 56, 61; Gaillon, 45, 46, **35**; Ponts-de-Cé, 20; Richelieu, 144; **153**; St. Pol, 17; the Tuileries, 112; Marly, 233; Les Baux, **41**; designs for in Palissy and Du Cerceau, 84, 89. *See also* casino
Payen (Deslandes-Payen), Pierre 148
Peiresc, Fabri de 178
Père Joseph, le, *see* Tremblay
Perelle, Adam 151, 155, 158; **68, 165, 184, 258, 261, 262, 265, 266, 274, 275**
Perelle, Gabriel 155, 158, 185; **108, 123, 166**
Perelle, Nicolas 155, 158
Perelle family, engravings by **137, 148, 149, 152, 155, 158, 159, 161, 162, 163, 168, 178, 192, 209, 210, 217, 219, 222, 223, 233, 235, 239, 252, 253, 257**
Perrault, Charles 201, 209, 244–245, 297n
Perrault, Claude 201
perspective, laws of, in Alberti 31, 34; applied to garden design, 100, 164, 242
Peruzzi, Baldassare 35, 64
Petit-Bourg, garden 167, 175; **185, 186**
Peyrat, Guillaume de 87
Philip II, duke of Burgundy (the Bold) 16
Philip III, duke of Burgundy (the Good) 16, 23
Picard, Abbé Jean 220
picturesque image, the 158
Pienza 34
Pierrevive, Marie de 79, 121
Piganiol de la Force 255
Pilon, Germain, sculptor 61
Pitti Palace, Florence 93, 121, 134
Pius II (Aeneas Silvius Piccolomini), Pope 34
plants and planting, plants used for ornament, 300–306; sixteenth century practice, 97–110; at Blois, 54; Chenonceaux, 71, 72; Fontainebleau, 57; Gaillon, 45, 46; Liancourt, 141; the Luxembourg, 134, 138; Marly, 234; Richelieu, 143; Rueil, 151, 154, 155; Saint-Germain-en-Laye, 130, 133, 239–240; Saint-Mandé, 189; Trianon, 228, 230, 232; the Tuileries, 112–115, 118, 178, 240–244; Versailles, 211, 212, 225–229; Villandry, 286, 291
Plato 31
Pliny the younger 33
Plotinus 30
Poggio a Caiano, villa 34, 293n; **25**
Poggio Reale, villa 35–36, 39, 41, 61, 68; **26**
Poiret, Nicolas, gardener at Fontainebleau 238
Poitiers, Diane de, *see* Diane de Poitiers
Pol de Limbourg 17
Pons, Antoine de 139
Pons, Antoinette de 139
ponds and lakes, at Berny, 169; Fontainebleau, 57; Meudon, 181; Palais Royal, 143; Rueil, 151; Versailles, 206, 213
Pontano, Giovanni 35
Ponts-de-Cé, manor of 20
Pope, Alexander 268
Porcher, Prior of Crécy 99
Portland, William Bentinck, duke of 253
potager (kitchen garden), as component of French Renaissance garden, 97–99; at Versailles, 221; ornamental planting of in Boyceau, 178–179; at Villandry, 288
Poussin, Nicolas 154, 185, 188
Pratolino 123, 124, 128, 129, 130, 295n, 296n; **119**
préciosité 175
Primaticcio, Francesco 52, 55, 59, 61
Pythagoras 31

QUARACCHI 293n
Quinteau de Richemont, Gaspard, gardener at Fontainebleau 238

RABEL, DANIEL 104; **76**
Rabelais, François 20, 52
Rambouillet, Catherine de Vivonne, marquise de 295n
Rambouillet, dairy 35, 275
Raon, J. sculptor 293n
Raphael 294n
Raray, château 29
Regnaudin, Thomas, sculptor 201, 216; **231**
Renard, Gilles 117, 242, 243
René, duc d'Anjou (Le Roi René) 18–21, 23, 33, 34, 267
Renée de France, duchess of Ferrara 34, 51, 83, 87, 89, 91
Renoult (Renoud) called Fondet, painter of grotesques 61
Repton, Humphry 276, 277
Richard, Claude 253
Richelieu, Armand, Jean du Plessis de, Cardinal 123, 143–147, 148, 155, 162, 181
Richelieu, château and garden 143–147; **147, 150–153**
Richelieu, hôtel de, *see* Palais Royal
Rigaud, J. 294n; **225, 287**
Ripa, Cesare 170, 216
Riquet, engineer 264
Robbia, Girolamo della 57
Robert, Hubert 213
Robert, Nicolas 104; **94, 102, 255**
Robertet, Florimond 41, 48, 49
Robillard, Claude 192
Robin, Jean 104, 110
Robin, Vespasien 104
Roche-Courbon, La, château and garden, 284; **304**
Roches, Monsieur des 155
rocks, artificial, at Le Lydieu, Gaillon, 46, 83; Fontainebleau, 82; the Luxembourg, 134; Rueil, 154; the Tuileries, 83; **38, 78, 79**
Roman de la Rose, Le, 13, 16, 17, 21, 23, 29, 42; **5**
Romorantin, château 51
Ronsard, Pierre de 82, 83
Rossellino, Bernardo 34
Rosso (Gian Battista di Jacopo) 59, 61
Roule, Le (La Pépinière du Roule) 225, 228, 298n
Rousseau, Jean-Jacques 275
Rousset, Firmin 61
Rucellai garden, Quaracchi 34, 293n
Rueil, château and garden 123, 148–158, 267, 296n; **148, 156–159, 161–163**
ruins, classical 23, 32, 34; gothic 158
Rungis aqueduct 127, 134, 137; **129**

SAINT-ANDRÉ, JACQUES D'ALBON DE, 54
Saint-Cloud, château and garden 79, 123, 148, 255–257; **154, 155, 268–273**
Saint-Germain-en-Laye, De L'Orme at 52–53, 93; 99, 100, 108, 121, 124, 129–133, 234; under Louis XIV, 239–240; **42, 132–137, 249–251**; grottes, 124, 127, 130, 133; **118**
Saint-James, Baudard de 272
Saint-James, Folie 272
Saint James's Palace, London 297n
Saint-Leger, château 225
Saint-Mandé, château and garden 183–184, 194, 243; **191**
Saint-Maur-les-Fossés 52, 79, 107
Saint-Pol, palace and garden 16
Saint-Simon, Louis de Rouvroy, duc de 232, 264
Sannazaro, Jacopo 33, 34, 35
Saugière, Robert, gardener at Fontainebleau 293n
Sauval, Henri 16
Sceaux, château and garden 259, 271, 272; **274–276**
Schomberg, Henri de 161
Schomberg de Nanteuil-le-Hardouin, Jeanne 139
Scudéry, Madeleine de 175, 183, 190, 192. See also *Clélie*
sculpture: at Berny, 169–170; Brécy, 166; Bury, 49; Chantilly, 249; Fontainebleau, 56, 61, 124, 237; the Luxembourg, 134, 137, 296n; Marly, 234; Richelieu, 143, 144–147; Rueil, 155; Saint-Cloud, 148; Saint-Mandé, 184; Vaux-le-Vicomte, 188, 190–192; Versailles, 170, 201, 203, 209, 211, 214–217
seats, turf 16, 19, 211; **6, 8, 95**
Sefton Park, Liverpool 277
Serlio, Sebastiano 35, 51, 52, 61–63, 64, 65, 84, 90
Serres family 99
Serres, Olivier de 16, 83, 99–100, 108; **99**
Servien, Abel 181–182, 193, 225, 261
Sevigné, Marie de Rabutin-Chantal, marquise de 175, 183, 206
Sforza, Ludovico 39, 40
Shaftesbury, Anthony, Ashley, Cooper, third Earl of 291
Shenstone, William 9, 272, 299n
Silvestre, Israel 29, 61, 113, 115, 117, 230, 139, 155, 158, 164, 169, 181, 185, 190, 202, 237, 239, 243, 261, 279; **34, 35, 45, 51, 53, 69, 71–73, 89, 105, 112, 113, 115, 117, 121, 124, 133–135, 139, 140, 143–146, 154, 157, 171, 172, 183, 189, 190, 193, 195–199, 203, 206, 208, 216, 246–249, 254, 277, 300**
Smith, P. 175
Solario, Agostino 46
Sommier, Alfred 279, 297n
Sommier, Edmé 297n
Songe de Poliphile 29, 63, 292n; **17–19, 21, 22.** See also, *Hypnerotomachia Poliphili*
Stoopendael, Bastien 36; **26**
Stowe, 272
Style paysager 277, 288; **295**
Sucy-en-Brie, château 184
Sully, Maximilien de Bethune, duc de 114, 121, 124, 161
Surflet, Richard 99
Sybrayque, sculptor 298n

TALLEMANT DES RÉAUX 139, 161, 162
Tanlay, château and garden 162–164; **171–174**
Tapié, Victor 223
Tarquin, André and Bastien, gardeners at the Tuileries 114, 295n
Tasso, Torquato 33
Tè, Palazzo del, Mantua 33, 52, 59
temples, at Anet, 69, at La Bastie d'Urfé 55; **59, 69**
terraces at Ancy-le-Franc 63; Anet, 66, 68; Brécy, 166; Bury, 49; Chantilly, 74; Chenonceaux, 71; Gaillon, 45; Le Raincy, 185; Maisons, 173; Marly, 233; Meudon, 181; Montjeu, 161; Saint-Germain-en-Laye, 53, 93, 129, 133, 240; Sceaux, 259; the Tuileries, 115; Vaux-le-Vicomte, 190; Verneuil, 91; Versailles, 197, 200, 202
Tessin, Nicodemus 141
Tête d'Or, park, Lyon 277
Thomassin, Simon 297n
Thouin, André 299n
Thouin, Gabriel 277
Tissier de Mallerais, Martine 48
Tivoli 33; **88**. *See also* Este, villa d'.
tonnelles (*see also* berceaux) at Angers, 19; Ponts-de-Cé, 20; Saint-Pol, 17; in *trompe l'oeil* painting 61
topiary 27, 29, 34, 115; **20, 22, 23**
Torlonia, villa, Frascati 123; **122**
Tournelles, palace, Paris 79
trees, *see* plants and planting
trellis-work, uses and construction, 97–98; at Bury, 49; Chantilly, 249, 253; Chenonceaux, 71, 82; Gaillon, 46; Montargis, 95; Saint-Pol, 17; the Tuileries, 112; Versailles, 213, 225, 227. *See also* berceaux, pavilions, tonnelles
Tremblay, François Leclerc (Le Père Joseph) 148
Trianon 197, 220, 225, 272; gardens, creation of 200; flower garden and nursery, 228– 230; Michel Le Bouteux at, 225, 228; Le Nôtre at, 213, 230; Marie Antoinette's *Hameau* at, 33, 275; Trianon de Porcelaine, 228; **239, 240**; Trianon de Marbre (Grand Trianon), 228, 230; **236, 241**
Tribolo, Nicolo Pericoli, called 64
Trumel, Antoine, gardener at Vaux-le-Vicomte, Le Roule and Trianon 228, 243, 298n
Trumel, Laurens, gardener at Trianon 228
Trumel, Marin, gardener at Versailles 225
Tuby, Jean-Baptiste, sculptor 201, 203, 211; **213**
Tuileries, palace and garden, origins, 79; 112–118 *passim*; festival at, 83; grotto by Palissy at, 84, 87; designs for parterres at, 99, 107, 178; André Le Nôtre at, 117, 185, 234, 242–245; Mollet's archetypal French garden, 242; in modern Paris, 288; **73–75, 112–114, 116, 117, 252–254**
Turenne, Henri de la Tour d'Auvergne, vicomte de 197

URBAN IV (Jacques Pantaléon), Pope 16
Urfé, Claude d' 55
Urfé, Honoré d' 33, 158
Utens, G. van 34; **25, 57**

VAINUCOURT, PERRINET DE, gardener at Baugé 20
Valence, Pierre 46, 72
Valléry, château and garden 54, 89, 90; **43**
Vallet, Pierre 104, 110
Valois tapestries 83
Van Clève, Corneille, sculptor **232**
Varro, Marcus Terentius 13, 40, 97
Vasari, Giorgio 55, 59
Vatican, Cortile del Belvedere 41
Vauban, Sebastien le Prestre, Seigneur de 220
Vaultier, gardener at the *potager*, Versailles 225
Vaux-le-Vicomte, château and garden 123, 161, 173, 182, 184, 185, 188–194, 197, 206, 225, 247, 279; **193–203**
Vendôme, Louis-Joseph, duc de 69, 263, 267
Vera, A. 288, 299n; **312, 313**
Verneuil, château and garden 87, 89, 90, 91–93, 107; **87, 89**
Versailles, before Louis XIV, 121–123; structure of, 197–206; **205, 206** (from south, 1664), **207, 210** (from west before 1675); Allée Royale, 201, 213, 215; bosquets, 206–219, 225; **216, 217, 219, 220, 221, 222, 223, 224, 225, 233**; Grotte de Thétis, 201, 219, 220; **209**; Labyrinthe, 207, 209, 297n; Ménagerie, 200, 203; Orangerie, 181, 197, 202, 206, 209, 216, 225, 272; **215**; Parterre de Latone, 200, 203, 209, 217; **211, 212**; Parterre du Nord, 200; Petit Parc, 188, 197, 206, 213, 225; Pièce d'Eau des Suisses, 197, 206, 216, 221, 272; Potager du Roi, 197, 206, 221, 225; **235**; sculpture, 170, 190, 201, 203, 211, 213, 214–217; **213, 226–232, 296, 297**; water, 219, 220; Laugier's criticism of, 223
Viau, Théophile de 299n
Vigarini, Carlo 297n
Vignola, Giacomo Barozzi, called 52, 61, 65, 124
Villandry, château and garden 84, 95, 286–288, 291; **307–311**
Villars, Claude Louis Hector, duc de 194
Ville, baron Arnold de 220
Villeroy, Secretary of State 74
Villers-Cotterets, château and garden 52, 57, 95, 293n
Villette, château and garden 284; **305, 306**
Vincennes 79, 225
Vinet, Élie 97
Vitruvius, Pollio Marcus 31, 40, 63, 66, 84, 128
Voisins, château and garden 279–280; **298**
Vouet, Simon 185
Vredemann de Vries, Hans 61, 89; **52**

WALPOLE, HORACE 271
Wars of Religion 77
water 9, 10, 33, 42, 123; aesthetic value of 9, 203, 284. *See also* canals, cascades, fountains, ponds and lakes
water gardens 129, 188, 234
water organs 128, 201
water parterres 130, 158, 202–203, 247, 257
water stairways 234, 284
Watteau, Antoine 158, 232; **167**
Whately, Thomas 272
Wideville, château and garden 127, 137, 144, 162, 163; **128**
William III 197, 220
Wimbledon House 297n
Windsor 267

YOLANDE D'ARAGON 18, 20

ZUCCARI, Palazzo (Rome) 296n